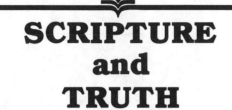

SCRIPTURE
and
TRUTH

SCRIPTURE
and
TRUTH

Edited by

D. A. Carson
and
John D. Woodbridge

Academie
Books Grand Rapids, Michigan
Zondervan Publishing House

Academie books are published by Zondervan Publishing House,
1415 Lake Drive, S.E., Grand Rapids, Michigan 49506

SCRIPTURE AND TRUTH
Copyright © 1983 by The Zondervan Corporation
Grand Rapids, Michigan

Library of Congress Cataloging in Publication Data

Main entry under title:
Scripture and truth.

Bibliography: p.
Includes indexes.
1. Bible—Evidences, authority, etc.—Addresses, essays, lectures. 2. Bible—
Inspiration—Addresses, essays, lectures. Carson, D. A.   II.   Woodbridge, John D.

BS480.S346   1983   220.1'3   82-20074
ISBN 0-310-43791-1

Edited by Gerard Terpstra
Designed by Louise Bauer

Printed in the United States of America

85   86   87   88   89 / 9   8   7   6   5   4   3   2

Contents

Preface

Twin dangers confront the Christian concerned with defining and promulgating biblical truth. The first is pugnaciousness. The line between contending for the faith and being contentious about the faith is extremely thin. A Christian can almost unknowingly develop a boisterous rhetoric and a caustic spirit, neither of which are helpful for the advance of the kingdom. The evangelical community suffers when its members lack humility and grace.

The second danger is less easy to recognize, but is not less insidious. It is a kind of arrogant apathy that bolsters a mindset less interested in the truth than in its pursuit. It involves a fine balancing of all opinions in such a way that a person is somehow impolite to insist that one opinion has the ring of truth, and, conversely, the others are to that degree false.

To read Luther makes one conscious of the first error; to read many modern theologians makes one conscious of the second. The comparison is not wholly fair, because Luther must be read against the backdrop of his contemporaries' intemperate speech, and moderns should be accorded a similar courtesy. Nevertheless, gaining a historical perspective helps us discover the cultural shadows of our own age with greater sensitivity than could otherwise be the case. Despite large pockets of believers who apparently yield to the first error, it must be admitted that the contemporary tide is toward the second.

That observation puts the writers of this book in an awkward position; for in the best sense of the word, this volume of essays is apologetical. Each contributor, of course, is responsible only for his own work; but taken collectively, their writings contend (that word again!) that the Bible is the Word of God written. We hold that what the Scriptures teach is infallibly true and that this belief is not only patient of reasoned defense but is extremely important for the well-being of the church.

A spate of books has appeared within recent years challenging this traditional evangelical perspective. Jack Rogers and Donald McKim's *Authority and Interpretation of the Bible* (New York: Harper and Row, 1979) is but one in a train of those that have done so. This present book is intended to respond to some of the issues raised by these volumes, to advance beyond those issues, and to do so without substituting careless rhetoric for careful argument.

In this book we have not been content merely to repeat received opinions. Some of the chapters treat again in modern form questions thrashed out by previous generations. This is valuable in its own right. Too few Christians are aware, for instance, of the strong evidence inherent in the Scripture's self-attestation for the position this book defends, even though such evidence has been assembled before in other forms. But several chapters break new ground, either in the clarification of a well-considered doctrine of Scripture or in the analysis of historical and critical problems.

The book is divided into three sections. The first is concerned with distinctively biblical questions as they are being raised today. Some of the issues treated by contemporary biblical scholars have fostered the suspicion that the classic understanding of Scripture has been rendered obsolete. We prefer to think that as the Arian controversy helped the theologians of Athanasius's day grapple with biblical christology without (we would argue) transmuting the biblical christological categories into something qualitatively innovative, and as the Reformation recovered and refined (among others) the doctrines of grace and Scripture, so the modern controversies regarding Scripture may help Christians formulate with increased perspicuity what the Bible itself teaches about its own nature. The aim is to achieve this without binding the conscience of believers with more than what Scripture requires and, equally, without succumbing to various forms of unqualified unbelief. Each of the five chapters in this first section could have been developed into a book. But even in short compass, they provide valuable insights concerning the contemporary debate. Our hope is that they may point the way to increased understanding of and faithfulness to the Bible as the infallible Word of God.

The second section responds to new directions taken by certain recent historical studies. Some scholars (like Jack Rogers, and Charles Briggs before him) have argued that neither the Reformers nor the Fathers held to an "infallible" or "inerrant" Scripture (as these words are used by conservatives), since such categories were not among their interests or concerns. Therefore modern conservative formulations, dating from the Princetonians at the end of the last century, are an aberration that should not be read back into, say, the Reformers. This claim needs to be examined, for a priori one must suspect that the modern proclivity to deny absolutes may equally be read back into the Reformers and Fathers. If it is wrong to read Warfield into Calvin, it is equally wrong to read Barth or Berkouwer into Calvin. What is required is dispassionate, even-handed, and comprehensive analysis of the primary sources.

At this point, it may be worth discussing a definition of "error" that is increasingly in vogue. It is too restrictive to understand error to entail "self-conscious deceit." With such an understanding of error, one could plausibly agree that the Bible is "inerrant," because no human author self-consciously set out to deceive; but there may remain all kinds of errors not covered by the definition—accidental lapses of memory, false information, mistaken judgments, and the like—none of which involves self-conscious, purposeful deception. But four objections challenge the legitimacy of this approach: (1) Biblical understanding of *truth*, involving factuality, faithfulness, and completeness (see chapter 10, by Nicole) is too comprehensive to allow so restricted a definition of *error*. (2) Until modern times the church has never operated with so narrow a definition. For instance, Augustine's correspondence with Jerome is most telling in this regard (see his correspondence of A.D. 405, Letter 82:3–4). Augustine writes that no one would ascribe to Jerome any self-conscious deceit in his own writings and points out that the Scriptures bear an authority beyond the writings of Jerome because the latter may have unwitting errors whereas the former have none. (3) Scripture's self-attestation, as Grudem has demonstrated in chapter 1, requires the view that whatever the *mode* of inspiration, God so superintended the writing of Scripture that He preserved it in truth; and God cannot be deceived or accidentally mistaken. To appeal to the "humanness" of Scripture in this regard is a methodologically suspect step, for if "to err is human," so also would it be true to say that "to deceive is human." The humanness of Scripture, by Scripture's own attestation, does not consist in deceit or error, and the participation of God in the inscripturation of the biblical revelation positively rules out such an approach. (4) To restrict error to self-conscious deceit raises new hermeneutical problems. The remaining accidental "errors" are not tagged for us. How then would the reader of Scripture eliminate the possibility that Paul, say, was *accidentally* in error about some aspect of the atonement? Or about the physical reality of the resurrection? Or about the exclusiveness of the gospel? C. H. Dodd, after all, was heard to exclaim over one atonement passage in Romans, "What rubbish!" But Dodd would surely not ascribe *deceit* to Paul.

We are learning, then, that historical considerations are assuming a large part in the contemporary debate over Scripture; and if revisionist historians are challenging us to reexamine the traditional historical understandings of earlier generations, we judge it not less urgent to scrutinize the historiography of the revisionist historians themselves.

The third section is composed of three chapters loosely labeled "theological." It is useless to speak of the "truth" of Scripture unless the term be defined. Having come to an agreed definition, we must still examine *how* one comes to the place where it is possible to say, "I believe that the Word of God is infallibly true" or the like. Moreover, an alert Bible student should analyze the relationship between an authoritative Bible and the role of hermeneutics—not least because the two categories are commonly confused.

Many more worthwhile topics could have been discussed in this volume. The reasons for this selection were hammered out in detail. In brief, we invited our distinguished colleagues to write on subjects that would either directly address the modern debate or raise afresh arguments and evidence too long ignored. We believe that the various chapters do focus on some of the more important issues that Christians will discuss in the 1980s concerning biblical authority. Our earnest prayer is that the selection may strengthen the church of the One reported to have said (and that almost casually!), "The Scripture cannot be broken" (John 10:35).

Soli Deo gloria!

The Editors

PART I
BIBLICAL ESSAYS

SCRIPTURE'S
SELF-ATTESTATION
AND THE PROBLEM
OF FORMULATING
A DOCTRINE OF SCRIPTURE

Wayne A. Grudem

Wayne A. Grudem

Wayne A. Grudem is Assistant Professor of New Testament at Trinity Evangelical Divinity School. He is a graduate of Harvard University (B.A.), Westminster Theological Seminary (M.Div.) and the University of Cambridge, England (Ph.D.). He was for four and one-half years Assistant Professor of Theology at Bethel College, St. Paul, Minnesota. He has written one book, *The Gift of Prophecy in I Corinthians* (1982), and numerous articles for periodicals. He is preparing to write a book on the Bible and economic decisions and a commentary on 1 Peter. He is a member of the Evangelical Theological Society, the Institute for Biblical Research, the Tyndale Fellowship for Biblical Research, and the Society of Biblical Literature.

SCRIPTURE'S SELF-ATTESTATION
AND THE PROBLEM OF FORMULATING
A DOCTRINE OF SCRIPTURE

In what sense is the Bible the Word of God for Christians today? And in what way should we perceive the nature and character of the Bible as we read it today? More specifically, how should we today think of the truthfulness of the Bible?

In order to answer those questions it will be profitable first to look at the Old Testament text on its own terms, asking initially not the theological question, "What should we believe today?" but the literary and historical question, "What views of God's word(s) are presented in the Old Testament text itself?" Then we can ask, "What views of the Old Testament text and of the emerging New Testament writings are found among the New Testament authors?"

After those questions have been answered in some detail, we can go on to attempt the formulation of a doctrine of Scripture, asking whether or not it it possible to decide what Christians today should think about the nature and character of the Bible, with particular focus on the question of the truthfulness of the Bible.

OLD TESTAMENT REPORTS OF DIRECT SPEECH
FROM GOD TO MEN AND WOMEN

The Old Testament records several instances of speech from God to individual people. The most familiar instance is probably the giving of the law on Mt. Sinai:

> And God spoke all these words, saying, "I am the LORD your God, who brought you out of the land of Egypt, out of the house of bondage.
> "You shall have no other gods before me.
> "You shall not make for yourself a graven image . . ." (Exod. 20:1–4).[1]

But there are many other examples, such as the speech by God to Adam and Eve both before and after the Fall (Gen. 1:28–30; 3:9–19), the call of Abram (Gen. 12:1–3), subsequent lengthy conversations with Abram in which God's covenantal provisions are established (Gen. 15:1–21; 17:1–21; note also Abraham's remarkable conversation with the Lord in Gen. 18:1–23), the extensive dialogue between God and Moses at the burning bush (Exod. 3:1–4:23), the revelation to Samuel concerning the doom of Eli's house (1 Sam. 3:10–14), the conversation with Elijah at Mount Horeb (1 Kings 19:9–18), God's detailed (and poetic) response to Job (Job 38–41), and frequent conversations between

God and the prophets (Isa. 6:8–13; Jonah 1:1–2; 3:1–2; 4:1–11, et al.). In addition, large sections of the legal code found in the Pentateuch are represented as words spoken directly by God to Moses (see, for example, Exod. 20:22–23:33).

This list could be greatly expanded, especially from passages in the Prophets, but enough examples have been given to establish two points. First, the Old Testament frequently portrays God as communicating with people by using actual spoken words, not simply by communicating ideas or thoughts somehow apart from individual words. This concept of verbal communication from God was quite often opposed by scholars of a previous generation,[2] so much so that James Barr in 1963 said in protest:

> Direct verbal communication between God and particular men on particular occasions ... is, I believe, an inescapable fact of the Bible and of the OT in particular. God can speak specific verbal messages, when he wills, to the man of his choice.... If we persist in saying that this direct, specific communication must be subsumed under revelation through events in history and taken as subsidiary interpretation of the latter, I shall say that we are abandoning the Bible's own representation of the matter for another which is apologetically more comfortable.[3]

Second, these passages never view human language as a barrier to effective communication by God. There is no hint that some inadequacies inherent in human language may be used as a legitimate reason to disbelieve or to disobey anything God has said. The appropriate response, according to the Old Testament writers, is, "All the words which the LORD has spoken we will do" (Exod. 24:3). Similarly, Abram's belief in God's seemingly impossible promises is commended: "And he believed the LORD; and he reckoned it to him as righteousness" (Gen. 15:6).

So the Old Testament text speaks frequently of direct verbal communication from God, communication that demands absolute belief and absolute obedience. God is viewed as the Creator and Lord of human language ("Who has made man's mouth?" [Exod. 4:11]), who is able to use language however He wills in order to accomplish His purposes.

OLD TESTAMENT REPORTS OF PROPHETIC SPEECH (GOD'S WORDS SPOKEN BY MEN)

PROPHETS ARE VIEWED AS AUTHORITATIVE MESSENGERS OF GOD

The Old Testament prophets are most frequently pictured as messengers sent by God to speak God's words to people.[4] James F. Ross lists several discernible characteristics of a "messenger speech" (*Botenspruch*) in the Old Testament narratives:[5] an introductory formula ("thus says Yahweh"), a standard conclusion ("says Yahweh"), the frequent use of the verb *šālaḥ* ("send") to indicate that the prophet is *sent* by God,[6] and a commissioning narrative in which Yahweh tells the prophet, "Go and say to _____, 'Thus says Yahweh....'" Ancient Near Eastern parallels, especially those found in the Mari and Ras Shamra texts, provide additional examples of prophets as messengers of a god. (However, the evidence from such sources is not completely unambiguous.)[7]

It is characteristic of this kind of messenger that his words possess not merely his own personal authority but the authority of the one who sent him. So it is with the Old Testament prophets: their words carry the authority of Yahweh Himself, because He has called them as authoritative messengers who will speak for Him.[8]

Lindblom is no doubt correct when he points to the "council [*sôd*] of Yahweh" as a reference to the source of a prophet's speech: "That the prophets are in possession of the divine word depends on the fact that they are admitted to the *sôd* of Yahweh.... Thus the words of the prophets are words which they have heard directly from Yahweh."[9] But more basic even than this council to Old Testament thought is the simple hearing-speaking pattern Lindblom describes: "Yahweh speaks to the prophet, the prophet hears what Yahweh says, and then he pronounces what he has heard to the listening people."[10]

The Old Testament text, then, together with parallels in Ancient Near Eastern literature, portrays the prophets as messengers sent by God and bearing God's authority in the message He has given them to deliver.

"THUS SAYS THE LORD" AS A ROYAL DECREE FORMULA

The frequent use of the introductory formula ("thus says Yahweh [or the LORD]") or its equivalent is a further indication of the high degree of authority and reliability claimed for the words the prophets spoke in God's name.[11] This formula is one that would have been used in the Ancient Near East to introduce an edict issued by a king to his subjects.

An extrabiblical parallel to this phrase is seen by J. S. Holladay in the Neo-Assyrian phrase "*Amāt šarri ana* _____" ("Word of the king to _____"). This phrase is "almost invariable in the letters of the king to his subjects," says Holladay. "That *amāt šarri* is an especially authoritative, compelling mode of address (equivalent to 'edict of the king') is shown (a) by the fact that it appears as an introductory formula only in the king's letters ..., (b) by the fact that, when the king addresses his letters to presumed equals ... he invariably uses the introductory formula normally reserved for more personal or familial communication."[12]

In the Old Testament text itself, this royal decree formula is used in an interesting conflict between Sennacherib, the king of Assyria, and Yahweh, the king of Israel, in Isaiah 36–37. The Rabshakeh's statement:

"Thus says the great king, the king of Assyria . . ." is set against Isaiah's statement: "Thus says Yahweh, the God of Israel . . ." (Isa. 36:4; cf. 36:13–14, 16; 37:6, 21). The "messenger verb" *šālaḥ* is used several times (Isa. 36:2, 12; 37:14 of Rabshakeh; cf. 37:21).

On another level, Hezekiah is the king who sends (*wayyišlaḥ*, Isa. 37:2) messengers to Isaiah saying, "Thus says Hezekiah" (Isa. 37:3).

Royal messengers from Ben-hadad also use this introductory formula in 1 Kings 20:2 (3), 5: "Thus says Ben-hadad." There is a response in kind to Ahab the prophet (1 Kings 20:13, 14, 28). However, once Ben-hadad has been defeated, he cannot use the royal decree formula, but instead sends messengers who say, "Your servant Ben-hadad says" (1 Kings 20:32)!

The formula is also used by Pharaoh's taskmasters to report Pharaoh's edict to the people (Exod. 5:10; note that the Lord sends messengers to speak to Pharaoh in the same way: Exod. 4:22; 5:1, et al.). In Jeremiah 28:2, 11, however, a false prophet uses the formula with disastrous consequences (v. 17).

The formula "Thus says the Lord," appearing hundreds of times in the Old Testament,[13] is a royal decree formula used to preface the edict of a king to his subjects, an edict that could not be challenged or questioned but simply had to be obeyed. God is viewed as the sovereign king of Israel, and when the prophets speak, they are seen as bringing the divine king's absolutely authoritative decrees to His subjects.

IT IS THOUGHT THAT EVERY WORD THE PROPHET SPEAKS IN GOD'S NAME MUST COME FROM GOD

The distinguishing characteristic of a true prophet is that he does not speak his own words or "words of his own heart," but words that God has sent (*šālaḥ*) him to deliver (Deut. 18:18–20; Jer. 14:14; 23:16–40; 29:31–32; Ezek. 13:1–19; cf. Num. 16:28).[14] Throughout the Old Testament there is an emphasis not simply on the general content of prophetic speech as coming from God, but on the very words themselves. God says to Moses, the archetypal Old Testament prophet,[15] "I will be with your mouth and teach you what you shall speak" (Exod. 4:12; cf. 24:3). The same is said of other prophets: "I will put my words in his mouth" (Deut. 18:18; cf. vv. 21–22); "I have put my words in your mouth" (Jer. 1:9); "The word that God puts in my mouth, that I must speak" (Num 22:38; cf. 23:5, 16); "You shall speak my words to them" (Ezek. 2:7; cf. 3:27).

This emphasis on the actual words spoken by the mouth of the prophet indicates something more than a conviction that ideas have been given by God to the prophet, who will then express the ideas in his own words. Not just the general message but also the very words in which it is expressed are seen as coming from God. Any prophet who spoke a word "not from the mouth of the Lord" (Jer. 23:16) was a false prophet. And "the prophet who presumes to speak a word in my name which I have not commanded him to speak . . . shall die" (Deut. 18:20). The people refused to listen to "the words of the LORD which he [the LORD] spoke through [*beyad*] Jeremiah the prophet" (Jer. 37:2). Many similar examples could be given (see 1 Kings 16:34; 2 Kings 9:36; 14:25; 17:23; 24:2; 2 Chron. 29:25; Ezra 9:10–11; Neh. 9:30; Zech. 7:7, 12, et al.), but the point is clear: When a prophet speaks, the people are to think of the words as words that God Himself is speaking to them.

WHAT THE PROPHET SAYS IN GOD'S NAME, GOD SAYS

One more indication of the absolute divine authority attributed to prophetic speech is seen in the frequency with which God is referred to as the speaker of something a prophet said. In 1 Kings 13:26, "the word which the LORD spoke to him" is the word the *prophet* had spoken in verse 21. Similarly, Elijah's words in 1 Kings 21:19 are referred to in 2 Kings 9:25–26 as the oracle that "the LORD uttered . . . against him," and Elijah is not even mentioned. To obey "the words of Haggai the prophet" is equivalent to obeying "the voice of the LORD" (Hag. 1:12; cf. 1 Sam. 15:3, 18).

An Old Testament Israelite listening to the words of a prophet, then, viewed the words as not merely words of a man but also words that God Himself was speaking through the prophet. The Old Testament text indicates that these words were to be accorded the same status and character as direct speech from God. For God to speak through a prophet was to use a different means of speaking to people than when He spoke directly to the people with a voice out of heaven at Mt. Sinai (Exod. 20:22; Deut. 5:22–26). But the speech that came forth was exactly the same in terms of its character and status. Whatever could be said about the authority, power, truthfulness, or purity of one form of divine speech could also be said about the other.

PROPHETS OFTEN SPEAK FOR GOD IN THE FIRST PERSON

If the Old Testament prophets are seen as God's royal messengers, and if they speak as though they are delivering unchallengeable edicts from a divine King to His people, and if it is frequently claimed that the very words of their messages have been given them by God, then it is not surprising that the prophets often speak for God in the first person (2 Sam. 7:4–16; 1 Kings 20:13, 42; 2 Kings 17:13; 19:25–28, 34; 21:12–15; 22:16–20; 2 Chron. 12:5, and the Latter Prophets, passim). The manner in which the prophet's words are so completely identified with Yahweh's words is seen when the prophet says things like, "You shall know that I am the LORD" (1 Kings 20:13), or, "I am the LORD, and there is no other, besides me there is no God" (Isa. 45:5). Clearly no Israelite would have thought that the prophet was speaking his own words in such cases; he was simply repeating the words of the one who had sent him.[16]

GOD IS OFTEN SAID TO SPEAK "THROUGH" THE PROPHET

This identification of the prophet's words with Yahweh's words is so strong in the Old Testament that often we read of God's speaking "through" a prophet. That is, the prophet himself is speaking, but his words are also thought to be words that God is speaking to the people. Israel mourned for Jeroboam's son, "according to the word of the LORD, which he [the LORD] spoke by [*beyad*] his servant Ahijah the prophet" (1 Kings 14:18). Zimri destroyed the house of Baasha, "according to the word of the LORD, which he [the LORD] spoke against Baasha by Jehu the prophet" (1 Kings 16:12).

TO DISBELIEVE OR DISOBEY ANYTHING A PROPHET SAYS IS TO DISBELIEVE OR DISOBEY GOD

If prophetic words are viewed as God's words in the Old Testament, then we would expect to find some indications of moral obligations placed on the hearers, obligations to hear these words and unquestioningly believe them and obey them. In fact, several indications of this sort are found in the Old Testament.

According to Deuteronomy 18:19, the LORD says of the coming prophet who would be like Moses: "Whoever will not give heed to my words which he shall speak in my name, I myself will require it of him" (Deut. 18:19).

When Saul disobeyed Samuel's command to wait seven days at Gilgal "until I come to you and show you what you shall do" (1 Sam. 10:8), Samuel rebuked him: "You have done foolishly; you have not kept the commandment of the LORD your God, which *he commanded you* . . . now your kingdom shall not continue . . . because you have not kept what *the LORD commanded you*" (1 Sam. 13:13–14). To disobey the prophet's words is to disobey God.

In 1 Samuel 15:3, God spoke through Samuel and commanded him to destroy the Amalekites, and to "utterly destroy all that they have." Again when Saul disobeyed, Samuel asked, "Why then did you not obey the voice (*qôl*) of the LORD? . . . .Because you have rejected the word of the Lord, he has also rejected you from being king" (1 Sam. 15:19, 23).[17]

To disobey a command of one of "the sons of the prophets" who is speaking "by the word of the LORD" (1 Kings 20:35) is to disobey "the voice of the LORD," and can lead to sudden death (1 Kings 20:36). When the people demand a king instead of Samuel the prophet, God says to Samuel, "They have not rejected you, but they have rejected me from being king over them" (1 Sam. 8:7): To reject God's prophet is to reject God.

The parallelism in 2 Chronicles 20:20 indicates an equivalence between obeying God's prophets and obeying God:[18]

"Believe the Lord your God, and you will be established;
believe his prophets, and you will succeed."

In fact, to reject a prophet's words is to invite certain destruction by God (2 Chron. 25:16; Isa. 30:12–14; Jer. 6:10–11; 16:19; 36:29–31).[19]

In summary, the words that a prophet speaks in God's name are throughout the Old Testament said to be words that God also speaks. What the prophet says in God's name, God says. To disbelieve or disobey anything a prophet says in God's name is to disbelieve or disobey God.

WRITTEN WORDS FROM GOD

In addition to Old Testament records of direct speech by God, and of God's words spoken by men and women, there are several accounts of the writing of words that were then taken to be God's words in written form. Once again, the evaluation of the character of these words (they are both human and divine) and of their truth-status (they must be believed and obeyed) seems indistinguishable from the evaluations of direct divine speech and of divine speech spoken by people.

There is first the account of the giving of the two stone tablets by God to Moses: They were "tables of stone, written with the finger of God" (Exod. 31:18). "And the tables were the work of God, and the writing was the writing of God, graven upon the tables" (Exod. 32:16; cf. Exod. 34:1, 28; Deut. 4:13; 10:4). Clearly, these words are seen as having absolute divine authority. The written words on the tablets are God's own words.

But there are also reports of men writing down words that God told them to write, words that are then understood as God's words. In most of the following instances the attribution of authorship to a prophet seems also to be significant, especially when viewed through the eyes of an Old Testament Israelite who had the high regard for the divine authority of prophetic words that was outlined in the preceding section.

Exod. 17:14	"The Lord said to Moses, 'Write this as a memorial in a book.'"
Exod. 24:4	"And Moses wrote all the words of the Lord."
Exod. 34:27	"And the Lord said to Moses, 'Write these words; in accordance with these words I have made a covenant with you and with Israel.'"
Num. 33:2	"Moses wrote down their starting places, stage by stage, by command of the Lord; and these are their stages according to their starting places."
Deut. 31:22	"So Moses wrote this song the same day."
Deut. 31:24	"When Moses had finished writing the words of this law in a book, to the very end ..."

Josh. 24:26   "Joshua wrote these words [the statutes and ordi-
                 nances, and the words of covenant renewal, v. 25] in
                 the book of the law of God." (See 1 Kings 16:34; Josh.
                 1:5, 16–18, on Joshua as a prophet.)

1 Sam. 10:25   "Samuel told the people the rights and duties of the
                 kingship, and he wrote them in a book and laid it up
                 before the Lord."

1 Chron. 29:29   "The acts of King David, from first to last, are written in
                 the Chronicles [*diḇrê*] of Samuel the seer, and in the
                 Chronicles of Nathan the prophet, and in the Chroni-
                 cles of Gad the seer."

2 Chron. 9:29   "Now the rest of the acts of Solomon, from first to last,
                 are they not written in the Chronicles of Nathan the
                 prophet, and in the prophecy of Ahijah the Shilonite,
                 and in the visions of Iddo the seer concerning
                 Jereboam the son of Nebat?"

2 Chron. 12:15   "Now the acts of Rehoboam, from first to last, are they
                 not written in the Chronicles of Shemaiah the prophet
                 and of Iddo the seer?"

2 Chron. 13:22   "The rest of the acts of Abijah, his ways and his sayings,
                 are written in the story [*miḏraš*] of the prophet Iddo."

2 Chron. 20:34   "Now the rest of the acts of Jehoshaphat, from first to
                 last, are written in the Chronicles of Jehu the son of
                 Hanani, which are recorded in the Book of the Kings of
                 Israel." (Jehu the son of Hanani is called a prophet in
                 1 Kings 16:7.)

2 Chron. 26:22   "Now the rest of the acts of Uzziah, from first to last,
                 Isaiah the prophet the son of Amoz wrote."

2 Chron. 32:32   "Now the rest of the acts of Hezekiah, and his good
                 deeds, behold, they are written in the vision of Isaiah
                 the prophet, the son of Amoz, in the Book of the Kings
                 of Judah and Israel."

This brings us well into the period of the classical or "writing"
prophets.[20] The degree to which their speeches were primarily oral, or
both oral and written from the beginning, need not concern us here.[21]
But it is certain that there was at least some writing of prophecies either
before or immediately after the oral delivery, and sometimes transcription of the words during the delivery by the prophet's followers.

For example, God said to Jeremiah, "Thus says the Lord, the God
of Israel: Write in a book all the words that I have spoken to you" (Jer.
30:2). God commanded Isaiah concerning what had been revealed,
"And now, go, write it before them on a tablet, and inscribe it in a book,
that it may be for the time to come, as a witness forever" (Isa. 30:8; cf.
Jer. 29:1; 36:1–32; 45:1; 51:60; Ezek. 43:11; Hab. 2:2; Dan. 7:1). Lindblom

says, "We must, in fact, allow for the existence of both oral and written transmission from the beginning, though it may be that the former predominated in the earliest period."[22]

The purpose of this writing seems to have been intimately connected with the covenant relation between Israel and Yahweh. The words of the prophets were said to be written down as a witness to the covenant: an authoritative record of the provisions of the covenant, of the ratification by the parties involved, and of subsequent covenant-related behavior by Yahweh and the people. So the writing can be called "the book of the covenant" (Exod. 24:7; 2 Kings 23:2, 21; 2 Chron. 34:30), and Isaiah wrote in a book that it might be a witness against the people forever (Isa. 30:8; cf. Deut. 31:19, 26). The provisions of covenant behavior are often written in a book (Exod. 34:27; Josh. 24:26; 1 Sam. 10:25; Ezek. 43:11), and the historical narratives themselves may be seen as a record of activities performed by members of the covenant bond.[23] The latter prophets, then, are seen as covenant messengers of Yahweh reminding Israel of the terms of their covenant relationship and calling them to obedience to these terms.

This writing function is closely linked to the conception that the words of prophecy are God's words. As Lindblom says, since the prophets regarded their utterances as Yahweh's words, they thought they were significant for all times.[24] Furthermore, their written words seem to have been considered just as authoritative as their spoken words. When Moses read the book of the covenant to the people, they responded, "All that the Lord has *spoken* [*dibber*] we will do" (Exod. 24:7). Later in the Old Testament narrative, the law of Moses (presumably this refers to the written law) is said to have been commanded by the Lord (2 Kings 14:6; 2 Chron. 25:4; Neh. 8:14; Mal. 4:4). The written words are seen as God's words in every way that direct speech by God and God's speech through the mouths of people are seen as God's words. The form of communication differs, but the character, authority, and truth status of the words do not.

Regarding the introductory formula "the word of the Lord which was to Hosea" (Hos. 1:1; cf. Mic. 1:1; Zeph. 1:1), Procksch writes, "It certainly implies that the whole book is regarded as 'the word of the Lord.' In the written form no distinction is made between the divine voice in the prophet and its expression in poetry, saying, and address. We have here a transition to the final view that not merely the prophetic book, but in the last resort the whole of the Old Testament is the Word of God."[25]

FURTHER STATEMENTS ABOUT THE WORD OF GOD

Up to this point we have seen indications of the kind of status and authority attributed to three forms of God's word in the Old Testament account:

1. Direct speech by God to men
2. God's words spoken by men
3. God's words written, usually through the writing activity of prophets[26]

We have not yet tried to specify how much of our present Old Testament consists of records of these three types but only to define the characteristics attributed to each type by the Old Testament authors.

There are now some remaining texts that make further statements about the nature or character of "God's word" or "God's words." In each of these texts that follow, one must ask, to which words of God is the writer referring? The initial referent cannot be the entire Old Testament, for at the time these passages were written the Old Testament was not complete.

On the other hand, when the Old Testament authors made statements about the character of God's word they probably did not intend to distinguish among God's words written, spoken by men, or spoken directly by God. The same characteristics were applied to each (see above), and what could be said of one could be said of the others. Statements not further specified by context, therefore, can legitimately be thought to refer to God's words in all three forms.

Nevertheless, God's words directly spoken and God's words spoken by men were not available for repeated hearing and inspection by others, or even by the initial hearers, at any time subsequent to the initial utterance (except through secondary oral reports or written records). So it would be primarily God's word written that an Old Testament author would be able to read or hear, ponder, meditate on, and write about. This is relevant for our investigation, because we are attempting to discover attitudes toward God's word written in Scripture.

NUMBERS 23:19; 1 SAMUEL 15:29

Balaam said to Balak, "God is not a man, that he should *lie* [*kāzab*, Piel] or a son of man, that he should repent. Has he said, and will he not do it? Or has he spoken, and will he not fulfill it?" (Num. 23:19). The context shows Balak trying to get Balaam to curse Israel and thus nullify his earlier blessing (vv. 7–11). Although Balaam himself is not fully righteous in the entire episode (Num. 22:22, 34), he is certainly seen as a prophet who speaks God's words (Num. 22:35; 23:5, 12, 26; 24:2–4, 13, 15–16). The statement "God is not a man, that he should lie" is itself part of a prophetic utterance, spoken in response to the question in verse 17, "What has the LORD spoken?"

In this context, the purpose of saying that God does not lie is to tell Balak that there can be no falsehood in the previous prophecy that could be nullified by later prophecies. What God had predicted would certainly happen, for God does not lie.

This passage therefore refers to human words spoken by a

prophet in God's name as God's words. It further says of those prophetic words that the normal human proclivity for lying does not
apply to them; even though they were spoken by human lips they can
only rightly be assigned a truth-status that stands in clear contrast to
one that normally describes human speech: the words of people contain lies, but God's words spoken by people do not.[27]

Furthermore, Numbers 23:19 claims much more than the fact that
God did not lie in the prophecy of Numbers 23:7–10. For the statement
"God is not a man, that he should lie" is a general statement used to
demonstrate the specific fact that He did not lie in the prophecy of
verses 7–10. But as a general statement it speaks of the character of
God's speech in all circumstances. It is because God *never* lies that
Balak should be assured that God did not lie in the first prophecy.
(Otherwise Balak might hope that one of these rare exceptions where
God could lie would be in the first prophecy.) So Numbers 23:19 is an
affirmation that in any case in which God speaks through human lips,
there will be no "lie" or factually untrue statement in the speech. It will
be completely truthful, and will faithfully correspond to reality.[28] In
terms of its reliability and truthfulness it is to be treated as divine
speech, not human speech.

First Samuel 15:29 is a similar passage. Samuel, speaking as a
prophet, had told Saul that God had rejected him from being king of
Israel (v. 23). Saul begged Samuel to change the verdict (v. 25) and
grabbed Samuel's robe to prevent him from leaving (v. 27). The robe
tore, and Samuel reaffirmed the judgment (v. 27). Then he said, "And
also the Glory of Israel[29] will not lie or repent; for he is not a man, that
he should repent" (v. 29).

Once again the statement affirms the unchanging reliability of
God's words spoken by men. Once again there is a contrast between
human failure to live up to what one promises and divine faithfulness
to every promise. Once again a divine standard of reliability and truthfulness is applied to prophetic speech, and a human standard is
explicitly rejected.[30]

DEUTERONOMY 4:2; 12:32

Deuteronomy 4:2 records Moses as saying, "You shall not add to
the word which I command you, nor take from it; that you may keep
the commandments of the LORD your God which I command you."
Similarly, Deuteronomy 12:32 (13:1) says, "Everything that I command
you you shall be careful to do; you shall not add to it or take from it"
(cf. Deut. 32:46).

It is significant here that the words of God spoken by Moses and,
according to Deuteronomy 31:24, the words of God that Moses wrote
in the Book of Deuteronomy, are seen to be unique and important in
their entirety. The prohibition against adding to the commands indicates a unique kind of authority; no other words are fit to be added by

the people themselves, for no other words are seen as having an equivalent status; these words are unlike all other human words.

The prohibition against taking from the commands indicates a view that no parts of the spoken (or written) words of God are unimportant or insignificant. If anyone were to try to "take from" these words, it might often involve the taking of minor, less central or less significant details. Yet even that is forbidden, for all of God's words spoken or written through Moses are thought to be valuable.

PSALM 12:6 (7)

In the midst of despair over the faithlessness of people (Ps. 12:1–4), the psalmist exclaims:

"The words[31] of the LORD are words that are pure, silver refined in a furnace on the ground, purified seven times" (Ps. 12:6 [7]).

The term used to speak of God's words is not *dābār* ("word, thing"), but *'imrâh* ("word, utterance"), a term that places emphasis on the actual words spoken or written as opposed to the general content of a message.

What words is the writer referring to? The immediate reference is to the message of comfort and deliverance in the preceding verse. This is not a quotation from elsewhere in the Old Testament, nor is it likely that a prophet was nearby providing a ready answer to his plea for help. Apparently verse 5 (6) is direct speech from God that came to the psalmist in a manner for us unexplained. Yet even if the primary reference is to direct speech from God, the general statement is one that has implications beyond its immediate reference to the preceding verse. The psalmist knows that the comforting words of the LORD in verse 5 (6) are pure because he is convinced that in general the words of the LORD are pure. Whatever words can be called "words of the LORD" are, according to the psalmist, "pure."

This attribution of purity is exceptionally strong. The term *ṭāhôr* ("pure") is used to describe freedom from imperfections or impurities, as with pure gold (Exod. 25:11, 17, 24, et al.), a pure heart (free from evil motives and desires, Ps. 51:10 [12]; cf. *ṭāhēr* in Ezek. 36:25), or ritual purity or cleanness (Lev. 10:10, 14; 13:13, 17; Deut. 14:11, 20; Mal. 1:11, et al.). Here the psalmist compares the purity of God's words to the purity of silver that has been refined in a "furnace of clay" or a "furnace on the ground."[32] The extremely hot furnace would enable the silver to be purged of all impurities; so the metaphor is apt. In order to prevent us from missing the point, he adds the phrase "purified seven times." Using a number that probably indicates a "perfect" number of times,[33] the psalmist is expressing in a forceful way the concept of absolute purity, total freedom from impurity or imperfection.

Against the contrasting background of unfaithful and lying words spoken by "every one" among the "sons of men" (vv. 1–2), this affirmation of absolute purity acquires a clear epistemological aspect: All human beings' words contain lies and falsehood, but the words of the Lord do not, for they are absolutely free from any impurities in the sense of unreliable or untruthful speech. With respect to truthfulness, the words of the Lord are as pure as "silver refined in a furnace on the ground, purified seven times." There is no untruthfulness in them.

This conclusion indicates how foreign it would be to the thought of at least some Old Testament authors to argue, as some do today,[34] that because God's words come to us in human language and through human spokesmen the words may therefore contain some degree of untruthfulness, such as factual errors in areas unrelated to "faith and practice," or misstatements of fact in matters unrelated to or only distantly related to the central purpose. The psalmist takes care to point out the great *contrast* between the total truthfulness of God's words and the falsehoods found in all merely human words. It is *all* God's words, argues the writer in Psalm 12:6 (7), that are pure from falsehood: *Every* word God speaks, no matter on what subject and no matter how tangentially related to the central purpose of a particular message, is free from falsehood: His words are as pure as perfectly refined silver.

PSALM 18:30 (31) (= 2 SAM. 22:31); PSALM 119:140; PROVERBS 30:5

The same word (*'imrâh*) that occurred in a plural form in Psalm 12:6 (7) is here used in a singular form to affirm a similar statement: "The word of the LORD [*'imrat-YHWH*][35] is flawless. He is a shield for all who take refuge in him" (Ps. 18:30 [31], NIV). The "word" the psalmist refers to seems to be the written words of God, the "statutes" and "ordinances" that he claims to have continually looked at (v. 22). "The word of the LORD" seems to be used here in a collective sense (see BDB, p. 57) to refer to all the words of God, especially written words that the psalmist had available to him at that time.

To say that the word of the Lord is "flawless" is again to indicate its freedom from imperfection. The verb *ṣārap* commonly means "to refine, smelt, test," and is used to refer to the refining of silver by fire (Ps. 12:6[7]; Jer. 6:29–30; Zech. 13:9). The passive participle (*ṣᵉrûpâh*) used in Ps. 18:30 [31] indicates that God's words are words from which all impurities have been removed: the words are "pure," or "flawless."

The context again emphasizes the reliability of God's words as the aspect of purity that the psalmist is especially concerned with. God had promised to reward righteous living and obedience to Himself, and in verses 20 and 24 there is a recounting of God's faithfulness to these promises. Again, the idea of "purity" suggests that according to the writer of this Psalm, there was nothing in God's word that could not be relied on or trusted: God's words are pure, and no unreliable statements can be found in them.

Psalm 119:140 says, "Your word is very pure [ṣᵉrûpâh] and your servant loves it." As in Psalm 18:30 (31), the word referred to is the written word of God. That is even more clear in this Psalm, since the subject of the entire Psalm is the law of God, the "statutes," "commandments," "ordinances," etc., that the psalmist has available for meditation and repeated inspection (vv. 6, 15, 18, 23, et al.). As in Psalm 18, the word of God is said to be "pure"; in fact, here it is said to be "very pure." This emphasis indicates that the psalmist saw no element of untruthfulness or unreliability in the written words of God to which he had access, even though they were in human language and written by imperfect human beings. Ordinary human error did not attach to these words; unlike all other human words, these were "very pure."

This affirmation is even stronger in Proverbs: "Every word of God is flawless; he is a shield to those who take refuge in him" (Prov. 30:5–6). The first line again uses ṣᵉrûpah to indicate the flawlessness and purity of God's words. The range of reference is more explicitly broad here: it is "every" word of God (that is, every utterance or speech from God to men), that is free from imperfection. According to the writer of this proverb, God always speaks in words that are pure, and no impurity exists in any part of His speech.

The next line, "he is a shield to those who take refuge in him," suggests the trustworthiness of God's words: to rely on every word spoken by God is to rely on God Himself, who will not fail those who trust Him. It is significant that in most contexts where the purity of God's speech is emphasized, this element of reliability lies near at hand. This fact suggests that the kind of purity intended is a purity from error, falsehood, or deception, elements that would make God's words unreliable. Other kinds of purity that might be imagined—a "mechanical" purity in the flawless copying of manuscripts, for example, or a "sophisticated grammatical purity" in the polished use of academically acceptable grammatical constructions, or a "stylistically uniformitarian purity" in the use of one impersonal, unvarying style of writing throughout all of God's written words—are not in view in the contexts we have examined. These considerations do not appear to have been of interest or concern to the Old Testament authors; in fact, there is no indication that these authors would have thought of such kinds of "purity." The purity is rather in regard to reliability or truthfulness.

I must emphasize that the Bible's insistence that God speaks pure words and is always truthful does not preclude Him from using a wide diversity of literary and/or oral devices: parable, phenomenological language, metaphor, hyperbole, and so forth. "True words" can include hyperbolic words, for instance; but they must be recognized as such and interpreted within that framework. If a narrative (for example, the story of the prodigal son) is not *historical* narrative, but belongs to some other genre, then the truthfulness of the narrative is measured by its conformity to reality once it has been interpreted within the framework of the genre to which it gives evidence of belonging. These are hermeneutical issues largely dealt with by another chapter in this volume. In this chapter, I assume that these hermeneutical cautions are understood and do not have to be repeated constantly, and I recognize that in some instances they are difficult to apply. But once granted, they do not adversely affect the main point of this chapter but contribute to its applicability to all of the various literary styles and forms found in Scripture.

On the other hand, there is no hint from these Old Testament passages that the flawless reliability or truthfulness of God's words are limited to certain matters, such as matters of "faith and practice," or the "main points" of each message, or certain kinds of "revelatory" material. It is "every word" of God that is flawless (Prov. 30:5), not just some words, and these words are "flawless" and "pure," not marred by impurities in unreliable statements about minor details. Far from having small parts that are untruthful, God's words are said to be "very pure" (Ps. 119:140), "like silver refined in a furnace on the ground, purified seven times" (Ps. 12:6). This kind of statement excludes the possibility of any untruthfulness on seemingly minor details.

PSALM 119:89

Psalm 119 is an extensive discussion of the qualities of the written words of God that are available to the psalmist (see above, p. 32). In this context, he says, "For ever, O LORD, your word is firmly fixed in the heavens" (Ps. 119:89). This is an unusual statement, because the context shows that "your word" refers to God's written words. How could he say that the words he reads are forever fixed in the heavens?

The word *niṣṣāb* ("fixed," a Niphal participle from the root *nṣb*) means "to stand, to be stationed," and here means "to stand firm."[36] God's word stands firm forever in the heavens, the place of God's abode. This implies that according to the psalmist God's written words are actually a copy of words that God in heaven has permanently decided on and has subsequently caused to be committed to writing by men. Briggs writes of this verse, "The divine Law was everlasting, preexistent in heaven before it came down to earth as the latter rabbins understood it . . . immutable for all future time in generation after generation of mankind."[37]

This immutability and perpetual establishment in heaven of these written words of God surely implied total reliability and truthfulness to the mind of the psalmist. For he was convinced that God hated all falsehood and untruthfulness (Ps. 119:43, 69, 86, 160, 163; cf. Ps. 62:4; Prov. 13:5; Zeph. 3:13, et al.). Therefore, he could see God's written words remaining forever in heaven by God's pleasure only if they were words wholly devoid of falsehood, words that would forever remain as a reminder of God's love for absolute truthfulness in speech.

PSALM 119:96

"I have seen a limit to all perfection, but your commandment is exceedingly broad," writes the psalmist. The contrast is between all the human or creaturely works that he observes and God's written commandments, the subject of the psalm. The perfection (*tiḵlâh*) of all that he sees has an end or limit (*qēṣ*), but God's commandment is different: he can see no limit, so far-reaching is its perfection. It is unlimited in its perfection. Once again the author sees a qualitative contrast between God's written words and all other works, including all other human words. God's written words are unlimited in their perfection; no other words can be assessed in that way.

PSALM 119:160

"The sum of your words[38] is truth, and every one of your right-eous ordinances endures forever" (Ps. 119:160). The second clause is similar in meaning to Psalm 119:89, except that it specifies "every one" of God's ordinances rather than calling them collectively God's "word."

The first clause speaks of the truth of God's words. "Sum" is used elsewhere to refer to the total of a census count (Exod. 30:12; Num. 1:2, 49, et al.). It here represents the result obtained by combining and evaluating all of God's words: the result is "truth." The word used here (*'emet*) is the most common word for "truth" in the Old Testament and can signify both epistemological truth (truth as opposed to lies and falsehood, Deut. 13:14 [15]; 17:4; 22:20; 1 Kings 22:16; 2 Chron. 18:15; Ps. 15:2) and ethical truth (truth or faithfulness as opposed to sin, Gen. 24:49; 49:29; 1 Kings 2:4; 3:6, et al.). In this context the subject is the written words of God, but the emphasis is on their relationship to human behavior. So neither sense can be legitimately excluded.

When the psalmist adds together all the words of God, the result is truth: they are all reliable, truthful, firm, able to be trusted and depended on. There is no falsehood or unreliability in them. The NIV translates Psalm 119:160, "All your words are true."

Yet something more than the truth of all the individual words may be implied here. If the sum of them is truth, then there is affirmed an internal consistency to God's words as well: they do not contradict each other or show other words of God to be false.

PROVERBS 8:8

Wisdom is pictured here as saying to people: "All the words (*'imrê*) of my mouth are righteous; there is nothing twisted or crooked in them" (Prov. 8:8). The close connection of wisdom with God's eternal purposes in Proverbs 8:22–31 implies that to the mind of the writer the words of wisdom's mouth (v. 8) are probably words that God Himself has spoken. (Even if this is not so, the words of wisdom are very wise human words whose purity and truthfulness certainly cannot be less than that of God's words. In either case, therefore, there is in this verse a characterization that can rightly be applied to God's words.)

Once again this verse indicates the total reliability of all parts of the words spoken by God. Nothing in them needs to be improved or straightened out because there is nothing "twisted" (*pātal*, Niphal) or "crooked" (*'iqqēš*, "twisted, perverted") in them. Although the emphasis is on moral guidance (the words are righteous), it should not be overlooked that the writer here affirms the total purity of these words in all their parts. The reader is encouraged never to suspect any element of these words, never to be "on guard," thinking that some minor imperfections will have to be filtered out because they are unworthy of full and complete trust. No untrustworthy words are ever spoken by this mouth of God's wisdom.

ISAIAH 66:2

According to the following prophecy of Isaiah, God speaks to describe the kind of attitude that is pleasing to Him: "This is the man to whom I will look, he that is humble and contrite in spirit, and trembles at my word" (Isa. 66:2). This prophecy advocates a response to God's word (*dābār*) that is appropriate only when responding to God Himself: to tremble in reverence and awe. This is an exhortation to respond to God's word exactly as if one were responding to God Himself. In terms of this text, it seems that to respond to God's word *is* to respond to God.

Furthermore, "trembling" suggests a complete acceptance of that word, an unwillingness to think any of it unworthy of trust or obedience, and a refusal to challenge or call into question any of that word. To tremble before God's word is to submit to it and accept it, to believe it and obey it absolutely.

SUMMARY

We have by no means exhausted all the relevant Old Testament texts on this subject. Many other passages speak of loving God's words, of meditating on them day and night, treasuring them in one's heart, living by them, etc. But these few passages have at least given us a glimpse of the attitudes of several Old Testament authors toward God's words, especially God's words as spoken and written by men. These words are viewed consistently by the Old Testament authors as different in character and truth status from all other human words; in character, they are God's words, not merely man's. What these words say, God says. In truth status they are seen as being different from all other human words, for human words invariably contain falsehood and error (Ps. 116:11), but these do not; they are spoken by God who never lies (Num. 23:19; 1 Sam. 15:29). They are completely truthful (Ps. 119:160) and free from impurity or unreliability of any kind (Ps. 12:6 [7]; 18:30 [31]; 119:89, 96, 160; Prov. 8:8; 30:5–6). The appropriate response to God's word is to tremble before it (Isa. 66:2).

There is not yet an indication of how much of our present Old Testament would be included in the intention of these authors when they speak of "God's words," especially God's words in written form. A final determination of that question is difficult to find within the limits of the Old Testament text itself, although some help can be found in later Jewish literature.[39] For our purposes, however, it is enough to note at this point that these categories of divine words (spoken directly, spoken through men, and written) were commonly acknowledged, and to note the extremely high view of the purity and truthfulness of whatever words were thought to be included in any of those categories.

EXTRABIBLICAL LITERATURE

Space allows only a brief mention of the high views of the Old Testament Scriptures found in Jewish literature in the period after the completion of the writings now considered canonical. When the rabbis speak of Scripture, their views are every bit as strong as those found in the Old Testament when it spoke of prophets who were messengers of God. This is especially true of the supreme prophet, Moses, and his writing, the Torah. We read in the Talmud:

> Another[40] taught, "Because he hath despised the word of the Lord" (Num. 15:31)—this refers to him who maintains that the Torah is not from Heaven. And even if he asserts that the whole Torah is from Heaven, excepting a particular verse, which (he maintains) was not uttered by God but by Moses himself, he is included in "because he hath despised the word of the Lord." And even if he admits that the whole Torah is from Heaven, excepting a single point, a particular *ad majus* deduction or a certain *gezerah shawah*—he is still included in "because he hath despised the word of the Lord" (*b. Sanh.* 99a).

Views such as this are common in rabbinic literature.[41]

G. F. Moore writes that for the rabbinical schools "it was an uncontested axiom that every syllable of Scripture had the veracity and authority of the word of God."[42] For a similar example in the targums, see Targum Onkelos on Exodus 14:31, where the Masoretic text speaks of believing in the Lord but the targum interprets this to mean believing in the word (*mymr'*) of the Lord.

Josephus shows a similar high esteem for the authority of the Old Testament prophets. Where an Old Testament narrative simply reports that "God said to [David, et al.]," Josephus understands that the Old Testament author is thinking of a prophet through whom God spoke, and so he often introduces a prophet into the narrative (*Antiq.* 7:72, 294, 371; 8:197; 9:139; cf. Loeb edition, vol. 5, p. 677, n.b.). So he apparently sees no difference between direct speech from God and speech through a human prophet.[43] On the other hand, Josephus can say of something that had been foretold through a prophet, "God prophesied it" (*Antiq.* 9:145; 10:126). He says that the prophets alone had the privilege of writing the history of their people under the inspiration (*epipnoia*) of God. As a result, their books do not conflict with each other but are a clear and accurate record (*Ag. Ap.* 1:37–38). Then, after thus attributing the Old Testament to the work of the prophets, he reiterates the common Jewish attitude toward the Scriptures:

> We have given practical proof of our reverence for our own Scriptures. For, although such long ages have now passed, no one has ventured either to add, or to remove, or to alter a syllable; and it is an instinct with every Jew, from the day of his birth, to regard them as the decrees [*dogmata*] of God, to abide by them, and, if need be, cheerfully to die for them (*Ag. Ap.* 1:42).

Regarding Old Testament prophecy, Philo had a stronger view than that found in the Old Testament or any of the other literature we have examined. For, according to Philo, the human prophet contributed virtually nothing.

> For indeed the prophet, even when he seems to be speaking, really holds his peace, and his organs of speech, mouth and tongue, are wholly in the employ of Another (*Quis Her.* 266).

> For no pronouncement of a prophet is ever his own, but he is an interpreter prompted by Another in all his utterances (*Spec. Leg.* 4:49).

When the prophets speak, it is God who is speaking, for Philo wrote that God prophesied through the mouth of the prophets. Philo then quotes Jeremiah 2:13 (*Fug.* 197; cf. *Spec. Leg.* 2:189). The writings of the prophets, the sacred Scriptures, "are not monuments of knowledge and vision, but are the divine commands and divine words" (*Q. Gen.* 4:140).[44]

NEW TESTAMENT PERSPECTIVES
ON THE OLD TESTAMENT

The high view of the trustworthiness and reliability of God's words written by human authors that is seen in the Old Testament writings is reflected in many ways in the writings of the New Testament authors as well. This is especially clear in their use of the Old Testament.

MANY OLD TESTAMENT WRITINGS ARE THOUGHT OF AS GOD'S SPEECH

Throughout the New Testament there are citations of Old Testament texts that indicate that the Old Testament writings are considered God's speech. It is impossible here to discuss each text at length, but many are noted briefly in the following list.

Matthew 1:22: Isaiah's words in Isaiah 7:14 are cited as "what the Lord had spoken by the prophet."

Matthew 4:4: Jesus says to the devil, "Man shall not live by bread alone, but by every word that proceeds from the mouth of God." In the context of Jesus' frequent citations from Deuteronomy to answer every temptation, the words that proceed "from the mouth of God" are here best understood to be the written Scriptures of the Old Testament.

Matthew 19:5: The words of the author in Genesis 2:24, not attributed to God in the Genesis narrative, are quoted by Jesus as words that God "said."

Mark 7:9–13: What Jesus calls "the commandment of God" in verse 9 is cited in verse 10 as "Moses said." But in verse 13, what Moses said is called "the word [*logos*] of God." If we accept Markan priority here, it is significant that instead of "Moses said," Matthew 15:4 has "God commanded."

Luke 1:70: In Zechariah's prophecy, God is said to have "spoken [*elalēsen*] by the mouth of his holy prophets" in the Old Testament.

Luke 24:25: Jesus calls the disciples "foolish men" because they did not believe "all that the prophets have spoken [*elalēsan*]." This is then taken to refer to "all the scriptures" (v. 27). Moral culpability seems therefore to attach to not believing the Old Testament Scriptures. This suggests that they are viewed as God's words.

John 5:45–47: Speaking of the writings of Moses, Jesus says, "If you do not believe his writings, how will you believe my words?" (v. 47). Apparently, Moses' writings and Jesus' words are thought to have the same authority to compel belief.

Acts 1:16: "The Holy Spirit spoke beforehand [*proeipen*] by the mouth of David" (the words of Pss. 69:25; 109:8). Words of Scripture are said to be spoken by the Holy Spirit.

Acts 2:16–17: In quoting "what was spoken by the prophet Joel" in Joel 2:28–32, Peter inserts "says God," thus attributing to God words written by Joel.

Acts 3:18: God "foretold [*prokatēngeilen*] by the mouth of all the prophets" the sufferings of Christ.

Acts 3:21: "God spoke [*elalēsen*] by the mouth of his holy prophets from of old."

Acts 4:25: The prayer of the church is addressed to God who "spoke" (*eipen*) the words of Psalm 2:1–2 "by the mouth of ... David ... through [*dia*] the Holy Spirit." (The sentence is complex and has led to some variation in the text, but the sense is clear: God through the Holy Spirit spoke through David's words.)

Acts 13:47: Isaiah 49:6 is quoted by Paul and Barnabas as something that "the Lord commanded us." An Old Testament prophecy is seen not only as God's command, but also as one that places moral obligation on first-century Christians.

Acts 28:25: Paul says that the Holy Spirit spoke through (*elalēsen dia*) Isaiah the prophet.

Romans 1:2: The gospel is something that "God promised beforehand through his prophets in the holy scriptures."

Romans 3:2: The Jews are entrusted with the oracles (*ta logia*) of God. The Old Testament Scriptures, which the Jews cared for and preserved, were the oracles spoken by God.

Romans 9:17: Paul quotes God's speech in Exodus 9:16 as what "scripture says to Pharaoh." Apparently there is in Paul's mind an equivalence between the nature of what Scripture says and the nature of what God says.

First Corinthians 9:8–10: The "law" of Deuteronomy 25:4 is something that God now "speaks" (*legei*, present tense) for our sake (v. 10). Written words of the Old Testament are seen by Paul as words that God not only spoke in the past but continues to speak in the present.

Second Timothy 3:16: "All scripture is God-breathed [*theopneustos*]."[45] Here "scripture" (*graphē*) must refer to the Old Testament written Scripture, for that is what *graphē* refers to in every one of its fifty occurrences in the New Testament.[46] Furthermore, it is the "sacred writings" (*hiera grammata*) of the Old Testament that Paul has just referred to in the previous verse.

Paul affirms that all of the Old Testament writings are *theopneustos*, breathed out (compare *pneō* in the sense of "breathe out": BAG^2, p. 679) by God. Since it is writings that are said to be "breathed out," this breathing must be understood as a metaphor for speaking. This verse thus states in brief form what has been evident in many other passages so far: the Old Testament writings are regarded as God's words in written form. God is the one who spoke (and still speaks) them, although using human agents to write them down.

Hebrews 1:1–2: "In many and various ways God spoke [*lalēsas*] of old to the fathers by [*en* + dative] the prophets; but in these last days he has spoken to us by a Son [*elalēsen hēmin en hyiō*]." God's speech through the prophets is spoken of in the same way as His speech through Christ. This suggests an equivalence in character and authority for the words of Christ and those of the Old Testament prophets.

It is also significant to notice the vague way in which the manner of Old Testament inspiration is referred to: "many [or, many parts] and various ways." This is characteristic of both the Old Testament and the New Testament: while there is an abundance of evidence to affirm that the words of Scripture *are* God's words, there is almost no discussion of the *process* by which these words came to be written.

John J. Hughes is certainly correct at this point to call attention to the imprecise methodology of Jack Rogers and G. C. Berkouwer in their criticism of biblical inerrancy:

Both Rogers and Berkouwer fail adequately to distinguish the *mode of revelation* (dream, vision, dictation, etc.) from the *manner of inspiration* (the employment of various literary techniques and genres), from the *result of inspiration* (what Scripture says, God says), and the *purpose* of inspiration (to make us wise unto salvation). Apparently, they believe that to affirm both the purpose and manner of inspiration precludes affirming the result of inspiration.[47]

Hebrews 1:6–7: In quoting Deuteronomy 32:43 (LXX)[48] and Psalm 104:4, the author twice affirms that God "says" (*legei*) them.

Second Peter 1:21: Speaking of the prophecies of Scripture (v. 20), which means at least the Old Testament Scriptures to which Peter encourages his readers to give careful attention (v. 19), Peter says that none of these prophecies ever came "by the impulse [*thelēma,* "will"] of man," but that "men moved [lit. "carried along," *pheromenoi*] by the Holy Spirit spoke from God." It is not Peter's intention to deny completely human volition or personality in the writing of Scripture (the writers "spoke"), but rather to say that the ultimate source of every prophecy was never man's decision about what he wanted to write, but rather the Holy Spirit's action in the prophet's life, carried out in ways unspecified here or elsewhere in Scripture. This is similar to the Old Testament warnings against prophesying words of one's own mind, rather than words that God had given (Deut. 18:18, 20; Jer. 23:16, et al.). It indicates a similar belief that all of the Old Testament prophecies (and, in light of verses 19–20, this probably includes all of the written Scripture of the Old Testament) are spoken "from God."

INDIVIDUAL WORDS AND LETTERS OF THE OLD TESTAMENT ARE RELIED ON

Consistent with the view that the Old Testament writings are God's own speech is a willingness on the part of New Testament authors to rely on individual words or even letters of the Old Testament. Jesus' affirmation of the abiding validity of every "iota" and "dot" of the Old Testament law (Matt. 5:18) indicates such confidence. So also does the statement of Jesus in Luke 16:17: "It is easier for heaven and earth to pass away than for one dot of the law to become void." This is not foreign to New Testament thought: heaven and earth have been created by God and will one day be destroyed (Matt. 24:35; Heb. 1:10–12), but God's word reflects His unchanging veracity and eternal determination to speak exactly what He wills; thus, His word is, in the words of Psalm 119:89, forever "fixed in the heavens."

In Matthew 22:44–45 (Mark 12:36–37; Luke 20:42–44), Jesus proves that David calls the Messiah "Lord" from Psalm 110:1, "The Lord said to my Lord, sit at my right hand. . . ." Two different persons are implied by the two uses of the word *Lord:* the first is God the Father whom the Jews acknowledged; the second is the Messiah, whom David calls "my Lord" (NIV). In order for this argument to work, Jesus relies on the fact that Psalm 110:1 has David calling the Messiah "*my* Lord." Otherwise the text would not prove that the Messiah was David's Lord.[49]

Now the word *my* is signified by only one letter (י) in the consonantal Hebrew text: "my Lord" is אדני. A slight lengthening of the final consonant to ו would make "his Lord"; a bit more lengthening to ך would make "your Lord." In either case, the argument would no longer work. Here Jesus' argument depends on the reliability of one letter of the written Old Testament.

This is not a unique instance: many others are cited by R. Nicole, "New Testament Use of the Old Testament," in *Revelation and the Bible*, ed. Carl F. H. Henry (Grand Rapids: Baker, 1958), p. 139.

MINOR DETAILS OF OLD TESTAMENT PROPHECIES ARE SEEN TO BE FULFILLED IN CHRIST'S LIFE

Also indicative of a high regard for the reliability of all of the Old Testament is the frequent reference to a seemingly obscure detail of an Old Testament prophecy that was fulfilled in Christ's life. The following list is not exhaustive, but it does give enough examples to indicate an unwillingness to think of any detail of the Old Testament as "unreliable" because it was not crucial to the "main point" of the prophecy.

Micah 5:2	Matthew 2:5	He was born in Bethlehem.
Zech. 9:9	John 12:14–15	He rode to Jerusalem on a donkey.
Psalm 41:9	John 13:18	His betrayer ate bread with Him.
Psalm 22:18	John 19:24	Lots were cast for His garments.
Psalm 69:21	(John 19:28–30)[50]	He was given vinegar to drink.
Psalm 34:20	John 19:36	None of His bones were broken.
Zech. 12:10	John 19:37	He was pierced with a sword.
Isaiah 53:9	(Matt. 27:57–60)[50]	He was buried in a rich man's grave.

The ways in which the New Testament "fulfills" the Old Testament, or the interpretive patterns bound up with typology (for instance), do not affect the main point. What is here at issue is not how the New Testament writers perceived that this or that Old Testament passage pointed to Christ (which is a separate issue), but that they often focused on relatively obscure Old Testament details.

MINOR HISTORICAL DETAILS OF THE OLD TESTAMENT ARE TREATED AS TRUSTWORTHY AND RELIABLE

While it is often argued today that the truthfulness of the Bible need not extend to every historical detail,[51] the New Testament authors give no indication of any unwillingness to trust even the smallest historical details of the Old Testament narrative. In the following list are some of the historical details cited by New Testament authors. If all of these are matters of "faith and practice," then every historical detail of the Old Testament is a matter of "faith and practice." On the other hand, if so many details can be affirmed, then it seems that all of the historical details in the Old Testament can be affirmed as true.

Matthew 12:3–4 (Mark 2:25–26; Luke 6:3–4)	David ate the bread of the Presence.
Matthew 12:40	Jonah was in the whale.
Matthew 12:41 (Luke 11:30, 32)	The men of Nineveh repented.[52]
Matthew 12:42 (Luke 11:31)	The Queen of the South came to hear Solomon.
Matthew 23:35 (Luke 11:51)	Zechariah[53] was murdered between the sanctuary and the altar.
Luke 4:25–26	Elijah was sent to the widow of Zarephath.
Luke 4:27	Naaman the Syrian was cleansed of leprosy.
Luke 17:29	On the day Lot left Sodom fire and brimstone rained from heaven.
Luke 17:32	"Remember Lot's wife" (who turned to salt for looking back at Sodom).
John 3:14	Moses lifted up the serpent in the wilderness.
John 4:5	Jacob gave a field to Joseph.
Acts 13:17–23	Several details of the history of Israel are cited by Paul.
Romans 4:10	Abraham believed and received the promise before he was circumcised.
Romans 4:19	Abraham was about a hundred years old.
Romans 9:10–12	God told Rebecca before her children were born that the elder child would serve the younger.
Romans 11:2–4	Elijah spoke with God, as recorded in 1 Kings 19:10, 18.
1 Corinthians 10:11	The people of Israel passed through the sea, ate and drank spiritual food and drink, desired evil, sat down to drink, rose up to dance, indulged in immorality, grumbled, and were destroyed (vv. 1–11).
	Then Paul says that these things "happened" (*synebainen*, v. 11). The verb *synbaino* is commonly used to refer to historical events that "took place" or "happened" (Luke 24:14;

Acts 3:10, 20:19, 21:35; 1 Peter 4:12; 2 Peter 2:22).[54] Paul has no hesitancy in affirming that even extremely obscure details of the Old Testament ("the people sat down to eat and rose up to dance") both *happened* and were written down for our instruction.

Hebrews 7:2	Abraham gave a tenth of everything to Melchizedek.
Hebrews 9:1–5	Detailed descriptions of the Old Testament tabernacle are reported.
Hebrews 9:19–21	Moses sprinkled the people and the tabernacle vessels with blood and water, using scarlet wool and hyssop.
Hebrews 11:3	The world was created by the word of God. This is not a "minor" detail, but it is useful as an example of a "scientific" fact that is affirmed in the Old Testament. The author says that we know this scientific/historical fact "by faith." Faith here is explicitly said to involve trust in the truthfulness of a scientific and historical fact recorded in Old Testament Scripture.
Hebrews 11, passim	Many details of the lives of Abel, Enoch, Noah, Abraham, Moses, Rahab, and others are recounted as events that actually happened.
Hebrews 12:16–17	Esau sold his birthright for a single meal, and later sought it back with tears.
James 2:25	Rahab received the spies and sent them out another way.
1 Peter 3:20; 2 Peter 2:5	Eight persons were saved in the ark.
2 Peter 2:6–7	God turned Sodom and Gommorah to ashes but saved Lot.
2 Peter 2:16	Balaam's donkey spoke.

This list indicates a willingness on the part of the New Testament writers to rely on the truthfulness of any part of the historical narratives of the Old Testament. No detail is too insignificant to be used for the instruction of New Testament Christians. There is no indication of any thought that there was a certain category of Old Testament statements that were unreliable and untrustworthy (such as "nonrevelational statements"[55] or "historical and scientific" statements, as opposed to doctrinal and moral passages).

In fact, the statement of the purpose of Scripture in 2 Timothy 3:16 certainly is not intended to limit the types of statements in the Old Testament that can be relied on; it is "all scripture" that is "profitable for teaching, for reproof, for correction, and for training in righteousness." For the instruction and edification of the early Christians the New Testament authors were willing to use *any* historical (or "scientific")[56] statement of the Old Testament, to affirm that it happened as God said in His written words, and to draw lessons from it for contemporary hearers. "All scripture," every detail of Scripture, is useful for this purpose, says Paul.

Moreover, against the background of the idea of the permanence of Scripture (Ps. 119:89; Matt. 5:18; Luke 16:17), Paul's affirmation of the usefulness of every part of Scripture becomes even more significant. For it to be eternally useful for edification, God's word must be an abiding testimony to the veractiy of God's speech: Untruthful statements would be unprofitable and bring dishonor to God by portraying Him as one who at times speaks untruthfully, and they would serve as an encouragement to people to imitate God and sometimes speak untruthfully as well. This would be morally destructive, not edifying. In order to be fully and perpetually profitable, and in order always to bring glory to God, all the statements in God's written words must be trustworthy.

HOW MUCH OF THE OLD TESTAMENT IS SAID TO BE WORTHY OF BELIEF BY NEW TESTAMENT CHRISTIANS?

The citations listed above from all parts of the Old Testament are enough to indicate inductively that all of the Old Testament was treated by the New Testament authors as (1) words that God Himself spoke and (2) reliable in whatever they represented as having happened. But there are also several passages that state this reliance on the Old Testament explicitly.

In Luke 24:25, the disciples are rebuked for not believing "*all* that the prophets have spoken." Then in verse 27, Luke reports Jesus as using "*all* the scriptures" to teach about Himself. Although it is difficult to define the limits of the Old Testament canon from data within the Old Testament itself, it is not difficult to demonstrate that for first-century Jews the canon of the Old Testament included exactly the books of the Protestant Old Testament today.[57] It is "all" of these that are said to speak about Christ. This categorization is made more explicit in Luke 24:44 where Jesus speaks of the necessity for the fulfillment of all that was "written" about Him "in the law of Moses and the prophets and the psalms."

Peter said that God foretold the sufferings of the Messiah by the mouth of "*all* the prophets" (Acts 3:18).

Paul, standing before Felix, said that he worshiped God while (or by) "believing *everything* [*pisteuōn pasi*] laid down by the law or written in the prophets" (Acts 24:14).

Romans 15:4 reaffirms the value of everything written in the Old Testament: "Whatever [*hosa*] was written in former days was written for our instruction, that by steadfastness and by the encouragement of the scriptures we might have hope."

These statements affirm in a general way what was evident from the many specific references quoted earlier: to the New Testament authors, every part of the Old Testament was God's very word, and was worthy of absolute trust.

THE NEW TESTAMENT AS WORDS OF GOD

At last we come to a consideration of the New Testament writings themselves. Did the New Testament writers consider their writings equal to the Old Testament Scriptures in character and truth status? There are several indications that they did.

First, it is evident that the New Testament authors thought it possible for God to speak directly to people in human language, for there are recorded instances of such direct speech from God at the baptism of Jesus (Matt. 3:17; Mark 1:11; Luke 3:22), the Transfiguration (Matt. 17:5; Mark 9:7; Luke 9:35; 2 Peter 1:17–18), the voice from the Father speaking to Jesus (John 12:28), the conversion of Saul (Acts 9:4; 26:14–18, from the risen Lord), the instructions to Ananias (Acts 9:11–16), Peter's vision (Acts 10:13), events during Paul's journeys (Acts 18:9–10; 23:11), and the revelation to John (Rev. 1:11–3:22).

Furthermore, there is abundant evidence of God's speech through human lips, both in the words of Jesus (Matt. 5:22, et al.; Luke 5:1; John 3:34 ["he whom God has sent utters the words of God"]; 6:63, 68; 8:47; 12:48, 49–50 ["the Father who sent me has himself given me commandment what to say and what to speak"]; 14:10; 14:24 ["the word which you hear is not mine but the Father's who sent me"]; 15:22; 17:8, 14) and in the words of the apostles (Matt. 10:19–20; Luke 10:16; John 17:8; Acts 2:41; 4:29, 31; 2 Cor. 13:3; Gal. 1:8–9, 10–11,[58] 1 Thess. 2:13).

But were the New Testament writings thought to be God's words in the same sense as the Old Testament writings? Using only the data of the New Testament itself, we are in a situation analogous to that which arose with the Old Testament: It is possible to show that *some* of the New Testament writings are thought to be God's words, but one cannot prove conclusively that all of the New Testament writings were so regarded, at least not by using the data of the New Testament alone.

Nevertheless, the authors' claims that they are writing God's words are quite strong. There is a hint of that claim in John's record of the promise of Jesus that the Holy Spirit would bring to the remembrance of the disciples all that Jesus said to them (John 14:26).[59] Those who believe are to keep (or obey, *tēreō*) the disciples' words just as they keep Jesus' words (John 15:20). The Spirit of truth will guide them into all the truth (John 16:13).

A related statement about the authority of apostolic writings is found in 2 Peter 3:2, where the readers are told to remember not only the Old Testament prophets,[60] but also "the commandment of the Lord and Savior through [their] apostles." Since this is a "reminder" to the readers (v. 1), it is probably—though not certainly—written commands that he exhorts them to remember. This would make the apostolic commands mentioned in verse 2 parallel in form to the writings of the Old Testament apostles also mentioned in that verse.

Further support for this view can be found in 2 Peter 3:16. There the author shows not only an awareness of the existence of written epistles from Paul but also a clear willingness to classify "all of his [Paul's] epistles" with "the other scriptures [*tas loipas graphas*]." Since *graphē* in the New Testament always refers to the Old Testament Scriptures, which both Jews and Christians held to be the authoritative words of God, it is noteworthy that Peter here classifies all of Paul's epistles as *graphai*. This is an indication that very early in the history of the church Paul's epistles were considered to be God's written words in the same sense as the Old Testament texts.

Paul's writings themselves show some evidence of a claim to write "words of God": "This is what we speak, not in words taught by human wisdom but taught by the Spirit, interpreting spiritual things in spiritual words (1 Cor. 2:13).[61]

The verse is occasionally taken to refer to believers generally, but the more common view is that it refers to Paul or to Paul and his companions. The latter explanation is preferable for several reasons: (1) The context is one of Paul's defense of his own ministry. (2) The subsequent rebuke of the Corinthians for being unable even to *receive* more advanced teaching (3:1–4) makes it virtually impossible that they would be included among those who could speak of it or teach it to others. (3) The *laloumen* ("we speak") in verse 13 refers to the same speaking as the speaking (*laloumen*) of wisdom in verse 6, with which Paul began the passage. This is a speaking "among those who are mature," and Paul excludes the Corinthians (who were like "infants" [3:1]) from this category.[62] Thus, the Corinthians themselves are not included in the "we" of verse 13.

Whether the "we" of 1 Corinthians 2:13 is a reference to Paul alone or to a wider group of mature Christian preachers cannot be conclusively determined from the context. The clear "I" sections in 1:17; 2:1; 3:1 argue in favor of restricting it to Paul alone, while the switch to the first person plural in 2:6–16 may imply that Paul is speaking of general truths applicable to more than himself alone. (However, note Paul's changes from first person singular to plural in 2 Cor. 10:1, 11; cf. also 10:13 with 12:1).

What is clear is that at least for himself, and at most for some limited group of Christian preachers, Paul claims (1) to have received information from God by revelation (*apekalypsen*, v. 10), and (2) to speak of this revelation concerning the things given by God (v. 12) in words taught by the Spirit.[63]

The picture of Paul's being "taught" words by the Holy Spirit is similar to the Old Testament picture of a prophet's hearing a message from God and then speaking it to the people. Also in a manner similar to that of the Old Testament prophets, Paul singles out the words themselves, not simply the general content, as is evident from the fact that the question of eloquent speech is under consideration.

One objection to a parallel between Old Testament prophets and New Testament apostles might be brought from 1 Corinthians 7:12, where Paul distinguishes his words from those of the Lord: "To the rest I say, not the Lord. . . . " It is undeniable that such a distinction is made, but it must be evaluated in the light of verses 25 and 40. In verse 25 Paul says he has no command (*epitagē*) of the Lord concerning the unmarried, but will give his own opinion. This means at least that he had possession of no earthly word of Jesus on this subject and probably also that he had received no subsequent revelation about it. In verse 12, then, the meaning must be that in this area Paul had no earthly words of Jesus that he could quote.

It is remarkable therefore that Paul can go on in 1 Corinthians 7:12–15 to give several specific ethical standards, apparently with the full expectation that he will be believed and obeyed by the Corinthians. The explanation is found in the fact that Paul has obtained mercy from the Lord to be trustworthy (v. 25), and by this statement he seemingly implies that his considered judgments were able to be placed on the same authoritative level as the words of Jesus.[64] Nor could the Corinthians claim that Paul was acting contrary to the Holy Spirit when he assumed such authority. In a classic example of ironic understatement, Paul says, "And I think that I have the Spirit of God" (v. 40).

There is a difference here between Paul and the Old Testament prophets, but it is not one that establishes a lesser authority for his words. Rather, 1 Corinthians 7:12 shows that Paul exceeded all of the Old Testament prophets in at least one respect: He had been given such reliable judgment and insight into God's will that at times he needed no specific revelation to speak with divine authority.

In 1 Corinthians 14:37–38, Paul writes, "If anyone thinks that he is a prophet, or spiritual, he should acknowledge that what I am writing to you is a command of the Lord [*ha graphō hymin hoti kyriou estin entolē*].[65] If anyone does not recognize this, he is not recognized."[66]

So Paul claims here that what he writes to the Corinthians is itself a command of the Lord. How much of the preceding discourse is comprehended by the phrase "the things I write to you" is perhaps impossible to determine with certainty, but we can note that it comes exactly at the end of the discussion of spiritual gifts (chapters 12–14) and would seem most naturally to apply to the entire section. It might be argued that this statement refers only to the preceding sentence, or to the directive about women (vv. 33–35). However, it is so general and is made so indefinite by the use of the plural that such a restriction appears highly artificial. Paul's purpose is to conclude the discussion and at the same time to bar the way for any prophet at Corinth to propound "in the Spirit" new rules that would contradict those given by Paul. Certainly this concern applies to the whole range of directives for worship, reaching back to chapters 12 and 13, and perhaps even to chapter 11.

But this means that in 1 Corinthians 14:37 there is a very strong statement of the authority of Paul's written words. For it is inconceivable that all the instructions in 1 Corinthians 12–14 are based on words of the earthly Jesus handed down to Paul through oral or written tradition (otherwise we would certainly have echoes of such a large group of "*charismata–logia*" elsewhere in the New Testament). Rather, Paul has here instituted a number of new rules for church worship at Corinth and has claimed for them the status of "commands of the Lord."[67]

In 1 Thessalonians 4:15 Paul says, "For this we declare to you in a word of the Lord" (trans. mine). C. Masson argues that his was not a saying of the earthly Jesus preserved in tradition, because it is unthinkable that the evangelists would have possessed such a decisive word on so burning an issue in the early church without recording it.[68] Additional difficulty for the view that this is an "earthly" saying is raised by use of the first person for believers remaining alive (vv. 15, 17) and the reference to the Lord in the third person (vv. 16, 17). At most it would have to be an allusion to a saying of Jesus, but this hardly seems to call for the strong introduction: "For this we declare to you in a word of the Lord" (literal translation).

Furthermore, the idea of speaking "in a word of the Lord" has an Old Testament counterpart that always suggests prophetic speech: *bidḇar YHWH* ("in a word of the Lord").[69] Thus, the most likely solution is to understand Paul as claiming in 1 Thessalonians 4:15 that he himself[70] is speaking words that were also the very words of the Lord.[71]

In 1 Timothy 5:18 Paul[72] writes, "For the scripture [*graphē*] says, 'You shall not muzzle an ox when it is treading out the grain,' and, 'The laborer deserves his wages.'" The first quotation is from Deuteronomy 25:4, but the second occurs nowhere in the Old Testament. It does occur, however, in Luke 10:7, in exactly the same words cited by Paul. This means that Paul is quoting Luke's Gospel as *graphē* ("Scripture").[73] Since *graphē* in the New Testament always is used of the Old

Testament Scripture (fifty out of fifty times), we have here an instance of Paul's putting Luke's Gospel in the same category as Old Testament Scripture.

In brief, we have strong evidence that the early church soon began to receive some New Testament writings as "words of God" equal to the Old Testament.

Revelation 22:18–19 contains an inscriptional curse, warning of severe punishment from God for anyone who adds to or takes away from the words of "this book." In the first instance, "this book" refers to the book of Revelation itself, and the prohibition against tampering with the words implies that the writer wants his readers to think of the book as words of God (cf. Deut. 4:2; 12:32; Prov. 30:6).

But perhaps it is possible to make one further observation about this inscriptional curse. For one who believes that God oversaw the compilation of the New Testament, the fact that these verses occur at the end of this particular book cannot be seen as a mere coincidence. Revelation is the book that primarily describes for us the distant future and it most naturally belongs at the end of the canon, just as Genesis, which describes the distant past, belongs at the beginning. Therefore, it may not be inappropriate to think of Revelation 22:18–19 as having a secondary application to the whole of the Bible that precedes it. Understood in this way, these verses both close the canon and simultaneously warn all future generations that all the words that go before are God's very words, and to add to them or take from them is to invite eternal death.

OTHER STATEMENTS ABOUT THE CHARACTER OF SCRIPTURE

Once it is clear (1) that all of the Old Testament writings are considered God's words, (2) that the written words of God are thought by both Old Testament and New Testament authors to be equal in character and truth-status to God's words spoken directly to men, and (3) that the New Testament writings, as they became accepted as "Scripture," were thought to be just as fully God's words as the words of the Old Testament, then any New Testament passage that speaks of some characteristic of God's words can properly be applied to all of the Old Testament and to as much of the New Testament as is accepted as Scripture. For to the New Testament authors, Scripture *is* God's words, and to say something about the character of God's speech is to say something about the character of Scripture.

Thus it is appropriate to apply Titus 1:2 to written Scripture: It speaks of the "hope of eternal life which God, who never lies [*ho apseudēs theos*, 'the unlying God'], promised ages ago." Because God never lies, because His character is that of an "unlying God" who cannot speak a lie (*pseudēs*), therefore His promises can always be trusted. These of course were written promises in Scripture. But if all of Scripture is spoken by God, as both Old Testament and New Testament authors believed, then Scripture also must be "unlying" (*apseudēs*). There can be no falsehood or untruthfulness in Scripture.

Hebrews 6:18 mentions two unchangeable things (God's oath and His promise) "in which it is impossible for God to lie" (NIV). Once again the total truthfulness of all that God promises is strongly affirmed; in fact, the author says not merely that God does not lie, but that it is *not possible* for him to lie. Although the immediate reference is only to oaths and promises, if it is impossible for God to lie in these utterances, that certainly must imply that it is impossible for Him ever to lie.[74] Once again, then, we have an affirmation that can be seen as more evidence that the New Testament authors saw all of Scripture as truthful and completely reliable.

Further evidence of a similar sort is seen in John 17:17, where Jesus says to the Father, "Thy word is truth [*alētheia*]."[75] It is also very plain in John 10:35, where Jesus says, "Scripture cannot be broken [*lythēnai*; here, 'annulled, made void']." Jesus is here making a statement about "Scripture" in general. It is a characteristic of Scripture that it cannot be thought untrue or wrong. Since that is true of Scripture as a whole, it is true, according to Jesus, of one particular word in Psalm 82:6: the word *gods* in reference to human judges. If Jesus would thus use the absolute reliability of Scripture as a whole to establish the correctness of one particular word chosen to apply to human judges (certainly not one of the "central doctrines" of the Bible), then should we not follow His example and affirm that the absolute reliability of Scripture establishes the correctness of *every* word of Scripture?

Several passages therefore indicate that God never lies and that it is appropriate to apply these descriptions of God's unlying character to the words of Scripture as well. Furthermore, the fact that God never lies and cannot lie means not merely that He always acts in a morally right way or that He never speaks falsehood for a bad purpose. "To lie" (*pseudomai*) often means to affirm in words something that is untrue, that does not correspond to reality, no matter whether the intentions are good or bad, and no matter whether one's conduct of life is morally good or bad apart from the affirmation (Matt. 5:11; Acts 5:3–4; Rom. 9:1 [good intentions were not in doubt]; 2 Cor. 11:31; Gal. 1:20; Col. 3:9; 1 Tim. 2:7; cf. *pseudos* [of speech] in Eph. 4:25 and the description of "truth" as correspondence to reality in Luke 1:4; John 8:17; 10:41; 19:35; 21:24). For the New Testament writers to say that God does not lie was to say that Scripture, which was to them God's words, never affirms anything that is contrary to fact.

The contrast between Satan, who is "father of lies" (John 8:44), and God, who "never lies," is reflected in other passages that speak of God's love for truthfulness in speech and His hatred of falsehood and of the imitation of those qualities in His children (John 8:44, 55; Col. 3:9–10; 1 Thess. 2:3; 1 Tim. 1:10; 2:7; Rev. 2:2; 21:8). God loves truthfulness and hates falsehood in speech, and this fact seems to give even greater certainty that He will never speak something that is untrue.

THE QUESTIONS OF IMPRECISE STATEMENTS, FREE QUOTATIONS, AND DESCRIPTIVE LANGUAGE

At the end of this analysis of texts that speak of the Bible's truthfulness it is important to distinguish this claim to truthfulness from three other possible claims that the Bible does not make for itself. Such a distinction must be made when considering the questions of imprecise statements, free quotations, and descriptive language about the natural world.

It must be remembered that there is a difference between precision and truthfulness. To argue for the total *truthfulness* of Scripture is certainly not to argue for technical *precision* at every point, for a statement can be imprecise and still be completely true. Consider the following statements: (1) "My home is not far from my office." (2) "My home is about one and a half miles from my office." (3) "My home is 1.6 miles from my office." All three statements are absolutely true (or "inerrant"). All three are completely free of falsehood; they contain no errors. Even though (3) is much more precise then (1), it is not more "true" than (1). Both (1) and (3) are completely true, even though they have different degrees of precision. (And a land surveyor could presumably make a statement that is even more precise than statement [3].)

Similar considerations apply to the matter of quotations. The statement "I said, 'My home is not far from my office,'" would be a verbatim quotation of statement (1) above and the quotation would be completely true. But the statement "I said that I lived near my place of work," though using several different words, would still be (in ordinary conversation at least) a perfectly acceptable and truthful report of what I had said.

In the Bible we sometimes find, for example, round numbers or approximations in measurements and in battle figures. These statements are not highly precise, but they can still be completely true. We also find in the New Testament quotations of the Old Testament or quotations of Jesus that are not verbatim quotations of the type we find in precise scholarly writing today, but that are closer to the kind of indirect quotation mentioned in the example above. Even though they do not report the exact words used, they faithfully represent the content of the person or text cited.

These instances of nontechnical reporting should not be urged as counterexamples that contradict the many texts that affirm the Bible's total truthfulness, for they are merely instances of a lack of highly technical precision, not instances of falsehood or error. The emphasis of the many texts cited above is on the *truthfulness* of God's speech in the Bible. No texts were found to claim any particular level of precision in measurement or any adherence to one certain style of quotation.

The question then arises, How imprecise can a statement be and still be true? In the example given above, the statement "My home is four miles from my office" would be false, as would the statement "I said that my home was very far from my offiice." But between what would clearly be true and what would clearly be false there is a wide range of possible statements. The degree of imprecision that would be acceptable as "truthful" speech would vary according to the situation in which I was speaking, the degree of precision implied by my statements, and the degree of precision that would ordinarily be expected by my hearers in that particular context. It would be difficult to define in advance what degree of precision would be required in order for speech to be truthful, for one would need more information about each individual situation in question.

When we ask what degree of precision is necessary for biblical statements to be completely *true*, an analysis of individual texts in Scripture will be very helpful to us (see, for example, chapter 5 concerning the New Testament use of the Old Testament). We should not expect to find one particular level of precision throughout the whole Bible (such as "round off to the nearest hundred soldiers killed") but degrees of precision that will vary according to the different kinds of purpose, subject matter, historical setting, and literary type that characterize the different parts of Scripture.

What is important for our purposes in this chapter is to emphasize the differences between imprecision and untruthfulness. In contemporary discussions about biblical "inerrancy" the question is not whether the Bible contains statements that lack technical precision (all agree that it does) but whether it contains clearly false affirmations (on this there is disagreement). There may be some texts about which some will say they contain not imprecision but actual falsehood, while others will say they contain only imprecision. Those cases will have to be dealt with on an individual basis. (In most cases these are not the really crucial texts in the "inerrancy" discussion anyway.) My purpose here is only to point out the difference between precision and truthfulness and to emphasize that it is the total *truthfulness* of Scripture that is affirmed again and again in Scripture itself.

One further distinction must be made. Statements that describe the natural world can be completely truthful even though they are stated in ordinary descriptive or observational language, not in terms of twentieth-century scientific knowledge. The Bible says that the sun "rises" and "goes down" (Gen. 15:12; 19:23; Ps. 50:1; Matt. 5:45, et al.). These are descriptions of what the speaker observed, and they are accurate descriptions from the speaker's perspective. One might object that from a vantage point somewhere else in our solar system, perhaps from the vantage point of the sun, the sun does not really "rise" or "go down," for the earth rotates. But from the same vantage point the rain does not really go "down"; rather, it is pulled by gravity toward the center of the earth, even though at any given moment it may be going "up" or "sideways" from the standpoint of a viewer out in space. But from the observational standpoint of a person here on earth, the rain does indeed "fall" and the sun does indeed "rise" and "go down." These are accurate and truthful descriptions of what he observes and, with respect to that person, they are true.

It is important to remember again at this point that the Bible emphasizes that its statements are *true*, *not* that the human authors had omniscience or that they were given special insight into future scientific knowledge. (The latter may or may not have been true at some points, but it is not our present concern and it is not taught in the passages we examined.) For their statements to be truthful, it is necessary only that the biblical authors accurately observed and recorded what they saw, and that they did not go beyond those observations to affirm speculative but false theories about what they could not themselves observe. (Thus, the Bible is remarkably free from affirmations that the sun goes around the earth, or that the earth is flat, or that the earth rests on a giant turtle or elephant, and so forth.)

In summary, it is important to note that the Bible repeatedly affirms its own *truthfulness*, but that this affirmation does not imply a claim to a very high level of *precision* or to a practice of *verbatim quotation* or to the possession of *future scientific knowledge*. These elements are not essential to complete truthfulness in speech and writing.

THE QUESTION OF "ACCOMMODATION" TO HUMAN ERROR

Before an attempt is made to summarize and define clearly the conclusions that can be drawn from the texts examined above, it will be useful to consider one particular view of the nature of God's words in Scripture, a view that is quite widely held at the present time. This viewpoint can be called the concept of "accommodation"; that is, the view that "the God who lovingly willed to communicate revelational truth to men deliberately *accommodated* his language in nonrevelational matters to the way the original readers viewed the world about them, so as to enhance the communication of revelational truth, by which alone men could be saved."[76] Those who advocate such a concept also argue that this accommodation can include the statement of, and at least the incidental affirmation of, factual details in historical or scientific matters that are untrue (in the sense that they do not correspond to reality) but that are generally believed by the hearers or readers.[77] Although the advocates of this position may deny that such statements are "affirmed" in one sense (because they do not belong to the main purpose of the author), for purposes of discussion it is important to recognize that such statements are "affirmed" in another sense, namely, that they are repeated by the author in such a way that no indication of disbelief in their truthfulness is communicated by the author to the original readers or hearers. In fact, that is the purpose for such "accommodation"; if any suggestion of disbelief in these supposed facts were to be communicated, it would hinder communication by causing needless distraction of attention from the author's main point (according to the advocates of accommodation). Such an affirmation, in the second sense specified above, I will call "incidental affirmation"; it refers to something incidental to the main purpose of the author.

The question is this: Did God in Scripture ever make an incidental affirmation of a "fact" that was untrue? In other words, does the Bible contain any incidental affirmations of error, particularly when dealing with subjects other than our faith and our moral standards ("faith and practice")? Specifically in the areas of minor historical details and of "scientific" facts,[78] did God intentionally "accommodate" His speech in Scripture to make incidental affirmations of popularly held false beliefs in order to "enhance communication"? (It should be noted that the position that is being analyzed here is formulated in terms of divine, not human, activity in the writing of Scripture. Therefore that will be the focus of the following comments as well.) The following six considerations indicate a negative answer to these questions, and suggest that this concept of "accommodation" is not consistent with the testimony of Scripture.

1. Accommodation would be contrary to the unanimous witness of the Old Testament and New Testament authors concerning the truthfulness of Scripture. As the preceding sections have indicated, whenever Old Testament and New Testament authors speak of the truthfulness of Scripture, their unanimous witness is not to the absolute veracity and reliability of Scripture only when it speaks on certain subjects; it is not to the total veracity of Scripture with regard only to its main points or major purposes; it is not to the absolute reliability of *some* of Scripture or even *most* of Scripture. Rather, the authors of both the Old Testament and the New Testament repeatedly affirm the absolute veracity, reliability, and purity of *every word* of Scripture (Ps. 12:6; 18:30; 119:96, 140; Prov. 8:8; 30:5; Matt. 22:44–45; Luke 24:25; John 10:35; Acts 24:14; Rom. 15:5, et al.). Accommodation would indicate that there are some words of Scripture that are not absolutely reliable, and would therefore be contrary to these passages.

2. Accommodation would imply a denial of God's lordship over human language. As many passages in the Old and New Testaments have indicated,[79] the limitation of human language does not make it impossible for God to communicate both effectively and with total truthfulness. Whether God speaks directly to people, through the lips

of His spokesmen, or through written words, He is viewed as the sovereign Lord of human language who is able to use it however He wills to accomplish His purposes.

Those who argue for the concept of accommodation do not seem to have answered satisfactorily the following question: Was it *necessary* for God to accommodate His speech to human error in order to communicate effectively? If the answer is yes, then the full implications of such a conclusion must be faced honestly: If it was necessary for God to give incidental affirmation to human error in order to communicate effectively, then *all* of Scripture where there is "effective communication" is necessarily tainted with error. The only parts free from error would then be those parts where God's communication is ineffective.

On the other hand, someone might respond that such accommodation was not *necessary* for effective communication, but that it was merely "helpful"; it "enhanced" the communication; it made it better or more effective. Yet this response is not greatly different, for it is only saying that accommodation was necessary for the most effective communication. The result then would be that all those parts of Scripture where there is the best kind of communication necessarily have incidental affirmations of error, and the only parts free from error are those where communication is not the most effective. In either case, to affirm that accommodation to historical or scientific error was necessary implies that there is error in most or all parts of Scripture.

But if an advocate of the concept of accommodation responds that accommodation was *not necessary* for effective communication, but that God did it anyway, then we would have to answer that this theory makes God out to be unwise, for He then would have chosen to affirm falsehood when He did not have to in order to accomplish His purposes. If accommodation was not necessary for effective communication, then we would be better off to abandon the concept and follow instead the repeated affirmations in Scripture about the total truthfulness of every word of God's speech. At least up to the present time, the theory of accommodation has not been established by using one or two (or more) supposedly clear examples of accommodation in Scripture, for no example has been clear enough to compel assent from those who do not accept the theory of accommodation.[80] For every example that has been suggested, there is at least one, and often more than one, alternative and entirely possible explanation in the commentaries.[81]

In order to do justice to the Old Testament and New Testament proclamation of the lordship of God over human language, it seems proper to conclude that this lordship allows God to communicate effectively without ever affirming any of the historical or scientific errors that may have been held by people during the time of the writing of Scripture. Free from the limitations of finitude and sin to which we are subject, God can and does communicate to us without such accommodation. According to Scripture, this is precisely the difference between God's speech through human agents and all other human speech.

3. Accommodation would imply that God had acted contrary to His character as an "unlying God" (Num. 23:19; Titus 1:2; Heb. 6:18). It is not helpful to divert attention from this difficulty by repeated emphasis on the gracious condescension of God to speak on our level. Yes, God does condescend to speak our language, the language of humans. But no passage of Scripture teaches that He "condescends" so as to act contrary to His moral character. He is never said to be able to condescend to affirm even incidentally something that is false. If God were to accommodate Himself in this way, He would cease to be the "unlying God"; He would cease to be the God the Bible represents Him to be.

4. Accommodation would make Scripture an eternal witness to the lack of perfect truthfulness in God's speech. As noted above, Scripture is said to be unchanging and eternal (Ps. 119:89, 160; cf. Matt. 5:18). As such, one of its purposes is to serve as an eternal testimony to the absolute veracity of God in all that He says. Those who understand it will give glory to God for always speaking what is true, in contrast to man (Num. 23:19; 1 Sam. 15:29). But if there were accommodation in Scripture to the point of incidental affirmation of factual error, then for all eternity God's veracity would be impugned by Scripture and the glory God would receive from the response of people to Scripture would be diminished.[82]

5. Accommodation would create a serious moral problem for us. We are to be imitators of God's moral character (Lev. 11:44; Luke 6:36; Eph. 5:1; 1 Peter 5:1, et al.). With regard to truthfulness in speech, Paul says that it is *because* in our new natures we are becoming more like God (Eph. 4:24) that we should "put away falsehood" and "speak the truth" with one another. We imitate God's truthfulness in our speech.

But if the accommodation theory is correct, then God intentionally made incidental affirmations of falsehood in order to enhance communication. Therefore, would it not also be right for us to intentionally make incidental affirmations of falsehood whenever it would "enhance communication"? Yet this would be tantamount to saying that a minor falsehood told for a good purpose (a "white lie") is not wrong. Such a position is contradicted by the Scripture passages cited on pages 49–51, yet it is a position implied by the accommodation theory.

Furthermore, accommodation creates a moral problem with the obligation people have with respect to God. The original readers or hearers of any passage in which there was accommodation to human error would have been unable to know that God was incidentally affirming falsehood that He did not intend them to believe (it was something they would have thought to be true). To them it would have been indistinguishable from all other parts of what God said. Since these words came to the hearers as God's words, the hearers would have been under moral obligation to believe all of them. Therefore, according to the concept of accommodation, God would have been requiring His people to believe falsehood.

6. Accommodation would misuse a summary statement about the purpose of Scripture. To say that the major purpose of Scripture is to "make us wise unto salvation" or teach us in matters of "faith and practice" is to make a useful and correct summary of God's purpose in giving us the Bible. But it is only a summary and it includes only the most prominent purpose or purposes of God in giving Scripture.

Therefore it is incorrect to use that summary to deny that it is part of the purpose of Scripture to tell us about minor historical details, or about some aspects of astronomy or geography, and so forth. A summary cannot properly be used to deny one of the things it is summarizing! To use it this way would simply show that the summary is not detailed enough to specify the items in question.

It is better to say that the whole purpose of Scripture is to say everything it does say, on whatever subject. Every one of God's words in Scripture was deemed by Him to be important for us, whether or not we understand all of that importance at any one time. Thus, God issues severe warnings to anyone who would take away even one word from what He has said to us (Deut. 4:2; 12:32; Rev. 22:18–19): We cannot add to God's words or take from them, for all are part of His larger purpose in speaking to us. Accommodation would use a summary of the Bible's purpose to exclude from God's purposes some matters on which God has in fact chosen to speak to us.

For these six reasons, the concept of accommodation seems to be an unsatisfactory way to formulate a conclusion about the texts we have analyzed concerning the statements of the Old and New Testaments about the truthfulness of the Bible.

THE POSSIBILITY OF FORMULATING A DOCTRINE OF SCRIPTURE

The texts we have examined have indicated clearly a few themes that must contribute to what Christians today believe about the nature and character of Scripture.

1. What has traditionally been called "verbal inspiration"— namely, the view that all the words of Scripture are spoken by God—is clearly taught by many passages in both the Old Testament and New Testament. In fact, it is "plenary" verbal inspiration,[83] in that it includes every word of Scripture. The evidence is so great that it hits one, as Warfield said, like an avalanche, demonstrating that what Scripture says, God says.

2. The method of revelation from God to the authors of Scripture

is seldom discussed. There is historical research (Luke 1:1–4), memory (John 14:26), the use of one's own good judgment (1 Cor. 7:12), revelation in being caught up into heaven (2 Cor. 12:1–4), and dictation (Rev. 1:11–3:22). But for the most part the method of revelation is not specified. Scripture clearly was written by many different human authors, each employing his own vocabulary, style, and literary sense. Yet the emphasis of Scripture is not on the process but the result. By whatever process, every word written was exactly the word God wanted written, so that Scripture is not only the words of men but also the words of God.

3. The Old and New Testament authors clearly teach that Scripture is infallible—if that word is taken to mean that Scripture will never lead us astray in what we are to believe or obey ("matters of faith and practice"). It is as trustworthy and reliable as the God who speaks in it (Ps. 119:160; 2 Tim. 3:16).

4. Yet any attempt to find in the Bible some encouragement to restrict the areas in which Scripture is reliable and truthful will surely fail, for the implication of literally hundreds of verses is that God's word is reliable in every way: It is free from all impurities (Ps. 12:6); it is eternal and unchanging in heaven (Ps. 119:89); it has unique and unlimited perfection (Ps. 119:96); it proves true in every word (Prov. 30:5); it is not only true in each part, but it is also "truth" when the parts are added together (Ps. 119:160). It is not limited to the truthfulness of man, but is as truthful as God Himself (Num. 23:19; 1 Sam. 15:29). We are to tremble before it (Isa. 66:2). Any historical detail in the Old Testament narrative can be cited with a confidence that it both "happened" and "was written down for our instruction" (Rom. 15:4; 1 Cor. 10:11), because every word of Scripture has been spoken by God who never lies (Titus 1:2) and for whom lying is impossible (Heb. 6:18). God's word is not only "true"; it is "truth" (John 17:17). To say that Scripture is truthful in everything it says is to say that it is "inerrant"; it does not affirm anything that is contrary to fact.

Certainly, truthfulness is not the only characteristic of Scripture associated with its divine authorship. It is also powerful and beautiful and necessary for awakening and sustaining our spiritual life. We are to tremble at its warnings, rejoice in its promises, receive with faith the salvation it offers, and speak the praises it contains. Yet the focus of this particular study was the authority and truthfulness that the authors of Scripture claimed for it.

It is evident from the New Testament that one cannot legitimately separate "matters of faith and practice" or "revelatory matters" from other matters in Scripture: The New Testament authors readily quote and rely on anything written in the Old Testament text, for "all Scripture ... is profitable" (2 Tim. 3:16). Perhaps it has not been stated emphatically enough that *nowhere* in the Old Testament or in the New Testament does any writer give *any* hint of a tendency to distrust or consider slightly unreliable any other part of Scripture. Hundreds of texts encourage God's people to trust Scripture completely, but no text encourages any doubt or even slight mistrust of Scripture. To rely on the "inerrancy" of every historical detail affirmed in Scripture is not to adopt a "twentieth-century view" of truth or error; it is to follow the teaching and practice of the biblical authors themselves. It is to adopt a biblical view of truth and error.

5. Once we have understood what these texts say about the Bible's truthfulness, it is necessary to move from the academic exercise of examining scriptural texts to the personal question each person must ask himself: Will I believe this? Will I believe that the words of Scripture are the words of my Creator, the words of One who cannot lie, and that they are even now speaking to me?

To believe that all the words of the Bible are God's words and that God cannot speak untruthfully will significantly affect the way in which one approaches a "problem text" or an "alleged error" in Scripture. To seek for a harmonization of parallel accounts will be a worthy undertaking.[84] To approach a text with the confident expectation that it will, if rightly understood, be consistent with what the rest of the Bible says, will be a proper attitude. To allow less clear passages of Scripture to be interpreted with the help of passages that speak more clearly on the same subject will be a reasonable procedure. In all of this, the basis of such procedures will be the fact that one has learned something true from an inductive study of the Bible and that that truth is a conclusion drawn from careful observation of the data. But such a conclusion will now also function as a basis on which further investigation can proceed and further discoveries can be made. If we really believe what the Bible says about itself, can we do anything else?

UNITY AND DIVERSITY
IN THE NEW TESTAMENT:
THE POSSIBILITY
OF SYSTEMATIC THEOLOGY

D. A. Carson

D. A. Carson

D. A. Carson is Professor of New Testament at Trinity Evangelical Divinity School. He is a graduate of McGill University (B.Sc.), Central Baptist Seminary in Toronto (M.Div.), Cambridge University (Ph.D.), and has studied at Regent College and in Germany. He has served both as a church planter and as a pastor and lectures frequently in Canada, the United States, and the United Kingdom. Before moving to Trinity, he taught at Northwest Baptist Theological College and Seminary in Vancouver. He is editor of the *Trinity Journal* and the author or editor of several books, including *Divine Sovereignty and Human Responsibility* and *From Sabbath to Lord's Day*, and many articles. He holds membership in *Societas Novi Testamenti Studiorum*, Society of Biblical Literature, Canadian Society of Biblical Studies, Tyndale Fellowship for Biblical Research, and the Evangelical Theological Society.

UNITY AND DIVERSITY
IN THE NEW TESTAMENT:
THE POSSIBILITY OF SYSTEMATIC THEOLOGY

STATEMENT OF THE PROBLEM

One might well ask, in the contemporary climate of academic theology, why a student whose prime focus of scholarly interest is the New Testament documents should meddle with questions concerning the foundations of systematic theology. The reasons are many, and few of them easy. We live in an age of increasing specialization (owing in part to the rapid expansion of knowledge), and disciplines that a priori ought to work hand in glove are being driven apart. More important, there is a growing consensus among New Testament scholars that any systematic theology that claims to summarize biblical truth is obsolete at best and perverse at worst. Any possibility of legitimate systematic theology presupposes that the discipline will look elsewhere for its norms, or begin from some center smaller than or different from the Christian canon.

It is important to grasp the proportions of the modern dilemma. At its center stand several close-knit assumptions: the New Testament is full of contradictions, it embraces many different theological perspectives that cannot be arranged into one system, its diversity is not only linguistic but conceptual, and it is made up of documents that come from so long a time span that major developments have rendered obsolete the theological positions of the earlier documents. The conclusion to be drawn from this cluster of propositions is that a systematic theology of the New Testament is impossible, let alone one that embraces both Testaments. In that sense, one cannot legitimately speak of "New Testament theology" but only of "New Testament theologies." The former category, "New Testament theology," may be considered an appropriate designation for the discipline of studying such theology as may be found in the New Testament, but not for referring to some supposed unified structure of theistic belief. As a result, it is not too surprising that of the ten major New Testament theologies published between 1967 and 1976, no two scholars agree on the nature, scope, purpose, or method of the discipline.[1]

It is not my purpose to trace the rise of these developments. Their roots stretch far back into the Enlightenment; and my knowledge of their growth is sufficient only to assure me that I do not possess the detailed understanding of history required to untangle them. My more modest goal is to focus on a number of representative works, first with description and then with criticism, and, following this, to offer some reflections that may be of use to the student who is persuaded that the New Testament documents are nothing less than the Word of God, yet who cannot in all integrity fail to grapple with their substantial diversity. For convenience I will limit myself largely to the New Testament, although similar analysis could be extended to the Bible as a whole. I will not address directly the question of whether a transcendent/personal God can use the languages of finite men[2] nor wrestle with current developments in hermeneutics that argue for disjunction between the author's intent and the reader's understanding.[3] Such questions, though related to this inquiry, are of sufficient complexity to deserve separate treatment.

We may profitably begin with the enormously influential book by Walter Bauer, *Orthodoxy and Heresy in Earliest Christianity.*[4] The question Bauer sets himself is whether the church early embraced a clearly defined doctrinal corpus that enabled it to reject false belief, or whether the distinction between orthodoxy and heresy is a rather late development. Methodologically, Bauer abandons the New Testament evidence because it is so disputed and conducts his readers on a whirlwind tour of second-century Christianity. He concludes that from the beginning so-called heretical and orthodox churches existed side by side, the latter frequently in the minority; and the reasons why the "orthodox" groups eventually won out have less to do with self-conscious theological incompatibility than with what we might call politics. The implication of all this is that even *first*-century Christianity was no different: highly diverse and even mutually exclusive beliefs were tolerated without embarrassment.

This reconstruction of early church history is very popular among New Testament scholars today. It wielded enormous influence on Bultmann and his disciples, but to one degree or another its impact was also felt in much wider circles. In an appendix to the 1964 edition of Bauer's book, G. Strecker developed the argument further and concluded that Jewish Christianity in the first century was not only diverse but was, by later "orthodox" standards, itself heretical.[5] A similar point of view is developed in Elaine Pagels's recent book, where it is argued that the theological options of the first two centuries, finally judged heretical, were not so lightly esteemed in their own time and should therefore be explored afresh as valid options for us today.[6] E. P. Sanders presupposes that at some point divisions between the "heretical" and the "orthodox" began to take place, but that this "shift in the consciousness of the Christian community" did not occur until the second and third centuries.[7] Stephen S. Smalley examines the Gospel and Epistles of John and concludes that even there great diversity exists, so much so that this corpus "can hardly be regarded as consciously orthodox *or* heretical; it is neither one nor the other."[8]

In short, Bauer's work has established a new critical orthodoxy on this point, and recent studies tend to follow this direction.[9] From such a perspective, it is not difficult to exclude the possibility of a systematic theology based on the New Testament documents. One writer tells us that "the Bible is not a unified writing but a composite body of literature";[10] at some level this disjunction is surely false. Another tells us that "the New Testament is a repository of many *kerygmas*, not one,"[11] while a third rejoices that there are many contradictions in Scripture because they constitute "an aid in establishing chronology and in discerning the use of sources or the development of traditions, and through this an aid to historical reconstruction in general."[12]

This critical reconstruction of early church history, coupled with other developments that equally depreciate the truthfulness of the New Testament have generated a host of writings exploring the nature of New Testament theology. Lost confidence in the unity of the New Testament stretches back a long way,[13] but the results are much with us. Scholars now ask if a New Testament theology is possible;[14] or they develop esoteric, narrow, and extrabiblical criteria for what such theology might include;[15] or, in the case of Roman Catholics, they frankly appeal to the authority of the Catholic church as the only way out of the dilemma.[16]

The solution to the post-Enlightenment epistemological crisis that Gabler proposes—viz., to distinguish sharply between systematic and biblical theology, the latter alone being recognized as a historical discipline[17]—has largely petered out. The biblical theology movement enjoyed its heyday from roughly 1930 to 1960; but its decline has been chronicled.[18] Even those who plaintively insist that the death notice is premature[19] do not provide any solid solutions, for in reality the movement has always lacked unity. It was useful in encouraging nuanced study of the various corpora that make up Scripture, but it was largely incapable of forging a consensus regarding what should be preached in the churches. Its proponents could not even agree that "theology" was a proper term, since it implies a coherent system, at least within each corpus.

The malaise is profound. Sensitive Bible scholars have come to recognize that the loss of confidence in the unity of the New Testament entails some kind of pick-and-choose method when it comes to preaching; and very often it is preaching that reveals our deepest theology. Ernst Käsemann advocates a "canon within the canon,"[20] but there is no possibility of establishing broadly agreed criteria for delineating such a minicanon. As radical as he is, Käsemann is troubled by the loss of control and comments elsewhere, in an oft-repeated quote: "The main virtue of the historian and the beginning of all meaningful hermeneutic is for me the practice of hearing, which begins simply by letting what is historically foreign maintain its validity and does not regard rape as the basic form of engagement."[21] The problem is that Käsemann continues to practice rape as, if not the basic, then at least a primary, form of engagement. A fairly conservative critic like Peter Stuhlmacher wants to be open to "the possibility of transcendence" and to every method and every truth, but he cannot bring himself to accept everything the New Testament says because it includes (he argues) numerous contradictions—like that between Paul and James.[22] The net result of such hesitations is a deeply disturbing subjectivity, a subjectivity that among at least some New Testament scholars has a frankly atheistic structure.[23] At the end of the day the only kind of authority the New Testament can enjoy in this climate is some kind of latitudinarian "functional" authority.[24]

It should not be thought that there have been no positive voices. Ronald A. Ward insists that the New Testament presents a unified plan of salvation.[25] The New Testament theology written by Ladd has received wide circulation,[26] but though Ladd handles admirably the vast literature and competently traces out the main themes in each corpus, he does not attempt the promised unification of the results of his theology. Hasel's survey of problems relative to New Testament theology is extraordinarily useful,[27] but when it comes to delineating the unity of the New Testament, he is surprisingly hesitant.[28] The center of the New Testament, he says, is simply Jesus Himself;[29] this statement is true but it scarcely tackles the problem before us. R. P. Martin, in a recent essay, surveys the field and opts to use "Paul and his disciples" as the central touchstone (by this rubric he manages to include the entire Pauline corpus while denying Pauline authorship to some of the epistles ascribed to him);[30] but when one inquires on what basis Paul is selected, the answer is, "Paul towers over the terrain of the apostolic community—in so far as we can judge from the surviving documents —as the great champion of the divine initiative in salvation."[31] The theme to pursue is *reconciliation*, "found principally in Paul but embracing all stages of the trajectory that runs from pre-Pauline Christianity by way of the apostle himself to his disciples in the post-Pauline period."[32] One cannot help but wonder on what basis such choices are made. No exegetical or theological defense is proffered. Why not a completely different theme?

This chapter is designed to outline the seriousness of the problem and does not give consideration to other influential contributors to the debate, such as William Wrede, Adolf Schlatter, and Rudolf Bultmann. Nor have I traced the rise of canon criticism since, unless I am greatly mistaken, it suffers at the moment, in its various forms, from the same epistemological problems afflicting much of the biblical-theology movement.

By far the most influential recent work on the topic of this chapter is the latest book by J. D. G. Dunn, *Unity and Diversity in the New Testament: An Inquiry into the Character of Earliest Christianity.*[33] Far longer and more sophisticated than its near contemporary, J. L. Houlden's *Patterns of Faith: A Study in the Relationship between the New Testament and Christian Doctrine,*[34] Dunn's book deserves special treatment, not least because it comes from the pen of one who aligns himself with so conservative a professional association as the Tyndale Fellowship for Biblical Research.

WORKING DEFINITIONS

Before I enter into specific criticisms of Dunn's book and offers constructive suggestions, however, it is necessary to pause momentarily and define some terms that are variously treated by different authors. I am referring to *biblical theology* and *systematic theology*.

The vagueness of the categories is in part responsible for the high degree of uncertainty regarding what these disciplines are or should be. Warfield pointed out a long time ago that at one level "systematic theology" is "an impertinent tautology."[35] Surely any theology worthy of the name is in some sense systematic. If the study is merely confusingly impressionistic or thoroughly incoherent, it can scarcely be classified as "theology" at all; and if it is theology, it must perforce be in some sense systematic. "Biblical theology" does not fare much better, for what systematician would like to think that his work is *un*biblical?

In the light of such ambiguities, some have argued that "biblical theology" should be used to refer to any theology that seeks to be true to the Bible and to relate the parts fairly and honestly with one another, using biblical categories.[36] By contrast, "systematic theology" emerges from the study of Scripture when alien philosophical frameworks are utilized,[37] or, alternatively, when pure biblical theology is applied to some later culture and its problems and questions.[38] Some prefer to eliminate the "systematic theology" category entirely and to use "biblical theology" to refer to all of the above save the theology that imparts an alien philosophical framework, for the latter is considered illegitimate.[39] Others are comfortable with "systematic theology" but would like to displace "biblical theology" with "history of special revelation" or the like.[40]

My own use of these labels may be briefly stated. First, although *theology* can relate to the entire scope of religious studies,[41] I use the term more narrowly to refer to the study of what the Scriptures say. This includes exegesis and historical criticism, the requisite analysis of method and epistemology, and the presentation of the biblical data in orderly fashion. I therefore exclude apolog   cs and ethics, except insofar as such topics are treated in Scripture.[42] By *biblical theology* I refer to that branch of theology whose concern it is to study each corpus of the Scripture in its own right, especially with respect to its place in the history of God's unfolding revelation. The emphasis is on history and on the individual corpus. By *systematic theology* I refer to the branch of theology that seeks to elaborate the whole and the parts of Scripture,[43] demonstrating their logical (rather than their merely historical) connections and taking full cognizance of the history of

doctrine and the contemporary intellectual climate and categories
and queries while finding its sole ultimate authority in the Scriptures
themselves, rightly interpreted. Systematic theology deals with the
Bible as a finished product.

These definitions do not avoid overlap: biblical theology must be
systematic, even if it focuses on the historical place and significance of
each corpus; and systematic theology, if it turns on fair exegesis, must
perforce rely on historical considerations. But the distinctions I have
drawn are clear enough and are not novel.[44] Warfield offers an analogy
that despite its limits, is worth repeating:

> The immediate work of exegesis may be compared to the work of a
> recruiting officer: it draws out from the mass of mankind the men who
> are to constitute the army. Biblical Theology organizes these men into
> companies and regiments and corps, arranged in marching order and
> accoutered for service. Systematic Theology combines these companies
> and regiments and corps into an army—a single and unitary whole,
> determined by its own all-pervasive principle. It, too, is composed of
> men—the same men who were recruited by the Exegetics; but it is com-
> posed of these men, not as individuals merely, but in their due relations
> to the other men of their companies and regiments and corps. The simile
> is far from a perfect one; but it may illustrate the mutual relations of the
> disciplines, and also, perhaps, suggest the historical element that at-
> taches to Biblical Theology, and the element of all-inclusive systematiza-
> tion which is inseparable from Systematic Theology.[45]

The "simile" is indeed weak at several points. All the recruits get taken
up into the army; and the army qua people is not more than the sum
of the recruits. By contrast, not every exegetical scrap goes into systematic theology; yet, as we will see, systematic theology may at certain points be more than the sum of the exegetical data. Numerous
other distinctions spring to mind, but if the analogy, like any analogy,
has its limits, it also helps to clarify the distinction between biblical
theology and systematic theology.

It follows, then, that questions concerning the unity and diversity
of the New Testament affect both biblical theology and systematic
theology. For example, if it be argued that a particular writer or book is
inconsistent, owing to oversight, later redaction, the incorporation of
incompatible sources, or the like, then it is impossible to develop a
biblical theology for that corpus. At most one could practice the *discipline* of biblical theology and demonstrate thereby that the corpus in
question embraces divergent biblical theolo*gies*. Similarly, the possibility of developing a systematic theology turns on finding that none of
the books of the New Testament are inconsistent (whether such consistency is hammered out in logical, historical, functional, or other
categories). If there is insurmountable inconsistency, then the *discipline* of systematic theology may remain, but no single systematic
theology qua end product would be possible. The individual sys-

tematician would become free to pick and choose whatever elements of the biblical data he preferred. The resulting system would not in any primary sense be dictated by the Scriptures themselves but would be definitively shaped by outside considerations, using the biblical data as nothing more than disparate building blocks.

Granted the internal coherence of each corpus, it is theoretically possible to develop a biblical theology for each corpus, yet fail to find the consensus needed for systematic theology. If, however, a unified systematic theology is possible, biblical theology itself achieves new dignity, for one entailment of the systematic theology would be the certainty that the contributing corpuses are coherent if rightly organized in the historical framework of biblical theology.

If the definitions and relationships I have sketched in be permitted to stand, it follows that the legitimacy of pursuing a systematic theology depends on the unity of the New Testament. Such wide diversity as there is must not involve logical or historical contradiction. Conversely, if New Testament diversity is as sweeping as is often alleged, we ought forthwith to abandon the pursuit of a systematic theology, and those who write theology ought to tell us by what criteria they choose to include this or that dictum or make this or that value judgment.

CRITIQUE

What remains to be done is both negative and positive. Negatively, I propose to survey rapidly a few of the more telling responses to Walter Bauer and to interact in some detail with the recent work by J. D. G. Dunn. Positively, I propose in the next section to set forth some reflections in defense of preserving the unity of the New Testament while recognizing its diversity.

When Bauer's *Orthodoxy and Heresy in Earliest Christianity* appeared,[46] most reviews were overwhelmingly positive. There were thoughtful caveats and hesitations, but few frontal assaults.[47] This changed when A. M. Hunter published *The Unity of the New Testament*.[48] Hunter argued in considerable detail that whatever diversity the New Testament embraces, its writers exhibit a basic unity in their commitment to one Lord, one church, and one salvation.

More important yet was H. E. W. Turner's 1954 Bampton Lectures.[49] Turner examined Bauer's work in ruthless detail and exposed its repeated arguments from silence, its sustained misjudgments concerning the theological positions of such figures as Ignatius and Polycarp, and its incautious exaggerations on many fronts. Turner demonstrated that the church's understanding of its theology antedates the attempt to work the Scriptures into a religious whole: "Christians lived Trinitarily long before the evolution of Nicene orthodoxy."[50]

Various brief essays have been penned more recently. I. H. Mar-

shall demonstrates that in virtually all of the New Testament documents, early or late, there is unambiguous recognition of the fact that
certain beliefs are incompatible with the truth, and even damning.[51]
This does not prove that all such stances can be made to fit together,
but it does demonstrate that Bauer's central thesis—that the very
concepts of orthodoxy and heresy are late developments and motivated by less than religious concerns—are false. J. F. McCue argues
persuasively that Bauer's understanding of the Valentinian Gnostics is
seriously deficient.[52] The Valentinians did *not* develop as an independent branch of Christianity but set themselves over against the
orthodox. Moreover, early Valentinians use the books of the orthodox
New Testament in a way that suggests they emerged from within an
orthodox matrix.

Such considerations as these make Bauer's case untenable; yet his
influence is broadly felt to this day—not least in the recent book by
J. D. G. Dunn.[53] Dunn stakes out his territory for exploration on the
assumption that Bauer is basically correct. "Bauer has shown," he
says, "that second-century Christianity was a very mixed bag. There
was no 'pure' form of Christianity that existed in the beginning which
can properly be called 'orthodoxy.' In fact there was no uniform concept of orthodoxy at all—only different forms of Christianity competing for the loyalty of believers."[54] It may be doubted whether Bauer is
correct in any of his main theses, but Dunn, building on this foundation, now attempts to push the inquiry back into the first century, and
more or less along the same lines.

Dunn gives the first two-thirds of his book over to a discussion of
diversity in the New Testament. In successive chapters he treats the
kerygma ("Kerygma or Kerygmata?"), the primitive confessional formulae, the role of tradition, the use of the Old Testament, concepts of
ministry, patterns of worship, the sacraments, the place of the Spirit
and experience, and Christ and christology. In each chapter he is
concerned to demonstrate the diversity surrounding these themes in
the pages of the New Testament. The final third of the book reverses
procedures and searches for whatever unity may be found among
such diverse groupings as Jewish Christianity, Hellenistic Christianity,
Apocalyptic Christianity, and early catholicism.

The final chapter summarizes Dunn's findings and raises some
questions about the function of the canon. Dunn concludes that the
diversity of first-century Christianity is very pronounced, indeed that
"there was no single normative form of Christianity in the first century."[55] By this, Dunn does not mean to say only that there were
various complementary theological insights and diverse ecclesiastical
structures (although he affirms both of these things), but that there
were mutually incompatible theologies and no consciousness of a
fundamental orthodoxy/heterodoxy tension. The primary unifying feature, according to Dunn, is the common acknowledgment of the unity

between Jesus the man and Jesus the exalted one. Dunn tends to trumpet this finding as if it were a major breakthrough, a glorious discovery; but the value of even this minimal confession is rather mitigated by his observation that the mode of the unity between Jesus the man and Jesus the exalted one is rather disputed and uncertain.

The crucial question arising from all this concerns the canon. What authority can the New Testament documents exercise if Dunn's reconstruction is correct? Dunn denies that the New Testament writings "are canonical because they were *more inspired* than other and later Christian writings" (emphasis his).[56] The evidence, he argues, shows rather that early Christian communities, functioned, in effect, each with its own "canon within the canon," and therefore what the New Testament does is establish the validity of diversity. "To affirm the canon of the NT," Dunn states, "is to affirm the diversity of Christianity."[57] The New Testament may also establish the *limits* of legitimate diversity; but what Dunn self-confessedly wants to do is to serve as a sort of broker between liberalism and conservatism, challenging each side to recognize the legitimacy of the other. With this end in view he attempts to formulate the essential, the irreducible, Christian message:

> Christianity begins from and finally depends on the conviction that in Jesus we still have a paradigm for man's relation to God and man's relation to man, that in Jesus' life, death, and life out of death we see the clearest and fullest embodiment of divine grace, of creative wisdom and power, that ever achieved historical actuality, that the Christian is accepted by God and enabled to love God and his neighbour by that same grace which we now recognize to have the character of that same Jesus. This conviction (whether in these or in alternative words) would appear to be the irreducible minimum without which "Christianity" loses any distinctive definition and becomes an empty pot into which men pour whatever meaning they choose. But to require some particular elaboration of it as the norm, to insist that some further assertion or a particular form of words is also fundamental, would be to move beyond the unifying canon within the canon, to erect a canon on only one or two strands within the NT and no longer on the broad consensus of the NT writings as a whole. It would be divisive rather than unifying. It would draw the circumference of acceptable diversity far more tightly than the canonical writings themselves justify.[58]

I confess I do not recognize much of the Christian gospel in this summary. Instead of perceiving complementary truths in various parts of the canon, Dunn hunts for the lowest common denominator. The result is a "gospel" that makes no mention of sin, gives no thought to the incarnation or the atonement, presents Jesus primarily as a "paradigm" instead of a Savior (Why can't we have both?), and has no more authority behind it than what can be salvaged from Dunn's reconstruction of history—all of which prompts me to wonder why his reconstruction should be thought any more compelling than that of any other scholar whose predisposition is to dismiss most of the evidence.

This is not to say that Dunn's book does not have many admirable features. Dunn displays an enviable breadth of learning, a massive knowledge of the secondary literature, and an admirable clarity and felicity of expression. Unfortunately, however, the sweep of material that impresses the reader with its breadth is simultaneously a distorting compression that, as Dunn's most perceptive reviewer has noted, "results both in indigestion and in apparently cavalier generalizations and one-sided treatments."[59] To cite but one of scores of examples: Dunn concludes, after a mere three-page discussion, that Jesus was not, in His own teaching, the object of faith—a conclusion attained by ignoring most of the evidence in the Gospels and dismissing the rest as anachronistic.

Many of the reviewers highlight not only the strengths but also the recurrent weaknesses of Dunn's book,[60] and they need not be repeated here. What might be more useful in this essay is to focus briefly on one chapter as a sample of Dunn's argument and to offer some suggestions as to possible lines of rebuttal. Rigorous detail cannot be provided in the brief compass of this section, but the shape of the confrontation can be nicely delineated.

In chapter 2, titled "Kerygma or Kerygmata?" Dunn attempts to show the diversity of *kerygmata* in the New Testament. The method Dunn adopts is to "make an aerial survey of the most important proclamations of the Gospel in the NT, concentrating on picking out the characteristic features of each kerygma [Doesn't such phraseology already prejudge the issue?] rather than attempting a fully balanced treatment of the whole."[61] Dunn begins with the kerygma of Jesus. He excludes the evidence in the fourth Gospel on the grounds that it does not use the word κηρύσσω, κήρυγμα, εὐαγγελίζομαι, or εὐαγγέλιον,[62] and thereby he eliminates a substantial part of the evidence. The kerygma of Jesus, according to the synoptic Gospels, then, is summed up in several statements. First of all, Jesus proclaimed the imminent kingdom of God but was mistaken in that His own expectations failed to materialize. Second, Jesus called for repentance and faith (in God, not in Himself) "in face of the end-time power and claim of God."[63] Third, Jesus offered forgiveness and participation in the messianic feast of the new age, and on this built the ethical corollary of love.

I am sure critical orthodoxy will be pleased, but the effrontery is astounding nonetheless. Dunn does not here discuss the parables with their repeated emphasis on grace (e.g., servants hired at various hours) and their picture of delay before the Parousia (e.g., wheat and tares). He is silent regarding the Lord's Supper and its forward-looking stance to His own death and the community's continued memory (before the Parousia: "till I come"!) of that death, specific sayings rich in pregnant significance (e.g., Mark 10:45, the so-called ransom saying), the acceptance of obeisance, the utter lack of any consciousness of sin coupled with the willingness and ability to forgive sin, the specific references to His church in Matthew and the dozens of passages where the community is presumed to continue, and much more. Dunn treats many of these things elsewhere but he does not treat them as if they have any reference to an understanding of Jesus' kerygma. By eliminating much evidence as anachronistic and parceling up sections of the synoptic Gospels into mutually exclusive categories, Dunn arrives at his minimalistic conclusion. Nor does he explore Jesus' place in salvation history or the consequences such exploration might have in the way Jesus expresses Himself.

Dunn then goes on to consider the kerygma in Acts. Positively, Dunn states, the kerygma in Acts proclaims the resurrection of Jesus and the need for a response characterized by repentance and faith in Jesus, issuing in the promise of forgiveness, salvation, and the Spirit. Negatively, Acts is characterized by the absence of any theology of the death of Jesus and of the tension between fulfillment and consummation ("completely lacking," Dunn says),[64] and by a subordinationist christology. To encourage faith in Jesus rather than in God is already a shift from Jesus' preaching, Dunn insists; but as we have seen, he has eliminated the relevant evidence in the Gospels. True, there is *more* emphasis on faith in Jesus in Acts than in the Gospels, but this is largely due to the new perspective brought about by the cross, resurrection, and exaltation: the stance in salvation history is now a little further advanced, and it is clearer than before just who Jesus is. In fact, Acts reveals a *growing* awareness of the implications of Jesus' death and resurrection, implications progressively developed through the earliest preaching, the ministry of Stephen, the admission of Samaritans and then of Gentiles, the developing consciousness of a new relation to Old Testament law, and so forth; but such major salvation history perspectives Dunn does not consider at this point. The Spirit is promised the believer, he says, but he does not consider how this blessed gift is climactically poured out at Pentecost and how at least some further manifestations have to do with validation of the newly converted community before the Jerusalem church. How may one legitimately treat the kerygma in Acts *without* considering such things?

And is it true that Luke has no theology of the death of Christ? Dunn notes the places where Jesus' death is referred to but always finds some other explanation. Even 20:28 is dismissed because it "remains more than a little puzzling and obscure."[65] The treatment of this subject by W. J. Larkin, who gives some indication of the atonement theology presupposed in Luke-Acts, is much to be preferred.[66] And if Larkin and others are right, then 20:28 can be dropped into the text casually and without comment precisely because it was an accepted item of belief. Dunn repeatedly warns us against reading all of

Galatians and Romans into passages in Acts (e.g., Acts 5:30 and 10:39), and his warning is to the point. But he pushes this warning so hard that he adopts a methodologically indefensible stance. Must everything be said about every doctrine on every occasion? Must silence or deemphasis signify ignorance or disagreement? From the point of view of credible historical methodology, might it not be argued that allusive references to a doctrine explicitly expounded elsewhere presuppose such a doctrine as easily as deny such a doctrine? Could it be that Luke focuses more attention on the resurrection than on the atonement precisely because he is so interested in his witness theme and the part that it played in the earliest preaching? (The apostles could witness the death of Christ and the resurrected Christ but not, in the deepest sense, the atonement of Christ.) Is there no significance to the fact that the Luke who penned Acts also wrote Luke 21:28; 24:21?[67] Does not this fact prompt suspicions that some, at least, of the relative silence regarding the atonement in Acts springs *not* from ignorance or disavowal but from other considerations? And why is there not so much as a mention of Leon Morris's substantial and responsible treatment of this subject from a perspective very different from that of Dunn?[68]

In the area of christology, Dunn fares no better. It is true that there is a substantial "subordinationist" strand in the christology of Acts, but Dunn's conclusions are not entailed by this fact. Equal subordinationism can be found in the fourth Gospel,[69] a document that also embraces the highest christology. One might legitimately conclude, therefore, that some early Christians, at least, saw no necessary incompatibility between the two strands. What is needed therefore is an analysis of the way these true strands complement each other.[70] Moreover it is surely illegitimate to treat the christology of Acts without again considering the flow of salvation history and the church's rising understanding of the Christ event. The question is whether or not such doctrinal development introduced categories that annulled their earlier understanding. If not, there is development, but not contradiction; growth in comprehension and theological awareness, but no clashing confessions or kerygmata. At least some attempts to analyze the earliest developments in christology have proceeded along these lines,[71] but Dunn does not interact with them or show where they are in error. Why not?

The limitations of space prevent me from embarking on even a cursory response to Dunn's treatment of the kerygma in Paul and in John. The same problems abound there, coupled with two or three magnificent non sequiturs, the best of which is the following (italicized for emphasis in Dunn): "Where the very concept of and claim to apostleship was the subject of controversy, what meaning can we give to the phrase 'the apostolic faith'?"[72]

Dunn is a very competent scholar, and I have no doubt he could defend his position a little better if he tackled in depth any of the areas he treats in this book. Of course, I must not criticize him for not writing a book he did not intend to write, but in all fairness it must be said that this book could win only those who have already bought into the critical orthodoxy of the age without pausing to consider the alternative options that cry out to be heard on almost every page of Dunn's work. There is an important place for superficial books, but it is sad to see a superficial book claiming to present a profound argument.

POSITIVE REFLECTIONS

I do not propose to *demonstrate* the unity of the New Testament, except incidentally. To do so would require several books and far more time and skill than I have at my disposal. I propose instead to attempt something much more modest. I will simultaneously assume a high view of Scripture (based not least on Scripture's self-attestation)[73] and that the diversity of the New Testament documents is to be taken seriously. Beginning with these twin assumptions, I will offer a number of reflections relative to the possibility of establishing a systematic theology on the basis of such diverse documents. These reflections are neither original nor profound but they may help provide an introductory framework both for the Evangelical who is attempting to establish his theology on the Scriptures and for the non-Evangelical who seeks to understand why Evangelicals continue to hold that a systematic theology grounded on the Bible is important.

1. *First, it is important to recognize that virtually every person not an atheist adopts some kind of systematic theology.* This is not to say that every systematic theology is good, useful, balanced, wise, or biblical; it is to say nothing more than that most people adopt *some* kind of systematic theology.

Consider, for example, the person who says that he doesn't believe the Bible is the Word of God, that it is full of errors and contradictions, and that many of its teachings are at best obsolete. If he is not an atheist, he nevertheless believes *something* about God (or gods, but for convenience we will assume he is monotheistic). In his own mind he adopts a number of beliefs that he holds to be consistent. Even a dialectician thinks his beliefs are *ultimately* reconcilable.

It may be, of course, that some of his beliefs are not consistent with other components of his belief system. But no one will consciously adopt such logical inconsistencies, except perhaps in the sense that he might temporarily hold several in tension while he tries to sort them out. He may maintain a core belief system about which he entertains few doubts and a wider circle of beliefs about which he is less certain, but unless he is insane, he will press for maximum logical consistency. This is true even when he springs from a culture in which people like to think in pictures rather than in abstract propositions, for it is a universal apperception that behind the pictures stand realities, however dimly perceived. If someone presents a structure of theology that conflicts sharply with his own system, then even if that structure is presented in pictures it will evoke a negative reaction.

What this means is that it ill suits anyone to scoff at systematic theology or to minimize its importance, for the scoffer inevitably embraces some kind of systematic theology of his own. Relevant discussion therefore does not call into question the legitimacy of systematic theology per se, but the data base on which it is built; the methods admitted to its construction; the principles that pronounce exclusion of certain information; the language and felicity in which it is phrased; and the consistency, cogency, and precision of the results.

Consider, first, the data base. What propositions about God—His nature, characteristics, functions, relationships—do we admit into our system? Where do we find them? Which ones do we exclude? How do we verify them? What place does revelation have in providing data? Is revelation merely personal, merely propositional, or is it both personal and propositional? If merely personal, how closely do human descriptions of that personal revelation correspond with the reality?

I am not suggesting that everyone thinks through his personal theology by asking himself these questions but rather that these questions lurk unrecognized behind every systematic theology. That is why sophisticated treatments like those of, say, Hodge, Litton, and Henry devote a considerable amount of attention to introductory questions of method.[74]

If these reflections are valid, then a J. D. G. Dunn, for instance, has his own systematic theology. He has admitted as much in that he has attempted to determine the common core of the New Testament. He may believe other things in the New Testament and adopt them into his reconstructed core, but he cannot adopt all that the New Testament has to say, because he is convinced the full set of New Testament data is inconsistent and will not cohere historically or logically. But Dunn has his own systematic theology nevertheless. The crucial question in Dunn's attempt to write Christian theology is the basis on which he selects his data. Why do some New Testament truths, and not others, become central for him? On what basis are some traditional Christian beliefs rejected?

The point I am trying to make is that it is not the validity of systematic theology qua discipline that is called into question, but the cogency of one's critical tools. *Christian* systematic theology cannot be done without reference to the Bible, but what role should the Bible play? And should all of it play a role?

The data base of systematic theology is not the only consideration. Systematic theology, to be coherent to its contemporary culture, must use contemporary language and at least *some* of the paradigms of that culture (or offer astute reasons for rejecting them). Finite and sinful as every human being is, there will no doubt be some diversity in the theologies of the various systematicians. But nothing is as important as the data basis that is permitted, for this is a question of authority and legitimation, not of hermeneutics. It follows that everyone who presents a case for this or that systematizing of theology owes it to his followers to explain as unambiguously as possible what he will and will not admit into his system. He may of course go much further and justify his data base, but he must at least identify it.

Dunn's work, at least in part, is an attempt to justify his extremely limited data base. Unfortunately, it is precisely at this point that his book is so weak. Dunn adopts many current, critical *shibboleths* but he does not take the time to subject them to rigorous scrutiny, or even to consider whether his approach to the canon, his literary tests, his historical reconstructions, and his failure to wrestle with the alternative options offered even by those who use the same tools may not unwittingly exclude all kinds of data that should be admitted.

2. *The data base to be urged upon systematic theologians is the entire Bible, the canonical sixty-six books; and the validity of this choice depends on the adoption of four positions.*

The *first* position is that all of Scripture is trustworthy, and this of course presupposes that Scripture is truthful. If certain parts are not trustworthy, then they should not be used as data for the systematic theology.

What is objectionable about Dunn's approach is not so much that he detects errors here or there, as false (in my judgment) as his detection is, but that apart from a minimalistic common denominator he is prepared to baptize as Christian some structures of thought that in his view are mutually contradictory. This preserves, he argues, the validity of diverse theologies. But which, if any, is *true*—that is, which corresponds to historical and spiritual reality? Which, if any, is *trustworthy*? If they are mutually contradictory on any point, not more than one, and perhaps none, is true. Defending the validity of diversity in christology, for instance, may be helpful if the various christologies are mutually complementary; but if they are mutually contradictory, a defense of the diverse reduces to a defense of diverse error and untrustworthiness.

This first position, that all of Scripture is trustworthy, can be competently defended on wide grounds: the Scriptures' self-attestation, the approach of Christ to the Scriptures, the amazing reliability the Bible manifests where it is historically testable, and so forth. Some of these grounds are produced elsewhere in this volume. My concern at the moment is simply to set forth in brief form positions on which a systematic theology of the canonical Scriptures must be based, and, implicitly, to show how opposing systematic theologies need to clarify their own approaches.

The *second* position presupposed by my approach to systematic theology is that the basic laws of logic—such as the law of noncontradiction or the law of the excluded middle—are not *inventions* of Aristotle or formulations of some other *savant*, but *discoveries* to do with the nature of reality and of communication. They do no more than affirm that certain relationships obtain if communication is possible and coherent, and if any truth whatsoever may be known. If anyone denies this, I reply that the true import of his denial is the opposite of what he says; and I cannot possibly be *logically* (if I may be forgiven for using the word) refuted. The substratum of *any* communication, whether between two individuals or two ages, is simple logic, regardless of the literary genre in which the communication is embedded. The "inner logic of divine revelation," to which some have appealed as a substitute, sounds devout, but either it is a way of saying that the relationships among divinely given truths in the Scripture must be established by Scripture (in which case it is difficult to see how this is opposed to logic) or else it is a way of appealing to fideism of the irrational variety.

It will not do to respond by citing Isaiah 55:8–9: "'For my thoughts are not your thoughts, neither are your ways my ways,' declares the Lord. 'As the heavens are higher than the earth, so are my ways higher than your ways and my thoughts than your thoughts.'" The context makes it evident that the categories do not concern competing logic systems or the like; rather, they are essentially moral. The preceding verse exhorts, "Let the wicked forsake his *way* and the evil man his *thoughts*" (55:7). Man's thoughts are to be brought into conformity with God's thoughts not by abandoning logic but by repentance.

Similarly, it is no real objection to this point to spread out the Bible's use of paradox, hyperbole, parable, and other literary forms and devices. None of these things endanger logic in the slightest, but they do caution us as to how logic is to be applied.

Logic can produce a false answer if, for instance, the premises are wrong, or if insufficient data are considered, or if a paradox is not recognized for what it is. But such failures do not threaten logic itself so much as faulty conclusions grounded in poor premises. To pit Scripture against logic is simply incoherent. Rogers and McKim thoroughly misrepresent Calvin on this matter when they say:

> Calvin knew the value of logic as one of the human sciences.... But the law of noncontradiction, which dialectics taught, did not, for Calvin, have precedence over the teachings of Scripture. The power of truth to persuade us through faith was a greater value for Calvin with his humanist background. He commented, for example, on Matthew 27:43, "He trusts in God, let God deliver him now...." He condemned as "Satan's logic" any interpretation that applied logic to God's providence and then concluded that God does not love us because we suffer. Calvin accepted that God had given logic along with physics, mathematics, and other worldly

disciplines "that we may be helped ... by the work and ministry of the ungodly." But if logic was used to drive persons away from faith in the truths of Scripture, then it was to be categorically rejected.[75]

Rogers and McKim use the phrase "Satan's logic" as if to suggest that Calvin presents logic as if it were in the peculiar domain of Satan. In fact, Calvin says that Satan attempts to drive us to despair by "this logic," that is, "this logical argument," viz., that since God watches over the safety of His people it appears He does not love those whom He does not assist. Calvin calls Satan's ruse "this logic" because it has the form of logical argument, but he then goes on to argue that Satan's argument is false, *not on the grounds that logic must take a back seat to Scripture*, but on the grounds that the premises are inadequate. God's love cannot be reduced to the present instant, Calvin says, and God may demonstrate His love in the long haul. Moreover, God often uses adversity to train His people in obedience. In short, Calvin argues that Satan uses a prejudicial selection of the data in constructing his argument. Rogers and McKim are mistaken when they say Calvin rejected "any interpretation *that applied logic* to God's providence and then concluded that God does not love us because we suffer."[76] On the contrary, the cogency of Calvin's response depends entirely on the logic that he himself applies to the same problem, using a broader selection of data. There is not the slightest suggestion, either in his commentaries or in the *Institutes*, that Calvin ever considered logic itself as something that could, in and of itself, "drive persons away from faith in the truths of Scripture" and was therefore "to be categorically rejected."[77] The real problem is that Rogers and McKim characteristically read historical evidence through the spectacles of their own reconstruction of history and thereby treat it anachronistically.[78]

These two positions bring us to a *third*. If the Scriptures are trustworthy, and if the basic laws of logic are not inventions of dubious worth but discoveries of the basic relationships that make both coherent communication and knowledge of truth possible, then for systematic theology to be based on the Bible also requires that the documents that constitute the Bible deal with the same general topic. For instance, a written analysis of Elizabethan English and a text on the quantum behavior of quarks may conceivably be equally trustworthy, but it would be extremely difficult to develop a consistent synthesis from these two literary pieces. By the same token, a systematic theology based on the Bible requires that the biblical books be close enough in subject matter to cohere.

It is important to observe carefully the limits of this position. I am not saying that the Bible is like a jigsaw puzzle of five thousand pieces and that all the five thousand pieces are provided, so that with time and thought the entire picture may be completed. Rather, I am suggesting that the Bible is like a jigsaw puzzle that provides five thousand pieces along with the assurance that these pieces all belong to the same puzzle, even though ninety-five thousand pieces (the relative figures are unimportant for my analogy) are missing. Most of the pieces that are provided, the instructions insist, fit together rather nicely; but there are a lot of gaping holes, a lot of edges that cry out to be completed, and some clusters of pieces that seem to be on their own. Nevertheless, the assurance that all of the pieces do belong to one puzzle is helpful, for that makes it possible to develop the systematic theology, even though the systematic theology is not going to be completed until we receive more pieces from the One who made it. And meanwhile, even some systematicians who believe that all the pieces belong to the same puzzle are not very adept puzzle players but sometimes force pieces into slots where they don't really belong. The picture gets distorted somewhat, but it remains basically recognizable.

Finally, although good systematic theology must be phrased in the language of the present and interact with and speak to contemporary concerns,[79] it must be controlled by the biblical data. "Any number of supposedly biblical theologies in our day are so heavily infected with contemporary personalist, existential, or historical thinking as to render their biblical basis highly suspect," comments one critic,[80] and the remark is even more relevant to current systematic theology. That the control should run in this direction is an epistemological requirement that depends on the revelatory status of the Bible.[81] If this be not so, the kind of systematic theology being advocated here is impossible, and the attempt to develop such should forthwith be abandoned.

In short, I am concerned to show the positions implicitly adopted when an Evangelical maintains that the proper data base for systematic theologians is the Bible, the canonical sixty-six books, and to offer some brief comments on their reasonableness. From now on, by "systematic theology" I will refer only to systematic theology based on the canon, unless I explicitly state otherwise. It is in this narrow sense of the designation that the subtitle of this chapter is to be taken: "The Possibility of Systematic Theology."

My focus from this point on will be the New Testament rather than the entire canon, for no other reason than that the immensity of the problems and the literature requires that I reduce the field a little. The substantial questions concerning the *diversity* of the New Testament documents I have not yet directly addressed. To compare systematic theology with a jigsaw puzzle with many pieces not present begs a host of methodological questions, and to these we must now turn.

3. *Progressive revelation must be treated with all seriousness, but appeal to progressive revelation in order to exclude inconvenient components along that revelation's alleged trajectory is illegitimate.*

The term "progressive revelation" is a slippery one. Coined first in liberal circles to describe an evolutionary approach to understanding the Bible,[82] it has subsequently often been taken over and given another meaning, the meaning I wish to adopt. By "progressive revelation" I refer to the fact that God progressively revealed Himself in event and in Scripture, climaxing the events with the death-resurrection-exaltation of Christ and climaxing the Scriptures with the closing of the canon. The result is that God's ways and purposes were progressively fulfilled not only in redemption events but also in inscripturated explanation. The earlier revelation prepares for the later; the later carries further and in some way explicates the earlier.

The most dramatic canonical shift is the shift from Old Testament to New.[83] Yet even within the New, the amount of development is astounding. Chronologically, it covers less than a century, but it moves from Judaism and the slaughter of the innocents under Herod the Great, through the preaching of John the Baptist, the public ministry of Jesus (characterized by Jesus' personal submission to Old Testament law [though He often broke with tradition], along with a host of His sayings that could adequately be comprehended only after His death and resurrection),[84] the early Jerusalem church, the progressive self-consciousness within the church that recognized the obsolescence of the temple and, because of the gift of the Spirit, the admission of believing Gentiles into a common fellowship with shared Savior and God, the rapid evangelization of the Mediterranean world, and the growing rift between Judaism and Christianity.

Of the various models used to describe this development, the organic one (seed leads to plant) is no doubt the best analogy.[85] We are dealing with the growth of a single specimen, not transmutation into new species. It follows that systematic theology is possible, in the same way that the botanical description of a tree is possible. That there is growth and development in revealed truth within the canon requires, not the abolition of systematic theology, but treatment that is sensitive to the nature of the object being studied.

Even so, there are certain characteristics of the diversity in the New Testament that have to be borne in mind. Just as certain parts of the seed are not taken up in the plant it produces, so certain parts of the old covenant under which Jesus lived are not continued under the new covenant He inaugurated (e.g., Mark 7:19; much of Hebrews). Any systematic theology cannot escape such historical considerations. Inasmuch as it is the systematician's concern to synthesize in *contemporary* terms the truth of Scripture, he must summarize not only what God has required in the past, but especially what He requires in his own present. In that sense he must take special pains to discover how the earlier revelation relates to its later fulfillment and applies to himself and his contemporaries.[86]

A second characteristic of New Testament diversity lies in the fact that even after the Spirit-age begins at Pentecost the full implications of this new age take some time to be understood (as Jesus Himself suggested they would; cf. John 16:12–15),[87] and this understanding comes only in degrees, unevenly, haltingly, cautiously. The significance of the descent of the Spirit on Cornelius and his household (Acts 10–11), both to Peter and to Luke, is that the charismatic phenomena accompanying this baptism validated the reality of Gentile salvation to the Jerusalem church. But his does not prevent the circumcision crisis from precipitating the Jerusalem Council (Acts 15). According to Paul, both Peter and Barnabas failed on one occasion to live up to their own confessed understanding of the gospel (Gal. 2). Such events tend to support notions of human fallibility and sinful inconsistency, rather than the notion that there were highly diverse parties in the church with major doctrinal differences. It is not only in the present that people sometimes fail to live up to their best insights or refuse to see the entailments of their professed positions.

Can there be development within the writings of one particular author? One must distinguish between the development of a writer's subject matter, which he records and interprets (e.g., Luke–Acts), and the development of the thought of the writer himself.[88] The best test case of the latter is Paul. Most writers follow in the line of an influential pair of essays by C. H. Dodd[89] and affirm unhesitatingly that they can trace development in Paul's thought. The most careful of them, however, confess that there are formidable hurdles to overcome if any real objectivity is to be attained.[90] Quite apart from questions of authenticity, it is not easy to date all of the Pauline correspondence with certainty. Many of the epistles' different emphases stem from diverse pastoral concerns (a point to which I will return). Moreover, it is important to recognize that Paul had been a believer for a solid fifteen years or more before he penned the first letter recognized as canonical, and that is time enough to develop some pretty stable beliefs. All of Paul's canonical writing took place in a single span of fifteen years, long after he had become a mature teacher, and that is not a lengthy period in which to develop major new theological shifts.

There is little reason to doubt that Paul sees himself growing in understanding and maturity, including theological maturity (cf. 1 Cor. 13:8–12; Phil. 3:12–16). But there is not the slightest evidence that Paul perceived himself to be abandoning any position he had formerly maintained in his writings.[91] It remains important that we interpret Paul by Paul,[92] not only for the sake of systematic theology but also for the sake of understanding Paul.

What must be avoided are the simplistic reconstructions of earliest church history that manufacture straight-line developments everywhere and then force the only primary data we have, the New Testament documents themselves, into some Procrustean bed. Attempts are made, for instance, to show how Paul moved from a futurist eschatology to a realized eschatology,[93] despite the fact it has been repeatedly shown that both elements are there from the beginning.[94] It is still common to argue that Acts must be late because Luke so nicely exemplifies *Frühkatholizismus*, even though it has been convincingly argued that Luke–Acts betrays *both* "early catholicism" and "enthusiasm."[95] Theology, like life, is complex. Most of us have learned to live with the "already/not yet" tension in the New Testament; why, then, do we find it so difficult to accept the "early catholicism/ enthusiasm" tension? If Acts is taken seriously, there is order and discipline, not to mention recognized elders, from the earliest years of the church.

The problem for the Evangelical systematician is already difficult enough when he confronts the diversity of the New Testament without having to face the dogmatic reorganization of the evidence along the lines of critical orthodoxy. While various critics are accusing him of constructing a rigid systematic theology that forces him to distort his exegesis, he may perhaps be forgiven if he finds that his critics are reconstructing church history and developing what I have elsewhere called "histmatics,"[96] thereby distorting their exegesis far more seriously.

More difficult to assess is the kind of development in Paul suggested by Murray J. Harris in his published works.[97] Harris thinks 2 Corinthians 5:1–10 is a watershed in Paul's theology, reflecting change in his eschatological thinking because of a brush with death in Asia (cf. 2 Cor. 1:8–11). He now no longer thinks of the resurrection in terms of a corporate phenomenon experienced by all deceased Christians at the Parousia, but in terms of a personal transformation of each Christian at death so as to receive a "spiritual body" comparable to Christ's at that time.

This, of course, is very different from what Paul has expressed in 1 Corinthians 15 and 1 Thessalonians 4. With some hesitation, I would argue that it is an inadmissable example of "development" in Paul. Considerations that bear on my judgment include the following: (1) The New Testament presupposes a real continuity between Jesus' prepassion body and His postresurrection body. Otherwise why the stigmata, and where did the dead body go? Inasmuch as Jesus' resurrection is the firstfruits of the harvest, how different from Jesus' resurrection may the harvest be? (2) Was the Asian experience as traumatic as all that? Second Corinthians 11 makes it clear how often Paul faced suffering and death. Is it likely therefore that one more such experience could effect so major a change in the thinking of a mature and seasoned theologian? (3) Surely the "not . . . but" construction in 2 Corinthians 5:1–10 is a Semitic way of expressing fundamental preference rather than absolute antithesis. (4) Is it possible that the crucial verses, 2 Corinthians 5:3–5, are included by Paul to cover himself against the Corinthian errorists, already confronted in 1 Corinthians 15, who might still be prone to think of verse 2 in immaterial terms? (5) If we grant that 2 Corinthians 10–13 was written after 2 Corinthians

5, then there is evidence that Paul still held to an anthropology that could conceive of human existence apart from the body (2 Cor. 12:1–10), even if it was not the ultimate mode of existence. (6) The exegetical evidence in 2 Corinthians 5:1–10 makes Harris's view possible; it by no means requires it. But Harris's view faces not only the above challenges, but a question from the vantage of systematic theology. The progress of revelation in this instance is interpreted by Harris to involve so massive a change of view that Paul's earlier teaching (esp. in 1 Thess. 4) was *wrong*. That earlier teaching did not simply point forward, serve as a shadow pointing proleptically to the reality in another covenant, or constitute a part of the truth now being fully developed; rather, it was in error. For all these reasons, I am reluctant to side with Harris without seeing much more exegetical warrant.[98]

I have tried to show how the systematic theologian must be aware of questions concerning progressive revelation and I have suggested a few things that might serve as helpful limits. One fairly common application of progressive revelation I confess I reject. This is exemplified by David Kelsey.[99] It attempts to plot the development in theology reflected in Scripture (usually on the basis of a doubtful critical orthodoxy) and then uses the *patterns thus developed*, not the Scripture itself, as normative. In fact, the events of Scripture are inseparable from their interpretation,[100] and the "patterns" Kelsey and others detect are so subjectively grounded that it is difficult to imagine how they could achieve normative status as anything more than interesting paradigms.[101] Progressive revelation must be taken in all seriousness, but appeal to progressive revelation in order to exclude inconvenient components along that revelation's alleged trajectory is illegitimate.

4. *The diversity in the New Testament very often reflects diverse pastoral concerns, with no implications whatsoever of a different credal structure.*

It is easy to find *formal* inconsistencies and contradictions in the New Testament. "Carry each other's burdens," Paul says to the Galatians, "and in this way you will fulfill the law of Christ" (Gal. 6:2). This does not prevent him from advising them, a few verses farther on, that "each one should carry his own load" (Gal. 6:5). Most commentators have no trouble explaining how these verses could come from the pen of one man within one paragraph, and what they mean.[102]

When we move to two different epistles by the same author, however, the situation is rather different. There is still, for instance, a tendency to pit Galatians against 1 Corinthians. In two of the more recent treatments, those by Drane and Richardson,[103] much more allowance is made for the distinctive pastoral problems Paul is facing in the two cities; but even so, Drane in particular is still inclined, in my judgment, to see rather more of a change in Paul's thinking than the evidence allows. Drane sees an early Galatians denouncing attempts to impose law-keeping on Gentile believers. Unfortunately, Drane suggests, some of Paul's converts developed this theme too far, and in the permissive city of Corinth they sank into licentiousness and immorality based on a crude antinomianism. This, according to Drane, prompted Paul to write 1 Corinthians, which imposes far more rules than the Paul of Galatians could have envisaged. In fact, Paul was in danger of overreaction. Later, however, Paul penned 2 Corinthians and Romans and found the right balance.

This analysis presupposes that Galatians and 1 Corinthians are unbalanced and cannot be taken to reflect Paul's mature thought. From a methodological point of view, I would be curious to know how Drane would support his structure over against one that explains the differences in terms of the pastoral problem confronting Paul. This is not to deny that Paul's personal understanding of the dangers might not have improved with experience; but it is to deny that Paul would later have withdrawn any word from Galatians or 1 Corinthians if he had had to face those same problems again. The clues Drane finds to distinguish between the two paradigms (e.g., he argues that the Corinthians had read the epistle to the Galatians) I do not find entirely convincing.

Unfortunately, there is not space to probe this question in detail, but it is important to remember that, as one writer puts it, the epistles "are occasional documents of the first century, written out of the context of the recipients."[104] F. F. Bruce has traced a number of tensions in Paul's letters[105] and, although his synthesis is not convincing in every case, he approaches the diversity with methodological sensitivity.[106]

Part of the problem, I suspect, is that Paul, like Jesus before him, tends to absolutize the language used in addressing the current problem. Granted that Matthew 6 and Luke 18 retain authentic material, it is intriguing to note that in the former passage Jesus seems to be arguing for brief prayers that avoid both pomp and repetition, while in the latter passage he tells a parable with the express purpose of showing his disciples "that they should always pray and not give up" (Luke 18:1). Formally, the two stand in mutual contradiction. In reality, the Matthean passage addresses itself to those whose prayers are merely for show, and to those who think that by their much speaking they can manipulate God. By contrast, the Lukan passage addresses itself to the sins of the doubting and the apathetic. There is no real contradiction whatsoever once the circumstances being addressed are properly understood. Jesus, preacher that He is, regularly uses strong, antithetical language to tackle *each* side of a complex question.[107] One of the values of systematic theology, therefore, is that Jesus' or Paul's approach to a host of issues is likely to receive more balanced scrutiny than by the reductionist methods of those who pit Jesus against Jesus and Paul against Paul.

The question of the diverse circumstances that call forth New Testament writings becomes more controversial yet when author is compared with author—Paul with James, for instance, or John with Paul. Not all New Testament diversity can be accounted for by appealing to diverse circumstances; but a surprising amount of it is surely influenced by such considerations. If the "faith of Abraham" is used by Paul to teach that people are justified by grace through faith and by James to teach that faith without works is dead, it does not necessarily follow that the two authors are ignorant of the other's work or in disagreement with it.[108] In the areas of eschatology and christology, C. F. D. Moule has cogently argued that varied circumstances have prompted much of the New Testament diversity.[109] His work, though widely cited, is still far too infrequently used and treated with the seriousness it deserves.[110] What we need, as E. E. Lemcio has put it, only half facetiously, is the rise of a new sensitivity to "Circumstantionsgeschichte."[111]

Even confessional formulae must be inspected in this light. In 1 Corinthians 12:3 Paul can affirm that "no one can say, 'Jesus is Lord,' except by the Holy Spirit." In 1 John 4:2–3 John insists, "Every spirit that acknowledges that Jesus Christ has come in the flesh [or, as I would prefer, "that Jesus is Christ come in the flesh"] is from God, but every spirit that does not acknowledge Jesus is not from God." The two confessions are not mutually exclusive, nor do they reflect divergent groups of Christians whose christological statements have developed along rather different and perhaps mutually exclusive paths. Rather, in the Corinthian situation with its claims from many lords, the Pauline formulation was both necessary and sufficient. In John's historical context, in which docetists were attempting to divide Jesus from Christ, the Johannine formulation is both necessary and sufficient. But Paul's formulation is inadequate to exclude heretics in John's situation, and John's formulation is inadequate to exclude heretics in Paul's situation. Both formulations—and a number of others, for that matter—are *necessary;* but it does not follow that any one of them is *sufficient* in *every* context (notwithstanding the simplistic use of the confession "Jesus is Lord" by some elements of the WCC!).

W. L. Lane argues that such diversity (he does not use this particular example) reflects a changing theological expression based on a given creedal structure.[112] There is a sense in which he is right, even though I am unhappy with his terminology. But one must go beyond that observation to note that our *only* access to the assumed credal structure of the earliest church is the New Testament documents. Because this is so, and also because those documents are themselves inspired, it will not do to try to recover the early creedal structure while ignoring that structure's specific and diverse exemplifications. Rather, it is precisely at this point that systematic theology is necessary, not only for an adequate exposition of the Christian faith in contemporary terms but also as the only adequate tool to handle the confessional diversity in a responsible way and thereby sketch in the creedal structure.[113]

The alternative is ironic. From all sides New Testament scholars are warned against trying to find a systematic theology in the New Testament. In fact, what these critics are doing is establishing a large number of systematic theologies in the New Testament and then pitting them against each other. A confession is isolated from the historical setting that limits its *sufficiency* (but not its *necessity*) in other settings and is built into a large structure that is set over against some other manufactured structure. Part of this procedure depends on dubious historical reconstructions, something I have already briefly discussed in this chapter, but part of it turns on an irresponsible approach to historical data, an approach that, while decrying systematic theology, is busily systematizing the diversity it finds instead of being sensitive to the mutually complementary nature of the occasional documents that constitute the New Testament.[114]

5. *The diversity in the New Testament documents very often reflects the diverse personal interests and idiosyncratic styles of the individual writers.*

No one of any theological sophistication argues that the Holy Spirit's work in inspiring the Scriptures imposed a literary sameness on all the parts. John still sounds like John, Matthew like Matthew, and so forth.

The same phenomena afford us another view of the unity and diversity problem. The language, style, and interests of the individual writers are all to some extent idiosyncratic; and one must therefore be very careful about arguing that such and such a New Testament writer does not believe this or that simply because he does not mention it or perhaps emphasize it. This is especially important when we remember what New Testament scholars have been telling us all along, viz. that the New Testament writers are not attempting to write systematic theology. Would we attempt to delineate the entire theological structure of some modern religious thinker on the basis of two or three occasional monographs called forth in part by his own focused interests and in part by some pressing pastoral concern?

Terminology may differ from writer to writer. As is well known, Matthew uses "call" to refer to a general invitation to the lost, whereas Paul uses "call" to refer to an effectual action by God; but whereas the terminology differs, this does not itself constitute evidence that Paul denies that God invites the lost or that Matthew disbelieves in election.

Brice Martin has compared Matthew and Paul with respect to the relationship between Christ and the law.[115] His major conclusion is that Matthew and Paul are utilizing two quite different sets of categories and that they therefore constitute noncontradictory, noncomplementary, but compatible, perspectives. His exegesis is not always convincing and he underplays the importance of other considerations (such as the role of salvation history). Worse, it is difficult to see exactly what "noncomplementary but compatible perspectives" means. If both are dealing with the same God and the relationships of men with that God, their perspectives must be complementary in some ways. Martin has imposed alien philosophical categories on the material. Yet, once stripped of such antithetical language and softened by other considerations, his argument still has a point: different New Testament writers may focus on different aspects of truth and from quite different perspectives, whether for apologetic or personal reasons, and such diversity must be taken into account.

Part of the contemporary dilemma lies in the fact that many New Testament scholars who decry systematic theology are busy *over*-theologizing (if this barbarism may be forgiven) the New Testament. Every utterance, every epistle, every literary scrap, must be prompted by explicit *theological* concerns. These concerns (it is alleged) override historical considerations and personal interests. A New Testament writer is always engaged in refuting some theological opponent. Few allow for the possibility that one of the reasons why a particular pericope is admitted may be because the writer found the story interesting. It is with a sigh of relief that we turn to Morna Hooker's cheeky article, "Were There False Teachers in Colossae?"[116]

I do not mean to argue that the New Testament writers are but seldom refuting false notions or that the inclusion of this or that list of material is to be accounted for purely on the grounds of idiosyncratic preference. I mean, rather, to point out that the rich diversity of the New Testament—diversity in genre, style, confession, perhaps liturgy, even content and focus[117]—must not be interpreted solely in the categories of antithetical *theological* formulations. The evidence itself cries against it. But when such evidence is taken into account, it is difficult to see why a deep underlying theological unity is impossible, or even unlikely.

6. *On the basis of these reflections it must be insisted that there is no intrinsic disgrace to theological harmonization, which is of the essence of systematic theology.*

In fact, one might even argue that there is disgrace attached to the failure to make the attempt. Are the assumptions of critical orthodoxy all that unshakable? There was more communication in the ancient world than we sometimes recognize and much more fundamental agreement among the apostles and apostolic writers than is often allowed. The modern notion of well-nigh hermetically sealed communities doing their own theology and touching up their own traditions in splendid isolation, all to produce some New Testament document by multiple authors, is gross exaggeration; and to the extent it reflects any truth at all, we must frankly admit, with Hengel,[118] that we know virtually nothing of such communities. On the positive side, there is evidence that a beginning New Testament canon was recognized very early, during the fifties, when many eyewitnesses were still alive.[119] This suggests greater agreement and harmony among the early Christians than is commonly affirmed.

Critics of systematic theology, of course, are afraid that these arguments will force the New Testament documents into an artificial conformity. That danger is certainly present. But in one sense the approach I have been following encourages theological exploration that, far from being rigid and narrow, encourages work not otherwise possible. "There is ... a sense in which every New Testament writer communicates to Christians today more than he knew he was communicating, simply because Christians can now read his work as part of the completed New Testament canon."[120] This is not an appeal to *sensus plenior*, at least in any traditional sense. Rather, it is an acknowledgment that with greater numbers of pieces of the jigsaw puzzle provided, the individual pieces and clusters of pieces are seen in new relationships not visible before.

What, then, is the proper place for the *analogia fidei*, the "analogy of the faith"? Can we safeguard our exegesis from an untoward usage of systematic theology? The answer, I fear, is, "Not entirely." It would be convenient if we could operate exclusively along the direction of the following diagram:

Exegesis →Biblical Theology →[Historical Theology]→Systematic Theology

(The brackets around the third element are meant to suggest that in this paradigm historical theology makes a direct contribution to the development from biblical theology to systematic theology but is not itself a part of that line.) In fact, this paradigm, though neat, is naïve. No exegesis is ever done in a vacuum. If every theist is in some sense a systematician, then he is a systematician *before* he begins his exegesis. Are we, then, locked into a hermeneutical circle, like the following?

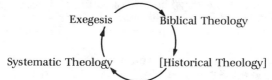

No; there is a better way. It might be diagramed like this:

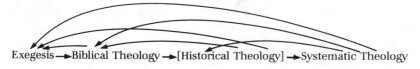

That is to say, there are feedback lines (and more lines going forward, for that matter). It is absurd to deny that one's systematic theology does not affect one's exegesis. Nevertheless the line of final control is the straight one from exegesis right through biblical and historical theology to systematic theology. The final authority is the Scriptures, the Scriptures alone. For this reason exegesis, though affected by systematic theology, is not to be shackled by it. Packer is right when he argues:

> The maxim that exegesis and biblical interpretation are for the sake of an adequate systematic theology is true, yet if one stops there one has told only half the story. The other half, the complementary truth which alone can ward off the baleful misunderstanding that a particular rational orthodoxy is all that matters, is that the main reason for seeking an adequate systematic theology is for the sake of better and more profound biblical interpretation.[121]

Even so, it is important, first, to recognize that the final control is in the Bible, and the Bible alone, and, second, to be self-consciously aware what kind of appeal is being made at each stage of the enterprise, in order not to confuse the lines of control.

If anyone objects that this is giving far too significant a place to systematic theology, I insist that in one sense my strongest opponent is doing the same thing, and perhaps less self-critically than I, for he has adopted his own kind of "systematic theology" in adopting various notions about how the New Testament can or cannot fit together. Often, in fact, such a critic will be particularly vulnerable to his own structured thought precisely because he doesn't believe it influences him unduly. My model is valid only if Scripture is trustworthy, but for various reasons I believe that it is. My concern, then, is to legitimate the harmonization implicit in systematic theology and show that such harmonization, properly handled, enriches biblical interpretation without distorting it.

There are one or two specific dangers in appealing to the *analogia fidei* that should be mentioned. Quite apart from the question of the ultimate line of control, one must beware of handling the *analogia fidei* anachronistically. This does not mean that for every revelatory text one should develop an *analogia fidei* based exclusively on *earlier* revelatory material[122] (although such a method has its own usefulness in tackling certain problems), for that would mean no really new revelation could ever be admitted. It means, rather, that the *analogia fidei* should be used cautiously as an outer limit and as a final consideration,[123] rather than as the determining device.

A second illicit procedure is that exemplified by P. K. Jewett in his book *Man as Male and Female*.[124] As Jewett develops his appeal to *analogia fidei*, it becomes clear he is in fact operating with a "canon within the canon." He isolates (at least to his own satisfaction) the central teachings of the Scriptures on his chosen subject and on that basis excludes Paul's argument in 1 Timothy 2:11–15 on the ground that it does not cohere with the *analogia fidei* he has constructed *on the basis of his now-limited canon.* This is a novel appeal to *analogia fidei* indeed, one that is methodologically indistinguishable from the approach of Ernst Käsemann or anyone else who chooses to go with a restricted canon.[125] If Jewett wishes to follow that line of argument, that is his business; but it is illicit to christen it with the *analogia fidei* argument, which traditionally assumes that the canon is the given. In fact, one of the methodological advantages of working with systematic theology is that, rightly executed, it eliminates the pick-and-choose kind of theologizing that enables the theologian to say pretty much what he wants to say. Systematic theology carefully handled can help ensure us that we still hear the Word of God, and not just the pre-selected answers to carefully limited questions.

In short, with care, there is no disgrace to the theological harmonization that is of the essence of systematic theology, but there are numerous pitfalls to be avoided.

7. *Systematic theologians should be careful to note how various truths and arguments function in Scripture and they should be very cautious about stepping outside those functions with new ones.*

"When considering apparently divergent passages, it is important to look at the purpose of the wording before pronouncing on the details of the language."[126] That advice is sound not only in exegesis but also in systematic theology.

Two or three rapid examples will flesh out the force of this reflection. It is as illicit to conclude from the fact that women were last at the cross and first at the tomb that therefore they should be ordained as elders as it is to conclude from the fact that all of the Twelve were men that therefore women should not be ordained as elders. Again, although the New Testament confesses that Jesus Christ is simultaneously God and man and that God cannot be tempted, it does not necessarily follow that Jesus Christ cannot be tempted.

There are two reasons why we need to be extraordinarily hesitant about stepping outside the example of Scripture in such matters. First, to ascribe certain functions to various truths or events in Scripture even though Scripture does not make use of those same truths and events to develop such functions may involve us in a prejudicial selection of data from the data base. We may fail to learn how certain truths function at a *pastoral* level, or we may unwittingly draw a conclusion that contradicts some of the primary data.

The second reason lies in the fact that a number of fundamental Christian beliefs involve huge areas of unknowns. Take, for instance, the Incarnation, or the Trinity, or the relationship between God's sovereignty and man's responsibility. In each of these areas, it is possible to demonstrate that there is no necessary logical contradiction; but it does not seem possible at the moment to provide an exhaustive account of how these fundamentals of the faith cohere. We are dealing with the suprarational[127] (but certainly not with the irrational or the illogical), with a painful shortage of information at crucial points. But it is surely worth observing, for instance, that God's sovereignty functions in Scripture to engender confidence in His people (e.g., Rom. 8:28) and to ensure final judgment, but it never functions to reduce man to the status of an irresponsible robot. Similarly, man is encouraged to believe, choose, obey, repent, and so forth, but his responsibilities in these areas never function in the Scriptures (as they sometimes do in other Jewish literature) to make God fundamentally contingent.[128]

These cautions, I hasten to add, do not call into question the value of logic. Rather, they highlight the complexity of the data and the fact that certain data we might desire are not to be found in Scripture. To limit oneself primarily to copying the functions found in Scripture is to adopt a methodological control that will ensure that one's systematic theology is a little more biblical than might otherwise be the case.

CONCLUSION

The one thing I am here to say to you is this: that it is worse than useless for Christians to talk about the importance of Christian morality, unless they are prepared to take their stand upon the fundamentals of Christian theology. It is a lie to say that dogma does not matter; it matters enormously. It is fatal to let people suppose that Christianity is only a mode of feeling; it is virtually necessary to insist that it is first and foremost a rational explanation of the universe. It is hopeless to offer Christianity as a vaguely idealistic aspiration of a simple and consoling kind; it is, on the contrary, a hard, tough, exacting, and complex doctrine, steeped in a drastic and uncompromising realism. And it is fatal to imagine that everybody knows quite well what Christianity is and needs only a little encouragement to practise it. The brutal fact is that in this Christian country not one person in a hundred has the faintest notion about what the church teaches about God or man or society or the person of Jesus Christ.[129]

So writes Dorothy Sayers, and I think she is basically right. This chapter has dealt with technical articles and critical judgments, but in the final analysis what is at stake is not some purely academic dispute, but what we preach.

I am not persuaded, either by Bauer or by Dunn, that the early church was characterized by such tepid toleration and unconcern for truth that it would have put up with basic theological liberalism. As I read the evidence, I perceive great diversity in emphasis, formulation, application, genre of literature, and forms of ecclesiastical administration. But I also perceive that there is a unity of teaching that makes systematic theology not only possible but necessary, and that modern theology at variance with this stance is both methodologically and doctrinally deficient. It is difficult to conceive how systematic theology of the sort defended in this chapter is possible unless the New Testament documents (and the Old Testament documents as well, for that matter) are true and trustworthy; and it is difficult to conceive how the same documents can be true and trustworthy without finding systematic theology both possible and necessary.

There are many questions surrounding the unity and diversity of the New Testament that I have not broached here, not least the relationship of the New Testament to the Old; but if the main lines of the argument are sound, then Evangelicals have every reason to ignore the demurrals and get on with writing systematic theology and training systematic theologians. And perhaps such highly desirable goals constitute sufficient reason for a student of the New Testament to step outside the area of his relative expertise.

ON THE FORM, FUNCTION, AND AUTHORITY OF THE NEW TESTAMENT LETTERS

Richard N. Longenecker

Richard N. Longenecker

Richard N. Longenecker is Professor of New Testament at Wycliffe College, University of Toronto. He is a graduate of Wheaton College (B.A.), Wheaton Graduate School of Theology (M.A.), and New College, University of Edinburgh (Ph.D.), with further study at the University of Basel and Cambridge University. Formerly he taught at Wheaton College, Wheaton Graduate School of Theology, and Trinity Evangelical Divinity School. Dr. Longenecker is the author of *Paul, Apostle of Liberty* (1964), *The Christology of Early Jewish Christianity* (1970), *The Ministry and Message of Paul* (1971), *Biblical Exegesis in the Apostolic Period* (1975), "The Acts of the Apostles" in *The Expositor's Bible Commentary*, vol. 9 (1981), and over thirty articles in periodicals and symposia. He is a member of Studiorum Novi Testamenti Societas, the Society of Biblical Literature, the Evangelical Theological Society, Tyndale Fellowship for Biblical Research, the Institute for Biblical Research, and the Canadian Theological Society. He is also a member of the Committee for Bible Translation for the New International Version of the Bible.

ON THE FORM, FUNCTION, AND AUTHORITY OF THE NEW TESTAMENT LETTERS

Of the twenty-seven New Testament writings, twenty-one are letters. The four Gospels, of course, are not letters; neither are the Acts of the Apostles and the Apocalypse of John. Within the Acts and the Apocalypse, however, there are nine more letters: one from the Jerusalem church to Gentile Christians in Antioch, Syria, and Cilicia (Acts 15:23–29); one from the commander Claudius Lysias to the governor Felix (Acts 23:26–30); and seven from the exalted Christ through John the Seer to seven churches in western Asia Minor (Rev. 2–3).

The letters of the New Testament, together with the Gospels, Acts, and the Apocalypse, have been accepted by the church as the touchstone for Christian faith and practice and therefore are designated "canonical" (i.e., "authoritative," "officially approved"). Most orthodox Christians receive them as the revelation of God and view them on a par in authority with the Hebrew Scriptures, the so-called Old Testament. But orthodox Christians also affirm that they are fully human writings as well, in that they were written in specific historical situations with particular purposes in mind, using the literary forms then current. As we hold, then, to both their divine inspiration and their human provenance, questions naturally arise as to the impact of the divine on the human and of the human on the divine in the composition of the New Testament letters.

Our purpose here is to consider certain aspects of the latter point, asking about the impact of the literary forms used by the letter writers of the New Testament on the authority claimed by and/or attributed to their writings. Since form and content, in varying degrees, are inseparable in the study of any body of literature, it is necessary to give attention not only to what is said but also to how it is said—viz., to the form used to convey meaning and to the function served by that particular form.

LETTERS IN ANTIQUITY

The letter form is almost as old as writing itself, reaching a high point of development in Greco-Roman times. An emphasis on education, the need to administer far-flung peoples and provinces, and increased travel made letter writing among Greeks and Romans common. Extensive correspondence was in vogue in the imperial courts of Rome, with facility in the art considered of great importance in a young man's training.

Most of the extant Greek and Roman letters are business letters expressing the interests and concerns of commerce. Even receipts, reports, contracts, wills, and land surveys were written up in letter form. Private letters dealing with all sorts of matters are common from the period as well, as are also official letters on political, judicial, and military themes. In addition, there were public letters written for political purposes and tractate or essay-type letters for literary and educational purposes. Isocrates (436–338 B.C.) and Plato (427–347 B.C.) were two of the earliest practitioners of the art of the public letter, addressing their appeals to kings and populace. The Roman statesman Cicero (106–43 B.C.) was famous for his use of the letter to influence public opinion, with 931 of his letters being published either during his lifetime or after his death. The twenty-four letters attributed to Hippocrates, written by the Hippocratic school during the first century B.C., are good examples of public letters for educational purposes. And Seneca's (4 B.C.–A.D. 65) Letters to Lucilius are classic examples of the tractate type of letter, with their moralistic advice on "how to live."

Letter writing among the Jews during the Greco-Roman period is a more difficult matter to document, simply because the Jewish impulse toward preservation was directed elsewhere and therefore very few Jewish letters remain. Acts 28:21 implies that Jewish officials sent letters when necessary, and the Talmud speaks of rabbis carrying on correspondence with Jewish communities in the Diaspora.[1] The letters of which the Talmud speaks were pastoral letters, in which rabbinic authorities responded to questions from Jews outside Israel and gave counsel. In addition, there were tractate-type letters circulating within Israel, such as the Letter of Aristeas and the Epistle of Jeremy.

The letter form was popular in antiquity for the same reason that it remains so today, viz., its stress on "presence"—the presence of the writer with those being addressed, even though physically separated. This feature was of great importance, not only for writers of private and pastoral letters, but also for those who wrote commercial, official, public, and tractate letters. For personal letters, "friendly relationship" was at the fore in this feature of "presence"; for pastoral letters, a past relationship and present authority were highlighted; for letters of a more public or official kind, "presence" conveyed authority; and for tractate or essay-type letters, the conversational dialogue of spoken instruction was continued.

PASTORAL LETTERS

As is well known, Adolf Deissmann was so impressed by the correspondence in form between Paul's letters and the "true letters" of the nonliterary papyri—i.e., letters arising from a specific situation and intended only for the eye of the person or persons to whom they were addressed and not for the public at large or with the studied art of the "literary epistles" of the day—that he concluded, "I have no hesitation in maintaining the thesis that all the letters of Paul are real, nonliterary letters. Paul was not a writer of epistles but of letters; he was not a literary man."[2] What Deissmann was attempting to highlight by this distinction were (1) the genuine, unaffected religious impulse that can be seen in Paul's letters and (2) the definite, unrepeatable situations to which they spoke. But laudatory and helpful as his thesis was at the time, it was also misleading. As Milligan pointed out:

> The letters of St. Paul may not be epistles, if by that we are to understand literary compositions written without any thought of a particular body of readers. At the same time, in view of the tone of authority adopted by their author, and the general principles with which they deal, they are equally far removed from the unstudied expression of personal feeling, which we associate with the idea of a true letter. And if we are to describe them as letters at all, it is well to define the term still further by the addition of some such distinguishing epithet as "missionary" or "pastoral." It is not merely St. Paul the man, but St. Paul the spiritual teacher and guide who speaks in them throughout.[3]

And scholarship today agrees that Paul's letters are not merely private, personal letters—at least, not "private" and "personal" in the usual sense of those terms. They were written to Christian believers for use in their common life, by one who was self-consciously an apostle and therefore an official representative of early Christianity. Quite correctly Selby writes:

> These letters are not, strictly speaking, private letters. As their character clearly shows, they were written to be read before the congregation to which they were addressed. The second personal plural, the allusions to various persons, and the greetings and salutations make them group communications.[4]

Paul's letters are the principal New Testament writings coming closest to the standard form of nonliterary "true letters" in the Greco-Roman period. That form may be outlined as follows:

1. An introduction, prescript, or salutation, which included the name of the sender, the name of the addressee, greetings, and often a wish for good health.
2. The body or text of the letter, introduced by characteristic formulae.
3. A conclusion, which included greetings to persons other than the addressee, a final greeting or prayer sentence, and sometimes a date.

All of the thirteen letters bearing Paul's name conform in their structure and idiom to this standard form. Only the apostle's thanksgiving sections (often with a prayer for his converts) before the body of the Letter (except in Galatians) and his parenthetic sections that follow the central body sections go beyond the common form of the day. But those features probably derive from Christian preaching and may have had parallels in Jewish pastoral letters now extinct. Romans and Ephesians, while in form like the rest, in content exceed the limits of a strictly pastoral letter and in tone suggest something more of a tractate letter. But of the rest—1 and 2 Corinthians, Galatians, Philippians, Colossians, Philemon, 1 and 2 Thessalonians, 1 and 2 Timothy, Titus —their structure, idiom, contents, and tone are those of what can appropriately be called a pastoral letter. This is true also of the writings known as 2 Peter, 2 and 3 John, and Jude.

We must speak later of tractate letters, amanuenses, anonymity, and pseudonymity. Here our purpose is to point out that the pastoral letters of the New Testament took their form from the conventions of the day, were written as substitutes for being present in person, and were meant to convey the apostolic presence, teaching, and authority. Their form was that of the Greco-Roman world from the third century B.C. to the third century A.D.; their function was parallel to that of Jewish pastoral letters; and their authority was that of Christian apostles, to whom was given the right to teach and govern the church of God. As pastoral letters, they were to be read widely in the churches (cf. their salutations and such verses as Col. 4:16; 1 Thess. 5:27). Yet as letters arising from a particular situation and speaking to that situation, their message was more circumstantially than systematically delivered. They are not tractate- or essay-type letters. They are real letters dealing pastorally with issues then current, and they must be interpreted accordingly.

TRACTATE LETTERS

What is not often enough recognized is that in addition to pastoral letters the New Testament contains tractate-type letters. Their purposes, of course, are also broadly pastoral, and their form is in many respects that of ordinary letters. But their content and tone suggest that they were originally intended to be more than strictly pastoral responses to specific sets of issues arising in particular places. And at times, one or more of the extant texts or some ecclesiastical tradition gives us a hint of this difference.

The Letter to the Romans, for example, is the longest and most systematic of Paul's writings and more a comprehensive exposition of the apostle's message than a letter as such. A great many proposals have been made as to its purpose and audience, with that whole discussion becoming more intense of late.[5] Probably, however, we should view the body of Romans (1:18–15:13) as something of a précis of Paul's preaching in Jewish synagogues of the Diaspora and at Jewish-Gentile gatherings, with that précis during the course of his missionary activities having become more and more polished in literary form and having been used by his converts at various times as a kind of missionary tractate giving a résumé of his message, and which, when directed to Rome, was supplemented with an epistolary introduction (1:1–17) and the personal elements of chapters 15 and 16 (esp. 15:14–16:24, allowing the possibility of a separate provenance for most of chapter 16 and viewing the doxology of 16:25–27 as part of the original tractate). Such a view would explain the internal differences of content and tone between 1:18–15:13 and 1:1–17; 15:14ff. It would also go far to explain the uncertainties within the early church regarding the relation of the final two chapters to the rest of the writing, the absence of "in Rome" at 1:7 and 15 in some minor manuscripts, and the presence of two doxologies at 15:33 and 16:25–27, with the Western and Byzantine Texts adding a third at 16:24.

The so-called Letter to the Ephesians also has the appearance of a tractate letter, particularly if we accept the testimony of the earliest extant texts (Aleph, B, P[46]) and omit the words "in Ephesus" at 1:1. It may be an introduction by an early disciple of the apostle to the letters of Paul, as E. J. Goodspeed and others have argued. More likely it was originally meant to be a précis of Paul's teaching on redemption in Christ and the nature of the church, and was sent out as something of a circular tractate letter to churches in the Roman province of Asia, of which Ephesus was the capital.

The Letter to the Hebrews has less of a letter form than any New Testament epistolary writing considered so far, being exceeded in this respect only by James and 1 John. Without salutation, without stated author, without specified address, it is almost entirely an expositional and hortatory tractate. Only at the close of the final chapter is there the form and idiom of a letter: in asking for the prayers of its addressees (13:18–19), in a rather eloquent benediction (13:20–21), and in a personal subscription (13:22–25). Just who wrote it and to whom it was written have been continuing questions that probably will never have a final answer—though I believe that Apollos to Jewish Christians with an Essene-type background is as good a guess as any. The original recipients of the letter undoubtedly knew who the author was, probably through a messenger authorized to deliver the composition. Nevertheless, whatever its provenance, Hebrews is in form a tractate letter, and that fact has some bearing on its interpretation.

Likewise, three of the seven so-called Catholic or General Epistles are identifiable as tractate letters. The Letter of James begins with a salutation typical of a letter (1:1), but thereafter it is a collection of moral maxims and exhortations. Probably the writing was first a sermon representative of James's teaching—perhaps extracts drawn from a number of his sermons—and only later given a salutation and circulated widely as a tractate letter. First Peter also seems to be a compendium of Petrine sermonic and catechetical materials (1:3–4:11), to which has been added the salutation of 1:1–2, the exhortations of 4:12–5:11, and the personal subscription of 5:12–14. In the

form sent out to Christians in the five provinces of northern Asia Minor
and preserved for us in the New Testament, the work is genuinely
epistolary. But in that it incorporates earlier material representative of
Peter's preaching—perhaps even an early baptismal hymn (3:18–22)
used by Peter in his sermons and liturgical practice—it has the
character of a sermonic tractate with an attached letter. So too 1 John
probably was originally a compendium of John's characteristic teaching. At no point does it have the form or idiom of a letter, though 2 and
3 John may have served as covering letters in two instances.

The designation "Catholic" or "General" originated on the assumption that these writings were intended for Christians "universally" or "generally," in contrast to those of Paul that were addressed
to specific congregations or persons. But it is becoming increasingly
clear, particularly because of their affinities with the Qumran materials, that these writings are in reality Jewish-Christian compositions
that circulated at first primarily within the Jewish-Christian cycle of
witness in the church. Like their Jewish compatriots who collected
representative teachings of prominent rabbis, Jewish Christians seem
also to have been interested in the characteristic teachings of their
three most prominent leaders—Peter, James, and John—and to have
wanted this material disseminated widely, particularly to Jewish-
Christian congregations of the Diaspora. The tractate-type letter was
the form selected—either the more conventional tractate letter (as
James), a tractate with an attached letter (as 1 Peter), or a tractate with
a covering letter (as 1 John, with 2 and 3 John) —for it not only made
known the apostolic teaching but also conveyed the apostolic presence and authority.

AMANUENSES

The extant nonliterary Greek papyri, the bulk of which (some
40,000 to 60,000) were found during the 1890s in the Fayum of Egypt,
indicate quite clearly that an amanuensis or secretary was frequently,
if not commonly, used in the writing of letters in the years before,
during, and after the first Christian century. Literary men of the day
may have preferred, as did Quintillian (c. A.D. 35–95), not to use an
amanuensis for their personal correspondence, or they may have
agreed with Cicero (106–43 B.C.) that dictation to a secretary was an
expediency necessitated only by illness or the press of duties. But the
papyrus materials show that a common practice for more ordinary
men was to use an amanuensis to write out their letters, after which
the sender himself would often—though not invariably—add in his
own hand a word of farewell, his personal greetings, and the date.
Frequently the presence of an amanuensis is obvious by a difference of
hands in a letter: the salutation, body, and conclusion being written in
a more regular and practiced hand, with what follows more crudely

put down. Sometimes the involvement of an amanuensis is directly stated; at times it can be inferred from what is said; and at times it may be assumed by the more official nature of the contents and the quality of the syntax, as well as by a more literary hand writing. A number of papyrus letters state that an amanuensis was used because the sender was "unlettered" (μὴ ἴδοτες γράμματα or ἀγράμματος) or "wrote slowly" (διὰ τό βραδύτερα γράφειν), though probably the difficulty of procuring the necessary materials for writing and the relatively low cost of hiring a secretary—who would not only do the actual writing but also have at hand all that was necessary for the task—helped to make the use of an amanuensis both fashionable and practical, even for those for whom writing itself was no problem.

Writing skills of amanuenses undoubtedly varied. A third-century A.D. Latin payment schedule reads: "To a scribe for best writing, 100 lines, 25 denarii; for second-quality writing, 100 lines, 20 denarii; to a notary for writing a petition or legal document, 100 lines, 10 denarii."[6] The Greek biographer Plutarch (c. A.D. 46–120) credited Cicero (106–43 B.C.) with the invention of a system of Latin shorthand, relating how Cicero placed a number of scribes in various locations in the senate chamber to record the speeches and taught them in advance "signs having the force of many letters in little and short marks"[7]—though it may have been Tiro, the freedman of Cicero, who actually was the inventor, for inventions of slaves were often credited to their masters. The reference by Seneca (4 B.C.–A.D. 65) to slaves having invented among their other notable accomplishments "signs for words, with which a speech is taken down, however rapid, and the hand follows the speed of the tongue"[8] seems to support Tiro, or someone like him, as the originator and to suggest that at least by A.D. 63–64, when Seneca's Letters to Lucilius were written, a system of Latin shorthand was widely employed. The earliest comparable evidence for the existence of a system of Greek shorthand is contained in P. Oxy. 724, dated March 1, A.D. 155 ("the fifth of Phamenouth in the eighteenth year of the emperor Titus Ailios Hadrian Antonius Augustus Eusebius"), wherein a former official of Oxyrhynchus by the name of Panechotes binds his slave Chaerammon to a stenographer named Apollonius for a term of two years in order to learn shorthand from him. Though Panechotes' letter is a second-century writing, the developed system of shorthand that it assumes and which Chaerammon was to take two years to learn presupposes a workable system of Greek shorthand prior to this—at least in the first Christian century, and probably earlier.

The extent of freedom that amanuenses had in drafting letters is impossible to determine from the evidence presently at hand, and it undoubtedly varied from case to case. Amanuenses may have written a client's message word-for-word or even syllable by syllable; they may have been given the sense of the message and left to work out the wording themselves; or they may even have been asked to write in the sender's name on a particular subject without being given explicit directions as to how to develop the topic, especially if the sender felt his amanuensis already knew his mind on the matter. Scholarly opinion as to what the evidence indicates on this is sharply divided. Roller, for example, believed that ancient amanuenses had a great deal of freedom and that dictation of a word-for-word variety was rare,[9] whereas Hitchcock drew exactly the opposite conclusion.[10] But whatever method or methods may have been used in the writing of any particular letter, the sender often added a personal subscription in his own hand, thereby attesting to all that was written. At times he even included in that personal subscription a résumé of what had been written, thereby acknowledging further the contents and details.

Although we possess no autograph of any of the New Testament letters, it may be assumed that their authors followed current letter-writing conventions in their use of amanuenses as well—though in this case, amanuenses were probably more apostolic companions than trained scribes. In 2 Thessalonians 3:17 Paul says explicitly that it was his practice to add a personal subscription to his letters in his own handwriting, thereby attesting to what was written and assuring his converts that the letter was really from him. Such a statement fits well the literary convention of the day and alerts us to the likely presence of other such personal subscriptions in his own handwriting within the Pauline corpus, though it provides no guidance as to how to mark them off precisely. Likewise, the words of 1 Corinthians 16:21 and Colossians 4:18 ("I, Paul, write this greeting in my own hand") give reason to believe that the personal subscriptions in these letters were also distinguishable by their handwriting from their respective texts—necessitating, of course, the involvement of amanuenses in what precedes the subscriptions. The words "I, Tertius, who wrote this epistle in the Lord" in Romans 16:22 cannot be understood in any way other than that an amanuensis was involved to some extent in Paul's letter to Christians at Rome (or, as some suggest, to believers at Ephesus). Galatians 6:11, while admittedly allowing some uncertainty as to the precise extent of the reference, recalls certain features observable in the subscriptions of Greek letters when it declares, "See what large letters I use as I write to you with my own hand!" And Philemon 19 may well be the beginning of such a personal subscription with its words, "I, Paul, am writing this with my own hand," thereby attesting what has been said in verses 1–18 and going on to restate a willingness to assume all Onesimus's debts to Philemon.

Of the non-Pauline materials in the New Testament, 1 Peter among the Epistles and John among the Gospels (to go for a moment beyond just letters) are most plausibly to be viewed as written by amanuenses. As Milligan observed, "In the case of the First Epistle of St. Peter, indeed, this seems to be distinctly stated, for the words διὰ Σιλουανοῦ, 'by Silvanus,' in c. v. 12, are best understood as implying that Silvanus was not only the bearer, but the actual scribe of the Epistle. And in the same way an interesting tradition, which finds pictorial representation in many mediaeval manuscripts of the fourth Gospel, says that St. John dictated his Gospel to a disciple of his named Prochorus."[11]

Just how closely amanuenses were supervised in the writing of the canonical pastoral and tractate letters is impossible to say. As we have seen, the responsibilities of amanuenses could be quite varied, ranging all the way from taking dictation verbatim to "fleshing out" a general line of thought. Paul's own practice probably varied with the circumstances encountered and the companions available. Assuming, as Roller proposed, that amanuenses were often identified in the salutations (particularly if they would be known to the addressees), more might be left to the discretion of Silas and Timothy (cf. 1 Thess. 1:1; 2 Thess. 1:1) or to Timothy alone (cf. 2 Cor. 1:1; Col. 1:1; Phil. 1:1; Philem. 1) than to Sosthenes (cf. 1 Cor. 1:1) or Tertius (cf. Rom. 16:22) —and perhaps much more to Luke, who alone was with Paul during his final imprisonment (cf. 2 Tim. 4:11). And if in one case an apostle closely scrutinized and revised a letter, at another time he may have allowed it to go out practically unaltered.

A high view of New Testament authority does not demand that everything was actually written by an apostolic man himself, nor does the recognition of an amanuensis at work in a writing diminish our access to the mind of the writer or lessen our confidence in its message. Historically, in all extant letters from antiquity—as well, of course, as in all modern letters, unless there is a disclaimer—it is assumed that the sender is responsible for everything written at his direction and attested by his hand, however the actual composition took place. And theologically, a doctrine of inspiration refers to the original writing as finally produced and faithfully reproduced, whatever methods and procedures were used in its formulation. The recognition of amanuenses at work in the New Testament writings keeps us from being wooden in either criticism or interpretation, but it does nothing to detract from the New Testament's authority. Rather, being sensitive to the methods used in the writing of canonical letters, we gain a new appreciation for their message, for we are able to interpret a message better by understanding not only its linguistic features and historical context but also its literary conventions.

ANONYMITY AND PSEUDONYMITY

While the involvement of amanuenses in the writing of New Testament letters poses no threat to their authority, many view their anonymity (Hebrews, 1 John, and probably Ephesians) and possible pseudonymity (e.g., the Pastoral and General Epistles) as doing just that. With F. E. D. Schleiermacher, J. G. Eichhorn, W. M. L. de Wette, and F. C. Baur, a new literary category of "canonical pseudepigrapha" arose in nineteenth-century criticism and has been commonplace in New Testament scholarship ever since.

The issue is usually treated by claiming that pseudonymity was merely a literary convention of the day—an innocent literary device under no onus of deception, forgery, or blame—and was therefore acceptable to early Christians, as it was to others in antiquity. Appealing for support to the fact of numerous anonymous and pseudonymous writings in antiquity, the proponents of such an approach are mainly interested in the psychology underlying the production of such materials and not in their acceptance. But Candlish long ago aptly disputed the relevance of an appeal to ancient historiography as a justification for the innocence and acceptability of pseudonymity, concluding from a study of the evidence

> that in the early Christian centuries, when any work was given out as of ancient or venerable authorship, it was either received as genuine, which was done with very great facility of belief, or rejected as an imposture; that such fictions, though very common, were regarded, at least by the stricter Christian teachers, as morally blameworthy; and that the notion of dramatic personation as a legitimate literary device is never mentioned, and seems never to have been thought of as a defence of such compositions. If any author wrote a pseudonymous book in such a way, he must have been very unsuccessful in his purpose; for it was generally taken as a genuine work, or else rejected as feigned and worthless."[12]

Aland has recently proposed an eschatological and theological explanation for these issues.[13] He argues that with the expectation of an imminent Parousia and the experience of the Spirit's active presence in the church, there was no impulse among Christians to assign authors' names to their writings, but with the abating of eschatological enthusiasm and the loss of a consciousness of the Spirit's activity, there arose an awareness of history that called for the assigning of authors to the describing of events that accompanied revelations. So in the earliest period of the Christian movement a notion of anonymity dominated, but some time around the beginning of the second century the ascription of authorship became important—and with that later interest pseudonymity arose. Paul's letters, of course, do not fit into such a pattern, but Aland identifies them as real letters to be distinguished from literary epistles and so does not consider them in opposition to his thesis. Yet it must be asked (1) if Aland has not inadvertently resurrected Deissmann's overdrawn distinction between letters and epistles in the interests of his thesis; (2) why Paul was able to manifest the Spirit's activity and also identify his authorship, whereas others could not; and (3) whether the picture of the early church as drawn by Aland and others who stress the effects of "Parousia Delay" and the rise of "Early Catholicism" is really accurate.

A better approach, I believe, is to recognize (as I have done above) that there are features that distinguish pastoral letters from tractate letters in the New Testament—even though both types are broadly pastoral in purpose and of the same genus in form—and to relate the questions of anonymity and pseudonymity to these two species of related writings. The issues are somewhat different for each, and therefore we must deal with them separately.

Eleven of the Pauline letters and four of the General Epistles we have called pastoral letters, and of this lot 1 and 2 Timothy, Titus, 2 Peter, and Jude are most commonly identified as canonical pseudepigrapha. Yet a good case for the internally claimed and traditionally accepted authorship of each is by no means impossible. With Schleiermacher's 1807 attack on the genuineness of 1 Timothy and Eichhorn's 1812 widening of that criticism to include all three so-called Pastoral Epistles, the category of canonical pseudepigraphy was born. Principally on the basis of their more formal tone and the high frequency of words not found elsewhere in the acknowledged writings of Paul, these three letters were discounted and have been set aside by many as not being by Paul but a later Paulinist. But taking into consideration the difference of topic in these letters, the altered situation presupposed by them for the apostle at the time of writing, and the probable use of an amanuensis, such features need not be considered fatal to Pauline authorship. In fact, scholarship of late has begun to return to a consideration of the authenticity of these letters as a live possibility—largely along the lines of Otto Roller's 1933 vindication of them on an amanuensis hypothesis, as witness the treatments by J. Jeremias (1949), J. N. D. Kelly (1963), and C. F. D. Moule (1965).

The absence of any reference to an amanuensis in 2 Peter may be the key to its stylistic and conceptual differences from 1 Peter. Perhaps this is how Peter himself wrote when not aided by Silas (1 Peter 5:12), Mark (*à la* Papias on the composition of Mark's Gospel), or Luke (cf. Peter's preaching in Acts). And the departure from the LXX in its one Old Testament quotation in 2:22, evidently translated directly from the Hebrew of Proverbs 26:11, suggests a Hebraic background for 2 Peter. Likewise, a circumstantial case can be made for Jude. Paul's reference to "brothers of the Lord" carrying on an itinerant ministry (1 Cor. 9:5) suggests that Jude's conversion and prominence in the early church was no more impossible than was James's. "It is not inconceivable," as Beasley-Murray points out, "that after the death of James, Jude should have addressed a similar circle of readers as his brother to safeguard them from new perils."[14] The reference to 1 Enoch in verse 14 and the allusion to the Assumption of Moses in verse 9 seem to relate the author and his readers to the category of Jewish Christians. And it is difficult to see why a pseudonymous writer would assume the name of Jude to commend his work when a more prominent figure would surely have served better.

Anonymity is principally an issue for what we have called tractate

letters in the New Testament. But tractate letters were undoubtedly
not anonymous to their original recipients, being introduced by messengers who delivered them and/or covering letters from their authors.
Thus Hebrews, while anonymous, was probably introduced by the one
who delivered it, with its personal subscription of 13:18–25 validating
the messenger's statements and emphasizing the author's "presence."
Likewise, 1 John was probably delivered by someone who could speak
regarding its provenance, and it may have had covering letters (2 and 3
John) attached on two occasions. Romans, James, and 1 Peter, while
probably formulated first as tractates, were sent out as letters and in
this manner circulated widely. And the hypothesis that Ephesians was
authored by Paul at about the same time as the Colossian letter and
meant to be something of a tractate or circular letter to Christians in
the Roman province of Asia is as good an explanation for its
peculiarities of style, structure, and contents as any other.

Anonymity may be a frustrating phenomenon for us today as we
seek to reconstruct situations and purposes, but it is doubtful that it
was to the original authors and recipients. Messengers, covering letters, and incorporated personal references all served in various ways
to provide these details and to strengthen the feature of "presence."
Ecclesiastical tradition has attempted to preserve these details; and
while we may not be prepared to accept everything that tradition tells
us on these matters, it is folly to refuse everything simply because it is
traditional. Anonymity, therefore, it may be assumed, had no necessary adverse effect on authority for the original recipients of the canonical tractate letters, and it need not be a disparaging factor for us
either.

SELECTED BIBLIOGRAPHY

Aland, Kurt. "The Problem of Anonymity and Pseudonymity in Chris-
    tian Literature of the First Two Centuries," *Journal of Theological
    Studies* 12 (1961): 39–49; also in *The Authority and Integrity of the
    New Testament* (SPCK Theological Collections 4). London: SPCK,
    1965. Pp. 1–13.
Bahnsen, Gregory L. "Autographs, Amanuenses and Restricted Inspira-
    tion," *Evangelical Quarterly* 45 (1973): 100–110.
Bahr, Gordon J. "Paul and Letter Writing in the First Century," *Catholic
    Biblical Quarterly* 28 (1966): 465–77.
————. "The Subscriptions in the Pauline Letters," *Journal of Biblical
    Literature* 87 (1968): 27–41.
Deissmann, Adolf. *Light From the Ancient East*, trans. L. R. M. Strachan.
    London: Hodder and Stoughton, 1909.
Doty, William G. *Letters in Primitive Christianity*. Philadelphia: For-
    tress, 1973.

Exler, Francis X. J. "The Form of the Ancient Greek Letter: A Study in Greek Epistolography." Dissertation, Catholic University of America, 1923.

Funk, Robert W. "The Letter: Form and Style," in *Language, Hermeneutic, and Word of God.* New York: Harper and Row, 1966. Pp. 250–74.

──────. "The Apostolic *Parousia:* Form and Significance," in *Christian History and Interpretation. Studies Presented to John Knox,* ed. W. R. Farmer, C. F. D. Moule, and R. R. Niebuhr. Cambridge: Cambridge University Press, 1967. Pp. 249–68

──────. "The Form and Structure of II and III John," *Journal of Biblical Literature* 86 (1967): 424–30.

Guthrie, Donald. "The Development of the Idea of Canonical Pseudepigrapha in New Testament Criticism," *Vox Evangelica* 1 (1962): pp. 43–59; also in *The Authority and Integrity of the New Testament* (SPCK Theological Collections 4). London: SPCK, 1965. Pp. 14–39.

Koskenniemi, Heikki. *Studien zur Idee und Phraseologie des griechischen Briefes bis 400 n. Chr.* Helsinki: Suomalaien Tiedeakatemie, 1956.

Longenecker, Richard N. "Ancient Amanuenses and the Pauline Epistles," in *New Dimensions in New Testament Study,* ed. R. N. Longenecker and M. C. Tenney. Grand Rapids: Zondervan, 1974. Pp. 281–97.

Mavrodes, George I. "The Inspiration of Autographs," *Evangelical Quarterly* 41 (1969): 19–29.

Milligan, George. *The New Testament Documents, Their Origin and Early History.* London: Macmillan, 1913.

──────. *Selections From the Greek Papyri.* Cambridge: Cambridge University Press, 1910.

Milne, H. J. M. *Greek Shorthand Manuals: Syllabary and Commentary.* London: Oxford University Press, 1934.

Moule, C. F. D. "The Problem of the Pastoral Epistles: A Reappraisal," *Bulletin of the John Rylands Library* 47 (1965): 430–52.

Pack, Roger A. *The Greek and Latin Literary Texts From Greco-Roman Egypt,* 2nd. ed. Ann Arbor: University of Michigan Press, 1965.

Roberts. C. H. *Greek Literary Hands, 350 B.C.–A.D. 400.* Oxford: Clarendon, 1956.

Roller, Otto. *Das Formular der paulinischer Briefe, ein Beitrag zur Lehre vom antiken Briefe.* Stuttgart: Kohlhammer, 1933.

Sanders, Jack T. "The Transition From Opening Epistolary Thanksgiving to Body in the Pauline Corpus," *Journal of Biblical Literature* 81 (1962): 348–62.

Schubert, Paul. "Form and Function of the Pauline Letters," *Journal of Religion* 19 (1939): 365–77.

Sherk, Robert K. *Roman Documents From the Greek East: Senatus Consulta and Epistulae to the Age of Augustus.* Baltimore: Johns Hopkins, 1969.

Stirewalt, M. Luther, Jr. "The Form and Function of the Greek Letter-Essay." A paper distributed to the Society of Biblical Literature Seminar on "The Form and Function of the Pauline Letter," 1971.

Turner, Eric G. *Greek Manuscripts of the Ancient World.* Princeton: Princeton University Press, 1971.

Wendland, Paul. "Die urchristlichen Literaturformen," in *Handbuch zum Neuen Testament*, I. 3. Tübingen: Mohr, 1912. Pp. 339–45.

White, John L. *The Form and Function of the Body of the Greek Letter: A Study of the Letter-Body in the Non-Literary Papyri and in Paul the Apostle.* Missoula: Scholars, 1972.

REDACTION CRITICISM:
ON THE LEGITIMACY
AND ILLEGITIMACY
OF A LITERARY TOOL

D. A. Carson

D. A. Carson

D. A. Carson is Professor of New Testament at Trinity Evangelical Divinity School. He is a graduate of McGill University (B.Sc.), Central Baptist Seminary in Toronto (M.Div.), Cambridge University (Ph.D.), and has studied at Regent College and in Germany. He has served both as a church planter and as a pastor and lectures frequently in Canada, the United States, and the United Kingdom. Before moving to Trinity, he taught at Northwest Baptist Theological College and Seminary in Vancouver. He is editor of the *Trinity Journal* and the author or editor of several books, including *Divine Sovereignty and Human Responsibility* and *From Sabbath to Lord's Day*, and of many articles. He holds membership in *Societas Novi Testamenti Studiorum*, Society of Biblical Literature, Canadian Society of Biblical Studies, Tyndale Fellowship for Biblical Research, and the Evangelical Theological Society.

REDACTION CRITICISM: ON THE LEGITIMACY AND ILLEGITIMACY OF A LITERARY TOOL

INTRODUCTION

A British journal recently published a short series of articles under the general title "Slippery Words."[1] Contributors treated such terms as *myth, eschatology,* and the like. No doubt the editor could have enlarged the list of entries had he chosen to do so; but for whatever reason, he did not. One expression that could lay large claim to consideration in any expanded list is "redaction criticism."

The ambiguity is partly denotative and partly connotative. At the denotative level, "redaction criticism" can refer to a surprising range of literary activity. It can refer to the study of how an author who depends on an earlier document has used that document—e.g., changing order, editing, polishing, transforming emphases. Elsewhere, when the source document is no longer available, "redaction criticism" can serve as a comprehensive category that includes source criticism and tradition criticism, since it is very difficult to say much about redaction until one has some idea of what is being redacted. Others use the expression in a much weaker sense to refer to the study of an author's particular emphases and tendencies.

The connotative ambiguities are not less diverse. To scholars with antisupernatural presuppositions, the practice of redaction criticism both confirms those presuppositions and serves as a tool for expressing them.[2] On the other hand, more than one conservative Evangelical has expressed strong (not to say, heated) reservations about the legitimacy of *any* use of redaction criticism.[3]

Before I can say anything useful about the legitimacy and illegitimacy of this literary tool, therefore, I will have to sketch in a little background. Having done this, I will offer a number of criticisms of the most common kinds of redaction criticism and provide a couple of examples. None of this material is original or comprehensive but it forms the necessary backdrop to the final section, in which I will suggest some guidelines for the use of redaction criticism by those who have a high view of Scripture. In other words, at that point I will offer some programmatic suggestions aimed both at advancing the debate among Evangelicals a little further and at demonstrating to non-Evangelicals that the reservations we maintain concerning redaction criticism are reasonable and that our use of the tool is not necessarily perversely idiosyncratic and inconsistent.

But first, something must be said about the development of the tool.

THE DEVELOPMENT OF REDACTION CRITICISM

The synoptic problem was widely recognized in the early church. The first known systematic attempt at harmonization is that of Tatian (c. 110–172); but for our purposes the fact that he made the attempt is more important than his solutions, for it is evidence of an awareness of some of the problems.

The synoptic problem, however conceived, involves some literary dependence; that is, some New Testament authors are using literary sources. That should not surprise us. Luke (1:1–4) tells us as much, and there is solid evidence of literary dependence elsewhere (e.g., 2 Peter/Jude). Assured that there were literary sources, modern critics of the past one hundred years or so have expended enormous amounts of energy on retrieving literary sources whose independent existence is not attested anywhere. Source criticism became one of the dominant interests of many New Testament critics at the turn of the century; and this, coupled with the prevailing rationalism, prompted many to date the Gospels (especially Matthew and Luke) rather late and to assess their historical trustworthiness as minimal (by conservative standards).

How, then, could very much be said about the historical Jesus? Once having removed the general reliability of the Gospels, scholars could not easily locate the historical Jesus. Based in part on source criticism and in part on a complete restructuring of first-century history, their studies produced highly diverse models of Jesus. Von Harnack constructed the classic liberal Jesus;[4] and many scholars accepted this Jesus as indeed historical, retrieved from the Gospels by judicious source criticism and post-Enlightenment insight. Schweitzer, however, demonstrated how subjective this historical reconstruction really was. The quest for the historical Jesus was leading down blind alleys. Yet Schweitzer's own reconstruction depended heavily on another selective ordering of the evidence: he thought the historical Jesus was an apocalyptic but misguided itinerant Palestinian preacher.[5] It all depended on the "sources" retrieved and the nature of the history that had been worked up by the scholar. The general effect of Schweitzer's work on radical criticism was nothing less than the tolling of the death-knell over the quest for the historical Jesus. The quest, hitherto judged difficult, was now deemed impossible.

In this environment, form criticism appeared and began to flourish. Developed in a systematic way by Hermann Gunkel for use in history-of-religions research into the Old Testament,[6] form criticism was rapidly and rigorously applied to the New Testament, in particular to the Gospels, by K. L. Schmidt,[7] M. Dibelius,[8] and Rudolf

Bultmann.[9] Form criticism was a way of getting behind the written materials to the oral sources. Using the studies of folklorists and anthropologists concerned with the passing on of oral tradition in primitive cultures, the form critics theorized that various kinds of story, each with its technical name ("miracle story," "apophthegm," or whatever)[10] necessarily tended to assume a certain shape or form in the course of being passed on from hearer to hearer. It was thought that if the form of any particular pericope in the Gospel is identical with the ideal form, that is solid evidence for a stable transmission of the story. If it breaks form, there have probably been a number of additions by later transmitters of the tradition or by the final redactor, who was no doubt motivated by theological concerns.

The early form critics went further, especially in two respects. First, they theorized regarding what situations in the early church (i.e., what "life-settings" or *Sitze im Leben*) would *generate* such stories. The church, then, does not merely pass on stories about Jesus; it *creates* them to meet various theological needs. Second, in the case of Bultmann in particular, his handling of form criticism was so tied up with his general historical reconstructions regarding pre-Christian Gnosticism and his presuppositional antisupernaturalism that the net effect of his studies was the conclusion that one could know almost nothing about the historical Jesus.

If such form-critical understanding of the formation of the Gospels is even approximately correct, then the Evangelists (i.e., those who put the four Gospels into their present form) were little more than compilers of discrete stories. Careful study of the Gospels, in this view, discovers very little about Jesus and a great deal about the life-settings of the church—or, more precisely, of various churches, since the churches behind the diverse Gospel pericopae were not thought to be much concerned with mutual conformity and consistency. The effect of this theory on Bultmann's two-volume *Theology* is a mere thirty pages devoted to Jesus (and those thirty pages say little that is positive) as compared with one hundred pages devoted to the beliefs of the Hellenistic communities. Many scholars abandoned the quest for the historical Jesus.

If several Gospels preserve the same story, but with changes in emphasis and form, then it becomes theoretically possible to plot the changes in the tradition as the story gets passed along. By this means one can chart a *trajectory* of the form and its changing content. As is well known, the German word *Formgeschichte* is poorly rendered by "form criticism." It might better be translated "form history" or "history of form." Because of adopted convention, I will continue to use the term *form criticism*, but the German term opens a window onto what is entailed when this literary tool is used.

In time, it came to be noticed that the Evangelists (i.e., the final compilers) were not simply collectors of nice stories. Coupling form criticism with literary dependence, it was argued that the Evangelists shaped the traditions that came to them; that is, they omitted things; added details; and changed emphases, specific utterances, and locale. They were *redactors*; that is, they edited this inherited material to express their own theology and their own view of the materials they were passing on. They were creative theologians in their own right.

Of course, this view of the Evangelists' task introduces a new problem. One must now distinguish between what is redactional and what is traditional—that is, between what the Evangelist has received in the tradition that has come to him and what he has added or changed himself. Discovering this distinction is the task of redaction criticism. Traditionally, if redaction criticism determines that some word or phrase is redactional, then even if it is ascribed to Jesus in the text it cannot possibly be authentic; that is, it cannot possibly derive from the historical Jesus in the days of His flesh. If, on the other hand, redaction criticism determines that some word or phrase is traditional, then at least it stretches back beyond the redactor. This does not guarantee its authenticity; it simply makes authenticity a live option. This slender distinction between redaction and tradition sparked off a new round of interest in the historical Jesus. The resulting pictures were still pretty minimalistic, but they offered more than Bultmann did.

The task of the redaction critic is to distinguish between what is redactional and what is traditional. To do this he establishes a number of criteria (some of which I will briefly consider in the next section). Hence, the validity of this initial distinction turns entirely on the validity of his chosen criteria, and redaction criticism itself turns in part on the validity of form criticism. Moreover, the expression "redaction criticism" came quickly to be used not only in the study of those places in the synoptic Gospels where there are literary parallels, but also in parts of the Gospels where there are no parallels, and in other kinds of documents (e.g., the letters of Paul). At that point redaction criticism is implicitly involved in source criticism and form criticism, because until something is known about the alleged source, not very much can be said about the way it is being redacted. In practice, source criticism, form criticism, and redaction criticism collapse methodologically into one procedure, and the procedure is still called "redaction criticism." But it needs to be pointed out that such redaction criticism is rather different from that practiced on passages that boast close literary parallels.[11]

This rather potted history of the rise of redaction criticism is fairly well known and is detailed with rigor elsewhere.[12] The only detail I must add is that in the present discussion the expression "redaction criticism" is being used in much broader ways that are rather divorced from these methodological and philosophical roots. The expression is often taken to refer to the study of the particular emphases of the

Evangelist (or other author) in question. For example, Mark character-istically uses εὐθύς and εὐθέως, whereas John uses κόσμος; how much do these linguistic distinctives reflect not *Jesus'* usage but the respec-tive *Evangelists'* usage? How does the topical ordering of material and the selection of *this* pericope over *that* affect the thrust of each Evangelist's message? Such questions begin to do justice to the contri-bution made by each Evangelist without necessarily bringing along the radical skepticism of the pioneering form critics and redaction critics. Moreover, methodologically the attempt to wrestle with such con-cerns was already well demonstrated in the careful and thought-provoking work of Ned B. Stonehouse.[13] Although he never used the expression "redaction criticism," he pioneered in developing what is in fact a rather conservative redaction criticism.

What should be clear at this point is that to comment on the legitimacy and illegitimacy of this particular literary tool raises a host of problems of definition. Osborne, for instance, aware of these prob-lems, wants to use redaction criticism to distinguish between "tradi-tion" and "redaction," but in his use of the terms, the question of historicity does not arise. Both redactional material and traditional material are authentic, but the former refers to what the Evangelist added or changed or reworded, whereas the latter refers to the form of the tradition he received.[14] The distinction that Osborne maintains assists him in detecting peculiar emphases and interests on the part of the Evangelists; but Osborne, especially in his most recent essay, at-tempts to distance himself from using redaction criticism to deter-mine authenticity.

Between this conservative use of redaction criticism and the radi-cal one, which developed the tool, stand a number of middle-of-the-road positions.[15] Whatever their individual merits or demerits, one cannot escape two facts: redaction criticism is here to stay and it means different things to different people. Especially the latter fact must be borne in mind when we attempt to synthesize an evangelical position.

COMMON CRITICISMS LEVELED AGAINST REDACTION CRITICISM

Before attempting to synthesize an evangelical position, I will note some of the charges against various kinds of redaction criticism. This list is neither exhaustive nor, for the most part, original; and the entries are not in any particular order. But if we are to assess the legitimacy and illegitimacy of this literary tool, we must take rapid note of some of its widely acknowledged weaknesses.

1. A majority of New Testament scholars still hold that the most likely solution to the synoptic problem is the two-source hypothesis. If it is correct, then one may legitimately speak of the ways in which

Matthew has changed, added to, or omitted something from Mark. With increasing frequency, however, the old Griesbach hypothesis has been dusted off and set up as an alternative option.[16] For those who hold it to be the correct solution, it is illegitimate to speak of Matthew changing Mark; one must speak of Mark changing Matthew. In my view, both solutions are too simple: there is more probably a certain amount of *inter*dependency. Perhaps Mark relied on an early (Aramaic?) Matthew, and Matthew relied on a finished Mark; I am uncertain. But certain parallel accounts can be more readily accounted for by assuming Mark borrowed from Matthew than vice-versa (e.g., the parable of the sower),[17] even if, taken as a whole, the two-source hypothesis is more believable. If the situation is complex, one may legitimately speak of the differences and emphases peculiar to Matthew, Mark, or some other Evangelist; but only with some hesitation may one speak of one Evangelist changing or modifying the work of another.

2. It is common knowledge that the comparative studies of oral tradition (e.g., on the Maori civilization) deal with periods of three hundred years or longer. By contrast, the Gospels were written within at most sixty years of the events they purport to describe. The effects of this restriction have not been adequately considered. Some dates offered for the Gospels are improbably late; but early or late, the Gospels stand in relation to the life of Christ more or less as we stand in relation to World War II or the Great Depression—*not* as we stand in relation to, say, the Restoration in Britain, the flourishing of the *coureurs de bois* in Canada, or the settling of New Amsterdam. There were *witnesses* still alive when the New Testament documents were written; but the way many form critics write one would think that all witnesses to the life, death, and resurrection of Christ had been mysteriously snatched away the moment after the Ascension, and a new group had to begin all over again.[18]

3. Gerhardsson and Riesenfeld have argued for a stability in the tradition owing to memory patterns in instruction shared by Jesus and the rabbis.[19] Even if they overstate the case, their most eloquent critic concedes there is something to it.[20]

4. Recent research has argued for *written* records that go back to Jesus' ministry.[21] Patterns in *oral* tradition have no parallel in *written* tradition. The form-critical hypotheses are beginning to appear increasingly dubious.

5. A good case can still be made for Matthean authorship of the Gospel of Matthew.[22] If that were once conceded, even as a possibility, then the first Evangelist, even if he relied on Mark (and why shouldn't he?), was also an eyewitness. The wedge between redaction and tradition would become worthless as far as questions of authenticity are concerned.

6. Radical form criticism assumes we have a much greater knowl-

edge of the life-settings of the church than we do. All we think we know of such settings is derived from speculation based on form-critical theories and fertile imaginations. Of course, such speculations *may* be sound, but they are *at best* nothing more than speculations.[23] As Humphrey Palmer has rather trenchantly remarked, whether or not the early church was adept at thinking up stories about Jesus to fit church settings, the form critics have certainly been adept at thinking up church settings to fit the stories about Jesus.[24]

7. The radical reconstruction postulates postresurrection believers who cleverly think up a lot of profound sayings and then ascribe them all to Jesus. This is psychologically unconvincing. Worse, it tilts against the evidence, for the Gospel writers claim to be able to distinguish between what Jesus says before the Cross and what the disciples understand after that event (e.g., John 2:20–22).[25]

8. The criteria that have been established to distinguish between redaction and tradition are for the most part so imprecise as to be not much more than silly. The criterion of dissimiliarity is the worst of these; that is, an authentic teaching of Jesus (it is argued) is one that can be paralleled neither in the early church nor in surrounding Judaism. This criterion has been ruthlessly shredded in several essays[26] but it is still defended in some circles. At *best* it might produce what is idiosyncratic about Jesus' teaching but it cannot possibly produce what is characteristic about it. Is any method more silly that requires that a historical person say nothing like what is said around him, and that, granted he is the most influential person of all time, so little influence his followers that no thought of theirs may legitimately be traced to him—even when those same followers deliberately make the connection?

To respond by saying that the criterion of dissimilarity at least has the advantage of affording the critic bedrock certainty regarding the authenticity of a few sayings out of the total complex of difficult material is nevertheless to agree with my point: the criterion is hopelessly inadequate for the task assigned it. Worse, there is an irresistible temptation to reconstruct the teaching of Jesus on the basis of this select material, and the result cannot possibly be other than a massive distortion.

9. The criterion of dissimilarity is doubly ridiculous when placed alongside the criterion of coherence. Unbounded subjectivity must be the result.[27] Moreover, the other criteria for distinguishing redaction from tradition do not fare much better.[28]

10. Redaction criticism hangs far too much *theological* significance on every changed καί and δέ. Literature is not written that way. In any case, even if we suppose that Matthew used Mark as a source and effected his changes for various reasons, it is illegitimate to conclude (1) that only the changes reflect what Matthew believed, for if he used a source and left it unaltered, then surely he did so because it

expressed what he wanted to say, and therefore one may legitimately deduce what Matthew believed only from his entire work, and not merely from the changes, and (2) that all changes are necessarily prompted by theological interests rather than an entire range of concerns. Redaction critics far too often see the knots on the trees; only occasionally do they see the trees. Rarely indeed do they perceive the forest.[29]

11. We speak of redaction criticism as a *tool*, a word that somehow conjures up images of scientific precision. In fact, a glance at the available redaction critical works on any Gospel reveals how terribly subjective these literary tools usually are. "Of course," Hooker comments, "NT scholars recognize the inadequacy of their tools; when different people look at one passage, and all get different answers, the inadequacy is obvious, even to NT scholars! But they do not draw the logical deduction from this fact"[30]—viz., that the tools are incapable of providing an entirely neutral and agreed judgment as to what is authentic.

12. It is methodologically irresponsible to pit history against theology as if the two could not be compatible.[31] Moreover, the oft-repeated claim that faith is independent of history is reasonable *only if* Christianity is reduced to purely existential categories. If, however, Christianity is grounded in what God in Christ did *in history* and if faith is related in some way to propositions about God's acts *in history*, then even if historical recital or historical evidence is not *sufficient* to call faith to life, yet nevertheless faith under such premises is so bound up with historical events that an ahistorical faith is both nonsensical and heterodox. Paul certainly thought so (see 1 Cor. 15:1–11).

13. It is too often forgotten that whatever else Jesus was, He was an itinerant preacher. As anyone who has done much itinerant preaching knows, minor variations of the same messages or rearrangements of them come out again and again. Form and redaction critics have developed no methodology for distinguishing between, on the one hand, similar sayings in separate Gospels that do reflect a trajectory of interpretation and, on the other, similar sayings in separate Gospels that are actually *both* authentic.[32]

14. It is illegitimate to reject a priori as unhistorical all that is abnormal, the more so if the context has prompted the reader to expect the abnormal.[33]

15. Individuals, not communities, write books (or chapters of books) and think creatively. No doubt the community is *one* of the factors that help to shape an individual, but that is not what the radical critics are saying. If it were, they would need to distinguish between what the hypothetical community believed and what the writer thought and make suggestions as to the methodological problem involved in distinguishing how much of the writer's content springs from community influence and how much from other sources of influence.

16. Radical form criticism arbitrarily limits the genuine teaching of Jesus to basic simple sentences. The most influential mind in the history of the world was, as France nicely puts it, "apparently incapable of any complexity of thought or care in composition, any word of explanation or development of a theme, all of which are freely credited to his followers."[34]

17. Form and redaction criticism have not established adequate criteria for distinguishing between elements of a story that break with the theoretical standard form because they are late additions and elements of a story that break with the theoretical standard form because they are *early reminiscences* that have not yet been whipped out of the account by the process of oral transmission. A careful reading of any twenty pages of Bultmann's *History of the Synoptic Tradition* brings to light numerous examples in which the learned Marburger proceeds by way of arbitrary declaration on this point, rather than by way of explanation. But if the distinction is incapable of rigorous justification, the plotting of entire trajectories is nothing more than arbitrary.

18. Similarly, inadequate thought has been given to criteria that might distinguish in the church between a *Sitz im Leben* that *creates* a story and one that *preserves* an authentic story. Unless unambiguous criteria are established to make this distinction, the results are arbitrary.

19. In any case, the suggestion that one can jump from a form to a particular creative setting in the church has been shown to be false. "Judgments about the Sitz im Leben of a pericope have often differed considerably.... Recent research into oral tradition points to a ... flexible situation. Almost every 'form' of oral tradition may be used in a wide variety of ways. Similarly, any given situation can utilize very different forms."[35]

20. Current interest in literary criticism and structuralism is calling into question the validity of any approach that focuses so narrowly on a pericope, a phrase, or a word that the broad literary unit, the Gospel itself, is overlooked. These new critics are far more interested in how each phrase or word or symbol in, say, Mark functions within the context of the entire Gospel of Mark.[36] In his recent study of this Gospel, D.H. Juel adopts just such an approach and notes in passing that if we begin to treat Mark as a piece of literature, it is very difficult to distinguish between tradition and redaction.[37] The point seems pretty obvious but it is regularly overlooked by the redaction critics. This is not to say that these new literary critics are concerned to maintain the historicity of the Gospels. Quite the contrary: the most influential of them suspect that the redaction critics are finding more bedrock history than is really there.[38] But it is to say that other approaches that treat the Gospels in a more unified fashion are available; and they call into question the piecemeal approach of mainstream redaction criticism.

These are some—by no means all—of the criticisms that have been raised against redaction criticism and its necessary progenitor, form criticism. It must not be thought, however, that redaction criticism has been used solely in the service of skepticism. Evangelicals have recently written two massive commentaries that owe much of their volume to a mild form of redaction criticism.[39] Other scholars have used the tool to one degree or another to distinguish peculiar emphases in the individual passion narratives,[40] to argue for the essential unity of the Matthean birth narratives,[41] and much more.

What, then, may be said in a programmatic or methodological way concerning the legitimacy and illegitimacy of redaction criticism? Before turning to such considerations, I would like to illustrate what has been written so far by examining two New Testament passages.

TWO EXAMPLES

I propose to offer a few observations (not thorough redactional studies) on two passages from Matthew. The first wrestles with questions of authenticity, and the second with questions of harmonization and emphasis. I will make no attempt to present in detail the meaning and/or history of the passages. Instead, my focus is exclusively on the italicized words, phrases, and clauses.

A. MATTHEW 5:17–20

[17]*Do not think* that I have come to abolish the Law *or the Prophets;* I have not come to abolish them but to fulfill them. [18]*I tell you the truth,* until heaven and earth disappear, not the smallest letter, not the least stroke of a pen, will by any means disappear from the Law until everything is accomplished. [19]Anyone who breaks one of the least of these commandments and teaches others to do the same will be called least in the kingdom of heaven, but whoever practices and teaches these commands will be called great in the kingdom of heaven. [20]*For* I tell you that *unless* your *righteousness surpasses* that of the Pharisees and the teachers of the law, you will certainly not enter the *kingdom of heaven.*

I propose to comment briefly on a select few of the redaction critical judgments currently in vogue.

1. Some see the separate verses as originally four discrete sayings that have been put together by the Evangelist.[42] This does not seem compelling. Did Jesus speak only in one-liners? Despite the contention of Banks,[43] the connecting words like γάρ and οὖν constitute no proof that the sayings were once separate; in fact if they had been joined together, would there not have been a need for connecting particles? What criteria can be offered to distinguish the one case from the other?

2. Some hold that the words "Do not think that" are a late rhetorical device that does not go back to Jesus (so also in a structurally

similar verse, Matthew 10:34).[44] What external evidence is there that this is a *late* rhetorical device? How does one explain that both here and in 10:34 Matthew ascribes these words to Jesus? *If* it is a late rhetorical device, and Jesus does not say precisely these words (in Aramaic or Greek), how does one methodologically distinguish between the possibility that Matthew made this part up and the possibility that even if the expression is Matthean the essential truth-content is to be traced to Jesus?

3. Several see the words "or the prophets" as a Matthean addition, since the disjunctive "or" occurs in thirteen other instances in this Gospel; and of these, nine are probably due to Matthew's redactional activity. Moreover, it is agreed that eight of these betray a similar construction, viz., a conjunction followed by a noun.[45] However, it must be noted that (1) this is not a rare construction in the New Testament; (2) the nine *probable* redactional instances of "or" are not entirely indisputable; (3) "nine out of thirteen" provides a statistical basis with a massive margin for error (or, otherwise put, the ratio is not demonstrably significant); and (4) *even if* Matthew added the term to his tradition (What tradition, precisely, if he was an eyewitness?), the joint expression may mean no more than the simpler expression, since "law" *can* refer to the entire Old Testament Scriptures (e.g., John 12:34; 15:25; 1 Cor. 14:21).

4. The words "I tell you the truth" are rejected as unauthentic by some[46] on several grounds: (1) in the parallel saying in Luke 16:17, this clause is missing; (2) the clause might well have arisen in Greek-speaking Judaism, and (3) Matthew is the only New Testament writer to use this particular formula with γὰρ (ἀμὴν γὰρ λέγω ὑμῖν). But in response we may well ask: (1) Does Luke's parallel seem to come from the same occasion? Is it certain the utterance was unattached in the tradition and nailed down in one place by Matthew and in another by Luke? How can this hypothesis be distinguished from the more plausible one—that an itinerant preacher says similar things on many occasions? And *if* the two accounts have the same source, how may we know Matthew added it, rather than supposing Luke dropped it? (2) *Perhaps* the clause arose in Greek-speaking Judaism, but *perhaps* not. Note the transliterated word ἀμήν. What does that suggest? And *if* the expression arose in such circles, *perhaps* Jesus was trilingual and invented it. And perhaps not. What *methodological* control is there to enable one to respond to any of these questions? (3) If Matthew is the only one to associate γάρ with the clause, might this not just as easily mean that only γάρ was added as that the entire clause is redactional? Is it not remarkable that only Jesus in the New Testament uses ἀμήν at the *beginning* of clauses—would this not argue for authenticity? In any case, though it is true that Matthew is the only New Testament writer to use γάρ with this expression, he does so in only four of thirty-two occurrences. That means he uses the expression without

γάρ twenty-eight times, but Mark uses the expression (without γάρ) only thirteen times, and Luke a mere six. Perhaps, it may be argued, if Mark or Luke had used the expression more, they too would have slipped in the odd γάρ. In any case, since I am not worried about the *ipsissima verba* of Jesus but only about His *ipsissima vox*, might it be that where γάρ does appear there is simply a Matthean connection that reveals a connection that Jesus Himself made, whether by contextual implication, logic, explicit statement (in Aramaic?), or some other means? How does one methodologically *eliminate* such possibilities?

5. Banks argues that the italicized words, *for, unless, righteousness, surpasses,* and *kingdom of heaven* are probably all unauthentic and that the verse as a whole, though traditional, is probably not authentic. However, he insists that Matthew is nevertheless not imposing something essentially alien to Jesus' intention but is simply drawing out some practical implications from the attitude Jesus maintains.[47] My problem with this approach is in part akin to my hesitations in all the other passages; but I will press on and ask a broader question. Did Matthew (according to Banks) simply make deductions about Jesus' general *attitude* without ever hearing Jesus deal with this subject? If he *did* hear Jesus deal with it, might he not be giving the gist of what Jesus said (*ipsissima vox*)? And how, methodologically speaking, can Banks (or anyone else) distinguish between these two cases?

I must hasten to add that these reflections in no way *prove* the authenticity of this snippet or that. I am at the moment concerned only with the methodological problems inherent in redaction criticism; and I am trying to demonstrate that at least in this passage redaction criticism is *intrinsically incapable* of dealing believably with questions of authenticity. It is not really a "tool" in any precise sense: it is freighted with subjective judgments; it is based on too many implausible assumptions; and, worst of all, in each judgment it makes it ignores numerous questions that are not only relevant but that expose its fundamental weakness.

It is also fairly clear, in this example at least, that the distinction between redaction and tradition is often not only unhelpful but misleading when it comes to weighing probabilities of authenticity. "Redactional" comments *may* be prompted by purely theological considerations but equally they *may* be prompted by stylistic concerns or even by additional information springing from further research (Luke 1:1–4). This fundamental point is disappointingly overlooked in Jeremias's last book on Luke.[48] Despite the formal rigor of the work, not only is there some *methodological* weakness in the attempt to distinguish tradition from redaction, but, far worse, Jeremias maintains the *theoretical* distinction between the two, maintaining that Luke is heard only in the redaction and that authenticity is possible only in the tradition. Such bifurcation is without methodological justification.

B. MATTHEW 19:16–21 AND PARALLELS

This is the first part of the parable of the rich fool. It is a particularly difficult example of somewhat divergent synoptic accounts of the same incident:

Matthew 19:16-20	*Mark 10:17-21*	*Luke 18:18-22*
[16]Now *a man* came up to Jesus and asked, "Teacher, *what good thing* must I do to get eternal life?"	[17]As Jesus started on his way, *a man ran up to him and fell on his knees before him.* "*Good teacher*," he asked, "what must I do to inherit eternal life?"	[18]*A certain man* asked him, "*Good teacher*, what must I do to inherit eternal life?"
[17]"Why do you *ask me about what is good?*" Jesus replied. "There is only One who is good. If you want to enter life, obey the commandments."	[18]"Why do you *call me good?*" Jesus answered. "No one is good—except God alone.	[19]"Why do you *call me good?*" Jesus answered. "No one is good—except God alone.
[18]"Which ones?" the man inquired. Jesus replied, "'Do not murder, do not commit adultery, do not steal, do not give false testimony, [19]honor your father and your mother,' and 'love your neighbor as yourself.'"	[19]You know the commandments: 'Do not murder, do not steal, do not give false testimony, do not defraud, honor your father and mother.'"	[20]You know the commandments: 'Do not commit adultery, do not murder, do not steal, do not give false testimony, honor your father and mother.'"
[20]"*All these I have kept,*" the *young man* said. "*What do I still lack?*"	[20]"Teacher," he declared "*all these I have kept since I was a boy.*"	[21]"*All these I have kept since I was a boy,*" he said.
[21]Jesus answered, "If you want to be perfect, go, sell your possessions and give to	[21]Jesus looked at him and loved him. "*One thing you lack,*" he said. "Go sell every-	[22]When Jesus heard this, he said to him, "*You still lack one thing.* Sell everything

the poor, and you will have treasure in heaven. Then come, follow me."	thing you have and give to the poor, and you will have treasure in heaven. Then come, follow me."	you have and give to the poor, and you will have treasure in heaven. Then come, follow me."

The account of the rich young ruler according to the three synoptic Gospels plays a central role in the history of Gospel criticism. It is often taken as one of the few stories in which doctrinal development is unambiguous, and therefore it functions in much critical thought as a central justification for very elaborate schemes.

The questions raised are too complex for exhaustive treatment here; but the following observations bear directly on the concerns of this chapter:

1. The parallels cited above are from a much larger pericope: Matthew 19:16–30; Mark 10:17–31; and Luke 18:18–30. Mark's account, with 279 words, is longer than the other two: Luke's has 202, and Matthew's, 270. The last figure is reduced to 225 if we eliminate Matthew 19:28, which has no parallel in the others. These figures are interesting insofar as they suggest that, given Markan priority, Matthew and Luke are not simply gratuitously *expanding* a simple account.

2. There are numerous minor variations from account to account. Only Matthew has ἰδού ("behold"; or, in the NIV, "Now . . . "). Matthew refers to the questioner as "one" (εἷς), but later tells us he was young (19:20). Mark likewise calls him "one" (εἷς; NIV, "a man"); but though he says nothing about this "one's" age, he provides a little detail regarding the encounter: it was *while Jesus was setting out on His way* that a man *ran up* to Him and *knelt before Him*. Luke, like Matthew, provides neither of these details, but he mentions that the questioner was "a certain ruler" (τις ἄρχων). Mark and Luke have the questioner reply, "All these things I have kept since I was a boy"; but in Matthew the statement is briefer: "All these I have kept." The reference to youth is preserved only in the fact that the man himself is described as "young." In Mark and Luke, it is Jesus who says, "One thing you lack" (with some variation in the words—Mark: ἕν σε ὑστερεῖ; Luke: ἔτι ἕν σοι λείπει); But Matthew puts these words as a question on the young man's lips: "What do I still lack?" Farther on (beyond what I have cited), in the resulting interchange with His disciples, Jesus speaks of the one who gives up family and goods "for me and the gospel" (Mark 10:29), or "for my sake" (Matthew 19:24), or "for the sake of the kingdom of God" (Luke 18:29). There are other less significant minor changes in grammar, word order, and the like.

It is difficult to see how some of these changes are anything other than stylistic. There is not much difference between ἕν σε ὑστερεῖ (Mark) and ἔτι ἕν σοι λείπει (Luke). The force of ἰδού in Hellenistic

Greek is so weakened that its presence changes nothing of substance. It *may* give an impression (in Matthew) that this story happens hard on the heels of the previous one; but this is doubtful. In short, some of these changes are of minimal significance.

Other changes clearly add something or take something away. Mark's statement "ran up to him and fell on his knees before him" has disappeared in Matthew and Luke; but with their shorter accounts, it appears that they are trimming and condensing a little. They certainly are not concerned to *deny* that the questioner ran up to Jesus and fell to his knees before him. Luke's added information that the questioner was "a certain ruler" does not derive from Matthew or Luke. If we may assume the two-source hypothesis, then these words are certainly redactional. However, three points must be noted: (1) Luke himself assures his readers (1:1–4) that his research has included many written and oral sources, including eyewitnesses. It is therefore entirely gratuitous to leap to the conclusion that because the words are redactional they must not refer to what is historically true. Even the suggestion that Luke guesses the man was a ruler because he knows that he was rich is rather simple-minded. Were all synagogue rulers (or members of the Sanhedrin—the expression could mean either) rich? Were they the only ones who were rich? In the light of Luke's description of his approach to writing the third Gospel, it is far more probable that Luke is relying on additional information for this redactional addition. (2) It is very difficult to detect theological significance in the change. It is historiographically responsible to read the three accounts and conclude that the questioner was a young, rich ruler. However, even if Luke had made something of the fact that he was a ruler, it would not necessarily follow that the additional information was not historically based. It might only mean that Matthew and Mark did not know this point, or that if they did, they chose not to make any capital out of it. What *methodological* way is there for distinguishing these options from one another? (3) It can hardly be overlooked that we have detected this redactional addition solely on the basis of the comparative passages and the assumption of the reliability of the two-source hypothesis. If at this point only Luke had preserved the narrative, there would have been no way to detect that ἄρχων was redactional; for the usual method, based on determining what words are particularly Lukan, yields false results in this case: Matthew uses the word thirteen times; Mark, twenty-eight; and Luke, thirty-one (which is proportionately fewer than Mark's usage).

The other minor variations from Gospel to Gospel are no more difficult than these, provided we remember that the Evangelists do not purport to give verbatim quotes, that they do summarize, and that they use their own language to provide an accurate impression of the historical substance. It is difficult to justify radical criticism on the basis of the variations "for my sake," "for me and the gospel," and "for the sake of the kingdom of God," since all of the Synoptists tie together Jesus, the gospel, and the kingdom as the ultimates for which a person must give up everything. Luke's "for the sake of the kingdom of God" (18:29) may be a conscious assimilation to 18:25 in order to promote literary unity in the narrative; and Matthew's brief "for my sake" may reflect the abbreviating of Mark's account characteristic of several other verses. Whether the young man asks, "What do I still lack?" (Matthew), or Jesus says, "One thing you lack," is scarcely a problem at all. It is possible that both the question and the answer were uttered: but if not, it is entirely within the range of reliable reporting to understand that the young man *in fact* was asking this question (with or without the words) by coming to Jesus with his dilemma and subsequent self-justification. He quite clearly thought of himself as perfectly obedient to the law, yet knew he was lacking something. No eyewitness would fail to perceive that he was in fact asking just this question, "What do I still lack?" whether he phrased it this way or not. Similar remarks could be made about Jesus' response. It is difficult to see how any of the three accounts says anything at this point that is not implicit in the other two.

The final minor variation I have mentioned in this section is the contrast between "All these I have kept since I was a *boy*" (νεότης, Mark and Luke), and Matthew's "All these I have kept," followed by the notice, "the young man [νεανίσκος] said." Schweizer says this is a "recasting"[49] of Mark's account. To what end, he does not suggest. Historically, the questioner would no doubt have put himself under the law in a formal way when he was twelve years old, when Jewish boys assumed the yoke of the commandments and were held responsible for them (Ber. 2:2; cf. Luke 2:42). This is necessary background behind all three synoptic accounts; so it is difficult to perceive any theological reason why it should be omitted, unless Matthew thought either that it was not particularly interesting or relevant, or that it was already well known. It is puzzling that Matthew should add ὁ νεανίσκος *only if we assume* that he had no information of the event other than what he could glean from Mark. If on the other hand we allow for the likelihood that he had other information and for the possibility that he was himself an eyewitness, there is no reason to suppose that his information is not true.

3. Up to this point, I have dealt with the minor variations and avoided the pair of major variations. I must now turn to the latter. In Mark and Luke, the questioner asks, "Good teacher, what must I do to inherit eternal life?" Jesus responds, "Why do you call me good? No one is good—except God alone." In Matthew, however, the questioner opens the exchange with "Teacher, what good thing must I do to inherit eternal life?" Jesus responds, "Why do you ask me about what is good? There is only One who is good." It is commonly taken for granted that Matthew introduces a change in Mark's wording because

he represents a later stage in the development of the church's doctrine when the church could no longer tolerate even the suggestion that Jesus might be sinful.[50]

The differences between Mark/Luke and Matthew at this point are indeed quite remarkable; but once acknowledged, this christological explanation for the differences must nevertheless not be adopted too hastily. Even if Matthew avoids the suggestion that Jesus was not "good," he nevertheless preserves the saying, "There is only One who is good"—an obvious reference to God. The alteration therefore "implies nothing about Jesus' status in relation to God," as David Hill has put it.[51] Stonehouse has argued at length, and convincingly, that christological concerns are not in this instance at the heart of any of the synoptic accounts.[52] Rather, in the way the story develops in the ensuing discussion with the disciples, there is a move in all three synoptic Gospels toward recognizing "the indispensability of the sovereign action of divine grace for discipleship as one of the most foundational elements in this story."[53] More telling yet, becoming perfect and *following Jesus* (not God) are seen as one act (Matt. 19:21); and farther on, the eschatological blessing is promised to those who have left all for *Jesus'* sake (Matt. 19:29). And it is Matthew alone who describes the session of the Son of Man (19:28). When to these salient points is added the fact that in all of the Synoptics Jesus most frequently is concerned with God's glory, God's kingdom, God's truth, God's will, and God's judgment and presents Himself as the Lord's anointed, then perhaps there is good reason for thinking that the alteration in wording is not motivated by christological concerns. Jesus in the days of His flesh manifested Himself progressively, allowing those around Him to perceive only gradually who He really was, speaking in terms and categories that unveiled His splendor best in the hindsight gleaned after the Cross and the Resurrection.[54] It is a mark of the fidelity of the Synoptists (Matthew included) to the historical situation that they have preserved this intrinsically more ambiguous self-revelation.

It must also be pointed out that the christological explanation for Matthew's alteration depends on a historical reconstruction that, however popular, takes constant liberties with the only text we have. Fair treatment of the New Testament documents does not support the view that a high christology was invented rather late.[55] The question is too large to be explored here; but it is surely a point for pause to note that Luke, apparently written *after* Matthew, does not detect any christological difficulty in Mark. Why then must we be so certain that Matthew's alteration is due to anything more than whatever prompted the change that placed the words "What do I still lack?" on the lips of the young man?

In point of fact, several different suggestions for the alteration have been offered.[56] Harmonization by mere addition ("*Good* master, what *good* thing ...?" followed by Jesus giving *both* answers), though logically possible, is not very convincing as a historical reconstruction —not least because of the kinds of changes the Evangelists have made elsewhere in the narrative. Pedantic precision and verbatim quotation do not seem to be their goals. Yet those same changes warn us against facile accusations that the writers are introducing errors of fact or substance. Just as a modern writer might condense a lengthy discussion and tell of it in his own idiom and in a fraction of the total number of words actually spoken, without being charged with lies, inventiveness, distortion, or deceit, so the Gospel writers must be allowed the same freedom. This is the nature of reportage, even reportage designed to make theological and historical points.

The question, then, is whether there is a likely reconstruction of the historical event that could have generated *both* Mark/Luke and Matthew on this point. To phrase the problem in this way presupposes that Matthew had access to knowledge regarding the event other than that gleaned from Mark; but I believe that is (to say the least) highly probable. If this assumption is correct, it is historiographically irresponsible *not* to attempt a reconstruction.

Suppose, then, as one possible reconstruction among several that I can think of, that the original question was something like this: "Good teacher, what must I do to inherit eternal life?" Such a way of addressing a teacher was (as far as we can tell) extraordinary, but both the form of address and the question itself reveal the young ruler had no proper understanding of what absolute goodness, God's goodness, really involved, nor of the need for divine initiative in order for a person to gain eternal life. If this were the opening remark, the idea of the *good* action or *good* deed is not spelled out, but is certainly bound up with the question as it stands; it is inconceivable that the ruler was asking about what *neutral* thing or *wicked* thing he would have to do to gain eternal life!

Suppose, further, that Jesus' answer was something like this: "Why do you ask *me* [with *me* emphatic] questions regarding the good? There is only One who is good, namely God." Such a statement, like many of Jesus' aphorisms, could purposely be a trifle ambiguous, precisely because it bears on the ruler's question in several complementary ways. It recognizes that the ruler's concern is what good thing he must do, even though he has not thought about absolute goodness; and it recognizes that the man is addressing Jesus as good, equally without giving thought to the absolute nature of God's goodness (cf. 1 Chron. 16:34; 2 Chron. 5:13; Ps. 106:1; 118:1, 29). The fact that the man did not in any ultimate sense wish to ascribe goodness to Jesus is revealed rather pathetically by the fact he did not wish to obey Him; and the same evidence shows his unconcern for ultimately good deeds. The root of the problem in all three synoptic Gospels is not christological, but an abysmal failure on the part of the ruler to recognize what kind of goodness is required in order to inherit eternal life. Jesus would not allow the fuzzy categories to stand.

If this reconstruction has any plausibility, then the alteration by Matthew is no more theologically significant than the other alterations he offers in this pericope. There is in Matthew a bit more emphasis against the merit theology presupposed by the ruler's question as recorded in *all* the Synoptics, but the general thrust of the account remains the same in each Gospel. I am not arguing that this must have been what happened, still less that we should preach theoretical reconstructions (my own or anyone else's). We must preach the Scriptures as they stand, for they, and not my reconstructions, constitute the Word of God written. On the other hand, I am certainly arguing that redaction criticism, which might legitimately find some small change of emphasis from Gospel to Gospel in this account, cannot be thought to have unearthed a major christological development. Such a theory requires the implausible notion that Matthew had no source other than Mark. Even if we accept such an unlikely suggestion, the exegesis of Matthew as the text stands does not encourage this kind of christological explanation, given the specific theological concerns Matthew preserves.

Christians, of course, might detect in Jesus' response, recorded in Mark and Luke, a tacit identification of Jesus with God. But this is to go beyond what the texts actually say.[57] I think the response may be part of a pattern of replies by Jesus that betray His own self-consciousness of His true identity; but in relatively few instances do such christological self-affirmations spring unambiguously from Jesus' lips. The subject is in any case too large to broach here; but it must be admitted that while radical critics have sometimes moved way beyond what the Synoptics actually say in this pericope, conservatives have sometimes done the same, if in an opposite direction.

The point of this lengthy section and its two Matthean examples is that redaction criticism is simply an inadequate tool for establishing authenticity; and although it is adequate for making a contribution to the study of an author's particular interests, even there it is not a neutral tool. It is used in connection with a broad range of reconstructions, theories, and exegetical decisions. But these observations bring me to the central question of this chapter.

SUGGESTED GUIDELINES FOR THE USE OF REDACTION CRITICISM

How legitimate, or illegitimate, is redaction criticism as a literary tool?

If its application to questions of authenticity depends on its roots in radical form criticism, the answer must surely be that redaction criticism is well-nigh useless. It can pick out eccentric bits here and there; but even then the distorted picture of Jesus thus drawn varies enormously from scholar to scholar. Redaction criticism that ignores the brevity of time between Jesus and the Evangelists, that utilizes comparative studies of oral tradition over centuries when it is dealing with a combination of written and oral tradition over decades at most, that disallows any firm connection between Jesus and Judaism or Jesus and the church, that depends on dogmatic certainties regarding the synoptic problem, and that disallows the *ipsissima vox* just be-cause the idiom is that of the Evangelist is methodologically bankrupt and should be abandoned forthwith by all.

More recently, however, there have been efforts by some, notably Osborne and Stein,[58] to use the criteria of redaction criticism not so much to disallow the authenticity of certain sayings as to establish the authenticity of at least some of Jesus' sayings. Stein's important essay allows four of the eleven criteria he suggests to function negatively; the rest, he argues, may legitimately function only positively. This means that when a particular saying is not demonstrably authentic according to the criteria Stein lists, it still does not follow that the saying is *not* authentic, because the positive criteria are simply incapable, methodologically speaking, of making a negative judgment. Stein's negative criteria *could* disallow the authenticity of some saying; but in my view, the application of those negative criteria is fraught with extra difficulties he does not discuss (and which, unfortunately, I cannot detail here).

The entire approach of Stein (and other conservatives who oper-ate this way even if they do not spell out their method as clearly as Stein) has much more to be said for it than the radical redaction criticism to which we have become accustomed. Nevertheless, two important cautions must be adopted rather urgently. The first is that even Stein's positive criteria are based, to a rather alarming extent, on a view of the descent of the tradition that still embraces critical or-thodoxy but may well be called into question at point after point. If this criticism is basically sound—and my primary motive for including the earlier sections of this chapter was to demonstrate its reasonable-ness, at least in a preliminary way—then the conservative use of re-daction criticism advocated by Stein and practiced by others must tread very cautiously lest it discover to its chagrin and danger that it has a tiger by the tail.

The second caution springs from the first. If conservative Evangel-ical scholars adopt redaction criticism of the conservative variety and, believing that it is an objective tool, ignore the doubtful historical assumptions that make up at least part of its pedigree, they are likely to find themselves in an intensely embarrassing position. Suppose, for instance, that in the defense of a high view of Scripture they use redaction criticism apologetically to establish the authenticity of this saying or that. What happens when they come to some saying where there are inadequate grounds to claim authenticity (on the grounds of this conservative redaction criticism) and perhaps some grounds, following Stein's negative criteria, to plead *un*authenticity? There are but three options:

(1) He may abandon the traditional conservative position. When that happens, the scholar should clearly admit it and not play games with the creeds to which he has hitherto affixed his signature. In my view, he is following current critical orthodoxy on very weak grounds, methodologically speaking; but I respect his integrity if he tells us frankly where he is going. (2) He may call into question his understanding of the power of redaction criticism and become more a critic of the tool than a practitioner—at least as far as the tool's application to questions of authenticity is concerned. (3) He may wind up using redaction criticism only when it supports his high view of Scripture and appeal to other arguments when it seems to go against him. This leaves him open to the trenchant attack of James Barr,[59] who claims Evangelicals do this regularly and thereby demonstrate a serious want of scholarly integrity. Barr has a point, unless the scholar who is pursuing this option does so for purely apologetic reasons (in which case he has retreated to the second position). However, as long as a scholar feels that the results of redaction criticism are sure and reliable, he does not have the right to discount them because of his other beliefs. He must reconcile his disparate beliefs, abandoning those that engender contradiction,[60] or else he is open to the charge that he is not playing the redaction critical game with integrity. Embarrassing as it may be, Barr's charge is often valid.

Part of the problem is that redaction criticism has so much come to the fore in questions of authenticity that older methods are ignored or even cursorily dismissed as out of date. The kind of argument developed by Grudem in chapter 1 of this volume is by and large unwelcome in the scholarly world; but it is important nevertheless. The approach that tests an author against outside sources—e.g., archaeology, knowledge of the times, historical details—wherever possible and, finding that author reliable in the testable areas, concludes he is reliable elsewhere is largely passed by in silence. Harmonization of parallel accounts (by which I do *not* necessarily mean the simple addition of both accounts!)[61] is deprecated with the adjective *easy*. But surely only *glib* harmonizations ought to be dismissed; *easy* harmonizations ought to be given the most serious consideration. To adopt glib harmonizations is historiographically irresponsible, but refusal to adopt easy harmonizations is equally irresponsible.[62] Of course, when someone dismisses a harmonization as "easy," what he means is that it is glib. Nevertheless, my objection is more than semantic; for the underlying historiographical question—viz., When are harmonizations permissible, or even mandated?—gets buried under the euphemism "easy," so that somehow harmonization is rejected as a cop-out, something that scholars who recognize how *difficult* (as opposed to *easy*) the material is will eschew.

Why have these and other tools, for many scholars, become out of date? They are certainly no weaker than radical redaction criticism; indeed, I would judge them much stronger. Like any literary and historical tool, they can be abused; but to fail to use them and give them grades at least as high as redaction criticism betrays a sort of contemporaneity chauvinism. To use a multiplicity of methods, to adopt several competing literary tools, is a necessary safeguard. Part of the problem with redaction criticism rests on the sad fact that, as often used, it disqualifies results from older methods as if those methods were invalid. The use of many tools is cumbersome; but the more qualified and nuanced results that emerge protect the scholar from Barr's charges that the grounds for depending or not depending on redaction criticism are shifting and subjective. Far from it. Our reasons for adopting this or that conclusion turn on a multiplicity of methods and tools that are mutually limiting, and therefore there is *methodological* reason for doubting the results of *one* of these many tools at some particular point.

The one place where redaction criticism may offer considerably more help, and where it may function with some legitimacy, is in aiding us to discern more closely the Evangelists' individual concerns and emphases. In one sense, of course, interpreters have always been interested in such questions. In the broadest sense, therefore, redaction criticism is nothing new. But if the examples in the last section of this chapter are typical, then even here redaction criticism must tread softly. The distinction between what is traditional and what is redactional is not a happy one; it is too fraught with overtones of "authentic" and "unauthentic." And even when some snippet is demonstrably redactional, it does not follow that any particular alteration owes its existence to theological concerns. Moreover, if the method presupposes the entire package of radical form criticism and a simplistic adoption of the two-source hypothesis, then the results will inevitably prove not only slanted but ephemeral: a new scholarly fad is bound to shake one or both of these theories in years to come, jeopardizing a vast amount of current work.

It seems best, then, if redaction criticism as applied to discerning distinctive emphases is to produce work of lasting importance, that it should not take its pedigree too seriously and it should not speak too dogmatically, for instance, of Matthew's change of Mark but rather of the variations between the two.

A brief example may be helpful. A comparison of Matthew 8:18 with Mark 4:35 shows that Matthew departs from Markan sequence: in Mark, the crowd in question surrounds Jesus after His *second* period of ministry in Capernaum, but in Matthew this is still Jesus' *first* period. Matthew does not explicitly rule out Mark's sequence, but one could not possibly reconstruct it simply by reading Mark. Why, then, does Matthew follow the order he does in chapter 8? The reasons are many, and the literary dependences complex, but one quite certain conclusion is that Matthew at this point is interested in developing the theme of Jesus' authority. Jesus' authoritative teaching is stressed in 7:28–29, and the second of the two healings at the beginning of Matthew 8 lays some emphasis on Jesus' authority as a healer (8:9). Such authority extends to many diseases and to exorcism of demons and stands in fulfillment of the Scriptures (8:16–17). There is personal lowliness attached to Jesus' authority, yet at the same time it brooks no half-hearted followers (8:18–22). It is so embracing that it extends to the realm of nature (8:23–27), the spirit world (8:28–34), the last judgment (8:29), and even to the forgiveness of sins (9:2–8)—a prerogative belonging to God alone. There are other themes holding these pericopae together, but it is clear that Matthew's topical arrangement of his material forges certain themes that some other arrangement would not so explicitly reveal. Redaction criticism devoted to such study can be of genuine service to the interpretation of the Scriptures, provided the reservations already expressed are not ignored.

If redaction criticism is applied with these kinds of reservations to the study of the Gospels, it will certainly help us discern more precisely the distinctive witness of each Evangelist to Jesus Christ and may legitimately take its place along side other literary tools. But precisely because "redaction criticism" is in the category of slippery words, qualifications and reservations are needed to keep us from worshiping before a shrine that has decidedly mixed credentials.

APPENDED NOTE

Like so many other problems in the study of Christianity (or any other topic, for that matter), the role of redaction criticism is bound up with epistemology. Epistemological questions are addressed directly elsewhere in this volume, but perhaps the connection with redaction criticism should be briefly explored here.

At a learned society meeting some months ago, a young and gifted evangelical scholar told me that he uses redaction criticism as a neutral tool and that when he uses it he does not assume the inerrancy of Scripture. Up to that point, he asserted, he had discovered nothing that called his traditional belief into question. My reservations regarding the reliability of redaction criticism have already been expressed; I need not repeat them. But the next question to ask is how many times this scholar needs to find his beliefs taught or reinforced before he can treat them as functional nonnegotiables.[63] Everyone develops such nonnegotiables. Would he remain similarly "neutral" regarding certain points in christology or any and every other basic creedal point? Surely not. Then why this one?

Everyone, I have said, develops functional nonnegotiables of various strengths. For finite persons this is both desirable and unavoidable. These nonnegotiables can be overthrown (or else no one could ever change his "position" on anything), but such an overthrow is not easy. Our finiteness and our sinfulness combine to guarantee that our knowledge is always partial and frequently faulty, and therefore we need to walk humbly. But it is as reprehensible not to adopt certain nonnegotiables that are apparently taught again and again as it is to refrain from overthrowing nonnegotiables that do not stand up under close scrutiny.

In the traditional view, the knowledge that God is omniscient and without sin encourages us to believe that what He has revealed, though not exhaustively true, is nevertheless completely true. The person who holds this view thereby establishes an epistemological base of some strength. But how does he come to know this?

I hold (but cannot here defend my view) that such knowledge derives from a mixture of evidence, training, predisposition, and the secret work of the Spirit of God. The latter ingredient should not be taken as being necessarily *apart* from the others, since the Spirit may use any or all of them. The problem as I see it is partly paralleled by the well-known tension between Cornelius Van Til and Francis Schaeffer. The former establishes an essentially biblical epistemology but then wrongly demands a presuppositionalist apologetic. The latter often uses a modified evidentialist apologetic, but then comes perilously close (especially in *He Is There and He Is Not Silent*)[64] to an evidentialist epistemology and unwittingly falls into Lessing's ditch. There is no necessary connection between epistemology and apologetics, for the evidences are surely things that the God of all truth uses to change predispositions. Such evidences *by themselves* do not guarantee that any particular individual will come to the truth, but this does not foreclose on our responsibility to appeal to evidences (as witness the apostles in Acts, or Paul in 1 Cor. 15). So also with respect to the doctrine of Scripture (or any other doctrine): the evidences per se (and there are many) guarantee nothing, just as a well-witnessed resurrection from the dead will not convince everyone of who Jesus is. Nevertheless the display of evidences is important, and the cool analysis of counterarguments not less so. The traditional view of Holy Scripture, which in my view is correct, can withstand the roughest scrutiny; but even so, it must be remembered that this view holds that the Bible is the infallible Word of God, not that our doctrine of the infallibility of the Word of God is infallible.[65]

THE NEW TESTAMENT USE
OF THE OLD TESTAMENT:
TEXT FORM AND AUTHORITY

Moisés Silva

Moisés Silva

Moisés Silva is Associate Professor of New Testament at Westminster Theological Seminary in Philadelphia. He is a graduate of Bob Jones University (B.A.), Westminster Theological Seminary (B.D., Th.M.), and the University of Manchester, England (Ph.D.). He also did graduate work in Semitics at Dropsie University. Prior to his present position he taught for nine years at Westmont College, where he also served as chairman of the Department of Religious Studies.

He has written two books—*New Testament Survey* and *Biblical Words and Their Meaning*—and articles for such periodicals as *Westminster Theological Journal* (of which he is currently editor), *New Testament Studies, Zeitschrift für die neutestamentliche Wissenschaft,* and *Biblica.*

He is a member of the Society of Biblical Literature and the International Organization for Septuagint and Cognate Studies.

THE NEW TESTAMENT USE
OF THE OLD TESTAMENT:
TEXT FORM AND AUTHORITY

Most Christians, I suspect, have at some point or another in their spiritual pilgrimage been seriously disturbed by the statement "Such-and-such a word is not found in the better biblical manuscripts." To hear that kind of a remark for the first time with reference to the Holy Scriptures is most surely a rude introduction to textual criticism. It would be altogether different, of course, if we grew up learning, along with our multiplication tables, that the great plays of Aeschylus, for instance, have come down to us in a hundred or so corrupt manuscripts—the earliest of which was copied a millennium and a half after the original was composed—and that not infrequently we are at the mercy of imaginative scholars who must make educated guesses ("conjectural emendations") as to what the tragedian might really have said, every available manuscript having failed us.

Even a superficial acquaintance with the processes involved in the transmission of any literature would lead us to *expect*, rather than be surprised at, the kinds of scribal errors present in all biblical manuscripts. And only a moment's reflection would then persuade us of the implausibility, indeed the absurdity, that it might be otherwise. If an enemy of Christianity took it in hand to copy a biblical book, must God prevent him from distorting the material? More to the point: did our Lord ever promise that any fool who wished to copy some portion of Scripture would automatically be kept from error? Dare a modern printer, for that matter, forego proofreading when producing copies of the Bible?

Both skillful and unskillful scribes, but none infallible, have produced biblical manuscripts. It is merely in recognition of that fact that affirmations regarding the infallibility of Scripture are normally qualified by some such phrase as "in the original manuscripts." Unfortunately, what is intended only as an acknowledgment of the realities of textual transmission has become for many a basis for ridicule. What is the use, we are told, of "inerrant autographs" if we do not have them? Why fuss about infallible documents if only errant ones are available to us? The simple answer is that, with regard to the bulk of Scripture, we *know* what the autographs said. To be more specific: the possibility of textual variation hardly ever affects those passages that are claimed by some to teach error or falsehood. If we made a list of the really controversial portions of Scripture (Adam's creation, Paul's teaching on women, etc.), we would be hard pressed to find any in which textual variation becomes a factor; that is, no one really doubts what the original writers said concerning these matters—though we may disagree on what they meant! Occasionally, let us grant, scholars might debate whether a particular error should be attributed to the original or to its transmission; but when it comes to virtually every issue of substance, we are as certain as it is possible to be regarding what the autographs said.[1]

It should be stressed, incidentally, that this last statement applies, with minor qualifications, to most of the ancient literature that has survived. For example, we have only about a half dozen truly valuable manuscripts of Aristotle's *Metaphysics*, two of which date back to the tenth century (the others to the twelfth and fourteenth centuries). At hundreds of points the text is uncertain, but the vast majority of the variations do not materially affect the meaning of those passages; certainly no significant Aristotelian doctrine hangs on a textual variant![2] If this principle holds true even for the average piece of ancient literature, how shall we react to the richness of textual attestation characteristic of Scripture? Greek manuscripts of the New Testament are so early and numerous—to say nothing of supporting ancient translations and patristic quotations—that no other writing of antiquity begins to compare with it.[3] Textual evidence for the Hebrew Old Testament is of a peculiar character, with a few books (notably Samuel–Kings) presenting special difficulties; still, the extraordinary faithfulness of medieval scribes (the Massoretes), combined with the independent evidence of the Dead Sea Scrolls on the one hand and of the Greek versions on the other, results in a truly formidable set of materials. Yet long before most of these materials were available, the Westminster divines had already sufficient evidence to speak of "the singular care and providence" of God in preserving His Word.[4]

The editors of this volume, however, have asked me to discuss how the concept of biblical authority is affected, not by textual transmission in general,[5] but by those variations found in a very special subset of texts: Old Testament quotations in the New Testament. When studying these quotations, we are faced with the further complications of determining the transmission of one text *within* the transmission of another; and this factor happens to complicate matters in the manner of geometric progression—much in the same way as the addition of, say, a fourth child enlivens the household by approximately sixteenfold.

But this is not all. It would be more accurate to say that we are dealing with transmission-within-transmission-within-transmission. For the New Testament authors, writing in Greek, could not quote the Old Testament in Hebrew; they had to translate the Old Testament passages right then or, more often, use some existing Greek version. And, as it turns out, this "bridging" element is the most perplexing of all. Indeed, the textual transmission of the Greek Old Testament, when set against any other piece of ancient literature, almost certainly ranks first in complexity.[6]

In addition to all these *textual* problems, our difficulties are further intensified by the issue of apostolic hermeneutics. Even a superficial reading of the quotations found in the New Testament reveals that its authors felt no need to quote the Old Testament verbatim; their concern for interpretation and application led, through paraphrase, to formal changes (whether or not it led to *substantive* changes is a question that will soon occupy us). Not surprisingly, the mere presence of inexact quotations has been used to argue that the apostles had no view of "verbal inspiration"; but this argument can hardly be taken seriously. It is not even quite adequate to infer that the New Testament writers were more interested in ideas than in words.[7] Loose quotations and paraphrases may readily be found also in the writings of modern authors who fight tooth-and-nail for the doctrines of inerrancy and verbal inspiration.

It has often been pointed out that the ancients had no clear-cut system of identifying direct quotations, yet it continues to be difficult for us to appreciate how deep and pervasive are the changes in writing convention that have taken place over the centuries. The availability of quotation marks, ellipses, question marks, exclamation points, dashes and parentheses, a variety of type faces, footnotes and precise bibliographic information, chapter-and-verse references, standard critical texts with apparatus—all of these create a frame of mind and a set of expectations far removed from those of ancient writers and their readers. To read a document with all the words run together, and with almost none of the punctuation helps listed above,

CREATESAVERYDIFFERENTI
MPRESSIONFROMTHATWHICHW
EREUSEDTOWOULDNTYOUAGREE

It may not be altogether possible, or even beneficial, for us to shed our modern perspective; but surely every effort should be made not to expect from an ancient writer what we are accustomed to read.

In any event, the fact that the New Testament authors often do not quote verbatim (for theological reasons),[8] in addition to the textual problems previously mentioned, presents a need for detailed, technical research, much of which is yet to be done. Clearly, then, there can be no question in this one article of attempting a definitive solution to our problem. We know enough, however, to lay out the choices available to us, to reject certain facile solutions, and to suggest promising avenues of approach.

A TEST CASE—HEBREWS 11:21

We can lay out some of these choices quite clearly by dealing with a relatively simple problem that has come up in discussions of inerrancy. In Hebrews 11:21 we read that Jacob, when he was at the point of death, blessed Joseph's sons "and worshiped upon the top of his staff." These words are an exact quotation from the Septuagint (LXX) of Genesis 47:31 (*kai prosekynēsen Israēl epi to akron tēs rhabdou autou;* Hebrews 11:21 omits *Israēl* because Jacob has already been identified in the first part of the verse). The difficulty arises when we check our English versions of Genesis, which say nothing about a staff; rather, they speak of Israel (Jacob) as bowing down on the head of his *bed.* Now the Hebrew word in question, which consists of the three consonants *mth*, can be vocalized in two different ways. At the time the LXX was produced, no system for marking vowels (or doubling consonants) was available; so the translator had to supply them in his mind (not a difficult task for a fluent speaker of Hebrew). The LXX translators assumed that the word was *maṭṭeh*, meaning "staff." When the Masoretes (medieval Hebrew scribes) designed a system of vowel notation, they marked this word in Genesis 47:31 differently: *miṭṭāh*, "bed." Most scholars seem agreed that the Masoretes were right (thus the rendering in the standard English versions) and the Greek translators wrong. It might appear, then, that the author of Hebrews, having been misled by the LXX, misquoted the Old Testament. If this interpretation of the facts is accurate, we would have to agree that the author has made a mistake (i.e., he is affirming something that happens to be false) and that we should in all honesty renounce any doctrine of inerrancy or verbal inspiration.

But this is not the only reasonable interpretation of the facts. Problems of this type, in fact, can be handled in many ways. Most of the possible solutions may not apply to this particular instance, but it will be useful to list them for illustration.

1. The first possibility to be considered is that of *corruption in the transmission of the Hebrew text.* In other words, when we encounter a textual difference between our Hebrew Bibles (= the Masoretic Text) and the LXX, we cannot assume that the former *must* be right. This consideration, however, is not really applicable to the problem in Genesis 47:31, where the difference is due to interpretive rather than textual reasons.[9]

2. Second, we may consider whether there is a *textual corruption in the transmission,* not of the Hebrew text, *but of the LXX.* Is it possible that the Greek translators rendered *mth* with the Greek word for "bed" but that later copyists changed the word to "staff"? The gifted and erudite Puritan theologian, John Owen, took this position, not only with reference to Genesis 47:31 but more generally whenever the LXX differed significantly with the Masoretic Text (MT) while agreeing with a New Testament quotation. His theory was that late copyists, familiar with the New Testament, were likely to change LXX manuscripts at those points where they differed from apostolic citations of the Old Testament.[10] In principle, this kind of textual development is quite

possible; indeed, we *know* that many variants in LXX manuscripts can be accounted for in some such fashion. Owen, however, had no access to a great deal of information available today and his proposed solution cannot be sustained. In particular, none of the many surviving LXX manuscripts of Genesis has the reading "bed"; we cannot doubt, then, that "staff" was the original Greek translation.

3. We are therefore led to consider the possibility of *textual corruption*, not in the Hebrew text nor in the LXX, but *in the Epistle to the Hebrews* itself. It is theoretically possible that the author used the Greek word for "bed" in conformity with the Masoretic understanding of Genesis, but that a later copyist, familiar with the LXX reading, suspected that his master copy was mistaken and therefore changed the word to "staff." Once again we may say that, in principle, there is nothing far-fetched about such a process. This is precisely what has happened, for instance, in Acts 7:32, where the original reading, "the God of Abraham and of Isaac and of Jacob," has been changed, in conformity with the LXX of Exodus 3:6, to "the God of Abraham and the God of Isaac and the God of Jacob" (this corrected reading appears in the great majority of New Testament manuscripts). In Hebrews 11:21, however, the evidence clearly points in a different direction, since no manuscript, to our knowledge, gives the variant "bed."[11] Furthermore, the author of Hebrews is known to cite the LXX even when it differs from the Hebrew. We are therefore as certain as it is possible to be that "staff" was the reading in the autograph of the epistle.

4. So far we have considered the possibility of textual corruption in each of the three documents that concern us and we have concluded that, though the attempt to isolate such corruption is legitimate and may work in some places, the problem in Hebrews 11:21 cannot be solved by an appeal to variation in the manuscripts. Assuming then that our texts are well established, we may turn to other considerations. For example, we may reconsider the difference between the MT and the LXX, this time focusing on the interpretive, rather than the textual, issue. Since both the translators' text and that of the Masoretes read the same consonants, the question is not, which *text* is more accurate, but *whose interpretation is more probable?*

The Masoretes, we should keep in mind, were masters of the Hebrew language; so their opinions on lexical and grammatical problems should be set aside only on the basis of very weighty evidence. Still, they were not inspired, infallible scribes; furthermore, since they lived many centuries after the Scriptures were composed, some of their information was faulty. Almost all modern commentators on Genesis agree with the Masoretic interpretation, "bed." It would be gratuitous, however, to suggest that nothing at all can be said in support of the LXX rendering. To begin with, it may be necessary to point out that the decision to translate "staff" can certainly *not* be attributed to ignorance or carelessness, for two verses later they translate Hebrew *miṭṭāh* with Greek *klinē*, "bed." Second, we cannot forget that the Hebrew construction is not free of difficulty.[12] It has been suggested, though one cannot easily verify it, that the Alexandrian (LXX) translators may have been influenced by Egyptian customs or by the fact that Hebrew beds had no head.[13] However that may be, the Greek rendering was thoughtfully considered. Quite probably, the significance of Jacob's staff, as brought out in Genesis 32:10, influenced their decision; it is also possible that they were reflecting some Jewish tradition that emphasized the staff (see below).

We must admit that the weight of probability lies on the side of the Masoretic interpretation. In other words, we can, but probably should not, try to solve the problem in Hebrews 11:21 by claiming that the LXX is correct after all. In particular, we should resist the strong temptation to assume that quotations in the New Testament, having been written by inspiration, must determine the form of the Old Testament passages; as we have already noted, the New Testament writers often introduce intentional changes. Still, the view that the LXX translators were right remains a possible, even if unlikely, solution.

5. Another proposed solution is to suggest that *both the MT and the New Testament are correct*. We can support this proposal in one of two ways: (1) by arguing that the author of Hebrews is referring to a different event, or (2) by suggesting, with John Owen, that Jacob bowed toward the head of the bed while supporting himself on his staff. We could also justify this approach by pointing out that the author does not explicitly say he is quoting (e.g., by the use of some introductory formula, such as in Hebrews 3:7, "the Holy Spirit says"). There are, however, two serious problems with this approach. In the first place, it gives the impression of grasping at a straw for the sake of harmonization. Although the picture of an aged patriarch leaning on his staff while bowing toward the head of his bed is convincing enough, and though in theory almost anything is possible,[14] we should normally aim for hermeneutical sobriety! Second, it stretches one's credulity to assume that the author received by revelation this bit of trivial information, especially in view of the fact that elsewhere he clearly depends on the LXX. Easy solutions of this sort must be resisted.

6. Assuming, then, that the MT is correct and that the author of Hebrews is intentionally quoting the LXX, we could argue that, precisely because he is quoting, *a trivial error in the quotation should not be attributed to him*. Calvin, Leupold, and, at least implicitly, many others apparently take this position.[15] There are two distinct, though related, issues involved here. One is that of *triviality*; the other has to do with whether the author is *affirming* everything that is part of the quotation. In this section we will consider the second issue, which hinges on the distinction between conventional (or culturally conditioned) statements and positive teachings. It is agreed on all sides that a phrase such as "the four corners of the earth," though used by

the authors of Scripture, does not constitute an affirmation regarding the shape of the earth; rather, it belongs to a class of acceptable expressions found in all languages.[16] A special subclass consists of quotations. The statement "There is no God" is made by an author of Scripture (Ps. 14:1), but no one attributes error or falsehood to the psalmist, since the comment is introduced by the words "The fool says in his heart." Unfortunately, the problem in Hebrews 11:21 is not analogous, for the author of the epistle clearly regards his quotations as authoritative. Perhaps it is possible to argue that the authoritative element is only the act of worship on Jacob's part and that the reference to the staff, while naturally included to remind the readers (themselves familiar with the LXX) of the event in view, is not part of the author's affirmation. This approach is hardly distinguishable from 7.3 below.

7. What about the appeal to the *trivial nature* of the problem? Unhappily, such an appeal can suggest different things to different people. (1) It may reflect a relaxed (or, depending on one's point of view, careless) attitude toward details. One must admit that there is a certain wholesomeness to the insistence that we should refuse to "major on the minors." Yet one must ask whether an aversion to details really serves to protect "the majors." The most insignificant sin in the life of Christ would destroy the central truth of His sinlessness; as far as *that* doctrine is concerned, one need not discover some gross, immoral act. Can we consistently hold the central truth that *all* Scripture is God's very breath if we allow for a series of minor errors? When we add the further consideration that one man's mountain is another man's mole hill, it appears that this solution is no solution at all.[17]

(2) But to speak of trivialities may suggest a slightly different approach, namely, the supposed need to distinguish between revelational and nonrevelational matters in Scripture.[18] In this approach, the distinction does not lie between important fact and insignificant detail, but between matters that affect salvation and those that do not. We are faced here, however, with a disturbing dichotomy between the religious (the sphere of faith) and the nonreligious (the sphere of scientific research), and it is very doubtful whether this general approach can be made to work.[19]

(3) More satisfactory is the position that takes "trivial" to mean something like *nondidactic*, so that we are back to the matter discussed above (section 6). In this section, however, my comments are not tied to the fact that Hebrews 11:21 happens to be a quotation. All responsible formulations of inerrancy have recognized that the Scriptures may, for example, use imprecise (i.e., round) numbers and that this fact does not disturb any meaningful understanding of infallibility.[20] If a writer intends—so far as intention can be exegetically determined—to give precise numbers, yet fails to do so, his failure would indeed entail error or falsehood. If, on the other hand, he states

(or implies), "I am giving round numbers for convenience," we all accept his figures as "true." Again, Jesus' well-known comment that the mustard seed is the smallest of all seeds was certainly not *intended* as an absolute scientific statement, but as an appeal to such knowledge as was available to his Palestinian audience—the statement was true within that defined context.[21]

Such appears to be the consideration that led Calvin to comment that the writer of Hebrews accomodated himself (on a point that did not materially affect his *teachings*) to the Greek translations available to his Hellenistic Jewish readers.[22] Of the possibilities we have thus far surveyed, this one may be the least objectionable; but it is not entirely convincing, since the problem in Hebrews 11:21 is not strictly analogous to the previous examples. If Jacob did *not* in fact "worship on the top of his staff," then to say that he did should probably be interpreted as positive error rather than as imprecise statement. Furthermore, it is not at all clear that the reference to the staff was as insignificant as is often suggested. The possibility that the author saw some special significance in this detail leads us to our next consideration.

8. Otto Michel comments on this passage that both the LXX and the Epistle to the Hebrews "presuppose a haggada concerning Jacob's staff" as the symbol of "wandering."[23] The haggada to which Michel refers is found in various forms in several rabbinic documents. We may summarize the legend as follows: Toward the end of the sixth day of creation, God created ten special objects, one of which was *the rod*, hewn from the sapphire of God's throne. God gave this rod to Adam and it was transmitted to Enoch, Noah, Shem, Abraham, Isaac, and Jacob. (According to one tradition, Jacob took the rod away from his brother Esau. As he was fleeing from Esau, he used this rod, his only possession [cf. Gen. 32:11], to divide the waters of the Jordan.) Jacob brought it to Egypt and gave it to Joseph. After Joseph's death, the Egyptians took it. Jethro, Moses' father-in-law, stole it from the Egyptians and eventually it came into Moses' possession. Aaron used it to perform miracles in Egypt. After miraculously blossoming (Num. 17), it was placed in the Ark of the Covenant. David used it in his encounter with Goliath, and it remained in the possession of his descendants until the destruction of Jerusalem, when it mysteriously disappeared. In the future, however, Elijah will give it to the Messiah.[24]

Now it is impossible to determine how much, if any, of this tradition existed at the time the LXX was composed; but that it was *in substance* known to the author of Hebrews and to his readers seems likely. Moreover, we may be sure that the significance of the staff did not escape the author: he makes reference to "Aaron's rod that budded" (9:4) and, more important, to the royal messianic scepter (1:8, same Greek word, *rhabdos*, translating Ps. 45:6). Of immediate significance to our passage, however, is the emphasis that chapter 11 places on the *wandering* patriarchs who looked for a city without foundations (v. 10). They were believers who recognized their status as exiles and who desired a better, heavenly country (vv. 13–16).[25] In the light of these facts, it appears doubtful that the reference to Jacob's staff was insignificant or even incidental. Rather, it would seem that the author deliberately used the LXX rendering to make a theological point. In other words, he makes a conscious hermeneutical decision in order to lay stress on Jacob's faith as a wanderer who longed for the messianic hope!

But does this approach solve our problem? Does it not rather intensify the difficulty? Do the New Testament writers feel free to change the original for theological reasons? Some conservative scholars would prefer almost any view to the one I am proposing. For example, S. Lewis Johnson, Jr., argues that the doctrine of inerrancy, without demanding verbatim quotations, "requires that the meaning the New Testament author finds in the Old Testament and uses in the New is really in the Old Testament."[26] Many evangelicals would agree with this statement, and perhaps it is accurate. But how do we determine whether or not it *is* accurate? Is it a criterion we have obtained from scriptural teaching or only an assumption that informs our way of thinking? At this point I merely wish to leave open the possibility that the author of Hebrews deliberately and for theological reasons used the LXX reference to Jacob's staff and that such a use of the Old Testament—though it incorporates nonbiblical Jewish traditions—is not necessarily incompatible with the doctrine of inerrancy.

The rest of this chapter consists largely of an elaboration of that possibility. First, however, we need to assess where we have come in the argument so far. The reader, remembering my earlier reference to Hebrews 11:21 as a "relatively simple problem," may by now have lost all confidence in my credibility. Let me stress, therefore, that if we were interested only in that particular quotation, the discussion would have been considerably briefer, since several of the proposals were either inapplicable or unworthy of serious consideration, while some others, though possible, seemed very unlikely; of the suggested solutions, only three (4, 7.3, and 8) should be seriously considered. But our interests are not limited to that verse. The solutions that I have rejected for it are often applicable to other passages. Indeed, there are some additional considerations (particularly "subtypes" of the first three proposals) that provide persuasive answers for a number of Old Testament quotations. For example, the presence of Targumic text forms in first-century Palestine is known to have influenced the New Testament writers.[27] Again, the possibility of typological interpretation helps to solve still other problems.[28] In short, we may have as many as fifteen or even twenty distinct approaches to the difficulties raised by the New Testament writers' use of the Old Testament, though only a couple of them may be applicable at any one time. It is clear, therefore, that we should avoid quick solutions and simplistic answers. But it is no less clear that the tendency, in some quarters, to point out biblical difficulties without acknowledging the great complexity of the issues and without giving a sympathetic hearing to the wide range of possible solutions available to us, far from promoting intellectually honest inquiry, obstructs it.

APOSTOLIC AND RABBINIC INTERPRETATION

During the past decade or two, biblical scholarship has shown a growing obsession with the issue of *hermeneutics*, a harmless enough word, but one occasionally used as a euphemism for "the skill of all but totally ignoring the Bible while appearing to accept it." Although one may be excused for feeling irritated at the way the word is thrown about as the ultimate panacea, it would be a grave mistake to dismiss the issue altogether. It is so easy for us to read the evening paper and understand it—that is, interpret it accurately—that we tend to think of interpretation as an eminently simple process. In reality, we depend on a massive framework of assumptions slowly formed by innumerable experiences.[29] As a result, those aspects of interpretation that appear to us to be the most obvious are often the ones that cause us the greatest difficulty. In particular, when we confront a text written by someone whose "framework of assumptions" differs significantly from ours, how can we possibly bridge the two? The attempt to answer that question is what hermeneutics is all about.

The contemporary discussion has relevance to this chapter for the simple reason that textual differences in Old Testament quotations cannot be accounted for by merely appealing to the mechanical aspects of text-critical work. Indeed, some of the most perplexing quotations are those that, *without exhibiting textual changes*, are used by the New Testament writers in ways foreign to us; for example, "Out of Egypt I have called my son" (Hosea 11:1) is applied in Matthew 2:14–15 to what appears to be a different and unrelated event. The literature on this general subject is immense,[30] and we cannot hope to do full justice to it here. Nevertheless, the following suggestions may prove helpful for our concerns.

Perhaps the most basic, yet often overlooked, consideration is quite simply that the New Testament writers used the Old Testament at different times in different ways for different purposes. Although in principle everyone might agree with that statement, it seldom seems to make any practical difference. A scholar, for example, might offer a general judgment on whether Paul's use of the Scripture is compatible with modern exegetical principles yet fail to specify just where in Paul's letters that judgment happens to be applicable. For truly even the most negative critic will have to admit that at least some of Paul's Old Testament quotations do not at all conflict with our grammatico-historical interpretation of the corresponding Old Testament passages.

In particular, we need to rid ourselves of the almost universal assumption that whenever a New Testament writer uses the Old Testament, he intends to prove a theological point. It may turn out, of course, that the assumption is correct, but this has to be demonstrated; does the doctrine of inspiration demand that the New Testament writers may refer to the Old Testament for dogmatic reasons only? Most of us balk at the possibility we are considering because it seems to open the door to abuse, as in the case of modern works that appear to make careless references to the Scriptures. For example, Edith Hamilton's popular book on Greek culture abounds with allusions to biblical passages that, she believes, illustrate some point or another of ancient literature. In a discussion of Pindar's poems to athletic heroes she quotes Hebrews 12:1; she describes Sophoclean tragedy in the words, "Lo, I come to do thy will"; Paul's comment that "the invisible must be understood by the visible" is regarded as the basis of all great art; Ephesians 6:12 becomes illustrative of the view that the most divisive human conflicts are those waged "for one side of the truth to the suppression of the other side."[31] One's immediate reaction is to smile condescendingly or express indignation that the true meaning of Scripture is being perverted. This judgment may well be valid, but is it so in every case?

Some time ago I asked a prominent evangelical scholar to evaluate an article I had written; with undue modesty, he prefaced his criticisms with the qualification that, in regard to the subject matter of the article, he was like *ho anaplērōn ton topon tou idiōtou*, "one who occupies the place of the unskilled," a quotation from 1 Corinthians 14:16. Now it would not occur to anyone to accuse this scholar of violating grammatico-historical exegesis or of adopting a low view of Scripture. Is it then completely out of the question that the New Testament writers, intimately acquainted as they were with the Scriptures, might make relatively casual references to the Old Testament? If they did, these casual references would reveal nothing about their exegetical method, much less about their doctrine of inspiration.

It must be admitted, of course, that in the very nature of the case casual allusions are unlikely. The New Testament documents are not casual letters, but eminently serious and often urgent. It is indeed doubtful whether one could come up with a really persuasive example, though we might consider 2 Corinthians 13:1, where Paul, having announced his *third* visit to Corinth, quotes Deuteronomy 19:15, "Everything shall be established by the mouth of two or three witnesses."[32] That Paul is thereby threatening his opponents with a formal trial seems improbable; this view fails, among other things, to appreciate that the quotation ("three witnesses") must be related to the remark about three visits. On the other hand, one must seriously doubt the suggestion (in spite of its impressive pedigree—it goes back to Calvin) that three visits by *one* person constitute fulfillment of the

judicial requirement. Barrett comes closer to a satisfactory interpretation when he comments that "Paul does not use his quotation as a
proof (there is no 'as it stands written'—contrast iv.13; viii.15; ix.9), but
says, in effect: You have had due warning, as prescribed; I am now
about to take action."[33] Some have objected that this approach makes
Paul appear whimsical in a very serious context. Yet the very seriousness of the matter leads Paul, more than once, to use irony and
ridicule (cf. "super-apostles" in 11:5; note also Gal. 5:12). We should
therefore not be too quick to dismiss the possibility that the reference
to a third visit has reminded Paul of a well-known Jewish principle
and that he proceeds to use it, not in order to demonstrate a theological or ethical point, but purely for its emotional impact. We should
immediately remind ourselves, however, that even if this approach is
correct, one could hardly accuse Paul of a loose view of Scripture or
conclude that this passage betrays his principles of interpretation.

Yet again, we may consider the possibility that some quotations are
neither purely illustrative (as I have just suggested) nor used for proof,
but somewhere in between. Perhaps an expression such as "shifts in
application"[34] accurately describes what I have in mind here. Notice, as
a possible example, Romans 15:21, where Paul quotes the words of
Isaiah 52:15 ("what they were not told, they will see, and what they have
not heard, they will understand") in connection with his missionary
method of working where Christ has not been preached. Now it is clear
that the prophet himself did not have Paul in mind. Furthermore, we
cannot here be satisfied with an appeal to divine authorship ("Maybe
the prophet didn't know, but God did"). While the principle may be
valid in certain situations, it is often abused, and here it is simply
inadequate. Granted that God in His omniscience and sovereignty
foresaw Paul's missionary labors among the Gentiles, that factor alone
does not account for the peculiar application of the passage.

Paul is in effect explaining why he has not yet visited Rome: since
a Christian community has already been established there, he must
give priority to other, unevangelized fields. Do we need to believe that
Paul considered the words in Isaiah a set of instructions concerning
the arrangement of his missionary travels? Does Paul suggest that if he
had gone to Rome the prophecy would not have been fulfilled? It
would seem more reasonable to see in this passage something analogous to what modern Christians do when they apply to a present situation a biblical statement that clearly does not speak *directly* to that
situation. Interestingly, Charles Hodge, while favoring the view that
Paul was acting on the basis of a prediction, allows for my suggestion:
"There is, however, no objection to considering this passage as merely
an expression, in borrowed language, of the apostle's own ideas."[35] In
short, we should be open to the possibility that the New Testament
writers may in some instances quote the Old Testament, not because
they understand their use of it to correspond with the original writer's

intention (or even God's original intention), but because their minds would naturally turn to passages that might have some kind of association, even a purely formal one, with the subject at hand.

Third, we may consider whether some passages that give every appearance of being dogmatic proofs, may turn out to reflect *an opponent's position*. Herman Ridderbos, we should note, has persuasively argued that Paul's hostile tone when speaking of the law should be understood in the light of the synagogue's handling of the law.[36] That factor alone alerts us to the possibility that a particular quotation may in fact be a short-hand pointer to the Judaizers' interpretation of that passage. Consider Galatians 3:11–12, where Paul apparently opposes Habakkuk 2:4 to Leviticus 18:5, as though the Old Testament taught two mutually exclusive approaches to salvation. One of many attempts to solve the problem is to suggest that Leviticus 18:5 was something like the Judaizers' motto, so that Paul's use of that passage would have been understood by his readers as a reference to the Judaizing point of view.[37] Even if we disagree with this particular interpretation of Galatians 3, is there a principial reason to set aside such an approach? From a slightly different standpoint, and with particular reference to Galatians 4:21–31, C. K. Barrett argues that Paul often refers to "passages that have been used by his opponents, correcting their exegesis, and showing that their Old Testament prooftexts were on his side rather than theirs."[38]

We have seen, then, that the New Testament authors may well have used the Old Testament in at least three ways, none of which requires an understanding of the quotations as proof texts. Let us now turn our attention to those—no doubt a majority—that are indeed used for doctrinal demonstration. What do we learn from them regarding apostolic exegesis? Or, to ask a more specific question, What are the similarities and differences between apostolic and rabbinic interpretation?[39]

First of all, the differences. If we compare the bulk of quotations in the New Testament with the bulk of quotations in rabbinic literature, we cannot but be struck by the greater sensitivity of New Testament writers to the original context. As we will see shortly, the rabbinic approach may not be so faulty as it appears at first sight; nonetheless, a sympathetic study of the relevant New Testament passages reveals a notably sane, unfanciful method. Thus, C. H. Dodd, as is well known, argued that the early Christians normally quoted Old Testament passages

> rather as pointers to the whole context than as constituting testimonies in and of themselves. At the same time, detached sentences from other parts of the Old Testament could be adduced to illustrate or elucidate the meaning of the main section under consideration. But in the fundamental passages it is the *total context* that is in view, and is the basis of the argument.[40]

Dodd himself believed that the New Testament contained "a fringe of questionable, arbitrary or even fanciful exegesis," but that

> the main line of interpretation of the Old Testament exemplified in the New is not only consistent and intelligent in itself, but also founded upon a genuinely historical understanding of the process of the religious ... history of Israel as a whole.[41]

In other words, Dodd was not at all interested in the possibility of inerrancy—he believed that the New Testament authors did engage in some faulty use of Scripture. But instances of such use, being rare and atypical, were disregarded by him. In his judgment, the *distinguishing* feature was the New Testament authors' reasonableness. With some qualifications, Dodd's viewpoint has been widely accepted.[42]

But, we may ask, if the New Testament writers were characterized by sane interpretation, should not that very factor shed light on the apparent exceptions? Significantly, one of the reasons Barrett credits the Judaizers with the initial use of the Sarah-Hagar "allegory" is that Paul's treatment in Galatians 4 is quite unusual for the apostle.[43] We need *not* follow Dodd in speaking of fanciful exegesis unless we have first considered whether the few passages at issue may be classed in one of the three categories previously discussed or whether they may be understood along lines yet to be set forth in this article.

So much for the differences. While it is certainly true that the New Testament compares favorably with rabbinic literature, we must also recognize the deep affinities between the two. In particular, we are interested in the possibility that, as is the case with rabbinic hermeneutics, certain citations may simply reflect accepted interpretations. One need not find it difficult to see that, in the absence of chapter-and-verse references, a writer may quote a verse when he in fact means to draw our attention to a rather long passage. Would it be very different to quote a verse and mean not just the verse of the passage but an interpretive framework associated with this verse? One of the great difficulties in reading the Mishnah—particularly in the Hebrew rather than in a helpful translation—is the extreme compression of the argument. Brief citations from the Scriptures or from "the sages" are clearly intended to evoke sizeable theological structures apart from which the material is unintelligible.[44]

Some appreciation of that factor can temper our attitude toward rabbinic interpretation. It is very easy to reduce an audience to hysterics by reading some examples of Jewish exegesis.[45] I suspect that, in some cases at least, the joke might be on us. For consider: How does one account for the fact that intelligent people, indeed scholars, should come up with interpretations that have nothing to do, so far as we can tell, with the original passage? The only reasonable answer is that the connection between text and interpretation *does* exist, only that time and tradition have obscured it.

The process of biblical interpretation is very ancient—it goes back to the Old Testament itself. For example, the author of the books of Chronicles certainly made use of the books of Samuel–Kings, and it is obvious that in using the earlier material he has reworked *and interpreted* it.[46] Any interpretation or application of a passage, even the most legitimate, necessitates some degree of *contextual separation.* Thus, for instance, it may be valid to appeal to Ephesians 4:30 ("Do not grieve the Holy Spirit") as proof for the personality of the Spirit, but in its context the verse is rather making a point about the Christian life; moreover, even this last statement is now found in the new context of "The New Testament Use of the Old Testament"!

Now the process of interpretation that began in Old Testament times grew through oral (and sometimes written) tradition over many centuries, with the New Testament writers right in the middle of the process. Even the wildest talmudic application may be the result of layer upon layer of deduction, so that *we* cannot see the connection between the beginning and the end. It may be that the New Testament writers, without rejecting such a hermeneutical process in principle, avoid its extreme application. It may be, indeed, that the difference between biblical and rabbinic interpretation, in this respect, is quantitative rather than qualitative.[47] If so, we need not be surprised at the presence of difficult passages in the New Testament that reveal similarities to rabbinic methods.[48]

CONCLUDING OBSERVATIONS

We may now return to our test case, Hebrews 11:21, and to the suggestion that the author, perhaps influenced by Jewish traditions about Jacob's staff, deliberately used the LXX rendering to make a theological point. In light of the complex hermeneutical issues we have briefly surveyed, it would seem facile to dismiss this proposed solution on doctrinal grounds. Serious consideration should be given to the possibility that it does *not* conflict with the doctrine of inerrancy.

Several obstacles stand in our way of accepting this suggestion. For example, we find it difficult to dissociate the results of inspiration (an infallible Scripture) from the process of inspiration (involving that writer's subjective experience). While everyone would agree in principle that inspiration is not deification,[49] we often assume, unwittingly, that it does entail omniscience. With regard to Hebrews 11:21, do we *need* to assume, if we wish to preserve the doctrine of inerrancy, that the author must have been acquainted with the Hebrew and that he was therefore aware of the apparent discrepancy between it (or rather its probable interpretation) and the LXX? Do we need to assume, as John Owen did, that the author was conscious of revealing (or confirming) a historical fact not recorded in the Hebrew text, namely, Jacob's use of the staff when he worshiped? These and similar questions remind us that many important issues are well beyond our power to explain, and our ignorance in turn suggests that accepting a particular interpretation must not depend on unproved assumptions regarding those issues.

Another obstacle consists of a different set of assumptions, this time with regard to historiography. The rise of "scientific" history-writing in modern times has conditioned us to expect certain standards of any author who purports to deal with facts. Consciously or not, we assume that the failure of an ancient author to conform to such standards necessarily implies falsehood or error. The point we are making is, of course, easily abused. The differences between ancient and modern methods have often been exaggerated, sometimes with the insinuation that ancient authors did not care at all about facts. It is perfectly evident, however, that the ancients recognized, and indeed emphasized, the difference between fact and fiction.[50]

What we need to appreciate is that *in the reporting* of historical events ancient authors were seldom concerned about verbatim quotations and precise information. Furthermore, it is clear that in Judaism haggadic interpretations were closely linked with those historical events—to refer to the one was almost necessarily to refer to the other. We ourselves may be reluctant to admit it, but even our own appeals to Scripture are in effect appeals to some *interpretation* of Scripture, even if it is a fairly obvious one (but obvious to whom?).[51] May not the New Testament writers appeal to (a particular understanding of) a particular Scripture by citing, in effect, a generally received tradition? In short, Hebrews 11:21 may be interpreted merely as an appeal to a particular interpretation of Jacob's act and not necessarily as an affirmation regarding the historicity of Jacob's bowing on his staff.

One final objection to our proposed interpretation must be considered, and that is the question whether Hebrews 11:21 could then be regarded as a model for *our* exegesis. The significance of this question can hardly be overestimated. Indeed, the word "authority" in the title of this chapter faces its most serious challenge right here. For what is the use of affirming infallibility if the apostles' very handling of Scripture proves invalid for us?

Articles and books that touch on this general subject often conclude with a remark to the effect that, though the New Testament writers' use of the Old Testament can be appreciated and in some respects defended, we have no business copying it.[52] Others, recognizing the fundamental inadequacy of such a conclusion, affirm that we *must* pattern our interpretation after that of the apostles, though one is not always clear how it is possible to do so.[53] Perhaps more realistic is Longenecker's attempt to deal with the seriousness of this issue without playing down the difficulties accompanying it. His answer[54] is that, first, we *cannot* follow the apostles when their exegesis "is based on a revelatory stance"[55] or when it is culturally conditioned (midrash, allegory, *ad hominem*); and second, we *can* reproduce their exegesis when it follows that line of grammatico-historical exegesis.

Longenecker's approach advances the discussion in several respects; for example, in his recognition that the various Old Testament quotations in the New Testament do not follow a uniform pattern and in his reminder that we normally agree to distinguish between the descriptive and the normative in theological discussions. His formulation, however, appears to me to be less than persuasive. Indeed, we may question both the negative and the positive features of his solution—the former because it is too negative, the latter because it is "too positive." (Perhaps another way to phrase my concern is to say that his formulation assumes too sharp a contrast between what biblical writers used to do and what we do today.)

With regard to the culturally conditioned statements, Longenecker's formulations imply that the apostles' handling of Scripture was indeed faulty at times, and this faultiness in turn suggests that their argumentation was sometimes invalid. Possibly this is not what he means (my own position, as we will see, may not be very far removed from his), but one may question the appropriateness of his description.

But why should we further suggest that his positive evaluation is "too positive"? In a sense, Longenecker gives the apostles more credit than is wise or necessary. Modern exegesis involves a series of skills that in the very nature of the case, were unavailable before modern times. For example, *we* cannot very well do responsible exegesis without relying on precise, scientific philological information. Further, we are all agreed that the Bible is no more a textbook of philology (or of textual criticism, form criticism, source analysis, etc.) than it is a textbook of zoology. The fact that the biblical writers (though *authoritative*) had a "prescientific" understanding of the animal world is no reason for us to remain prescientific and burn our modern zoology textbooks. Similarly, it is hardly a troubling thought that the apostles had no scientific literary hermeneutics—unless we decide that inspiration does entail omniscience after all. The authority and validity of apostolic interpretation, therefore, do *not* depend on its conformity to modern exegetical method.[56]

Perhaps I can best illustrate my point with a *contemporary*, though still "prescientific," example. On Saturday evening, May 17, 1980, riots broke out in a Black community in Miami, Florida. The following morning Mount St. Helens erupted, producing one of the most sensational natural phenomena of our generation. Almost immediately, political cartoons all over the country took advantage of this fortuitous combination and editorials appeared with such titles as "A Black Cloud Over Miami." One might, I suppose, protest that the two events had no scientific connection—how could journalists be so ignorant? But of course, we all understand, accept, and even appreciate such associations. They may have no scientific validity, yet they have validity (even in our scientific age) at a different level, functioning usefully within established social and literary expectations.[57]

Well, then, if God wished to reveal something of the significance of the Old Testament through His inspired apostles, would He do so through "scientific" methods that were to take twenty centuries to develop and would therefore have been totally incomprehensible to first-century readers? Might He not rather use those very associations and interpretive clues that would awaken the intended human response? Just as the use of *imperfect* human languages like Hebrew and Greek can prove an adequate channel for conveying divine truth unmixed with error,[58] so does prescientific apostolic exegesis serve to communicate, infallibly, the teaching of the Old Testament.

It also follows, however, that just as we are not required to write in Greek (as the author of Hebrews did) in order to produce valid exegesis, so are we not *required* to use Jewish haggadic tradition to communicate our understanding of Scripture. But to say that much is not for a moment to suggest that we can dispense with apostolic interpretation. Quite the contrary. If we refuse to pattern our exegesis after that of the apostles, we are in practice denying the authoritative character of their scriptural interpretation—and to do so is to strike at the very heart of the Christian faith.

What I wish to point out is that adherence to this basic principle does not entail indiscriminate imitation, any more than faithfulness to the pattern of apostolic evangelism requires us to board ships rather than airplanes or to make Antioch the headquarters for modern missions.[59] While we are committed to discover and *pursue* the interpretive framework that characterized apostolic interpretation, we need not suppose that such a commitment compels us to reproduce it in all its features. With particular reference to Hebrews 11:21, our decision to accept the solution proposed in this chapter should not depend on whether we are required to reproduce the precise method of exegesis used by the author of the epistle.[60]

In conclusion, I may anticipate a general objection to my suggestions. Are we not playing with words when we insist on "inerrancy" or some equivalent? Are we not stretching these words beyond their reasonable limits—or, conversely, narrowing the sense of "error" so that practically nothing will fit its meaning? This kind of objection, though often heard, and though it may evoke considerable sympathy, reveals a failure to understand the concerns that gave rise to the modern formulations of inerrancy in the first place. For clearly, our better theologians assumed from the beginning that because of the human form in which Scripture was given the claim that the Scriptures teach only truth would be measured according to the usual canons of veracity, not according to some artificial criterion of "absolute truth" (i.e., absolute precision, exhaustive and verbatim reports, etc.). It makes no more sense to accuse the New Testament writers of error or falsehood in their use of the Old Testament than to hurl the same charge at the journalists who linked the Miami riots with Mount St. Helens' eruption.

PART II

HISTORICAL ESSAYS

THE TRUTH OF SCRIPTURE
AND THE PROBLEM
OF HISTORICAL RELATIVITY

Philip Edgcumbe Hughes

Philip Edgcumbe Hughes

Philip Edgcumbe Hughes is a graduate of the University of Cape Town (B.A., M.A., D.Litt.), the University of London (B.D.), and the Australian College of Theology (Th.D.). He is a clergyman of the Episcopal Church and is Visiting Professor of Westminster Theological Seminary, Philadelphia; Professor Emeritus of Systematic Theology, Trinity Episcopal School for Ministry, Ambridge, Pennsylvania; and Associate Rector, St. John's Episcopal Church, Huntingdon Valley, Pennsylvania.

His publications include *A Commentary on the Epistle to the Hebrews*, *Commentary on Paul's Second Epistle to the Corinthians*, *Theology of the English Reformers*, *Interpreting Prophecy*, and *Hope for a Despairing World*.

Dr. Hughes is a member of *Studiorum Novi Testamenti Societas*, Renaissance Society of America, and the American Society for Reformation Research. Formerly he was Vice-Principal of Tyndale Hall, Bristol, England, Executive Secretary of the Church Society, London, and Editor of *The Churchman* (London).

THE TRUTH OF SCRIPTURE
AND THE PROBLEM
OF HISTORICAL RELATIVITY

The Bible is a collection of documents belonging to a period of history now long past. The most recent of its writings, those that comprise the books of the New Testament, are nineteen hundred years removed from the age in which we live. It can be stated without exaggeration that the remarkable scientific and technological advances of our day would have been inconceivable to persons living less than a century ago, let alone in the first century of the Christian era. To these people our world with its nuclear power and its computerization, its man-made satellites orbiting the earth, and its landing of men on the moon would have seemed like some legendary other planet. There is every justification, then, for asking what possible relevance the ancient writings of a bygone prescientific and unsophisticated age can possibly have for modern man.

Such a question, however, is less momentous than at first sight it appears to be. A large proportion of our much-vaunted twentieth-century world may accurately be described as to all intents and purposes prescientific and unsophisticated. Let us restrict the question accordingly to that portion of our planet's population that is able to enjoy, because it can afford, the benefits of our advanced technological inventions. (I say nothing here about the terrible blight of death and destruction that modern "progress" has brought with it.) Yet even granting this qualifying restriction, the scenario is still far from realistic. Two other modifications of our present world situation should not be left out of account. First, a moment of reflection will suffice to show that the great majority of the millions who daily use the wonderful gadgets and appliances of our electronic civilization are, except for the fact that they take these conveniences for granted, hardly more scientifically minded than the underprivileged masses who know no power other than that of muscles and mules. The expertise of our "civilized" society is limited, in the main, to turning switches on and off. The prevailing ignorance and incompetence become starkly apparent when the machines in common use break down or function erratically. Even the multitudes who now travel by air with a display of sophistication, being devoid of any knowledge of aeronautics, are adept only at taking seats in jet planes—an achievement inferior to that of riding a camel over the sands of the Sahara. Second, it is no less evident that the members of "simple" and "backward" societies are equally capable of learning to turn switches on and off, to make use of

modern machinery, and rapidly to become as technologically sophisticated as the average members of an "advanced" society. Moreover,
those who are so inclined can readily be taught the technicalities of
assembling and maintaining our modern inventions. In short, the
technological distance between the "first" and the "third" worlds, and
by the same token between the twentieth and the first centuries, is
more apparent than real insofar as human powers of adaptability are
concerned.

In the unfolding of history man is naturally a constant focal point
because it is with the affairs of mankind that history is concerned. But
there is another constant, superior to man. God, as the Creator of all
things, sovereignly overrules the course of history by His exercise of
providence, judgment, and redemption. Made in the image of God and
entrusted with the mandate to have dominion, under God, over the
rest of the created order, man is the divinely appointed agent through
whom, in the unfolding of history, the purpose for which all things
were created is carried forward to its fulfillment. The fundamental
tragedy of history is that man, by reason of his self-induced fallenness,
has perverted the potential implicit in this mandate. That this potential has not been destroyed is evident in man's cultural and scientific
achievements. The tragic perversion of that potential is seen in the
ever-present propensity to put these achievements to ungodly and
inhuman uses. Technological progress has certainly not brought ethical improvement. Man is no better today, no more loving and compas-
sionate, than he was two thousand or four thousand years ago.

Now of course the Bible is not free from historical relativity. The
New Testament, for example, was written in the Greek language of the
first-century Mediterranean world, not in classical or modern Greek.
The cultural conventions of those originally addressed by the New
Testament authors were certainly not those that prevail in the twentieth century; and even those conventions varied from community to
community, depending on whether they were predominantly Jewish,
Greek, Roman, or barbarian. It is plain that the apostle Paul was well
aware of these variations in the cultural norms and backgrounds of
those he was evangelizing and adjusted his approach accordingly.

> To the Jews I became like a Jew, to win the Jews [he wrote]. To those
> under the law I became like one under the law (though I myself am not
> under the law), so as to win those under the law. To those not having the
> law I became like one not having the law (though I am not free from God's
> law but am under Christ's law), so as to win those not having the law. To
> the weak I became weak, to win the weak. I have become all things to all
> men so that by all possible means I might save some (1 Cor. 9:20–22).

When speaking to Jews it was Paul's custom to demonstrate the
truth of the Christian gospel by proving that in it there was a complete
fulfillment of the promises and prophecies of the Old Testament Scrip-

tures, which they knew and venerated. In the synagogue of the Jews at Thessalonica, for instance, "he reasoned with them from the Scriptures, explaining and proving that the Christ had to suffer and rise from the dead, and saying, 'This Jesus I am proclaiming to you is the Christ'" (Acts 17:1–3). But shortly afterward, in Athens, when he was given the opportunity of addressing a group of Epicurean and Stoic philosophers, who were ignorant of the Old Testament Scriptures, he followed a different line, speaking to them as sophisticated religious inquirers and even attempting to establish rapport by quoting from their own philosopher-poets, but without compromising the essential gospel. He declared to them the true God, hitherto unknown to them, who has revealed Himself redemptively in the incarnation, death, and resurrection of Jesus (Acts 17:16–31). Subsequently, no doubt, those who believed were carefully instructed in the witness of the Scriptures. But by adjusting his presentation to the cultural formalities and preferences of his audiences, and showing himself sensitive to their degree of sophistication, Paul effectively pursued the objective "by all means to save some."

This objective, we should notice, is ever the same: *to save some.* Whether they be religious Jews or philosophical Greeks or imperialistic Romans or unpolished barbarians, whether they be kings and rulers or just the ordinary everyday men and women in the street, all are human beings and all are sinners in desperate need of the saving grace of God, and therefore all share the one basic necessity of being evangelized. Hence the apostle's protestation: "I am compelled to preach. Woe to me if I do not preach the gospel!" (1 Cor. 9:16). And "to save some" is also the primary purpose of Holy Scripture, which is so designed that it is "able to make [us] wise for salvation through faith in Christ Jesus" (2 Tim. 3:15). The Bible belongs integrally within the divine scheme of redemption. That is why its central message, which does not vary from age to age, is not at all culturally conditioned and why, precisely because it is directed to the heart of the human predicament, which also does not vary from age to age, it is unfailingly relevant to mankind in every period of history.

This means that the cultural environment within which the biblical writings first saw the light of day is not of central significance. But it would be wrong to conclude that it is of no significance. Our understanding of the language of the New Testament, for example, has been enhanced by knowledge acquired from the study of nonliterary material still available to us from the first century; and the discovery of the Dead Sea Scrolls has added an important dimension to our comprehension of Jewish thought and interpretation in the age of the apostles. The more we know of the period and its culture, in all its manifestations, the better equipped we are to penetrate to the sense of the biblical text. Such intellectual advances, however, do not change the central message of the Scriptures, which is unmistakably clear for all to see, with or without linguistic and archaeological training. The scholarly specialist is able to give valuable aid to the ordinary reader who is unskilled in the original languages and social background of the Bible.

But, as is plain from the evangelistic purpose of Holy Scripture and as the history of the spread of the Christian faith shows, *the Bible is for everyone*. It is not the preserve of the specialist. To allow it to become the book of the expert, on whose pronouncements the average person is dependent, is an abuse and inversion that can lead only to disastrous results. The effect is to take the Bible out of the hands of those for whom it is intended, that is, the totality of mankind. Whatever the difficulties and obscurities associated with particular passages (on which the expert may be able to throw some light), not only is the Bible's central message, in all its plainness and constancy, addressed to everyone, but it is also accessible to everyone. It is especially pertinent to the one who recognizes in himself or herself the sinner for whom Christ died, and therefore the one who needs above all else to hear and heed the good news of redemption and reconciliation in Christ. The apostle John's explanation of the purpose of his Gospel provides also a perfect epitomy of the primary purpose of Scripture in its entirety: "These are written that you may believe that Jesus is the Christ, the Son of God, and that by believing you may have life in his name" (John 20:31).

This was a lesson that P. T. Forsyth, himself an academic and an expert, had to learn. Once he learned it, the whole thrust of his theological perception was reshaped.

> The authority of the Bible [he wrote] speaks not to the critical faculty that handles evidence but to the soul that makes response. The Bible witness of salvation in Christ is felt immediately to have authority by every soul pining for redemption. It is not so much food for the rationally healthy, but it is medicine for the sick, and life for the dead. All the highest interpretation of the Bible comes from that principle of grace.[1]

The Bible, Forsyth has said in another place,

> is not a history of Israel, but it is a history of redemption. It is not the history of an idea, but of a long divine act.... [The] first value of the Bible is not to historical science but to evangelical faith, not to the historian, but to the gospeller.[2]

This insistence is of course congenial to the evangelical mind, which, while it welcomes the advances in understanding resulting from scholarly research, is unwilling, as a matter both of principle and of experience, to concede that the absolute truth of revelation can in any way become outmoded or invalidated by the changing relativities of the historical situation. We live in a day, however (as did Forsyth), when many academic "experts" are intent on persuading us that a radical restructuring of the central message of Scripture is necessary. They demand a change not merely at the periphery but at the very heart of the Christian faith. They argue that teaching conditioned by and appropriate to a historical context now long past is meaningless and unacceptable to modern scientific man.

For more than fifteen hundred years the authority and authenticity of the Bible as the infallibly inspired Word of God was a fixed and uncontested belief of the Christian church. The widespread departure from this position in the modern era is symptomatic of the abandonment by many of the distinctive teaching of Christ and His apostles, and this development is responsible for the present ecclesiastical crisis of authority. At the same time it is symptomatic of the attempt to secularize the church by the removal of its ancient landmarks on the part of those who wish to accomodate it to the spirit of the age and thus to win the world's favor. The ground was prepared for the questioning of the relevance of past history to present faith by the leaders of the intellectual movement of the eighteenth century known as the Enlightenment, whose roots reached back into the deistic soil of the preceding century. Naturalism, which left little or no room for the presence of the supernatural; rationalism, which affirmed the self-adequacy of human reason; and confidence in the essential goodness and freedom of man were the characteristic tenets of this movement. God, if His existence was allowed, was regarded as little more than an uninvolved spectator remote from the course of this world's affairs. The philosophical skepticism that became fashionable for members of the Republic of Letters inevitably cast a shadow over theological beliefs hitherto held sacrosanct.

Against this background Hermann Reimarus (1694–1768), a Hamburg schoolmaster, composed, privately, and avowedly for the purpose of quieting his own conscience, a manuscript of considerable length to which he gave the title *An Apology or Defence on behalf of the Rational Worshippers of God*. Not long after the author's death the work came into the possession of Gotthold Lessing (1729–1781), who decided to proceed with its publication, though designating it an anonymous composition (Reimarus had not intended to make it public). Lessing alleged that he had discovered it at Wolfenbüttel in the collection of the Duke of Brunswick, by whom he was appointed librarian in 1770. Accordingly, between the years 1774 and 1778 Lessing brought out a number of excerpts, calling them *Fragments by an Anonymous Person* (also known as the *Wolfenbüttel Fragments*), in which the teachings of the New Testament were quite radically "demythologized," the figure of Jesus being reduced to that of a merely human Palestinian Jew, and the account of His resurrection from the dead and His significance as the world's redeemer being dismissed as inventions of His apostles, who, it was averred, had succeeded in spiriting His corpse away, thus leaving His tomb empty. The appearance of the *Fragments* aroused a storm of denunciation. In 1778 Lessing responded with an essay *On the Proof of the Spirit and of Power*—a title borrowed from 1 Corinthians 2:4. That text had long, though not necessarily accurately, been interpreted as referring to the fulfillment of prophecy (spirit) and the performance of miracles (power). It was Lessing's contention that, even if the factuality of prophetic and miraculous events was accepted, once prophecies had been fulfilled and miracles performed, their force and significance were exhausted. Though their occurrence might be historically true, the report or record of their occurrence afforded no proof that Christianity was true, since the logical demonstration of historical truth was an impossibility. Only the one to whom particular events happened could possess the proof and the knowledge that they were true. Absolute truth, it was contended, cannot rest on contingent events of the past, or, as Lessing put it, "accidental truths of history can never become the proof of necessary truths of reason," for between the two there is an "ugly broad ditch" that cannot be bridged.

It was in this way that Lessing postulated the irrelevance of past history to Christian faith and reason. Occurrences, then, like the virgin birth of Jesus, His death on the cross, and His bodily resurrection, even if they were actual historical events, could not validate present faith, which must be founded in reason. This is the subsoil of twentieth-century existentialism, for the effect of such theorizing is not only to individualize man but also to isolate him, and to isolate him not merely from the past but even from God.

It is little wonder that Lessing succeeded in persuading himself that it is not by the possession of the truth but by the search for the truth that man finds his true worth. "Is it not a fact," Karl Barth pertinently asked, "that Lessing's man is self-sufficient, and has no need of God in any event?"[3] The Reimarus-Lessing reassessment represents a radical departure from the central perspective of Scripture. The very essence of the biblical gospel is its indissoluble connection with particular historical events proclaimed as the acts of God Himself sovereignly intervening in the midst of human history for the purpose of reconciling the world to Himself. Hence the further observation of Karl Barth that "it is precisely the Protestant doctrine of Scripture that Lessing is trying to juggle away."[4] Despite his professed hostility to rationalism and liberalism, however, Barth's own thought did not free itself from Lessing's intellectual motives: he too, with his distinction (learned from Martin Kähler) between *Historie* and *Geschichte*, adopted the "ditch" mentality, and with his illuministic theory of Scripture came close to existential individualism. To relax one's hold on the objectivity of the great biblical absolutes can only result in the vacuous speculations of finite subjectivism.

Impressed by Lessing's views, Immanuel Kant (1724–1804) formulated his philosophical system in which the principle of keeping history separate from faith was given an important place. Redemption, for

Lessing, consisted in respecting the divinely given laws of morality, in doing better than previously, in cancelling wrong with right, in doing for ourselves what Christ our fellow had done for Himself. Kant, in turn, developed this theme. He asserted the universal givenness of what he called practical reason, that is to say, the rational moral awareness in every person of the "categorical imperative," the absolute sense of duty, which lays on us both the obligation and the ability to fulfill the dictates of that ultimate and unconditioned law which alone engenders unity between God and man. Thus defined, practical reason is both prior and superior to the happenings of history. Indeed, in his treatise *Religion within the Limits of Reason Alone*, published in 1793, Kant postulated not just an "ugly ditch" but a "mighty chasm" between objective facts of history (which would include the supernatural events of the Gospel accounts) and the subjective constant of reason. He insisted that finite man is totally incapable of grasping the Infinite One by means of revelation—that is to say, revelation as biblically understood, which involves reception and handing down as a historical faith. The only true revelation, according to Kant, is the God within ourselves who speaks to us through our own reason and whom we worship in the duty of honoring our moral obligations. The authority of the Bible is experienced by interpreting it in a manner that harmonizes with this inward moralistic revelation. Not surprisingly, the celebrated Kantian scholar Edward Caird accused Kant of "saving his morality at the expense of his religion" and objected that the defect of Kant's position lay precisely in the sharp line he drew

> between rational and revealed religion, or in other words between the essential elements in religion and the accidents of its historical form ... for the division between the ideal and the real, the subjective and the objective, which Kant adopted from the individualism of his time, makes him cast away as part of the external form much that belongs to the very essence of religion.[5]

A movement of religious romanticism (which also had roots in previous centuries) developed in reaction to the intellectualism of the Enlightenment. But it left Lessing's ditch or Kant's chasm unbridged. Rejecting the moralistic rationalism of Lessing and Kant, though like them opposing dogmatic formulations of Christianity, Friedrich Schleiermacher (1768–1834) insisted that feeling was the heart of religion, and in particular man's feeling of absolute dependence and his sensation of oneness with God. Lessing, as a matter of fact, had also placed considerable emphasis on feeling. Part of his argument against historicism was that the Christian feels that Christianity is true quite independently of historical testimony to its truth. He granted that if one's personal feeling of experience of truth happened to coincide with historically communicated truth, then, but only then, could the accidental truth of the latter convey the force of proof and become one with the necessary truth of reason: it must be *my* truth, not someone else's. In this teaching, once again, we hear the genuine ring of existentialism two hundred years before our day. Schleiermacher's argument followed a different line. However, he arrived at a similar conclusion regarding the relevance to contemporary man of the historical witness of the Bible. He would not allow that "faith in Jesus as the Christ or as the Son of God and the Redeemer of men" could be based on the authority of Scripture. He contended that if Scripture were treated as authoritative in this way it would place reason before faith, so that unbelieving hearts might be persuaded, even though they felt absolutely no need of redemption. Schleiermacher's perspective betrayed an unfortunate misunderstanding of the purpose of Scripture (2 Timothy 3:15 and John 20:31 again!) and a failure to recognize that it is only to the believing heart that Scripture authenticates itself in the deepest sense (John 5:39–47).

The Bible, in Schleiermacher's view, may be useful without being indispensable for the Christian faith. As the apostles' faith was prior to the New Testament, so ours may be independent of it. Schleiermacher held that "the grounds of our faith must be the same for us as for the first Christians," in whose souls faith was awakened by "a direct impression." Their description of Jesus, now embodied in the writings of the New Testament, "was only an expression of this faith." It may indeed move us to faith, "but in no sense conditionally on the acceptance of a special doctrine about these writings, as having had their origin in special divine revelation or inspiration." For Schleiermacher, then, there is no necessity of Scripture but only of "faith itself, present in a feeling of need (in whatever source that feeling may have originated)." Scripture may be adduced, he says, "only as expressing the same faith in detail."[6] The destination reached by Schleiermacher is that of his starting point, namely, one of subjective individualism.

Limitations of space preclude the possibility of discussing the significant contributions to the articulation of nineteenth-century liberalism made by other notable scholars and theorists such as Ferdinand Christian Baur and the Tübingen School that he founded, David Friedrich Strauss, and Albrecht Ritschl; or the remarkable influence of the Hegelian dialectic on theological as well as philosophical minds; or the powerful, though delayed, impact in our own century of the anti-Hegelian "existential" thought of Sören Kierkegaard. The twentieth century has seen the rise of existentialism as a philosophy that has for the most part been atheistic and unconcerned with Christian presuppositions. In the light of the formulation of liberal theology over the past two centuries, with its heavy emphasis on subjectivity, it should not be found surprising that contemporary reductionists have embraced existentialism as though it were a blood relative. The rejection of objectivity leaves no alternative but to seek the meaning and the worth of things entirely within oneself, and in existentialism the isolation of the individual has been carried to the extreme.

There is, indeed, this difference between the subjectivism of the past two centuries and that of our own day: the former was conceived and formed by unbounded confidence in the rational and ethical powers of man, whereas the latter is the offspring of desperation. The ghastly carnage of two world wars and the disorientation of society in general gave a painful check to the optimism of the past and caused widespread disillusionment. The modern existentialist, feeling himself engulfed by meaninglessness, sought to make some sense of life by passionately asserting the meaning of his own existence in the face of futility and to affirm his own dignity even by choosing that over which he had no choice, including the ultimate negation and absurdity of his own death. For him there is only one history that has meaning, and that is his own history. The future is black nothingness. He is solely a man of the present, and that present is solely his own individualistic present. Not all forms of contemporary existentialism are stamped with such utter hopelessness. In some there is a place for the numinous, and in those that have been "christianized" the relevance of Jesus and the existence of God are postulated in one way or another. But all forms, whether present or past, have this in common: they are expressions of humanistic egocentricity.

The outstanding exponent of the amalgamation of theology and existentialism is Rudolf Bultmann (1884–1979), whose writings have been remarkably influential. Insisting that the New Testament was filled with mythological notions and elements unacceptable to modern scientific man, he propounded a procedure of demythologization that cut away from the Gospel accounts every aspect of the supernatural. Bultmann portrayed Jesus as a merely human figure who lived and died in first-century Palestine, himself the exemplary existentialist. In their recollection of him, his disciples found existential worth and inspiration. His value to them was given graphic expression by their embellishment of his story with miraculous (and mythical) additions, such as his deity, his preexistence, his virgin birth, his sinlessness, his vicarious sacrifice, his resurrection and ascension, and his heavenly glory and future return. All this was not a reprehensible falsification of history but an honorable attempt to find symbols and put into words the significance he had for them. We now know, of course, on the authority of Bultmann, that the church was mistaken in thinking for so many centuries that such supernormal elements could be or were intended to be literally believed—and that we who live in the age of man's maturity must make allowances for the fact that those were the naïve, prescientific centuries.

The gospel history, as Bultmann sees it, is the history of subjective moments of encounter effected through the agency of preaching. Far from being events of past history, the incarnation and resurrection of

Jesus are eschatological events that come to pass every time that the message preached meets with the faith of the hearer. Indeed, Bultmann speaks of the Word of God becoming incarnate in the preacher: "For the incarnation is likewise an eschatological event and not a datable event of the past; it is an event which is continually being re-enacted in the event of the proclamation."[7] Again, he has written elsewhere: "Jesus Christ cannot be objectively established as an Eschatological Event, so that one could there and then believe in him. Rather he is such—indeed, to put it more exactly, he becomes such—in the encounter—when the Word which proclaims him meets with belief." Revelation, too, has to be understood as belonging, not to a divine action of the past, but to the immediate, present moment or encounter: "It is only revelation as an event in the present, that is, where he [Jesus] confronts me at any time with what he preached and what he is—as the act of God to me or to us."[8] E. L. Mascall has tartly commented that Bultmann has succeeded in substituting magic for myth.[9]

Bultmann's method turns out to be a game of words—words without moorings, words in a vacuum, words about the deity, incarnation, and resurrection of a mere man long since dead and buried, who was not God and was not incarnate and did not rise from the dead and is not a savior. What possible sense could there be in my believing them? And in any case why connect them especially with the man Jesus? Why not with anyone else who made extravagant claims for himself—Simon Magus, for example? And why the New Testament? Why should not any other book of inspiring thoughts produce the same existential response from me? Bultmann, who has subjectivized everything to the ultimate degree, can only suggest that a christological pronouncement about Jesus is a pronouncement about myself, simply a value-judgment of his significance at a particular moment to me. Jesus, I am told, does not help me because he is the Son of God (that would be to objectify him) but he is the Son of God because he helps me. Bultmann explains that "the sentence 'And we believe and are sure that thou art that Christ, the Son of the living God' (John 6:69) would be quite simply just a confession of significance for the 'moment' in which it was uttered, and not a dogmatic pronouncement."[10] This, of course, is Bultmann's dogmatic christological pronouncement.

We may readily acknowledge that the message of the gospel, as it is read in Scripture and heard in preaching, is thoroughly existential. There is indeed such a thing as a dynamic moment of encounter, when the message meets with faith and becomes truly and transformingly present and the Bible leaps to life in the experience of the believer as the authentic Word of God. But this is not the same thing as the illuminism of Karl Barth, according to which a fallible word of man may at a given moment become the veritable Word of God to me; nor is it compatible with the humanistic egocentrism of Rudolf Bultmann, which tears the heart out of the gospel record and makes the value of Scripture dependent on the judgment of my experience of its worth. What is at stake is the actual *truth* of the biblical witness; not in the first place its truth *for me*—though, as we have agreed, this is important because the message of the gospel is addressed to me—but its truth as coming *from God.* In other words, the objective character of Scripture as truth given by God comes before and validates my subjective experience of its truth. A person may willfully shut his eyes and deny that the sun is shining, and in doing so he is truly in darkness, both physical and intellectual; but once he opens his eyes, the sun's brightness will transform his outlook. Though it is at that moment that his darkness is dispelled, the sun has never ceased objectively to be the sun and to radiate forth its brilliance. The objectivity of the light of biblical truth has not only been a classical doctrine of the Christian church but was also fundamental in the teaching of Christ and His apostles, for whom the word of Scripture was identical with the Word of God. It should be added that the believer's experience of the truth of the biblical witness within himself is not solely a subjective experience, because it is concomitant with and effected by the dynamic working of the Holy Spirit in the heart of his being, so that in this respect it is objective in character, and the experience in its fullness is an indivisibly objective-subjective event. Thus the apostle John says, "Anyone who believes in the Son of God has this testimony in his heart. Anyone who does not believe God has made him out to be a liar, because he has not believed the testimony God has given about his Son (1 John 5:10; cf. Rom. 8:16; Gal. 4:6).

It can be taken for granted that scholars who nowadays offer for our approval their own attempts at the "reconstruction" of the Christian faith are in fact busily engaged in the demolition of historic orthodoxy. A recent contribution of this *genre* is a symposium of essays by seven British academics with the title *The Myth of God Incarnate.*[11] The authors, who rightly "make no pretence to originality," prepare the ground for the radical change they wish to advocate by maintaining that Christianity has ever been a "changing movement." They point to "two major new adjustments" of the nineteenth century, namely, the recognition that man must now be naturalistically understood as having "emerged within the evolution of the forms of life on this earth" (ignoring the fact that evolutionism is scientifically highly vulnerable), and the realization that the books of the Bible "cannot be accorded a verbal divine authority" (ignoring the fact that the majority of Christendom still believes otherwise). Then, contending that the doctrine of the incarnation was not an element of the original faith of Christian believers, they express their conviction "that another major theological development is called for in this the last part of the twentieth century," namely, the abandonment of belief in the Incarnation. "The later conception" of Jesus, they explain, "as God incarnate, the Second Person of the Holy Trinity living a human life, is a mythological or poetic way of expressing his significance for us" (once more simply a matter of subjective value-judgment!). For those who think that this would be the betrayal of something essential to the faith once delivered they throw in the assurance that "modern scholarship has shown that the supposed unchanging set of beliefs is a mirage," with the result that "'Orthodoxy' is a myth."[12] These academics are in fact hoping to persuade us that historic orthodoxy is actually heterodoxy and that their heterodoxy is after all these centuries of ecclesiastical incomprehension the original orthodoxy.

Accordingly, it is the atonishing claim of these authors that they have "come full circle back to the primitive faith of the church."[13] If this is really so, what, we may ask, has happened to the insistence on the necessity for constant change? Apparently the changes of the centuries, elsewhere said to be so integral a part of the church's life, now need to be eradicated. The only change to be made is that of the elimination of change, so that we may return to a pristine faith. However, this is a faith that the first Christians would have found unrecognizable and unworthy of the name, and certainly so paltry and powerless that there could have been no point in living and dying for it. The distinctive character of this "primitive faith" is that it is totally natural and human; there is no place in it for the dimension of the supernatural or for divine intervention. This is a most happy discovery, because in our modern sophisticated world, too, "there is no room for God as a causal factor in our international, industrial or personal lives."[14] What we are invited to return to, then, is "a 'deabsolutized' scripture" which, we are instructed, "is of infinitely greater religious value than the flat oracle of fundamentalism"; and "a 'deabsolutized' Jesus" who "can be recognized as revealing God to us in much more complex ways than the Christ of Chalcedon."[15] Indeed, we are warned that "Chalcedonian christology could be a remote ancestor of modern unbelief"![16] It is even contended that these regrettable changes and additions to the simple "primitive faith" were made not only by the Nicene and Chalcedonian fathers but by the apostles themselves.[17] Evidently these latter-day theologians have transferred to their own pronouncements the dogmatic infallibility that the church always believed to be a distinctive mark of the teaching of the apostles.

Nonetheless, careless of contradiction, they approve of change as a beneficial necessity inseparable from the relativities of the historical perspective. Thus they draw attention to "the great cultural gap which separates Jesus and his contemporaries from all things 'modern.'"[18] and assure us that, while "the idea of supernatural divine intervention was a natural category of thought and faith" and "supernatural causation was accepted without question" in the first century, such notions have become "simply incredible" for most people in this twentieth century, including "the main body even of convinced believers."[19] This, in fact, is a tendentious and misleading assertion, since millions of convinced believers in our modern world find these notions anything but incredible. One can only wonder at the puny god, deprived of the power of causation and intervention, that these reductionist academics have formed for themselves. For them to assure us, further, that "the raising of the dead to life, understood in the most literal sense, did not at that time and in those circles seem so utterly earth-shaking and well-nigh incredible as it does to the modern mind"[20] flies in the face of all the evidence. Since the apostles themselves, let alone the rest of their first-century world, thought that the death of Jesus meant the end of Jesus and of their hopes in Him. They were at first completely incredulous when it was reported that He was alive from the dead. But, attributing the resurrection appearances of Jesus to "the power of hysteria within a small community,"[21] the symposiasts will have none of this. For them, the measure of our sophistication must provide the canon of our christology. Christ, they stress, can remain a figure of inspiring significance to our world only "if he is an ever-changing figure. Just as he changed greatly between apostolic and Nicene times, so he has changed down the generations and must continue to change if, as cultural change accelerates, he is to continue to mediate the nature, grace and demands of God to succeeding generations."[22]

The faith of the New Testament is secure and immutable precisely because it is founded on absolutes. But now with their plea for the deabsolutization of Christ and the Scriptures the authors of *The Myth of God Incarnate* are inviting the church to engulf itself in the quagmire of relativism. We are told that we must bid farewell to the uniqueness of the Christian faith and see it as merely sharing a place, pluralistically, with the other religions of the world. We are informed, as though it were a matter no longer open to question, of "our new recognition of the validity of the other great world faiths as being also, at their best, ways of salvation." Consequently, our witness to Christ can only be relativistic, no more than a part contributed to the whole of religious reality, and the answer given to the question, "Should *our* revelation of the Logos, namely in the life of Jesus, be made available to all mankind?" is, "Yes, of course; and so also should other particular revelations of the Logos at work in human life—in the Hebrew prophets, in the Buddha, in the *Upanishads* and *Bhagavad Gita*, in the *Koran*, and so on."[23]

In brief, we are being urged to abandon the uniqueness of the Christian gospel and to subjectivize the Christian faith (on the understanding that any other religion or none will serve the purpose equally well). No wonder the obligatory prerequisite for doing so is the "deabsolutization" of Christ and Bible, for it would be most inconvenient if the dominical pronouncement "No one comes to the Father except through me" (John 14:6), the apostolic admonition that "salvation is found in no one else" (Acts 4:12), and the Pauline anathema thundered against any who should preach a different gospel (Gal. 1:6–9) were to remain unobliterated. But to remove the church's landmarks in order to render it completely open and congenial to all and sundry of whatever persuasion is to lose the Christian faith, for it requires the dismantlement of the gospel. Those who are willing to pay that price have no right to the name of Christians. "The final tendency of 'advanced theology' is backwards," P. T. Forsyth once pointedly observed. "Like Molière's ghost, it has improved very much for the worse."[24]

As we have seen, it is the contention of modern liberal scholars that the Bible is historically and culturally conditioned not only in its provenance but also in the course of its interpretation across the centuries. Because the mentality of the first century was supposedly anything but commensurate with the mentality of the twentieth century, a radical reinterpretation is now being demanded as a necessity for the church. Their battle cry, like that of the militant evolutionists of a former generation, is "Change or perish!"—though always with the proviso that the change must be one of which they approve, that is to say, of a reductionist nature. For example, they deplore as a change for the worse the transition that they postulate took place from the understanding of the primitive church to that of the Chalcedonian Definition of the Faith in the fourth century. This is a judgment that I believe to be mistaken in respect, first, to there being a change and, second, to there being a change for the worse.

That there have been differing interpretations of the biblical text throughout the history of the church is an undeniable fact. But it is wrongheaded to adduce this as evidence that demonstrates either that the authority of Scripture (which can be made to mean different things by different people) is an illusion or that biblical interpretation is subject to historical relativity. It is not the comparatively few difficult and obscure passages that are in question here; precisely because of the uncertainty of their meaning, these passages naturally evoke a variety of judgments and explanations. Nor, for that matter, is it a question of those places where there are gaps in our knowledge rather than exegetical difficulties in the text. In this connection it is somewhat ironical that the earliest Christians were much better informed than we are. They knew, for instance, which languages Jesus spoke on different occasions, whether Paul realized his desire to carry the gospel as far west as Spain (Rom. 15:24, 28), who wrote the Epistle to the Hebrews, and the identity and location of its recipients, and they had the answer to numerous other matters now in dispute on which much intellectual energy in scholarly research and speculative ingenuity has been expended.

Our concern here, rather, is with straightforward passages whose sense is plain for all to see and that nonetheless have had a variety of interpretations imposed on them. This is not the place for a survey of hermeneutics, but it is well known that in the history of biblical exposition a fourfold scheme of interpretation (comprising the literal, allegorical, tropological, and anagogical senses) was long prevalent in church circles. For all practical purposes, however, these four senses amounted basically to two main senses, namely the literal and the allegorical—the literal being the natural or surface sense, and the allegorical the "spiritual" or deep sense. In the early Christian centuries two rival schools of interpretation appeared: the Antiochene, which insisted on the primacy of the literal sense, and the Alexandrian, which championed the allegorical sense, with Theodore of Mopsuestia as a leading exponent of the former and Origen of the latter. The allegorical method may be traced back to Greek intellectualism that prior to the Christian era had become accustomed to interpret the Hellenic mythology and the Homeric epics in an allegorical manner. Alexandria had for some considerable time enjoyed a reputation as a center of Greek culture. It was there that Philo, the Jewish philosopher and contemporary of the apostles, constructed his platonic allegorization of the events and personages of the Old Testament. But the allegorical method of biblical interpretation was not limited to a particular city or a restricted period of time. It had many exponents throughout the church from the subapostolic generation for fifteen hundred years. The method in fact persists right up to the present day in some Christian circles. Therefore it cannot be categorized as a phenomenon of historical relativity.

The principle behind the allegorizing method is nonetheless a pernicious one. It presupposes that under the surface of the text, hidden from the sight of the multitude, there lies a profound "spiritual" sense that only the expert is capable of discerning. This inevitably fosters an attitude of disdain and disregard for the plain, natural sense of the text and reduces the Bible to a book of intellectual word puzzles. It also leads to the spinning out of exegesis of the most elaborate and fantastic character that is as unedifying as it is fanciful. And, worst of all, it has the effect of taking the Bible out of the hands of the common people and making it the preserve of inventive academics. The two rival schools of Alexandria and Antioch have been mentioned, but it would be an oversimplification to imagine that the theory of either was invariably matched by its practice. The Antiochene exegetes pursued the saner course, allowing that different senses were present in Scripture and holding that any of these senses—whether historical, allegorical, ethical, or heavenly—might, depending on the nature of the passage and its context, be the proper or literal sense. They acknowledged also that a particular passage might well be susceptible of more than one sense. Thus, for example, it was certainly not illegitimate to see christological significance in much of the history of the Old Testament. But even these commentators occasionally succumbed to the temptation to indulge in allegorization of a questionable nature.

Allegorical esotericism is an abuse of Scripture. Its practitioners disclose deep secrets and arcane significances that were never there to begin with and never entered the mind of the author. The same results could be produced by the application of their ingenuity to virtually any other text of whatever kind, religious or irreligious. Moreover, as Luther remarked, "allegories of this sort prove nothing, and it is better to teach these things at their proper places, for it is hazardous to change meanings in this way and to depart so far from the literal meaning."[25] In general, the allegorizers "discovered" truths that were explicitly taught and constituted the literal sense elsewhere in the Bible; hence Luther's admonition that "it is better to teach these things at their proper places." In other words, the church's allegorizers were inherently orthodox: it was not their intention to develop their technique as an instrument for the propagation of heterodoxy.

The point I am making here is that, until modern times, the church always had a clear and acknowledged line of orthodoxy. However much corrupt and unspiritual practices might infiltrate into its ranks, the standard of orthodoxy remained constant, and that standard was the doctrine of Holy Scripture. We cannot afford to overlook the significance of the church's recognition of Scripture as *canon*, or measuring rod, to whose teaching all faith and practice, if they are to be genuinely Christian, must conform. Furthermore, the church formulated the ecumenical creeds as controls for the assents of its members, not, however, as additions or alternatives to the biblical canon, but as summary statements of central beliefs directly derived from Scripture, and authoritative precisely for that reason. The same is true of the Chalcedonian Definition of 451, which as a filling-out or amplification of the original Creed of Nicea was avowedly the church's affirmation of the authentic apostolic faith of the New Testament. It did not create a departure from or alteration of the primitive Christian position (though some modern academics, as we have seen, would like to persuade us otherwise).

This consideration, however, should not be taken to imply that the church is immune to pressures arising from specific historical situations. Undoubtedly there was a strong temptation for the early church to accommodate its formulations to the idiosyncrasies of Greek thought then prevalent. But the orthodox leaders resolutely resisted this temptation. To maintain, as it is now fashionable to do in some academic circles, that the creedal documents of Nicea and Chalcedon represent a capitulation to Greek thought and the Hellenization of the church is to turn things upside down. As Greek was the language used, the articles of belief were expressed in Greek terms. But it is precarious to argue that the presence of Greek terminology means the adoption of Greek philosophy. Equally precarious is the conception, also fashionable, that there is a radical difference between Hebrew and Greek ways of thinking and that this radical difference is actually ingrained in the Hebrew and Greek languages. Hebrew thought/language, we have been assured a thousand times, is dynamic and concrete, whereas Greek thought/language is static and abstract, so that one might wonder how it could ever be possible to translate the one into the other. James Barr nailed the lid on the coffin of this scientifically disreputable canard in his book *The Semantics of Biblical Language*,[26] but the misconception obstinately persists. The authors of *The Myth of God Incarnate*, for example, explain that the original (subjective) "poetry" hardened later into (objective) prose "and escalated from a metaphorical son of God to a metaphysical God the Son."[27] Moreover, Rudolf Bultmann speaks of the early church as having sought a solution to the christological question "in an inadequate way by means of Greek thought with its objectivizing nature, a solution which indeed found an expression that is now impossible for our thought, in the Chalcedonian formula."[28]

Far from Greek philosophical notions being readily absorbed into the Christian system, it was precisely *against* the Hellenization of the faith that the leaders of the early church waged unrelenting warfare. Seen in its historical perspective, the Chalcedonian affirmation of Christ's incarnation, death and resurrection, and double *homoousios* ("truly God and truly man, ... of one substance with the Father as regards his Godhead, and at the same time of one substance with us as regards his manhood") was a categorical rejection of the Greek philosophical mind, to which an affirmation of this kind was totally unacceptable. The battle actually began in the time of the apostles who emphatically opposed the threat to the gospel posed by docetism. The philosophical principle of docetism was the dualistic spirit/matter antithesis whose ancestry went back at least as far as Pythagoras and that continued its existence as the core of the more complicated forms of gnosticism elaborated in the postapostolic period. For those whose thought was governed by this principle the incarnation was an impossibility. So also the roots of Arianism, whose subtle formulations caused a crisis in the church of the fourth century, can be traced back to the theories of Greek philosophy. It was such Hellenizing movements that were decisively denounced and repudiated as heretical by the church's first four general councils. In short, *the real Hellenizers were the heretics!* And the orthodox leaders of the church opposed them so resolutely because they saw clearly that the alien notions they wished to import attacked the heart of the gospel itself and that therefore the survival of authentic Christianity was at stake. It may well be that to some degree the statement of christological truth could benefit from a limited revision of the ancient terminology, but only with the proviso that this truth, being unique and ageless, is not itself compromised or subjected to revision.

The Chalcedonian Definition did not mark the end of the battle of truth against error. It was, however, the culmination of the church's efforts in these early centuries to provide for all persons, and for all time, a statement of theological (and especially, because of the nature of their struggle, christological) orthodoxy that preserved the integrity of the gospel and faithfully set forth the teaching of Holy Scripture. The situation has been presented in admirable perspective by Aloys Grillmeier, who has expressed his conviction that "the simple, original proclamation of Christ, the revealer and bringer of salvation, the proclamation of Christ the Son of God can be heard in undiminished strength through all the *philosophoumena* of the Fathers." He continues:

> These *philosophoumena*, these technical concepts and formulas (*though their "technical" character should not be exaggerated*), are not an end in themselves. They have a service to perform for the faith of the church. They are intended to preserve the Christ of the gospels and the apostolic age for the faith of posterity. In all the christological formulas of the ancient church there is a manifest concern not to allow the total demand made on men's faith by the person of Jesus to be weakened by pseudo-solutions. It must be handed on undiminished to all generations of Christendom. On a closer inspection, *the christological "heresies" turn out to be a compromise between the original message of the Bible and the understanding of it in Hellenism and paganism. It is here that we have the real Hellenization of Christianity.*[29]

Now again, in our day, the christological battle lines are drawn. As in the apostolic age, so once more in ours the warfare is quite simply between Christianity and antichristianity, between the authentic faith and a philosophical counterfeit, between divinely revealed truth and humanistic speculation. The admonition of the disciple whom Jesus loved is just as urgent in our twentieth century as it was when it was first written: "Many deceivers, who do not acknowledge Jesus Christ as coming in the flesh, have gone out into the world. Any such person is the deceiver and the antichrist. Watch out. . . . Anyone who runs ahead and does not continue in the teaching of Christ does not have God" (2 John 7–9).

In the perennial struggle against heterodoxy there has frequently been, perhaps not surprisingly, a tendency for the orthodox mind to lose the theological equilibrium that rightly belongs to the fullness of Christian truth. Preoccupation with the defense and affirmation of a doctrine that is under attack is understandable and necessary. In such a situation, however, the temptation is always there to allow the threatened doctrine so to dominate the orthodox perspective that other important doctrines, just as firmly believed, are not given due prominence. This leads to imbalance. The christological controversy of the fourth and fifth centuries provides an illustration of this sort of overreaction. The erroneous constructions placed by the Arians on certain texts, which they cited as proof that Christ was not the eternal

Second Person of the Trinity but a creature of some kind, were in some cases countered by the champions of orthodoxy with interpretations that themselves were questionable. Thus it was agreed that the assertion of Psalm 2:7, "Thou art my Son, today I have begotten thee" (RSV) had christological significance. This passage, according to the Arian explanation, meant that there was a day when the Son was begotten and therefore a time when He came into being. Anxious to maintain the eternal deity of the Son, the majority of the orthodox theologians responded by asserting that the "day" in question was the everlasting day of God's eternity and thus that the text implied not the temporal creatureliness but the eternal generation of the Son. They would, however, have done better to be guided by the apostolic interpretation according to which this verse was fulfilled in the resurrection of Jesus, the incarnate Son, from the dead (Acts 13:32–33; Rom. 1:4; Heb. 1:5): the resurrection day was the day of the begetting or rebirth, in Christ, of the humanity He had taken to Himself. It was not as though the orthodox were dependent on the exposition of this text in a particular way for the establishment of their case. But in this and other instances their zeal for the doctrine of Christ's eternal sonship caused them to engage in a less-than-satisfactory form of polemical exegesis. This, though, was no more than a tendency—an example, one might say, of the pressure of "historical relativism." The unfailing loyalty of these advocates of the authentic faith was to the truth divinely revealed in Scripture, and it would be unpardonable to leave out of account the great number of passages legitimately adduced and interpreted by them to the confusion of their opponents.

Still today this tendency is discernible in the ranks of orthodoxy. In the face of current christological reductionism, which cuts the figure of the historic Jesus Christ down to the paltry dimensions of a mere man, dead and buried for nearly two millennia (psilanthropism), there has rightly been an emphatic insistence on His divine and eternal existence. But at the same time, and largely because of this, there has been an inadvertent neglect or misplacing of the rich biblical doctrine of the humanity of Christ and the absolutely fundamental significance for the believer of the human life, death, and glorification of Christ, since it was *our* humanity that He took to Himself in the incarnation in order that He might redeem it and bring it to its destined glory, which is *His* glory.

Likewise the modern humanistic determination to destroy the authenticity and therefore the authority of Holy Scripture, leaving no more than a mutilated corpse of a document, has rightly spurred those who have experienced the saving power of the Bible's message to reaffirm with passion the truth of the Scriptures as the genuine and binding Word of God. But, challenged with the necessity for asserting the "divinity" of the Bible, some orthodox voices have remained silent about its "humanness." There has been an unwillingness to acknowledge that the phenomenon of Scripture is a *mystery*. That the infinite God should condescend to us, in the sense of His coming down to our finite level, whether by the eternal Word's becoming flesh and dwelling among us as man with man and for man, or by the communication of His truth, and in particular *this* truth, to us in the frail form of human language, is something so marvelous that it is beyond the limited grasp of our comprehension—though not, thanks to divine grace, beyond our experience. This condescension is humiliation, self-humbling. But it is humiliation with a purpose, and that purpose, being *God's* purpose, is achieved with absolute adequacy and indefectibility.

Thus again today orthodox Christians are feeling the pressure of "historical relativity" as fresh and fierce assaults are launched against the bastion of Holy Scripture. In the heat of the conflict there is a strong temptation, when insisting on the "divinity" of Scripture, to thrust aside its "humanity," and this can only be at the expense of upsetting the balance of the paradox and ignoring the mystery. There is then, inevitably, resort to rationalization, which in itself is a form of reductionism (even though this is the last thing that is intended) as the level is lowered to the capacity of human thought by putting the emphasis on one pole of the paradox. This tendency is sometimes displayed in the postulation that inerrancy belongs only to the original autographs, which (as far as we know) are no longer in existence. It is seen also in the deduction from this premise that we now possess only errant copies of these autographs. To be assured that these copies, though errant, are nonetheless infallible is far from helpful. The use of language in this confused and confusing manner is hardly conducive to sound reason and understanding. It creates, rather, the impression of verbal acrobatics.

Here I must state plainly that I certainly do not regard the original text as unimportant or as only relatively important. Obviously, full authenticity belongs only to the autograph or to a completely faithful copy of the autograph. This is the first principle of all textual and literary research, secular as well as religious. Obviously, too, in our reconstruction of the authentic biblical text we will favor the text that, to the best of our judgment, approximates most nearly to what was originally written—hence the painstaking process of textual criticism —and we will reject variant readings that we judge to be unoriginal. By the same token, we will welcome that translation that most accurately reproduces the meaning of the original (or, as we do not possess the original, the text closest to the original)—though a merely literalistic translation, word for word, would be altogether pitiful and inadequate (as a reference to any interlinear Hebrew-English or Greek-English Bible will show), since it is not a sequence of isolated words that have to be translated, but rather words in context and in combination as sentences and ideas and idioms. The points I wish to stress are these: (1) that even without possessing the autographs we have the Word of

God, whether in Hebrew or Greek or in the form of a translation; (2) that the Scriptures are translatable without ceasing thereby to be the authentic Word of God; (3) that the term *inerrancy* is sometimes used in an ambiguous and confusing manner; (4) that the distinction between *inerrancy* and *infallibility* as between superior and inferior concepts is open to serious question; (5) that the "humanity" of Scripture, the fact that it involves the "weakness" inseparable from the finiteness of human language, must not be left out of account, even though by God's grace it adequately fulfills its revelatory and redemptive purpose and there is a true harmony in the union of the "human" and the "divine"; (6) that thanks to the providential control and guidance of the Holy Spirit throughout the course of the church's history the integrity of the Scriptures has been essentially preserved in the transmission of the text; and (7) that even if the autographs were to be discovered tomorrow, though this would display the authentic text and mean the end of all textual criticism, the problems and perplexities that puzzle us now would remain unresolved—the chronological questions regarding passion week, for example, or the difference in the order of Christ's temptations as given by Matthew and Luke. Thus, much though we would like to have the original autographs, we are not at a disadvantage for not having them. No good purpose is served by taking refuge in unavailable autographs, and it is much healthier for us to speak simply, positively, and confidently of the Bible as the Word of God without any qualification.

Rather than stretch out the arm of our human reason to steady the ark of Scripture when it seems to be in danger of falling, we should approach the Bible with simplicity, reverence, and expectancy, and always with thankfulness, knowing it to be that inexplicable mystery that is the Word of God written. As such we acknowledge its teaching to be absolutely true and supremely authoritative. We shall not depend on our limited powers of logic or on the testimonies of experts and scholars (valuable though these may be in their place) for our persuasion that Scripture is indeed the Word of God, for it is only by the inner working and witness of the Holy Spirit that this conviction becomes unshakably established in our hearts and minds. And this is a certainty, as Calvin has observed, that is primary because it is "higher and stronger than any human judgment."[30] We must not allow "the certainty of *faith* to be supplanted by the certainty of *intellect*."[31] Moreover, the certainty of faith confirms to us the understanding that the Holy Spirit who first sovereignly gave the truth of Holy Scripture also sovereignly superintends the transmission of the Word of grace from generation to generation, kindling simultaneously in our hearts the response of belief in the gospel and the recognition that Scripture is indeed the dynamic Word of God. Thus throughout the course of history the written Word, precisely because it is God-breathed, accomplishes the purpose of its giving and prospers in the thing for which it was sent (Isa. 55:10). The Holy Spirit is indeed the *primary* author of Scripture, but we may also say, with Abraham Kuyper, that He is the *perpetual* author of Scripture as He graciously writes its revitalizing truth in the hearts and lives of believers from one age to another.[32] Apart from the light He brings, the Scripture remains, because of our sinful blindness, as lusterless as a diamond in the dark.[33] God's Word will not and, by virtue of its being *God's* Word, cannot return to Him empty. Its truth is eternal, its message is infinite grace, its power is to bring us from death to life through faith in Jesus Christ. That is why the truth of Holy Scripture triumphantly transcends and transforms all relativities of human history.

We who cherish the orthodox and evangelical faith have become *too defensive* about the Bible; we have grown accustomed to jumping from a worthy premise: "The Bible is the Word of God," to a conclusion negative in form: ". . . therefore it is inerrant." This, of course, is not wrong in itself, but I suggest that it reflects the position into which we have allowed ourselves to be maneuvered. We must move on to the offensive, boldly wielding this powerful weapon that we know to be the sword of the Spirit (Eph. 6:17), as we *positively* (and, I believe, more biblically) proclaim to the world that the Bible is the Word of God and therefore is living, dynamic, penetrating, and unfailingly effective as it cuts with the edge of redemption for the believer and with the edge of condemnation for the unbeliever (Heb. 4:12).

In much contemporary writing about hermeneutics, or the interpretation of Scripture, there seems to be a preoccupation with methods of understanding that may variously be described as humanistic, relativistic, or existentialist (self-centered). It is quite legitimate to recognize that there are significant differences between the horizon of the biblical author and the horizon of the modern interpreter and to take this difference into account; but, as Anthony Thiselton has pointed out, "historical method becomes anthropocentric when the interpreter's own experience of life becomes the test of all historical truth."[34] Besides, as I have said earlier, the radical predicament of man remains unaltered through the centuries, and the authentic force of God's Word, precisely because it is *God's* Word, continues undiminished.

THE CHURCH FATHERS
AND HOLY SCRIPTURE

Geoffrey W. Bromiley

Geoffrey W. Bromiley

Geoffrey W. Bromiley is Senior Professor of Church History and Historical Theology at Fuller Theological Seminary, Pasadena, California. He has served as pastor in the Anglican dioceses of Carlisle and Edinburgh and also as Vice-Principal of Trinity College, Bristol, England. In addition to writing several articles, reviews, and books, including *Introduction to Historical Theology* and *Introduction to the Theology of Karl Barth*, he has been co-editor of Barth's *Church Dogmatics* in English, has translated the *Theological Dictionary of the New Testament* and *Helmut Thielicke's Evangelical Faith*, and is currently general editor of the revision of the *International Standard Bible Encyclopedia*.

THE CHURCH FATHERS
AND HOLY SCRIPTURE

THE FACT OF SCRIPTURE

THE OLD TESTAMENT

The early church arose in a situation in which Holy Scripture already existed as a fact. Jesus and the apostles belonged to the people through whom and to whom God had given the Old Testament in what became the threefold form of the Law, the Prophets, and the Writings. Not only had they no reason to dispute the divine uniqueness of this literary legacy; they also perceived in Christ's own life and ministry its culmination and fulfillment. From the very beginning, then, they gave Holy Scripture to the infant church and taught the first believers, both Jews and Gentiles, to accept, read, study, revere, quote, and commend it as the written Word of God. Innumerable examples could be culled from the writings of the apostolic fathers and the second-century apologists to show how well the Christians learned this basic lesson.

The only uncertainty concerned the compass of the Old Testament. This had come down in two forms. In the original Hebrew it consisted of twenty-two (or twenty-four) books usually grouped in the three traditional divisions. It had also been translated into Greek (the Septuagint) for the Jews of the Dispersion. In this form it included the additional works commonly known as the Apocrypha. When the church underwent its rapid expansion outside the borders of Palestine, the Greek Translation very naturally became the most widely known and used version of the Old Testament. Hence it is no surprise that writers like Barnabas quoted the book of Wisdom as Scripture[1] and that Irenaeus,[2] Tertullian, Clement of Alexandria, and Origen all used the Apocrypha in the same way as they did the Law, the Prophets, and the Writings of the narrower Hebrew canon.

Nevertheless, even in the second century a sense of distinction may be observed. Melito of Sardis contended firmly that only the Hebrew original constitutes the true canon.[3] Origen, with his Hebrew scholarship, moved in the same direction[4] even though he did not scruple to quote the Apocrypha. The later Eastern Fathers, represented by Athanasius,[5] Cyril of Jerusalem,[6] and John of Damascus,[7] rejected the full authority of the Apocrypha, although rather oddly the Antiochenes Theodoret and Chrysostom took a different path and all the Fathers continued to use and quote the Apocrypha for its edificatory value. In the Western church Hilary,[8] Rufinus,[9] and especially Jerome[10] restricted the canon to the Hebrew works, from which alone they believed the church may derive its authoritative teaching. By and large, however, the West took the broader position, which found an able advocate in Augustine.[11] A synod held at Carthage in 397 recognized the enlarged canon, and Innocent I added Roman endorsement to this view in a letter dated 405. From that point onward the canonical status of the Apocrypha went virtually unchallenged in the West until the Reformation, and even then, although the Reformers sided with the early Eastern church and Jerome, the Council of Trent, followed by modern Roman Catholicism, continued to sponsor the addition of the Greek works to the original Hebrew.

Four points may be noted in relation to this issue. Historically, it may reflect a difference between Palestinian and Dispersion Judaism in their approach to the whole concept of the canon (although scholars differ on this point).[12] Intellectually, it brings to light a deficiency in the scholarship of the West from which even the great Augustine suffered and which it could ill afford, namely, a lack of linguistic expertise and a resultant dependence on translations. Doctrinally, not a great deal is at stake, although support has been found in the Apocrypha for prayers for the dead and a measure of justification by works. Pragmatically, division in the matter has tended to lead to an overuse of the Apocrypha on the one side and its undue disparagement on the other in place of the healthy balance whereby it is excluded from canonical rank but its merits as religious literature are properly appreciated and exploited.

THE NEW TESTAMENT

If the church inherited the Old Testament from Judaism by way of Jesus and His first disciples, the same cannot be said about the New Testament. No ready-made canon of the New Testament existed when the earliest Christian communities came into being. Not for many years, in fact, would there be a set number of books that could be listed alongside the works of the Old Testament and accorded the same status and authority. Nevertheless, as the writings that we now know as the New Testament were being composed and circulated, the church was again confronted with a fact. Epistles and gospels either deriving directly from the apostles or having apostolic associations and bearing the apostolic message became part of the life and legacy of the first believers. They began to quote these writings in their own oral and written communications and they soon realized, subconsciously perhaps at first but then with rapidly increasing consciousness, that they had to reckon with the normative ranking of these writings no less than with that of the familiar Old Testament canon.

Already in Clement of Rome and Polycarp one may find extensive quotations from works that now belong to the New Testament. The first generation, it is true, did not introduce these quotations with the type of formula ("It is written ... ") that they had inherited for Old Testament citations. But the apostolic works quickly received even this formal recognition, as one may see in the well-known "another scripture saith" of 2 Clement[13] and similar statements in Justin Martyr.[14] By the end of the second century Irenaeus plainly accorded to the New Testament (or at least the Gospels) the same authority as he did to the Old Testament,[15] Clement of Alexandria began to speak of "the new Testament,"[16] and Tertullian balanced the evangelical and apostolic books (the Gospels and Epistles) over against the Law and the Prophets.[17]

In the case of the New Testament, too, an issue of expansion arose. Some groups, as may be seen from the so-called Muratorian Canon, attributed the *Shepherd of Hermas* to the New Testament Hermas and were ready to recognize and quote it as an apostolic writing. Others were promoting and using pseudepigraphical works (e.g., the Gospel of Thomas), usually in the interests of the Gnostic versions of the gospel that invaded the churches during the second century. Even a writing of the status of 2 Clement could adduce supposedly dominical sayings that are generally thought to come from the noncanonical Gospel of the Egyptians.[18] If the church confronted the fact of authoritative apostolic literature, it soon had to face the problem of differentiating the true New Testament canon from the false.

The problem was one of illegitimate restriction as well as expansion. Marcion, in Tertullian's famous phrase,[19] was using the knife and not the pen, and the result of his activity was the elimination of the whole of the Old Testament, of all the Gospels apart from certain portions of Luke, and of all the rest of the New Testament apart from ten expurgated epistles of Paul. This radical reduction of the canon did not rest, of course, on historical or literary considerations but on the theological principle of an antithesis of law and grace. Yet it combined with the unwarranted expansion of the canon to force the church of the later second century to wrestle with the question of authentic apostolicity and to seek an agreed consensus on what should be acknowledged and commended as the true New Testament canon.

The church responded forcefully to the challenge. Irenaeus not only defended the four Gospels but gave some (admittedly strange) reasons why there should be no more and no fewer than four.[20] Tertullian, writing against Marcion, included in his list of authoritative works the four Gospels, the thirteen epistles of Paul, Acts, Hebrews, 1 John, and Revelation.[21] The Muratorian Canon, usually thought to be a Roman list of the same date, recognized all the books of the present New Testament apart from Hebrews, James, 1 and 2 Peter, and 3 John, although it also included Wisdom and the Apocalypse of Peter.[22] In the period that followed, three groups of writings tended to emerge: first, those of whose canonicity the church entertained no doubts; second, writings like Hebrews and the smaller General Epistles, which some groups treated with suspicion but which were gradually receiving universal recognition; and third, fringe writings like the Didache, the Shepherd, and the Apocalypse of Peter, which enjoyed some initial support, which might still be quoted by many authors, but which the church could not finally include in the canonical list.[23] Athanasius, who had a habit of making history, took a step whose significance, perhaps, was not at first realized when in his Easter Letter of 367 he became, so far as we know, the first to endorse officially the canonicity of twenty-seven New Testament books. His lead was followed in the next centuries by every church and father until a consensus was achieved that not even the doubts of Martin Luther or the revised datings of liberal scholarship could seriously disturb.

Face to face with the New Testament canon and the slow and tortuous story of its recognition by the Fathers, can we speak accurately about a fact that confronted the church? Do we not have instead a fact that the church itself created? From one standpoint, of course, this is a circular question and therefore a pointless one. The authors of the New Testament undoubtedly belonged to the church and to that extent the church undoubtedly created the fact of the canon. Yet inasmuch as these authors played a unique role in composing their writings, the church at large found itself confronted by a quasi-extraneous fact in its encounter with these writings. It gave evidence of this in its awareness that the definition of the canon was not just a matter of giving some of its own productions the preference over others, but rather of the recognition of an authoritative status that some works enjoyed by objective and inherent right. The church had no authority to make its own canon. It had to recognize, endorse, and proclaim a canon that was already there.

It could do this, of course, only if it had a criterion by which to do it. Apostolicity provided this criterion. Apostolicity had two related aspects: a historical and a doctrinal. The aspects were related because the early church wanted to know (1) in what works the apostles had transmitted their message and (2) what this apostolic message was in order that it might itself transmit it faithfully. Historically, apostolicity meant credible authorship either by an apostle (e.g., Peter, Paul, or John) or by someone closely associated with an apostle (e.g., Mark or Luke). Doctrinally, it meant conformity to the emergent consensus of apostolic teaching.

The historical aspect obviously involved the early church in a measure of scientific investigation. Its members did not enjoy, of course, the skills and resources of modern scholarship in pursuing this task. On the other hand, they were closer to the sources than we are and they could not afford to be too credulous in the face of the flood of pseudepigraphical works that might have been acceptable as a literary genre but that could only cause confusion in view of their divergent teachings. The reserve with which the early church treated even many of the pieces that were finally approved bears testimony, not to a readiness to attach an apostle's name to any or every writing, but to a desire for certainty that ought to cause many modern scholars to take more seriously than they do the external testimony to New Testament authorship.

The doctrinal aspect supplemented historical inquiry by focusing on apostolicity of content. Works of whose apostolic derivation little or no doubt existed provided a body of teaching—coincident with what was also taught orally in the churches—that could serve as a check on writings that were circulated as apostolic or proposed for acceptance into the canon. In this regard, of course, the danger of moving in a circle arises. A work, it might be believed, is or is not apostolic merely because it does or does not teach what the other apostolic writings teach. Yet there are safeguards against this, for the doctrinal aspect does not rule out historical inquiry nor does a consensus in essentials preclude a certain variety in detail.[24] Furthermore, the early church very obviously did not fall into the trap of first deciding what the apostolic message ought to be and then evaluating the early literature in accordance with this preconception. While it was undoubtedly influenced by what was traditionally preached and taught in the churches, it also made a sincere effort to discern the apostolic message by objective study, to take into account the historical credentials of supposedly apostolic works,[25] and only then to apply the test whether a particular work spoke with an authentic apostolic voice.

In the last resort the early church had to deal with the fact of a New Testament as well as an Old Testament canon because it had no real power—and it realized that it had no real power—either to make or to unmake the canon. Irrespective of its judgment, the writings that came down in and to it were either apostolic or not, and, like the church in every age, it could only try to reach a judgment that would correspond to the objective reality. In this regard it functioned in much the same world as the artistic world that, when confronted by the alleged painting of a great master, can neither make a false work authentic nor an authentic work false but can only come to considered (and usually reliable) judgment according to the external and internal evidence available and its own experience in assessing it. As the early church perceived it, certain works had been written to give the apostolic message a more permanent form in writing. These works constituted the fact of the New Testament canon. The church's task was to recognize these works, to differentiate them from others, and to give them the public endorsement that would mean their agreed use and authority in the churches.

THE ORIGIN OF SCRIPTURE

THE DIVINE ORIGIN

Awareness of the facticity of the canon was linked in the early church to a very definite recognition of the divine origin of the canonical literature. The Old Testament, it is true, was inherited historically from Judaism, yet here, too, a special act of God had led to the creation of this particular body of literature. Israel could not be regarded as its true author any more than the church could be regarded as the true author of the New Testament. Scripture, as a fact, was also a gift. It was not a gift from one human being to another, or from one group of human beings to another. It was a gift from God made primarily to the people of God but to be passed on by this people to the world. If it confronted the early church as a fact, it did so ultimately because it had its origin, not just in the prophets and apostles, but in God.

That the Fathers accepted the divine inspiration of Holy Scripture, whether as the Old Testament or the New, may be demonstrated with the greatest of ease. Irenaeus was not surprised that the Bible could sometimes be obscure—he found the explanation in its "wholly spiritual" nature.[26] Theodore of Mopsuestia, while differentiating various types of inspiration, attributed all Scripture to the operation of the one Spirit.[27] Gregory of Nyssa, following the apostle Paul, descried the hand of the Holy Spirit in every statement of the Bible.[28] Augustine found in both the Old and the New Testaments the gift of the Holy Spirit by way of the sacred writers.[29]

Even the problems that readers encountered in Holy Scripture did not deter the Fathers from a strong belief in its inspiration. Origen was convinced that a divine purpose lay behind passages that the intelligence might have initial difficulty in accepting.[30] Chrysostom deduced from the inspiration of Scripture, and regarded as evidence of it, the fact that even the most trivial biblical statements have more than superficial value.[31] Jerome argued that only the ignorant fail to see the wisdom in a simple letter like Philemon.[32] Augustine did not allow textual or historical difficulties to affect in the least his belief in divine inspiration.[33]

Emphasis on the divine authorship of Holy Scripture could lead sometimes to a certain depreciation of the role of the human writers. Athenagoras is perhaps the best-known representative of this tendency with his reference to the ecstatic nature of prophesying and his comparison of the Holy Spirit to a flutist.[34] The passivity of the Montanist prophets and prophetesses, who claimed that they spoke directly in the name of God, accorded with the same understanding.[35] In spite of the rejection of Montanism, Irenaeus offered something of a parallel to it with his statement that Scripture is dictated by the Spirit.[36] Chrysostom spoke of the Holy Spirit stroking the lyre of the work written by John, the humble fisherman, although in this instance the reference seems to be to the present ministry of the Holy Spirit in the hearers rather than to His initial ministry in the writer.[37] Augustine in a famous passage stated that Christ has in fact given us written materials Himself, since He used His disciples for this purpose as if they were His own hands.[38] Gregory the Great summed up this whole line of thought when he bluntly affirmed that the question of human authorship is of little relevance. If we know who is the true author of each work and we understand what He says to us, why should we be curious to learn what pen imprinted the divine words on the page?[39]

THE HUMAN ORIGIN

Nevertheless, the early church hesitated to commit itself to a theory of divine inspiration by ecstasy or dictation. If Hippolytus on occasion could use a musical comparison, he also claimed that an important part of the ministry of the Holy Spirit was to teach and illumine the human authors.[40] Origen, too, believed that the Holy Spirit, far from transporting the mind into an ecstatic state, gave instead a fuller and clearer apprehension of truth.[41] Epiphanius differentiated sharply between the experiences of the Old and New Testament writers and those of the inauthentic Montanist ecstatics.[42] Chrysostom, while looking for more than human wisdom, keenly appreciated the way in which the individual writers made their own contributions.[43] Jerome engaged in some historical and literary research into the settings of the various books.[44] Augustine did not allow his description of the disciples as the hands of Christ to reduce their role to one of pure passivity, for he argued that under the superintendence of the Holy Spirit, the writers of the Gospels used materials of which they themselves had personal knowledge.[45] Even Gregory the Great, when he uttered his famous dictum, was referring in fact to the Book of Job, a work whose authorship is unknown and cannot, therefore, be of any relevance in objective interpretation. With the Fathers, as with other theologians, one has to be on guard against taking a saying out of context and elevating it to the level of a dogmatic axiom or all-controlling principle. The Fathers realized plainly enough that God had not caused Holy Scripture to come down directly from heaven nor used the human writers merely as automatic instruments for the recording of the divine words. The Holy Spirit had taken selected human beings and given the prophetic and apostolic testimony through their human gifts in the historical circumstances in which they were set. In some instances our knowledge of the human aspect might be scanty and in any case investigation of the human aspect could never yield the fullness of truth that Scripture was intended to convey. This did not entail, however, an elimination or even a serious disparagement of the human element either in principle or in general practice.

The Fathers did not, of course, probe deeply into the difficult question of the relationship between the divine author and the human authors. As previously noted, Theodore of Mopsuestia, who had a keen interest in the historical aspect of Scripture, attempted a distinction between the modes of inspiration discernible, as he thought, in the Prophets and the Writings.[46] Augustine, too, found a clarification of the mind in some instances and an immediacy of vision in others.[47] Origen had earlier engaged in some literary criticism in trying to establish the similarities and differences between Hebrews and the epistles of Paul.[48] He had also noted the variety of genres in the biblical writings, especially the mixing together of literal and figurative elements.[49] Behind this, however, he discerned a divine rather than a human purpose.

Whatever the mode of operation, for all the Fathers the use of human writers by the Holy Spirit did not entail any loss of infallibility in the finished products. On the contrary, the ministry of the Spirit guaranteed the freedom of the authors from ordinary human error.[50] If the Fathers did not give any particular emphasis to the term *inerrancy*, they undoubtedly expressed the content denoted by the word. To be sure, they were not so interested in technical historical accuracy as modern readers tend to be. On the other hand, they were plainly aware of apparent discrepancies and difficulties. Even so, they were still convinced, as Augustine put it, that truth is present in Scripture "absolutely."[51] The Scripture cannot lie.[52] It may be described as "sacred, and infallible, and absolutely trustworthy."[53] Although the exact nature of the relation between the Holy Spirit and the human author could not be understood or stated in detail, they confidently assumed that the Holy Spirit overruled human imperfection in such a way that what was written could be accepted as in every sense true and reliable.[54]

Not incorrectly, patristic discussion focused on the divine origin of Scripture. This, after all, is its unique feature. Other books are all of human derivation. They may contain valuable features. In some respects they may be compared to Scripture. One might even claim that all of them—or all that are of worth—owe their origin in the last resort to the general inspiration of the divine Spirit. Yet Scripture alone of all human books enjoys the special inspiration whereby it comes to us as the Word of God with all the force of divine truth and all the promise of grace and life from God. It was right, then, that the Fathers should give priority to this aspect. To have directed attention primarily to the human elements would have been to miss the distinctiveness of Scripture and to fail to grasp its final significance.

At the same time, it would be hard to deny that in general the Fathers tended to minimize unduly the human factors that the Holy Spirit used in producing the works that constitute the written Word. One can hardly complain, or course, that they did not solve the mystery of the divine and human operation. God Himself has not explained the process of inspiration to us and all attempts to elucidate it have thus far proved to be unsatisfactory in some respect. Nevertheless, the Fathers incontestably tilted the balance far too much in favor of the divine element, were attracted unduly by the mantic concepts of inspiration current in their day, and displayed neither the interest nor the skills necessary for a full appreciation of the human factors. The consequences, which are serious but not fatal, come to light most vividly in their attempts at exposition and interpretation.

Yet the patristic emphasis had its positive side. It produced a strong concept of the status of Scripture. It also initiated the church into an understanding of its central meaning.

THE STATUS OF SCRIPTURE

BIBLICAL AUTHORITY

As the Word of God given by the Spirit of God, Scripture had for the Fathers the status of a primary authority in the life, teaching, and mission of the church. Deriving from God and enshrining the truth of God, it had indeed the authority of God Himself. This applied to the Old Testament in virtue of its prophetic testimony to the Christ who was still to come. It applied to the New Testament in virtue of its apostolic witness to the Christ who had already come in fulfillment of the promises.

From an early date, but especially with the emergence of the New Testament canon, the Fathers clearly affirmed the authoritative status of Scripture. Irenaeus described it as the foundation and pillar of our faith.[55] Tertullian argued that whatever it teaches is true and we must accept its teachings and abide by them.[56] Clement of Alexandria called it the first principle of instruction, which is first apprehended by faith and then gives demonstration of itself, since in it we hear the voice of the Lord, which is more to be relied on than any demonstration.[57] Origen, for all his speculative bent, regarded the Bible as the norm of doctrine and tried to find a biblical starting point for even his wildest flights of fancy.[58] Cyril of Jerusalem refused to countenance any teaching that did not have biblical support; he based his instruction on the creed because he regarded the creed as a summary of biblical truth.[59] Chrysostom constantly directed his congregations to Scripture and urged the people to get their own copies and read and ponder them frequently at home.[60] Hilary of Poitiers exerted himself to refute Arianism on a biblical basis, the problem being not only to expound correctly the texts adduced by the Arians but also to show that the term *homoousion*, while not itself biblical, does in fact embody a biblical concept.[61] Augustine described Scripture as founded on "the highest pinnacle of divine authority."[62] John Cassian argued for the normativity of the creed only because he regarded the creed as an epitome of the biblical message, which was itself more than adequate for every purpose.[63]

SECONDARY AUTHORITIES

Without reducing the status of Scripture, the Fathers referred to other authorities that might suitably be described as the context of biblical authority. Chief among these was the apostolic tradition. By tradition they did not mean, of course, the unwritten practices (e.g., using the sign of the cross) to which Tertullian made reference[64] and which he himself did not equate directly with the tradition.[65] When Irenaeus appealed to tradition in his controversy with the Gnostics,[66] he obviously had in view the testimony of the apostles as it was being openly and unanimously handed down in the proclamation of the churches. In the middle of the second century, prior to the more precise definition and endorsement of the New Testament canon, the oral and written forms of the apostolic testimony stood in greater equipoise than they would later, when the written form would increasingly come to serve as a check on the more fluid and therefore the more easily corrupted oral form. In face of the Gnostic reinterpretation of Scripture, and its associated claim to a secret tradition deriving from the apostles,[67] the proponents of apostolic orthodoxy found it helpful and effective to adduce the common teaching of the apostolic churches—the tradition—not to oppose or correct or supplement Holy Scripture, but to bring its true message into focus. The appeal to tradition was in fact an appeal to the very apostolicity that formed the main criterion of New Testament canonicity. Tradition and Scripture were two forms of one and the same thing, as indeed they should be in every age if the church faithfully discharges its commission to proclaim God's Word. They were the Word preached on the one side and the Word written on the other. Irenaeus himself made this clear both formally when he described the New Testament as written tradition[68] and materially when he did in fact make considerable use of the New Testament as well as the Old (cf. his exposition of John 1:1ff.)[69] in his refutation of the Gnostics.

What may be said of tradition may be said also of the so-called canon of truth (Irenaeus)[70] or rule of faith (Tertullian).[71] If this can hardly be identified as an early creed, its contents undoubtedly resemble the developing creeds inasmuch as they epitomize the gospel and thus constitute a summary of the living tradition of the church. For Tertullian the rule of faith performed an important hermeneutical function.[72] To engage in simple exegetical debate with Marcion and the Gnostics was useless. They simply misinterpreted Scripture to their own advantage.[73] What was needed was an interpretative key, and Tertullian found this in the rule of faith, which contained all the important teachings found in each and all the apostolic churches. Superficially this might seem to exalt the authority of the rule above the authority of Scripture itself. Plainly, however, Tertullian did not intend to do this, for as he saw it the rule was a compendium of what the Bible also taught, so that the Bible was being interpreted in terms of its own essential message. The central point here is that, while the rule might have developed in the ongoing ministry of the church, it had not developed in independence of the New Testament or in competition with it. Behind the twofoldness of the form lay a unity of content, so that in its hermeneutical role the rule functioned only as the analogy of faith did for the Reformers of the sixteenth century. Everything depended, or course, on the identity of Scripture and the rule, on the correctness of their equation, but if the rule served as a key to the interpretation of Scripture, Scripture also acted as an important check on the content of the rule.

In the later patristic period less was said about the canon or rule of faith, except for a period in the Alexandrian school. Instead, the church itself increasingly emerged as a distinctive authority in the totality of its apostolic testimony. The Arian controversy of the fourth century helped to give contours to this amorphous phenomenon, for at this period the church began to take form in ecumenical synods and their rulings, and in defense of the essential deity of the Son and the Holy Spirit the Nicene Fathers appealed not merely to Holy Scripture but also to the creeds, to the prior teaching of the churches, and even to liturgical practices such as baptizing in the triune name.[74] Later, of course, the Fathers appealed to the Nicene formulae themselves, and Cyril of Alexandria, in his condemnation of Nestorius, quoted from earlier Fathers as well as from Holy Scripture.[75] Behind this procedure lay the conviction that, while the Bible itself constitutes the primary rule of teaching, the church and its formulated dogma offer an authoritative interpretation. This line of thinking received a particular twist in Rome, where forceful bishops like Damasus, Innocent I, and Leo the Great argued for the Petrine supremacy, for the resultant primacy of the Roman See, and for the hermeneutical authority not merely of the church at large but more specifically of the Roman pontiff as its temporal head. Augustine advanced a different though not unrelated concept when he stated bluntly that the church, too, possesses the crown of authority,[76] that it guarantees Holy Scripture,[77] and that we should even not believe Holy Scripture except as we are moved to do so by this authority.[78] It is no surprise, then, that Augustine also contended for the established interpretation of Scripture, for the canonical rules laid down by the church's exegetes, and for a rejection of all expositions that are not compatible with the catholic faith.[79]

In passing it may be noted that many of the Fathers also found a place for reason in their discussion of authority. The whole enterprise of the second-century apologists depended in part on an appeal to reason. So, too, did the work of the Alexandrians, as may be seen from Clement's decision to attempt a commendation of the gospel in nonbiblical terms and concepts.[80] Nor did Tertullian abandon reason, as is often supposed, for his authorities included nature and discipline as well as Scripture,[81] and reason, although probably in a more specialized legal sense,[82] played an important part in his interrelating of the three. Augustine, of course, made a more direct apologetic plea for the use of such natural reason as would influence unbelievers and help believers in their evaluation of beliefs.[83] In patristic theology as a whole, however, the secondary status of reason is everywhere apparent. Even the Alexandrians realized that there can be no attaining to the knowledge of God apart from the gracious revelation to which God has given a written form in holy Scripture. Clement might surmise that Greek philosophy had also served as a preparation for the gospel, but it could never have done so had not God Himself ordained and used it for this purpose,[84] and it could not itself supply the truth that comes through the divine work of revelation and reconciliation.

If the authority of reason did little to affect the normative status of Scripture, the same cannot be said so easily for the developing appeal to the church. In this respect, however, one must be particularly on guard against facile or polemical judgments. Historically, no doubt, the decisions made by the Fathers and the patterns of thought that they established contributed in the long run to the crisis of authority that led to the Reformation and evoked the reaffirmation of the uniqueness of biblical authority that this entailed. The supremacy of the authority of Scripture did indeed tend to be weakened, not so much perhaps by the tumult of conflicting voices, but by the increasing development of the hermeneutical authority of the church, whether in terms of its established dogma or in terms of its ongoing mission and ministry. The point would be reached when some Fathers (e.g., Jerome) defended doctrines that had no biblical basis at all.[85] Nevertheless, two compensating factors must also be considered.

First, the Fathers clearly did not intend to deprive Scripture of its authoritative status. No less than the most vociferous proponents of *sola scriptura*, they realized that the gospel comes from God by revelation and that God has caused the Old and New Testaments to be written as the normative prophetic and apostolic witness to it. They desired neither to shape Scripture to their own ends nor to depart from it, nor indeed to impose ecclesiastical authority on it in the form of normative dogmatic interpretation. As they perceived it, they were championing Scripture itself when they championed the correct understanding either proclaimed in the churches or agreed on in their synods. The possibility of a conflict between Scripture and church might have been a real one, but it was not a possibility that they themselves envisioned, except as a temporary phenomenon as in the semi-Arian years, when various segments of the church might try to enforce dubious statements that were rightly resisted and finally had to be abandoned. In these circumstances, they could view with equanimity the rise of a dogmatic tradition, look confidently to the church of past and present for authentic biblical interpretation, and still believe that they were magnifying rather than impugning the primary authority of Holy Scripture. Even the grounding of secondary doctrines on nonbiblical foundations did not seem to institute a direct challenge to biblical authority, though in fact it would finally come to be this.

It should be remembered, too, that the Fathers were dealing with real problems of authority—problems that arise in every communion and cannot be dismissed by the mere mouthing of slogans. In the age of Irenaeus and Tertullian the Gnostics quoted Scripture, just as the orthodox did, and they did not stop doing so merely because Tertullian rhetorically informed them that they were trespassers to whom Scripture did not rightly belong.[86] During the same period the New Testament canon, while not nonexistent, had not yet come to full recognition, so that even in the formulation of the canon itself the apostolic tradition necessarily played a role of enhanced importance. Even when the canon received more explicit and ecumenical recognition, the proclamation of the gospel continued to be a task of the church alongside the publication of Scripture, so that the question of the relationship between oral and written testimony persisted either openly or tacitly, as it has in fact persisted in every age and every communion. At the same time Scripture did not regulate, or intend to regulate, everything that might be said and done in the church. Inevitably, therefore, the church developed customs and verbal patterns for which no written authority could be found, and though they might not be of absolute authority for all time, a certain normative status might well be claimed for them. At an even deeper level, successive waves of heresy beat upon the shores of the church as it wrestled with the problems of interpretation and attempted to put its teaching in the language and thought forms of the world around it. The hermeneutical and dogmatic task could hardly be left to individual believers to pursue in isolation. For all the differences that might arise in detail, the common body worked out a general line of understanding that it regarded (on good grounds) as the correct interpretation of Scripture and the orthodox mode of presentation. The church had to uphold this in order to safeguard Scripture itself, even it it unavoidably conferred on the church a measure of hermeneutical and dogmatic authority. No communion—not even one that deliberately avoids explicit secondary standards—can in fact evade the problem the Fathers faced thus in paradigmatic fashion. As questions and differences arise, every communion is forced into some measure of at least implicit interpretative and doctrinal consensus that will salutarily exclude a chaos of conflicting exegesis and opinion. Confronting the question of the meaning of Scripture and the proper way to express that meaning in a contemporary setting, the church must certainly make every effort to avoid imposing its own authority on the authority of Scripture. It must always be prepared for a fresh scrutiny of the most ancient and hallowed of its exegetical and dogmatic traditions. It must recognize that its own relative expression of biblical truth does not have the same normativity as biblical truth itself. It must resist the temptation to consider itself of equal authority with Scripture. Nevertheless, it cannot evade the responsibility of assuming and upholding a measure of hermeneutical and dogmatic authority, not for the purpose of rivaling or restricting the authority of Scripture, but for the purpose of upholding and enhancing it.

THE MEANING OF SCRIPTURE

CHRISTOLOGICAL EXEGESIS

The hermeneutical problem, of course, was not solved by the early church without a good deal of discussion and dissension. A continuing series of heresies and schisms tested out the patristic interpretation, and within orthodoxy itself different groups tried different approaches. One should not, however, confuse the external and internal controversies. At issue in relation to heresies and schisms was the differentiation of an agreed interpretation of Scripture from conflicting and competing understandings. At issue in relation to the varied approaches were differences within the agreed interpretation.

In presentations of patristic hermeneutics attention is often focused so sharply on the inner differences that the strong element of agreed understanding, while not, of course, denied, does not receive its proper due. Yet a cursory acquaintance with the Fathers quickly reveals that for all the exegetical variations, they undoubtedly shared the same basic understanding. Relative to both the Old Testament and the New, this understanding might very well be summarized under the rubric of prophecy (or promise) and fulfillment. Taught by Christ and the apostles, the church found in the gospel of Christ's life and death and resurrection and in the outpouring of the Holy Spirit a striking fulfillment of the Old Testament Scriptures, so that not only was a distinctive meaning found for these Scriptures, but the Old Testament and the New Testament were seen together in indissoluble unity as the one book of the one God inspired by the one Spirit and testifying to the one Son.

The Christian interpretation of the Old Testament and the concept of the unity of the Old Testament and the New found frequent expression during the patristic period. Justin Martyr told Trypho the Jew that Scripture belongs more to Christians than to Jews because the latter read it but do not understand it.[87] Justin himself was particularly impressed in his reading by the way in which detailed prophecies had found fulfillment in Christ, but beyond that he also discerned a broader pattern as in the witness of Isaiah 53 to the vicarious suffering of Jesus as the Lord's true Servant.[88] Under pressure from Marcion and the Gnostics, who either rejected the Old Testament or divided it into different categories and if necessary resorted to allegory, Irenaeus recognized a certain progression in the divine revelation, but the hand of the same God was over it all.[89] Many passages that caused superficial difficulty carried a deeper meaning that the fullness of revelation disclosed, and the prophets in particular gave a full account of the teaching and ministry of Christ in a symbolical form that the events themselves had finally elucidated.[90] Tertullian used the metaphor of the seed and its fruit,[91] and Origen that of a symphony,[92] to illustrate the relation between the Testaments, and both insisted that, while the mode of presentation changed, the content remained substantially the same.[93] Augustine summed up this whole line of patristic thinking in his famous dictum that the New Testament is latent in the Old and the Old Testament is patent in the New.[94] This implied, on the one hand, that the prophetic word of the Old Testament came to clear fulfillment in the teaching and events recorded in the New Testament. It implied, on the other hand, that while the New Testament cannot be understood apart from the Old, the converse also holds good and one must not only read the New Testament but also begin with it[95] if one is to attain to a proper understanding of the Old.

The themes of unity and fulfillment found their focus for the Fathers in the conviction that Christ Himself is the true and final subject of Scripture. Whether they looked at the individual prophecies of the Old Testament or at the themes and factors that figured prominently in its history and message, the Fathers saw all the lines converging on the incarnate Son who, with the Father and the Holy Spirit, formed the core of Christian faith and proclamation. The Epistle of Barnabas, in its more restrained typology, discerned in Christ and His work both the true temple and the true Sabbath.[96] Irenaeus found in Christ the higher righteousness intimated but not yet declared in the law.[97] Origen pointed to the sacrifice of Christ as a fulfillment of the ceremonial sacrifices of the Mosaic system.[98] Chrysostom saw a need to dig deeply into Scripture because the meaning is not expressed on the surface and it is only as we attain to the profounder sense that we can see and appreciate the christological testimony.[99] Augustine pointed out that Christ Himself had shown His disciples how He had fulfilled all the prophecies.[100] The fact that this christological interpretation is a commonplace of patristic hermeneutics should not blind us to its significance. As Judaism perceived, it formed the very heart of Christianity itself. It explained why the church so easily adopted the Old Testament canon. It also constituted in a sense the justification of the canonizing of the New Testament, which so patently involved this christological interpretation of the Old. Furthermore, it ruled out the dissolution of the unity of Scripture, which Marcion thought to be necessary in the interests of grace.[101] Christ in fact provided the hermeneutical key that enabled patristic exegetes to see the whole of

Scripture in its divinely given unity and to achieve a convincingly integrated understanding.

The Fathers realized plainly enough that not all readers of the Old Testament, nor indeed of the New, enjoyed the same understanding as they did. Jews on the one side and pagans on the other either failed to see the Bible as the book of Christ or obstinately refused to do so. Difficult though individual portions of Scripture might be, this could hardly be ascribed to an ultimate obscurity of the divinely inspired message. The Fathers, then, were led to another important hermeneutical principle, namely, that only as people read the Bible in the enlightening power of the Holy Spirit, with faith and a spiritual understanding, can they come to a true appreciation of its meaning. Justin had something of this in mind—though he put it in more "Pelagian" form—when he told Trypho that Christians let themselves be persuaded as they read.[102] Clement of Alexandria combined the ideas of the attraction of the Holy Spirit[103] and a necessary openness of mind to the totality of the biblical message.[104] Chrysostom pleaded for faith in the reading of Scripture so that one may hear the voice of the Spirit and thus be enabled to perceive heavenly things.[105] Augustine saw a need for the spiritual understanding that only the Holy Spirit can give.[106] The letter kills; the spirit gives life,[107] but to find the spirit we must come with prayer and piety as well as reason and intelligence.[108] When we do this, we not only find the way of salvation plain but we can also pierce through to the deeper mysteries that constantly remind us that we are only beginners in biblical study.[109]

ALLEGORICAL AND HISTORICAL EXEGESIS

Consensus reigned among the Fathers that Holy Scripture, inspired and illumined by the Spirit, is in its unity and totality the book of Christ. Not the christological principle, but the details of its outworking, gave rise to the main disagreement in patristic exegesis, namely, the disagreement between the Alexandrians and their successors, who favored a more allegorical line, and the Antiochenes and their supporters, who pleaded for a more strictly historical interpretation. The depth of the division between the two schools can hardly be concealed, but it should be emphasized again that fundamentally they shared a common christological understanding in the face of Jewish opposition and pagan blindness or ridicule. To differing degrees the theologians of Antioch as well as those of Alexandria found a place for typology as the New Testament itself obviously demanded. The difference, then, did not relate to the general christological understanding of the Bible but in part to the legitimate compass of typology and in part to its supplementation or replacement by a broader and more arbitrary allegorizing.

The wilder possibilities opened up by a Christian reading of the Old Testament found early realization in the Epistle of Barnabas when its author managed to discern a testimony to Christ and His work on the cross in the number of the servants of Abraham (318) who helped him in his fight with the five kings.[110] Along similar lines the letter of the Gnostic Ptolemaus to Flora was prepared to salvage some parts of the Mosaic Law by giving to it a purely spiritual significance.[111] Influenced by Plato, and following the example of Philo, Origen adopted allegorizing for various reasons. First, the New Testament interpretation of the Old Testament seemed to offer a model. Second, many passages in the Bible demanded a figurative sense.[112] Third, Scripture had been given by God not merely to the simple but also to the more intellectual and spiritual, so that it carried three senses—the historical, typological, and devotional—corresponding, as it were, to the human body, mind, and spirit.[113] Fourth, Scripture must be understood in a way that is in keeping with the Holy Spirit who inspired and interprets it.[114] Displaying an enviable ingenuity in practice, Origen established a mode of approach that appealed to many who succeeded him. Even the scholarly Jerome did not reject the threefold method,[115] while Augustine, who in his early Christian period achieved an inventiveness comparable to that of Origen, expanded the threefold sense into a fourfold: the historical, etiological, analogical, and figurative.[116] Yet Augustine recognized the danger of unchecked speculation. He thus advanced some important safeguards. All allegorical interpretation needs the support of other plain passages of Scripture.[117] It must also correspond to the rules of faith and love.[118] Within these limits, however, allegorizing could still flourish as Augustine's fourfold division developed into the familiar historical, allegorical, moral, and anagogical senses of the Middle Ages. In passing it may be noted that not even the Antiochenes avoided allegorization completely, at least in their homiletical practice, as may be seen from some of the less sober interpretations of Chrysostom.

Nevertheless, the exegetes of the Antioch school—Diodore of Tarsus, Theodore of Mopsuestia, and Theodoret—offered an important theoretical and practical alternative to the Alexandrian excesses. They agreed that Scripture has a spiritual message and that the aim of exposition is to perceive this behind the historical expression.[119] They accepted, then, the validity of typology, the type being for them a form of prophecy.[120] They insisted, however, on strict adherence to the historical form in biblical exposition, even in the discernment and unfolding of the type.[121] Nor would they accept an arbitrary imposition of types where none seemed to exist. Some passages must be taken solely in their historical sense. Allegory meant the introduction of a supposedly hidden meaning to the detriment of the natural sense and was thus to be differentiated from the authentic typology of, e.g., the brazen serpent or the story of Jonah.[122] In their commentaries—e.g., on the Minor Prophets, the Psalms, and the Song of Songs—the Antiochenes made a serious effort to put the various pieces in their historical settings, to explain the primary meanings of the texts, and to bring out their prophetic significance only where it was plainly indicated either by direct reference in the New Testament or by the general tenor of the Christian message.

While the tension between allegorical and historical exegesis rightly stands in the foreground in a depiction of patristic hermeneutics, it should not be forgotten that all patristic theologians indulged in a good deal of "proof-texting" in the great doctrinal controversies that afflicted the church in this whole era. The Arians in particular made this use of Scripture almost unavoidable with their marshaling of favorite verses and their attempts to deduce the Arian propositions from them by logical inference. Allegorizing itself could be pressed in the service of "proof-texting." Origen showed this when he discovered the eternal generation of the Son in Jeremiah.[123] The common equation of Christ with Wisdom initiated a violent debate in the light of Proverbs 8:22. Hilary, who dealt patiently with all the Arian verses as well as adducing a set of his own in favor of the Nicene position,[124] regarded the verse from Proverbs as "the most powerful wave of their storm."[125] Confronted by isolated texts, the Fathers did not think that they could simply appeal to tradition or ask for a broader hermeneutical approach. They might do these things too, but they also felt some constraint to meet the challenge of heresy head-on in a direct battle of conflicting verses. The redeeming feature in this procedure was that behind the tedious "proof-texting" lay a broader theological understanding drawn from the totality of Old and New Testament history and teaching.

In similar vein the early church, notwithstanding its taste for allegory, could sometimes be surprisingly literal in its reading of Scripture. The Didache, for example, recommended fasting on Wednesday and Friday on the ground that Christians should not fast in the same way (on the same days!) as the hypocrites.[126] The Didache also supported the restriction of communion to believers by the saying that we are not to give what is holy to the dogs.[127] The young Origen in his zeal not only went about barefoot but reportedly emasculated himself in order to make himself a eunuch for the kingdom's sake—does this in part explain his later enthusiasm for allegory? The whole monastic movement, which became so powerful in the fourth century, rested on a literal acceptance of the counsels of chastity and poverty, and in its corporate form on the model set by the primitive community in Jerusalem. Under the Benedictine rule the practice of holding a midnight service and then observing the seven liturgical hours derived from the texts in the Psalms that refer to praising God at midnight and then seven times a day.[128] Nor did a literal reading of Scripture influence only the monastic side of life in the early church, for many canons, e.g., those forbidding usury,[129] had a basis in biblical injunctions. The Fathers realized, of course, that they could not adopt the legislation of

Scripture in its totality, either for individuals or for churches. Yet they were not prepared for a complete elimination or evasion of the text by spiritualization. Where verses or passages seemed to be applicable, they brought them to bear with full force, and in the strictest possible sense, on Christian problems and practices.

CONCLUSION

Perhaps the main weakness of the Fathers in their doctrine and use of Scripture was their failure to give full weight to its human and historical aspect. One cannot attribute this to a simple lack of opportunity, for linguistically, intellectually, and temporally the Fathers were much closer to the Bible than we are. Their age had, of course, less of a historical and scientific interest and the techniques of literary and historical research had yet to be developed in a way that would make fuller investigation possible. Yet antiquity had its own interest in humanity and its affairs, so that responsibility for the weakness cannot be assigned simply to the more general background of patristic thinking. The truth is that the Fathers seem not to have appreciated the real significance of the human dimension nor to have grasped the possibilities of a better exegesis that lexical, literary, and historical inquiry would present. They made some beginnings along these lines, but these were modest indeed compared to the achievements they might have made. The tide of allegorizing, to which an emphasis on the suprahuman aspect of Scripture contributed, not only overpowered the less exciting historical activity, but virtually obliterated its influence and results for long periods in the church's later history.

Second only to the depreciation of the human aspect of Scripture was the incontestable tendency of the Fathers to let the authority of Scripture be merged into that of tradition and the church. This tendency, as we have seen, should not be attributed to a deliberate intention to reduce the status of Scripture. It developed out of the original coexistence of oral and written forms of the tradition and the use of an epitome of apostolic teaching not only for instruction but also for the rebuttal of heresy. The Fathers realized clearly enough that prophetic and apostolic Scripture has a normative function in the church, and the experience of the semi-Arian period showed incontestably that councils could reach erroneous or ambiguous conclusions on important doctrinal issues. Yet the concept emerged and persisted that in and through every deviation the church will finally reach a right decision, so that the church's teaching office may be relied on in its interpretation of Scripture and a body of doctrine is established that is so true to Scripture that it has itself what is tantamount to the same authority. To the extent that the early church did in fact achieve a true understanding, the development had some justification. Yet it carried with it four dangerous challenges to the supremacy of Holy Scripture:

first, the confidence that the church would always be right; second, the assumption that doctrinal decisions, which put biblical truth in a particular historical setting, are virtually equivalent to biblical truth itself and never need to be resubmitted to biblical scrutiny; third, the acceptance in principle as well as practice of the ongoing expository normativeness of oral proclamation; and fourth, the readiness to accept dogmas that had only the backing of tradition and not of Scripture.

Compensating the weaknesses of the Fathers are their corresponding positive qualities. Over against the lack of appreciation of the human aspect of Scripture one may set a full commitment to its divine derivation and authority. The Fathers believed without hesitation that God had caused the Bible to be written. They accepted without cavil both its inspiration and its reliability. Where they encountered individual difficulties, they either suspended judgment or sought explanation in a way that would preserve biblical infallibility. Believing that Scripture came from God, they construed it as a coherent and consistent divine message, not abstractly, but in relation to the work of God that had begun in the Old Testament and in accordance with prophetic intimation had reached its climax in the New. They achieved a good sense of the unity of the Bible with Christ as the focus and center. They learned to interpret it, not as a source-book that might advance historical knowledge and promote academic careers, but as a message from God that, centered in Christ and applied by the Holy Spirit, could bring salvation and renewal to individuals and society. They understand that, while the statements of Scripture are for the most part plain, penetration to its deeper message comes only by the Holy Spirit to people of faith and prayer. If their concern for a spiritual meaning led sometimes to extremes of allegorizing, they avoided the sterile inquiry that produces only an unsatisfactory history of Israel and its religion or a bafflingly incomplete biography of Jesus or a fanciful reconstruction of the primitive community and its problems. In all essential matters of biblical understanding the Fathers went to the heart of the matter. It is no mean tribute to their insight that some of the more recent movements in biblical theology and exegesis have led back at important points to the themes of patristic presentation.

Nor should it be forgotten that the Fathers were far from wrong, either in fact or in principle, when they refused to isolate Holy Scripture from its churchly context. God had in fact given the Old Testament in and through Israel to be used, expounded, and applied in the life of the divine community. Similarly, He had caused the New Testament to be written from within the infant church, in concert with the apostolic preaching, for use in the church's own life and for commendation to the pagan world. Accepting the primary status of Scripture, the Fathers rightly perceived its context too, neither isolating it from other factors nor bringing it into open competition with them, but facing the problems of authority as they arose with the fulfillment of their mission of proclamation and their settling of dogmatic and practical issues. Naturally the existence of the listening, teaching, and preaching church, also under the Holy Spirit, poses a potential threat to the authority of Scripture. But no less dangerous is the illusion that Scripture can reign in isolation—an illusion that avenges itself when this isolated Scripture is shackled either by unrecognized tradition on the one side or unbridled individualism on the other. The Fathers confronted the facts. Scripture had come forth out of the church and was committed into its hands. The church in particular has the task of expounding it and passing on its message. Discharging this ministry, the church necessarily builds up a structure of agreed interpretation. In no sense can it avoid either its divinely given commission or the responsible development of its own thinking and teaching in fulfillment of it. The Fathers show us that there can be no theology of Holy Scripture in a vacuum. *Sola scriptura* is true enough inasmuch as the Bible is the supreme court of appeal, but it does not remove or invalidate all other authorities. Every church in every age has to face up to the existence of these other authorities and both in its life and thought to relate them properly, not only to Holy Scripture but also in the last resort to God Himself, the ultimate authority from whom every other authority derives its authorization.

In this regard four final points may be made that the Fathers sensed but did not always formulate as explicitly as one could desire. First, the coexistence of the oral and written Word or tradition must not mean their equation, for the two must be differentiated as well as identified and the former subordinated to the latter. Second, the presence of the Holy Spirit in the life and work of the church does not imply the church's exemption from the control of Holy Scripture, for it is by the latter that the Holy Spirit rules the church and discharges His ministry. Third, although Christianity cannot abandon its constitutive understanding of Scripture without abandoning itself, no agreed interpretation, however ancient or assured, can be described as definitive, for under the Spirit the new investigation that is demanded may necessitate important modifications, especially in detail. Fourth, the dogmas of the church do not form, even at the hermeneutical level, a body of teaching comparable in status to Holy Scripture, for while they may stand up to rigorous biblical scrutiny and commend themselves to successive generations of believers, they are always historical interpretations and as such they can have only a relative normativeness and not the absolute normativeness that, under God, Holy Scripture itself enjoys.

220 Geoffrey W. Bromiley

A SELECTED BIBLIOGRAPHY

Barth, K. *Church Dogmatics*, I,2 (Edinburgh: T. and T. Clark, 1956).
Sections 19–21.

Berkhof, H. *Christian Faith* (Grand Rapids: Eerdmans, 1979). P. 16.

Bray, G.L., *Holiness and the Will of God* (London: Marshall, Morgan and Scott, 1979). Chap. 4.

Bromiley, G. W. *An Introduction to Historical Theology* (Grand Rapids: Eerdmans, 1978). Part I.

Farrar, F. W. *History of Interpretation* (Grand Rapids: Baker, 1961).

Grant, R. *A Short History of the Interpretation of the Bible.* Rev. ed. (New York: Macmillan, 1966).

Kelly, J. N. D. *Early Christian Doctrines* (New York: Harper and Row, 1959). Chaps. 2–3.

Polman, A. D. R. *The Word of God According to St. Augustine* (Grand Rapids: Eerdmans, 1961).

Ramm, B. *Protestant Biblical Interpretation* (Boston: W. A. Wilde, 1950). Chap. 2.

Stevenson, J. *A New Eusebius* (London: SPCK, 1960).

Vawter, B. *Biblical Inspiration* (Philadelphia: Westminster, 1972).

Wilkinson, J. *Principles of Biblical Interpretation* (London: Epworth, 1960).

BIBLICAL AUTHORITY
IN THE SIXTEENTH
AND SEVENTEENTH
CENTURIES:
A QUESTION OF TRANSITION

W. Robert Godfrey

W. Robert Godfrey

W. Robert Godfrey is Professor of Church History at Westminster Theological Seminary in California. He is a graduate of Stanford University (B.A., M.A., and Ph.D.) and Gordon-Conwell Theological Seminary (M.Div.). He is a minister in the Christian Reformed Church. He has contributed to the books *Discord, Dialogue, and Concord: Studies in the Lutheran Reformation's Formula of Concord* and *John Calvin, His Influence in the Western World* and to various periodicals. He is a member of the American Society for Reformation Research, the American Historical Association, and the Conference on Faith and History.

BIBLICAL AUTHORITY IN THE SIXTEENTH
AND SEVENTEENTH CENTURIES:
A QUESTION OF TRANSITION

Sola Scriptura was one of the ringing cries of the Protestant Reformation. This affirmation spoke to the issue of religious authority and summarized the Protestant conviction that religious truth could be known with certainty, not from popes and councils, but from the Bible alone. As the declarations *sola fide* (by faith alone), *sola gratia* (by grace alone), and *solus Christus* (Christ alone) summarized the essence of the gospel, *sola Scriptura* pointed to the reliable source for all knowledge of that gospel.

Both historians and theologians have sought to understand the meaning of *sola Scriptura* for Protestants in the sixteenth and seventeenth centuries. Recently they have given special attention to change and development in the understanding of the nature and authority of the Bible in this period. Most interpreters have seen a basic agreement and continuity between sixteenth-century Reformers and seventeenth-century orthodox theologians that the Bible was God's Word and was absolutely reliable in all it said.[1]

Some theologians and historians in the past fifty years, often influenced by neoorthodoxy,[2] have stressed the discontinuity between the Reformation and the following period of Protestant orthodoxy. This scholarship has argued that the contemporary evangelical belief in the absolute reliability or inerrancy of the Bible is a betrayal of the position of the early Reformers and grows instead from an innovation of seventeenth-century orthodoxy.

In the past decade, however, the stress on the discontinuity between the Reformation and the period of orthodoxy has been increasingly challenged. New studies have demonstrated that the lines of continuity between the Reformation and the period of orthodoxy are very strong and that the processes of change were much more gradual than had previously been seen.[3] There were indeed changes: new enemies to be answered, old theological debates to be refined in ever more meticulous terms, and the perceived need for the more precise language of dialectics. But the fundamental theological direction remained the same.

This chapter will demonstrate that the continuity between sixteenth- and seventeenth-century theologies presented in recent scholarship applies to the question of biblical authority and that the period of orthodoxy faithfully received and maintained the basic position of the Reformation. While there were shifting emphases in the transition from Reformation to orthodoxy and while both eras may warrant criticism for some particular conclusions, Reformers and orthodox were one in their basic conviction about the Scriptures. For both the Bible is the only ultimate authority for Christians, and it is inerrant.

Examining in a single chapter the attitudes about biblical authority in two centuries requires that sharp limits be established. For this reason it will be useful for me to develop this chapter as a critique of one book that represents the position of those who deny that the Reformers accepted inerrancy and who see a belief in inerrancy as one of the bad products of orthodoxy. This recent book, Jack B. Rogers and Donald K. McKim, *The Authority and Interpretation of the Bible: An Historical Approach*,[4] is an important one that demands careful evaluation. Rogers and McKim present a clear statement of the thesis that the Reformers did not accept the inerrancy of the Bible, a contention that must be tested against the primary and other secondary literature that reveals attitudes in the sixteenth and seventeenth centuries toward biblical authority.

Rogers and McKim develop their thesis on the foundation of a strict distinction between the function and the form of Scripture. They argue that church history bears eloquent testimony that the Bible is unfailing and absolutely reliable as it fulfills its function of presenting the message of salvation in Christ. They deny, however, that that infallible function is linked to an inerrant form. Indeed they insist that the greatest Christian thinkers, including the early Reformers, fully recognized errors in the form of the Bible while maintaining the faithful fulfillment of its function. They insist that by focusing on the function of the Bible the early Reformers (and the English Puritans until the time of John Owen) made Christ central and kept theology practical. The Reformers maintained Augustine's view that one must believe in order to understand. They achieved this by recognizing that God had accommodated Himself to man. God's Word is incarnated in man's words. Errors are inevitable in such a process, Rogers and McKim maintain, but in no way detract from the saving function of the Bible.

According to Rogers and McKim, concern about an inerrant form is a serious departure from the position of the Reformers. Such concern reflects a loss of concern for the functon of Scripture. In particular it means a loss of Christcenteredness, an exaltation of abstract theology, a failure to understand God's act of accommodation in Scripture, and a return to the Aristotelian scholasticism that insists that one must understand in order to believe.

This chapter will demonstrate the inadequacy of the Rogers-McKim thesis in the light of the evidence in five key areas: (1) Luther's thought, (2) Calvin's thought, (3) the Reformed confessions and catechisms, (4) English Puritanism, and (5) continental Reformed orthodoxy.

LUTHER

Martin Luther (1483–1546) is one of the most heroic and fascinating figures of history. His reforming message radiated far beyond the pulpit and classroom of Wittenberg in electoral Saxony and continues to attract and stimulate students of his thought. There can be no doubt that his theology was profoundly centered in Christ and that he stressed that Christ was the message of the Scriptures. As Luther declared, "Christians receive Christ, the Son of God, as the central content of Holy Scripture. Having learned to know him, the remainder becomes meaningful to them and all scripture becomes transparent."[5] Thus Luther undeniably does stress the saving function of Scripture.

Luther does not accept, however, a dichotomy between the function and the form of the Bible as Rogers and McKim and others have suggested. Luther is concerned about questions relating to the form of Scripture, and his position on the form of Scripture is stated clearly: The Bible is inerrant. The following statements from Luther show his concern about inerrancy in matters of form: "But everyone, indeed, knows that at times they [the Fathers] have erred as men will; therefore, I am ready to trust them only when they prove their opinions from Scripture, which has never erred."[6] Also, "The Word of God is perfect: it is precious and pure: it is truth itself. There is no falsehood in it."[7] His concern for form is also expressed in terms of particulars: "Not only the words but also the expressions used by the Holy Spirit and Scripture are divine."[8] Luther argues further that "one letter, even a single tittle of Scripture means more to us than heaven and earth. Therefore we cannot permit even the most minute change."[9]

Even in his most famous words Luther bore testimony to his concern for the form of Scripture. When Luther appeared at the Diet of Worms in 1521 before Emperor Charles V and the powers of this world, he pointed to the Bible as the religious authority that formed the foundation of the gospel that he preached. He declared, "Unless I am convinced by testimony from Scripture or evident reason—for I believe neither the Pope nor the Councils alone, since it is established that they have often erred and contradicted themselves—I am conquered by the writings cited by me, and my conscience is captive to the Word of God; I cannot and I will not recant anything, since it is neither safe nor honest to do aught against conscience."[10] Inherent in this statement is Luther's conviction that the Word of God, which holds him captive, does not contradict itself and does not err.

Luther also used his commitment to the absolutely reliable form of Scripture in his theology. Particularly in defending his eucharistic theology Luther showed his trust in the precise words of Scripture. In answering the Zwinglians he pressed the form as well as the function of the words of Scripture:

> Therefore you can joyfully say to Christ, both at your death and in the Last Judgment: My dear Lord Jesus, there has arisen a strife about Thy words at the Last Supper. Some want them to be understood differently from what they say. However, since they cannot teach me anything certain, but only lead me into confusion and uncertainty ... I have remained with Thy text as the words stand. If there should be an obscurity in them, Thou wilt bear with me if I do not completely understand them, just as Thou didst forbear with Thine apostles when they did not understand Thee in many things—for instance, when Thou didst speak to them about Thy suffering and resurrection, and yet they retained Thy words and did not alter them. As also Thy dear mother did not understand when Thou didst tell her, Luke 2, "I must be about my Father's business," and yet she kept these words in her heart and did not alter them: Thus, I also have remained with these Thy words: This is my body, etc. Lo, no enthusiast will dare to speak thus with Christ.[11]

Luther was quite willing to rest one of his major theological concerns on the precise form of the little word *is* because he believed that every word of the Bible is God's Word.

The analysis of Luther's theology by Rogers and McKim argues, contrary to Luther's own testimony, that the great Reformer was not concerned about the form of Scripture. They point to Luther's stress that God has accommodated Himself in speaking to man in the Scriptures. The Scriptures are accommodated to man in a way analogous to the incarnation of the Eternal Word. For Rogers and McKim this accommodation means that the Bible is written in "weak and imperfect human speech."[12] They cite Luther's words, "Holy Scripture possesses no external glory, attracts no attention, lacks all beauty and adornment."[13]

Rogers and McKim, however, seriously misuse the concept of accommodation in regard to Luther and others in their book. They assume, without real examination, the absolute truth of Seneca's maxim: "To err is human." If God accommodated Himself to human language in the Bible, then, they assume, it must contain errors. But is error absolutely inevitable in all things human? This question comes to sharpest focus when the principle of accommodation is related to the Incarnation. Is the incarnate form of Jesus Christ irrelevant to His saving function? Is not Jesus' person (His form) foundational to His work (His function)? Is not the human speech of Jesus Christ without error? There is nothing in the principle of accommodation as used by Luther that conflicts with biblical inerrancy. In fact just the opposite is true.

Luther's comments on the lack of beauty in the Scriptures also are in harmony with a doctrine of inerrancy. Luther wrote in the context of the Renaissance's revived knowledge of ancient literature. Luther like others noted the Scripture's commonness and lack of beauty when compared to Ciceronian eloquence. But Luther denied that the plainnesss and simplicity of the Bible detracted from the clarity, efficacy, or authority of its revelation of Jesus Christ. Luther's recognition that Scripture does not speak with the eloquence of this world was not at all a recognition of error in the Bible. Lack of stylistic grandeur is not an error.

Further, Rogers and McKim refer to specific instances in which Luther supposedly recognized errors in the details of the Bible. Their list of errors is taken from the one-page discussion of this subject in Reinhold Seeberg's *History of Doctrines*.[14] Curiously they do not take serious account of several important secondary sources that argue a position very different from their own.[15] For example, Paul Althaus in his highly respected work *The Theology of Martin Luther* summarizes Luther's position: "Scripture never errs. Therefore it alone has unconditional authority."[16] A. Skevington Wood in *Captive to the Word, Martin Luther: Doctor of Sacred Scripture* concludes that "Luther's doctrine of inspiration is inseparably linked with that of inerrancy."[17] M. Reu in his very careful study *Luther and the Scriptures* reaches the same conclusion.[18]

Those who try to deny inerrancy in Luther use other arguments as well. Often they refer to Luther's questions on the canonicity of certain books. But such an argument is not relevant. Canonicity and inerrancy are quite separate theological subjects. However, Luther's concern with questions of canonicity does show his concern for the form of Scripture, indeed it shows that he ties form and function (canon and the gospel message) closely together.

Sometimes Luther's recognition of problems in harmonizing Gospel accounts is cited as evidence of his rejection of inerrancy. One notable example is Jesus' cleansing of the Temple, which Matthew places at the end of Jesus' ministry and John places near the beginning.[19] Several scholars refer to Luther's statement that the failure to harmonize this difference between Matthew and John cannot undermine one's faith in Christ.[20] In the context, however, Luther's statement does not show either an indifference to form or a recognition of error in the Bible. Luther in this instance first suggested different possibilities of harmonization. He then suggested his own preferred solution to the problem. Yet he did not insist on his solution, acknowledging, "These are problems and will remain problems. I shall not venture to settle them. Nor are they essential."[21] He explained that such problems remain, in part, because the Evangelists do not necessarily intend to give a chronological order and because Christian faith does not require full knowledge of chronological details: "All the evangelists agree on this, that Christ died for our sins. But in their accounts of Christ's deeds and miracles they do not observe a uniform order and often ignore the proper chronological sequence."[22] But the lack of chronological order is not an error for Luther as he shows in another place where he dealt with a problem of harmonization: "St. Luke testifies at the beginning of his Gospel that he wanted to record all things from the beginning in order. . . . Therefore there is no question that Matthew did not retain the exact order, but Luke has obligated himself to do so and does so in fact."[23] It is clear that Luther, in facing his problems of harmonizing certain texts and in recognizing different methodologies used by different Gospel writers, was indeed concerned about the form of the Scriptures and was not ascribing error to the Bible.

In concluding this brief look at Luther's view of biblical authority, one must remember that Luther was influenced by Renaissance humanist study of literature. He recognized differences of style and was sensitive to the context in studying Scripture. He applied the best scholarly tools to the study of the Bible. But his commitment to scholarship was not based on a separation of function and form as Rogers and McKim suggest: "Luther's faith, therefore, was in the subject matter of Scripture, not its form, which was the object of scholarly investigation."[24] Luther rejected any such dualism. Reason and scholarship are helpful tools in understanding the Scripture, but must be used with true faith and must ultimately submit to the form as well as the function of Scripture: "Believing and reading scripture means that we hear the Word from Christ's mouth. When that happens to you, you know that this is no mere human word, but truly God's."[25]

CALVIN

John Calvin (1509–1564) was the most brilliant light of the second generation of the Reformers. He came from quite a different background from that of Martin Luther. He was raised in an upper-middle-class family in northern France. He received a fine humanist education in the classics and in the law. He was not steeped in scholastic theology as Luther had been. His life's work was done largely in a Swiss city-state. While Luther wrote largely on specific theological topics or detailed and extended commentaries, Calvin was more a systematic theologian (as shown by his *Institutes of the Christian Religion*) and a commentator on many biblical books in his style of "lucid brevity."

Despite such divergent personal histories, Calvin saw his own theology as very similar to that of Luther. While there were differences, especially on the Lord's Supper, Calvin saw himself as part of the theological movement that Luther had pioneered. This unity certainly existed in their theology of biblical authority. Calvin, like Luther, stressed the primary importance of the Bible's saving function: "This is what we should in short seek in the whole Scripture: truly to know Jesus Christ, and the infinite riches that are comprised in him and are offered to us by him from God the Father."[26]

Calvin, again like Luther, did not separate function from form in his doctrine of Scripture. The form as well as the function were from

God Himself, as Calvin's famous words in the *Institutes* show: "Hence the Scriptures obtain full authority among believers only when men regard them as having sprung from heaven, as if there the living words of God were heard."[27] He could speak of the apostles as "sure and genuine scribes of the Holy Spirit, and their writings are therefore to be considered oracles of God."[28] In another clear statement Calvin linked the certainty of faith and the saving message of Scripture to the absolute truthfulness of its form:

> Now, therefore, we hold faith to be a knowledge of God's will toward us, perceived from His Word. But the foundation of this is a preconceived conviction of God's truth. As for its certainty, so long as your mind is at war with itself, the Word will be of doubtful and weak authority, or rather of none. And it is not even enough to believe that God is trustworthy, who can neither deceive nor lie, unless you hold to be beyond doubt that whatever proceeds from Him is sacred and inviolable truth.[29]

In his commentaries Calvin also gave testimony to his belief in the truthfulness of Scripture in words that show a confidence in the inerrancy of its form. In speaking of the praise of the law in Psalm 119:105, Calvin noted, "Let us, then, be assured that an unerring light is to be found there, provided we open our eyes to behold it."[30] In commenting on 2 Timothy 3:16 Calvin distinguished yet bound together the form and function of the Bible as he spoke of its authority and its profit:

> First he [Paul] commends the Scripture because of its authority, and then because of the profit that comes from it. To assert its authority he teaches that it is *inspired of God*, for, if that is so, it is beyond all question that men should receive it with reverence.... This is the meaning of the first clause, that we owe to Scripture the same reverence as we owe to God, since it has its only source in Him and has nothing of human origin mixed with it.[31]

His absolute confidence in the form of Scripture is shown in his reliance on the details of the Bible. After noting the differences of style between 1 Peter and 2 Peter and acknowledging that some in the ancient church denied the canonicity of 2 Peter, Calvin concluded, "If it [2 Peter] be received as canonical, we must allow Peter to be the author, since it has his name inscribed, and he also testifies that he lived with Christ: and it would have been a fiction unworthy of a minister of Christ, to have personated another individual."[32] Indeed Calvin judged that those who find fault with God's Word have a serious moral problem:

> And he affirms that his love to God's word was not a rash, or a blind and inconsiderate affection, but that he loved it, because like gold or silver which has been refined, it was pure and free from all dregs and dross.... How few are there who are not guilty, either by their distrust, or waywardness, or pride, or voluptuousness, of casting upon God's word some

spot or stain! The flesh then being so rebellious, it is no small commendation of revealed truth, when it is compared to gold well refined, so that it
shines pure from all defilement.[33]

Against such evidence as that cited above, Rogers and McKim, like
others, have sought to show that Calvin did not accept the inerrancy of
Scripture. Their procedure is to present various kinds of evidence that
they believe shows that Calvin did not hold to inerrancy. Some of this
material is similar to that cited from Luther. They note that Calvin saw
God accommodating Himself to man in Scripture and they assume,
without demonstration, that Calvin believed that the Bible was written
in "imperfect language."[34] As argued above in reference to Luther, the
principle of accommodation does not entail error.

Rogers and McKim also note Calvin's recognition that the Bible
was not always written in an exalted style,[35] but they wrongly infer
that this shows Calvin's lack of concern for Scripture's form. Calvin,
like Luther, referred to the common style of Scripture, not to accuse it
of error, but to defend it from Ciceronian humanist critics.

Rogers and McKim also present new lines of argument and evidence from what was discussed in relation to Luther. They point out
that Calvin recognized that some New Testament quotations from the
Old Testament were paraphrases rather than exact quotes. They infer
that Calvin saw these as "imperfect" and as "inaccuracies."[36] But Calvin did not say that, and it is far from self-evident that a paraphrase is
an error. Indeed Calvin recognized the legitimacy of the paraphrases
precisely to vindicate the form the apostolic writings took and to preserve them from the charge of error. So too when Calvin noted that
some New Testament uses of Old Testament texts were not full expositions but were rather allusions to or applications of those texts, Rogers
and McKim believe that Calvin was recognizing an error. But in Calvin's words, cited by Rogers and McKim, he made such observations to
show that "there is nothing improper"[37] in that apostolic practice.
Calvin did not regard such practices as erroneous.

Another kind of error recognized by Calvin, Rogers and McKim
argue, is in the area of science. They refer to Calvin's argument that
Moses wrote in Genesis not as a scientist, but as a theologian.[38] Calvin
was arguing the propriety of a theologian talking of scientific matters
in popular language, oriented to human observation of natural phenomena (e.g., "The sun rises") rather than in the language of scientific
exactness. Calvin was arguing that such a procedure was proper and
involved no misrepresentation of the truth. Calvin was not accepting a
dualism by which "scientific" truth could be set in opposition to revealed statements of Scripture. While the vocabulary, purpose, perspective, and fullness of the discussion of natural phenomena would
differ for the theologian and for the scientist, both were teaching the
same truth, according to Calvin. In this area too, there is no evidence
that Calvin perceived errors in the Bible.

Still Rogers and McKim offer one more piece of evidence that seems decisive: "In his commentary on Acts 7:16, Calvin declared that Luke had 'made a manifest error.' . . . "[39] In this instance, however, the error is that of Rogers and McKim. Calvin actually said, "But when he [Luke] goes on to say that they were buried in the sepulchre which Abraham had bought from the sons of Hamor, it is obvious that an error has been made in the name of Abraham. . . . This verse must be amended accordingly."[40] Calvin did indeed recognize an error in the text at Acts 7:16 and insisted that the text be changed. But he did not explicitly attribute the error to Luke. Indeed in the context it is likely that Calvin meant something quite different. Two paragraphs earlier Calvin wrote on Acts 7:14:

> In saying that Jacob came into Egypt with seventy-five people, Stephen does not agree with Moses, whose reckoning is only seventy. . . . Therefore I conclude that this discrepancy arose by an error on the part of copyists [of the Septuagint]. But this was not such an important matter that Luke should have confused the Gentiles over it, when they were used to the Greek reading. And it is possible that he himself did write down the true number, but somebody erroneously changed it from the verse of Moses. . . . If anyone is to persist in disputing this, let us allow him a superiority of wisdom. Let us remember that it is not for nothing that Paul forbids us to be troubled and curious about genealogies (Titus 3:9).[41]

Several points emerge from these quotations. First, Calvin did not believe that one should be unduly troubled by problems of harmonization. Vain curiosity is a danger to the spiritual life. Second, in recognizing his problem in harmonizing the text, he did not conclude that Luke had made an error in his writing. Calvin was not indifferent to the form of the text but on Acts 7:14 he spent a long paragraph investigating various ways of accounting for and understanding the form of the text. Third, his own solution in Acts 7:14 was that copyists had made an error. It is most probable therefore that he assumed the same origin for the error in Acts 7:16. Indeed his insistence that the text of Acts 7:16 should be amended almost certainly means that he attributed the error to a copyist. Rogers and McKim want to conclude from such evidence that Calvin acknowledged "historical inaccuracies"[42] in the text. But that simply is not the case.[43]

In concluding this brief look at Calvin's doctrine of biblical authority, it is useful to reflect on John Leith's stimulating observation: "Scholars disagree whether Calvin believed in verbal inerrancy. The evidence seems to point to a more liberal understanding than verbal inerrancy connotes today, though Calvin did certainly insist that the words of Scripture are the very words of God. The question can probably never be answered, for Calvin never faced the question in the way in which any man who has encounted critical historical studies must ask it. . . . For this reason it is futile to find answers in Calvin's writings to new questions raised by modern historical consciousness."[44] Leith is right to insist that Calvin did not face modern criticism of the Bible. He may be right that some modern inerrantists would have problems occasionally with Calvin's approach to a problem of harmonization.[45] And Calvin certainly cannot be expected to have anticipated all specific questions raised by modern critics of the Bible. But when the "modern historical consciousness" rejects the Bible in part or wholly as God's Word, when it stands in judgment of the Bible's complete truthfulness and reliability, the position of Calvin is clear and relevant. The "words of Scripture are the very words of God." Calvin would insist that the modern Christian as well as the sixteenth-century Christian must submit every thought to the Word of God and allow the Bible to stand as judge of man's truth and even of man's historical consciousness. Calvin was committed to the best of scholarship, but rejected all dualism between a saving function of the Bible, which is the concern of the pastor, and the form of Scripture, which is the concern of independent scholars.[46] Calvin believed that every word of the Bible was God's Word and that every word was true in all that it says. In Calvin then is clearly found a belief in biblical inerrancy.

REFORMED CONFESSIONS AND CATECHISMS

The Reformed confessions and catechisms stress the saving message of the Scripture, for that was a principal distinctive of Protestants over against the Roman Catholic church. The Reformers maintained that the Bible contained the complete and clear message of salvation and that Christians did not need the additions of tradition or the authoritative interpretations of the church. The Reformers had no dispute with Rome over the truthfulness of the whole Bible. Thus defense of the Scripture's reliability does not figure prominently in the confessions and catechisms. Still the confessions do assert a commitment to the full truthfulness of the Scripture. A few examples serve to demonstrate this commitment to an inerrant Bible.

Calvin's Catechism of the Church of Geneva (1545) declared that one profits from Scripture when "we lay hold on it with complete heartfelt conviction as nothing less than certain truth come down from heaven."[47] The French Confession of 1559, which Calvin helped write, declared that the Word of God is "the rule of all truth."[48] The Belgic Confession (1561) is more extensive in its statements. It confessed that the Scriptures, "against which nothing can be alleged,"[49] are the "infallible rule"[50] of Christians who believe "without doubt, all things contained in them."[51]

The Heidelberg Catechism makes the same confession in its definition of faith (A. 21): "I hold for truth all that God has revealed to us in his Word." Zacharias Ursinus, one of the authors of the Catechism, in commenting on this statement, wrote that an essential element of faith "is to yield assent to every word of God delivered to the church."[52] He insisted that the faithful Christian "believes that every thing which the Scriptures contain is true, and from God."[53]

ENGLISH PURITANISM

English Puritanism has attracted many interpreters because of its great formative influence, particularly because of its place in the development of American church history. Puritanism was a theological movement with its own distinctive characteristics because of the unique environment in which it developed. Puritanism grew up within the Church of England, a church that was Reformed in doctrine, but according to the Puritans, not fully Reformed in practice. As a result the Puritans often focused their theological interests on matters of ecclesiastical and personal practice. Puritan theology had a distinctively practical cast to it.

Rogers and McKim emphasize the distinctiveness of Puritan theology as the foundation for their thesis that English Puritanism represents an exception to the early triumph of scholasticism in seventeenth-century Reformed theology. They argue that the practical, nonscholastic character of Puritan theology, flowing out of the unique ecclesiastical politics and philosophical orientation of England,[54] preserved Puritanism from excessive concern about the form of Scripture and from the doctrine of inerrancy.

The distinctive interaction of Puritan theology with its environment, however, does not actually provide a foundation for the approach Rogers and McKim take.[55] Both Puritans and continental Reformed theologians saw themselves as members of a cooperative international Reformed community. The English, for example, participated fully in the Synod of Dort,[56] and Puritans like William Ames hailed Dort's theological statements. English Puritans and continental Reformed theologians shared most theological viewpoints, including a belief in inerrancy.

Even more important than the unique ecclesiastical politics in England, Rogers and McKim argue, were the unique philosophical conditions. Among English Puritans the philosophy of Peter Ramus was dominant. This philosophical approach retained more of the Augustinian, rhetorical tradition and claimed to reject Aristotle. Rogers and McKim maintain that it was Ramus who kept English Puritanism focused on the message of the Scripture and free of concern about an inerrant form of Scripture.

Ramism, however, was not as theologically determinative as Rogers and McKim claim. The methodology of Ramism often yielded the same theological conclusions as the methodology of Aristotle. For example, the Ramist Arminius sharply attacked the Ramist Perkins for his strong supralapsarian views, while the Aristotelian Gomarus defended Perkins. Neither did Ramism necessarily keep one from rationalism as Rogers and McKim imply. For example, Moise Amyraut was very much influenced by the Ramist tradition,[57] but he was at the same time a rationalist: "Amyraut was a rationalist in the sense that he submitted all truths to the test of reason."[58]

William Ames is the strongest example of the inadequacy of Rogers and McKim's efforts to show that the Puritans did not accept inerrancy. Ames was a militant Puritan (a nonconformist) and a Ramist. He wrote one of the most influential Puritan handbooks of theology, *The Marrow of Theology* (third edition, 1629). Yet in his *Marrow*, contrary to what one would have expected according to Rogers and McKim, Ames clearly teaches inerrancy. Writing of the manner in which the authors of the Bible were inspired, Ames stated:

> Some things were known by a natural knowledge and some by a supernatural. In those things that were hidden and unknown, divine inspiration was a work by itself. In those things which were known, or where the knowledge was obtained by ordinary means, there was added the writers' devout zeal so that (God assisting them) they might not err in writing.
>
> In all those things made known by supernatural inspiration, whether matters of right or fact, God inspired not only the subjects to be written about but dictated and suggested the very words in which they should be set forth. But this was done with a subtle tempering so that every writer might use the manner of speaking which most suited his person and condition.[59]

This statement shows that Ames was indeed concerned about the form of Scripture and that he did explicitly proclaim the inerrancy of the Bible.

REFORMED ORTHODOXY

Reformed orthodoxy, as noted in the introduction to this study, has been the object of considerable scholarly investigation and debate. Many more thorough studies will be needed before more exact lines of continuity and discontinuity can be established between the early Reformers and the period of orthodoxy. Such investigation must be attentive to the new historical situation that seventeenth-century orthodox theologians faced. The particulars of orthodox theology cannot be examined in the abstract. Nor can the adequacy of its constructs be fully determined without considering the historical context that produced seventeenth-century orthodoxy.

Rogers and McKim enter this scholarly discussion with their chapter on Protestant orthodoxy.[60] The first part of that chapter examines various stages and elements in the development of Protestant orthodoxy and the second part examines Francis Turretin, who epitomizes Reformed scholasticism. Rogers and McKim insist that the development of orthodoxy represents a steady erosion of the Reformation teaching on the centrality of Christ, faith, and the saving message of the Scripture. They argue that orthodoxy represents the progressive triumph of matters of form over the saving function of the Bible. In this era of decline, they argue, the doctrine of the inerrancy of Scripture arose in Protestantism.

Within the brief scope of this study it is impossible to examine all of the assertions of Rogers and McKim in this area.[61] What should emerge from this study, however, is clear evidence that the orthodox remained concerned for the centrality of the saving message of the Scripture just as the early Reformers had been concerned about the inerrant form of the Scriptures. Also it should be clear that the orthodox discussion of the formal authority of Scripture retained most, if not all, of the emphases of the early Reformers. In this chapter I will discuss orthodoxy with a brief methodological observation first and then with a more extensive analysis of the work of Francis Turretin.

Methodologically Rogers and McKim begin by rightly recognizing the important new threats to Protestantism posed by the rise of Socinianism and of a revived Roman Catholicism in the late sixteenth century.[62] But they fail to appreciate the seriousness of these threats. They seem quickly to forget that these heirs of the Reformation had new challenges to answer that necessitated theological development. Those new challenges were often in the area of formal authority of the Scripture: the Socinians insisting on a determinative role for reason and the Roman Catholics pressing the refined arguments of Robert Bellarmine and others for an authoritative church. The orthodox Protestants necessarily responded by refining and elaborating their arguments for the sole authority of a completely reliable Bible. But in their legitimate, scholarly concern for the form of Scripture the orthodox were only continuing the work begun by the early Reformers. The evidence also shows that the orthodox continued to insist on the importance of the saving message of the gospel.[63]

Francis Turretin (1623–1687) was born in Geneva to a Reformed family of Italian refugee stock. His father was a minister and a professor of theology. He received an education in Geneva from orthodox theologians and himself became a pastor and served as a professor of theology in Geneva from 1653 to 1687. His most noted work was his great systematic theology, *Institutio Theologiae Elencticae*.

For Rogers and McKim, Turretin epitomizes the deadly interest of Reformed scholasticism in the inerrant form of Scripture. They maintain that "Turretin apparently realized that Calvin's approach to Scripture was antithetical to his own."[64] They particularly focus on Turretin's understanding of the role of the Holy Spirit and of reason in attesting to the authority of Scripture. They also critique his scholarly approach to the Scripture and the role of the concept of accommodation in his theology of the Bible. While this study cannot offer a complete study of the historical forces bearing on Turretin or an exhaustive study of Turretin's views of Scripture, it can demonstrate serious deficiencies in Rogers and McKim's line of approach.[65]

Rogers and McKim criticize Turretin for not resting the authority of the Bible's message—its saving function—on the internal witness of the Spirit. They see Turretin limiting the Spirit to the realm of belief in the inerrant form of Scripture.[66] But Turretin could speak strongly of the role of the Spirit:

> The Holy Spirit, the supplier, by whom believers should be God-taught, Jer. 31:34, John 1:43, 1 John 2:27, does not render the Scripture less necessary; because he is not given to us in order to introduce new revelations, but to impress the written word on our hearts; So that here the word must never be separated from the Spirit, Isa. 59:21. The former works objectively, the latter efficiently; the former strikes the ears from without, the latter opens the heart within: The Spirit is the Teacher, Scripture is the doctrine which he teaches us.[67]

The doctrine or message of Scripture to which Turretin referred is not some formal matter but the content of the Bible, which he could summarize elsewhere as

> the wonderful *sublimity* of the *mysteries*, which could have been discovered by no sharp sightedness of reason; such as the Trinity, Incarnation, the Satisfaction of Christ, the Resurrection of the dead and the like. The *holiness* and purity *of the precepts*, regulating even the thoughts, and the internal affects of the heart, and adapted to render man perfect in every kind of virtue and worthy of his maker. . . .[68]

Contrary to Rogers and McKim,[69] it is also clear that Turretin did not derive the authority of the Bible from its inerrant form. He did indeed argue that a Bible with errors would not be authoritative and labored at length to demonstrate the inerrancy of the Bible. But he was clear that its inerrant form was a result of its divine authority and origin: "Upon the Origin of Scriptures, which we have just discussed, depends their authority, for just because they are from God, they must be authentic and divine." And further, "When the Divinity of the Scriptures is proved, as in the preceding question, its infallibility necessarily follows."[70]

Turretin also discussed in some detail how man could know that the Bible was God's Word. He said clearly that only the Spirit could convince a person of the Bible's divine origin. In harmony with Calvin, Turretin argued that the Spirit does this convincing, not by the testimony of the church, but by the Scripture itself: "But concerning the *Argument* or principle motive which the Spirit uses in persuading us of its truth," it is not "the inartificial argument of the testimony of the church, as the Papists say," but it is "the artificial, derived from the marks of the Scripture itself, which we hold."[71] Turretin further claimed that not only the Bible's claims about itself (its autopistic character) established its authority, but also the marks of the Scripture establish it:

The Bible proves itself divine, not only *authoritatively* and in the manner of an inartificial argument or of testimony, when it *proclaims itself God-inspired:* which although it may be well used against those Christians who profess to believe it, yet cannot be employed against those who reject it. But *ratiocinatively,* by an artificial argument, from the *marks* which God has impressed upon the Scriptures and which furnish indubitable proofs of divinity. For as the works of God exhibit visibly to our eyes by certain marks the incomparable excellence of the Artificer himself, and as the sun makes himself known by his own light; so he wished in the Bible, which is an emanation from the Father of lights and the Sun of righteousness, to send forth different rays of divinity, by which he might make himself known.[72]

Turretin in his discussion of the marks of the Bible distinguished between the external and the internal marks, of which the internal are the more persuasive.[73] The external marks include the antiquity and survival of the Bible, the weakness of the authors who produced such a work, and the witness of the martyrs and all people.[74] The internal marks are the matter of Scripture (Christ and the gospel), the style, the form (the harmony of the doctrine), and the end (the glory of God and the salvation of men).[75]

Turretin's discussion of the possibility of proving the Bible by its marks is wholly in harmony with Calvin. Calvin insisted, "True, if we wished to proceed by arguments, we might advance many things that would easily prove—if there is a god in heaven—that the law, the prophets, and the gospel come from him."[76] Calvin even listed some such evidence: "What wonderful confirmation ensues when, with keener study, we ponder the economy of the divine wisdom, so well ordered and disposed; the completely heavenly character of its doctrine, savoring of nothing earthly; the beautiful agreement of all the parts with one another—as well as such other qualities as can gain majesty for the writings."[77] Calvin also discussed other confirmations such as the antiquity of the Scriptures, the miracles that accompanied the revelation, and the testimony of the whole church and the martyrs.[78] Calvin's list of confirmations is very similar to Turretin's list of marks.

There is one significant difference, however, between Calvin and Turretin on the usefulness of these marks. Calvin insisted that one believes the Bible without marks or proofs. He declared passionately:

For even if it [the Bible] wins reverence for itself by its own majesty, it seriously affects us only when it is sealed upon our hearts through the Spirit. Therefore, illumined by his power, we believe neither by our own nor by anyone else's judgment that Scripture is from God; but above human judgment we affirm with utter certainty (just as if we were gazing upon the majesty of God himself) that it has flowed to us from the very mouth of God by the ministry of men. We seek no proofs, no marks of genuineness upon which our judgment may lean; but we subject our judgment and wit to it as to a thing far beyond any guesswork! This we do, not as persons accustomed to seize upon some unknown thing, which under close scrutiny displeases them, but fully conscious that we hold the unassailable truth! . . . we feel that the undoubted power of his divine majesty lives and breathes there. By this power we are drawn and inflamed, knowingly and willingly, to obey him, yet also more vitally and more effectively than by mere willing or knowing.[79]

While Calvin was not speaking of some irrational mysticism here, he did claim that acceptance of the Bible's authority is more profound than knowing: it is feeling. He seems to be speaking of a direct intuition of the Bible's truth: "As to their question—How can we be assured that this has sprung from God unless we have recourse to the decree of the church?—it is as if someone asked: Whence will we learn to distinguish light from darkness, white from black, sweet from bitter?"[80] For Calvin proofs were "very useful aids,"[81] but only to those already accepting the Bible.

Turretin went beyond and to some extent against Calvin in arguing that marks or proofs *can* (but do not have to) be useful in coming to an acceptance of the Bible. He maintained:

Although faith may be founded upon the authority of testimony, and not upon scientific demonstration, it does not thence follow that it cannot be assisted by artificial arguments, especially in erecting the principles of faith: because before faith can believe, it must have the divinity of the witness to whom faith is to be given, clearly established, from certain true marks which are apprehended in it, otherwise it cannot believe. For where suitable reasons of believing anyone are wanting the testimony of such a witness cannot be worthy of credence.[82]

Turretin said, as Calvin would have, that faith must have something to believe before it can believe, but further Turretin argued, as Calvin would not have, that rational demonstration can be used to support what needs to be believed.

While there is a difference between Calvin and Turretin here, this difference is not directly relevant to the subject of inerrancy. Both Calvin and Turretin agree with the doctrine of inerrancy and disagree only on the usefulness of the proofs of the Bible's authority in bringing one to trust the Bible. This disagreement *may* represent a greater role for reason and for Aristotle in Turretin than in Calvin, but does not represent some fundamental betrayal of the Reformation perspective as Rogers and McKim seem to suggest.[83]

Further Turretin's orthodoxy did not lead him away from the humanistic principles of interpretation developed in the early Reformation. He did not treat the Scripture simply as a series of propositions or proof texts laid out for the convenience of systematic theologians.[84] He insisted on taking the context of any Scriptural text seriously:

To ascertain the true sense of the Scriptures, *Interpretation* is needed, not only of the *words*, which are contained in the versions, but also of *the things....* But for this, after fervent prayer to God, there is need of an inspection of the sources, the knowledge of languages, the distinction between proper and figurative words, attention to the scope and circumstances, collation of passages, connexion of what precedes and follows, removal of prejudices, and confirmation of the interpretation of the analogy of faith.[85]

He also fully recognized that the authors of Scripture selected and ordered their material in various ways: "For these histories are not written so in detail as to contain every circumstance; many things were undoubtedly brought into a narrow compass, other things which did not appear to be so important, omitted."[86]

Turretin also accepted the legitimacy of other scholarly opinions than his own in dealing with apparent errors in the Bible. He certainly did not hang faith on only one theory in this matter.[87] He taught:

Others again think that a few very slight errors have crept into the Scriptures, and even now exist, which cannot be corrected by any collation of Manuscripts, not to be imputed, however, to the sacred writers themselves, but partly to the injuries of time, partly to the fault of copyists and librarians.... Thus Scaliger, Cappellus, Amamus, Vossius and others think. Finally others defend the integrity of the Scriptures and say that these various contradictions are only apparent.[88]

Turretin held to the latter opinion and argued vigorously for it, but recognized the former as orthodox.

In a related area, many have criticized Turretin for his prominent role in the preparation and propagation of the Formula Consensus Helvetica (1675). They point especially to these words of the Consensus: "But, in particular, the Hebrew Original of the Old Testament, which we have received and to this day do retain as handed down by the Jewish Church, ... is, not only in its consonants, but in its vowels—either the vowel points themselves, or at least the power of the points—not only in its matter, but in its words, inspired by God...."[89] They claim that these words demonstrate the intellectual absurdities into which proponents of inerrancy are led. Two observations are important here. First, in Turretin's day the position of the Consensus was not absurd and was one defensible scholarly theory.[90] Turretin and other supporters of the Consensus reasserted their conviction that they possessed the true text of the Scripture both in its consonants and in the force of the vowels. They were continuing a humanistic emphasis on the importance of the original sources. They believed that they had a reliable copy of the original Hebrew text and so rejected emendations of that text by an appeal to translations.[91] They believed that the Masoretic vowel pointing faithfully presented the force of the vowels for the original text and so rejected criticism of that vocalization.

The second observation is that modern scholarship has indeed shown that the position of the Consensus on these matters of text is wrong. Turretin's belief that he possessed a fully reliable copy of the Hebrew original cannot be maintained. But modern rejection of Turretin's view of the Hebrew text does not demonstrate that his commitment to biblical authority was absurd. Turretin did regard his views on the Hebrew text as an element in his defense of the Bible's inerrant authority. He argued that Christians possessed inerrant copies of the inerrant original. But the collapse of that one element of his defense, does not make the doctrine of the inerrancy of the original autographs untenable either for Turretin or for those who continued to share his concerns.

For Rogers and McKim Turretin's formalization of Scripture's authority climaxes in his abandoning the idea of accommodation. They declare that accommodation "was entirely absent from Turretin."[92] But here again Turretin is misrepresented. He declared clearly, "When God understands, he understands himself, as he is infinite, and so infinitely; but when he speaks, he speaks not to himself, but to us, i.e., in accommodation to our capacity, which is finite, and cannot take in many senses."[93] He also recognized this principle in other ways: "God is called *the Ancient of days.... Days*, therefore, and *years* are not ascribed to him properly, but after the manner of men, because we, who live in time, can conceive nothing unless by a relation to time, in which we are,"[94] and: "Repentance is attributed to God *after the manner of men*, but must be understood *after the manner of God.*"[95]

Rogers and McKim criticize Protestant scholasticism in general because the practical concerns of theology are swallowed up in an excessive concern for an abstract and speculative theology: "Precision replaced piety as the goal of theology."[96] Here again Turretin does not fit such a description. Turretin defined theology as a mixed discipline partly theoretical and partly practical, concluding that "it is more practical than theoretical."[97] He insisted on theoretical elements (which he defined as the knowledge of matters like the Trinity and the Incarnation) in theology in opposition to the Socinians and Remonstrants. He believed that a purely practical theology was moralism. He warned "that Socinians and Remonstrants ... say that Theology is so strictly practical, that nothing in it is positively necessary to salvation, unless what pertains to moral precepts and promises.... Their object is evidently to take away the necessity of the knowledge of the doctrines of the Trinity, Incarnation, etc."[98] But his commitment to theology as mixed did not lead him away from piety. Rather he had a vision of a vital theology in both its theoretical and practical elements, as the following statement demonstrates:

> That theology is mixed, that is, partly theoretical and partly practical, the
> following proofs may be given. 1. The *object*, God to be known and worshipped, as the first truth and the highest good. 2. The *subject*, man to be
> made perfect in the knowledge of the truth, by which his understanding
> may be enlightened, and in love of good, by which the will may be

adorned, in *faith*, which is extended to credible, and in *love*, to practical things. 3. The *principle*, both *external*, the *word of God*, which embraces the Law and the Gospel, the former setting forth the things to be done, the latter those to be known and believed, hence called the *mystery of godliness* and the *word of life;* and *internal*, the *spirit*, who is a spirit of truth and sanctification, of knowledge and of the fear of the Lord.[99]

The preceding discussion of Turretin is by no means definitive. There are doubtless other elements in his thought that represent differences with the early Reformers than what have been highlighted here. What is clear, however, is the striking agreement of Calvin and Turretin on the basics of the doctrine of Scripture. Both stress the work of the Spirit in establishing the authority of Scripture. Both believe that the majesty and divinity of Scripture can be proved. Both recognize the accommodated, historical nature of Scripture. Both see the message of Scripture as central. For neither Calvin nor Turretin do concerns for the form of Scripture undermine the gospel message. Both teach the inerrancy of Scripture.

CONCLUSION

Exegesis and theology form the center of the battleline for champions of the inerrancy of the Bible. The strength of that center will ultimately determine the outcome of the struggle to understand the nature of the Scriptures. Yet in this conflict the history of the church's attitudes toward the Bible has become an important flank of the battleline. Various skirmishes have contested whether inerrantists can legitimately claim the history of the church as one of their allies. Hopefully the foray represented by this study of the sixteenth and seventeenth centuries will advance the discussion and help reassert the conviction that inerrancy is a vital element of historic Christianity.

THE PRINCETONIANS
AND BIBLICAL AUTHORITY:
AN ASSESSMENT OF THE
ERNEST SANDEEN PROPOSAL

John D. Woodbridge
and Randall H. Balmer

John D. Woodbridge

John D. Woodbridge is Professor of Church History at Trinity Evangelical Divinity School, Deerfield, Illinois. He is a graduate of Wheaton College (B.A.), Michigan State University (M.A.), University of Toulouse (Doctorat de Troisième Cycle), and Trinity Evangelical Divinity School (M. Div.). He has received fellowships from the Fulbright Commission, the National Endowment for the Humanities, the American Council of Learned Societies, the Centre Nationale de la Recherche Scientifique (Paris) and the Herzog August Bibliothek (Wolfenbüttel, West Germany).

Dr. Woodbridge is the author of *Biblical Authority: A Critique of the Rogers and McKim Proposal.* He is also the co-author or co-editor of four other books: the present volume, *Scripture and Truth* (co-editor), *The Gospel in America* (co-author), *The Evangelicals* (co-editor), and *Richard Simon Additions aux 'Recherches curieuses sur la diversité des langues et religions' d'Edward Brerewood* (co-editor). He has contributed articles to several periodicals and is a member of learned societies both in the United States and Europe.

Randall H. Balmer

Randall H. Balmer holds the master's degree in religion from Princeton University where he is currently a doctoral student. He earned the B.A. at Trinity College and the M.A. at Trinity Evangelical Divinity School, where his thesis on nineteenth-century Princeton theology was given the Professor T. B. Madsen Award. The former editor of *Voices*, his scholarly articles have appeared in the *Journal of Presbyterian History*, *Trinity Journal*, *De Halve Maen*, and *Westminster Theological Journal*.

THE PRINCETONIANS AND BIBLICAL AUTHORITY: AN ASSESSMENT OF THE ERNEST SANDEEN PROPOSAL

For some years now students of American religion have sought to understand better that elusive movement known as Fundamentalism.[1] The publication of Ernest Sandeen's *Roots of Fundamentalism: British and American Millenarianism 1800–1930* (1970; reprint ed., Grand Rapids: Baker, 1978) constituted an important milestone in their enterprise. It provided the scholarly community with one of its most provocative and instructive interpretations of that movement's origins.[2] According to Professor Sandeen, the primary nineteenth-century roots of Fundamentalism were planted in the teachings of millenarianism (especially John Darby's Dispensationalism) and in the instruction dispensed by the Old School Presbyterian teachers at Princeton Theological Seminary. In the second half of the century, Dispensationalists and Princetonians joined in a common cause: the desire to defend a high view of biblical authority against those who in their opinion were advocating inferior or defective perspectives.[3] From contacts between these two parties, the Fundamentalist movement was born, having its numerical strength in the northeast.[4]

Sandeen's interpretation of the origins of Fundamentalism prompted at least some commentators on American religion to abandon stereotypic evaluations. Authors of texts in American history had frequently described Fundamentalists in sociological terms, with scant reference to their theological concerns. Fundamentalists were portrayed as rural Americans who rejected "urban values." They could not adjust to the significant social and intellectual changes that the twentieth century brought to the United States. In his well-known college text *The American Nation: A History of the United States*, John Garraty wrote, "Educated persons had been able to resolve apparent contradictions between Darwin's theory and religious teachings easily enough, but in rural backwaters, especially in the southern and border states, this was never the case. Partly, Fundamentalism resulted from simple ignorance; where educational standards were low and culture relatively static, old ideas remained unchallenged."[5] In a certain measure Sandeen's study disputed such appraisals.[6] It summoned scholars to do more careful research concerning the theological factors that helped shape the Fundamentalist movement.

Several of the principal theses in Sandeen's work have gained particular notice. While appreciating the richness of Sandeen's fine-textured interpretation, Professor George Marsden of Calvin College has engaged in polite debate with him. Marsden believes that Sandeen has overemphasized the importance of millenarian thought for the Fundamentalist movement.[7] Marsden suggests that many roots nourished the tree that became Fundamentalism.[8] Moreover he proposes that a correct methodology for analyzing Fundamentalism begins with an assessment of its manifestations in the 1920s; only when the 1920s trunk is carefully examined can one sort out the movement's tangled roots.[9] According to Marsden, Sandeen did not follow this procedure in his research; rather, he isolated the root of millenarianism from the history of nineteenth-century Evangelicalism without sufficient regard to what Fundamentalism represented in the 1920s.

While Marsden has critiqued these aspects of Sandeen's work, many scholars have accepted without serious scrutiny another one of Sandeen's interpretations: his analysis of the attitudes of nineteenth-century professors at Princeton Theological Seminary toward Holy Scripture.[10] Professor Sandeen suggests that the Princetonians A. A. Hodge and B. B. Warfield engaged in doctrinal innovation by elevating the belief in the "inerrancy of Scriptures in the original documents" to the rank of a doctrinal commitment for some Presbyterians. They did so in a joint essay, "Inspiration," published in 1881. Eventually their formulation spread through the ranks of Fundamentalists.[11] The belief eventually took on great importance for conservative Evangelicals who did not comprehend that this "doctrine" they defended so stoutly was not only a doctrinal innovation of relatively recent vintage but also a betrayal of the teachings of Reformed Christians ranging from the Westminster divines to John Calvin himself. Given the import of Sandeen's proposal, it is indeed odd that the interpretation has not come under closer scrutiny.

Scholars ranging from James Barr in his book *Fundamentalism* (1977) to Jack Rogers and Donald McKim in their study *The Authority and Interpretation of the Bible* (1979) have incorporated much of Sandeen's discussion about the Princetonians in their broad criticism of conservative Evangelicals and "Fundamentalists."[12] Other members of the academic community at large have accepted Sandeen's analysis.

Because his study did not receive what Sandeen evidently considered to be telling rebuttals, the author published the 1978 Baker edition without serious revisions: "The text of this edition is identical with that of the first except that typographical and factual errors in eight passages have been corrected" (from the preface).[13] In the preface to the new edition Sandeen expressed the hope that a large group of "Fundamentalist pastors, seminary students, and laymen" might become acquainted with his book and therefore understand better their own backgrounds.[14] His writing, then, did not lack for a missionary impulse.

In this chapter we will examine Sandeen's contentions concerning the Princetonians' alleged innovation of creating the doctrine of inerrancy in the original autographs. By focusing our attention on this one aspect of his interpretation, our task becomes more modest and more manageable. And yet it retains a certain significance, for the credibility of Sandeen's basic interpretation depends in some measure on the accuracy of his analysis of the Princetonians' views of Scripture. In the first section we set forth in broad strokes Sandeen's proposal concerning the Old Princetonians' views of Scripture. In the second section we present some specific criticisms of his proposal. And finally, in the third, we make some remarks about why a revision of his important interpretation might be appropriate. We contend that the subject of biblical authority in nineteenth-century America has not yet found its historian.

THE SANDEEN PROPOSAL

Professor Sandeen's proposal is based on the premise that American Protestants did not have a well-considered doctrine of biblical authority before the second half of the nineteenth century. Writes Sandeen:

> A systematic theology of biblical authority which defended the common evangelical faith in the infallibility of the Bible had to be created in the midst of the nineteenth century controversy. The formation of this theology in association with the growth of the millenarian movement determined the character of Fundamentalism.[15]

In this light Sandeen sees the emergence of one such well-defined doctrine of biblical authority at Princeton. He argues that Archibald Alexander (1772–1851), the first professor at Princeton Seminary, had not dogmatically stated that the Bible's inspiration extends to words.[16] Archibald Alexander's student Charles Hodge (1797–1878) began to stress verbal inspiration, but still remained reticent about affirming biblical inerrancy dogmatically.[17] In his *Systematic Theology* (1871) Charles Hodge minimized what import little errors might have on biblical authority by presenting his famous "flecks in the Parthenon" illustration.[18] A. A. Hodge, Charles Hodge's son, did not maintain this flexible stance. Buffeted by the findings of higher criticism and developmental science, A. A. Hodge (1823–1886), along with B. B. Warfield (1851–1921), advocated the doctrine of inerrancy in the original autographs in their joint article, "Inspiration" (1881).[19] Writes Sandeen: "One could no longer dismiss them [errors] as had Charles Hodge—as flecks of sandstone in the Parthenon marble. Hodge and Warfield retreated."[20] Sandeen scored this retreat to "lost and completely useless autographs" as a calculated dodge.[21] No one could ever demonstrate that the Bible was errant, because the original autographs had long since been lost. The Princetonians' apologetic was constructed to be impregnable. In reality, it was built on shifting sands.

For Sandeen, the Princetonians' formulation "inerrancy in the original autographs" represents a doctrinal innovation. Neither Calvin nor the divines at the Westminster Assembly, who were the standard bearers of the Reformed tradition, defended this formulation. Sandeen insists, "This doctrine [inerrancy in the original autographs] did not exist in either Europe or America prior to its formulation in the last half of the nineteenth century."[22] B. B. Warfield in particular departed from Reformed teachings by emphasizing the "external evidences" for the Bible's authority rather than accenting the witness of the Holy Spirit within the believer to confirm that authority.[23] Innovative though it was, this doctrine became a benchmark for Northern Presbyterians until the 1920s. It also became the essential ingredient of Fundamentalism's teaching about biblical authority.[24]

A CRITIQUE OF PROFESSOR SANDEEN'S PROPOSAL

Professor Sandeen's proposal, bold and trenchant as it is, falters at several points: (1) it presupposes a misconstrued version of the history of biblical authority in the Reformed tradition, (2) it presents a misleading portrait of the development of the doctrine of biblical authority at Princeton Theological Seminary during the nineteenth century, and (3) it tends to separate the Princetonians' teachings about the infallibility of the original autographs from the wider context of American and European evangelical thought. Each one of these points deserves further elaboration.

TWO REPRESENTATIVES OF THE REFORMED TRADITION OR BIBLICAL AUTHORITY: WILLIAM WHITAKER AND WILLIAM AMES

To review the intricacies of Reformed thought concerning biblical authority in brief compass is a perilous if not impossible task.[25] Perhaps we would be better served if we sample the thinking of two individuals who greatly influenced the theology of Anglo-Saxon Protestants concerning biblical authority. They are William Whitaker (1547–1595) and William Ames (1576–1633). By studying Whitaker and Ames, we will observe that the concept of complete biblical infallibility, what we today call biblical inerrancy, was no new creation of the late nineteenth century and that earlier Protestants who were not so-called scholastics advocated the position.[26]

Roman Catholic apologists acknowledged that William Whitaker's *Disputation on Holy Scripture* (1588) constituted one of the seminal Protestant books about biblical authority. Nearly a century after its publication, the famous biblical critic Richard Simon (1638–1712) remarked in his *Histoire critique du Vieux Testament* (1678):

> In addition, I have gone into more detail about the sentiments which Whitaker had of Bellarmine and other Jesuits, because that ought to serve

as a key for understanding countless books which have been written thereafter by Protestants of France, England, and Germany against the books of Bellarmine.[27]

In the second half of the sixteenth century Bellarmine was the most influential Roman Catholic who disputed Protestant claims about *sola Scriptura*, and Whitaker was his chief opponent.[28] Bellarmine apparently admired Whitaker so much that he kept the Englishman's portrait in his study.[29] Not well known to us today, Whitaker, a Cambridge professor, crafted the most extensive Protestant book on biblical authority in Elizabeth's England.[30] Moreover he was a very godly man, held in high esteem by his contemporaries.[31]

In his *Disputation on Holy Scripture*, Whitaker, who was known for his Puritan sympathies, affirmed his belief in complete biblical infallibility. He cited Augustine as an authority who had earlier maintained this same stance:

> We cannot but wholly disapprove the opinion of those, who think that the sacred writers have in some places, fallen into mistakes. That some of the ancients were of this opinion appears from the testimony of Augustine, who maintains, in opposition to them, "that the evangelists are free from all falsehood, both from that which proceeds from deliberate deceit, and that which is the result of forgetfulness."[32]

Whitaker suggested that, whereas Erasmus and perhaps even Saint Jerome had allowed for small errors due to "slips of memory," "it becomes us to be so scrupulous as not to allow that any such slip can be found in scripture."[33] Whitaker continued:

> For, whatever Erasmus may think, it is a solid answer which Augustine gives to Jerome: "If any, even the smallest, lie be admitted in the scriptures, the whole authority of scripture is presently invalidated and destroyed."[34]

Whitaker denied specifically, for example, that Stephen had made an error in Acts 7:16:

> Stephen, therefore, could no more have been mistaken than Luke; because the Holy Ghost was the same in Luke and in Stephen.... Therefore we must maintain intact the authority of Scripture in such a sense as not to allow that anything is therein delivered otherwise than the most perfect truth required.[35]

Whitaker, like Augustine, believed that "errors" in the biblical texts would constitute a telling blow against biblical authority. His own advocacy of complete biblical infallibility was straightforward indeed.

Nor was Whitaker a "scholastic," basing his commitment to biblical authority on the cumulative impact of a well-structured rational apologetic. Certainly, Whitaker did set forth a detailed defense of *sola Scriptura*, against the claims of Bellarmine and Stapleton, who appealed to the added authority of the church's "Tradition." But like

Calvin, Whitaker ultimately based his own commitment to biblical authority on the confirming work of the Holy Spirit:

> These topics may prove that these books are divine, yet will never be sufficient to bring conviction to our souls so as to make us assent, unless the testimony of the Holy Spirit be added. When this is added, it fills our minds with a wonderful plenitude of assurance, confirms them, and causes us most gladly to embrace the scriptures, giving force to the preceding arguments. Those previous arguments may indeed urge and constrain us: but this (I mean the internal testimony of the Holy Spirit) is the only argument which can persuade us.[36]

Whitaker viewed himself as a Reformed theologian, faithful to Augustine and Calvin.

The Cambridge professor also argued that only those Scriptures that were immediately inspired by the Holy Spirit were truly "authentic":

> For authentic scripture must proceed immediately from the Holy Ghost himself ... (2 Tim. 3:16); now Jerome's translation is not divinely inspired: therefore it is not authentic scripture.[37]

Any conceivable error that found its way into the extant biblical text was due to the negligence of copyists:

> These then are the passages which Bellarmine was able to find fault with in the originals; and yet in these there is really nothing to require either blame or correction. But, even though we should allow (which we are so far from doing, that we have proved the contrary) that these were faulty in the original, what could our adversaries conclude from such an admission? Would it follow that the Hebrew fountain was more corrupt than the Latin streamlets, or that the Latin edition was authentic? Not, surely, unless it were previously assumed, either that canonical books of scripture cannot be erroneously copied sometimes by transcribers....[38]

The Cambridge professor held a position that could be fairly categorized as "complete biblical infallibility in the original documents."

The Puritan William Ames, a philosophical Ramist, believed much the same way as did William Whitaker.[39] In his *Marrow of Sacred Divinity* (1624, 1627, 1629), an influential text used at Harvard College in the seventeenth century, Ames set forth his stand about complete biblical infallibility:

> 2. Only those could set down the rule of faith and conduct in writing who in that matter were free from all error because of the direct and infallible direction they had from God....

> 4. They also wrote by the inspiration and guidance of the Holy Spirit so that the men themselves were at that point, so to speak, instruments of the Spirit....

5. But divine inspiration was present among those writers in different ways. Some things were altogether unknown to the writer in advance, as appears in the history of past creation, or in the foretelling of things to come. But some things were previously known to the writer, as appears in the history of Christ written by the apostles. Some things were known by a natural knowledge and some by a supernatural. In those things that were hidden and unknown, divine inspiration was at work by itself. In those things which were known, or where the knowledge was obtained by ordinary means, there was added the writers' devout zeal so that (God assisting them) they might not err in writing.

6. In all those things made known by supernatural inspiration, whether matters of right or fact, God inspired not only the subjects to be written about but dictated and suggested the very words in which they should be set forth. But this was done with a subtle tempering so that every writer might use the manner of speaking which most suited his person and condition.[40]

Moreover Ames believed that the truly authentic Scriptures were the original "sources."

27. The Scriptures are not so tied to these first languages that they cannot and ought not to be translated into other languages for common use in the church.

28. But, among interpreters, neither the seventy who turned them into Greek, nor Jerome, nor any other such held the office of a prophet; they were not free from errors in interpretation.

29. Hence no versions are fully authentic except as they express the sources, by which they are also to be weighed. . . .

31. God's providence in preserving the sources is notable and glorious, for neither have they wholly perished nor have they been injured by the loss of any book or blemished by any serious defect—though today not one of the earlier versions remains intact.[41]

The Puritan Ames also held a position that could be categorized without essential distortion as complete biblical infallibility in the original autographs.

The stance of William Whitaker and William Ames on this matter is important. Both men predate the Westminster Assembly.[42] Neither was apparently a so-called scholastic.[43] Both saw themselves as faithful followers of Calvin, St. Augustine, and the teachings of Scripture about its own authority.

When Professor Sandeen claims that the concept of inerrancy in the original documents had not been entertained by Reformed or other theologians before the mid-nineteenth century, he apparently failed to consider the beliefs of Whitaker and Ames or, more generally, the intense debates between Roman Catholics and Protestants in the sixteenth century over the "authenticity" of the Vulgate and the authenticity of the biblical "originals."[44] He apparently overlooked the commitment of many of the early church fathers (see chapter 7 by Geoffrey Bromiley) and Reformers (see chapter 8 by Robert Godfrey) to complete biblical infallibility.[45] It appears that Sandeen's contention concerning the innovative character of the Princetonians' beliefs needs serious qualification, if not recasting. Even these brief comments about members of the "Reformed tradition" allow us to affirm this.

THE NINETEENTH-CENTURY PRINCETONIANS AND BIBLICAL AUTHORITY

Sandeen's proposal that the Princetonians as a group played a determinative role in promoting the doctrine of inerrancy in the original autographs also lacks persuasive force.[46] Extensive research in nineteenth-century books and periodicals on the subject of biblical infallibility yields relatively little evidence of exceptional Princetonian influence on this point (save in Presbyterian circles). As we will see, the belief in the "infallibility of the originals" was commonly advocated by spokesmen of various communions. Non-Presbyterian Christians did not need to look to the Princetonians for particular guidance concerning this teaching.

It is further to be questioned why Sandeen places so much emphasis on the joint 1881 "Inspiration" article by A. A. Hodge and B. B. Warfield as a culminating point in the Princetonians' doctrinal development.[47] By his own account the clause about the autographs, a supposed innovation, had been introduced earlier by A. A. Hodge in the 1879 edition of his *Outlines of Theology*.

Citing a study by Presbyterian historian Lefferts Loetscher, Sandeen argues that the article "Inspiration" was the first occasion in which the "new views" were expressed and that "after this date the Princeton Theology took a much firmer position on the inerrancy of Scriptures."[48] If indeed Sandeen is correct, it is perplexing that A. A. Hodge and B. B. Warfield did not sense that they were embarking on some major doctrinal adventure. One searches in vain through their correspondence during this period for clear indications that the authors believed they were offering to the theological world, in Sandeen's words, "a new formulation of the doctrine of the Scriptures." The attacks on Scripture, particularly by Robertson Smith, are what they regarded as new, not their own theological posture.[49]

Sandeen sets the stage for the purported doctrinal innovation by making the following claim: "The problems raised by biblical criticism demanded a new formulation of the doctrine of the Scriptures" and that

> the pressure of biblical criticism after 1870 became so strong that later Princeton scholars in reaction to that pressure made important modifications which moved the Princeton Theology still further from the reformed tradition.[50]

This leads him to the conclusion that "the Princeton doctrine of the Scriptures was refined and tightened in the face of growing critical opposition."[51] In a word, biblical criticism provoked the creation of the inerrancy-of-the-original-autographs hypothesis.

Attacks Against Biblical Infallibility Before 1870

Like several other studies, Sandeen's analysis suffers because it does not adequately take note of the serious and diverse kinds of attacks *against* complete biblical infallibility (inerrancy) before the 1870s.[52] From reading his proposal one might suppose that the Princetonians either did not keep abreast of these attacks taking place in Germany, England, and elsewhere or that they chose to ignore them until 1870 or so. Only when they awoke to this menace did they modify their theology to counter the pressures of higher criticism. This interpretation, however, runs counter to the Princetonians' perceptions of their changing theological world. The very charter of Princeton Theological Seminary, adopted by the General Assembly of 1811 and reprinted at least five times throughout the century, includes the following statement under Article IV, "Of Study and Attainments":

> Every student, at the close of his course, must have made the following attainments, viz: He must be well skilled in the original languages of the Holy Scriptures. He must be able to explain the principal difficulties which arise in the perusal of the Scriptures, either from erroneous translations, apparent inconsistencies, real obscurities, or objections arising from history, reason, or argument. . . . Thus he will have laid the foundation for becoming a sound biblical critic.[53]

This statement summoned students to prepare themselves to defend the authority of the Bible against detractors in the second decade of the nineteenth century.[54]

Charles Hodge took leave of his responsibilities at the seminary from 1826 to 1828 to continue his studies in Germany. He became familiar—indeed conversant—with the critical theories circulating on the Continent.[55] Back in Princeton, Archibald Alexander was only too aware of the trend of German scholarship. At the conclusion of a letter to Hodge, who was then studying in Europe, he penned the following:

> My dear sir, I hope while you [are apart] from your earthly friends you will take care to keep the communication with heaven open! Remember that you breathe a poisoned atmosphere. If you lose the lively and deep impression of divine truth—If you fall into scepticism, or even into coldness, you will lose more than you gain from all the German professors and libraries. May the Lord preserve you from error, and all evil! You may depend upon any aid which my feeble prayers can afford. Write as often as you can! Do not be afraid of troubling me.[56]

A lecture by Hodge, entitled "Inspiration" and dated September 23, 1850, includes extensive refutations of the inspiration views of Samuel

Coleridge, J.D. Morell, Thomas Arnold, and Schleiermacher. Special reference is made to the latter, whom Hodge refers to as "the Plato of modern Germany."[57] The writings of these thinkers worried the Princetonians and other American Evangelicals decades before they experienced discomfiture over Darwin's *Origin of Species* and the Graf-Wellhausen hypothesis.[58] And yet nowhere do we find in Sandeen's study extended discussions devoted to Samuel Coleridge, J. D. Morell, and Thomas Arnold. These three thinkers, among others, caused considerable consternation for churchmen in Britain by their attacks against complete biblical infallibility in the first half of the nineteenth century.[59] In his posthumously published *Confessions of an Inquiring Mind* (1841), Coleridge acknowledged that a commitment to complete biblical infallibility was widespread in England. He noted the remark of a "well-disposed" skeptic:

> I have frequently attended meetings of the British and Foreign Bible Society, where I have heard speakers of every denomination, Calvinist and Arminian, Quaker and Methodist, Dissenting Ministers and Clergymen, nay, dignitaries of the Established Church—and still I have heard the same doctrine,—that the Bible was not to be regarded or reasoned about in the way that other good books are or may be. . . . What is more, their principal arguments were grounded on the position that the Bible throughout was dictated by Omniscience, and therefore in all its parts infallibly true and obligatory, and that the men, whose names are prefixed to the several books or chapters, were in fact but as different pens in the hand of one and the same Writer, and the words the words of God himself.[60]

Coleridge continued, "What could I reply to this?—I could neither deny the fact, nor evade the conclusion,—namely that such is at present the popular belief."[61] The author himself wanted to argue for a faith that comes through hearing—a living faith. This faith did not need to be bound to the letter of the Scriptures and its complete infallibility.[62] For the Bible contains "all truths necessary to salvation." It is not in every way the Word of God.[63] Coleridge specifically criticized "bibliolatry" and the dictation theory of inspiration.[64] He believed that many of his contemporaries advocated the latter view.

In a letter dated January 24, 1835, to Justice Coleridge (Samuel's nephew), Thomas Arnold of Rugby commented about the explosive character of Coleridge's writings on Scripture:

> Have you seen your uncle's "Letters on Inspiration," which I believe are to be published? They are well fitted to break ground in the approaches to that momentous question which involves in it so great a shock to existing notions; the greatest, probably, that has ever been given since the discovery of the falsehood of the doctrine of the Pope's infallibility.[65]

In this letter Arnold was referring to Coleridge's criticisms of complete biblical infallibility.

In the 1840s several American theologians commented on the large following that Coleridge was attracting in this country. Noah Porter (1811–1892), professor of metaphysics at Yale College, penned a lengthy article entitled "Coleridge and his American Disciples" for the 1847 *Bibliotheca Sacra*. Porter noted the contemporaneity of Coleridge's provocative analysis of biblical inspiration as spelled out in *Letters of an Inquiring Spirit:*

> The questions involved in these Letters, are the great questions of the day. The whispers of thousands and tens of thousands of "inquiring spirits" plead with earnest intreaties, that they shall be fairly considered and fairly answered.[66]

Porter generally approved Coleridge's theory of biblical inspiration but disputed some of his theological proposals. Moreover Porter devoted five pages of his essay to a taxonomical analysis of Coleridge's many disciples.[67]

As late as a *Princeton Review* article of 1881, Charles Elliott struggled with the import of Coleridge's *Letters of an Inquiring Spirit* for "absolute biblical infallibility."

Thomas Arnold, whose son Matthew Arnold became a major personage in the world of letters during the Victorian era, also troubled certain Protestant spokesmen. Arnold did much to propagate Coleridge's thinking about Scripture. Evangelicals found it difficult to criticize him because his own Christian piety could not be gainsaid.[68] Matthew Arnold commented later on his father's role in making Coleridge more palatable to Englishmen:

> In papa's time the exploding of the old notions of literal inspiration in Scripture, and the introducing of a truer method of interpretation, were the changes for which, here in England, the moment had come. Stiff people could not receive this change, and my dear old Methodist friend, Mr. Scott, used to say to the day of his death that papa and Coleridge might be excellent men, but that they had found and shown the rat-hole in the temple.[69]

Thomas Arnold, then, helped to undermine confidence in complete biblical infallibility.[70]

Some churchmen also balked at J. D. Morell's *Philosophy of Religion*, in which the author attempted to introduce to his English readers the theology of Schleiermacher, including the German's teachings about Scripture. Morell defined revelation as "the act of God, presenting to us the realities of the spiritual world."[71] He declared, "Inspiration is the especial influence wrought upon the faculties of the subject, by virtue of which he is able to grasp these realities in their fullness and integrity."[72] Morell's definition of inspiration shifted its focus to an influence whereby the apostles were able to grasp revelation. Henry B. Smith observed that in this theory "the specific divine agency in respect to the production of the Scriptures is lost from view."[73] From the point of view of many Evangelicals, Morell's perception of biblical inspiration was deficient.

So concerned were some American and English authors about the works of Coleridge, Arnold, Morell, and Schleiermacher that they specifically singled out their writings as foils for their own studies. Theodore Bozeman takes note of the crisis that Coleridge, Morell, and others provoked for Old School Presbyterians and particularly their "Baconian" presuppositions:

> Then, during the 1830s, a fresh sense of intellectual emergency was created within Old School ranks by the emergence of an emphatically non-Baconian philosophical movement. Quickly replacing Unitarianism as the leading challenge to traditional belief was the new Transcendentalism, which troubled conservatives associated with J. G. Fichte, G. W. F. Hegel, Friedrich Schleiermacher, Samuel Taylor Coleridge, Ralph Waldo Emerson, J. D. Morell, and other figures. Presbyterian literature from the late 1830s teems with anxious and scathing references, book reviews, and full-scale attacks against what was called variously, "Pantheism," "Rationalism," and "Transcendentalism."[74]

Bozeman could well have added that Old School Presbyterians were also concerned about these thinkers' attacks on complete biblical infallibility.[75]

In his influential *Inspiration of Holy Scriptures, Its Nature and Proof* (1854) William Lee of Trinity College, Dublin, argued that a good number of Christians were uneasy about their views of inspiration and biblical infallibility because they identified their perspective with a mechanical dictation theory.[76] He noted that Coleridge's *Letters of an Inquiring Spirit* "has done more than any modern work to unsettle the public mind, in these countries, with respect to the authority of the Bible *considered as a whole.*"[77] He complained that even "well-informed persons" were accepting the teachings of Morell about inspiration.[78] In his own discussion of "inspiration" the author sought to allow for a greater element of human participation in the writing of Scripture. He believed that the arguments of Coleridge, Morell, and Schleiermacher would lose their force if complete biblical infallibility were associated with his concept of inspiration as "dynamic inspiration."[79]

Charles Hodge of Princeton Seminary reviewed Lee's volume favorably in two reviews in the *Biblical Repertory* (1857).[80] Like Lee, he roundly criticized Coleridge, Morell, Schleiermacher, and others whose views concerning the Bible and biblical inspiration he found wanting. Speaking of Lee's view of inspiration, Hodge commented:

> This is the old orthodox doctrine of plenary inspiration. This is what the German writers and their followers in England and America stigmatize as "the mechanical theory." This is the doctrine which Coleridge ridicules, and which Morell endeavors to refute. This is the doctrine which the whole school of Schleiermacher, in both its great divisions, the religious and the sceptical, represent as unphilosophical and untenable.[81]

At this date, Hodge apparently did not sense any overwhelming challenges stemming from ongoing "scientific studies."[82]

In his *Systematic Theology* (1871) Charles Hodge argued that Coleridge simply did not understand what the church believes about inspiration:

> Even a man so distinguished for knowledge and ability as Coleridge, speaks with contempt of what he regards as the common theory of inspiration, when he utterly misunderstands the real doctrine which he opposes.[83]

And Hodge critiqued Schleiermacher, Morell, and others on the same count.[84]

In his posthumously published study, *The Human Element in the Inspiration of the Sacred Scriptures* (1867), the American theologian T. F. Curtis echoed Lee's analysis on several points. He viewed Coleridge and Arnold as those among others who had prompted much debate about biblical infallibility. Curtis wrote about Coleridge's general influence:

> Coleridge may be said to have broken ground in this subject in England, and his Confessions of an Inquiring Spirit, published after his death, have produced a greater effect morally among thinking Christians, than all he had published during his life.[85]

Curtis observed that Arnold of Rugby, "the Apostle of Christian culture in Young England in its best form"

> openly exhibited a freedom from, and dislike to the current belief in the infallibility of the Inspiration of the Bible; while he foresaw in this, as he said, as great a shock to the feelings of Protestant Christendom as Roman Catholic Christianity had received three hundred years ago, from the downfall of the belief in the infallibility of the Church.[86]

Whereas Lee had discussed the human element in the inspiration of the Scriptures with a view to bolstering the concept of complete biblical infallibility, Curtis stressed the human element to demonstrate that the Bible was errant. He was very sensitive to the fact that his study challenged the common belief in complete biblical infallibility:

> But the Protestant world must now open its eyes upon another Reformation, and learn not only that the Church is fallible, but that the Scriptures, especially of the Old Testament, though truly and properly to be venerated as holy, inspired and sacred documents of the Christian faith, are not therefore to be esteemed, especially in matters of current opinion, as science and history, absolutely infallible, but as having partly received their color from the ages in which they were produced, and from the sincere yet fallible opinions of holy men, moved by the Holy Ghost, who wrote them.[87]

Like Coleridge, Curtis believed that Christians could abandon an infallible Bible without overthrowing the faith.[88] In fact their faith could withstand modern critics better if it were dissociated from an outmoded concept.

Professor Sandeen's hypothesis that American Protestants had no "systematic theology of biblical authority which defended the common evangelical faith in the infallibility of the Bible" in the first half of the nineteenth century needs certain qualifications. Evangelicals did debate the *mode* of inspiration as they attempted to skirt the inconveniences of the dictation theory that Coleridge, Morell, and others had successfully exploited.[89] But most Evangelicals did generally agree on the effects of inspiration: the Bible was completely infallible.[90] In the *Union Bible Dictionary* (1839) prepared for a popular audience by the American Sunday School Union, the article "Inspiration (2 Tim. iii 16)" reads:

> Nor is it necessary that the particular style and method of the writer should be abandoned. God may have wise purposes to answer in preserving this, while he secures, through his agency, an infallible declaration of his will. So that style, manner, etc., may be of the author's own choice, provided the facts stated and the doctrines taught as of divine authority, are stated and taught under an immediate divine influence, without the possibility of error. And even if it should appear that the copies of such a book now in the world have suffered from the injuries of time, and the carelessness of transcribers and printers, so that inaccuracies and discrepancies of unessential importance might be detected, still if the substance of the book, if the grand system of truth of duty revealed, is evidently, as a whole, the result of such divine inspiration, it is to be received, and may be entirely credited as an inspired book.[91]

This description resembles William Ames's discussion of inspiration in several ways. In addition, the article includes definitions of "inspiration of elevation" and "inspiration of suggestion," pointing out that "all these various degrees or kinds of inspiration are supposed to occur in our Scriptures." Interestingly enough, the editors of the *Union Bible Dictionary* claimed that "whatever could be regarded as sectarian by any denomination of evangelical Christians is, of course, scrupulously excluded."[92] That is, they assumed that Evangelicals generally concurred with this definition of inspiration as well as their other comments about doctrinal matters. Sandeen's hypothesis that Evangelicals had "no systematic theology" of biblical authority before 1850 is a substantial exaggeration.[93] It is his perception of their viewpoints based on his definition of systematic theology.[94] Many (but not all) Evangelicals believed that these nineteenth-century Evangelicals did possess a satisfactory theology, even if they differed with other Christians about the mode of inspiration.

Moreover Sandeen's contention that the Princetonians developed the doctrine of biblical inerrancy in the 1870s and 1880s to meet the challenge of biblical criticism simply does not accord with their earlier grave misgivings about various attacks against complete biblical infallibility (inerrancy) associated with what Charles Elliott called in 1881, the "subjective theory of inspiration" and linked to the names of Coleridge, Arnold, Morell, and Schleiermacher.[95]

Biblical Infallibility at Princeton Seminary: A Question of Development

In light of the above discussion we should study Sandeen's supposition that the earlier Princetonians such as Archibald Alexander and Charles Hodge did not believe in the complete infallibility of the original autographs. We recall that Sandeen declares that Archibald Alexander, the first professor at Princeton Theological Seminary, did not dogmatically affirm verbal inspiration:

> First, the Princeton theologians agreed that the "inspiration of the Scriptures extends to the words." Archibald Alexander did not feel obliged to be dogmatic about the point, but after Charles Hodge adopted the position, no change occurred at Princeton regarding verbal inspiration.[96]

In truth, Archibald Alexander was quite dogmatic about his commitment to verbal inspiration and to complete biblical infallibility. He defined inspiration as

> SUCH A DIVINE INFLUENCE UPON THE MINDS OF THE SACRED WRITERS AS RENDERED THEM EXEMPT FROM ERROR, BOTH IN REGARD TO THE IDEAS AND WORDS.
>
> This is properly called PLENARY inspiration. Nothing can be conceived more satisfactory. Certainty, infallible certainty, is the utmost that can be desired in any *narrative;* and if we have this in the sacred Scriptures, there is nothing more to be wished in regard to this matter.[97]

Moreover Alexander was a proponent of biblical infallibility for the original autographs. In his 1836 *Evidences* he conceded that "some slight inaccuracies have crept into the copies of the New Testament, through the carelessness of transcribers."[98] Continuing this same line of reasoning, he claimed that "the Scriptures of the New Testament have come down to us in their original integrity, save those errors which arose from the carelessness or ignorance of transcribers."[99] In his 1831 review of Leonard Woods's *Lectures on the Inspiration of the Scriptures* he was even more explicit in his allowance for copyists' errors:

> There are in the Bible apparent discrepancies which can easily be reconciled by a little explanation; and there may be real contradictions in our copies, which may be owing to the mistakes of transcribers. Now, when such things are observed, there should not be a hasty conclusion that the book was not written by inspiration, but a careful and candid examination of the passages, and even when we cannot reconcile them, we should consider the circumstances under which these books have been transmitted to us, and the almost absolute certainty, that in so many ages, and in the process of such numerous transcriptions, mistakes must necessarily have occurred, and may have passed into all the copies extant.[100]

For Alexander, therefore, inaccuracies of copies or versions in no way blemished the infallibility of the original texts of Scripture. Although he does not specifically use the phrase "original autographs" in his definition of inspiration, it is clear that Alexander's theory encompassed that idea.[101]

Charles Hodge, Alexander's student, also recognized the presence of errors in available biblical texts. In a discussion of discrepancies in the Bible he notes, "Many of them may fairly be ascribed to errors of transcribers" and adds that "they furnish no rational ground for denying [Scripture's] infallibility."[102] Hodge also acknowledges the errors of transcribers (or "interpreters") in his lecture notes on biblical criticism:

> That the interpreters were not inspired is abundantly evident from the errors into which they frequently fell; evidently mistaking one word for another, and often not giving a sense consistent with the true meaning of the original Hebrew.[103]

A fuller elucidation of Hodge's thoughts on the matter is found in his manuscript notes for a biblical criticism course. The introductory lecture, dated November 1822, contains the following:

> When we remember the period which has elapsed since the Sacred writings were originally penned, the number of transcriptions to which they must have been subjected, the impossibility of transcribers avoiding many mistakes, and the probability that interested persons would intentionally alter the sacred text, it really becomes a matter of considerable concern to enquire how the Bible has sustained these dangers and in what state it has survived to the present day. It is vain to fold our arms in security and take it for granted that it has not been materially affected by these and similar causes, that a kind Providence has carefully preserved it. This assumption will neither satisfy the enemies of the truth nor its enlightened friends.[104]

In the first volume of the *Biblical Repertory* (1825), an influential journal that he edited, Hodge published an essay by C. Beck entitled "Monogrammata Hermeneutices N.T." Beck, who cited the authority of previous German authors, pointed out the distinction between original autographs and copies and described the role of copyists' errors:

> The autographs appear to have perished early, and the copies which were taken, became more or less subject to those errors, which arise from the mistakes of transcribers, the false corrections of commentators and critics, from marginal notes, and from other sources.[105]

In a word, Charles Hodge was fully acquainted with the proposition that there were errors in the copies of the Scriptures and that the original autographs had been lost, as European scholars had also stated.[106]

Moreover Sandeen's suggestion that Charles Hodge treated lightly alleged "errors" in the Scriptures is not an accurate appraisal of the

Princetonian's beliefs. Sandeen attempts to sustain his contention by citing Hodge's "flecks in the Parthenon marble" illustration:

> The errors in matter of fact which skeptics search out bear no proportion to the whole. No sane man would deny that the Parthenon was built of marble, even if here and there a speck of sandstone should be detected in its structure. Not less unreasonable is it to deny the inspiration of such a book as the Bible, because one sacred writer says that on a given occasion twenty-four thousand, and another says twenty-three thousand, men were slain. Surely a Christian may be allowed to tread such objections under his feet.[107]

This one statement is the only documentation Sandeen proffers to demonstrate Hodge's laxness. According to Sandeen, A. A. Hodge, and B. B. Warfield could not maintain this "flexible" attitude of Charles Hodge, and thus they retreated to the "inerrancy in the original autographs" defense.[108]

Sandeen, regrettably, does not cite Charles Hodge's next lines following the Parthenon illustration.

> Admitting that the Scriptures do contain, in a few instances, discrepancies which with our present means of knowledge, we are unable satisfactorily to explain, they furnish no rational ground for denying their infallibility.[109]

Elsewhere in his theology text, Charles Hodge declares:

> The whole Bible was written under such an influence as preserved its human authors from all error, and makes it for the Church the infallible rule of faith and practice.[110]

In other words, Charles Hodge did not accept the possibility that the "errors" were genuine ones.

It is interesting to note that Charles Hodge had earlier discussed his attitude toward "alleged errors" in an important review of William Lee's "Inspiration of Holy Scripture, Its Nature and Proof," *Biblical Repertory* 29 (1857): 686–87. With regard to alleged contradictions that cannot be satisfactorily explained, he declared, "It is rational to confess our ignorance, but irrational to assume that what we cannot explain is inexplicable."[111] In his review Hodge gave a lengthy exposition of his belief in complete biblical infallibility.

As early as the 1880s some commentators cited Charles Hodge's Parthenon illustration as evidence that the well-known theologian, now deceased, had not believed in biblical infallibility. To this suggestion, B. B. Warfield responded in a categorical fashion:

> Dr. Charles Hodge justly characterizes those [alleged errors] that have been adduced by disbelievers in the plenary inspiration of the Scriptures, as "for the most part trivial," "only apparent," and marvelously few "of any real importance." They bear, he adds, about the same relation to the whole that a speck of sandstone detected here and there in the marble of the Parthenon would bear to the building.

[To this he adds in a footnote:] We have purposely adduced this passage here to enable us to protest against the misuse of it, which in the exigencies of the present controversy, has been made, as if Dr. Hodge was in this passage admitting the reality of the alleged errors. . . . How far Dr. Hodge was from admitting the reality of error in the original Biblical text may be estimated from the frequency with which he asserts its freedom from error in the immediately preceding context.[112]

Sandeen's presentation of Charles Hodge as one who entertained a flexible attitude toward alleged errors in the biblical text is not well substantiated by the Princetonian's writings.

Like his mentor Archibald Alexander, Charles Hodge acknowledged errors of transcription in present-day versions of the Bible, but these discrepancies in no way weakened his faith in the infallibility of the original autographs.[113]

Still another Princetonian who shared this view was Francis L. Patton. In 1869, four years after his graduation from the seminary and (according to Sandeen) fully ten years before A. A. Hodge first articulated the original-autographs theory, Patton published *The Inspiration of the Scriptures*. The chapter entitled "Explication of the Doctrine of Inspiration" opens with the following italicized statement: "*When it is claimed that the Scriptures are inspired, it must be understood that we refer to the original manuscripts.*"[114] Patton explains:

This remark is necessary in view of the objections which are based on the various readings of MSS. and on differences in translations. The books of the Bible as they came from the hands of their writers were infallible. The autographs were penned under divine guidance. It is not claimed that a perpetual miracle has preserved the sacred text from the errors of copyists. The inspired character of our Bible depends, of course, upon its correspondence with the original inspired manuscripts. These autographs are not in existence, and we must determine the correct text of Scripture in the same way that we determine the text of any of the ancient classics.[115]

Thus a third Princetonian—a graduate of the seminary who would later become a professor (1881) and president at Princeton (1902)—plainly argued that the inerrancy of the Bible extends only to the original autographs.[116]

When this background is taken into consideration, we can understand better why A. A. Hodge and B. B. Warfield did not view themselves as special innovators when they crafted their 1881 article on inspiration. They understood that their predecessors at Princeton held the doctrine of biblical infallibility in the original autographs as did Christians from other communions and other centuries.[117] Moreover, despite a modern-day assumption to the contrary, A. A. Hodge and B. B. Warfield did not use the word *inerrancy* in that article, but used the more traditional word *infallibility* and expressions like "without error."[118] And, irony of ironies given Sandeen's perspective, they were accused by a few conservative critics of having probably "let down the claims of inspiration too low."[119] Sandeen's suggestion that "the first reference to the original autographs in the Princeton Theology occurs in 1879" and his suggestion that the 1881 inspiration article represented the "formulation of a new doctrine" have a very definite misleading character.[120]

The Princetonians and the Witness of the Holy Spirit

Sandeen makes rather categorical claims about the role of the Holy Spirit in the theology of the Princetonians:

> The witness of the Spirit, though not overlooked, cannot be said to play any important role in Princeton thought. It is with the external not the internal, the objective not the subjective, that they deal.[121]

The Princetonians departed from Reformed thought by deemphasizing the Holy Spirit. They attempted to "adapt theology to the methodology of Newtonian science."[122]

Theodore Bozeman, who has studied the Old School Princetonians with care, cautions us concerning Sandeen's assessment:

> Ernest R. Sandeen's comment that "it is with the external not the internal" that Princetonian Old Schoolers dealt is a substantial exaggeration, as applied to the antebellum development.[123]

Sandeen's analysis is particularly misleading in its treatment of Charles Hodge. Sandeen rightfully proposes that the Westminster Confession insists that only the witness of the Holy Spirit can convince a person that the Scriptures are authoritative and come from God. But then he declares that Charles Hodge substituted a doctrine of inspiration for Westminster's witness of the Spirit.[124] For Hodge had written:

> The infallibility and divine authority of the Scriptures are due to the fact that they are the word of God; and they are the word of God because they were given by the inspiration of the Holy Spirit.[125]

Unfortunately, Sandeen has misunderstood both the Westminster Confession and Charles Hodge. The Confession does acknowledge that the Bible has its authority because it is the inspired Word of God, but it also proposes that we *recognize* the Bible's authority because of the confirming witness of the Holy Spirit within us. Chapter I, section IV of the Westminster Confession contains a statement that Sandeen fails to cite in his discussion of this matter:

> The authority of the holy Scripture, for which it ought to be believed and obeyed, dependeth not upon the testimony of any man or church, but wholly upon God (who is truth itself), the Author thereof; and therefore it is to be received, because it is the Word of God.[126]

Then chapter I, section V explains that our full persuasion and assurance of the infallible truths and authority of the Scripture are ultimately founded on the inward work of the Holy Spirit.[127] In brief, the Bible receives its authority from God Himself (it is God's Word); it does not become God's Word because we recognize its authority.

Charles Hodge understood the work of the Holy Spirit well. In his writings are pertinent discussions about the role of the Holy Spirit in confirming biblical authority. In his important article "Inspiration" (1857) Hodge declares:

> Faith therefore in Christ involves faith in the Scriptures as the word of God, and faith in the Scriptures as the word of God, is faith in their plenary inspiration. That is, it is the persuasion that they are not the product of the fallible intellect of man, but of the infallible intellect of God. This faith, as the apostle teaches us, is not founded on reason, i.e. on arguments addressed to the understanding, nor is it induced by persuasive words addressed to the feelings, but it rests in the demonstration of the Spirit. This demonstration is internal. It does not consist in the outward array of evidence, but in a supernatural illumination imparting spiritual discernment, so that its subjects have no need of external teaching, but this anointing teacheth them what is truth.[128]

In his *Systematic Theology* Hodge describes the role of the Holy Spirit in determining our theology:

> The effort is not to make the assertions of the Bible harmonize with the speculative reason, but to subject our feeble reason to the mind of God as revealed in his Word, and by his Spirit in our inner life.[129]

In a Sunday afternoon discussion with the students at Princeton Seminary (December 18, 1858), Hodge proposed that "faith is the conviction of the truth contained in the word of God founded on the testimony of the Holy Ghost."[130] Charles Hodge was well aware of the Holy Spirit's role in confirming the authority of the Scriptures to the believer. He emphasized this teaching in his instruction concerning spiritual illumination, a doctrine that Archibald Alexander also accented.[131]

A. A. Hodge, Charles Hodge's son, was committed to the same belief. Like John Calvin and the Westminster divines, A. A. Hodge took note of the external evidences for the Scripture's authority. But, also like his predecessors, Hodge argued that the witness of the Holy Spirit ultimately leads the believer to accept the Bible's authority:

> Yet . . . the highest and most influential faith in the truth and authority of the Scriptures is the direct work of the Holy Spirit on our hearts. The Scriptures to the unregenerate man are like light to the blind. They may be felt as the rays of the sun are felt by the blind, but they cannot be fully seen. The Holy Spirit opens the blinded eyes and gives due sensibility to the diseased heart, and thus assurance comes with the evidence of spiritual experience.[132]

As judged by this forthright statement, A. A. Hodge does not appear to have minimized the import of the Holy Spirit in confirming the Bible's authority to the believer.

Built on a misreading of the Westminster Confession and of the Princetonians' own writings, Sandeen's discussion of their teachings about the witness of the Holy Spirit and Holy Scripture does not accurately reflect their viewpoints. However, Sandeen points out correctly that B. B. Warfield did tend to emphasize the external evidences for the Bible's authority.[133]

THE "INERRANCY OF THE ORIGINAL AUTOGRAPHS" IN THE WIDER CONTEXT OF AMERICAN AND EUROPEAN EVANGELICAL THOUGHT

Professor Sandeen's presentation of the Princetonians generally portrays them as innovators, theologically quite removed from "the Reformed tradition" and from other Christian communions. We have proposed earlier that in reality their commitment to biblical infallibility echoed the teachings of various Christians, from St. Augustine to Calvin to William Whitaker to William Ames. Moreover their emphasis on the infallibility of the original autographs was shared by other Evangelicals in the nineteenth century. These Evangelicals, like earlier Christian humanists, assumed that the textual critic should attempt to recover the originals to whatever extent it is possible to do so, and that the Bible's claims about its own inspiration applied only to the original writings.[134]

The Original-Autograph Hypothesis in England and America

Lest the impression be conveyed that only Princetonians held the doctrine of the complete infallibility of the original autographs, a brief examination of the views of their contemporaries is in order. An extensive—albeit incomplete—survey of books and periodical articles published between 1800 and 1880 in the United States and Great Britain reveals that no fewer than thirty-five writers expressed a view resembling the one articulated by the Princetonians.[135] Limitations of space prohibit the inclusion of references to all of these; nevertheless a representative sampling follows. These statements should be studied in their full contexts.

One of the earliest nineteenth-century articulations of this view was found in *An Essay on the Inspiration of the Holy Scriptures of the Old and New Testament*, published in 1800 by Scottish divine John Dick. He wrote:

> While we admire the care of divine providence in the preservation of the Scriptures, we do not affirm that all the transcribers of them were miraculously guarded against error. Various motives, among which a veneration for the sacred books may be considered as having exerted the chief influence, contributed to render them scrupulously careful; but that they were under no infallible guidance, is evident from the different readings, which are discovered by a collation of manuscripts, and the mistakes in matters of greater or less importance, observable in them all.

> A contradiction, which would not be imputed to the blunder of a transcriber, but was fairly chargeable on the sacred writers themselves, would completely disprove their inspiration.[136]

In a subsequent two-volume work, published posthumously in 1836, Dick warns that "no single manuscript can be supposed to exhibit the original text, without the slightest variation; it is to be presumed that in all manuscripts, errors more or fewer in number are to be found."[137]

In December 1803, the *Connecticut Evangelical Magazine* published an article entitled "On Inspiration" in which the author concludes "that the words of scripture are from God as well as the matter." He adds that because

> the scriptures were designed to be translated into different languages, this made it more necessary that they should be written, at first, with peculiar accuracy and precision. Men always write with exactness when they expect their writings will be translated into various languages. And upon this ground, we may reasonably suppose, that the Divine Spirit dictated every thought and word to the sacred penmen, to prevent, as much as possible, errors and mistakes from finally creeping into their writings by the translation of them into other languages.[138]

Thus was the importance of a perfect and error-free original underscored.

A short-lived periodical entitled *Spirit of the Pilgrims* and published in Boston from 1828 to 1833 carried an extended serialization called "The Inspiration of the Scriptures." The author, identified simply as "Pastor," was unequivocal in his belief that inspiration extends only to the original autographs of Scripture:[139]

> Instances of incorrectness in the present copies of the Scriptures, cannot be objected to the inspiration of the writers.
> How can the fact, that God has not infallibly guided all who have *transcribed* his word, prove that he did not infallibly guide those who *originally* wrote it? ... And if, in some instances, we find it necessary to admit, that in *the present copy* of the Scriptures there are *real* contradictions; even this cannot be relied on as a proof, that the original writers were not divinely inspired; because these contradictions may be owing to the mistakes of transcribers.[140]

Similarly an article in the *Christian Review* (1844) posits that

> the objection to the plenary inspiration of the Scriptures, from the inaccuracy of the translations, and the various readings of the ancient manuscript copies, is totally irrelevant. For what we assert is, the inspiration of the *original* Scriptures, not of the translations, or the ancient copies. The fact, that the Scriptures were divinely inspired, cannot be expunged or altered by any subsequent event. ... The integrity of the copies has nothing to do with the inspiration of the original.[141]

The author then adds the disclaimer frequently found in these other references as well: "It is, however, well known that the variations are hardly worthy to be mentioned."[142]

One of the more popular nineteenth-century works on inspiration was translated from the French as early as 1841. *Theopneusty, or, the Plenary Inspiration of the Holy Scriptures* by Louis Gaussen was reprinted many times, and the *Methodist Quarterly Review*'s description of Gaussen as "the ablest writer of our age on this subject" characterizes the esteem in which this work and its author were held by some, but not all, Evangelicals.[143] In his definition of inspiration, Gaussen says that the sacred books "contain no errors; all their writings are inspired of God" and the Holy Spirit guided the authors "even in the employment of the words they were to use, and to preserve them from all error, as well as from every omission."[144] As to the relative purity of translations, he asks:

> Who does not there perceive, at what an immense distance all these considerations place the original text from the translation, in respect to the importance of verbal inspiration! Between the translation of the divine thoughts into human words, and the simple version of these words into other words, the distance is as great as that between heaven and earth.[145]

For Gaussen, as for the Princetonians (who were familiar with his work), the Scriptures taught their own infallibility, which extended to the originals, not to translations or copies.[146]

A *Bibliotheca Sacra* review (1858) of William Lee's volume on inspiration includes the following clarifying statement regarding the divine originals:

> It should be understood, however, that when speaking of the inspiration of the sacred writings, we refer only to the original copies. We refer to them as they were when they came from the hands of the inspired penmen. We do not believe in the inspiration of transcribers, or translators, or interpreters.... We do not hold to the perfection of the Septuagint, or of our English version, or of any other version.[147]

In his *Inspiration of the Scriptures*, Alexander Carson argues that one can believe in the inspiration of the original and deny the inspiration of every translation.[148] David Dyer in his book *The Plenary Inspiration of the Old and New Testaments* (1849) writes:

> It is not a sound objection to this doctrine [of inspiration] *that there are found occasional inaccuracies in the statements of Scripture, or instances of apparent disagreement among its writers.* For these inaccuracies are, at best, but slight. They never refer to predictions, doctrines, or precepts, but to matters of limited application, and of comparatively little moment, and should be attributed to transcribers, and not to the original writers.[149]

Bishop J. C. Ryle's preface to the first volume of his *Expository Thoughts on the Gospels* is devoted to his convictions on the matter of inspiration. He writes:

> I feel no hesitation in avowing that I believe in the "plenary inspiration" of every word of the original text of Holy Scripture.... I grant the existence of occasional difficulties, and apparent discrepancies, in Scripture. They are traceable, in some cases, I believe, to the errors of early transcribers; and in others to our ignorance of explanatory circumstances and minute links and details.[150]

Ryle's preface was deemed important enough to be reprinted in the 1875 volume of a St. Louis–based periodical called *The Truth: or Testimony for Christ*.[151]

A final sampling illustrates that the currency of this view of inspiration extended across denominational and confessional barriers. An 1868 reviewer in the *Baptist Quarterly* states:

> Of course inspiration can be predicated only of the original Scriptures, because they only are the writings of inspired men. There is no evidence that these books have been miraculously preserved from errors of transmission.... Nor can translators and interpreters, or their work, claim exemption from human infirmity.[152]

The Baptist Alvah Hovey claims infallibility for the original autographs in his *Manual of Systematic Theology and Christian Ethics* published in 1877.[153] Concerning the present copies of Scripture, A. H. Kremer, writing in the *Reformed Quarterly Review* (1879), asks:

> Admitting some defects in the translations from the original, or some omissions, and even interpolations in the transcribing, is it not of infinite moment to have had a true and perfect original text?[154]

A treatise in the *Methodist Quarterly Review* (1868) defines the role of biblical criticism as "ascertaining the precise words of Holy Scripture as they stood in the original autographs of the sacred writers."[155] In 1855 Henry Boynton Smith delivered a sermon before the Presbyterian Synod of New York and New Jersey in which he gave this explication of the doctrine of inspiration as taught in 2 Timothy 3:16:

> We are to adduce the evidence that this position [on inspiration] holds true of the original, canonical Scriptures, that they are given by a divine inspiration, that they are the word of God, and, as such, an infallible and final authority for faith and life.[156]

Another Presbyterian opinion on the matter was expressed in the July 1851 issue of the *Southern Presbyterian Review*. The author affirms that the canonical books of Scripture are

> *really inspired*, and to such a degree that the writers were, by divine influence, infallibly secured from committing mistakes and errors in regard to their *ideas* and *words*, while they were discharging the duties of their office.[157]

Such influence, of course, extended only to the originals, and although

> various readings may be found, on comparing different manuscripts and translations; though alterations of letters and vowel-points may have

been made; and though some interpolations and errors, in consequence of the ignorance and carelessness of transcribers, or of their too scrupulous regard to calligraphy, may have been perpetrated; yet it is the decisive opinion of the most judicious, that the worst manuscript extant would not pervert a single article of faith, weaken the force of one moral precept, nor impair the credibility of any history, prophecy or miracle which these books record.[158]

The author notes, as did so many of his contemporaries, that what is truly remarkable is not the incidence of error in present-day copies, but that there are so *few* discrepancies after centuries of transmission.

The paragraphs above typify conservative views of inspiration in the nineteenth century. They cast serious doubt on Sandeen's assertion that the Princetonians created a "unique apologetic" by contending that the Scriptures were infallible in the original autographs.[159] Whatever else the Princeton doctrine of inspiration might have been—and Sandeen lays a number of charges at its feet—it clearly was not unique.

The Significance of Complete Biblical Infallibility: A Reconsideration

Sandeen argues that the article on inspiration (1881) by A. A. Hodge and B. B. Warfield marked still another innovation at Princeton: "Princeton in this article took its stand upon the absolute inerrancy of the Bible and, in a sense, seemed to risk the whole Christian faith upon one proved error."[160] By implication this stance was an obvious departure from those of earlier Princetonians and an aberration from the beliefs of other Christians.

A closer examination of Archibald Alexander's writings and those of other Evangelicals belies Sandeen's interpretation. Alexander, a Princeton founder and first professor, certainly did not take lightly the possibility of error in the Bible. In his review of Leonard Woods's "Lectures on the Inspiration of the Scriptures" published in the *Biblical Repertory*, Alexander writes:

> While it is evident, that contradictions merely apparent prove nothing against inspiration, it is equally certain, that real contradictions would furnish the strongest evidence against the inspiration of the words in which they were found.[161]

In his *Evidences of Authenticity, Inspiration, and Canonical Authority of the Holy Scriptures*, Alexander objects to the view of inspiration that posits

> that, while, in all matters of real importance, the penmen of the Scriptures were guided by a plenary inspiration, they were left to their own unassisted powers in trivial matters, and the relation of unimportant circumstances; and in such matters have, therefore, fallen into mistakes in regard to trivial circumstances.[162]

To this view Alexander responds that "it is in itself an improbable supposition, that the Spirit of God should infallibly guide a writer in some parts of his discourse, and forsake him in other parts."[163] He concludes:

> If we find a witness mistaken in some particulars, it weakens our confidence in his general testimony. And could it be shown that the evangelists had fallen into palpable mistakes in facts of minor importance, it would be impossible to demonstrate that they wrote any thing by inspiration.[164]

Princeton's founder, then, did not take lightly the possibility of error in the Scriptures, for the presence of such error would impugn the integrity of the entire text.

Other Evangelical Protestants had earlier expressed sentiments similar to those of A. A. Hodge and B. B. Warfield in their works. The influential Methodist theologian Samuel Wakefield wrote in his *Complete System of Christian Thought* (1869):

> But if it is once granted that they [the Scriptures] are in the least degree alloyed with error, an opening is made for every imaginable corruption. And to admit that the sacred writers were only occasionally inspired, would involve us in the greatest perplexity; because, not knowing when they were or were not inspired, we could not determine what parts of their writings should be regarded as the infallible word of God.[165]

The Lutheran C. F. W. Walther put the matter this way in 1858:

> He who imagines that he finds in Holy Scripture even only one error, believes not in Scripture, but in himself; for even if he accepted everything else as truth, he would believe it not because Scripture says so, but because it agrees with his reason or with his heart.[166]

Charles Finney, the famous evangelist, criticized an author who denied the infallibility of historical sections in the Bible:

> The ground taken by him is that the *doctrinal* parts of the New Testament are inspired, but the *historical* parts, or the mere narrative, are uninspired.
>
> Who will not see at first blush, if the writers were mistaken in recording the acts of Christ, there is equal reason to believe they were mistaken in recording the doctrines of Christ?[167]

Then again, we recall the sentiments of William Whitaker (1588), who cited Augustine:

> For, whatever Erasmus may think, it is a solid answer which Augustine gives to Jerome: "If any, even the smallest lie be admitted in the scriptures, the whole authority of scripture is presently invalidated and destroyed."[168]

To perceive a close relationship between complete biblical infallibility and biblical authority was not an innovative inference of A. A. Hodge and B. B. Warfield.[169]

SANDEEN'S INTERPRETATION OF THE PRINCETONIANS: THE NEED FOR A REVISION

Our reservations about Professor Sandeen's interpretation of the Princetonians' attitudes toward Holy Scripture are admittedly serious ones. Regrettably, they lead us to the conclusion that his interpretation should be thoroughly revised. First, it depends too much on the author's misconstrued perception of the history of Reformed theology. Second, the interpretation misleadingly posits the premise that the word *inerrancy* signified connotations for contemporaries different from connotations that they associated with the word *infallibility*. But Sandeen never fully explains how the meaning of the word *inerrancy* differed from the meaning of *infallibility*, nor does he explain his principles for evaluating the alleged doctrinal developments the use of *inerrancy* provoked.[170] Moreover we know that a contemporary such as the liberal Protestant William Newton Clarke apparently viewed the two words as synonymous.[171] Third, the interpretation unfairly paints the Princetonians into a corner. It does not situate them well in the broad sweep of Protestant discussions of the Bible in nineteenth-century America and England. The Princetonians' viewpoints and those of dispensationalists about complete biblical infallibility are made to appear parochial, whereas in fact Christians from diverse communions shared their perspective. And finally, it does not do justice to the Princetonians' teachings about the subjective character of truth as apprehended by the Christian believer through the witness of the Holy Spirit. Several of the Princetonians did strongly emphasize the "external" evidences for biblical authority, but they did not slight the witness of the Holy Spirit.

This brief study, itself more a sketch than a rich painting, points to the genuine need for historians to do well-considered studies concerning the complex question of biblical authority in nineteenth-century America. George Marsden's admirable volume *Fundamentalism and American Culture* (1980) points the way in this regard. Marsden suggests that other writers besides the Princetonians may have stimulated the commitment of many Fundamentalists to biblical inerrancy.[172] But he unadvisedly explains the nineteenth-century Princetonians' own concern for the infallible words of Scripture by arguing that "Baconianism" and Common Sense philosophy greatly conditioned this interest.[173] We should recall, however, that some Christians from Augustine to Calvin, who had not experienced these influences, viewed the very words of Scripture as important, while at the same time they acknowledged the great "truths" of the Bible (many becoming caught up in complex allegorical interpretations). And like John Vander Stelt, Marsden does not give adequate play to the Princetonians' teaching about the Holy Spirit, the doctrine of illumination (through A. A. Hodge), and the subjective character of truth.[174] His insightful study, then, makes its most significant contributions in sorting out the wide-ranging factors that prompted "Fundamentalists" from diverse denominations to live out their faith in the ways that they did. It does not advance our knowledge greatly concerning the Princetonians and truth.[175] Moreover with its wide-angle scope and its focus on other subjects it does not afford us a detailed analysis of biblical authority in the nineteenth century. That subject still awaits its historian or historians.

In this paragraph let us suggest several questions that may be suitable for exploration in any future comprehensive study of biblical authority as it relates to the Princetonians and other American Protestants. Is it possible, using the techniques now available to historians of the book trade, to determine the reading clientele of such popular works as William Lee's *Inspiration of Holy Scriptures: Its Nature and Proof* (1854), Louis Gaussen's *Theopneusty, or, the Plenary Inspiration of the Holy Scriptures* (1841; multiple editions), Samuel Wakefield's *Complete System of Christian Thought* (1869), and the theology texts and articles written by other European and American writers? If we determine the general nature of those who read these works, we might understand more fully the theological and denominational contexts for the Fundamentalists' and other Christians' commitment to biblical inerrancy. It would be helpful to learn also about the readership of works that were opposed to this doctrine.[176] We recall that A. J. Gordon advocated a doctrine of biblical inerrancy, citing Lee's and Gaussen's works and doing so with the "almost complete lack of references to the Princeton men."[177] How did the Princetonians (and other Evangelicals) reconcile their commitments to Common Sense philosophy and aspects of Baconian thought with their very real emphasis on the work of the Holy Spirit in confirming biblical authority and with their announced commitment to Reformed anthropology? How did their idea that theology was a science relate to their concern for personal religious experience?[178] What does research in the correspondence, books, and reviews of nineteenth-century Protestants from diverse communions reveal about their perceptions of the Princetonians? Did contemporaries perceive them as isolated loners, quite removed from the "mainstream" of evangelical Christianity, or is that an estimation placed on them by recent commentators? By finding answers to these questions, historians may help take the speculative edge off studies of the nineteenth-century Princetonians and their relationship to other nineteenth-century Christians and twentieth-century Fundamentalists. There is no lack of room for innovative question-framing and dispassionate analysis (using many tools) in this field of study.[179]

Although we are genuinely impressed by certain aspects of Professor Sandeen's study and applaud its ground-breaking character concerning the origins of "Fundamentalism," we do find very real weaknesses in the author's treatment of the Princetonians' attitudes toward Scripture. Even our preliminary investigations lead us to this evaluation. It might be argued that this assessment stems from our own biases on this subject. Historians do have their biases, more or less discreetly displayed. We have ours. It is our hope that those segments of this chapter that are obviously slanted by blind-sided prejudice or marred by simple ignorance will be dismissed as dross. But it is also our hope that open-minded scholars will be prepared to rethink their commitment to several of the categories of Sandeen's influential interpretation should our presentation be compelling at points. The academic community at large loses some of its credibility if it is not prepared to enter into the uncomfortable but important enterprise of reassessing its "assured givens," particularly if there is a good reason to suspect their accuracy.[180] And Christians suffer if they lessen their commitment to a doctrine because they incorrectly assume that it is an innovation of late-nineteenth-century vintage.

PART III
THEOLOGICAL ESSAYS

THE BIBLICAL CONCEPT
OF TRUTH

Roger Nicole

Roger Nicole

Roger Nicole is Andrew Mutch Professor of Theology at Gordon-Conwell Theological Seminary, where he has served since 1945. He is a graduate of The Gymnase Classique in Lausanne, Switzerland (A.B.); The Sorbonne, Paris (M.A.); Gordon Divinity School (B.D., S.T.M. Th.D.); Harvard University (Ph.D.); and Wheaton College, Wheaton, Illinois (D.D.). He has served as pastor of the French Baptist churches in Worcester and Manchaug, Massachusetts. He has taught as Visiting Professor and lectured in many different institutions in the United States, Asia, and Europe.

Dr. Nicole has written *Moyse Amyraut: A Bibliography;* he has been a joint editor for *B. B. Warfield: A Bibliography* and for *Inerrancy and Common Sense.* He has written numerous articles for symposia and periodicals. He is a member of the Evangelical Theological Society, the American Academy of Religion, the Phi Alpha Chi Society, and the International Council on Biblical Inerrancy.

THE BIBLICAL CONCEPT
OF TRUTH

What is truth?" Pilate asked (John 18:38), perhaps not as a serious question since he did not wait to hear Jesus' answer. Yet his question epitomizes an age-long query that arises in the human mind and has been the object of many discussions throughout the history of philosophy.

Pilate seemed in that moment to secure a kind of edge over Christ by dint of his sophistication, but perhaps he had not stopped to consider that his skeptical position would prove unstable and self-destructive, whatever answer Jesus might choose to give.

If Christ had replied with a definition, "Truth is such and such," then Pilate would have been embarrassed in discussing it, for either he would have had to concede the definition to be true, and that would spell the collapse of his skepticism, or he would have had to declare the definition inadequate, but that would have revealed a preexisting distinction in his mind between true and false, adequate and inadequate, and so on, and that would have proved that he was not truly entitled to his skepticism: you cannot discuss a definition of truth unless you take for granted a real distinction between true and false!

If Jesus had replied, "The truth is too great to be defined," Pilate would have been in trouble again if he had wished to disagree, for a challenge to this proposition presupposes that it is seen as false. But that presupposition once again implies the very distinction between true and false that Pilate wanted to erase.

If Jesus had replied, "You are right, Pilate; there is no such thing as truth, and no distinction between true and false," Pilate might have been pleased to hear this flattering concession, especially right after Jesus had stated that he "was born ... and came into the world to testify to the truth" (John 18:37). But what would have been the value of any concession, and indeed the significance of any statement, if there is no distinction between true and false? This would mean there is no meaning to language, and even those who would rejoice in that could find no appropriate word to express their feeling!

The same predicament applies to all who deny that, or even question whether, there is objective validity in verbal statements: They presuppose such validity at least for their denial (or question)!

As Charles Malik pointedly stated, "They tell you, there is no truth; it is all a matter of impression, or at best of probability and statistics. . . .

This is all false. If taken absolutely, then there is something absolute, namely, that there is no truth."[1]

In contrast to any such skepticism, we find the word *truth* used repeatedly in Scripture, and it is my purpose to analyze how it is used and what is the range and substance of meaning that it bears.

IN THE OLD TESTAMENT

In the Old Testament (kjv) the word *truth* occurs some one hundred twenty times, "true" some twenty-seven times, "truly" twenty-three times, and "verily" fifteen times. In the great majority of the cases this reflects the use of the Hebrew word *'emet* or some of its cognates.

The root meaning of this group appears to connote "support"[2] or "stability," and it is not difficult to see how both "faithfulness" and "truth" would develop as the implications of this rootage. Faithfulness is the quality that provides an appropriate ground for confidence, which gives support to trust on the part of those who depend on the faithful one. Truth is that firm conformity to reality that proves to be wholly reliable, so that those who accept a statement may depend on it that it will not turn out to be false or deceitful.

Thus in the Old Testament we see a twofold implementation of the concept of *'emet*. We note that these two dimensions are complementary rather than mutually exclusive.

FAITHFULNESS

In this category of meaning truth denotes faithfulness and reliability on the part of a person who can be depended on to perform according to a promise or a principle, usually in a way that is seen as favorable to the speaker or to those addressed. The opposite of "true" in this respect is "unfaithful," "unreliable," or "deceitful."

It is noteworthy that in a considerable number of cases falling within this category the NIV translates *'emet* by "faithfulness" or cognates.

In Exodus 18:21, there is a kind of definition by parallelism: "... men who fear God, trustworthy men [literally, men of *'emet*] who hate dishonest gain...." (Cf. also Neh. 7:2.)

1. In the Old Testament a strong emphasis is placed on the faithfulness of God. This is made especially apparent in the expression *ḥesed we 'emet* ("mercy and truth"), which is descriptive of God's attitude in a number of passages (Gen. 24:27; Gen. 32:10 [cf. Ps. 108:4]; Exod. 34:6; Josh. 2:14; 2 Sam. 2:6; Ps. 25:10; 40:10, 11; 57:3, 10; 61:7; 85:10; 86:15; 89:14; 115:1; 117:2; 138:2; Mic. 7:20).[3] Other passages refer to *'emet* as God's attribute:

> Neh. 9:33: "You have acted faithfully, while we did wrong."
> Ps. 30:9: "your faithfulness" (cf. Ps. 54:5; 71:22; 85:11; 91:4; 146:6; Isa. 38:18, 19; 42:3).

Isa. 61:8: "In my faithfulness I will reward them and make an everlasting covenant with them."

Zech. 8:8: "I will be faithful and righteous to them as their God."

What is stated of God as a person is projected also to His activity:

Ps. 69:13: "In your great love, O God, answer me with your *sure* salvation [salvation of *'emet*]."

Ps. 111:7–8: "The works of his hand are *faithful* and just; all his precepts are trustworthy. They are steadfast for ever and ever, done in *faithfulness* and uprightness."

Ps. 132:11: "The Lord swore an oath to David, a *sure* oath that he will not revoke."

When this usage applies to God's Word, the meaning passes naturally into that of truth and forms a connection between the two dimensions we are attempting to distinguish.

The whole concept may head up into the formulation that Yahweh is the God of truth (e.g., 2 Chron. 15:3; Ps. 31:5; Jer. 10:10), and here the implication is both that He is the only true God and that as God He sums up in Himself the fullness of faithfulness and truth.[4]

2. What is said of God can also be applied to human beings, for their faithfulness may reflect the faithfulness of God.

Josh. 24:14: "Fear the Lord and serve him *faithfully* with all your heart."

Ps. 145:18: "The Lord is near . . . to all who call on him *in truth*."

Isa. 48:1: "You who take oaths . . . but not *in truth* or righteousness."

Ezek. 18:8–9: "He . . . judges fairly between man and man. . . . He . . . *faithfully* keeps my laws."

Hos. 4:1: "There is no *faithfulness*, no love, no acknowledgment of God."

Zech. 8:16: "Render *true* and sound judgment."

This meaning may develop into a description of a course of action marked by integrity, as for instance, 1 Kings 2:4; 3:6; 2 Kings 20:3; 2 Chronicles 31:20; 32:1; Isaiah 38:3; 59:14, 15.

3. Finally, in this category we observe that the idea of faithfulness or reliability can actually be extended to objects that are not endowed with the capacity for decision:

Josh. 2:12: "a *sure* sign"

2 Kings 20:19: "peace and *security* in my lifetime" (cf. Isa. 39:8 and Jer. 33:6)

Esther 9:30: "words of goodwill and *assurance*"

Prov. 11:18: "a *sure* reward"

Jer. 14:13: "lasting peace" (literally, peace of *'emet*)

Jer. 32:41: "I . . . will *assuredly* plant them."

Zech. 8:19: "Therefore love *truth* and peace."

CONFORMITY TO FACT

A number of the examples of the preceding category are leading in the direction of the meaning of *'emet* in this section. Here the fundamental issue is that *'emet* represents that which is conformed to reality in contrast to anything that would be erroneous or deceitful.

1. Examples of this usage abound. We may start with passages like Deuteronomy 13:14; 17:4; 22:20, where the context is a legal investigation and the words "If it is true" mean "If the charge is substantiated." In Isaiah 43:9 the context is similar and the verdict "It is true" is sought in response to the hearing of witnesses.

In a number of passages we encounter expressions like "speaking the truth" (Prov. 8:7; Jer. 9:5; Dan. 11:2; Zech. 8:16). In Psalm 15:2 this is contrasted with "slandering," giving a false and malicious report. Passages in which someone's words are stated to be true are closely akin to this usage (Gen. 42:16; 2 Sam. 7:28; Ps. 119:160; Prov. 22:21 [twice]; Eccl. 12:10).

Similarly we read of a true report (1 Kings 10:6), a true vision (Dan. 8:26), a true message (Dan. 10:1). Prophets are summoned to speak "nothing but the truth" (1 Kings 22:16; 2 Chron. 18:15), and others may acknowledge the genuineness of their mission by saying, "The word of the Lord from your mouth is the truth" (1 Kings 17:24).

Scripture commends "truthful lips" (Prov. 12:19), truthful witness (Prov. 14:25; Jer. 42:5), true instruction (Mal. 2:6; literally, the law of truth).

"In truth" comes to mean "really" (Judg. 9:15, 16, 19; Isa. 10:20; Jer. 26:15; 28:9).

2. In close connection with what has just been said, we note that *'emet* may connote what is authentic, reliable, or simply "right."

      Gen. 24:48: "the right road"

      Jer. 2:21: "sound and *reliable* stock"

      Prov. 29:14: "judge *with fairness*" [literally "in truth"]

      Neh. 9:13: "just laws" [literally "laws of truth"]

      Zech. 7:9: "true justice"

      Jer. 4:2: "swear in a truthful, just and righteous way"

This meaning also appears perhaps in the expression "truth and peace" in 2 Kings 20:19; Isaiah 39:8; Jeremiah 14:13; Zechariah 8:19, in which a period of true prosperity is contemplated.

3. In line with what has developed thus far, and as an extension and fulfillment of it, *'emet* has come to mean "truth" as the embodiment of God's wise and merciful pattern for human life, designated by the terms *law, precepts, commandments, ordinances, judgment,* etc. This connotation is found especially in the Psalms but may be discovered elsewhere as well:

      Ps. 25:5: "guide me in your truth"

      Ps. 26:3: "I walk ... in your truth." Cf. also Ps. 86:11.

      Ps. 43:3: "let them [your light and your truth] guide me"

Ps. 51:6: "you desire truth in the inner parts"
(The exact connotation of "truth" here is debatable, but the passage fits well in this category.)
Ps. 119:43: "the word of truth"
Ps. 119:142: "your law is true"
Ps. 119:151: "your commands are true"
Ps. 119:160: "your words are true"
Prov. 23:23: "buy the truth and do not sell it"
Dan. 8:12: "truth was thrown to the ground"
Dan. 9:13: "giving attention to your truth"

Zechariah speaks of the "City of Truth" (Zech. 8:3) and Daniel of the "Book of Truth" (Dan. 10:21).

Thus we see two converging lines of meaning in the Old Testament. Neither is reducible to the other, yet they are not mutually conflicting. It is because truth is conformity to fact that confidence may be placed in it or in the one who asserts it, and it is because a person is faithful that he or she will be careful to make statements that are true. Meanwhile neither "factuality" nor "faithfulness" properly exhausts the meaning of *'emet*.[5]

Negatively, *'emet* stands in contrast to a number of terms variously rendered "deceit," "error," "falsehood," "guile," "lie," "vanity," and their cognates. These represent in the main eight different Hebrew roots occurring in the aggregate some three hundred times in the Old Testament. Almost uniformly there is condemnation of such practices, whether expressly, or in the instances in which people are presented as having recourse to lies. One notable exception is the case of Rahab, who lied in order to protect the "spies," but we should note that it is not her lie that is praised, but rather her faith in the God of Israel, which led her to make common cause with His people rather than with hers (Heb. 11:31; James 2:25).

Occasionally God is represented as leading people into some delusions (1 Kings 22:22–23; 2 Chron. 18:21–22; Jer. 20:7; Ezek. 14:9–10). In such passages it is important to note that it is not God Himself who actually takes the deceitful course, but some evil spirit who functions under the sovereign rule of God. Thus God's just retribution falls on those who incurred His displeasure (cf. Ps. 73:18; 81:12; Isa. 6:10; cf. in the same vein Rom. 1:26, 28; 2 Thess. 2:11).[6] The suggestion that God Himself could be a deceiver or a liar is contrary to the repeated and very express affirmations of Scripture in both the Old and the New Testaments.

Num. 23:19: "God is not a man that he should lie. . . ."
1 Sam. 15:29: "He who is the glory of Israel does not lie or change his mind."
Prov. 12:22: "The Lord detests lying lips, but he delights in men who are truthful."
John 3:33: "God is truthful."

Rom. 3:4: "Let God be true, and every man a liar."
2 Tim. 3:13: "He cannot disown himself."
Titus 1:2: "God, who does not lie. . . . "
Heb. 6:18: "It is impossible for God to lie."
1 John 1:5: "God is light; in him there is no darkness at all."

It is of course true that in many of the instances of Old Testament condemnation of lies, what is in view is some aggravated form of lying, such as lying under oath, or the spurious claims of false prophets pretending to have a message from God, or again the slanderous lies of false witnesses. Here the sins of perjury, blasphemy and grievous malice are added to that of falsehood, but the passages abound which condemn lying even without these complications (e.g., Ps. 5:7; 101:7; Prov. 6:17; 12:19, 22; Isa. 59:3). Lying is associated with some of the most glaring sins, such as robbery (Neh. 3:1), adultery (Jer. 23:14), murder (Isa. 59:3; cf. 7, 8), and pride (Ps. 119:69).

Thus the clear and insistent witness of the Old Testament in condemnation of all lies and deceit reinforces its strong commendation of *'emet* as faithfulness and veracity. Notably it provides impressive evidence to disprove the view sometimes advanced that "faithfulness" is the exclusive connotation of *'emet*. The combination of the positive and negative arguments appears well-nigh insuperable.

IN THE NEW TESTAMENT

As we pass from the Old Testament to the New we observe the shift from the Semitic mindset to the Greek idiom. Vrielink has cleverly quoted the prophecy of Noah in Genesis 9:27: "May Japheth live in the tents of Shem."[7]

We may note here three elements that provide a significant link between these two moments of special revelation. The first is the LXX translation that rendered *'emet* by the word *alētheia* and cognates in some six out of seven occurrences in the Hebrew canon. Etymologically this word has a more decidedly cognitive meaning than *'emet*. It is made up of the *alpha* privative and the root meaning "to be hidden," "to escape notice"; thus the etymological sense of *alētheia* could be expressed as "that which receives notice," "that which comes to be known," presumably by a correct perception of reality. Hence the idea of conformity to fact implicit in *'emet* becomes fairly naturally the key emphasis. The concept of faithfulness, on the other hand, which was a very important component of the meaning of *'emet* is now primarily represented by words of the family of *pistos*, "faithful," "reliable," "trustworthy." In a few cases words of this type actually are used by the LXX as the translation of *'emet*.[8]

A second connection between the Old and the New Testament is the use of expressions in which truth and grace are linked together, which reminds us of *ḥesed we 'emet* as noted above on page 288.

John 1:14: "full of grace and truth"
John 1:17: "Grace and truth came through Jesus Christ."
1 Cor. 13:6: "Love ... rejoices with the truth."
2 Cor. 6:6–7: "in sincere love; in truthful speech"
Eph. 4:15: "speaking the truth in love"
Eph. 5:9: "goodness, righteousness and truth"
Col. 1:6: "God's grace in all its truth"
2 Thess. 2:10: "They refused to love the truth [literally, they did not accept the love of the truth]."
1 Peter 5:12: "This is the true grace of God."
1 John 3:18: "Let us not love with words or tongue but with actions and in the truth."
2 John 1: "whom I love in the truth"
2 John 3: "Grace, mercy and peace ... will be with us in truth and love."
3 John 1: "Gaius, whom I love in truth"

A third feature that provides a tie between the Semitic idiom and the Greek of the New Testament is the use of the Hebrew word *"amen,"* which occurs at least 129 times in the New Testament.[9] Most of these (100) are found in the words of Jesus "Amen, I say to you" (Matthew 31 times, Mark 13 times, Luke 6 times, John [a double amen] 25 times). Twenty-seven more examples are found tied to doxologies or prayer.[10] The outstanding exception is Revelation 3:14, where Christ is called "the Amen, the faithful and true witness." Here we are reminded of Isaiah 65:16, where Yahweh is twice called "the God of amen," the God of truth. The maintenance of the Semitic "amen" in the midst of a text written in Greek (Τάδε λέγει ὁ ἀμήν, Rev. 3:14) manifests the impact of Hebraic concepts and language on the thought world and worship of the early church. The words *hallelujah*, *hosanna*, and *maranatha* and the occasions where the express words of Jesus are transcribed in the Gospels (Matt. 27:46; Mark 5:41; 7:34; 15:34) are other examples of this phenomenon.

The word *truth* and its cognates occur frequently in the New Testament, in fact 183 times.[11] As noted above, the connotation of "faithfulness," so common in the Old Testament, recedes into the background. In some cases the word *true* is actually linked with the word *pistos* "faithful" (Rev. 3:14; 19:11; 21:5; 22:6). The emphasis here is that the witness is speaking the truth and is worthy of confidence.

CONFORMITY TO FACT

The primary New Testament emphasis is clearly on truth as conformity to reality and opposition to lies or errors. This is seen in the use of the adverb *alethōs* ("truly") by which a genuine teacher, disciple, prophet, Israelite, etc., is distinguished from a spurious one, who appears under false pretense.[12]

Similarly the expression "in truth" contrasts what occurs in fact with what is imaginary or fallacious.[13] In Acts 12:9 the contrast is between factual reality and a dream or vision; in Philippians 1:18 it is between empty pretense and appropriate motivation; in 1 John 3:18 it is between mere verbal protestations of love and real love manifested by action.

That truth is viewed as factuality is made plain through expressions that combine "true" with "witness."[14] As Proverbs states (14:5), "A truthful witness does not deceive, but a false witness pours out lies."

In John 5:33 and 18:37 our Lord represents Himself as a witness *to* the truth. To give this witness is one of the purposes of His incarnation.

Moreover, several times we encounter expressions like "speaking the truth," "word of truth,"[15] sometimes reinforced by a statement that what is spoken is no lie.[16] This type of contrast is articulated in a number of ways:

> John 7:18: "[He] is a man of truth; there is nothing false about him."
> Rom. 3:7: "If my falsehood enhances God's truthfulness. . . . "
> 2 Cor. 6:8: "genuine, yet regarded as impostors"
> Eph. 4:25: "Put off falsehood and speak truthfully."
> James 3:14: "deny the truth" (literally, lie against the truth)
> 1 John 1:6: "If we claim to have fellowship with him [God] yet walk in the darkness, we lie and do not live by the truth."
> 1 John 2:4: "The man . . . is a liar, and the truth is not in him."
> 1 John 2:21: "No lie comes from the truth."
> 1 John 2:27: "real, not counterfeit"
> 1 John 4:6: "This is how we recognize the Spirit of truth and the spirit of falsehood."

Nowhere is this more forcefully presented than in the words of the Lord in reference to the devil: "He was a murderer from the beginning, not holding to the truth, for there is no truth in him. When he lies, he speaks his native language, for he is a liar and the father of lies" (John 8:44).

In sharp contrast to Satan, God is represented as true. The Father is the "true" God over against all idols or false gods (John 17:3; 1 Thess. 1:9; 1 John 5:20).[17]

God is not only the only genuine God, he is also one who is truthful.

> John 3:33: "God is truthful."
> John 7:28; 8:26: "He who sent me is true."
> Rom. 3:4: "Let God be true, and every man liar."
> Rev. 6:10: "Sovereign Lord, holy and true"

The truth is called God's truth (Rom. 1:25; 3:7; 15:8), for He has a stake in it. God's Word is truth (John 17:17; 2 Tim. 2:15; James 1:18). God's law is the embodiment of truth (Rom. 2:20). The gospel is the word of truth (Gal. 2:5, 14), which it is essential to know and accept in order to be saved (John 8:32; Eph. 1:13; Col. 1:5; 2 Thess. 2:13–14; 1 Tim. 2:4; 4:3; 2 Tim. 2:25; 3:7; Titus 1:1; Heb. 10:26) so that those who refuse to love the truth will perish (2 Thess. 2:10, 12).

Not only the Father, but also the Son is related to the truth. He came to witness to the truth (John 18:37); he was full of grace and truth (John 1:14); he is called faithful (or holy) and true (Rev. 3:7, 14; 19:11); he said "I am the truth" (John 14:6). Therefore the gospel is sometimes called the truth of Christ (2 Cor. 11:10; cf. Eph. 4:21). "The law was given through Moses; grace and truth came through Jesus Christ" (John 1:17).

Similarly the Holy Spirit is vitally interested in truth. He is called the Spirit of truth (John 14:17; 15:26; 16:13; 1 John 4:6). He will guide the disciples into all truth (John 16:13) and climactically He too is called "the truth" (1 John 5:6).

The close connection between Satan, darkness, and lying on one hand, and between God, light, and truth on the other hand (cf., e.g., 1 John 1:5–10) is probably the basis for a use of the word *truth* as connoting not merely conformity to fact, but that pattern of living that conforms to the revealed will of God.

Thus in 1 John 1:6 "to live by the truth" (literally "to do the truth") is the opposite of "to walk in darkness." The same contrast is found in John 3:20–21. Some passages speak of "obeying" (Gal. 5:7; 1 Peter 1:22) or "disobeying" (Rom. 2:8) the truth. James represents a wayward Christian as "wandering from the truth" (James 5:19). The "way of truth" in 2 Peter 2:2 corresponds to "walking in the truth" (2 John 4; 3 John 3–4). Perhaps the "belt of truth," mentioned in Ephesians 6:14 as a part of the Christian equipment for spiritual struggle, also fits into this category. Here we may also mention a request in Jesus' high-priestly prayer: "Sanctify them by the truth" (John 17:17; cf. v. 19), as well as the promise that the Spirit will guide the disciples "into the truth" (John 16:13). The immediate context may, it is true, emphasize a christological and eschatological content in this teaching, but the ethical is never far remote, and the distinction between dogmatics and ethics, while useful in the theological curriculum, is not to be pressed into a separation of doctrine and practice, which should always remain united.

COMPLETENESS

A notable group of passages, especially in the writings of John, exhibits a connotation of truth that goes beyond what has been discussed so far. Here the contrast is not so much between correct and false, but rather between complete and incomplete, definitive and provisional, full-orbed and partial.

> John 1:9: "the true light" (cf. 1 John 2:8)
> John 6:32: "true bread from heaven"
> John 6:55: "My flesh is real food and my blood is real drink."

John 15:1: "I am the true vine."

Heb. 8:2: "the true tabernacle set up by the Lord"

Heb. 9:24: "a man-made sanctuary that was only a copy of the true one"

In John 1:17 we read that "the law was given through Moses; grace and truth came through Jesus Christ." This does not deny the gracious character or the truth content of the Torah but it emphasizes that the administration of grace in its complete and ultimate form is the fruit of the incarnation of the Logos, "who came from the Father, full of grace and truth" (John 1:14). This category of meaning might also apply to John 4:23–24 where worshiping in "spirit and truth" is commended. This does not discredit the Old Testament worship in Jerusalem, mandated by God, but it presents this as only a foreshadowing of the full realization of worship made possible in the New Testament. Other possible examples of this usage may be found in 1 Corinthians 5:8 and 1 Peter 5:12.

The biblical view of truth (*'emeṭ-alētheia*) is that it is like a rope with several intertwined strands. It will not do to isolate the strands and deal with them separately, although they may be distinguished just as various lines in a telephone cable may be distinguished by color. *The full Bible concept of truth involves factuality, faithfulness, and completeness.* Those who have stressed one of these features in order to downgrade either or both of the others are falling short of the biblical pattern. Notably those who have stressed faithfulness, as if conformity to fact did not matter, are failing grievously to give proper attention to what constitutes probably a majority of the passages in which the word *truth* is used.

Truth, in the biblical sense, is ultimately associated with the triune God Himself as a perfection of His being. By His singular mercy truth is communicated in a finite though adequate measure to rational creatures, angelic and human, so they can distinguish between truth and error, veracity and mendacity, straightforwardness and deceptiveness. God is always on the side of what is true and right. Specifically He is always true to His word, so that faithfulness appears as a wondrous feature of His being, grounding full confidence on the part of the believers. In His faithfulness God will not stop with prefigurements and foreshadowings, but will provide to those who worship Him, true light, true bread, true life in Jesus Christ, the Savior full of grace and truth, who brought life and immortality to light through the Gospel (John 1:14; 2 Tim. 2:10).

A BRIEF ANNOTATED BIBLIOGRAPHY

Works marked with an asterisk are deemed particularly significant.

Berkouwer, G. C. and A. S. van der Woude, eds., *Wat is Waarheid?* Kampen: Kok, 1973. 194 pp. An interesting group of essays dealing with truth and verification.

*Blocher, Henri. "The Biblical Concept of Truth." *Themelios* 6/1 (1969): 47–61. An English translation of a French article that appeared in *Themelios* 4/2 (1967): 8–20; in *Ichthus*, and elsewhere. An excellent survey with the methodology of biblical theology with a careful delineation of the meaning of "truth" in various types of biblical literature.

Geisler, Norman L. "The Concept of Truth in the Inerrancy Debate." *Bibliotheca Sacra*, 137 (1980): 327–39. A trenchant advocacy of the correspondence view of truth.

Jepsen, Alfred. "*'aman*." In Botterweck and Ringgren, *TDOT*, 1:292–323. An extensive article on the Hebraic usage of all words in this category. Notable bibliography to 1970. This is a translation of the original German in *TWAT*.

Loretz, Oswald. *The Truth of the Bible*. New York: Herder, 1968. 182 pp. A well-documented volume advocating the authority and reliability of Scripture in spiritual matters only.

Maurer, J. H. *Wahrheit ist Richtigkeit und sonst-nichts?* Basel: n.p., 1966. A doctoral thesis for the University of Basel, with special emphasis on Anselm.

Müller, Eberhard, ed. *Der Gott der Wahrheit*. Berlin: Furche, 1936. 431 pp. A series of twenty-nine essays on various aspects of the subject from a variety of Protestant viewpoints.

Quell, Gottfried, Gerhard Kittel, and Rudolf Bultmann. "*Alētheia*." Kittel, ed. *TDNT*, 1:232–51. Quell deals with the Old Testament concept (232–37), Kittel with Rabbinic Judaism (237–38) and Bultmann with the Greek, Hellenistic, and New Testament usages (238–51). This is a thorough and helpful treatment, with some bibliography, notably an important article of R. Bultmann in *ZNW* 27 (1928): 113–63. In the original of *TWNT* this is found in 1:233–51.

Scott, Jack B. "*'aman*." In R. L. Harris, ed. *Theological Wordbook of the Old Testament*. Chicago: Moody, 1980. Vol. I, pp. 51–53. A brief but helpful summary.

*Thiselton, A. "Truth." In Colin Brown, ed. *NIDNTT*, III:874–902. A helpful and thorough discussion from an evangelical point of view, with a valuable discussion of various modern philosophical approaches (pp. 894–901). A substantial bibliography up to 1975 is appended. This is a greatly enlarged and developed version of the 1971 original by H. G. Link in L. Coenen, ed., *Theologisches Begriffslexikon zum N.T.* Pp. 1343–1355.

Thornwell, James H. *Discourses on Truth*. New York: Carter, 1855. 328
    pp. A series of chapel addresses by a prominent Presbyterian
    theologian of the South.
Thorson, Walter R. "The Concept of Truth in the Natural Sciences."
    Themelios. Vol. 5, no. 2 (1968), pp. 27–39. An interesting discus-
    sion from a scientist's point of view.
*Vos, Geerhardus. "'True' and 'Truth' in the Johannine Writings." *The
    Biblical Review* 12 (1927): 507–20. Reprinted in Richard Gaffin, ed.,
    *Redemptive History and Biblical Interpretation. The Shorter
    Writings of Geerhardus Vos*. Phillipsburg, N. J.: Presbyterian and
    Reformed, 1980. Pp. 343–51. A very insightful treatment by this
    penetrating exegete and theologian.
*Vrielink, J. H. *Het Waarheidsbegrip*. Nijkerk: Callenbach, 1956. 151 pp.
    A valuable thesis for the University of Utrecht.
Wildberger, H. "'*mn*." E. Jenni and C. Westermann, *Theologisches
    Handwörterbuch zum Alten Testament*. Munich: Kaiser, 1971. Vol.
    1, pp. 177–209. An unusually full and condensed treatment of
    this Hebrew root.

FAITH,
EVIDENCE,
AND THE SCRIPTURES

Paul Helm

Paul Helm

Paul Helm is a Senior Lecturer in Philosophy at the University of Liverpool, England, where he has taught since 1964. He is a graduate of the University of Oxford and has spent a year as a visiting professor at the University of Rhode Island. In addition to numerous articles in the philosophical journals, Mr. Helm has written *The Varieties of Belief, Divine Revelation,* and *Calvin and the Calvinists* and has edited *Divine Commands and Morality* and Jonathan Edwards' *Treatise on Grace.*

FAITH, EVIDENCE,
AND THE SCRIPTURES

Let us consider the following situation. Mrs. Jones is worried about her husband's loss of weight and his lassitude. With some difficulty (for her husband has never needed a doctor before) she persuades him to have a series of medical tests. The tests strongly support the view, the consultant tells her, that Mr. Jones has cancer. Mr. Jones says he has never felt fitter and that the consultant is probably incompetent.

In this situation there are three different kinds of questions that arise and need separate treatment: the question of whether or not Jones has cancer, the question of what evidence there is that he has cancer, and the question of what would persuade him to accept the diagnosis that he has cancer. These three questions are connected, but they are not the same question. Let us see why not.

The first question concerns what the facts are. If someone has cancer, this means that he has growths of a certain sort in his body, the presence of cancerous cells. This is what having cancer *is*. The second question concerns evidence. Cancer generally gives evidence of its presence, such as the development of certain lumps, loss of weight, and in certain cases the findings of x-rays or exploratory surgery. The two issues, whether someone has cancer and what the evidence for his having cancer is, are connected in the following way: Cancer normally or generally gives evidence of itself, and evidence of a certain sort is normally taken to be evidence for cancer. Cancer *normally* provides such evidence of itself; but it is necessary to allow for the possibility that there might be cancer but no evidence of it, or that there should be atypical evidence, or that there should be evidence of cancer but no cancer.

The third question concerns what will rationally convince someone that certain data are evidence for a certain condition—presumably such factors as attentiveness to the evidence, a willingness to accept its verdict however unpalatable, and so on. What *should* convince a person that he has cancer is enough evidence of the right kind. But often other nonrational factors (e.g., wants and predispositions of certain kinds) intervene to prevent this.

I

Exactly the same three questions arise about the Bible. Is the Bible the Word of God? What evidence is there for the Bible's being the Word of God? What evidence ought to persuade people that the Bible is the Word of God? These three questions, again, are distinct yet related. The first question is about the causal origins of the Bible. Does it come from God in a sense in which the *Times* or *Who's Who* do not come from God? In this chapter I am not going to dwell on what exactly is meant by the divine authorship of the Bible except to notice that the issue is basically a theological or metaphysical matter, bespeaking a relationship of a rather special kind between God, the Creator and ground of all being, and some aspect of His creation. The truth conditions of this are truths about God and His special relationship to certain human authors and not merely about the thought processes or literary habits of human authors. Perhaps it is fortunate that exploring the exact character of these truth conditions is not a matter that has to concern us.

What is going to concern us directly is the question, What evidence is there that the Bible is the Word of God? And also, though to a lesser extent, the question, What ought rationally to persuade someone to believe that the Bible is the Word of God? But although I will look at these questions directly I will not try to answer them directly by attempting to provide the evidence. Rather I will be concerned to ask what *sort* of questions these are and what *sort* of evidence might provide adequate answers.

The main thesis of this chapter is that the chief reasons for believing the Bible to be the Word of God are *religious* reasons. But "religious" here does not mean "subjective" or "irrational," but "concerning a person's bounden allegiance to God." Further, the evidence on which the Scriptures are to be considered to be the Word of God is chiefly *internal* evidence. The main part of the chapter will be concerned with setting out this thesis and defending it against certain objections. But first let us glance at certain other views, both in order to gain some perspective and to indicate the main deficiencies of such views.

The first view we can call *externalism*, which can be expressed as follows: the evidence of certain data that make no essential reference to the content of the Scriptures is logically necessary for the Bible's being accepted as the Word of God. The stress on logical *necessity* should be noted. External data are required to validate the Scriptures as the Word of God but they are not themselves sufficient to validate the Scriptures. Such a view does not hold that no attention needs to be paid to internal data but that such internal data are of no value unless they first meet certain tests.

The historical roots of this outlook, which has been very deeply entrenched in Anglo-American theology (to look no further), go back a long way. It was prominent in the writings of the eighteenth-century opponents of deism such as Joseph Butler and William Paley and even earlier in Thomas Aquinas.[1] But the actual example of this position that we will examine is that of Archibald Alexander (1772–1851), an influential Princeton theologian.

Alexander's approach, it must be remembered, is presupposed by what are, in his view, the convincing arguments of natural theology. Having established the existence and character of God by argument, the Christian apologist must then go on to establish that the Scriptures alone among all the books of the world are a credible revelation from God.

> That a revelation is possible, will not be called in question by any who believe in the existence of a God; nor can it be believed that there is anything in the notion of a revelation repugnant to the moral attributes of the Supreme Being. It cannot be inconsistent with the wisdom, goodness or holiness of God, to increase the knowledge of his intelligent creatures. The whole end of a revelation is to make men wiser, better, and happier; and what can be conceived more accordant with our ideas of divine perfection than this?[2]

Let us grant, for the sake of argument, both the legitimacy of the program of natural theology and its success. We can also grant the point made by Alexander in this quotation that the idea of revelation is logically consistent with the concept of God. Alexander goes on:

> Supposing a revelation to be given, what would be a satisfactory attestation of its divine origin? It must be some sign or evidence not capable of being counterfeited; something by which God should in some way manifest himself. And how could this be effected, but by the exertion of his power or the manifestation of his infinite knowledge; that is, by miracles, or by prophecies, or by both?[3]

Alexander is here considering the question of what sort of evidence there ought to be and he argues that initially at least the evidence ought to be external—miracles and prophecies. But notice the number of assumptions, which Alexander seems to regard as self-evident or at least perfectly reasonable, on which his argument rests:

1. The only satisfactory attestations of divine revelation are signs.
2. Such signs must be incapable of being counterfeited.
3. Only manifestations of divine power or infinite knowledge are sufficient to produce noncounterfeitable signs.
4. Miracles and prophecies are not counterfeitable.
5. Miracles and prophecies are the only noncounterfeitable signs and so they are the only satisfactory attestations of divine revelation.

None of these five propositions seems to be convincing, much less obviously true, and yet Alexander offers them as if they are unquestionable. Take 1, for example. May it not be true that great cheerfulness in the face of adversity, or financial prosperity, or inventiveness, or physical beauty are equally good attestations of divine revelation? And what about 2? It seems to be straightforwardly false, since miracles and prophecies have been and are counterfeited. And what about 3? May it not be the case that what is needed to produce noncounterfeitable signs is not *infinite* power, but just *very great* power?

The point of raising these questions is not to provide an alternative set of candidates to those Alexander produces and to argue that these are more reasonable than his, but to suggest two things about externalism. The first is that Alexander's argument relies on an extremely dubious appeal to what is obvious or reasonable; and second, that the form of the argument is badly conceived. The form of the argument—the strategy that Alexander, in common with all other externalists, uses—is that there is some obvious, unquestionable test or criterion of what is appropriate for a divine revelation and that the Bible, and only the Bible, meets it. But is this a properly conceived form of argument for the task in hand? Alexander does not argue that it is, but he assumes that it is. But, as we have seen, this form of argument is far from being self-evident.

We can see that a more general defect of externalism is the supposition that there is some a priori standard of reasonableness that the Scriptures must meet and do meet. But who is to decide what this standard is? And supposing that a standard can be agreed on, what is the force of calling it *reasonable*? The answer may be that what justifies our calling it reasonable is that there is some a priori likelihood that anything that will count as a revelation will meet this standard. But this would be ludicrous, for such a revelation is by definition (and by Alexander's own understanding of it) unique and unparalleled, a supernatural thing. Now some event or complex of events can be probable or improbable only *with respect to a given body of evidence.* So we say that the day is likely to be wet and windy on the evidence provided by other relevantly similar days.

But to what body of evidence is appeal being made when it is said that it is reasonable that anything counting as the Word of God must meet certain standards? We have not had experience of other revelations from God that would enable us to form a rule of generalization in the light of which we might judge that the next revelation has occurred. The trouble, then, lies with the form of the argument that gives rise to externalism; for it means that any criterion formulated in accordance with this form of argument is *bound* to be Procrustean. The air of reasonableness about such a position is totally spurious.

II

The other example of a type of argument that may be used to establish that the Scriptures are the Word of God is a version of *fideism.* But it is important to remember that "fideism" is the name of a family of positions. There are many differences between different members of the family. But broadly, as applied to the problem we are considering, the view is that the proof or evidence that the Bible is the Word of God is *not* to be found in a set of external criteria, but elsewhere. The contrast established by fideism is not necessarily between faith and reason but between faith and external proof. In order to see this more clearly it is necessary to distinguish between the following three positions:

1. The view that the Bible is the Word of God cannot be rationally defended. Accepting the Bible as the Word of God is a leap of faith.

2. The view that the Bible is the Word of God is not irrational as is shown by the inadequacy of arguments aiming to show that it is irrational.

3. The view that the Bible is the Word of God is a matter of its own evidence, and there are external arguments leading to this view.

These three positions (and others that we do not have space to consider) can be thought of as members of the fideistic family. But there are important differences between them. We shall not consider (1) any further, but concentrate on (2) and (3).

These positions may seem to be paradoxical, even self-contradictory. For, it may be asked, how can there be external arguments or reasons that lead to the conclusion that the Bible is God's Word and this *not* be what we have called externalism? Surely the whole point of something being self-justified is that it derives its justification from itself. If so, then what part can external reasons or arguments play? Have we not already considered and dismissed the view that acceptance of the Bible's being the Word of God is founded on external considerations?

But this question is based on a confusion, the confusion between

a. The only convincing reasons for accepting the Bible as God's Word are internal ones.

and

b. The Bible is God's Word.

The considerations that support *a* are not necessarily the same considerations that support *b*. Thus there may well be external reasons for accepting *a* that are not reasons for accepting *b*. For example, one reason for accepting *a* might be that any external considerations that are offered are empirically weak or logically flawed or theologically inadequate in some way. But these weaknesses or flaws are not positive reasons for accepting *b*, as they are of a wholly negative character. And so it may be argued that there are general considerations of an external kind, considerations that allow that the Scriptures may be their own evidence for being the Word of God.

One example of this sort of argument is that provided by Alvin Plantinga is his paper "Is Belief in God Rational?"[4] In this paper, he is concerned with the rationality of believing in the existence of God, whereas we are concerned with the rationality of accepting the Scriptures as God's Word; but the general issues are the same. Plantinga argues that classical natural theology—for example, the "Five Ways" of Thomas Aquinas (and also, incidentally, the natural theology of Archibald Alexander)—is *foundationalistic.* That is to say, classical natural theology is based on a view of human knowledge that claims that it has a foundation of self-evident beliefs, propositions that we all know, or can know, without having further evidence for them. The stock of such beliefs provides the foundations for knowledge. It is by reference to such foundational truths, propositions "evident to the senses" as Aquinas put it, that the existence of God may be rationally established.

Plantinga criticizes foundationalism on familiar grounds,[5] particularly on the ground that the notion of self-evidence on which foundationalism rests is suspect; for it may happen that what appears self-evident is not in fact true, and hence cannot be self-evident. And so the idea of knowledge being based on a self-evident foundation is dubious. But this is not to say, according to Plantinga, that knowledge is totally without foundations, but it is to deny that knowledge rests on a foundation of self-evident propositions. Knowledge has foundations, but not self-evident foundations, in Plantinga's view. Certain propositions are *basic* (but not self-evident) because a person commits himself to the truth they express and makes them the rational basis of all other propositions to which he rationally commits himself.

> If, with an older tradition, we think of reason as an organ, or power or faculty—the faculty whereby we discern what is self-evident—then the foundationalist commits himself to the basic reliability of reason. He doesn't do so, of course, as a result of (broadly speaking) scientific or rational investigation; he does so in advance of such investigation.[6]

If basic propositions are those propositions that a person commits himself to (and are not self-evidently true propositions) then there is no reason why a person should not commit himself to the existence of God as part of his intellectual foundations. "There is a God" would then be foundational for him.

> To accept belief in God as basic is clearly not irrational in the sense of being proscribed by reason or in conflict with the deliverances of reason. The dictum that belief in God is not basic in a rational noetic structure (structure of belief) is neither apparently self-evident nor apparently incorrigible. Is there, then, any reason at all for holding that a noetic structure including belief in God as basic is irrational? If there is, it remains to be specified.[7]

The form of Plantinga's argument might be expressed in this way:
1. There is no reason to suppose that *p* is not true (i.e., there is no reason to suppose that the proposition "God exists" may not form part of a person's foundational beliefs).

2. Therefore, *p* may be true (i.e., it is rational to hold that the proposition "God exists" may form part of a person's foundational beliefs).

Notice that on this argument there are and can be no *positive* reasons for accepting 2. There cannot be such reasons because otherwise the proposition that God exists could not be foundational in the required sense, for a proposition can be foundational only if in order rationally to believe it there need be no evidence for it. There could of course be *motives* for committing oneself foundationally to the proposition "God exists," but no *reasons*.

Interesting questions arise at this point. Are there any limits to the possibilities to which a person can commit himself foundationally? Could he commit himself foundationally to the existence of fairies and hobgoblins? Could he commit himself foundationally to the proposition that God does not exist? Presumably he could. Unfortunately we cannot go further into such questions here.

What we must consider are the consequences of someone taking this line of argument with respect to the proposition "The Bible is the Word of God." It seems possible that a person could commit himself to the Bible in this way. There appears to be nothing logically inconsistent in his doing so. But, once again, he would have no positive reason for doing so, and the idea that certain considerations might strengthen his confidence in the Scriptures as God's Word, and other considerations might weaken it, would be logically impossible. The only reply that the question, "Why do you accept the Bible as the Word of God?" could be met with is "For no reason . . . I have committed myself to the view that the Scriptures are the Word of God basically." And there seems nothing to stop others from doing exactly the same with *Science and Health, The Book of Mormon,* or *The Thoughts of Chairman Mao.*

This line of argument seems perfectly consistent, but it is awfully *thin.* What is thin is the idea that there are and can be no reasons *for* the view that God exists or that the Scriptures are the Word of God, only poor and inadequate reasons *against.*

III

Having looked at two types of argument or strategy that are unsatisfactory, we now come to the main thesis of this chapter: There are reasons for accepting the Scriptures as the Word of God and these reasons are chiefly to be found within the Scriptures themselves. This is a fideistic position of type 3, mentioned on page 307.

Perhaps we could express this more precisely as follows: It is a necessary condition of properly accepting the Bible to be the Word of God that one's main reasons for doing so arise out of the Scriptures themselves. In my defense of this position I hope to avoid, on the one hand, the externalism of Archibald Alexander and on the other hand the strong fideism of Alvin Plantinga. For all their obvious differences, what both arguments have in common is that they defend the divine authority of the Scriptures (in Plantinga's argument wholly, and in Alexander's partly) in abstraction from the actual content of the Scriptures.

The basic approach to the question of the origin and authority of the Scriptures must be a posteriori. It is wrong to decide such questions, either for or against, without considering the content of the Scriptures themselves. "Considering the content of the Scriptures" means not merely looking at what the Scriptures say about themselves but examining the force or impact of the Scriptures. Part of the reason for believing that a person is a king may be that he says that he is a king. But the evidence that he is a king is much stronger if he is seen exercising the prerogatives of a king. It is not simply that the Scriptures say that they are the revelation of God that is the evidence for their being so, but also that they function as the Word of God. Let us try to look at this in a little more detail.

We need, in the first place, to examine the basic "logic" of the meaning of the Scriptures. Though the Bible purports to provide its readers with information not available to them elsewhere, its basic stance is not merely that of an information-provider but that of a document that, on the basis of the information that it provides, makes claims on and offers invitations to its readers. Basic here is the idea of God's personal address to people, an address that calls for a response.

It is possible to break this down into a number of different elements. One element is the idea that the Bible purports to give an analysis or diagnosis of the reader. The Scriptures offer this diagnosis as the *truth* about the reader. Now if the Scriptures are what they claim to be, the Word of God, then one would expect that careful examination and self-scrutiny would reveal that the diagnosis "holds good" in the life of the reader. Connected with this is the power of the Scriptures to raise and satisfy certain distinctive needs in the reader, particularly the recognition of his sin before God and the enjoyment of forgiveness and reconciliation to God through Christ. Connected with this is the displaying in Scripture of excellent moral standards that focus and integrate the life of the reconciled person. And connected with *this* is the provision of new motivations to reach out for the newly set standards.

These ideas, briefly and inadequately expressed here, arise out of the meaning of the words and sentences of the Scriptures. They are briefly and inadequately expressed in that they need to be set in a fuller theological context than we are able to provide here and to be shown to be grounded in the data of Scripture. These are complex and never-finished tasks.

The peculiar logic of the situation might be expressed as follows: What has to be known in order for these biblical claims to be established is not merely something about the claims but also something about oneself. This may be partly what Augustine and especially John Calvin meant when they said that the knowledge of God and the knowledge of ourselves are conceptually intertwined.[8]

The data of Scripture, in which the divine authority of Scripture is grounded and which provide evidence for the Bible being the Word of God, are known a posteriori. Fundamental, therefore, to accepting the Bible as the Word of God is considering the relevant evidence for that claim honestly and seriously. This point cannot be overstressed, for it is common to find on both sides of this debate those who tell us what the Scriptures *must* be like without stopping to look and see if the Scriptures actually are like this.

The kinds of consideration that we have been discussing are not the only sort of internal evidence for the divine authority of the Scriptures, but they are the chief sort of evidence. I must now attempt to clarify this further by taking up additional aspects of the claim and then by trying to meet some objections. But there is one initial objection that arises, and that must be dispatched at once.

Someone may say that even if what has been said so far is acceptable, it is far from establishing the conclusion that the Scriptures are God's Word, for by "the Scriptures" is presumably meant the sixty-six canonical books of the Old and New Testaments. How do we get to the sixty-six books from the slender base that has been established? The short answer to this is that we get to it through the authority of Christ. It is because He endorses the Old Testament and makes provision for the New that both Old and New have this authority. He endorses these writings and sets the boundaries of what is authoritative, but of course these writings become authoritative in the sense of practically influencing the thinking and the conduct of those who accept them only when their teaching is actually submitted to and responded to. Perhaps we need to draw a distinction at this point between accepting the Bible as God's revelation and practically experiencing the "weight" of that authority. One may recognize the authority of the Scriptures in the first sense without recognizing it in the second sense in respect of some particular passage or book of Scripture either because one has not paid sufficient attention to it or because its "relevance" to one's situation is not apparent.

Would it be fair to say, on the view that is being defended, that the Scriptures are self-evident? "Self-evident" is an ambiguous expression, for it may mean, when applied to a proposition or set of propositions, that the proposition(s) are accepted as true on their own evidence, or it may mean that the evidence reaches a certain standard, that of being so evidently true that no other evidence could either make it more evident or less evident than it is. It has been argued that certain propositions such as 2 plus 2 equals 4, propositions that are believed to be true by everyone who understands them, and sincere utterances such as "I am in pain" are self-evidently true. Whether or not there are such self-evident truths, it is not the case that the previous argument about the Scriptures being the Word of God requires that there are. And so no claim is being made that the Scriptures are self-evident in the sense that it is impossible, rationally, to doubt their truth. For it is clearly possible to entertain doubts of a rational kind, doubts about the meaning and implications of the text, for example.

Similarly with the idea of self-witness. What I am arguing is not that Scripture witnesses to itself about its divine origin and that this witness rules out any rational doubt, but that Scripture witnesses about itself *to us* and that this witness may find confirmation or validation *in experience*, in the diagnostic and other work mentioned earlier. Emphasis does not fall on proving the existence of God and then proving by miracle and prophecy that this book of all books is God's revelation (the Alexander strategy) but it falls on proving God in experience and *a fortiori* establishing that He exists. God is proved by hearing and obeying Him and finding that He is as good as His word.

Thus the certainty of the Scriptures as revelatory documents lies in their being confirmed in experience and what this entails or renders probable. The experience is *not* a further revelation. To suppose that it were would lead to an infinite regress, for if it were a further revelation, it would need credentials for it to be rationally acceptable. But what could these credentials be other than a *further* revelation? And so on ad infinitum. Rather, the experience has to do with the *impact* of the revelation on the lives of those who receive it.

To clarify still further, the experience is not a different sort of evidence, ineffable or indescribable, that makes up for the inadequacy of the biblical evidence, but rather the discovery that the claims of the Scriptures bear the weight of experience.

"Self-evident" is also sometimes used as a rough equivalent to "axiomatic," and there is a sense in which our argument requires that the Scriptures be axiomatic, namely, theologically or religiously axiomatic; i.e., they provide the basic data and the basic set of "controls" from which theological conclusions are to be derived. They are theologically sufficient for such reflection.

How does what we have been arguing tie in with the theological doctrine of the internal testimony of the Holy Spirit? In the following way: What we have been describing, the power of the Scriptures to diagnose and "speak" is, in more theological language, the Spirit's internal testimony. The two are not different things but two different characterizations of the same thing. The internal testimony of the Spirit is not to be thought of as in some way short-circuiting the objective evidence or making up for the deficiencies in external scriptural evidence, nor as providing *additional* evidence, nor as merely acting as a mechanical stimulus, but as making the mind capable of the proper appreciation of the evidence, seeing it for what it is, and in particular heightening the mind's awareness of the marks of divinity present in the text in such a way as to produce the conviction that this text is indeed the product of the divine mind and therefore to be relied on utterly.

It is for this reason that our position cannot be ruled out as mere subjectivism, the idea that so-called religious or theological truth is merely about the believer's own state of mind. For while there is a subjective side of things, a believer, there is an objective side, the text and its meaning, something public and verifiable.

IV

Having tried to clarify what is meant by the self-evident truth of the Scriptures, we are now in a position to consider certain objections. (Incidentally, the very fact that I am taking objections seriously and am defending this view by contrast with the inadequacies of other views shows that the type of fideism I am defending is the type that argues for the existence of external arguments that lead to the conclusion that the proper evidence for the Bible's being the Word of God is the Bible's own evidence.)

1. The first objection is that this position is irrationalistic. If by this charge is meant that this view does not proceed from self-evident first principles by inductive or deductive argument, then the point is granted. By that austere standard the view being defended is irrational. The proper reply to this is not to say that few, if any, other views reach the same standard (for two wrongs do not make a right) but to doubt the truth of this brand of foundationalism. And there is plenty of reason to do this.[9] And if there are reasons for doubting the truth of foundationalism, it cannot be the mark of rationality in epistemology.

But to say that this position does not conform to the pattern of foundationalism is not to say that it is totally without reason. If anything, it conforms to a coherentist pattern of justification, for it is coherence with experience that forms the justification. Furthermore, in the face of doubts about the genuineness or reasonableness of the claim that the Bible is the Word of God there are ways in which such doubts may be met, by the clarification of meaning and the presentation of evidence, ways that are perfectly familiar from other rationally conducted disciplines. Thus, though the pattern of justification being offered is not foundationalistic, it does conform to that which obtains in interpersonal situations that each of us is familiar with.

A connected kind of irrationalism would be that the text simply causes or triggers some experience, as, for example, being in a crowded elevator might cause a claustrophobic to panic. But the words or propositions of the revelation are not the cause or occasion of the experience; rather, they engender it through the *meaning* of the propositions and their *force* (as commands, questions, invitations, or whatever) being appreciated.

2. The second objection that I wish to consider is that this view is logically circular. I am attempting to conclude that the Scriptures are the Word of God by appealing to the words of Christ as authoritative and so the words of Christ are already being taken to be, or are assumed to be, scriptural. Is this not to argue in a circle?

Certain arguments of this type would be circular. For example, it would be arguing in a circle to claim that the Scriptures are the Word of God because the Bible says so and the Bible is the Word of God and so must be believed. However, it is not clear that our argument is circular in this sense, nor indeed circular at all. For what is being argued is that the evidence for the Bible's being the Word of God is that the claims that the Bible makes are found to hold good. But these claims are not primarily, and certainly not only, that the Bible is the Word of God, but that certain promises, invitations, etc., hold good, and that the holding good of these in experience provides good inductive evidence for other claims, for example, the claims of Christ and His apostles that the Scriptures of the Old and New Testaments are the Word of God.

There is a logically contingent connection between the authority of Christ and the Old and New Testaments' being the Word of God in that it is possible for Christ to have been the Savior in circumstances in which only parts of the Old and New Testaments were the Word of God, or in which the Old Testament as a whole or large parts of it had not survived until the present day. Accepting the authority of Christ does not *entail* accepting the authority of the Old and New Testaments. What it does entail is the conclusion that there is good evidence that Christ is who He says He is, and hence is to be trusted in His teaching in general. And if He teaches that certain documents are the Word of God and are therefore to be trusted as He is to be trusted, then that is an additional matter.

But is not the Christ who is believed in the Christ of the Scriptures? No, He is (at best) the Christ of some of the Scriptures and also partly the Christ of human make-believe and tradition. Part of any Christian's task is to reform his ideas of Christ, to make them more and more consistently biblical.

3. Someone might argue that to base one's acceptance of the Scriptures on one's ability to diagnose the human condition and to provide new goals and new motivations in regard to the Scriptures is to build on a very slender base. For might there not have been a gigantic mistake or systematic self-deception? How can one be sure that one has been told the truth about oneself, given genuine promises and invitations? Could it not be that these are the product of one's imagination or of some source other than God? May they not be the effects of psychological weakness or, as Marx suggested, the product of adverse economic and social circumstances?

The answer to these questions is yes, such misconceptions are possible. Furthermore it is true that many people have come to believe that they are not merely possible, but actually so, and that the religion of their youth was make-believe. But the question is not whether there is the abstract possibility that the whole thrust of the Bible has been misunderstood, nor whether certain people have regarded themselves as having been duped, but whether *I* have reason to believe this. The history of thought is peppered with skepticisms of various kinds, both global and particular. Some have held, and do hold, that it is likely that we know nothing at all about anything, or exceedingly little. And it is logically possible that the whole of life is a dream, that I am not sitting at my desk typing this paper but that in fact my brain is being stimulated by some malicious superscientist into believing that I am typing when in fact I am eating (and should be enjoying) a very large chocolate nut sundae. These things are possible, but the relevant question is, have we reason to suppose that they are true? If it is said that it is impossible to defend our position against such possibilities, then the point must be granted, but it must also be granted that all other nonskeptical positions are in exactly the same boat.

So the general appeal to skepticism, if it proves anything at all, proves too much, consigning not only the view we are defending but all other claims to knowledge to the philosophical lumber room.

Yet it may be said that the fact that many have regarded the claims of Christ and of the Bible as fraudulent is surely some reason for caution. It is—in just the way in which the fact that some human friendships have been found to collapse when put under strain is a reason for caution about *this* friendship. But though caution is proper, doubt about the friendship of someone who shows every sign of being my friend would be neurotic and improper.

But surely this appeal to religious experience is purely subjective, isn't it? Not necessarily. If an engineer predicts the collapse of a bridge and it collapses, his prediction has physically objective confirmation. But physical objectivity is not the only kind of objectivity. Suppose Smith wonders whether Robinson really dislikes him. If Robinson does dislike Smith, then in a sense this is subjective, something about Robinson's state of mind. But in another sense it has objectivity. It has objectivity if, for example, it is sustained in varied sets of circumstances, if it is expressed in different ways. In the case of religious experience similar sorts of tests apply, and a person may become rationally convinced of the objectivity (i.e., the reality) of God's love, even though God does not have objective physical reality.

4. A fourth objection might be that we have left no place at all for the external evidence of the truth and trustworthiness of the Scriptures. For it might be said the Bible is a very diverse library of books, diverse in the sense that it contains not only moral and religious (in some narrow sense) claims, but also historical and metaphysical claims. Further, it might be said, not only are such claims made, but

they are not incidental, but central, to Christianity, which insists that God has acted in a decisive way in history. To say that God has acted in history makes the metaphysical claim that it is *God* who has acted, and it makes the historical claim that certain events have occurred as a result of divine agency. Surely these matters need to be investigated as a part of any project to validate the claims of the Bible to be the Word of God.

At this point it is necessary to use our earlier distinction between the truth conditions of certain claims and their evidence conditions. It is undoubtedly the case that as normally understood the central claims of the Christian faith involve the truth of certain historical propositions. (If someone objects to the use of "historical" in this connection because it implies certain things about historical *method*, then we can substitute the phrase "propositions expressing witness-able events.") If these claims are false, then Christianity is false. And further, in some sense these propositions form a part of the total evidence of Christianity, the set of propositions about the world that are true if Christianity is true.

But it does not follow from this that because a proposition is part of the total evidence for some claim that it has to be part of *my* evidence for this claim if my evidence is to be good evidence. Consider again the case of Mr. Jones, the victim of cancer. Part of the total evidence of Jones's being the victim of cancer is that there is some condition that causes or allows the growth of cancerous cells in his body. But it does not follow from this that in order for Jones or anyone else to have good evidence that he has cancer he has to know what causes or allows these growths. Nor does it follow that the cancer must be seen, for an expert might know by looking at Jones's history, together with certain tests, that he has cancer. He need not actually have direct evidence of the cancer itself.

The kind of "hold" the Scriptures have when they are understood in a certain way that implies the truth of certain historical happenings is prima facie evidence for the truth of the happenings in much the same way that the outcome of certain tests is prima facie evidence for cancer or a press report that a source near to the government has predicted a devaluation, followed by the devaluation, is good evidence that the source near to the government *had* predicted it.

But what if there is a *conflict* between the claims of the Scriptures and the findings of history? What happens if what has to be true, historically, for Scripture to be true is denied to be true by the consensus of competent historians? They might argue either in a straightfor-ward way that the events did not happen or in a more a priori manner that the documents are not to be taken at face value but are imaginative reconstructions by a group impressed by Jesus.

In the first of these circumstances it would be a legitimate strategy to investigate the historical evidence, to examine the data produced by the competent historians, to consider new evidence, and the like. In the second set of circumstances it would be legitimate to ask for the reasons that have led someone to take up the a priori view about the status of the documents.

What this shows about the place of historical evidence and research is that in order to establish that the Scriptures are the Word of God it is not necessary for one to investigate the historical reliability and trustworthiness of the Scriptures *before* placing confidence in them. Rather, if the one who accepts the God-givenness of the Scriptures is presented with prima facie damning evidence against his position, he or some competent person in the field is duty-bound to investigate it. At the very least, such an examination is relevant to the calling into question and to the ultimate overthrow of his position. So there is an important asymmetry here: historical evidence cannot by itself establish the divine authority of the Scriptures, but it could overthrow it. And the reason why it cannot establish it has already been given in our discussion of externalism.

Similarly with questions of logical consistency. If the Scriptures are the Word of God, then, properly interpreted, the sentences of Scripture will be at least logically consistent with each other. This follows from the fact that if the Scriptures are the Word of God, then, properly interpreted, the sentences are true. And if a set of propositions is true, the propositions must be consistent with each other. It follows from this that if anyone were plausibly to show that there is a self-contradiction in the Scriptures, or in some set of propositions implied by the Scriptures, then this is directly relevant to their truth and hence to their God-givenness. For if there is a genuine contradiction, then not both of the contradictory propositions can be true. In a parallel way, if it is alleged that there is a conflict between some properly interpreted sentence of Scripture and what is known on nonscriptural evidence, this also demands investigation. So, once again, though it is not the case that the consistency of Christianity has to be proved before it can be accepted as true, if its inconsistency were proved, this would be sufficient to sound its death knell, and if the charge of inconsistency is leveled against it, this represents a prima facie difficulty, requiring investigation.

These comments underline what has been said previously—that the position being defended is not mere subjectivism. Nor is it some form of reductionism according to which Christianity is really about something that is not dependent either on history or logic. History and logic are both relevant aspects of the complex web that makes up Christianity because the Christian revelation offers itself as something that is consistent and is essentially rooted in history. But this does not mean, as I have stressed, that all logical and historical problems ought to be solved before Christianity is credible or before the status of the Bible as the Word of God is credible any more than that all historical

and logical problems about Napoleon ought to be solved before anything about Napoleon's military career is credible. The existence of my
wife does not have to be established independently before I can be
sure that she loves me. Her existence is implied by her love for me.
This is not to say however, that there are no conceivable circumstances in which I might have to go about trying to establish that
she did in fact exist, as for example, if she had disappeared or I was
suffering from loss of memory.

5. It might be said that the view that I am defending, that the
evidence for the Scriptures being the Word of God is primarily internal
evidence, leaves that position formally similar to the position of the
truth claims of the myriad other religions and ideologies. In a sense
this is perfectly true. Christianity is in this position. There is no line of
argument that will prove to all, once and for all, that Christianity is true
and all other religions false. On this at least we must side with Plantinga against Alexander. It is an inevitable consequence of the denial of
natural theology and externalism.

However, in saying that Christianity is in a formally similar position to other religions and religious claims I am not saying that nothing can happen to break the deadlock. True, all empirical theories are
in a logically similar position with respect to the evidence, since the
evidence does not *entail* any one of them in preference to any other,
but this is not to say that there cannot be a rationally preferred theory,
one that is the simplest and most economical explanation of the data,
that generates correct predictions, and the like. In a parallel way the
Scriptures make promises and claims, offer diagnoses, etc., as we have
seen. And if a person is going to be rational in his approach to Christianity, he is going to have to do justice to these claims, to investigate
them, to allow himself to be open to them, and so forth. In a sense if
what the person who rejects Christianity has rejected is something
that does not contain these elements, then he cannot have rejected
Christianity, since these elements are vital to it and vital to a consideration of the God-givenness of the Scriptures on which Christianity
ultimately rests.

6. It might be objected from the theological side, which stresses
the importance for the authority of the Scriptures as the Word of God
of the Scriptures' "engaging" in the life and experience of the reader or
hearer, that we are in effect saying that under certain circumstances
the Bible *becomes* the Word of God.

This objection is based on fundamental misunderstanding. What I
have been exploring in the main part of this chapter are the conditions
under which a person may properly accept something as being the
revelation of God. I have not been concerned with what *makes* something the revelation of God, but with what evidence there is to conclude that it is the Word of God. To put the point theologically, it is
necessary to distinguish between *revelation* and *illumination*.[10]

There is a further point. In setting out the conditions under which someone might properly accept the Bible as God's Word, a distinction needs to be drawn between recognizing the evidence and accepting it. It does not follow from a person's recognizing the evidence that he accepts it. Otherwise it would follow that one person could not accept the same evidence rejected by another, and the idea of religious rejection and rebellion would have no application.

7. Finally, it might be said that the view being put forward here is different from that used by the apostles of Christ and therefore marks a degeneracy from primitive and pure Christianity.

There is a sense in which this can be granted, while in another sense it must be rejected. The basic pattern of justification is the same, but the details of the pattern are different, and necessarily so. The basic New Testament appeal is to the character of the work of God. The apostles do not appeal to the internal evidence of the entire canonical Scriptures, for this was not available to them; the arguments of the apostles are part of *our* evidence. We do not find them appealing to miracles or prophecies in abstraction, however, but to the coherence of both with the teaching and history of the Messiah and with their own experience of His power in their own lives and in the formation and life of the church.

Nevertheless, there are differences, but they are the sort of differences we might expect, because they arise out of their different epistemic positions. They were contemporaries or near-contemporaries of certain crucial divine acts. Therefore it is natural that they should appeal to eyewitnesses, as Paul does in 1 Corinthians 15. But it is impossible for us to do the same because no eyewitness of the resurrected Christ is available to us. It is implausible to suppose that in order for us to be justified in believing certain things it is necessary for us to have evidence available to us that *cannot* be available, for this would mean that we can never be justified in believing anything about the past more remote than a human lifetime. But we may do the next best thing: appeal to reports of the eyewitnesses, yet not, as I have stressed, to these reports in isolation, but to them as part of a web of history, prophecy, argument, claim and invitation, and human recognition and response.

V

I have been trying to argue that the chief evidence or reason for taking the Scriptures to be the Word of God is their own evidence, found to hold good in the life and experience of those who are serious and "open." Thus, in a sense, my approach is basically a fideistic one. Yet while I have distinguished it from externalism, I have also sought to distinguish it from two other kinds of fideism, the kind that says that no evidence or reason of any kind can or ought to be given for taking the Scriptures to be the Word of God, and the kind that says that since there are no convincing general arguments that force us to conclude we may *not* rationally take the Scriptures to be the Word of God, it follows that we may.

One final matter that needs to be appreciated is that I have been offering a theory or an account of why the Scriptures have had the place they have occupied in the life and experience of the Christian church. It is not a part of this exercise to make the *further* claim that in order for someone properly to appreciate the Scriptures as the Word of God that person must endorse my account, any more than that in order to be justified in thinking that the kettle is hot we need to know about and endorse theories about molecules. A person may be blissfully ignorant of this account (and of any of its rivals) and still exemplify in his life the state of affairs for which the theory is offered as an account.

INFALLIBLE SCRIPTURE
AND THE ROLE
OF HERMENEUTICS

J. I. Packer

J. I. Packer

    James I. Packer was educated at Oxford University (degrees in classics and theology; D.Phil.). He served as assistant minister at St. John's Church in England, Harborne, Birmingham, and then became Senior Tutor at Tyndale Hall, an Anglican seminary in Bristol. Then, after serving as Warden of Latimer House, an Anglican evangelical study center in Oxford, he returned to Bristol to become Principal of Tyndale Hall. When Tyndale Hall merged with two other evangelical colleges to become Trinity College, Bristol, he became Associate Principal. In 1979 he became Professor of Systematic and Historical Theology at Regent College, Vancouver.

    He has preached and lectured widely in Great Britain and America and is a frequent contributor to theological periodicals. Among his writings are: *'Fundamentalism' and the Word of God*, *Evangelism and the Sovereignty of God*, *Knowing God*, *God has Spoken*, and *Knowing Man*. He was an editor of the *Illustrated (New) Bible Dictionary*, and *The Bible Almanac*. With O. R. Johnston he translated and edited Luther's *Bondage of the Will*. He is currently at work on a number of books.

INFALLIBLE SCRIPTURE AND
THE ROLE OF HERMENEUTICS

THE CENTRALITY OF HERMENEUTICS TODAY

When some two thousand English evangelical leaders met in 1977, one session was given to hermeneutics. The preconference paper and the conference presentation were most competently done, yet many saw nothing of importance in the subject, and it became a conference joke to refer to "Herman Eutics" as the latest in a line of esoteric continental theologians. Maybe there are still Evangelicals for whom hermeneutics is a new and uncouth word denoting a latter-day academic triviality. But the theologically informed are likely to agree with Carl F. H. Henry's judgment: "The key intellectual issue for the '80s, as I see it, will still be the persistent problem of authority. It will concern especially the problem of hermeneutics."[1]

The truth is that ever since Karl Barth linked his version of Reformation teaching on biblical authority with a method of interpretation that at key points led away from Reformation beliefs, hermeneutics has been the real heart of the ongoing debate about Scripture. Barth was always clear that every theology stands or falls as a hermeneutic and every hermeneutic stands or falls as a theology, but it took others some time to catch up with this insight. In the English-speaking Protestant world the past hundred years appear as three eras of roughly equal length, during which the formal agenda for discussing the Bible has centred successively on inspiration (in the days before Barth),[2] revelation (in the heyday of Barth),[3] and interpretation (in the years since Barth).[4] Hermeneutics embraces this latter theme, integrating it into a theology of divine communication and God-given understanding through an appropriate intellectual process. The present-day awareness that hermeneutics is a matter of central theological importance began with Bultmann and his followers in the 1940s and since then has become steadily more marked in both Protestant and Roman Catholic scholarship.

This concentration on hermeneutics is from at least one standpoint healthy. By focusing on God's work of communicating with people here and now through the Scriptures it rules out that against which Barth so strongly battled—namely, highlighting the *givenness* of Scripture in a way that loses sight of its *instrumentality*. Honoring the Bible as embodying what God said to mankind long ago while failing to listen to it as God's word to us in the present will not do, said

Barth. Whether or not one finds this fault in the writers in whom Barth claimed to detect it (the seventeenth-century Protestant scholastics, for instance), and whether one accepts much or little of Barth's own account of Scripture,[5] there can surely be no question that he was right to make central the Bible's instrumental function of mediating God's revealed mind to each generation of the church. Now when Evangelicals have debated inspiration, revelation, and interpretation with exponents of liberalism and neoorthodoxy, they also have shown themselves anxious that Scripture be free to function, both in public worship and in the closet, as the means by which God's message is heard in pure and undiminished form, and it has been apparent that one main reason why they have joined battle has been their conviction that the positions they oppose would prevent Scripture from doing this. Motivationally, therefore, Barth and mainstream evangelicalism were not far apart, though each censured the other's views as tending to keep the Bible from so functioning.[6] Bultmann, too, shared with Evangelicals a concern that the Word of God be heard today, though Evangelicals have judged that his account of revelation makes this formally impossible.[7] So it seems to follow that the current avowed shift of the biblical debate to hermeneutics as its central focus, even if made under the influence of views that Evangelicals do not accept, is a move that Evangelicals can welcome, since it makes explicit their concern that the divine message be heard (something that Evangelicals themselves have not always managed to do) and calls on all parties to the discussion to identify with that concern.

For Evangelicals biblical authority does in fact mean Scripture communicating instruction from God about belief and behavior, the way of faith and obedience, and the life of worship and witness. The avowed rationale of evangelical controversy with liberalism on the one hand and catholicism on the other has always been that disbelief or misbelief of what Scripture actually says blots out some of that knowledge of God's grace and some of that understanding of His will, which better belief—truer belief, that is, about the Bible and its God—would bring. In other words, Evangelicals have been fighting not just for orthodoxy, but for religion; not just for purity of confession, but for fullness of faith and life; not just for God's truth as such, but for the godliness that is a response to it. Certainly, much of the recent argument has focused on whether skeptical theories about the origin and nature of biblical books are true and whether skeptical and incoherent exegeses of particular passages are sound, and no doubt some evangelical controversialists have been so bogged down in these debates that they have failed to articulate their concern for biblical godliness. No doubt, too, the heritage of seventeenth-century Protestant scholasticism, Lutheran and Reformed, with its characteristic if questionable stress on epistemological certainty as the basis of authority and on conceptual clarity as the basis of epistemological certainty, has had its effect in shaping evangelical responses to the anti-intellectual subjectivism of liberals and existentialists, making it seem on occasion that an intellectualist orthodoxy was all that Evangelicals cared about. But today's evangelicalism was not nurtured in last-century pietism for nothing, and the concern for godliness has always been there, whether or not it has always broken surface in debate.[8] The least acquaintance with the history of evangelical preaching and organizations for ministry and outreach over the past century shows this.[9] The concern continues and this is why Evangelicals continue to spend their strength contending for the authority of an infallible Bible as a basic principle of Christianity.[10]

THE BIBLICAL THEOLOGY OF EVANGELICALISM

I am generalizing in a broad way about evangelicalism; it will be well, I think, at this point to specify precisely what it is that I refer to. By evangelicalism I mean that multidenominational Protestant constituency within the world-wide church that combines acknowledgment of the trustworthiness, sufficiency, and divine authority of the Bible with adherence to the New Testament account of the gospel of Christ and the way of faith in Him. Characteristic of evangelicalism is its claim that the conceptual categories, arguments, and analyses in terms of which biblical authors present to us God, man, Christ, the Holy Spirit, Satan, sin, salvation, the church, and all else on which they give teaching are in truth God-taught and so have abiding validity. This is not to say that Evangelicals hesitate to acknowledge biblical imagery, symbols, parables, and other pictorial literary forms for what they are; in fact, they do not so hesitate;[11] but equally they do not allow themselves to forget that these literary forms are communicating *thoughts*, and the thoughts, whether indicative or imperative, evaluative, evocative, performative, or interrogative, are set before Bible readers by God Himself. Evangelicalism recognizes that all the church's formulations of God's truth, being to some extent culturally determined, are bound to lack finality and to need augmenting and qualifying from time to time. Evangelicalism recognizes too that God's revealed and universally valid teaching in Scripture, given as it was over many centuries in a slowly but surely changing Near Eastern cultural milieu, has to be unshelled from the local particularities in which we find it embedded in order that it may be reapplied today in terms of our own culture. Legal interpretation in a contemporary context of ancient but still binding statutes—for example, the British laws of 1677 and 1781 requiring public observance of the Lord's Day, or those of 1558 and 1698 forbidding public blasphemy, all of which are still invoked on occasion—present the nearest parallel to this reapplication procedure. But, while seeking to do full justice to both the above insights, evangelicalism rejects on principle all forms of dogmatic theological relativism, as the fruit of the fundamental mistake of not taking biblical instruction, as such, to be the Word of God.[12]

Evangelicalism's theology, with all its local and in-house variants, is (at least in intention and idea, if not always in perfect achievement) a body of tenets, attitudes, and approaches drawn from the biblical documents by allowing them to speak for themselves in terms of their own interests, viewpoints, and emphases; in other words, by a method that is thoroughly and consistently a posteriori. The method has been called "grammatico-historical," as a pointer to the techniques involved; it could equally well be called the a posteriori method, in virtue of its purpose of reading out of Scripture what is there in each author's expressed meaning and of avoiding reading into it at any point what is not there in that sense. Use of this method over four and a half centuries has produced a relatively stable form of theology that centers on the sovereign, speaking God; the divine, sin-bearing, risen, reigning, returning Christ; the divine forgiveness and reconciliation of sinners through Christ's cross, and their adoption into God's family; the work of the Holy Spirit mediating communion with God in Christ by faith through word and sacrament; the spiritual character of the church, as consisting in idea, at any rate, of born-again believers; and unending glory with Christ and His people as every Christian's sure and certain hope.[13] Yet while this theology is confessed and taught catechetically as if it were fixed and irreformable, Evangelicals know that it remains open to testing, correction, and augmentation by the light of those Scriptures whose message it seeks to focus. As a matter of fact, its faithfulness and fullness in spelling out the biblical message are constantly being reviewed and assessed by evangelical theologians,[14] and there are today many specific issues on which, despite their unity of method and approach, Evangelicals are far from being at one.

HAS SCRIPTURE ONE CLEAR MESSAGE?

Sometimes, however, the perception that Evangelicals have no perfectly unified answers to some questions of truth and duty is alleged to show, not that some (at least) of our minds are gripped by unbiblical a prioris and distorting influences, or are not well informed about that on which we try to pass biblical judgments,[15] but rather, of that, as liberal theology has long maintained, the method of appeal and submission to Scripture, no matter how carefully pursued, is intrinsically unable to produce certainty. Why not? *Either* (it is thought) because there is an ultimate pluralism in biblical teaching[16] *or* because it is really impossible for us to enter into and identify with the thoughts of people belonging to a past so remote from us as is the biblical period[17] *or* because modern insight into the hermeneutical process shows that different things are conveyed to different people by the same texts, depending on where those people are coming from and what experience and questions they bring with them[18] *or* (of course) for more than one of these reasons, perhaps all three together.

The idea that evangelical disagreements about biblical teaching might reflect some radical obscurity, or outright incoherence, or at least a Delphic sort of ambiguity, running throughout Scripture, cannot but disturb. Ought we then to conclude that when the Reformers affirmed the intrinsic clarity of Scripture in presenting its central message, they were wrong and that the many millions who down the centuries have lived and died by the light of what they took to be divinely taught certainties were self-deceived? Must we say that no such certainties are available to us, nor ever were to anyone? That is what this idea, if accepted, would imply. But the notion is gratuitous, as can be shown in a number of ways.

Granted, to start with, differences of conceptual resource and verbal expression do in fact mark one biblical writer from another, revealing differences in background, brains, and breadth of experience. But it has yet to be proved that things said in different ways at different times by different people are necessarily inconsistent with each other in substantive meaning. The appropriate test here is not whether the same vocabulary is used, but whether the logical and ontological implications of the different statements clash. It is, after all, possible to say the same thing in more than one way. Thus, Paul, John, and the writer to the Hebrews (for example) are three remarkably individual and strong-minded authors, each with his own distinctive way of putting things and not, so far as we can tell, dependent on either of the other two; yet the implications for thought and life of their three presentations of Christ prove to tally exactly. Plurality in presentation does not in this case involve pluralism in substance. The different theological accounts are complementary, not contradictory, and theories that affirm the opposite prove on inspection to be arbitrary and needless. The fashionable notion that different wording must always imply different and incompatible content should therefore be dismissed as a mistake.[19]

Granted again, different people in different situations find the same Scripture passages bringing them illumination from God in different ways and with different specific messages. (Think, for instance, of the many different human contexts in which down the centuries Psalm 23 will have brought reassurance from God.) But it has yet to be shown that the historico-theological meaning of each text that is applied for reassurance and guidance today does not continue to be identical. Some, to be sure, with Karl Barth, deny that Scripture offers general principles of truth for specific application and think rather in terms of a series of distinct divine "words" emerging from time to time through theological exegesis within the often wide parameters of meaning that texts prove to have when studied in the light of this or that student's questions, and in terms of canonical

Scripture as a whole.[20] But Barth's is not the only possible way to "model" the instrumentality of Scripture as God's means of communicating with us, and it may not be invoked a priori against the view mentioned earlier, which "models" this instrumentality by reference to the way in which ancient laws continue to be valid and applicable. What this latter view claims is that the historico-theological sense of each text, given and fixed by the thought-flow of which it is part, is illustration or application or apprehension (or, in some cases, misapprehension, recorded as such) of some universal truth about God which, once discerned, must then be reapplied today to yield evaluations and imperatives in our own situation. Applications vary with situations, but (so it is claimed) the core truths about God's work, will, and ways that each biblical book teaches, and that God Himself thereby teaches, remain both constant in themselves (for God does not change!) and permanently accessible to the careful exegete.

Thus, on this older, currently unfashionable but arguably truer view the manifold applications of the same Scriptures to different people do not in the least imply an ultimate pluralism in their teaching. But Barth's approach to exegesis, which appears to build on God's freedom to "say" different things to different people at different times out of the same words of human witness to Him, has naturally and inevitably led to what Kelsey calls "the unprecedented theological pluralism marking the neo-orthodox era."[21] This pluralism is something that, if I am right, future generations will see as the direct result of the hermeneutical Achilles' heel in Barth's epoch-making and formally correct reassertion of the authority of the Bible as God's channel of communication to sinful men.

Third, we may grant at once that there are in Scripture many points of exegetical detail on which a confident choice between competing options is almost if not quite impossible (whether, for instance, we should read Genesis 1 as matter-of-factly informing us that this planet was put into shape in 144 hours, or as allegorical science in which each "day" is a geological epoch, or as a quasi-liturgical celebration of the fact and quality of creation with no chronological and scientific implications at all). But it has yet to be shown that the theological content of this or any other part of Scripture as instruction to us from God about Himself and His relation to people and things is in any way rendered uncertain by the existence of more than one possibility of interpretation here and there.[22] One can master the argument of Kant's *Critique of Pure Reason* and still be unsure of the precise meaning of occasional sentences in it; and similarly with the Bible.

In the fourth place, we may also readily grant that the cultural trappings of the urbanized, technologized West of today are very different from those of the rural and pastoral Near East in the two millennia before Christ and also from those of Hellenistic towns in the first century A.D.—the worlds from which came our Old and New Testaments respectively. We grant too—indeed, we insist on our own account—that noting the distance between their worlds and ours with regard to manners, customs, expectations, and assumptions about life is very necessary in interpreting Scripture, just as it is in all study of ancient documents that present to us people of the past. To think of Jesus, or Socrates, or Julius Caesar, or the Buddha as if he were a man of our time and never to ask what was involved for him in being a man of his own time is bound to issue in grotesque misunderstanding.[23] There is good reason to inquire, as Dennis Nineham does, how deep, intellectually and emotionally, the convictional and attitudinal differences between people of ancient cultures and those of modern cultures go and to stress the human magnitude of these differences. It has yet, however, to be shown that the differences are so radical as to make Bible people and their writings unintelligible to us. This is what Nineham seems to claim,[24] but his claim is surely inadmissible.

Nineham's writing on this theme is consistently cloudy, for in it Nineham the disciplined and confident historical exegete is constantly at war with Nineham the impressionistic and skeptical theological phenomenologist. However, part of his thought plainly is that as children of a culture of positivist type, with antisupernatural, antimiraculous presuppositions (he would not say prejudices, though others might), we (he means people like himself) cannot see much of biblical theism as "making sense," that is, seeming to be true. To that it is surely proper to reply that one of the jobs the Bible does is to challenge and undercut "modern" positivistic deism, panentheism, and atheism, just as it challenged and undercut the then "modern" polytheistic paganism of the Greco-Roman world in the first Christian centuries. Presuppositional errors of cultures need to be nailed no less firmly than those of individuals. But it is also part of Nineham's view that any who suppose themselves to empathize genuinely with Bible folk and to identify with their outlook, struggles, trials, and triumphs are fooling themselves. Across so great a cultural divide as that which separates us from the New Testament community (let alone Old Testament believers), empathy is, so he says, for the most part impossible. We cannot by imagination put ourselves into their shoes; their experience, shaped by their culture, was too far outside ours; we cannot really conceive how they ticked, and when we read what they wrote, we cannot really enter into what they are expressing. This part of Nineham's thesis seems to be, to speak plainly, nonsense. Not only is there a lack of expert opinion from the field of sociology of knowledge to back it; not only is it incapable in principle of being proved (for there is no way to prove a universal negative); it also strikes at all who have ever claimed to understand any ancient religion or literature, whether Greek, Roman, Egyptian, Indian, Chinese, or whatever. For my part, I think it nonsense not only because I have heard and read so much modern material (including some pieces by Nineham!) that seems to me to show real empathy with Bible writers and real understanding of their minds; nor only because I seem to find in myself some small measure of this same empathy and understanding; but also because I seem to myself to empathize in a meaningful way with Catullus's experience of *eros* (to say nothing of that celebrated in Canticles!), with Aeschylus's vision of celestial *nemesis* for human *hubris,* with Sophocles' cosmic pessimism, with Homer's celebrations of heroism and fidelity, and with much else in classical literature—all of which is older than the New Testament, and none of which would I be able to enter into at all if Nineham's claim about cultural distance causing unintelligibility were right.

The truth seems to be rather that, as most people have always thought, what is deepest in human experience is also most universal and that such experiences as loving a spouse, admiring a hero, feeling the pity and terror of tragedy, and knowing the unchanging God are among the deepest of all, so that in principle they are the most fully communicable across historical and cultural divides to those who are capable of tuning in to such things (as in every generation everywhere some are and some are not).

I see no reason, then, to entertain Ninehamite skepticism about the possibility of understanding what the Bible writers expressed— that which, on the evangelical view, God is still showing and telling the world through their writings. I see only strong reasons to reject Nineham's idea as the sort of absurdity that it takes a very clever man to think of.

So we may conclude that such arguments as are currently offered to prove the intrinsic incoherence, ambiguity, or unintelligibility of Scripture, as instruction from God concerning God and life with Him, are very far from successful.[25]

The contention, however, that the hermeneutical process, as nowadays understood, makes it impossible to draw from Scripture universally valid truths and commands raises more issues than we have yet discussed, and to these we now turn.

THE CONCEPT OF HERMENEUTICS

What is hermeneutics? Since different hermeneuts today understand what they are doing in different ways (as is natural, since they are often in fact doing different things), only a formal definition can be offered at first. The formal definition is that hermeneutics is the theory of biblical interpretation or (putting it the other way round) the study of the process whereby the Bible speaks to us (from God, as Christians believe). Literary interpretation as such (and the Bible is, of course, literature) can be defined as the way of reading documents that shows their relevance for the reader. In line with this, biblical interpretation has always been conceived as the way of reading the historic Scriptures—a way that makes plain God's message being conveyed through them to Christians and the church. But as soon as it is asked what that message is, how it is related to the biblical text, and how people ever come to understand it, the ways divide. Hence the current tensions and uncertainties about hermeneutics, which we must now survey.

Before the nineteenth century no significant Christian thinkers questioned that Scripture is essentially a corpus of God-given instruction relating to Jesus Christ, and all interpretation proceeded on this basis. Bernard of Clairvaux's allegorizing of Canticles in the manner of Origen, and Calvin's practice of a posteriori historico-theological exegesis on Renaissance lines (so diligent that Old Testament commentaries were criticized as Judaic rather than Christian)[26] were at one here. The word *hermeneutic(s)*—from the Greek *hermēneuō*, which can mean verbalize, translate, and explain[27]—entered Protestant theology in the seventeenth century as a label for techniques of what would nowadays be called exegesis and exposition.[28] However, Kant's rationalistic dismissal of the idea of God-given instruction, followed by Schleiermacher's romantic reconceiving of theology even in the New Testament as a verbal expression of the church's corporate sense of God-relatedness, changed the scene in a fundamental way. Instead of seeking in Scripture the abiding message of the eternal God, interpreters now practiced reading the biblical books as human religious documents, as so many items in the ongoing flow of mankind's religious history. Schleiermacher, and Dilthey after him, urged that all literary hermeneutics, biblical interpretation included, is essentially the quest for an imaginative understanding of the author and that along with linguistic and historical knowledge for construing his scripts must go empathy with him, or else understanding is not gained. "Understanding" here, we should note, means something distinct from a logical grasp of the writer's assertions and their implications; these thinkers viewed it, rather, as a communion of souls across the ages (the very thing that Nineham regards as impossible).[29] The assumption was that when you could see how the writer ticked, and in that sense had got inside his experience, the interpretative task was done.

Now this assumption, though mistaken, should not be dismissed as if there was no truth in it at all. Empathy of the described sort is in fact extremely important in exegesis, since the way into the revealed mind of God is via the expressed minds of His human spokesmen and penmen, and feelings, attitudes, and dispositions are as much part of the personal "mind" that each of them expresses as are logical arguments and analyses. The affirmations about God and man made by biblical prophets, apostles, poets, and narrators may be logically detachable from their human and historical context, but to get their full force we have to appreciate them as the compound products of insight and ratiocination—temperamentally, emotionally, and attitudinally conditioned—which humanly speaking they are, and we must elucidate and learn from them accordingly. This is not, of course to deny the revelatory status of what the writers say. What is being affirmed is rather this, that what constitutes God's revelation is precisely what they themselves mean by their own statements in the total context and flow of their discourse, as distinct from the certainly narrower and perhaps unauthentic, anachronistic meaning that might be inferred from those statements if taken out of that context and set in a new one (say, a collection of texts from all over the Bible on one doctrinal theme). If, for instance, God's statement through Malachi, "I the Lord do not change" (Mal. 3:6), which in context is part of the faithful covenant-keeper's indignant plea to His inconstant people, were quoted as illustrating classical theism's developed metaphysical concept of God's intrinsic immutability, it would be a mistake.

What has been said carries important lessons. *First*, it shows the danger of citing proof texts without exegeting them in their context to make sure that they do in fact prove the point at issue. To be sure, there is nothing wrong with citing proof texts, indeed everything is right about it, provided that this caveat is observed. Those who criticize and eschew the practice of proof-texting seem to forget that in idea theology is neither more nor less than an analytical and applicatory echo of the given Word of God. But proof texts misapplied because their key words suggest to the student something other than what they mean in their own context are profitless.

Second, what was said shows the danger in the evangelical habit, now some decades old, of describing God's revelation as essentially propositional. This habit seems to have grown through negating the often-repeated claim of Emil Brunner and others that revelation is essentially not propositional but personal. The habit is dangerous, however, because revelation is (not less than, but) much more than propositional. It is in fact best, because truest, to agree with Brunner that revelation is indeed essentially personal, and then go on to say that this is why it is and had to be propositional: no person can make himself known to another without telling him things, and the God of Scripture does in fact appear as one who tells people things constantly.[30] To set propositional and personal revelation in opposition to each other is therefore to enmesh oneself in a patently false antithesis. And then, by accepting the thought that revelation is person-to-person communication (personal self-disclosure in and through the giving of information about oneself), we are enabled to recognize that revelation is embodied not only in propositions relayed by God's spokesmen on His behalf, but also in the attitudes, wishes, invitations, appeals, and reactions that they expressed by the way they put things. For these, no less than their propositional statements of fact, are revelations of God from God by God—to echo a famous formula of Karl Barth.

So divine revelation should not be thought of as if it were the kind of depersonalized conveying of information that one finds in official memoranda or company reports. Whether operating through verbal utterance, vision, sign, miracle, providence, or any other means, God's revelation was and is His personal self-disclosure, to which the only proper response is faith, worship, and obedience. Revelation is essentially God revealing *God*, as was said.

Now, the basic form of God's self-disclosure, as reported in Scripture, was His direct speech: speech to and through patriarchs and prophets (including apostles), who were no strangers to the prophetic experience of God's direct speech,[31] and supremely from the lips of His incarnate Son. In this direct speech God conveyed not only general truths about His work and will, but also His personal relational involvement in joy or sorrow, love or anger, with those to whom He spoke. When biblical historians and teachers wrote on God's behalf to edify their readers by instructing them about God's doings in creation, providence, and grace, and when biblical poets celebrated and responded to the glorious things that they knew about Him, seeking thereby to shape aright the faith, praise, and praying of God's people, it was of course, speaking grammatically, not God's direct speech but their own that they put on paper; yet the New Testament writers again and again cite this material, whatever its literary genre, as God's direct speech substantively, as if He were the historian, teacher, or poet, just as they cite prophetic oracles as God's direct speech.[32] Their view of the entire Old Testament clearly was that, as B.B. Warfield echoing Augustine put it, what Scripture says God says.[33] But to take this strand of biblical theology seriously obliges us to treat the writers' expressed feelings and attitudes to those to or about whom they wrote in God's name as reflecting God's own, just as it obliges us to treat their own expressed feelings and attitudes toward God as God-given models of dispositions that He wants us to cultivate, as honoring Him. In the case of the Psalms, at any rate, the worshiping church has always understood this, though the point has not always received clear theological formulation. In truth, however, it is a point that applies to all Scripture, as such.

It is thus a necessary part of the interpreter's task to understand each human writer's purpose of correcting and directing his readers as God's own purpose expressed through him, and to universalize each writer's attitudes toward the specific people to whom or of whom he writes as indicating God's own attitudes now as then toward all whose moral and spiritual dispositions correspond with theirs. To do this is simply to practice grammatico-historical interpretation as the great Reformers did, in a manner free from that cultivated detachment that became a cramping convention in academic Bible work, even that of the Reformers' most faithful heirs, about a century and a half ago. Called, or rather miscalled, "objectivity," this convention is based on the idea that the natural sciences provide a proper model for all historical and factual inquiry and that students can and should stand apart from all the existential involvements of those they study. To accept this idea (which really has nothing to do with the fact-finding and interpretative techniques of "critical" scholarship as such) is to cast a vote for the professorial ideal that Kierkegaard lampooned and against Kierkegaard's own ideal of "passion" in the sense of committedness. In fact, the convention of "objectivity" has blighted technical study of Scripture with theological unreality for too long; it is high time that awareness of the text as God here and now addressing us, its latter-day readers, and teaching us from it, challenging us by law and gospel, promise and command, gift and claim, should once more come to inform professional biblical studies in the church. The desire to recover this awareness fuels present-day hermeneutical discussion,[34] and we should be glad that it does. But if, as I am arguing, the first step in the actual receiving of God's instruction in these matters is to comprehend, not just the public facts but also the personal thoughts and feelings concerning them, both evaluative and reactive, that each writer expressed, then some measure of what I have called "empathy" (what Dilthey called *Verwandtschaft*, "affinity," and Fuchs refers to as *Einverständnis*) is certainly needed; and we may well applaud Schleiermacher for underlining its importance.

Unhappily, as has been noted, Schleiermacher predicated this insight on the belief that God's impact on people does not take the form of cognitive communication. Schleiermacher's God stirs our feelings but does not tell us things. Schleiermacher conceptualized the impact of biblical and later Christian language on the model of ritual incantation that casts an emotional spell rather than of person-to-person communication that informs. He read Scripture, dogma, and theology as religious feeling evocatively verbalized, just as his English contemporary and fellow-romantic William Wordsworth, in his preface to *Lyrical Ballads*, asked that his poetry be read as "emotion recollected in tranquillity." As a romantic valuing sensitivity of response to actual and potential experiences above all, and committed to vindicate religious awareness as part of the good life, Schleiermacher the theologian naturally drew his hermeneutical model from the world of art and aesthetics, and equally naturally turned his back on models from the worlds of philosophy and law, where the conveying of public facts, arguments, and lines of thought is the essence of the communicative process. In every hermeneutic, the questions, what is being conveyed and how is it being conveyed, are answered together; from this standpoint a hermeneutic is like an ellipse with two foci. For Schleiermacher and those who have followed him, the beginning of the answer to the first question is that biblical material, whatever else it is, is not at any point or in any respect the relaying of divinely uttered instruction, even when its writers think and claim the contrary.[35] And most of those who have in our day refocused attention on hermeneutics have done so on the basis of this same denial that Scripture is instruction about God from God, that it is, in other words, the Word of God in the sense in which all Christendom till the nineteenth century thought it was.

We inherit, therefore, a situation in which the phrase "the theory of biblical interpretation" means radically different things to different people.

Evangelicals, whose belief that Scripture is God's message Kant and his successors did not destroy, continue to think of hermeneutics essentially as it was thought of in the seventeenth century. How was that? It was thought of as the study of rules and procedures that enable us to grasp first of all what Scripture *meant* as communication from its human writers speaking on God's behalf to their own envisaged readers, and from that what it *means* for us—that is, how this instruction in faith, hope, and conduct, viewed as revelation from the unchanging God to all mankind, applies to our own present-day living, and what it tells us of God's eternal plan, His unchanging Christ, the abiding realities of discipleship and godliness, and the way to assess cultural shifts that make the worlds of biblical experience look different from our own. Understanding of what Scripture means when applied to us—that is, of what God in Scripture is saying to and about us—comes only through the work of the sovereign Holy Spirit, who alone enables us to apprehend what God is and see what we are in His eyes. (This is a different point from that made above: the empathy of which I spoke enables us to grasp what Scripture *meant*, but it takes the Spirit's enlightenment to show us what it *means*.) But this Spirit-given understanding comes by a rational process that can be stated, analyzed, and tested at each point. Therefore unanimity is always in principle possible, and in any age plurality of theological views, however inescapable and indeed stimulating in practice, must be seen as a sign of intellectual and/or spiritual deficiency in some if not all of God's learning people. All evangelical treatments of the way to gain understanding of Scripture take this general position more or less explicitly.

To the mixed multitude of Schleiermacher's spiritual children, however, hermeneutics means the study of an intrinsically enigmatic process whereby two separate-seeming things happen together. On the one hand we enter empathetically, so far as we can, into the personal existence of the Bible writers and the characters about whom they tell us, most notably Jesus Himself, who, despite the cultural gap between Him and us, which (so it is alleged) makes it impossible for us to endorse all His recorded beliefs—his view of Scripture, for instance, or of demons—nonetheless has significance for us as a model of basic ethico-religious attitudes.[36] On the other hand, a change takes place within us as (to echo some) we come to feel compelling authority in aspects at least of the church's sense of God and of the lifestyle that Jesus modeled, or (to follow the wording of others) we are met by God who changes our attitudes and commitments, our view of ourselves and of our world. Thus, in one way or another (so it is claimed) understanding dawns for us *through* the biblical text;[37] yet its relation to our understanding *of* that text, and to the different personal understandings professed by others who follow this same approach, remains forever problematical because of the lack of coherence between the understandings that the text triggers and that which it expresses.

But this means that each of the personal understandings that purport to have been sparked off by the biblical text is more or less arbitrary—unless, indeed, we take refuge in illuminism and claim for each of them the status of a private revelation—an extent to which no theologian in the Schleiermacherian camp, whether old-fashioned liberal, neoorthodox or reconstructed liberal, seems to want to go. And it also follows that an ultimate pluralism of personal understandings is inescapable in principle. This is partly because, as exponents of this viewpoint since Bultmann have insisted, our varied "preunderstandings" (on which see below) program us toward conclusions that are also varied; but more basically it is because, as our analysis above has shown, denial that the biblical text communicates information from God about God leaves us with no objective test for evaluating conclusions save our own capacity to develop them into coherent and more or less comprehensive systems, to be introduced with such words as "I feel," "it seems to me," or, more existentially, "my proposal is. . . ." (In fact, the most fitting introduction each time would be "I guess," for this approach reduces all thinking about God to guesswork in the final analysis.) Examples of such systems are: the reconstructed gnosticism of Paul Tillich, in which religions coalesce and "Christ" is the therapeutic symbol that induces "new being";[38] the modified deism of Maurice Wiles, whose Jesus is human but whose God is perceived in and through values;[39] the dynamic unitarianism of Geoffrey Lampe, for whom the incarnation of God is precisely the divine Spirit indwelling a man named Jesus;[40] the dualistic existentialism of Bultmann, whose God acts (noncognitively) in the individual's personal consciousness though not in the public, impersonal world of nature;[41] the process theology of John Cobb and others, for whom God is finite love undergoing development.[42] More examples could be given. It is plain that an endless succession of diverging personal theologies is unavoidable once the acknowledgment of Scripture teaching as revealed truth is given up.[43]

For both evangelical and Schleiermacherian hermeneutics, however, a major insight is focused by what Gadamer, following Heidegger, says of *horizons*.[44] The insight is that at the heart of the hermeneutical process there is between the text and the interpreter a kind of interaction in which their respective panoramic views of things, angled and limited as these are, "engage" or "intersect"—in other words, appear as challenging each other in some way. What this means is that as the student questions the text he becomes aware that the text is also questioning him, showing him an alternative to what he took for granted, forcing him to rethink at fundamental level and make fresh decisions as to how he will act henceforth, now that he has realized that some do, and he himself could, approach things differently. Every interpreter needs to realize that he himself stands in a given historical context and tradition, just as his text does, and that only as he becomes aware of this can he avoid reading into the text assumptions from his own background that would deafen him to what the text itself has to say to him.

Exegetes have noted that several of Jesus' parables have surprise endings that were meant to work in his hearers' minds like the punch line of jokes, unveiling facts that suddenly put the situation in a new light and call for a fresh assessment, exploding one's previous view of how things stood.[45] A joke that does this perfectly is the following gem, I think from Woody Allen: "My first wife was very neurotic. One day she came into the bathroom when I was in the bath and sank all my boats." Parables inducing the same sort of "double-take," a shock of assumptions confounded as new facts about God are revealed, include the Pharisee and the publican (who went home *justified*!), the laborers in the vineyard (to all of whom the owner was *equally generous*!), and the two sons (whose father rejoiced *more* at the return of the scapegrace than at the steadiness of the good guy!).[46] The devastating exchange into which Nathan drew David by telling him of the poor man's ewe lamb (2 Sam. 12:1–10) was a dialogue version of the same communicative device, as is every good preacher's regular trick of building up with seeming sympathy a description of the intellectual and moral position that his hearers occupy, in order then to fire off texts and arguments that slaughter it. This *dénouement* technique, as we may call it, is precisely a matter of getting the horizons of speaker and hearers suddenly to intersect in a way that forces on the latter a jolting reassessment of what before seemed clear, familiar, and fixed. It remains a block-busting resource for any communicator who knows how to use it. We thus can see that in focusing the fact that serious interpretation of anything, secular or sacred, involves dialoguing with and being vulnerable to the text, laying oneself and one's present ideas open to it and being willing to be startled and to alter one's view if what comes from the text seems so to require, Gadamer and those who follow him make a true and important point.

Important too is Gadamer's insistence that "distancing" must precede "fusing" of horizons; that is, that we must become aware of the differences between the culture and thought-background out of which the words of the text come and that of our own thought and speech. Only so can we be saved from the particular naïveté that H. J. Cadbury pinpointed when he wrote *The Peril of Modernizing Jesus.*[47] The naïveté consists of treating people and words from the past as if they belonged to the present, thus making it impossible to see them in their own world and have our own horizons extended or redrawn by the impact of what they actually meant. Popular Bible study and preaching easily go astray here—indeed one might almost say inherit a tradition of going astray here—and anyone who highlights the danger deserves our thanks.

Valuable however as these phenomenological (that is, descriptive and elucidatory) comments on the nature of the hermeneutical process are, they do nothing to narrow the theological Grand Canyon that yawns between the evangelical and the Schleiermacherian views of Scripture and hence of the knowledge of God that due interpretation of Scripture gives. In welcoming the insights that the current preoccupation with hermeneutics has yielded, it is important not to lose sight of the fact that "Scripture" is a word that to most of today's hermeneutical pioneers means something radically different from what it means to Evangelicals who gratefully learn from them.

THE "NEW HERMENEUTIC"

In our day the Schleiermacherian approach to Scripture, recast by Bultmann in existentialist form, has issued in the so-called "new hermeneutic" of Bultmann's disciples, Ernst Fuchs and Gerhard Ebeling.[48] Logically and psychologically it appears to be the very end of the Schleiermacherian road, the *ne plus ultra* of that approach, and as such it merits at least a glance at this stage of our argument.

The first thing to say about it is that it builds on the ontology of the later Heidegger.[49] On this view, the manner in which language yields understanding is not by directing our attention to objects (what semantic theory nowadays calls *referents*) in the way that mankind always thought. Understanding comes, rather, out of the heart or womb of language itself, and becomes ours through "letting language, *from within* language, speak to us."[50] For Heidegger, an antitheistic ex-Jesuit seminarian, self-disclosing being (*Sein*)—that is, being that consists precisely of what occurs in the event of its self-disclosure—is the final reality, and it is known and shown as such in the "primal thinking" and "primary speech" of "authentic" individuals. By this Heidegger means the sort of thought and speech found in poets, mystics, and Zen Buddhists,[51] people who have become (as he puts it) mouthpieces and guardians of being, through whom being speaks. The message of such utterance is apparently received by a kind of divination, as one realizes that in the words one is hearing being itself is "addressing me." Hermeneutics is thus the art of entry into the meaning of primary speech. It is remarkable how far Heidegger goes in ascribing ontological status to language as the "house" and "custodian" of being,[52] in conceiving of being activistically as event rather than in static terms, and in personalizing being as a speaker busy in self-disclosure, to whose voice we must open ourselves.[53] Perhaps this is another case of an odd view that only a very clever person would have been able to think up. Nonetheless, Heidegger's influence, to the point of guruhood, on young metaphysical nihilists longing for cosmic disclosures has been very great.

But Alan Richardson's comment is apt:

> What Heidegger in fact does is to provide modern man with a secular parody of the Christian religion. Instead of God he speaks of being; instead of a revelation through the word of God he gives us the disclosure of being through the voice of being. Instead of faith we have primal thinking. Instead of Christ we read of man as "the shepherd of being." Instead of a once-for-all victory over sin and death there is the individually repeated salvation from the dread of nothingness and from the futility of secondary thinking and unauthentic existence. Instead of the community of the redeemed there is a gnostic collection of individual primal thinkers. Instead of the fulfilment of man's destiny as the goal of history (eschatology) there is only a disclosure or "event" of being.[54]

It would seem safe to say that Heidegger's view of being and language, like the secular redemption-stories that Wagner wrote for his operas, would never have seen the light of day had not the author's imagination been haunted by the Christian faith he denied.

Now what Fuchs and Ebeling do is theologize this Heideggerian ontology, replacing being by God, or rather giving Heidegger's being the name of God, though otherwise leaving Him (it?) substantially unchanged. God is known, they say, in and by each "word-happening" (*Wortgeschehen*, Ebeling's term) or "language-event" (*Sprachereignis*, Fuchs's term) that the faith-full speech of the New Testament sparks off in those who read and hear it. Fuchs and Ebeling, like Bultmann, view preaching as the paradigm situation in which the word-event happens, and for them as for him the essence of it, when it does happen, is (not the receiving of instruction from God,[55] but) the birth of a new "self-understanding" (*Selbstverständnis*)—that is, a new way of relating to one's personal world. In Bultmann this "self-understanding" consisted of freedom from guilt and fear; Fuchs describes it as modeled on the faith of Jesus, by which he means Jesus' renouncing of all self-assertion and security, His submission to whatever came as coming from God, and His commitment to unqualified love. (Remember, when evaluating Fuchs's formula, that for him as for Bultmann Jesus is not God; faith is not cognitive, any more than it was for Schleiermacher; and the existentialist equation of individual committedness with authentic existence is axiomatic.) For both Fuchs and Ebeling theology is essentially hermeneutic, a mapping of the process whereby language-events happen and a delineating of the kind of "self-understanding" that results.

Fuchs complicates his picture by modeling the language-event exclusively on the way in which Jesus' words, especially in His parables, with their unexpected endings, shattered the assumptions of conventional religious persons in the days of His flesh. His development of this, as Thiselton notes, leaves him unable to find "room in his hermeneutic for tradition, the church, or history after the event of the cross"[56]—or for Jesus' historical resurrection (in which, as a good Bultmannian, he does not believe anyway). Faith to him is not and cannot be belief in Jesus as divine and risen, in the apostolic gospel as God's own teaching about Jesus who died and rose, and in the church as "pillar and foundation of the truth" (1 Tim. 3:15); in other words, it cannot be what it is in the epistles.[57] Fuchs thus sentences himself, as P. J. Achtemeier puts it, "to defend a view of faith based on some portions of the New Testament from a view of faith based on other portions,"[58] and to talk as if the word-event never happens except to folk who are not yet believers or who have lapsed from faith into a formalized, worldly religiosity. This is inept; yet the lopsidedness could perhaps be corrected without the collapse of Fuchs's whole scheme. But two more damaging questions now arise.

1. Can the new hermeneutic state the relation between what, on its view, comes to each individual from the biblical text in the language-event, and what the text meant historically—that is, what grammatico-historical exegesis finds in it? It seems not.

Fuchs is emphatic that in the word-event the interpreter is interpreted rather than the text.[59] Pinnock does not overstate when he writes that for Fuchs "the text is in motion!... It stands in dynamic, existential relation with its interpreter, and may be interpreted [that is, may strike sparks off him] in the opposite way from that which the writer intended."[60] Fuchs can say this not only because, as a radical historical critic, he holds that some of what the Gospels report about Jesus was misunderstood on the way and hence misrepresented by the evangelists; his more basic thought is that in any case what the writers of Scripture express within their subject-object frame of reference does not relate directly to the impact of Scripture on us in the word-event, where the subject-object frame of reference is transcended. Fuchs evidently wants to ride both horses and have the impact of the text emerge somehow from critical-historical study of it, but his Heideggerian insistence that the word-event is on a different plane from subject-object thinking robs him of the right to affirm that restrictive connection.

It is important to be clear on what Fuchs has got himself into at this point. "Subject-object thinking, they [Heidegger and Fuchs] believe, as well as distancing man from reality also sets in motion a vicious circularity by evaluating one set of human concepts in terms of another."[61]

Subject-object thinking, which was Heidegger's phrase for the "I–it" way of conceptualizing reality that was practiced from Plato on in the West, here means holding to the principle that apprehension of the text's message—the process that, with Gadamer and the new hermeneuts, we may well call the coming to speech of the reality (*Sache*)[62]—occurs within the limits and, one could say, on the rails laid down by what the text "objectively" means. ("Objectively" signifies historically, permanently, and publicly and "means" is a timeless present signifying "meant at and from the time of writing.") When the new hermeneuts insist that the text is not a *passive* object, we may agree: the whole New Testament (to look no further) is preaching on paper, written to call forth assent and obedience from all who read it, and in acknowledging it, with the Old Testament, as divinely inspired we recognize that it is not only man's preaching but God's also,[63] so that as the text's historical meaning is applied to us God Himself addresses us. Scripture is thus an *active* object, since God who speaks it—that is, speaks in and through it, saying what it says—is an active subject. But this way of understanding how Scripture speaks God to us is not open to those who have given up belief that what Scripture says, God says, and for whom it has become important to affirm that much of what Scripture says God does *not* say; and all hermeneuts of Bultmann's existentialist breed come in this category. They want to stress that God comes to people through Scripture to induce the new self-understanding, and one is glad that they do. But, since they think God is dumb and Scripture is only human witness, culturally determined, how can they give meaning and substance to their own point? Bultmann thought the new self-understanding would come as the New Testament was de- and re-mythologized according to his own announced rules. The snag in that, however, as is well known, was that it meant abandoning at the most crucial points the demonstrable meaning of the New Testament writers. Fuchs thinks the new self-understanding will emerge as the text is cut loose from the restraints of objective historical exegesis and thereby fully freed to interpret its interpreters. The snag in this, however, is that it sets us off and running along a path of fundamentally uncontrolled linguistic mysticism, in which, as it seems, almost anything could bring almost anything to speech. For the restraint of the text as object—i.e., as carrier of the precise meaning that its words are expressing—has been withdrawn, and Fuchs's own account of what Christian faith is, being no more, in terms of his own theory, than his own personal self-understanding, cannot be determinative for the rest of us. It is evident that Fuchs does not see this, but it is also evident that his account of the language-event as transcending the subject-object way of thinking makes the above conclusion logically inevitable.

It is hard to be enthusiastic about Fuchs's proposals. Surely it is arbitrary to treat as not significant for determining the nature of Christianity those major parts of the New Testament that consist of rational argument and systematic elucidation of theological concepts, in unambigously subject-object terms (Paul's letters, Hebrews, John's Gospel and first Epistle, for starters). Surely it is hazardous to assume that the New Testament interest in conceptualizing the faith was misdirected. Surely it is inadequate to reduce the whole New Testament message to the single formula: cease from self-assertion, practice and love instead.[64] By making this reduction, Fuchs in effect lines up with those horrendous preachers who manage to extract the same sermon from every text; but such skill is no more respectable in professors than it is in pulpiteers! And, finally, surely it is a recipe for spiritual disaster to deny that the text's historical meaning may be invoked to determine the authenticity or otherwise of the particular language-events of which people testify. This brings us to the next question.

2. Can the new hermeneutic provide any criterion of truth or value for assessing the new self-understanding(s) to which language-events give rise? Again, it seems not.

Remember where Fuchs has placed us. The criteria of correspondence with apostolic teaching in general and the historical sense of the text in particular have been denied us. What is now left? Is the mere fact of being more or less startling to us the criterion whereby new thoughts about ourselves and our lives are to be evaluated? Are we to judge the most startling to be the most authentic, or what? J. C. Weber asks, "In what way can we know that language does not bring to expression illusion, falsehood, or even chaos? If the criterion of truth is only in the language-event itself, how can the language-event be safeguarded against delusion, mockery, or utter triviality? Why cannot the language-event be a disguised event of nothingness? ... Fuchs' ontology is in danger of dissolving into a psychological illusionism"—meaning, presumably, an inducing of the sense that something significant happens when nothing significant happens.[65] There seems no counter to this criticism: Fuchs really has left us to sink in the swamps of subjectivist subjectivity, with no available criteria of truth and value at all for the language-events that came our way.

The new hermeneutic is in truth the end of the Schleiermacherian road. Its denial of the reality of revealed truth, linked with its rejection of the subject-object frame of reference for knowledge of God through Scripture, produces a state of affairs beyond which there is nowhere to go. Logically, the new hermeneutic is relativism; philosophically, it is irrationalism; psychologically, it is freedom to follow unfettered religious fancy; theologically, it is unitarianism; religiously, it is uncontrolled individualistic mysticism; structurally, it is all these things not by accident but of necessity. We leave it, and move on.

EVANGELICAL HERMENEUTICS

Over against what has been studied so far I will now offer a fuller evangelical account of the hermeneutical process.[66] Based on the beliefs about Scripture that were highlighted in the opening pages of this chapter, evangelical biblical interpretation proceeds by the following three stages: exegesis, synthesis, and application.

Exegesis means bringing out of the text all that it contains of the thoughts, attitudes, assumptions, and so forth—in short, the whole expressed mind—of the human writer. This gives the "literal" sense, in the name of which the Reformers rejected the allegorical senses beloved of medieval exegetes.[67] I call it the "natural" or "literary" sense, whereby the exegete seeks to put himself in the writer's linguistic, cultural, historical, and religious shoes. It has been the historic evangelical method of exegesis, followed with more or less consistency and success since the Reformers' time. (It is, of course, everybody's initial method nowadays.) This exegetical process assumes the full humanity of the inspired writings.[68]

In reaction from exegesis that concerned itself only with biblical events and ideas as parts of the global historical process, the plea is heard today for what Barth called *theological* and Brevard S. Childs calls *canonical* exegesis; that is, exegesis that is "churchly" (as opposed to "worldly") in that it (1) reads all Scripture as witness to the living God and (2) reads each book of Scripture as part of the total canon that bears this witness.[69] To practice canonical exegesis, in idea at any rate, is not to read into biblical texts what is not there, but to read them from an angle of vision that enables one to see what is there. This angle of vision is faith in the Bible's God—something that all the canonical writers shared and out of which they wrote. Evangelical exegesis has always been characteristically canonical in this sense.[70]

Synthesis here means the process of gathering up and surveying in historically integrated form the fruits of exegesis—a process that is sometimes, from one standpoint and at one level, called "biblical theology" in the classroom and at other times, from another standpoint and at another level, called "exposition" in the pulpit. This synthetic process assumes the organic character of Scripture.

Application means seeking to answer these questions: If God said and did in the circumstances recorded what the text tells us He said and did, what does He say and what is He doing and what will He do to us in our circumstances? If His promise and command then were thus and so, what is His promise and command to us now? Applicatory reasoning assumes the consistency of God and the essential identity of human nature and need from one age to another, along with the fact that "Jesus Christ is the same yesterday and today and for ever" (Heb. 13:8). Its basic thought is that as particulars of God's dealings recorded in the Old Testament have universal significance as paradigms for divine action under New Testament conditions (for samples of reasoning on this basis, see Rom. 4, 9; 1 Cor. 10:1–12; Gal. 3:6–14; Heb. 3:7–4:10, 10:26–12:29), so recorded particulars of God's dealings under New Testament conditions have universal significance as paradigms of how He will always now deal with His human creatures. Applicatory reasoning thus leads to Gadamer's distancing and fusing of horizons on a different level from that which Gadamer himself envisages; where Gadamer speaks of the intersecting of historically separate worlds of human thought, there evangelical application theory posits encounter with the revealed mind of the unchanging God whose thoughts and ways are never like those of fallen mankind in any era at all, and in whose hands each human being must realize that for better or for worse, as his own choice determines, he remains forever.

Ebeling is correct when he writes: "According to Luther, the word of God always comes as *adversarius noster*, our adversary. It does not simply confirm and strengthen us in what we think we are, and in what we wish to be taken for.... This is the way, the only way, in which the word draws us into concord and peace with God."[71] But this insight does not belong to Ebeling's new hermeneutic, in which "word of God" is a label for an event in which language impacts us with a creativity that is almost magical[72] even though God, being dumb, is never its speaker. Luther's insight belongs rather to his own hermeneutical world, the world of the old evangelical hermeneutic, where the exegete has constantly to reckon with the uncomfortable truth that what Scripture said about God to men of old times God says about Himself to us today. Law and gospel, promise and command, factual narration, theological generalization and prophetic vision, are all uttered afresh by God to us every time the Bible text faces us— uttered, that is, not in the once-for-all way in which they were uttered to the world when God first gave the text through His human penmen, but uttered in the applicatory sense of which we are now speaking, the sense that is modeled by Luther's *pro me* and by those minatory public notices that say, "This means *you!*" This is the sense that is felt after in the much-discussed Barthian formula that Scripture *becomes* the Word of God to its readers and hearers. The heart of the hermeneutical problem does not lie in the determining of the historical meaning of each passage (there are now many good commentaries that make that clear); it lies, rather, in seeing how it applies to you, me, and us at the point in history and personal life where we are now. That the application may be traumatic in its reproving and corrective thrust is not in dispute (cf. 2 Tim. 3:16–17!). My only point against Ebeling— which would certainly have been Luther's too, had Luther foreseen him—is that it is the present utterance of the living God, and nothing less, that is being applied; this means (putting it the other way around) that the applied teaching of Holy Scripture is in truth the message and instruction of God our Maker.

For two generations Protestant theology, especially that made in German, has focused on the question, How can the language of Scripture communicate the Word of God (whatever that is—views vary) across the cultural and historical gap that separates us from Bible times? Answers have been given in terms of a new word being spoken through the old words and of an existential impact being made by or via them. Nineham, as we saw, has given up the question, thinking that communication that is chronologically transcultural is simply impossible. (Would he say the same of communication that is geographically transcultural? Alas for the Christian missionary enterprise if so.) As a matter of observable fact, all who link the assertion that God genuinely communicates through Scripture with the denial that the written text as such is God's utterance become incoherent sooner or later. Only the evangelical theory of application remains rationally intelligible to the very end. On that theory, application is the last stage in the temporal process whereby God speaks to each generation and to individuals within each generation: God who gave His Word in the form of the rational narration, exposition, reflection, and devotion that Holy Scripture is, now prompts the making and receiving of rational application of it. This application is the Word of God to you and to me.

Evangelical theology affirms a correlation between the rational process whereby principles, having been established from biblical particulars, are applied to cases and persons, and the teaching ministry of the Holy Spirit, who enables our sin-darkened minds to draw and accept these correct conclusions as from God. Because correct application is a strictly rational process, most evangelical textbooks on interpreting Scripture say little or nothing about the Holy Spirit, Scripture's ultimate author, as the great hermeneut who by leading and enlightening us in the work of exegesis, synthesis, and application, actually interprets that Word in our minds and to our hearts.[73] The omission unhappily allows evangelical rationality in interpretation to look like a viciously self-reliant rationalism, while by contrast the regular neoorthodox appeal to the Spirit as interpreter (an appeal that appears on analysis to be an illuminist fig leaf donned to conceal disfiguring incoherence and arbitrariness in handling the text) looks like proper humility—and that is ironical indeed, since Evangelicals have in fact more to say than anyone else about the Spirit's work of enabling us to see, grasp, love, and live by God's revealed truth, just because they have more to say than anyone else about the spiritually blinding effect of sin on our minds.[74] It is to be hoped that future evangelical treatments of biblical interpretation will not fall short here.[75] If, as current need requires, they are written as treatments of hermeneutics, covering the whole process whereby we come to understand God's word to us from the texts through our being made the recipients of His communicative activity, explicit accounts of the

Spirit's witnessing, enlightening, and teaching ministry will have to be given, and the false impression will thereby automatically be corrected.[76]

BIBLICAL AUTHORITY AND THE HERMENEUTICAL CIRCLE

What has been said makes it clear that an overall view of biblical authority underlies and controls evangelical interpretation of Scripture. Is this view, in its function as a methodological principle, open to the charge of being an arbitrary and distorting a priori in the way that I have accused some other views of being? I think not, and will try to show the a posteriori nature of this control, as part of the total biblical faith, by adapting the concept of the "hermeneutical circle," which Bultmann first adapted from Heidegger.[77]

In the present context I use the phrase "hermeneutical circle" to express the truth (for truth it is) that our exegesis, synthesis, and application is determined by a hermeneutic—that is, a view of the interpretative process—that is determined by an overall theology, a theology that in its turn rests on and supports itself by exegesis, synthesis, and application. Thus defined, the circle is not logically vicious; it is not the circle of presupposing what you ought to prove, but the circle of successive approximation, a basic method in every science. From this standpoint it might be better to speak of the hermeneutical *spiral*, whereby we rise from a less exact and well-tested understanding to one that is more so. Within the circle, or spiral, two complementary processes take place: one is questioning the text and having one's questions progressively reshaped by what the text yields; the other is the reciprocal illumination of part by whole and whole by part in one's repeated traversings of long stretches of language (e.g., Deuteronomy, Romans, John's Gospel). Both processes are constantly involved in spiraling up to more precise and profound understanding. The point embodied in the circle-image is that we can understand only what in some way latches on to prior knowledge that we bring to it, so that what we bring to it will radically condition our understanding of it. The reason for preferring the spiral-image is that within the circle of presuppositionally conditioned interpretation it is always possible for dialogue and critical questioning to develop between what in the text does not easily or naturally fit in with our presuppositions and those presuppositions themselves, and for both our interpretation and our presuppositions to be modified as a result.

Now the evangelical theologian's method of seeking understanding is this: First, he goes to the text of Scripture to learn from it the doctrine of Scripture just as he goes to the text of Scripture to learn from it the doctrine of everything else it deals with. At this stage he takes with him as his presupposition, provisionally held (his "pre-understanding," Bultmann would call it), not, like Bultmann, a

Heideggerian anthropology, nor, like Barth, a Christomonist ontology, but an overall view of Christian truth and of the way to approach the Bible—a view that he has gained from the creeds, confessions, preaching, and corporate life of the church and from his own earlier ventures in exegesis and theology. By the light of his pre-understanding he discerns in Scripture material that yields an integrated account of the nature, place, and use of the Bible. From this doctrine of the Bible and its authority he next derives by theological analysis a set of hermeneutical principles; and, armed with these, he returns to the biblical text, to expound and apply its teaching on everything more scientifically than he could do before. If at any stage what appears to emerge from the texts appears to challenge his personal pre-understanding and/or call in question the tradition that was his personal springboard, he lets dialogue between the appearances develop, with the purpose of bringing his present understanding fully into line with biblical teaching once he sees clearly what this is. Thus he moves to and fro within the hermeneutical spiral. If his exegetical procedure is challenged, he defends it from his hermeneutic; if his hermeneutic is challenged, he defends it from his doctrine of biblical authority; if his doctrine of biblical authority is challenged, he defends it from biblical texts by exegesis, synthesis, and application. At no point does he decline to accept challenges to his present view of things, but at every point he meets them by renewed theological exegesis of relevant passages in the light of the questions that have been asked. It has been said that until Schleiermacher "hermeneutics was supposed to support, secure and clarify an already accepted understanding."[78] Whether this was ever really so for evangelical theology is arguable,[79] though there is no denying that defensive postures often made it look that way.[80] But in idea, at least, there are no a prioris in an Evangelical's theology, and nothing in it is "already accepted" in the sense of not being open to the possibility of theological challenge and biblical reassessment—not even his view of Scripture.[81]

INTERPRETATION, INFALLIBILITY, AND INERRANCY

What control does the hermeneutic that derives from the evangelical doctrine of Scripture place on one's interpretative practice? In a word, it binds us, first, to the grammatico-historical method in exegesis, second, to the principle of harmony in synthesis, and, third, to the principle of universalizing in application. Hints about all three have been scattered through this chapter; here I try to draw the threads together and state each point fully.

1. The grammatico-historical method of approaching texts is dictated not merely by common sense, but by the doctrine of inspiration,[82] which tells us that God has put His words into the mouths, and caused them to be written in the writings, of persons whose individu-

ality, as people of their time, was in no way lessened by the fact of their being thus overruled, and who spoke and wrote to be understood by their contemporaries. Since God has effected an identity between their words and His, the way for us to get into His mind, if we may thus phrase it, is via theirs; for their thought and speech about God constitutes God's own self-testimony. Though God may have more to say to us from each text than its human writer had in mind, God's meaning is never less than his. What he meant, God meant; and God's further meaning, as revealed when the text is exegeted in its canonical context, in relation to all that went before and came after, is simply extension, development, and application of what the writer was consciously expressing. So the first task is always to get into the writer's mind by grammatico-historical exegesis of the most thoroughgoing and disciplined kind, using all the tools provided by linguistic, historical, logical,[83] and semantic[84] study for the purpose.

2. Adherence to the principle of harmony is also dictated by the doctrine of inspiration, which tells us that the Scriptures are the products of a single divine mind. This principle branches into three. First, Scripture should be interpreted by Scripture, just as one part of a human teacher's message may and should be interpreted by appeal to the rest. *Scriptura scripturae interpres* was the Reformers' slogan on this point. Scripture must be approached as a single organism of instruction, and we must look always for its internal links and topical parallels, which in fact are there in profusion, waiting to be noticed. Second, Scripture should not be set against Scripture. Anglican Article XX forbids the church to "so expound one place of Scripture, that it be repugnant to another," and the principle applies to the individual expositor too. It is to be expected that the teaching of the God of truth will prove to be consistent with itself, and we should proceed accordingly. Then, third, what appears to be secondary, incidental, and obscure in Scripture should be viewed in the light of what appears to be primary, central, and plain. This principle requires us to echo the main emphases of the New Testament and to develop a christocentric, covenantal, kerygmatic exegesis of both Testaments; also, to keep a sense of proportion regarding what are confessedly minutiae, not letting them overshadow what God has indicated to be the weightier matters. These three principles together constitute what the Reformers called *analogia Scripturae*, and the analogy of Scripture, which for clarity's sake I have called the principle of harmony.

3. The principle of universality in application follows from the unchangeable consistency of the God whose particular words and deeds Scripture records. Since He does not change, devilish self-aggrandizement such as called forth His judicial hatred against Tyre (Ezek. 27–28) and Jerusalem (Isa. 1–5) and Rome (Rev. 17–18) will always and everywhere evoke the same hostility. Since the incarnate Son does not change (cf. Heb. 13:8), the compassion shown to the

penitent thief (Luke 23:43) and the Galilean prostitute (Luke 7:36ff.) and doubting Thomas (John 20:27ff.) continues to be there for all who know their need of it. Divine promises given in Scripture to Christians as such will be kept in every case, while the righteousness required of any is required of all; passage of time changes nothing in this regard. Watching how God dealt with people in Bible times, we learn how we may expect Him to deal with us. We see instanced in the particular events of the Bible story the universal principles of God's will and work, and the essence of our interpretative task is to unshell these from their immediate setting in order to reapply them to our own situations.[85] Barth's denial of revealed general principles is ultimately unconvincing, if only because in his own preaching he implicitly assumes them, as everyone who attempts to preach biblically does and must do. Historical exegesis, as practiced since the mid-nineteenth century, too often shrouds itself in ambiguity here: beliefs expressed in the text are formulated with poker-faced indifference as to whether they indicate what God might say to, think of, and do for us today. By contrast, the "theological" or "canonical" type of exegesis that was practiced more or less skillfully from the patristic period to the nineteenth century and that (thank God) is being cautiously recovered in many quarters today, accepts responsibility for identifying and applying the truth about the living God that Scripture yields. Thus it resolves into preaching, and rightly so. As Luther knew, the best and truest interpretation of "God's word written" (the phrase comes from Anglican Article XX) is achieved in the preaching of it.[86]

Shibboleths—test words indicating identity and allegiance (cf. Judg. 12:5–6)—are always suspect as obstacles to real thought, which indeed they can easily become. "Infallible" and "inerrant" as descriptions of the Bible function as shibboleths in some circles and so come under this suspicion in others. Individual definitions of both terms—minimizing, maximizing, and depreciating—are not lacking; it would be idle and irresponsible to speak as if there were always clarity and unanimity here. But if these words are construed, according to standard semantic theory, as carrying the meaning that they bear in general use among those who employ them and that appears, according to standard logical theory, in the expressive and communicative functions they perform, then they will be seen to be valuable verbal shorthand for conveying a fully biblical notion—namely, the total truth and trustworthiness of biblical affirmations and directives, as a consequence of their divine authenticity and as the foundation for their divine authority as revelation from God. They are in fact control words, with a self-involving logic: by affirming biblical infallibility and inerrancy, one commits oneself in advance to receive as God's instruction and obey as God's command whatever Scripture is already known to teach and may in the future be shown to teach. They entail no a priori commitments to specific views, whether of the nature of knowledge[87] or of the correct exegesis of biblical passages that touch on natural and historical events. They indicate only a commitment to the three interpretative principles set out above. As such, they have their own distinct usefulness.[88]

It should be added that in the task of interpreting Scripture theologically cognizant of, and encounter with, the historic Christian interpretative tradition, uniform or pluriform as at each point it may be, is of major methodological importance. Since Pentecost the Holy Spirit has been present and active in the church, and part of His ministry has been to teach God's people to understand the Scriptures and the message they contain (cf. Luke 24:44ff.; 1 Cor. 2:1–16; 2 Cor. 3:14–4:6; 1 Thess. 1:5, cf. 2:13; 1 John 2:20–27, cf. 5:20). That is why from the first it was expected, and rightly, that the doctrinal and ethical tradition stemming from the apostles—a tradition the bishops were set to guard and the ecumenical creeds came to enshrine—would prove on examination to be, so far as it went, true exposition of that which was central in the two Testaments. The medieval faith on this point could be summarized in the neat formula that Scripture is in tradition and tradition is in Scripture,[89] even though inroads of aberration had produced at certain points a state of affairs in which this faith could no longer be justified. When the Reformers' study of the Bible's literal sense (on which, according to Aquinas, all doctrine should rest) showed that with regard to the economy of grace (the way of salvation and the nature and role of the church) latter-day tradition and interpretation had gone radically wrong, the shock to Western Christendom was traumatic. In some Protestant bodies this trauma left behind it a neurotic fixation, as traumas tend to do—in this case, a fixed habit of suspecting that all tradition in those parts of the church that do not feel like home is always likely to be wrong; and one can point today to such groups whose interpretative style, though disciplined and conscientious, is narrow, shallow, naïve, lacking in roots, and wooden to a fault, for want of encounter with the theological and expository wisdom of nineteen Christian centuries.

The only course that the doctrine of the Holy Spirit in the church will sanction is to approach Scripture in the light of historic Christian study of it. Church tradition, in the sense of *traditio tradita*, that which is handed on, should be valued as a venture in biblical understanding by those who went before us, whom the Spirit helped as He helps us. It should not, indeed, be treated as at any point infallible, any more than our own ventures in biblical understanding should be, but rather as the product of honest scholarly endeavor for which the Spirit's aid was sought. Accordingly, we should expect to find it helpful as a guide, much more right than wrong. As we would think it perverse for a student of Scripture to refuse the help given by contemporary churchly scholarship in written commentaries, theologies, and manuals of various kinds, as well as in oral teaching, so we ought to think it perverse to refuse the help given by the churchly scholarship of the past. The former perversity would at once be diagnosed as that of a conceitedly self-sufficient person who fails to appreciate that the fellowship of the saints is the proper milieu for learning to understand the Bible; the latter perversity should be viewed in the same terms. Much of today's biblical study and exposition, even though conducted according to the three interpretative principles stated above, suffers through what C. S. Lewis somewhere called "chronological snobbery," the supposition that what is most recent will always be wisest and best, and that the latest word is nearer to being the last word than any that went before; those under the influence of this assumption do not seriously consult work done prior to our own time, and that is very much to our loss. Karl Barth characterized the tradition crystallized in creeds and confessions as a preliminary exposition of Scripture;[90] all Christian tradition should be seen in these terms and put to use in one's own mental dialogue accordingly. It is when Bible students are open to the Christian heritage of both present and past exposition and open also to the existential questions that arise for them out of the pressures of their times on their lives that interpretation and understanding may become profound, in a way that could not otherwise be.

HERMENEUTICS AND THE CONCEPT OF HOLY SCRIPTURE

To pull the threads yet closer together, it will be convenient to give summary answers to two questions, in the light of what has been said.

1. What conceptions of Scripture are hermeneutically invalid?— that is, unacceptable in the light of a posteriori exegesis of the recorded teaching of biblical authors, and particularly of Christ and the apostles, Christianity's normative teachers? Some theologians ignore the existence of a biblical doctrine of Scripture, and others, while noticing it, allow themselves to discount it; but it must be insisted that departure from the teaching of Christ and the apostles on this subject is as much a failure of discipleship as such a lapse on any other matter would be. The relevant biblical material cannot be paraded here,[91] but the following views may be listed as ruled out by it.

a. Views, such as those embraced by older generations of liberals and more recently by scholars like James Barr,[92] that see Scripture as a pluriform, multilayered testament of religious experience and/or insight, testifying only unevenly and fallibly to the God who was experienced and concerning whom the writers' convictions, true or false, were formulated.

b. Views, such as increasingly mark post–Vatican II Roman Catholic biblical work, that regard only that in Scripture which is necessary to salvation as having been infallibly and inerrantly delivered. Roman Catholic scholars who hold these views believe that the rest of Scripture (in the view of many, a very large amount) is every bit as uneven and fallible as liberal Protestants suppose.[93]

c. Views that, like those of Käsemann and Nineham, treat the body of canonical Scriptures as in their totality inconsistent, incoherent, or unintelligible; with or without the often-drawn corollary that whatever in Scripture seems significant to us should become our canon within the canon.[94]

2. What conceptions of biblical hermeneutics are hermeneutically invalid?—that is, out of line with proper principles of method for understanding Scripture? Variant hermeneutics among would-be theological exegetes in our day have led to widely differing accounts of how Scripture speaks and what it says, as we have already observed. But the following types of view may at once be decisively ruled out:

a. Views that hold that what God communicates in and through Scripture is something distinct from and perhaps unconnected with the writers' own expressed meaning and message in each case. All forms of nonliteral interpretation err here.

b. Views that regard God's communication through Scripture (if indeed such a thing may be affirmed at all) as noncognitive, in the sense that it conveys nothing that can be called factual information about God Himself. Schleiermacherians ancient and modern, including on this issue Bultmann and the exponents of the new hermeneutic, have gone astray at this point.

c. Views that assume that the way to understand the biblical message is to go behind the text to its supposed sources and exegete the material in relation to those sources rather than in its present canonical context, that is, as part of a whole book that is part of the whole Bible. Source-critical preoccupations have often led to disruptive exegesis of this kind.

d. Views that hold that events and circumstances may allow, indeed require, us to reorder the biblical message around a different center from that on which the New Testament focuses, namely knowing Jesus Christ as Savior from sin and spiritual death. Latin American liberation theology, which sees the bringing in of social and economic justice as the essence of what the Bible teaches that God's work today must be, is an example of this mistake.

PROSPECTS

It seems that, as was said at the start of this discussion, hermeneutical questions will continue to dominate theological debate in the world church for some time yet. Two considerations make this evident.

First, the most obvious, important, and tense differences between theologians today, the differences that most demand discussion and are, in fact, being most constantly discussed, are largely products of current hermeneutical pluaralism, which is therefore bound to stay central in debates about them. Take, for instance, Barthian theology, with its "Christomonistic" a priori whereby all truth about creation and the created order is swallowed up into the doctrine of Christ, and conceptions of election, reprobation, and redemption are formed that appear systematically to distort the plain sense of Scripture.[95] Or take Bultmannian theology, with its a priori that New Testament material that looks like historical testimony must be read as myth objectifying the transformed self-understanding of the writer. Or take process theology, with its a priori that though what biblical writers say of God's love should be taken as true, what they say of His triunity, eternity, and aseity (life in independence of His creatures) should not.[96] Or take the many current types of political theology, of which liberation theologies are only one, with their a priori that the *shalom* of socio-economic well-being in this world is what the biblical witness to God's saving work is really all about. It may be safely foretold that discussion of these things in the theological community will not soon expire.

Second, today's hermeneutical debate in theology is part of a larger debate about general or universal hermeneutics that has come to involve practitioners of the humanities *en masse*—philosophers, linguists, teachers of literature, lawyers, and historians of ideas among others. This discussion has been in progress on and off, mainly though not exclusively in Germany, ever since Schleiermacher in his character as a theologian of culture described literary interpretation as such as the art of divining and recreating the author's consciousness. During the past half-century, however, it has been influentially stoked up by the elaborate phenomenological accounts of hermeneutics—that is, of the mental process that genuinely receives what texts and works of art offer—that have been set forth in the writings of the philosophers Heidegger and Gadamer.[97] Both authors, in their different ways, tell us that what is offered via texts is not in fact found through any kind of study of the author's expressed mind (although it is not likely to be found without that study); what is offered is found, rather, in what the text "says" to us in the existential language-event, as the horizons we brought to the text fuse with horizons that emerge from the text itself. This "saying" is the emergence of genuinely new subject-matter, born of interaction between the text and the interpreter's prior consciousness. We saw earlier how this idea is put to service in the new hermeneutic. Heidegger and Gadamer are open to criticism for the wedge they drive between what the text meant in public, historical terms— that is, what was *given* in it—and what it says—*gives*—to its several interpreters in personal encounter. Like their disciples in theology, Fuchs and Ebeling, whom we reviewed earlier, Heidegger and Gadamer set us adrift without chart or compass on a sea of ultimately uncontrolled subjectivity.[98] History will probably view this as an un-balanced extreme of reaction against the interpretative objectivism that, starting with Descartes, ignored the individuality of the knowing subject and the heuristic importance of the questions he brings to the texts. What must be said at present, however, is that the flow of ideas from these men about the relation between text (source) and interpreter (the experiencing, knowing subject) has stirred up widespread discussion among scholars whose professions require them to interpret any kind of texts; and this will go on. It is to be hoped that Christian scholars, with their theological interest in the text-interpreter relation, will increasingly join in this wider debate.

Meantime, there is much here to enrich Christian thought on the knowledge of God via holy Scripture through the Spirit's work as illuminator and interpreter. Any evangelical who thought that after finding the weaknesses of Heidegger, Gadamer, Fuchs, and Ebeling there was no more to be said would be wrong. Maybe, indeed, the hermeneutical debate in theology has only just begun. Time will tell!

NOTES

Notes

SCRIPTURE'S SELF-ATTESTATION
AND THE PROBLEM OF FORMULATING
A DOCTRINE OF SCRIPTURE

Wayne A. Grudem

pages 19–59

[1]Scripture quotations in this chapter are usually from the RSV; however, in a number of cases I have used my own translation, usually then indicating in a footnote the reasons why I differ with the RSV at that point.

[2]See, for example, H. Knight, *The Hebrew Prophetic Consciousness* (London: Lutterworth, 1947), p. 116; S. Mowinckel, *The Old Testament as the Word of God*, trans. R. Bjornard (Oslo, 1938; reprint ed., Oxford: Blackwell, 1960), pp. 24–26; C. H. Dodd, *The Authority of the Bible* (London: Nisbet, 1928), p. 16; and, more recently, G. von Rad, *Old Testament Theology*, trans. D. M. G. Stalker, 2 vols. (Munich, 1960; reprint ed., London: Oliver and Boyd, 1962–65), 2:72 (a mixture of divine and human words).

[3]J. Barr, "The Interpretation of Scripture II: Revelation through History in the Old Testament and in Modern Theology," *Interpretation* 17 (1963): 201–2.

[4]James F. Ross, "The Prophet as Yahweh's Messenger," in *Israel's Prophetic Heritage*, ed. Bernhard W. Anderson and Walter Harrelson (London: SCM, 1962, pp. 98–107; J. Lindblom, *Prophecy in Ancient Israel* (Oxford: Blackwell, 1962), p. 104; Claus Westermann, *Basic Forms of Prophetic Speech*, trans. H. C. White (London: Lutterworth, 1967), pp. 98–128; Jörg Jeremias, "Die Vollmacht des Propheten in Alten Testament," *Evangelische Theologie* 31 (1971), p. 308; Rolf Rendtorff, "Nābî in the Old Testament," *Theological Dictionary of the New Testament* (hereafter, TDNT) VI, p. 810; Th. C. Vriezen, *An Outline of Old Testament Theology*, trans. S. Neuijen (Oxford: Blackwell, 1972), pp. 231–32; R. E. Clements, *Prophecy and Covenant* (London: SCM, 1965), pp. 24–25.

[5]Ross, "Messenger," p. 99.

[6]Ibid., n. 9, includes many such *šālah* verses. By contrast, to prophesy without being "sent" as God's messenger was to be a false prophet (Neh. 6:12; Jer. 14:14–15; 28:15; 29:9).

[7]Ross, "Messenger," pp. 100–101, and John S. Holladay, Jr., "Assyrian Statecraft and the Prophets of Israel," *Harvard Theological Review*, 63 (1970): 29–51, show positive parallels where the messengers are spokesmen either for a god or for a human king. A thorough summary of the research is in John F. Craghan, "Mari and Its Prophets," *Biblical Theology Bulletin* 5 (1975): 32–55. The year 1968 was a turning point in the study of Mari prophecy, since newly published tablets showed that not all the Mari prophets were messengers. It is safe to conclude that at times the Mari prophets were messengers of a god, and at other times not, since the texts show different kinds of functions (liturgical or cultic, political, private, public, etc.).

[8]Ross, "Messenger," pp. 101–5; Jeremias, "Vollmacht," p. 315; Sheldon H. Blank, "'Of a Truth the Lord Hath Sent Me': An Inquiry into the Source of the Prophet's Authority," in *Interpreting the Prophetic Tradition*, (Cincinnati: Hebrew Union College Press, 1969). J. B. Pritchard, *Ancient Near Eastern Texts*, pp. 103–4, gives a translation of a 14th-century-B.C. Egyptian text in which the god Nergal fails to show proper respect to the messenger of Ereshkigal, and therefore Ereshkigal seeks to kill Nergal. For later Jewish

and Christian views on the importance of a messenger, see *m. Ber.* 5:5 ("the representative of a person is like himself"); John 3:34; Ignatius, *Ephesians* 6:1.

[9]Lindblom, *Prophecy*, pp. 112–13 cf. Ross, "Messenger," pp. 102–3, and Jeremiah 23:18, 22; Amos 3:7.

[10]Lindblom, *Prophecy*, p. 110; cf. pp. 113–14. Otto Eissfeldt, *The Old Testament: An Introduction*, trans. P. Ackroyd (Oxford: Blackwell, 1965), p. 78, says that not all prophetic sayings go back to special moments of inspiration—some owe their origin to the "lasting prophetic consciousness of being the messenger of Yahweh and . . . can therefore with equal right as the others be set out as direct divine speech in the first person." However, it is doubtful whether the Old Testament attributes as much independence to the prophetic messenger as Eissfeldt suggests. In fact, to speak a word that Yahweh has not given makes one a false prophet (Deut. 18:20; Jer. 23:16, 18, 21, 22; Ezek. 13:1–7). The true prophet, as Yahweh's messenger, must confine his message to what Yahweh told him. There is also danger in overemphasizing the *sôd* of Yahweh when we have so few biblical data (only Jer. 23:18, 22; Amos 3:7; and, without the term being used, 1 Kings 22:19). We are on safer ground if we think primarily in terms of the hearing/speaking pattern mentioned by Lindblom and repeated consistently throughout the prophetic literature (cf. Exod. 7:1–2 with 4:15–16, which Lindblom takes as a paradigm of Old Testament prophecy [pp. 113–14]; 1 Sam. 3:10–14; 2 Sam. 7:14–17; 24:11–13; 1 Kings 14:5; 2 Kings 20:4–6; Isa. 6:9; 7:4; Jer. 1:4–19; Ezek. 2:1–3:27; Jonah 3:2; et al.).

[11]Walter Eichrodt, *Theology of the Old Testament*, trans. J. A. Baker, 2 vols. (London: SCM, 1961–67), 1:340.

[12]Holladay, "Assyrian Statecraft," p. 43, n. 54.

[13]A full listing is given in Mandelkern's concordance, but the compact format of these pages would make the obtaining of an exact count an extremely tedious task (S. Mandelkern, *Veteris Testamenti Concordantiae* (Tel Aviv: Schocken, 1941), pp. 532-33.

[14]Lindblom, *Prophecy in Ancient Israel*, pp. 109–10, 114; Westermann, *Basic Forms of Prophetic Speech*, pp. 94–95; W. F. Albright, *From the Stone Age to Christianity* (New York: Doubleday, 1957[2]), p. 308, n. 44; A. R. Johnson, *The Cultic Prophet in Ancient Israel* (Cardiff: University of Wales Press, 1962[2]), p. 37; Holladay, "Assyrian Statecraft," pp. 29–51; A. Heschel, *The Prophets* (New York: Harper and Row, 1962), p. 427–29; O. Procksch, "The Word of God in the Old Testament," TDNT 4:97; H. H. Rowley, "The Nature of Old Testament Prophecy in the Light of Recent Study," in *The Servant of the Lord and Other Essays on the Old Testament* (London: Lutterworth, 1952), pp. 123–24. Similar statements from more conservative scholars are found in G. Vos, *Biblical Theology* (Grand Rapids: Eerdmans, 1948), pp. 233, 239; E. J. Young, *My Servants the Prophets* (Grand Rapids: Eerdmans, 1952), p. 176.

[15]The superiority of Moses as the greatest prophet is a frequent theme in rabbinic literature; see *Lev. Rab.* 1:3, 14; 10:12; *Num. Rab,* 14:20; 23:5; *Est. Rab.*, proem 10; *b. Yebam.* 49*b*; b. *Ros. Has.* 21*b*; *Midr. Ps.* on Psalm 90:4, sec. 4. In the Old Testament itself, see Deuteronomy 18:15, 18; Hosea 12:13 (14).

[16]Nevertheless the prophets do not always speak for God in the first person. Note, for instance, the alternation between first and third person speech in 2 Kings 19:20–33; Jeremiah 23:15–21, et al.

[17]In 1 Samuel 15:24 to sin is to transgress the commandment of the Lord and the words of Samuel the prophet.

[18]The construction *ha '*a*mînû b*e- is the same in both clauses and should be translated in the same way to make the parallelism clear. "Believe in" would be acceptable in both cases, but simply "believe" is also possible (Exod. 19:9; 1 Sam. 27:12; Prov. 26:25; Jer. 12:6) and is perhaps more appropriate when the emphasis is not on the personal reliability of individual prophets but on the reliability of their words. There is a similar statement to 2 Chronicles 20:20 in Isaiah 7:9.

[19]Lindblom, *Prophecy*, p. 110, says, "Yahweh sends his words through the prop⸍

and then the people are willing to obey 'the voice of Yahweh,' their God (Isa. 42:6)."

[20]In view of the emphasis on writing among the records of the earlier prophets, however, it is somewhat misleading to restrict the term "writing prophets" to prophets from the eighth century onward. The Hebrew classification "Former Prophets" and "Latter Prophets" is probably more accurate.

[21]Lindblom, *Prophecy*, p. 424, has a discussion with bibliographical notes. Yehezkel Kaufmann, *The Religion of Israel*, trans. and abridged by Moshe Greenberg (Tel Aviv, 1937–48; reprint ed., Chicago: University of Chicago Press, 1960), pp. 354–56, argues strongly for the substantial completion of the texts in written form by the prophets themselves: "There are, then, no grounds for assuming that the literature ascribed to the prophets was cultivated by circles of disciples who eventually wrote it down, formulated it according to their lights. . . . We know nothing about 'circles' who could be credited with the cultivation and transmission of such traditions, written or oral" (p. 355). He concludes that the followers of a prophet preserved and transmitted the prophecies and wrote about the prophets, but did not themselves create prophecies (pp. 354, 356).

[22]Lindblom, *Prophecy*, p. 164.

[23]There is a large body of literature on the role of the prophets as covenant messengers. See Meredith Kline, *The Structure of Biblical Authority* (Grand Rapids: Eerdmans, 1972), pp. 58–62.

[24]Lindblom, *Prophecy*, p. 164. For the view that in Jeremiah 36 the prophet is deliberately creating a "holy book," see Martin Kessler, "The Significance of Jeremiah 36," *Zeitschrift für die alttestamentliche Wissenschaft* 81 (1969): 381–83.

[25]Procksch, TDNT, 4:96. This was clearly the view of later Judaism. George Foot Moore, *Judaism in the First Centuries of the Christian Era*, 3 vols. (Cambridge, Mass.: Harvard University Press, 1927–30), p. 238, says, "From the books of the prophet Moses and the books containing the oracles of prophets and bearing their names it was an easy and perhaps unconscious step to the position that all the books of the Bible were written by prophets, that is, by men who had the holy spirit."

[26]There is another form of God's word in the Old Testament, namely, God's word of creative power. "Let there be light" in Genesis 1:3 is one example. But since the Old Testament authors do not view that form as communication from God to man, it is not part of our present inquiry. For this classification of types of God's speech in Scripture, as well as for a very substantial formative influence on my own understanding of the doctrine of Scripture, I am grateful to John Frame of Westminster Theological Seminary.

[27]G. C. Berkouwer, *Holy Scripture*, trans. and ed. Jack B. Rogers (Grand Rapids: Eerdmans, 1975), mentions Numbers 23:19 once (p. 151), but does not consider its implications for evaluating the truth status of God's words spoken (or written) by men. In fact, he seems to deny the implications of Numbers 23:19 when discussing the "reliability" of Scripture, for he says, "All that is human seems to be quite open to error and lies" (p. 240). He goes on to support that statement in a strange kind of affirmation-by-denial of Psalm 116:11: "One need not even be caught up in a fear like that of the poet in Psalm 116 who exclaimed, 'All men are liars' (Ps. 116:11, ASV), in order to realize that" (ibid.). It is significant that the verse he cites, Psalm 116:11, uses the word *kāzāb* to say that all men are "liars." Yet this is the very word used in Numbers 23:19 to say that God's words spoken by men do not lie.

[28]The verb *kāzāb*, here translated "lie," refers to any speech that is factually untrue, that does not correspond to reality (2 Kings 4:16; Job 6:28; 24:25; Ps. 89:35 [36]; Prov. 14:5). The corresponding noun *kāzāb* has a similar sense (Judg. 16:10, 13; Prov. 6:19; 14:5, 25). It is significant to notice that neither word is restricted to falsehood told for sinful purposes: both can be used of falsehood spoken for a good purpose (2 Kings 4:16; Judg. 16:10, 13). Neither word is restricted to falsehoods concerning theological or ethical subjects, or to falsehoods in major points as opposed to minor details. Verses like "A faithful witness does not lie [*yᵉkazzēb*], but a false witness breathes out lies [*kᵉzābîm*],"

Proverbs 14:5, indicate a wide range of application, for in a trial, a false statement by a witness about any minor detail may be crucial to the outcome.

[29]The phrase *nēṣaḥ yiśrā'ēl* is used only here as a name for God. Most modern translations read "Glory of Israel," following the discussion in S. R. Driver, *Notes on the Hebrew Text and the Topography of the Books of Samuel* (Oxford: Clarendon, 1912²), pp. 128–29.

[30]The verb *šāqar*, here translated "lie," occurs only six times in the Old Testament. It sometimes means "to deal falsely or deceitfully" (Gen. 21:23; 63:8; cf. *Hebrew and English Lexicon of the Old Testament* [BDB], p. 1055). However, it can mean simply "to speak falsehood," at least in Leviticus 19:11 and 1 Samuel 15:29. Moreover, the corresponding noun *šeqer*, "lie," often refers to any kind of factually untrue speech (Exod. 20:16; Lev. 6:3; Deut. 19:12; 1 Kings 22:22–23; Prov. 6:17, 19; 21:6; 29:12) and is nearly synonymous with *kāzāḇ*, "lie." The noun *šeqer* is used of unintentional falsehood in Jereremiah 37:14.

[31]The translation "words" (NIV, NASB, KJV) is preferable to the RSV translation "promises," a restriction in sense that is not necessary with *'imrāh:* cf. BDB, p. 57; F. D. Kidner, *Psalms 73–150*, Tyndale Old Testament Commentaries (TOTC) (London: Inter-Varsity, 1975), p. 419.

[32]The phrase *lā'āres* would ordinarily signify "on the ground" (so RSV, NASB), but NIV has followed M. Dahood, *Psalms I*, Anchor Bible (Garden City, N.Y.: Doubleday, 1965), pp. 74–75, who argues that *'ereṣ* can mean earth as a material and that *l*ᵉ can take the sense of "from." See also D. Kidner, *Psalms 1–72*, TOTC (London: Inter-Varsity, 1973), p. 76.

[33]See E. D. Schmitz, s.v. "*Hepta*," *New International Dictionary of New Testament Theology*, ed. Colin Brown, 3 vols. (Grand Rapids: Zondervan, 1975–78), 2:690.

[34]See, for example, Berkouwer, *Holy Scripture*, p. 240. Also on page 17 he mentions those who argue that the words of Scripture should be evaluated according to divine standards of absolute reliability and truthfulness, not according to any human tendency to err. Berkouwer says that these people have taken their approach in order "so to cover over the human element by the divine that there was hardly anything relevant left of the human." Such a sentence is certainly an imprecise if not even a careless representation of the view he opposes, for those who hold such a view have given repeatedly a unanimous affirmation of the involvement of real human personalities and the use of intelligible, normal language in the writing of Scripture. These are certainly "revelant" human factors in Scripture. Berkouwer however seems to suggest here that to have "anything relevant ... of the human" element in Scripture we would need to have some factual error, some occasional untruthfulness of speech. Yet that is exactly what Psalm 12:6 (in the context of Ps. 12:1–2) denies.

In criticizing those who, according to Berkouwer, give "little significance" to the human character of Scripture, he speaks as follows of their position: "We can detect in this reaction a desire to depend on the *divine* as opposed to the *human* word" (p. 17; italics his). But should such a desire be criticized? The desire to depend on the divine instead of the human word is exactly the attitude expressed by the psalmist in Ps. 12:6 and given in Scripture as an example for us to emulate.

[35]Once again the translation "word" (NIV, NASB) is preferable to "promises" (RSV); see n. 31 above.

[36]BDB, p. 662, n. 4.

[37]C. A. Briggs and E. G. Briggs, *A Critical and Exegetical Commentary on the Book of Psalms*, International Critical Commentary (ICC), 2 vols. (Edinburgh: T. and T. Clark, 1906–07), 2:429.

[38]The RSV reads "thy word." The idea "sum" implies plurality, but the word itself is a collective singular: *d*ᵉḇārḵā ("your word").

[39]See Josephus, *Ag. Ap.* 1:41; 1 Macc. 4:45–46; 9:27; 14:41; *Prayer of Azariah* 15;

2 Baruch 85:3; *b. Yoma* 9*b*; *b. Soṭa* 48*b*; *b. Sanh.* 11*a*; *Cant. Rab.* 8:9:3. Str-B, 1:127 (b) also note *t. Soṭa* 13:2 and *j. Soṭa* 9:13 (24b, line 21); cf. also 1 QS 9:11.

See also R. Leivestad, "Das Dogma von der prophetenlosen Zeit," *NTS* 19 (1972–73), pp. 288–99; also W. D. Davies, *Paul and Rabbinic Judaism* (London: SPCK, 1970³), pp. 208–16; I. Abrahams, *Studies in Pharisaism and the Gospels: Second Series* (Cambridge: University Press, 1924), p. 121; J. Dunn, *Jesus and the Spirit* (London: SCM, 1975), p. 382, n. 81.

[40]The Soncino edition of the Babylonian Talmud at this point notes that "another" refers to a Baraitha—something excluded from the Mishnah (Nezkin, 3:672).

[41]Cf. *Kommentar zum Neuen Testament aus Talmud und Midrasch* (Str-B), vol. IV, i, pp. 443–51.

[42]G. F. Moore, *Judaism*, 1:239.

[43]Cf. Gerhard Delling, "Die biblische Prophetie bei Josephus," in *Josephus-Studien*, ed. Otto Betz et al. (Göttingen: Vandenhoeck und Ruprecht, 1974), p. 120.

[44]For other passages in Philo on the authority of Scripture see *Quis Her.* 259; *Spec. Leg.* 1:65; *Q. Gen.* 4:196. However, some freedom is attributed to the prophet himself in *Jos.* 95. Cf. H. A. Wolfson, *Philo*, 2 vols. (Cambridge: Harvard University Press, 1947), 1:140.

[45]The translation "All God-breathed scripture is also profitable ..." (a sense found in the NEB and the RSV mg.) is highly unlikely because it makes the *kai* ("also") awkward. In coherent speech, one must say that something has one characteristic before saying that it "also" has another characteristic. That is, "also" must indicate an addition to something that has previously been predicated. So *pasa graphē theopneustos kai ōphelimos* must be translated in a straightforward way: "All scripture is God-breathed and profitable...." Cf. G. Schrenk, "*graphō, ktl.*" TDNT 1:754: "This obviously means every passage of scripture."

[46]In at least two cases, 1 Timothy 5:18 and 2 Peter 3:16, *graphē* also includes some of the New Testament writings.

[47]John J. Hughes, review of W. W. Gasque and W. S. Lasor, eds., *Scripture, Tradition and Interpretation (Fs. E. F. Harrison)*, in *Westminster Theological Journal* (WTJ) 42:2 (Spring, 1980), p. 422. Hughes is correct in this criticism, for as this and many of the texts cited above indicate, the Old Testament and New Testament authors show great concern to affirm the result of inspiration, much less interest in specifying the purpose of inspiration, and very little interest in discussing the manner of inspiration or the mode of revelation (to use Hughes's phrases).

[48]See H. B. Swete, *An Introduction to the Old Testament in Greek* (Cambridge: University Press, 1900), p. 243. There is nothing in the Hebrew text that corresponds to the extra lines in the LXX. Yet for our purposes it is sufficient to note that for the author of Hebrews, it was Old Testament Scripture and therefore able to be cited as something that God "says." Whether this line is part of the correct text of Deuteronomy is a question of text criticism, not of theology proper. Hebrews 1:6 affirms that God said this, and to believe the New Testament would involve believing that God in fact did say these words. But Hebrews 1:6 does not affirm that the statement cited belonged to Deuteronomy or that Moses wrote it. It should not be thought impossible that in rare instances the biblical authors would say true facts but arrive at them for the wrong reasons (cf. the extreme instance in John 11:49–51). The text of Scripture affirms what the authors wrote, not necessarily every (unexpressed) reason they had for writing what they did.

[49]Note that the argument also requires Davidic authorship of Psalm 110 in order to be valid.

[50]These are not explicitly cited as fulfillments.

[51]See, for example, Jack Rogers, "The Church Doctrine of Biblical Authority" in Jack Rogers, ed., *Biblical Authority* (Waco: Word, 1977).

[52]Note that these same men who repented at Jonah's preaching "will arise at the judgment." These cannot easily be understood to be merely a literary creation: fictional characters are not people who will arise at the judgment. (It is unfortunate that this verse, probably the most relevant verse in the New Testament on the historicity of Jonah, is not discussed by Leslie Allen in his recent rejection of the historicity of Jonah: see Leslie Allen, *Joel, Obadiah, Jonah, Micah*, New International Commentary on the Old Testament (NICOT) (Grand Rapids: Eerdmans, 1976), pp. 175–81.

[53]In Matthew 22:35, *huiou Barachiou* is missing from Sinaiticus and at least four cursives; see B. F. Westcott and F. J. Hort, *The New Testament in the Original Greek: Introduction and Appendix* (London and New York: Macmillan, 1896), p. 17.

Several solutions have been proposed for the difficulty caused when we read in 2 Chronicles 24:21 that Zechariah the son of *Jehodiah* (not Barachiah) was killed, but the existence of a weak yet significant textual attestation to the omission of "son of Barachiah" raises an interesting question in the following manner:

If one decides (as some have done) that the only two really likely solutions to this verse are (1) that Matthew (or Jesus) made a mistake and spoke of the wrong Zechariah or (2) that "son of Barachiah" was not in the autograph, then this verse becomes an interesting "test case," for it requires that one decide which of two good convictions will weigh most heavily: the appropriateness of accepted procedures of text criticism (according to which the omission of "son of Barachiah" in the autograph is improbable) or the validity of the Bible's claims to its own truthfulness (according to which such an omission *is* probable). One or the other conviction will turn out to have priority.

Of course, one can always argue that "Zechariah the son of Barachiah" does not refer to the prophet Zechariah (a solution that seems to me even less likely than the textual solution I have suggested), but that is a rather similar solution to the same dilemma, for only a conviction about the total reliability of Scripture (or of Jesus' words) could persuade one to take such an otherwise unlikely solution.

It is not a case of "doctrine versus phenomena" of Scripture, however. It is a question of whether one's observations about *some* phenomena (the passages examined in this essay, for example) will be more convincing than one's observations about *other* phenomena (the way in which textual variants occur). (The RSV, NIV, and NASB have made somewhat similar choices for the weakly attested variant *echomen* in Rom. 5:1.)

[54]Cf. W. Bauer, W. Arndt, F. Gingrich, and F. Danker, *A Greek-English Lexicon of the New Testament* (Chicago: University of Chicago Press, 1979), p. 777.

[55]For the view that the "nonrevelational" statements of Scripture need not always be true (true, that is, in the sense that they correspond to reality), because the purpose of Scripture is "to make us wise unto salvation," not to inform us of facts that could be discovered apart from revelation, see Daniel P. Fuller, "Benjamin B. Warfield's View of Faith and History," *Bulletin of the Evangelical Theological Society* 11 (1968), pp. 75–83.

[56]"Scientific statement" here is used in a broad sense to refer to a statement about observable phenomena in the natural world.

[57]See n. 39 above. See also N. H. Ridderbos, "Canon of the Old Testament," *The New Bible Dictionary*, ed. J. D. Douglas (Grand Rapids: Eerdmans, 1962), pp. 186–94 (with bibliography).

[58]Peter's error that was corrected by Paul in Galatians 2:11–14 indicates something of the ordinary process of learning the application of the Christian faith to new situations that even the apostles experienced. Cf. Acts 11:2–18; 15:7 ("after there had been much debate"). The New Testament nowhere supports the idea that the apostles were free from sin in all their actions (or even that all their ideas were always correct), but rather that what they taught and wrote to the churches was, both in contents and words, God's speech as well as their own and thus completely reliable.

[59]There is in this passage some suggestion that the mode of revelation, at least in this instance, would be a kind of "supernatural" perfecting of a very "natural" process of

remembering: the disciples would remember clearly, accurately, and fully, because the Holy Spirit would empower their memories not to make mistakes in recalling what Jesus said.

[60]That Old Testament prophets are meant is evident (1) from 1:20–21 and 2:1, 16, where Old Testament prophets are in mind; (2) because the prophets are not connected with Christ or His words, as are the apostles; (3) because 2 Peter 3:1 makes it clear that a reference to 1 Peter is intended, and there the Old Testament prophets are in view (1:10–12); and (4) because in exhorting his readers to call certain words to mind, the author probably is thinking of written collections of words, of which there are many attributed to Old Testament prophets, but few or none attributed to New Testament prophets.

[61]The last phrase can be translated in various ways. "Interpreting spiritual things in spiritual words" (*pneumatikois* as neuter) and "interpreting spiritual things to spiritual men" (*pneumatikois* as masculine) and "combining spiritual things with spiritual words" (*synkrinō* as "combine") are all translations compatible with this interpretation. The second one is difficult because it makes Paul anticipate the thoughts of 2:15 and 3:1, that only "spiritual" people can understand these things. The first and third, however, make a nice summary of verses 12–13 ("what we learn from the Spirit we speak in words taught by the Spirit"). Since the context of interpreting things revealed is similar to the Old Testament context of interpreting dreams (*synkrinō* in this sense is found in Genesis 40:8, 16, 22; 41:12, 13, 15; Daniel 5:7, 12, 16 [of writing]; cf. *synkrisis* frequently in Daniel as "interpretation"), I prefer the first translation, but not strongly.

To take *pneumatos* as (human) "spirit" rather than "Spirit" (v. 13a, so NIV mg.) would be to ignore the strong contrast (*alla*) in the verse between "human wisdom" and "Spirit."

[62]It is unnecessary here to decide which verses of 1 Corinthians 2:6–16 are general truths applicable to all believers (probably 7b; perhaps 12, 16b), and which Paul intends to restrict to himself and perhaps his companions or the other apostles, for in either case the primary application of the truths is to Paul's own ministry, and it is in those verses that refer to his own speaking that this becomes most evident (2:6, 13; 3:1; 4:1). Cf. J. Kijne, "We, Us and Our in 1 & 2 Corinthians," in *Novum Testamentum* 8 (1966): 171–79.

The aorist *apekalypsen* in verse 10 suggests a single past experience of revelation, and is thus best restricted to Paul alone. Had he been referring to a continuing reception of "revelations" by all believers, Paul would have used the present tense.

[63]R. Scroggs, "Paul: *SOPHOS* and *PNEUMATIKOS*," in *New Testament Studies* 14 (1967–68): 52, says, "Paul here asserts that the language used to proclaim the wisdom teaching is itself taught by the spirit."

[64]Cf. O. Cullmann, "The Tradition," in *The Early Church*, ed. A. J. B. Higgins (London: SCM, 1956), p. 74.

[65]The reading *estin entolē* is to be preferred in verse 37. *Estin* alone, although shorter, is very unlikely because, with the exception of Origen, it is supported only by Western witnesses (D* G [it [d,e,g]] Origen [gr, lat] Ambrosiaster Hilary Pelagius), most of which are unreliable in other parts of this passage (D G it [d,e,g] and Ambrosiaster transpose vv. 34–35 to follow v. 40; Origen in the following verse gives three different readings). Also, the *entolē* could have been dropped to eliminate the awkward singular predicate nominative (*entolē*) following a plural subject (*ha*). The readings with *entolai* are best viewed as later attempts to conform to the plural *ha*. This leaves two alternatives, *entolē estin* (א*) and *estin entolē*; the latter has significant and diverse support (p [46] A B 048 1739 syr[pal] cop[bo] eth Augustine), and is thus the one I have chosen. *Contra* G. Zuntz, *The Text of the Epistles* (London: The British Academy, 1953), pp. 139–40.

[66]The textual variants in verse 38 do not materially affect my argument at this point. I have followed the RSV in translating verse 38.

[67]Cf. J. Héring, *The First Epistle of St. Paul to the Corinthians*, trans. A. W. Heathcote and P. J. Allcock (London: Epworth, 1962), p. 155.

[68]C. Masson, *L'Épître de Saint Paul aux Éphésiens*, in *L'Épître de Saint Paul aux Galates; L'Épître de Saint Paul aux Ephésiens*, by Pierre Bonnard and Charles Masson, CNT (Neuchâtel: Delachaux and Niestlé, 1953), pp. 62–63. *Contra* Joachim Jeremias, *Unknown Sayings of Jesus* (London: SPCK, 1958), p. 5.

[69]Cf. 1 Kings 20 (3 Kgdms. 21), 35–36; 1 Kings 13:2, 9, 17, 32; 2 Chronicles 30:12 with 36:16.

[70]For Paul's use of "we" to refer only to himself, note 1 Thessalonians 2:18; 3:1–2.

[71]This is not different from the authority claimed elsewhere (e.g., in 1 Cor. 2:13; 14:37), but as in those places the explicit statement of such a claim serves to emphasize that authority at a point where Paul must have thought such emphasis to be especially needed.

[72]Though I here cite Paul as author of 1 Timothy, it is not essential to the argument at this point. Those who hold a view other than that of Pauline authorship will still see in 1 Timothy 5:18 a very early instance of the citation of Luke's Gospel as "Scripture."

[73]One might argue that Paul is quoting from an earlier written collection of Jesus' sayings that was also used by Luke, but that would not affect my argument here, which is intended to show only that written New Testament materials very early began to be counted as "Scripture" on a par with the Old Testament.

In favor of the view that Luke's Gospel is being cited, however, are (1) the probability that Paul would have wanted to cite a text readily accessible to the Ephesians, or at least to Timothy, and that Luke's Gospel certainly could have been circulating by the time 1 Timothy was written; and (2) the fact that we have a Gospel that did circulate widely and does have those words, but we have no remaining "sayings source" that certainly circulated among the churches.

[74]Jesus harshly rebukes those who tell the truth only when under certain oaths (Matt. 5:33–37; 23:16–22).

[75]The use of the noun *alētheia* suggests that God's Word is here viewed not just as something that conforms to some other standard of truth but as being itself the final and ultimate standard against which all other claims to truthfulness must be tested. (2 Timothy 2:15 and James 1:18 call Scripture the "word of truth.")

[76]Daniel P. Fuller, "Benjamin B. Warfield's View of Faith and History," *Bulletin of the Evangelical Theological Society* 11 (1968): 81. A related but somewhat different position is represented by Jack Rogers and Donald McKim, *The Authority and Interpretation of the Bible* (New York: Harper and Row, 1979).

A similar position is also represented in the following statement by G. C. Berkouwer: "The supposition that limited human knowledge and time-boundness of any kind would cause someone to err and that Holy Scripture would no longer be the lamp for our feet unless every time-bound conception could be corrected, is a denial of the significance of historical development and of searching out as the unhappy business that God has given the sons of men to be busy with (Eccl. 1:13)" (*Holy Scripture*, p. 182). Berkouwer implies that there were always only two alternatives for God when speaking through Scripture: (1) to correct all the "time-bound" (presumably erroneous) conceptions of the hearers or (2) to affirm them. He fails to recognize a third possibility, namely, to correct those erroneous ideas that God deemed it necessary to correct and to remain silent concerning the others. In fact, this seems to be what happened. Certainly there were enough true ideas in any society to which Scripture was originally written for God to be able to communicate effectively without having to resort to the incidental affirmation of falsehood. (Fuller also fails to recognize this third possibility.)

Once again it must be emphasized that the Bible does not generally tell us exactly how this result came about (the method of revelation and inspiration). To say that the words of Scripture are exactly the words God wanted and that what Scripture says, God says, is clearly not to affirm mechanical "dictation." It is only to say that in the wise providence of God, through the use of the personalities and writing styles of the individual authors, the Bible came to be exactly what God wanted it to be.

[77]Ibid., pp. 81–82, where Fuller explains his view by use of the example of Matthew 13:32 and 17:20.

[78]"Scientific statement" is again used here in the broad sense to refer to a statement about observable phenomena in the natural world. To distinguish "science" in this sense from "history," we could further specify that science deals with constantly occurring or regularly repeatable phenomena, while history deals with the occurrences of unique events at certain points in time.

[79]The passages are too numerous to list again here, but the reader may refer to the earlier sections on God's speech directly to men, God's words spoken by men, and God's words in written form, both in the Old and the New Testaments.

[80]See below, n. 84.

[81]The case of the mustard seed, cited in Fuller, "Warfield's View," pp. 81–82, is a good example. The problem is that Fuller has adopted a definition of the word "seed" (*sperma*) that is foreign to the context of Matthew 13:32 and has thereby "discovered" in the text an error that really is not there. Fuller argues that "the mustard seed is not really the smallest of all seeds" (p. 81) and that therefore Jesus was not "as careful to be inerrant in this non-revelational matter" (p. 82) as He was in what Fuller terms "revelational" matters (those that make us wise unto salvation). Implicit in this argument is a rather specialized scientific sense of the word *seed*, something like the definition found in a modern dictionary: "A fertilized and ripened plant ovule containing an embryo capable of germinating to produce a new plant" (*The American Heritage Dictionary* [Boston: Houghton Mifflin, 1969], p. 1174).

However, Jesus and His hearers would have been unlikely to attach any such modern scientific meaning to *sperma*, "seed" (or to the Aramaic equivalent used by Jesus). In an agricultural society, "seed" would have meant to both Jesus and His hearers something like "that which people plant in the ground to grow crops." (*Sperma* takes this sense, for example, in Matt. 13:24, 27, 37, just a few verses before and after Matt. 13:32, and also in 1 Cor. 15:38; 2 Cor. 9:10.) This sense is further suggested by the preceding verse, which speaks of a mustard seed "which a man took *and sowed in his field*" (Matt. 13:31). In that sense of "seed," a sense common to the New Testament, Jesus' statement is in fact entirely accurate: the mustard seed is used in rabbinic writings when they needed a reference to the smallest perceptible object (Str-B cite *y. Ber.* 5.8d, 36; *b. Ber.* 31a; *Lev. Rab.* 31:9; *m. Nid.* 5:2; cf. O. Michel, TDNT, 3:810, n. 1) and therefore seems to have been the smallest seed cultivated by people in New Testament times. (The NIV has apparently adopted this meaning by translating "the smallest of all your seeds.") So there is not even an incidental affirmation of any factual error in Matthew 13:32, once an appropriate New Testament meaning is given to "seed," and the passage does not turn out to be a convincing example of "accommodation."

(If the mustard seed had in fact not been the smallest cultivated seed, many other options would have been available to Jesus with no diminution of effectiveness in communication: "Consider the mustard seed, how small it is! Yet . . . " or " . . . the mustard seed, such a tiny seed," etc. Even in such a case, accommodation that included the incidental affirmation of historical or scientific falsehood would not have been necessary, as Fuller on p. 82 suggests that it was to have highly effective communication.)

[82]To say that it will show the greatness of God in His willingness to accommodate Himself and affirm our errors is to misunderstand the purity and unity of God: He does not manifest greatness by acting in a way that contradicts His character.

[83]Because the terms *plenary* and *inspiration* have become somewhat obscure technical terms in theological study, I have tried to avoid using them up to this point and have attempted to use other words or phrases that allow my meaning to be more clearly specified. In this concluding paragraph I have used the terms in their traditional sense and have also explained what I mean by them.

[84]An analysis of various "problem texts" is itself a useful subject for study and is logically the next step after this discussion. Yet such a study has limited value in

formulating a doctrine of Scripture: I have looked at dozens of such texts, and in every single case there are possible solutions in the commentaries. If one accepts the Bible's claim to be God's very words, then the real question is not how "probable" any proposed solution is in itself, but how one weighs the probability of that proposed solution against the probability that God has spoken falsely. Personally I must say the "difficult texts" would have to become many times more difficult and many times more numerous before I would come to think that I had misunderstood the hundreds of texts about the truthfulness of God's words in Scripture, or that God had spoken falsely.

UNITY AND DIVERSITY IN THE NEW TESTAMENT: THE POSSIBILITY OF SYSTEMATIC THEOLOGY

D. A. Carson

pages 65–95

[1]Cf. G. Hasel, *New Testament Theology: Basic Issues in the Current Debate* (Grand Rapids: Eerdmans, 1978), pp. 9–10.

[2]Cf. R. L. Reymond, "Some Prolegomenous Issues Confronting the Systematic Theologian," *Presbyterion* 4 (1978): 5–23; J. I. Packer, "The Adequacy of Human Language," in *Inerrancy*, ed. Norman L. Geisler (Grand Rapids: Zondervan, 1979), pp. 197–226; Carl F. H. Henry, *God, Revelation and Authority*, 5 vols. (Waco: Word, 1976—), vol. 1.

[3]Cf. Henry, *God, Revelation and Authority* 4:463–66; D. A. Carson, "Hermeneutics: A brief assessment of some recent trends," *Themelios* 5, no. 2 (1979–80): 12–20; and especially A. C. Thiselton, *The Two Horizons: New Testament Hermeneutics and Philosophical Description* (Grand Rapids: Eerdmans, 1980).

[4]W. Bauer, *Rechtglaübigkeit und Ketzerei im ältesten Christentum* (Tübingen: Mohr/Siebeck, 1934). The English translation was based on the second editon (1964) and was edited by Robert A. Kraft and Gerhard Krodel (Philadelphia: Fortress, 1971).

[5]Bauer, *Orthodoxy and Heresy*, pp. 241–85.

[6]Elaine Pagels, *The Gnostic Gospels* (New York: Random, 1979).

[7]E. P. Sanders, ed., *Jewish and Christian Self-Definition*, vol. 1: *The Shaping of Christianity in the Second and Third Centuries* (Philadelphia: Fortress, 1980), p. ix.

[8]Stephen S. Smalley, "Diversity and Development in John," *New Testament Studies* 17 (1970–71): 276–92, esp. 279.

[9]E.g., R. A. Kraft, "The Development of the Concept of 'Orthodoxy' in Early Christianity," in *Current Issues in Biblical and Patristic Interpretation*, ed. G. F. Hawthorne (Grand Rapids: Eerdmans, 1975), pp. 47–59.

[10]James Barr, *The Bible in the Modern World* (New York: Harper and Row, 1973), p. 157.

[11]M. J. Suggs, "The Christian Two Way Tradition: Its Antiquity, Form, and Function," in *Studies in New Testament and Early Christian Literature*, ed. D. E. Aune (Supplement to Novum Testamentum XXXIII; Leiden: Brill, 1972), pp. 62–74.

[12]Nils A. Dahl, *Studies in Paul* (Minneapolis: Augsburg, 1977), p. 159.

[13]Cf. the collection of essays edited by G. Strecker, *Das Problem der Theologie des Neuen Testaments* (Darmstadt: Wissenschaftliche Buchgesellschaft, 1975).

[14]E.g., W. Lohff, "Zur Einführung: Über die Möglichkeit, Theologie im Überblick, darzustellen," *Wissenschaftliche Theologie im Überblick*, ed. W. Lohff and F. Hahn (Göttingen: Vandenhoeck und Ruprecht, 1974), pp. 5–12.

[15]E.g., D. Tracy, *Blessed Rage for Order: The New Pluralism in Theology* (New York: Seabury, 1975); R. T. Voelkel, *The Shape of the Theological Task* (Philadelphia: Westminster, 1968). Cf. also R. Morgan, *The Nature of New Testament Theology* (London: SCM, 1973), esp. pp. 1–67.

[16]E.g., A. Ziegenhaus, "Die Bildung des Schriftkanons als Formprinzip der Theologie," *Münchener Theologische Zeitschrift* 29 (1978): 264–83.

[17]J. Gabler, *De justo discrimine theologiae biblicae et dogmaticae regundisque recte utriusque finibus* ("On the proper distinction between biblical and dogmatic theology and the correct delimitation of their boundaries"). First delivered in 1787, this essay is available in a German translation in D. Merk, *Biblische Theologie des Neuen Testaments in ihrer Anfangszeit* (Marburg: Elwert, 1972), pp. 273–84, and in G. Strecker, *Problem*, pp. 32–44. Cf. the sensitive treatment of Gabler in Hendrikus Boers, *What Is New Testament Theology?* (Philadelphia: Fortress, 1979), pp. 23–38.

[18]In particular, cf. Brevard Childs, *Biblical Theology in Crisis* (Philadelphia: Westminster, 1970).

[19]E.g., James D. Smart, *The Past, Present, and Future of Biblical Theology* (Philadelphia: Westminster, 1979). Others besides Smart are optimistic; e.g., Klaus Haacker et al., *Biblische Theologie heute* (Neukirchen-Vluyn: Neukirchener Verlag, 1977).

[20]E. Käsemann, "Begrundet der neutestamentliche Kanon die Einheit der Kirche?" in *Das Neue Testament als Kanon*, ed. Ernst Käsemann (Göttingen: Vandenhoeck & Ruprecht, 1970), pp. 124–33. Käsemann does want more scriptural control than some of his contributors, but he draws no clear lines.

[21]E. Käsemann, "Zum Thema der urchristlichen Apokalyptik," *Zeitschrift für Theologie und Kirche* 59 (1962): 259.

[22]Cf. Peter Stuhlmacher, *Schriftauslegung auf dem Wege zur biblischen Theologie* (Göttingen: Vandenhoeck und Ruprecht, 1975). Part of this work has been recorded in English as *Historical Criticism and Theological Interpretation of Scripture*, tr. Roy A. Harrisville (Philadelphia: Fortress, 1977). Idem, *Vom Verstehen des Neuen Testaments: Eine Hermeneutik* (Göttingen: Vandenhoeck und Ruprecht, 1979).

[23]Cf. E. Rudolph, "Die atheistische Struktur der neuzeitlichen Subjektivität," *Neue Zeitschrift für systematische Theologie und Religionsphilosophie* 21 (1979): 119–38.

[24]Cf. especially David H. Kelsey, *The Uses of Scripture in Recent Theology* (Philadelphia: Fortress, 1975). Such authority rests not in what Scripture *says* (i.e., its content) but in its patterns. Which pattern or selection of patterns is chosen is entirely incidental. See the discussion in Henry, *God, Revelation and Authority*, 4:470–75.

[25]Ronald A. Ward, *The Pattern of Our Salvation: A Study of New Testament Unity* (Waco: Word, 1978).

[26]George E. Ladd, *A Theology of the New Testament* (Grand Rapids: Eerdmans, 1974).

[27]Hasel, *New Testament Theology*.

[28]Ibid., pp. 217–19.

[29]Ibid., p. 216. Cf. also H. Riesenfeld, "Zur Frage nach der Einheit des Neuen Testaments," *Erbe und Auftrag* 53 (1977): 32–45.

[30]R. P. Martin, "New Testament Theology: Impasse and Exit," *The Expository Times* 91 (1979–80): 264–69.

[31]Ibid., p. 267.

[32]Ibid., p. 268.

[33](London: SCM, 1977).

[34](London: SCM, 1977).

[35]B. B. Warfield, "The Idea of Systematic Theology," *The Presbyterian and Reformed Review* 7 (1896): 243; reprinted in *The Necessity of Systematic Theology*, ed. John Jefferson Davis (Washington: University Press of America, 1978), p. 99. All further quotes are from the latter.

[36]So, among others, Elmer A. Martens, "Tackling Old Testament Theology," *Journal of the Evangelical Theological Society* 20 (1977): 123–32; Gerhard F. Hasel, "The Future of

Biblical Theology," *Perspectives on Evangelical Theology*, ed. Kenneth S. Kantzer and Stanley N. Gundry (Grand Rapids: Baker, 1979), pp. 179–94.

[37]Ibid.

[38]This appears to be the working assumption of Hasel, *New Testament Theology*.

[39]R. B. Gaffin, "Systematic Theology and Biblical Theology," *Westminster Theological Journal* 38 (1975–76): 281–99; also printed in *The New Testament Student and Theology*, pp. 18–31, esp. p. 18.

[40]G. Vos *Biblical Theology: Old and New Testaments* (Grand Rapids: Eerdmans, 1948), p. 23; John Murray, "Systematic Theology, *Westminster Theological Journal* 26 (1963–64): 33–46, reprinted in *The New Testament Student and Theology*, pp. 18–31, esp. p. 18.

[41]Such an assumption stands behind the sophisticated treatment of Bernard Lonergan, especially in his book, *Method in Theology* (New York: Herder and Herder, 1972). Cf. the brief exposition by William Mathews, "Theology as Collaborative Wonder: A Portrait of the Work of Bernard Lonergan, S. J.," *The Expository Times* 91 (1979–80): 172–76. Despite the value of Lonergan's work, he does not attempt to answer unambiguously the precise nature of the authority Scripture has for him and how or to what extent it circumscribes all his endeavor.

[42]Of course, "theology" may also have a narrower sense, as in "theology proper"— what the Scriptures teach concerning God. But the usage does not interest us here.

[43]By relating systematic theology to the Scripture, I mean to exclude vague definitions. For instance, Stephen Sykes, *The Integrity of Anglicanism* (London: Mowbrays, 1978), laments the fact that systematic theology has been ignored in British universities and defines such theology as "that constructive discipline which presents the substance of the Christian faith with a claim on the minds of men" (p. ix). Superficially, I have no quarrel with the definition, but I wonder on what basis the "substance of the Christian faith" is to be determined.

[44]See, for instance, the similar recent treatment by Roger R. Nicole, "The Relationship Between Biblical Theology and Systematic Theology," *Evangelical Roots*, ed. Kenneth S. Kantzer (Nashville: Thomas Nelson, 1978), pp. 185–94.

[45]Warfield, "The Idea of Systematic Theology," p. 114.

[46]Cf. n. 4, *supra*.

[47]A convenient collection of these is found in an appendix to the English translation (cf. n. 4, *supra*).

[48](London: SCM, 1943).

[49]H. E. W. Turner, *The Pattern of Christian Truth: A Study in the Relations Between Orthodoxy and Heresy in the Early Church* (London: Mowbray, 1954).

[50]Ibid., p. 28.

[51]I. H. Marshall, "Orthodoxy and heresy in earlier Christianity," *Themelios* 2, no. 1 (1976–77): 5–14. The comparative "earlier" in Marshall's title is in reaction to Bauer who "had the effrontery to label the second century as '*earliest* Christianity'" (p. 6).

[52]J. F. McCue, "Orthodoxy and Heresy: Walter Bauer and the Valentinians," *Vigiliae Christianae* 33 (1979): 118–30.

[53]Dunn, *Unity and Diversity*; see n. 33, *supra*.

[54]Ibid., p. 3.

[55]Ibid., p. 373.

[56]Ibid., p. 386.

[57]Ibid., p. 377.

[58]Ibid., p. 376.

[59]R. T. France, in *Themelios* 5 (1979–80): 30–31.

[60]In addition to the review by France (cf. n. 59), cf. in particular the reviews in the following journals: *Theology* 81 (1978): 452–55; *Theology Today* 36 (1979): 116–21; *Catholic Biblical Quarterly* 49 (1978): 629–31; *Journal of Biblical Literature* 98 (1979): 135–37; *Andrews University Seminary Studies* 18 (1980): 111–13.

[61]Dunn, *Unity and Diversity*, p. 13.

[62]Ibid., p. 390, n. 4.

[63]Ibid., p. 16.

[64]Ibid., p. 18.

[65]Ibid.

[66]W. J. Larkin, "Luke's Use of the Old Testament as a Key to His Soteriology," *Journal of the Evangelical Theological Society* 20 (1977): 325–35. Cf. also A. George, "Le sens de la mort de Jésus pour Luc," *Revue Biblique* 80 (1973): 186–217; R. Glöckner, *Die Verkündigung des Heils beim Evangelisten Lukas* (Mainz: Matthias Grünwald, 1975), pp. 155–95; F. Schütz, *Der beidende Christus* (Stuttgart: Kohlhammer, 1969) pp. 93–94; and G. Voss, *Die Christologie des luckanischen Schriften* (Stuttgart: Kohlhammer, 1972), section 7.

[67]Cf. I. H. Marshall, "The Development of the Concept of Redemption in the New Testament" *Reconciliation and Hope*, ed. R. Banks (Exeter: Paternoster, 1974), pp. 153–69.

[68]Leon Morris, *The Cross in the New Testament* (Grand Rapids: Eerdmans, 1965), esp. pp. 63–143.

[69]Cf. especially C. K. Barrett, "'The Father is greater than I' (Jo 14, 28): Subordinationist Christology in the New Testament," in *Neues Testament und Kirche*, ed. J. B. Gnilka (Freiburg: Herder, 1974), pp. 144–59.

[70]I have attempted this for the christology of the fourth Gospel in one chapter of my *Divine Sovereignty and Human Responsibility: Some Aspects of Johannine Theology Against Jewish Background* (London: Marshall, Morgan and Scott, and Nashville: John Knox, 1980).

[71]See in particular I. H. Marshall, "The Development of Christology in the Early Church," *Tyndale Bulletin* 18 (1967), pp. 77–93; cf. also C. F. D. Moule, *The Origin of Christology* (Cambridge: University Press, 1977).

[72]Dunn, *Unity and Diversity*, p. 24.

[73]Cf. chapter 1 by W. Grudem in this book.

[74]Charles Hodge, *Systematic Theology*, 3 vols. (New York: Scribner, Armstrong, 1872), esp. 1:1–188; Edward Arthur Litton, *Introduction to Dogmatic Theology*, ed. Philip E. Hughes (London: James Clarke, 1960), esp. 1–40; Henry, *God, Revelation and Authority*.

[75]Jack B. Rogers and Donald K. McKim, *The Authority and Interpretation of the Bible: An Historical Approach* (New York: Harper and Row, 1979), pp. 90–91, citing *Commentary on Matthew* at 27:43 (Calvin Translation Society edition) and *Inst.* II.ii.16.

[76]Rogers and McKim, *Authority and Interpretation*, p. 91.

[77]Ibid.

[78]This is not a harsh or unfounded charge: see the detailed review article by John Woodbridge, *Trinity Journal* 1 NS (1980): 165–236. Moreover, Rogers and McKim constantly try to give the impression that distinctions re contradictions appear relatively late in the history of the church. In fact, it is not difficult to find passages like this one, where Justin rebukes Trypho for responding with a passage that almost suggests a contradiction: "If you spoke these words, Trypho, and then kept silence in simplicity and with no ill intent . . . you must be forgiven; but if [you have done so] because you imagined that you could throw doubt on the passage, in order that I might say the Scriptures contradicted each other, you have erred. But I shall not venture to suppose or to say such a thing; and if a Scripture which appears to be of such a kind be brought

forward, and if there be a pretext [for saying] that it is contrary [to some other], since I am entirely convinced that no Scripture contradicts another, I shall admit rather that I do not understand what is recorded, and shall strive to persuade those who imagine that the Scriptures are contradictory, rather to be of the same opinion as myself" (*Dial.* 65). Justin then goes on to give his own explanation of the troubling passage.

[79]"Evangelical theology is heretical if it is only creative and unworthy if it is only repetitious," comments Henry, *God, Revelation and Authority* 1:9.

[80]A. Dulles, "Response to Krister Stendahl's 'Method in the Study of Biblical Theology,'" *The Bible in Modern Theology*, ed. J. P. Hyatt (Nashville: Abingdon, 1965), pp. 210–16, esp. p. 214. Cf. also the warnings offered by K. Lehmann, "Über das Verhältnis der Exegese als historisch-kritischer Wissenschaft zum dogmatischen Verstehen," in *Jesus und der Menschensohn*, ed. R. Pesch and R. Schnackenburg (Freiburg: Herder, 1975), pp. 421–34.

[81]Cf. among others, Henry, *God, Revelation and Authority* 1:213–72.

[82]On the development of "progressive revelation," cf. J. I. Packer, "An Evangelical View of Progressive Revelation," in *Evangelical Roots*, ed. Kenneth S. Kantzer (Nashville: Thomas Nelson, 1978), pp. 143–58.

[83]Cf. especially Oscar Cullmann, *Salvation in History* (New York: Harper and Row, 1867).

[84]This is particularly clear in John's Gospel; cf. D. A. Carson, "Understanding Misunderstandings in the Fourth Gospel," *Tyndale Bulletin*, 33 (1982): p. 59–91.

[85]See, for instance, C. F. D. Moule, *Christology;* R. N. Longenecker, "On the Concept of Development in Pauline Thought," in *Perspectives on Evangelical Theology*, ed. Kenneth S. Kantzer and Stanley N. Gundry (Grand Rapids: Baker, 1979), pp. 195–207.

[86]This has been marked out in painstaking detail for the Sabbath/Sunday issue; cf. D. A. Carson, ed., *From Sabbath to Lord's Day: A Biblical, Historical and Theological Investigation* (Grand Rapids: Zondervan, 1982).

[87]Carson, "Understanding Misunderstandings."

[88]This distinction is overlooked by Longenecker, "Development in Pauline Thought," pp. 200–201.

[89]C. H. Dodd, "The Mind of Paul: Change and Development," *BJRL* 18 (1934): 69–110; idem, "The Mind of Paul: A Psychological Approach," *BJRL* 17 (1933): 91–105.

[90]E.g., Longenecker, "Development in Pauline Thought."

[91]This, of course, is disputed, especially by those who attempt to find major dislocations in the texts. See, for instance, J. C. Hurd, *The Origin of I Corinthians* (New York: Seabury, 1965), on which I will say more in the next reflection.

[92]Cf. C. F. D. Moule, "Interpreting Paul by Paul: An Essay in the Comparative Study of Pauline Thought," *New Testament Christianity for Africa and the World*, ed. Mark E. Glasswell and Edward W. Fasholé-Luke (London: SPCK, 1974), pp. 78–90.

[93]Charles Buck and G. Taylor, *Saint Paul: A Study of the Development of His Thought* (New York: Scribner, 1969).

[94]Most recently by John W. Drane, "Theological Diversity in the Letters of St. Paul," *Tyndale Bulletin* 26 (1976): 3–26.

[95]So Dunn, *Unity and Diversity*, pp. 356–58, even though he uses the same contrast elsewhere; A. Sand, "Überlegungen zur gegenwärtigen Diskussion über den 'Frühkatholizismus,'" *Catholica* 33 (1979): 49–62; and I. H. Marshall, "'Early Catholicism' in the New Testament," in *New Dimensions in New Testament Study*, ed. R. N. Longenecker and Merrill C. Tenney (Grand Rapids: Zondervan, 1974), pp. 217–31. Cf. E. Earle Ellis, "Dating the New Testament," *New Testament Studies* 26 (1979–80): 487–502, esp. 499–500. Ellis insists that the thesis/antithesis/synthesis model is equally

inappropriate in the modern reconstruction apocalypticism/delay of the Parousia/salvation history. Probably all three positions developed at the same time.

[96]D. A. Carson, "Historical Tradition and the Fourth Gospel: After Dodd, What?" in *Gospel Perspectives*, vol. 2, ed. David Wenham (Sheffield: JSOT, 1981), pp. 85–145.

[97]Murray J. Harris, "2 Corinthians 5:1–10: Watershed in Paul's Eschatology?" *Tyndale Bulletin* 22 (1971): 32–57; idem, "Paul's View of Death in 2 Corinthians 5:1–10," *New Dimensions in New Testament Study*, ed. R. N. Longenecker and Merrill C. Tenney (Grand Rapids: Zondervan, 1974), pp. 317–28. The restriction to published works is necessary, because in a private communication dated August 27, 1981, Dr. Harris told me that he no longer holds that Paul moved *from* believing that the spiritual body is received at the Parousia *to* the belief that the receipt occurs at death, nor does Harris now hold that Paul *substitutes* the notion of communion with Christ after death for the notion of sleep in the grave. In that sense, he can no longer speak of 2 Corinthians 5 as a "watershed" in Paul's eschatology. These changes will be thoroughly discussed in his forthcoming book *Raised Immortal*.

[98]Harris himself does not admit to a change in Paul's view such that Paul's earlier belief was in error; cf. Harris's treatment of this question in his chapter "Paul's View of Death in 2 Corinthians 5:1–10," in *New Dimensions in New Testament Study*, ed. R. N. Longenecker and M. C. Tenney (Grand Rapids: Zondervan, 1974), pp. 317–28, esp. pp. 322–23. But I am not convinced that he has successfully overcome the problem.

[99]David H. Kelsey, *The Uses of Scripture in Recent Theology* (Philadelphia: Fortress, 1975).

[100]On this most debated of themes, cf. most recently Donald Nicholl, "Historical Understanding," *The Downside Review* 97 (1979), pp. 99–113.

[101]Cf. the trenchant critique in Henry, *God, Revelation and Authority* 4:470–75.

[102]Even J. C. O'Neill (*The Recovery of Paul's Letter to the Galatians* [London: SPCK, 1972]), though he denies that these verses come from Paul, is not interested in denying that they come from one particular (and unknown) glossator.

[103]John W. Drane, *Paul: Libertine or Legalist?* (London: SPCK, 1975); and Peter Richardson, "Pauline Inconsistency: 1 Corinthians 9:19–23 and Galatians 2:11–14," *New Testament Studies* 26 (1979–80): 347–62. On Drane's work, see especially the reviews by R. N. Longenecker, *Journal of Biblical Literature* 96 (1977): 461–62 and by M. Silva, *Westminster Theological Journal* 40 (1977–78): 176–80.

[104]Gordon D. Fee, "Hermeneutics and Common Sense," *Inerrancy and Common Sense*, ed. Roger R. Nicole and J. Ramsey Michaels (Grand Rapids: Baker, 1980), p. 167.

[105]F. F. Bruce, "'All Things to All Men': Diversity in Unity and Other Pauline Tensions," in *Unity and Diversity in New Testament Theology*, ed. R. Guelich (Grand Rapids: Eerdmans, 1978), pp. 82–99.

[106]Compare E. P. Sanders, *Paul and Palestinian Judaism* (Philadelphia: Fortress, 1977), pp. 433, 518–23, who holds that though Paul is not a systematic thinker, he is a coherent thinker. I am not entirely happy with the distinction, since I am unsure how much the unsystematic (but not incoherent) factor finds its genesis less in Paul qua thinker than in the occasional nature of his writings. But even if Paul's thoughts are believed to "cohere," that is an adequate position from the viewpoint of this chapter.

[107]I have pointed this out at length in *The Sermon on the Mount: An Evangelical Exposition of Matthew 5–7* (Grand Rapids: Baker, 1978).

[108]Cf. especially Richard N. Longenecker, "The 'Faith of Abraham' Theme in Paul, James and Hebrews: A Study in the Circumstantial Nature of New Testament Teaching," *Journal of the Evangelical Theological Society* 20 (1977): 203–12.

[109]C. F. D. Moule, "The Influence of Circumstances on the Use of Christological Terms," *Journal of Theological Studies* 10 (1959): 247–63; idem, "The Influence of Cir-

cumstances on the Use of Eschatological Terms," *Journal of Theological Studies* 15 (1964): 1–15.

[110]E.g., Dunn, *Unity and Diversity*, p. 25 and n. 12.

[111]In private conversation.

[112]W. L. Lane, "Creed and Theology: Reflections on Colossians," *Journal of the Evangelical Theological Society* 21 (1978): 213–20. Cf. also Dunn, *Unity and Diversity*, pp. 359–60.

[113]One may wonder if R. P. Martin, "New Testament Theology," p. 266, takes these considerations into account adequately when he writes, "The use of the NT as a manual of systematic theology or a book of ecclesiastical rubric is no longer viable. 'Concepts of doctrine' (*Lehrbegriffe*) are not what the NT documents contain, though it is certainly a different question when we ask if we can in fact extrapolate Christian beliefs from what they comprise." In one sense, of course, the New Testament is *not* a manual of systematic theology. It does not come to us in that form; and systematic theology is therefore a derivative discipline. But it is not fair to the evidence to go so far as to say that the New Testament does not contain "concepts of doctrine." Quite the contrary: it contains not only a rich profusion of doctrines, but even sweeping "concepts of doctrine." What it does *not* contain is a very systematic treatment of these things.

[114]J. C. Hurd (*The Origin of First Corinthians* [Naperville, Ill.: Allenson, 1965]) offers a fine example of a really radical historical reconstruction in the service of demonstrating Pauline inconsistency. He uses 1 Corinthians to explore Paul's earlier dealings with the church in Corinth and concludes that the Corinthians had remained closer to the original Pauline gospel than Paul himself had done. According to Hurd, when Paul first came to Corinth, he maintained that a man should not touch a woman (1 Cor. 7:1). He encouraged celibacy and insisted that all things were lawful (10:23) and there was no harm in eating food offered to idols. Because believers all have knowledge (8:1), Paul behaved like one outside the law (9:21). He taught that baptism and the Lord's Supper hold death in check and would continue to do so until the end, expected very shortly. He said nothing of the resurrection from the dead, and he permitted women to go without veils. Then, according to Hurd, Paul changed his mind on a number of points, and these changes were reflected in the "previous letter" (cf. 5:9). It was written to enforce the Apostolic Decree (Acts 15: 29; 21:15), which now forbade eating meat offered to idols. Paul now required veils and urged separation from immorality. He recommended marriage as a safeguard against fornication and for the first time urged caution in the matter of speaking in tongues. Small wonder, argues Hurd, that the poor Corinthians were confused! Paul, therefore, wrote 1 Corinthians, a balanced missive that tried to sort it all out. Hurd says it is good to have this balance, but it would be nice to have the earlier enthusiasm as well. This entire reconstruction is thoroughly implausible. It supposes that Paul, after more than fifteen years of extensive ministry, was still sorting out the most elementary aspects of the faith and in fact reversed himself over a period of perhaps two years. Paul makes no mention of the Jerusalem Council. Moreover, it is difficult to believe that a man as pastorally sensitive as Paul would (even supposing so substantial a shift in his own thinking) impose those changes on new converts by a letter that could only have been confusing. Methodologically, Hurd has built his entire case on his reading of 1 Corinthians; and there are far more believable ways to explain the diversity found there, not least the one that pictures Paul as not only dealing with a host of issues brought up to him but also carefully handling the disunity and divergent opinions about all these matters found within the Corinthian church. Paul is therefore pastorally concerned not only to provide answers but to do so in such a way that he heals the breaches caused by the polarized opinions. This is not only a solid explanation for the kind of argumentation found in the epistle, but a further piece of evidence to confirm the pastoral (rather than merely theoretical) concerns that often prompted the apostle Paul to write. Moreover, many of the particular problems behind 1 Corinthians can be plausibly related to an overrealized eschatology and the entailed "enthusiasm"; cf. A. C. Thiselton, "Realized Eschatology at Corinth," *New Testament Studies* 24 (1977–78): 510–26.

[115]Brice L. Martin, "Matthew and Paul on Christ and the Law: Compatible or Incompatible Theologies?" (Ph.D. Diss., McMaster University, 1976); idem, "Some reflections on the unity of the New Testament," *Studies in Religion/Sciences Religieuses* 8 (1979): 143–52.

[116]Morna D. Hooker, "Were There False Teachers in Colossae?" *Christ and Spirit in the New Testament*, ed. B. Lindars and Stephen S. Smalley (Cambridge: University Press, 1973), pp. 315–31.

[117]Cf. R. P. Martin, "Approaches to New Testament Exegesis," in *New Testament Interpretation*, ed. I. H. Marshall (Exeter: Paternoster, 1977), pp. 220–51.

[118]Martin Hengel, *Acts and the History of the Earliest Christianity* (London: SCM, 1979).

[119]Cf. the important article by J. Carmignac, "II Corinthians iii. 6, 14 et le Début de la Formation du Nouveau Testament," *New Testament Studies* 24 (1977–78): 383–86.

[120]James I. Packer, "Preaching as Biblical Interpretation," in *Inerrancy and Common Sense*, ed. Roger R. Nicole and J. Ramsey Michaels (Grand Rapids: Baker, 1980), p. 198.

[121]Ibid., p. 188. Further on the *analogia fidei*, cf. R. C. Sproul, "Biblical Interpretation and the Analogy of the Faith," in *Inerrancy and Common Sense*, ed. Roger R. Nicole and J. Ramsey Michaels (Grand Rapids: Baker, 1980), pp. 119–35; and in its connections with biblical theology, cf. Daniel P. Fuller, "Biblical Theology and the Analogy of Faith," in *Unity and Diversity in New Testament Theology*, ed. Robert A. Guelich (Grand Rapids: Eerdmans, 1978), pp. 195–213.

[122]Contra W. C. Kaiser, Jr., *Toward an Old Testament Theology* (Grand Rapids: Zondervan, 1978), pp. 16, 18, 19, 190, 196, 219, 267. Kaiser prefers to speak of the analogy of antecedent Scripture.

[123]Cf., among others, Robert L. Thomas, "A Hermeneutical Ambiguity of Eschatology: The Analogy of Faith," *Journal of the Evangelical Theological Society* 23 (1980): 45–53.

[124]P. K. Jewett, *Man as Male and Female: A Study in Sexual Relationships from a Theological Point of View* (Grand Rapids: Eerdmans, 1975).

[125]E.g., in the area of New Testament ethics, cf. E. Schweizer, "Traditional ethical patterns in the Pauline and post-Pauline letters and their development (lists of vices and house-tables)," in *Text and Interpretation*, ed. Ernest Best and R. McL. Wilson (Cambridge: University Press, 1979), pp. 195–209.

[126]C. F. D. Moule, *The Epistles to the Colossians and to Philemon* (Cambridge: University Press, 1957), p. 60.

[127]Cf. Donald G. Bloesch, *Essentials of Evangelical Theology*, 2 vols. (New York: Harper and Row, 1978–79), 1:18: "At the same time the truth of faith cannot be translated into a finalized, coherent system which denies the mystery and paradox in faith. This is because the truth is suprarational as well as rational. Our human system must always be one that is open to revision in the light of new insights into the Word of God and the human situation. It can never be a closed, airtight, logically consistent, perfected system of truth." I can live with this judgment, provided "logically consistent" is being applied to a "perfected" and "airtight" system that presupposes, implicitly or explicitly, that God has revealed all there is to know—i.e., that we have all the pieces to the puzzle. In that case, our use of logic will fall under the fact that we labor under a false premise and correspondingly distort the evidence, trying to force pieces from the puzzle into slots where they don't properly fit. I reject the statement if it is written in defense of a logically inconsistent system.

[128]I have dealt with this problem at length in *Divine Sovereignty and Human Responsibility*.

[129]Dorothy L. Sayers, "Creed or Chaos?" in *The Necessity of Systematic Theology*, ed. John Jefferson Davis (Washington: University Press of America, 1978), pp. 15–32.

ON THE FORM, FUNCTION, AND AUTHORITY
OF THE NEW TESTAMENT LETTERS

Richard N. Longenecker

pages 101–14

[1]Cf. J. Neusner, *A Life of Yohanan ben Zakkai, Ca. 1–80 C.E.*, 2nd. ed. (Leiden: Brill, 1970), pp. 238–41.

[2]Adolf Deissmann, *Light From the Ancient East*, trans. L. R. M. Strachan (London: Hodder and Stoughton, 1909), p. 232; cf. pp. 224–46.

[3]George Milligan, *The New Testament Documents, Their Origin and Early History* (London: Macmillan, 1913), p. 95.

[4]Donald J. Selby, *Toward the Understanding of St. Paul* (Englewood Cliffs: Prentice-Hall, 1962), p. 239.

[5]Cf. K. P. Donfried, ed., *The Romans Debate* (Minneapolis: Augsburg, 1977).

[6]*Edictum Diocletiani de pretiis rerum venalium*, col. vii, pp. 39–41.

[7]Plutarch, *Parallel Lives* 23, on Cato the Younger.

[8]Seneca, *Ad Lucilium Epistulae Morales* XC. 25.

[9]Otto Roller, *Das Formular der Paulinischer Briefe* (Stuttgart: Kohlhammer, 1933), p. 333.

[10]F. R. M. Hitchcock, "The Use of *graphein*," *Journal of Theological Studies* 31 (1930): 273–74.

[11]Milligan, *New Testament Documents*, pp. 22–23; cf. pp. 160–61 and plate V.

[12]J. S. Candlish, "On the Moral Character of Pseudonymous Books," *The Expositor*, 4 (1891): 103.

[13]Kurt Aland, "The Problem of Anonymity and Pseudonymity in Christian Literature of the First Two Centuries," *Journal of Theological Studies* 12 (1961): 39–49.

[14]George Beasley-Murray, *The General Epistles* (New York: Abingdon, 1965), p. 73.

REDACTION CRITICISM: ON THE LEGITIMACY
AND ILLEGITIMACY OF A LITERARY TOOL

D. A. Carson

pages 119–42

[1]*The Expository Times* 89–90 (June–October 1978).

[2]See, e.g., W. H. Kelber, "Redaction Criticism: On the Nature and Exposition of the Gospels," *Perspectives on Religious Studies* 6 (1979): 4–16.

[3]E.g., John Warwick Montgomery, "Why Has God Incarnate Suddenly Become Mythical?" in *Perspectives on Evangelical Theology*, ed. Kenneth S. Kantzer and Stanley N. Gundry (Grand Rapids: Baker, 1979), pp. 57–65. At the meeting at which Montgomery read his paper (a slightly more trenchant version of his chapter), advocating that we not make use of redaction criticism at all, another conservative rose to his feet in the ensuing discussion and gently warned him about the danger of throwing out the baby with the bathwater. Montgomery replied, "Look, _____, you and I disagree. You think there's a baby in the bathwater, and I think it's all dirty bathwater."

[4]Adolf von Harnack, esp. in his *What Is Christianity?*, trans. Thomas B. Saunders (New York: Putnam, 1902).

[5]Albert Schweitzer's now-famous book was originally entitled *Von Riemarus zu Wrede* (1906) and later *Geschichte der Leben-Jesu-Forschung*. The English title is *The Quest of the Historical Jesus* (London: A. and C. Black, 1910).

[6]Cf., among others, Hermann Gunkel, *The Psalms: A Form-Critical Introduction*, trans. T. M. Horner (Philadelphia: Fortress, 1967); idem, *Genesis* (Göttingen: Vandenhoeck und Ruprecht, 1917).

[7]K. L. Schmidt, *Der Rahmen der Geschichte Jesu* (Berlin: Töpelmann, 1919).

[8]M. Dibelius, *Die Formgeschichte des Evangeliums* (Tübingen: Mohr, 1919; later editions to 1959); ET, *From Tradition to Gospel*, trans. B. L. Woolf, ed. W. Barclay (London: James Clarke, 1971).

[9]The English translation is *History of the Synoptic Tradition*, trans. John Marsh (Oxford: Blackwell, 1963).

[10]The technical designations vary somewhat from form critic to form critic.

[11]The distinction is clearly seen in recent discussions on the fourth Gospel. Recent commentators practice "redaction criticism" of the sort that separates out sources, distinguishes redaction from tradition, comments on the trajectory of the tradition, and expounds the significance of the retrieved redaction all in one step. By contrast, R. T. Fortna, in his *Gospel of Signs* (Cambridge: University Press, 1970), restricts himself to *source* criticism to isolate the principal source he thinks the Evangelist used, and then in later articles he proceeds to redaction criticism by analyzing the changes that have taken place in the (alleged) move from his (reconstructed) source to the Gospel as we have it. Cf. his "Source and Redaction in the Fourth Gospel's Portrayal of Jesus' Signs," *Journal of Biblical Literature* 89 (1970): 156–65; idem, "From Christology to Soteriology," *Interpretation* 27 (1973): 31–47. On recent source-critical approaches to the Gospel of John, cf. E. Ruckstuhl, "Johannine Language and Style," *L'Evangile de Jean*, ed. M. de Jonge (Leuven: University Press, 1977), pp. 125–47; D. A. Carson, "Current Source Criticism of the Fourth Gospel: Some Methodological Questions," *Journal of Biblical Literature* 97 (1978): 411–29.

[12]In addition to the standard introductions to the New Testament, cf. in particular the relevant sections of W. G. Kümmel, *The New Testament: The History of the Investigation of Its Problems*, trans. S. McLean Gilmour and Howard C. Kee (Nashville: Abingdon, 1972); Stephen Neill, *The Interpretation of the New Testament, 1861–1961* (Oxford: University Press, 1966); Norman Perrin, *What Is Redaction Criticism?* (Philadelphia: Fortress, 1970); G. E. Ladd, *The New Testament and Criticism* (Grand Rapids: Eerdmans, 1967); Stephen S. Smalley, "Redaction Criticism," *New Testament Interpretation*, ed. I. H. Marshall (Exeter: Paternoster, 1977), pp. 181–95.

[13]Cf. esp. Stonehouse's book *The Witness of the Synoptic Gospels to Christ* (Grand Rapids: Baker, reprint 1979 of two volumes, *The Witness of Matthew and Mark to Christ* and *The Witness of Luke to Christ*); idem, *Origins of the Synoptic Gospels: Some Basic Questions* (Grand Rapids: Eerdmans, 1963). Cf. also the perceptive pair of essays by M. Silva, "Ned B. Stonehouse and Redaction Criticism, Part I: The Witness of the Synoptic Evangelists to Christ," and "Part II: The Historicity of the Synoptic Tradition," *Westminster Theological Journal* 40 (1977–78): 77–78, 281–303.

[14]G. R. Osborne, "The Evangelical and Redaction Criticism," *Journal of the Evangelical Theological Society* 22 (1979): esp. pp. 311–12.

[15]Cf. esp. R. H. Lightfoot, *History and Interpretation in the Gospels* (London: Hodder & Stoughton, 1935), who, though dependent on the German form critics, actually anticipated the German redaction critics. See also many of the writings of Vincent Taylor, C. H. Dodd, and others.

[16]The many who have either moved toward the Griesbach hypothesis or else at the very least called into grave question the adequacy of the two-source hypothesis include E. P. Sanders, *The Tendencies of the Synoptic Tradition* (SNTSMS 9; Cambridge: University Press, 1969); W. R. Farmer, *The Synoptic Problem: A Critical Analysis* (Dillsboro, N.C.: Western North Carolina Press, 1976); idem, "Modern Developments of Griesbach's Hypothesis," *New Testament Studies* 23 (1977): 275–95; T. R. W. Longstaff, *Evidence of Conflation in Mark? A Study of the Synoptic Problem* (SBLDS 28; Missoula: Scholars, 1977);

Bernard Orchard, *Matthew, Luke and Mark* (Manchester: Koinonia, 1976); idem, "J. A. T. Robinson and the Synoptic Problem," *New Testament Studies* 22 (1975–76): 346–52; J. B. Tyson, "Sequential Parallelism in the Synoptic Gospels," *New Testament Studies* 22 (1975–76): 276–305; F. Neirynck, ed., *The Minor Agreements of Matthew and Luke against Mark* (Leuven: University Press, 1974); F. Neirynck, "Minor Agreements Matthew–Luke in the Transfiguration Story," in *Orientierung an Jesus (Festschrift* for J. Schmid; Freiburg: Herder, 1973), pp. 253–66; Roland Mushat Frye, "The Synoptic Problems and Analogies in Other Literatures," in *The Relationships among the Gospels: An Interdisciplinary Dialogue,* ed. William O. Walker, Jr. (San Antonio: Trinity University Press, 1978), pp. 261–302. Cf. also the discussions and diverse perspectives presented by B. Orchard and T. L. W. Longstaff, ed., *J. J. Griesbach: Synoptic and Text-Critical Studies, 1776–1976* (SNTSMS 34; Cambridge: University Press, 1978). Note, too, that far more complex theories have been advanced: e.g., Tim Schramm, *Der Markus-Stoff bei Lukas* (SNTSMS 14; Cambridge: University Press, 1971) argues that Luke appears to rely on some otherwise unknown source in some passages (e.g., Luke 21). Whether or not this suggestion is correct, Schramm shares the dissatisfaction of others with respect to the simple two-source hypothesis.

[17]Cf. esp. D. Wenham, "The Synoptic Problem Revisited: Some New Suggestions About the Composition of Mark 4:1–34," *Tyndale Bulletin* 23 (1972): 3–38; idem, "The Interpretation of the Parable of the Sower," *New Testament Studies* 20 (1974): 299–319.

[18]Cf. F. F. Bruce, "Are the New Testament Documents Still Reliable?" in *Evangelical Roots,* ed. Kenneth S. Kantzer (Nashville: Nelson, 1978), p. 55. Cf. the celebrated remark of Vincent Taylor (quoted also by Bruce) to the effect that if certain proponents of form criticism were right, "the disciples must have been translated to heaven immediately after the Resurrection" in his book *The Formation of the Gospel Tradition* (London: Macmillan, 1933), p. 41.

[19]B. Gerhardsson, *Memory and Manuscript,* trans. Eric J. Sharpe (Uppsala: Gleerup, 1964); idem, "Tradition and Transmission in Early Christianity" *Coniectanea Neotestamentica* 20 (1964); H. Riesenfeld, "The Gospel Tradition and Its Beginnings: A Study in the Limits of 'Formgeschichte,'" most readily accessible in *The Gospel Tradition* (Philadelphia: Fortress, 1970), pp. 1–29. Cf. also the more recent work by B. Gerhardsson, *The Origins of the Gospel Traditions* (Philadelphia: Fortress, 1979).

[20]Viz., W. D. Davies, *The Setting of the Sermon on the Mount* (Cambridge: University Press, 1966), App. XV, pp. 464–80, esp. p. 480: "[Gerhardsson and Riesenfeld] have made it far more historically probable and reasonably credible, over against the scepticism of much form-criticism, that in the gospels we are within hearing of the authentic voice and within sight of the authentic activity of Jesus of Nazareth, however much muffled and obscured these may be by the process of transmission." Cf. also Peter H. Davids, "The Gospels and Jewish Tradition: Twenty Years After Gerhardsson," *Gospel Perspectives,* vol. 1, ed. R. T. France and David Wenham (Sheffield: JSOT, 1980), pp. 75–99.

[21]Cf. esp. H. Schürmann, "Die vorösterlichen Anfänge der Logientradition," in *Der historische Jesu und der kerygmatische Christus,* ed. H. Ristow and K. Matthiae (Berlin: Evangelische Verlagsanstalt, 1961), pp. 342–70; Robert H. Gundry, *The Use of the Old Testament in St. Matthew's Gospel* (Supplement to NovTest 18; Leiden Brill, 1967); E. Earle Ellis, "New Directions in Form Criticism," in *Jesus Christus in Historie und Theologie,* ed. G. Strecker (Tübingen: Mohr, 1975), pp. 299–315; cf. Rainer Riesner, "Jüdische Elementarbildung und Evangelienüberlieferung," in *Gospel Perspectives,* vol. 1, ed. R. T. France and David Wenham (Sheffield: JSOT, 1980), pp. 209–23; and now his dissertation, *Jesus als Lehrer* (Tübinger: J. C. B. Mohr, 1981).

[22]Cf. esp. Stonehouse, *Origins,* pp. 43–47.

[23]Cf. among others, Humphrey Palmer, *The Logic of Gospel Criticism* (New York: St. Martin's, 1968), p. 193; Morna D. Hooker, "On Using the Wrong Tool," *Theology* 75 (1972): 570–81; C. S. Lewis, *Fern-seed and Elephants* (Glasgow: Collins, 1975), pp. 113–17.

[24]Palmer, *Logic,* p. 185.

[25]Cf. Hooker, "Wrong Tool," p. 576; D. A. Carson, "Understanding Misunderstandings in the Fourth Gospel," *Tyndale Bulletin* 33 (1982): 29–61.

[26]In addition to the essays by Hooker, "Wrong Tool," and Ellis, "Form Criticism," cited above, cf. esp. R. T. France, "The Authenticity of the Sayings of Jesus," *History, Criticism and Faith*, ed. Colin Brown (Leicester: InterVarsity Press, 1976), esp. pp. 110–14; David L. Mealand, "The Dissimilarity Test," *Scottish Journal of Theology*, 31 (1978): 41–50 (though Mealand gives the test high marks for affirming the trustworthiness of the irreducible minimum).

[27]Cf. Hooker, "Wrong Tool," p. 577.

[28]Cf., in addition to the major introductions, n. 26 and the literature cited there.

[29]For a fine example, cf. H. Conzelmann's redaction critical study, *Die Mitte der Zeit* (Tübingen: Mohr, 1964). On this, cf. Neill, *Interpretation*, pp. 264–65.

[30]Hooker, "Wrong Tool," p. 578.

[31]Cf. Morna D. Hooker, "In his own Image?" in *What About the New Testament?* ed. Morna Hooker and Colin Hickling (London: SPCK, 1975), pp. 28–44, esp. pp. 36–37, where she criticizes Perrin (see n. 12 above) for pitting history against theology. She charges Perrin with "a revealing comment" that he "makes on a study in Marcan theology written by Ernest Best, which he describes as 'a strange book in that the author combines redaction criticism with the assumption "that Mark believes that the incidents he uses actually happened"'! Now this is really an extraordinary statement. Why should the fact that Mark is a 'theologian' preclude him from writing about events which he thought had happened? Can a 'theologian' write only about imaginary events? This is obviously sheer nonsense. Against Perrin, we must quote Perrin himself: 'Mark has the right to be read on his own terms.' And what is the most obvious thing about Mark's method of writing? It is that he presented his theology in a form which 'misled' generations of scholars into believing that he was writing an historical account! This, says Perrin, 'is mute testimony to the skill of Mark as an author'. Mark may well be more skillful than has sometimes been allowed—but not if he succeeded only in concealing his purpose until the twentieth-century critic uncovered it! Was he perhaps using his skill to do precisely what he seems to be doing? He certainly gives the impression that he is writing *Heilsgeschichte*, and that theology and history are for him inextricably bound together. Is it not unlikely that he has chosen 'to introduce his particular theology of the cross' in narrative form because it is an exposition of what he understands to have actually happened?"

[32]Cf. D. A. Carson, *The Sermon on the Mount* (Grand Rapids: Baker, 1978), pp. 145–47.

[33]Cf. esp. France, "Authenticity," pp. 106–7.

[34]Ibid., pp. 117–18 and n. 45.

[35]Ibid., p. 118.

[36]Graham Stanton, "Form Criticism Revisited," in *What About the New Testament?* ed. Morna Hooker and Colin Hickling (London: SPCK, 1975), p. 23.

[37]D. H. Juel, *Messiah and Temple: The Trial of Jesus in the Gospel of Mark* (SBLDS 31; Missoula: Scholars, 1977). Cf. also J. Delorme, "L'intégration des petits unités littéraires dans l'Evangile de Marc du point de vue de la sémiotique structurale," *New Testament Studies* 25 (1979): 469–91.

[38]Cf. esp. Erhardt Güttgemanns, *Candid Questions Concerning Gospel Form Criticism: A Methodological Sketch of the Fundamental Problematics of Form and Redaction Criticism*, tr. William G. Doty (Pittsburgh: Pickwick, 1979).

[39]Viz., William L. Lane, *Commentary on the Gospel of Mark* (NICNT; Grand Rapids: Eerdmans, 1974); I. Howard Marshall, *Commentary on Luke* (NIGTC; Grand Rapids: Eerdmans, 1978).

[40]G. R. Osborne, "Redactional Trajectories in the Crucifixion Narrative," *The Evangelical Quarterly* 51 (1979): 80–96.

[41]M. J. Down, "The Matthean Birth Narratives: Matthew 1^{18}–2^{23}," *The Expository Times* 90 (1978–79): 51–52.

[42]E.g., J. Schniewind, *Das Evangelium nach Matthäus* (NTD; Göttingen: Vandenhoeck und Ruprecht, 1937), p. 53; R. Banks, "Matthew's Understanding of the Law: Authenticity and Interpretation in Matthew 5:17–20," *Journal of Biblical Literature* 93 (1974): 226–42.

[43]Ibid., pp. 233, 238.

[44]S. Legasse, "Jésus: Juif ou non?" *Nouvelle Revue Théologique* 86 (1964): 692; W. Trilling, *Das wahre Israel* (Münich: Kösel-Verlag, 1964), p. 171.

[45]Banks, "Matthew's Understanding," p. 228.

[46]Ibid., pp. 232–33. Cf. also E. Schweizer, *The Good News According to Matthew* (Atlanta: John Knox, 1975), p. 104.

[47]Banks, "Matthew's Understanding."

[48]J. Jeremias, *Die Sprache des Lukasevangeliums: Redaktion und Tradition im Nicht-Markusstoff des dritten Evangeliums* (Meyers Kritisch-exegetischer Kommentar Sunderband; Göttingen: Vandenhoeck und Ruprecht, 1980).

[49]E. Schweizer, *The Good News According to Matthew*, trans. David E. Green (Atlanta: John Knox, 1975), p. 388.

[50]E.g., Hugh Anderson, *The Gospel of Mark* (NCB; Greenwood: Attic, 1976), pp. 248–49; G. M. Styler, "Stages in Christology in the Synoptic Gospels," *New Testament Studies* 10 (1963–64): 398–409; R. Pesch, *Das Markusevangelium*, 2 vols. (Freiburg: Herder, 1977), 2:138.

[51]David Hill, *The Gospel of Matthew* (NCB; Greenwood: Attic, 1972), p. 64. Cf. his entire discussion, pp. 64–65.

[52]Stonehouse, *Origins*, pp. 93–112.

[53]Ibid., p. 103.

[54]Ibid., p. 105, and pp. 176–92 for an excellent discussion. I take this to have been necessary because of the exigencies of the salvation-historical setting.

[55]Cf. among others, H. D. McDonald, *Jesus—Human and Divine* (Grand Rapids: Zondervan, 1968); C. F. D. Moule, *The Origin of Christology* (Cambridge: University Press, 1977); I. Howard Marshall, *The Origins of New Testament Christology* (Downers Grove: InterVarsity, 1976).

[56]Cf. especially Vincent Taylor, *The Gospel according to St. Mark* (London: Macmillan, 1953), pp. 424–27. Taylor himself proposes a different solution to the one adopted here.

[57]Marshall, *Commentary*, p. 684. Moreover, I have not here mentioned the text-critical problems.

[58]G. R. Osborne, "The Evangelical and *Traditionsgeschichte*," *Journal of the Evangelical Theological Society* 21 (1978): 117–30; Robert H. Stein, "The 'Criteria' for Authenticity," *Gospel Perspectives*, vol. 1, ed. R. T. France and David Wenham (Sheffield: JSOT, 1980), pp. 225–63.

[59]James Barr, *Fundamentalism* (London: SCM, 1977), esp. pp. 120–59.

[60]Cf. the excellent discussion by George I. Mavrodes, *Belief in God: A Study in the Epistemology of Religion* (New York: Random, 1970), esp. pp. 97–114.

[61]Exemplified in an embarrassing way by Harold Lindsell, *The Battle for the Bible* (Grand Rapids: Zondervan, 1976), pp. 175–76.

[62]I cannot here raise other questions that affect authenticity, such as the literary genre of any book or pericope, or the position that posits that the church received words

from the resurrected Christ through Christian prophets and read them back into the historical Jesus—a view that questions the authenticity not of the sayings but of the settings. Nor may I here lay out the epistemological base on which I would build a high view of Scripture.

[63]I have developed these categories in "Historical Tradition and the Fourth Gospel—After Dodd, What?" *Gospel Perspectives*, vol. 2, ed. R. T. France and David Wenham (Sheffield: JSOT, 1981).

[64](London: Hodder and Stoughton, 1972).

[65]I would like to record my gratitude to Dr. David Wenham for offering helpful suggestions while I was preparing this chapter.

THE NEW TESTAMENT USE OF THE OLD TESTAMENT:
TEXT FORM AND AUTHORITY
Moisés Silva
pages 147–65

[1]To be sure, a number of related and interesting questions can be asked, such as, Why would God be concerned about inerrant autographs if they were not to survive? That very common question has probably been discussed more intensively than it is worth. Particularly interesting, and difficult, is the problem of identifying what we mean by "autograph" when the book in question has had a long history of development. For example, is the autograph of the Pentateuch the shape it had during Moses' lifetime (assuming Mosaic authorship), or its shape after his death when some "updating" took place, or its "canonical shape" (to use a fashionable expression)? This question is extremely complicated and calls for serious discussion.

[2]The reason for this phenomenon lies in the *redundancy* inherent in language. The meaning of most sentences can be captured even if we miss individual words; also, the main points of a discourse come through though we may occasionally daydream. I have treated this matter in *Biblical Words and Their Meaning* (Grand Rapids: Zondervan, 1983), chap. 6.

[3]Note some relevant statistics in Bruce M. Metzger, *The Text of the New Testament*, 2nd ed. (Oxford: The University Press, 1968), pp. 31–35.

[4]The Westminster Confession of Faith, I.viii.

[5]This subject has been treated by many writers. Note John H. Skilton, "The Transmission of the Scriptures," in *The Infallible Word*, ed. N. B. Stonehouse and Paul Woolley, 3rd ed. (Philadelphia: Presbyterian and Reformed, 1967), pp. 141–95. More recently, and with special emphasis on Old Testament problems, Douglas Stuart, "Inerrancy and Textual Criticism," in *Inerrancy and Common Sense*, ed. Roger R. Nicole and J. Ramsey Michaels (Grand Rapids: Baker, 1980), pp. 97–117.

[6]The primary reason for this complexity is that several Greek translations and revisions of the same Old Testament books were produced from the fourth century B.C. to the fourth century A.D., and that surviving manuscripts contain "mixed texts," making it almost impossible to identify the original translation. Cf. Robert A. Kraft's discussion of the "Earliest Greek Versions" in *The Interpreter's Dictionary of the Bible*, Supplementary Volume (Nashville: Abingdon, 1976), pp. 811–15.

[7]This inference does contain a measure of truth. Cf. Donald A. Hagner, "The Old Testament in the New Testament," in *Interpreting the Word of God: Festschrift in Honor of Steven Barabas*, ed. Samuel J. Schultz and Morris A. Inch (Chicago: Moody, 1976), pp. 78–104, esp. p. 90.

[8]It should be noted that we are not interested here in *exact* quotations that happen to be used in unusual ways—though this subject will necessarily demand our attention later on. See O. Palmer Robertson, "Genesis 15:6: New Covenant Expositions of an Old

Covenant Text," *Westminster Theological Journal* 42 (1979–80): 259–89, esp. p. 279.

[9]That is, the Hebrew text used by the LXX translators had the same three consonants found in the Masoretic text (*mṭḥ*). The translators and the Masoretes disagreed on which of two possible meanings was conveyed by that combination of consonants. A good example of *textual* variation is Jeremiah 23:9, "I have become like a drunken man." The work "drunken" translates the Hebrew consonants *škwr* (vocalized *šikkôr*). The LXX, however, must have used a Hebrew text that read *šbwr* (vocalized *šābûr*), for they translated it with a Greek word that means "broken."

[10]John Owen, *An Exposition of Hebrews*, 7 vols. in 4 (1855; reprint of Goold ed., Marshallton, Del.: National Foundation for Christian Education, 1969), 1:114–17.

[11]More often than not, New Testament copyists resisted assimilation with the LXX. See Kenneth J. Thomas, "The Old Testament Citations in Hebrews," *New Testament Studies* 11 (1964–65): 303–25, esp. pp. 303–4, n. 7.

[12]E. A. Speiser says that the usual translation and the LXX rendering are "equally implausible" (*The Anchor Bible: Genesis* [N.Y.: Doubleday, 1964], p. 327); cf. also G. von Rad, *Genesis: A Commentary*, rev. ed. (London: SCM, 1972), p. 414, "The meaning of the gesture . . . is not quite clear."

[13]See especially Moses Stuart, *A Commentary on the Epistle to the Hebrews* (London: Fischer, Fischer and Jackson, 1834), pp. 492–93. It is true that the expression *roʾš hammiṭṭāh* does not occur elsewhere in the Bible. The view that the LXX has translated correctly is supported by a few other conservative scholars, such as Philip E. Hughes, *A Commentary on the Epistle to the Hebrews* (Grand Rapids: Eerdmans, 1977), p. 489.

[14]For an interesting, real-life example of apparently contradictory reports that were surprisingly harmonized when additional information became available, see the Summer 1980 issue of *Update* (published by the International Council on Biblical Inerrancy), p. 3. Harmonization is a standard historical tool—I am concerned here about its possible abuse. See also my article, "Ned B. Stonehouse and Redaction Criticism," *Westminster Theological Journal* 40 (1977–78): 77–88, 281–303, esp. p. 79.

[15]John Calvin, *Commentaries on the Epistle of Paul the Apostle to the Hebrews*, tr. John Owen (Grand Rapids: Eerdmans, 1948), pp. 290–91; this particular edition includes an introduction by Ned B. Stonehouse, who commends Calvin precisely because of his interpretation of 11:21. H. C. Leupold, *Exposition of Genesis* 2 vols. (1942; reprint, Grand Rapids: Baker, 1950), 2:1141–42. Note also the standard conservative commentaries on Hebrews (e.g., Delitzsch, Westcott).

[16]For example, "The sun *rose* this morning at six o'clock." Some writers argue (e.g., H. Ridderbos, *Studies in Scripture and Its Authority* [Grand Rapids: Eerdmans, 1978], p. 30) that the parallel is not real, since the biblical writers *did* believe some of these things; but to raise the objection that these writers were in fact limited is to confuse inerrancy with omniscience. (See also below, n. 21.) I might add in this connection that Daniel P. Fuller's comments on "Benjamin B. Warfield's View of Faith and History," *Bulletin of the Evangelical Theological Society* 11 (1968): 75–83, esp. pp. 80–81, do not take into account Warfield's own clear qualification: "No one is likely to assert infallibility for the apostles in aught else than in their official teaching. And whatever they may be shown to have held apart from their official teaching, may be readily looked upon with *only that respect* which we certainly must accord to the *opinions* of men of such exceptional intellectual and spiritual insight" (emphasis mine). See his collection of articles, *The Inspiration and Authority of the Bible* (Philadelphia: 1893; reprint ed., Presbyterian and Reformed, 1964), pp. 196–97.

[17]One cannot help but recall the scorn with which the serious christological controversies of the fourth century have been described as "the whole world convulsed over a diphthong" (*homoiousios*). Interestingly, Stephen T. Davis, *The Debate About the Bible: Inerrancy versus Infallibility* (Philadelphia: Westminster, 1977), first defines infallibility by saying that "in matters of faith and practice [the Bible] does not mislead us" (p. 16), but later redefines it to include only "matters that are *crucially relevant* to Christian faith

and practice" (p. 118, emphasis mine). I suspect one could honestly present good arguments for an estimate that only 5 percent of the Old Testament material is *crucially* relevant for Christian faith and practice (for example, in Genesis 1 only verses 1 and 26 might qualify). Even more interestingly, Davis himself considers an error the biblical statement that God commanded the Israelites to kill the Canaanites (pp. 96–98). But is not the ethics of killing crucially relevant for Christian practice? It would seem that, according to Davis, the Bible does mislead us in gravely significant matters of practice. So much for the complaint that inerrantists worry too much about trivial details.

[18]This formulation is characteristic of Daniel P. Fuller; cf. his articles on Warfield (see above, n. 16) and on "The Nature of Biblical Inerrancy," *Journal of the American Scientific Affiliation* 24 (1972): 47–51. Unfortunately, it is not at all clear what he means. His attempts at clarification in *JETS* 16 (1973): 67–69 would suggest that his view belongs, not here, but in the next item, 7.3. If so, his terminology is unfortunate. Cf. also Davis's evaluation, *The Debate About the Bible*, pp. 37–48.

[19]Though overstated, Montgomery's criticisms on this matter are generally on target; see *God's Inerrant Word: An International Symposium on the Trustworthiness of Scripture*, ed. J. W. Montgomery (Minneapolis: Bethany Fellowship, 1974), pp. 29–30.

[20]Cf. the quotations gathered by Ned. B. Stonehouse in *Origins of the Synoptic Gospels: Some Basic Questions* (Grand Rapids: Eerdmans, 1963), p. 110n. In what follows, my use of the word "intention" should be distinguished from that of Daniel P. Fuller, who emphasizes the *general* salvific purpose for which the Scriptures were given. My only concern is that the meaning of specific passages must be exegetically determined before we proceed to state what those passages infallibly teach.

[21]Even scholars hostile to any notion of infallibility have long recognized this elementary hermeneutical factor. One must therefore consider it a disturbing retrogression in the contemporary debate when Davis insists that Jesus' comment about the mustard seed contains "at least some sort of error" (*Debate*, p. 101). This statement is not only bad exegesis; it also erects a straw man by implying that inerrancy entails some artificial (= unnatural to human communication) standard of absolute truth.

[22]See above, n. 15.

[23]*Der Brief an die Hebräer*, 11. Aufl. (Göttingen: Vandenhoeck und Ruprecht, 1960), p. 270. Cf. also C. Spicq, *L'Épître aux Hébreux*, 2 vols. (Paris: J. Gabalda, 1952–53), 2:355, who states that, according to the LXX, the staff was a sign that Jacob professed faith in the future city—"or, at least, that his people would leave Egypt to possess the Promised Land."

[24]This material is most accessible in Louis Ginzberg, *The Legends of the Jews*, 7 vols. (Philadelphia: The Jewish Publication Society, 1912–28), 1:83, 347; 2:291ff.; 3:306–7, with corresponding notes; see also 2:34 for the view that the staff was a symbol of messiahship. Cf. Friedrich Schröger, *Der Verfasser der Hebräerbriefes als Schriftausleger* (Biblische Untersuchungen 4; Regensburg: Friedrich Pustet, 1968), p. 221.

[25]Cf. Ernst Käsemann, *Das wandernde Gottesvolk. Eine Untersuchung zum Hebräerbrief,* 2. Aufl. (Göttingen: Vandenhoeck und Ruprecht, 1957), esp. chap. 2, though the author does not comment on 11:21.

[26]S. Lewis Johnson, Jr., *The Old Testament in the New: An Argument for Biblical Inspiration* (Grand Rapids: Zondervan, 1980), p. 66. He makes this statement concerning the use of "body" (instead of "ears") in Hebrews 10:5. In a note, p. 104, he mentions the view of Simon Kistemaker, an Evangelical, that the author of Hebrews used the LXX precisely because it lent itself to his interpretation. Johnson responds that this suggestion "raises questions concerning the biblical doctrine of inspiration, to which [Kistemaker] has not addressed himself."

[27]One common example is the quotation of Isaiah 6:10 in Mark 4:12; among other details, the verb "be healed" is changed to "be forgiven," in correspondence to the Targum (Aramaic translation) of Isaiah. With regard to the importance of the Syriac

tradition, see Earl Richard, "The Old Testament in Acts: Wilcox's Semitisms in Retrospect," *Catholic Biblical Quarterly* 42 (1980): 330–41.

[28]Cf. Johnson, *The Old Testament in the New*, chap. 4, and the literature cited by him. O. Palmer Robertson, "Genesis 15:6: New Covenant Expositions of an Old Covenant Text," *Westminster Theological Journal* 42 (1979–80): 259–89, says concerning the quotation of Hosea 11:1 in Matthew 2:15 that "the 'fulfillment' envisioned involves the 'bringing of fruition' of a principle of redemptive history that had an earlier manifestation" (p. 285).

[29]For a comprehensive review, see Anthony C. Thiselton, *The Two Horizons: New Testament Hermeneutics and Philosophical Description* (Grand Rapids: Eerdmans, 1980), esp. chap. 4.

[30]Note the survey by Anthony J. Saldarini, "Judaism and the New Testament," in *The Bible and Its Modern Interpreters*, III (forthcoming). The basic issues are clearly laid out by E. Earle Ellis, "How the New Testament Uses the Old," in *New Testament Interpretation: Essays on Principles and Methods*, ed. I. Howard Marshall (Grand Rapids: Eerdmans, 1977), pp. 199–219. Also useful is C. K. Barrett, "The Interpretation of the Old Testament in the New," in *The Cambridge History of the Bible*, vol. I, ed. P. R. Ackroyd and C. F. Evans (Cambridge: The University Press, 1970), pp. 377–411.

[31]*The Greek Way* (1930; reprint, New York: Avon, 1973), pp. 69, 187, 208, 247.

[32]This example, among others, has been used by Anthony T. Hanson, *Studies in Paul's Technique and Theology* (Grand Rapids: Eerdmans, 1974), pp. 173–74, though his approach is in some respects different from mine.

[33]C. K. Barrett, *A Commentary on the Second Epistle to the Corinthians* (New York: Harper and Row, 1973), p. 333.

[34]I mean by this phrase something quite different from C. H. Dodd's similar term, "transposition," in *According to the Scriptures: The Sub-Structure of New Testament Theology* (Digswell Place: James Nisbet, 1952), p. 130.

[35]*Commentary on the Epistle to the Romans* (1886; reprint, Grand Rapids: Eerdmans, 1968), p. 441. Concerning the quotation in Romans 10:18, Hodge similarly remarks that Paul "is not to be understood as quoting the Psalmist as though the ancient prophet was speaking of the gospel. He simply uses scriptural language to express his own ideas, as is done involuntarily almost by every preacher in every sermon" (p. 349).

[36]*Paul: An Outline of His Theology* (Grand Rapids: Eerdmans, 1975), pp. 154ff.

[37]See Daniel P. Fuller, *Gospel and Law: Contrast or Continuum?* (Grand Rapids: Eerdmans, 1980), p. 98; see also Doublas J. Moo's critical review in *Trinity Journal* 3NS (1982): 99–103.

[38]"The Allegory of Abraham, Sarah, and Hagar in the Argument of Galatians," in *Rechtfertigung. Festschrift für Ernst Käsemann zum 70. Geburtstag*, ed. J. Friedrich et al. (Tübingen: Mohr, 1976), pp. 1–16, esp. p. 6.

[39]Strictly speaking, "rabbinic interpretation" describes the approach evident in works that date no earlier than the second century of our era. We are not interested, however, in whether a *particular* method (say, one of the supposed rules of Hillel) or line of interpretation existed in the first century; rather, we are concerned with a *basic approach* to Scripture. No one imagines that "the rabbinic mind" appeared *ex nihilo* after A.D. 70; indeed, the general features that have a bearing on our topic go back at least to the second century B.C. Note J. Weingreen, *From Bible to Mishna: The Continuity of Tradition* (Manchester: The University Press, 1976), passim, and my review article, "The Pharisees in Modern Jewish Scholarship," *WTJ* 42 (1979–80): 395–405, esp. pp. 402–3. Note also J. Weingreen et al., "Interpretation, History of," in *The Interpreter's Dictionary of the Bible*, Supplementary Volume, esp. pp. 436–48; and G. Vermes, "Bible and Midrash: Early Old Testament Exegesis," in *The Cambridge History of the Bible*, 1:199–231.

[40]Dodd, *According to the Scriptures*, p. 126.

[41]Ibid., p. 33.

[42]Note, however, James Barr, *Old and New in Interpretation: A Study of the Two Testaments* (New York: Harper and Row, 1966), p. 142, n. 2. Ernst Käsemann, *Commentary on Romans*, trans. Geoffrey W. Bromiley (Grand Rapids: Eerdmans, 1980), p. 86, accuses rabbinic exegesis *and* Paul of taking passages out of context.

[43]Barrett, "The Allegory," p. 10.

[44]Herbert Danby, *The Mishnah* (Oxford: The University Press, 1933), p. xxvi, n. 2, tells us that the ten opening words of *Arakhin* 4 required, for translation, seventy-seven English words (even so, many English readers would no doubt find the translation quite perplexing). For a taste of the complexities involved, see Jacob Neusner, *Invitation to the Talmud: A Teaching Book* (New York: Harper and Row, 1973).

[45]Franklin Johnson argued that the resemblance between Jewish and biblical interpretation "is chiefly in appearance; when the reader pierces below the surface, he finds but little of it; and it vanishes wholly when he searches in the New Testament for the obscurities, the superstitions, the cabalisms, the puerilities, the absurdities, the insanities, which stare at him from every page of the rabbinic interpretations of the sacred writings"; see *The Quotations of the New Testament from the Old, Considered in the Light of General Literature* (Philadelphia: American Baptist Publication Society, 1896), p. 379. More sober scholars, while avoiding such extremes, still tend to overemphasize the differences; cf. the highly regarded study of Robert H. Gundry, *The Use of the Old Testament in St. Matthew's Gospel, With Special Reference to the Messianic Hope* (Supplements to Novum Testamentum 18; Leiden: Brill, 1967), p. 205, which speaks of Qumran and rabbinic interpreters as "supremely oblivious to contextual exegesis whenever they wish." For a different viewpoint, see J. W. Doeve, *Jewish Hermeneutics in the Synoptic Gospels and Acts* (Van Gorcum's Theologische Bibliothek 24; Assen: Van Gorcum, 1954), p. 89.

[46]Notice how the phrase, "the king went to Gibeon" (1 Kings 3:4, right after a negative comment on Solomon's worship) becomes a five-verse apologetic in 2 Chronicles 1:2–6, where emphasis is put on Solomon's obedience to the instructions of Leviticus 17:1–7. (I owe this observation to Dr. Raymond B. Dillard, who is preparing a commentary on 2 Chronicles; cf. his article, "The Chronicler's Solomon," *Westminster Theological Journal* 43 [1980–81]: 289–300.) Important works on the chronicler's theology include T. Willi, *Die Chronik als Auslegung* (Göttingen: Vandenhoeck und Ruprecht, 1972), and H. G. M. Williamson, *Israel in the Books of Chronicles* (Cambridge: The University Press, 1977). More controversial is the question whether the Evangelists felt free to modify Jesus' deeds and teachings with a view to bringing out their significance; note my article "Ned B. Stonehouse," *Westminster Theological Journal* 40 (1977–78): 281–303, esp. pp. 289ff., and the massive development of this idea by Robert H. Gundry, *Matthew: A Commentary on His Literary and Theological Art* (Grand Rapids: Eerdmans, 1982).

[47]Needless to emphasize, there are qualitative differences, particularly in the christological perspective of New Testament writers. My statement does not have reference to *all* aspects of interpretation, but only to the question of "distance" between text and interpretation. Moreover, I do not wish to deny the possibility that some rabbinic interpretations were developed "to justify long-established usage not expressly ordained or permitted by Scripture" (Danby, *The Mishnah*, p. xv).

[48]Hanson, *Studies*, pp. 129 and 146–47, has stressed his view that what appears to us, at first blush, arbitrary Pauline interpretation often turns out to be established contemporary exegesis. Hanson takes things too far, however, as when he approvingly (p. 203) quotes Doeve's opinion that "there is no essential difference between rabbinic and New Testament use of Scripture."

[49]As Ridderbos, *Studies* (see above, n. 19), p. 25, rightly argues, although his own distinction between Scripture and the Word of God runs afoul of 2 Timothy 3:16.

[50]Cf. my comments in *Westminster Theological Journal* 40 (1977–78): 295n.

[51]Weingreen, *From Bible to Mishna*, repeatedly alludes to the Talmudic saying (*B. Kiddushin* 49a): "What is Tora? It is the exposition of Tora." In her famous article "Midrash" for the *Dictionnaire de la Bible*, Renée Bloch emphasizes the positive aspect: midrash is not to be understood as fable, but as an amplification intended "to show the full import" of Scripture, including its present adaptation. "So long as there is a people of God who regard the Bible as the living Word of God, there will be midrash: only the name might change. Nothing is more characteristic in this regard than the use of the Old Testament in the New Testament: it always involves midrashic actualization." See *Approaches to Judaism: Theory and Practice*, ed. William Scott Green (Brown Judaic Studies 1; Missoula: Scholars, 1978), pp. 29, 32. Note also Brian M. Nolan, *The Royal Son of God: The Christology of Matthew 1-2 in the Setting of the Gospel* (Orbis biblicus et orientalis, 23; Göttingen: Vandenhoeck und Ruprecht, 1979), pp. 52ff. For a valuable survey and bibliography, see M. P. Miller, "Midrash," *The Interpreter's Dictionary of the Bible*, suppl. vol., pp. 593–97.

[52]Cf. C. Dietzfelbinger, *Paulus und das Alte Testament* (München: Chr. Kaiser, 1961), p. 41, quoted by Marcus Barth, who responds: "I am not yet convinced that the hermeneutical methods developed since the enlightenment have yielded results so superior to those employed by the authors of the New Testament that we are entitled to put their hermeneutics on a *Schandpfahl* [pillory] or into a museum for good." See "The Old Testament in Hebrews: An Essay in Biblical Hermeneutics," in *Current Issues in New Testament Interpretation: Essays in Honor of Otto A. Piper*, ed. William Klassen and Gordon F. Snyder (New York: Harper and Row, 1962), pp. 53–78, esp. p. 78.

[53]Johnson, *The Old Testament in the New*, p. 67, is undoubtedly correct in remarking that "if the apostles are reliable guides in biblical teaching, then they surely are reliable guides in the doctrine of interpretation, and we must follow them." One must wonder, however, whether Johnson himself uses Scripture in a manner comparable to that in which, say, Matthew 2:15 uses Hosea—or whether he would approve of preachers who do!

[54]Richard N. Longenecker, *Biblical Exegesis in the Apostolic Period* (Grand Rapids: Eerdmans, 1975), p. 218.

[55]Here Longenecker has in mind particularly *pesher*-type interpretation: "This is the fulfillment of that." One wonders whether Clement of Rome was overstepping his bounds when he used *pesher* in addressing the Corinthians as follows: "All glory and enlargement was given to you, and that which has been written was fulfilled, 'My beloved ate and drank, was enlarged and made fat, and he kicked'" (1 Clement 3:1, quoting Deut. 32:15). We may here recall G. Vos's insistence that Christians, though not inspired, stand *with* Paul in their redemptive-historical perspective, so that the interpretive tasks are the same; see the discussion by Richard B. Gaffin, Jr., *The Centrality of the Resurrection: A Study in Paul's Soteriology* (Grand Rapids: Baker, 1978), pp. 23ff.

[56]Longenecker says as much; my own concern is to clarify what a phrase such as "conformity to modern exegesis" does and does not imply.

[57]Cf. C. S. Lewis's discussion of "second meanings" in *Reflections on the Psalms* (New York: Harcourt, Brace and World, 1958), pp. 99ff. The question of *sensus plenior* should probably be related to the present discussion. Unfortunately, I have nothing to contribute to this very complicated issue. For a firm denial of any kind of allegorizing, see Walter C. Kaiser, Jr., "The Current Crisis in Exegesis and the Apostolic Use of Deuteronomy 25:4 in 1 Corinthians 9:8–10," *JETS* 21 (1978): 3–18.

[58]Cf. John Frame, "God and Biblical Language: Transcendence and Immanence," in *God's Inerrant Word* (see above, n. 19), pp. 159–77.

[59]Cf. Longenecker's reference to the descriptive over against the normative, p. 219.

[60]It may be worthwhile to point out again that I do not regard this proposal as the only possible (or even necessarily the best) solution, but as an approach that should not be summarily dismissed by evangelicals.

THE TRUTH OF SCRIPTURE AND THE PROBLEM OF
HISTORICAL RELATIVITY

Philip Edgcumbe Hughes

pages 173–94

[1]P. T. Forsyth, *The Person and Place of Jesus Christ* (London: Hodder and Stoughton, 1909), p. 178.

[2]P. T. Forsyth, *Positive Preaching and the Modern Mind* (New York: A. C. Armstrong, 1907), pp. 10, 13.

[3]Karl Barth, *Protestant Thought: From Rousseau to Ritschl* (New York: Harper & Row, 1959), p. 148.

[4]Ibid., p. 146.

[5]Edward Caird, *The Critical Philosophy of Immanuel Kant* (Glasgow: J. Maclehose, 1889), 2:574–75.

[6]Friedrich Schleiermacher, *The Christian Faith* (Edinburgh: T. & T. Clark, 1928), §128, pp. 591–93. (The German work was first published in 1821/22.)

[7]Rudolf Bultmann, in *Kerygma and Myth*, ed. H.-W. Bartsch (London: SPCK, 1953), p. 209.

[8]Rudolf Bultmann, *Essays Philosophical and Theological* (New York: Macmillan/London: SCM, 1955), pp. 286–87.

[9]E. L. Mascall, *The Secularization of Christianity* (London: Darton, Longman and Todd, 1965), p. 11.

[10]Bultmann, *Essays*, p. 280.

[11]John Hick, ed., *The Myth of God Incarnate* (London: SCM, 1978).

[12]Ibid., pp. ix–x.

[13]Ibid., p. 61.

[14]Ibid., p. 31.

[15]Ibid., p. 141.

[16]Ibid., p. 143.

[17]Ibid., p. 60.

[18]Ibid., p. 192.

[19]Ibid., pp. 4, 31.

[20]Ibid., p. 170.

[21]Ibid., p. 59.

[22]Ibid., p. 200.

[23]Ibid., pp. 180ff.

[24]Forsyth, *Person and Place*, p. 133.

[25]Martin Luther, *Lectures on Genesis* (on Gen. 14:18).

[26]Oxford: University Press, 1961.

[27]Hick, ed., *Myth*, p. 176.

[28]Bultmann, *Essays*, p. 286.

[29]Aloys Grillmeier, *Christ in Christian Tradition*, vol. 1, *From the Apostolic Age to Chalcedon*, 2nd ed. (London: Mowbrays, 1975), p. 555.

[30]John Calvin, *Institutes* I. vii. 1.

[31]Abraham Kuyper, *Principles of Sacred Theology* (English trans., 1898; reprint ed., Grand Rapids: Eerdmans, 1965), p. 550.

[32]Ibid., p. 402.

[33]Ibid., p. 551.

[34]Anthony Thiselton, *The Two Horizons: New Testament Horizons and Philosophical Descriptions* (Grand Rapids: Eerdmans, 1980), p. 78.

THE CHURCH FATHERS AND HOLY SCRIPTURE
Geoffrey W. Bromiley
pages 199–220

[1]Epistle 6, 7.

[2]Cf. Heres. 4, 26, 3.

[3]Cf. Eusebius Eccles. Hist. 4, 26, 13f.

[4]Cf. Epist. to Afric. 4f.

[5]Ep. heort. 39.

[6]Catechet. Lect. 4, 33f.

[7]Orthodox Faith 4, 17.

[8]Psalms Prol. 15.

[9]Comm. on Creed 38.

[10]Epist. 53, 8; 107, 12

[11]Christ. Instruction 2, 13.

[12]On this question see G. L. Robinson and R. K. Harrison, Art. "Canon of the OT," ISBE I (1979), pp. 591ff.; N. H. Ridderbos, Art. "Canon of the OT," NBD (1962), pp. 186ff.

[13]2 Cl. 2, 4.

[14]E.g., Dial, Trypho 49, 5

[15]Heres. 4, 9, 1.

[16]Pedagogue 1, 59, 1.

[17]Prescription 36.

[18]2 Cl. 4, 5; 5, 2ff.; 12, 2ff.

[19]Prescription 40.

[20]Heres. 3, 11, 11.

[21]c. Marcion 4–5.

[22]See J. Stevenson, *A New Eusebius* (London, 1960), pp. 144ff.

[23]In Origen's threefold classification spurious works were put in the third category. Eusebius refined this system by dividing the disputed books into those that were accepted and those that were not.

[24]See the passage on the agreement and differences of the Gospels in the Muratorian Canon.

[25]See the Muratorian Canon on the date of *The Shepherd:* "It was written quite lately in our times by Hermas, while his brother Pius, the bishop, was sitting in the chair of the church of the city of Rome."

[26]Heres. 2, 28, 2.

[27]Comm. on Nah. 1, 1.

[28]c. Eunom. 7.

[29]Cf. City of God 20, 230.

[30]Cf. Princ. 4, 3, 1; Hom. on Jerem. 39, 1.

[31]In illud, Vidi dom.hom. 2, 2.

[32]In Philem. Prol.

[33]Faith and Creed 2.

[34]Leg. 7.

[35]Epiphanius Heres. 48, 1ff.

[36]Heres. 2, 28, 2.

[37]Hom. on John 1.

[38]Harmony 1, 35, 54.

[39]Morals Pref. 2.

[40]Christ and Antichrist 2.

[41]c. Cels. 7, 3–4.

[42]Heres. 48, 1ff.

[43]Hom. on Gen. 7, 4; 12, 1.

[44]Prol. to Is.; Jer.; Amos.

[45]Serm. 246, 1.

[46]Comm. on Job.

[47]On Gen. 12, 1ff.

[48]Cf. Eusebius Eccl. Hist. 6, 25, 11–12.

[49]Princ. 4, 3, 1.

[50]Cf. Augustine Instruction 1.

[51]Believing 6.

[52]Sermon 257.

[53]City of God, 2, 6; 15, 23.

[54]Cf. Augustine Letters 82.

[55]Heres. 3, 1, 1.

[56]Flesh of Christ 6.

[57]Strom. 7, 16, 95ff.

[58]Princ. 1 Pref. Cf. his basing of universalism on the "this day" of the Lord's Prayer in Prayer 26, 13ff.

[59]Catechetical Lectures 4, 17; 5, 12.

[60]Hom. on John 11.

[61]Trinity 9f.

[62]Letters 82.

[63]Incarn. 6, 3; Common. 2.

[64]Soldier's Crown, 3, 4

[65]I.e., "the one tradition of the selfsame rule of faith," Prescription 20.

[66]Heres. 3, 3, 1ff.

[67]Ibid. 3, 3, 1; Tertullian Prescription 25.

[68]Heres. 3, 1, 1.

[69]Ibid. 3, 11, 1.

[70]Ibid. 1, 2–3.

[71]Prescription 13.

[72]Ibid. 13ff.

[73]Ibid. 40.

[74]Basil of Caesarea argued for the deity of the Holy Spirit on this basis (Holy Spirit 26; 28), though it should be noted that the practice rests on the baptismal command of Matthew 28:19.

[75]Adv. Nestor. 4, 2.

[76]Believing 17.

[77]Confessions 7, 7.

[78]c. Manich. 5, 6.

[79]City of God, 15, 26; cf. Athanasius c. Arian, 3, 58.

[80]Strom. 7, 1, 1.

[81]Veiling of Virgins 16, 1–2.

[82]Cf. G. L. Bray, *Holiness and the Will of God* (London: Marshall, Morgan and Scott, 1979), pp. 113ff.

[83]Sermon 212.

[84]Strom. 1, 5, 28ff.

[85]c. Lucif. 8

[86]Prescription 37.

[87]Dial. Trypho 29.

[88]Cf. Apol. 153.

[89]Heres. 3, 12, 14; 4, 13.

[90]Ibid. 1, 10, 1.

[91]c. Marcion 4, 11.

[92]On John 5:8.

[93]c. Marcion 4, 39; Comm. on Matt 14, 4.

[94]Quest. on the Hept. 2 qu. 73; cf. City of God 20, 4.

[95]City of God 20, 4.

[96]Ep. Barn, 15–16.

[97]Heres. 4, 12–13.

[98]Hom. on Lev. 1, 4–6.

[99]Hom. on John 11.

[100]Jews 7.

[101]Cf. Irenaeus Heres. 1, 25, 1ff.

[102]Dial. Trypho 29.

[103]Strom. 7, 29.

[104]Ibid. 7, 16, 93ff.

[105]Hom. on John 1.

[106]Conf. 5, 14.

[107]Ibid. 6, 4.

[108]Instruction 2, 42.

[109]Letters 137, 1, 3.

[110]Ep. Barn. 9.

[111]Cf. Epiphanius Heres. 33, 3ff.

[112]Princ. 4, 3, 1.

[113]Ibid. 4, 2, 4.

[114]Ibid. 4, 2, 2.

[115]Ep. 120.

[116]Cf. Instruction 3, 27, 38, etc.

[117]Loc. cit.

[118]R. Grant, *A Short History of the Interpretation of the Bible* (New York: Macmillan, 1966), p. 111.

[119]*Theoria* was the key to the spiritual meaning.

[120]Cf. Severion on Creation 4, 2.

[121]Diodore Praef. in Pss.

[122]Theodore on John Pref.

[123]Hom. on Jeremiah 9, 4.

[124]Trinity 9.

[125]Ibid. 12.

[126]Didache 8, 1.

[127]Ibid. 9, 5.

[128]Cf. Benedictine Rule 16.

[129]Cf. Elvira 20; Nicea 17.

BIBLICAL AUTHORITY IN THE SIXTEENTH AND SEVENTEENTH CENTURIES:
A QUESTION OF TRANSITION

W. Robert Godfrey

pages 225–43

[1]See, for example, Richard Lovelace, "Inerrancy: Some Historical Perspectives," in *Inerrancy and Common Sense*, ed. Roger R. Nicole and J. Ramsey Michaels (Grand Rapids: Baker, 1980), pp. 21–25; Geoffrey W. Bromiley, *Historical Theology: An Introduction* (Grand Rapids: Eerdmans, 1978), pp. 327–28; Edward A. Dowey, Jr., *The Knowledge of God in Calvin's Theology* (New York: Columbia University Press, 1952), pp. 99ff.; see also studies by Robert Preus and John Robinson.

[2]See, for example, John Warwick Montgomery, "Lessons from Luther on the Inerrancy of Holy Writ," in *God's Inerrant Word*, ed. John Warwick Montgomery (Minneapolis: Bethany, 1974), p. 69.

[3]See, for example, Jill Raitt, *The Eucharistic Theology of Theodore Beza* (Chambersburg: Pa., American Academy of Religion, 1972); John S. Bray, *Theodore Beza's Doctrine of Predestination* (Nieuwkoop: De Graff, 1975); W. Robert Godfrey, "Tensions Within International Calvinism: The Debate on the Atonement at the Synod of Dort, 1618–1619," Ph.D. dissertation, Stanford University, 1974.

[4]Jack B. Rogers and Donald K. McKim, *The Authority and Interpretation of the Bible: An Historical Approach*, (San Francisco: Harper & Row, 1979).

[5]*D. Martin Luthers Werke, kritische Gesamtausgabe*, ed. J. F. K. Knaake et al. (Weimar, 1883—) (hereafter cited as *WA*), vol. 44, p. 510, cited by Willem Jan Kooiman, *Luther and the Bible*, (Philadelphia: Muhlenberg, 1961), pp. 235–36.

[6]*Luther's Works*, edited by Jaroslav J. Pelikan and Helmut T. Lehmann, vol. 32 (Philadelphia: Fortress, and St. Louis: Concordia, 1955—) (hereafter cited as *LW*), p. 11, cited by Paul Althaus, *The Theology of Martin Luther* (Philadelphia: Fortress, 1966), p. 6.

[7]*LW*, 23, 236 cited by A. Skevington Wood *Captive to the Word* (Grand Rapids: Eerdmans, 1969), p. 144.

[8]*WA*, 40, iii, 254, cited by Wood, *Captive to the Word*, p. 143.

[9]Ibid., ii, 52, cited by Wood, *Captive to the Word*, p. 145.

[10]Cited by M. Reu, *Luther and the Scriptures* (Columbus, Ohio: Wartburg, 1944), p. 28.

[11]Cited by Herman Sasse, *This Is My Body: Luther's Contention for the Real Presence in the Sacrament of the Altar* (Minneapolis: Augsburg, 1959), pp. 109–10.

[12]Rogers and McKim, *Authority and Interpretation*, p. 79.

[13]Ibid., p. 78.

[14]Reinhold Seeberg, *The History of Doctrines*, vol. 2 (Grand Rapids: Baker, 1977), p. 300.

[15]Rogers and McKim, in a footnote (p. 133, n. 115), dismiss some of this secondary literature, particularly the work of M. Reu, by citing Otto Heick's brief discussion of Luther on inerrancy in *A History of Christian Thought*, vol. 2 (Philadelphia: Fortress, 1965), pp. 347–48. Heick's list of errors parallels that of Seeberg. Heick does not offer any evidence for his rejection of Reu's work. Reu was a recognized Luther scholar who carefully analyzed the context of Luther's statements which allegedly ascribe errors to the Bible. Reu very convincingly shows that in context the kinds of references cited by Seeberg, Heick, and Rogers and McKim do not in fact show Luther ascribing any error to the Bible.

[16]Althaus, *Theology of Martin Luther*, p. 6.

[17]Wood, *Captive to the Word*, p. 144.

[18]Reu, *Luther and the Scriptures*, pp. 65–76, 103. See also Montgomery, "Lessons from Luther," pp. 88–90, for a review of Kooiman's work; he generally praises it, but warns against some of his conclusions on the question of inerrancy.

[19]*LW*, 22, 218–19.

[20]Rogers and McKim, *Authority and Interpretation*, p. 87; Kooiman, *Luther and the Bible*, p. 228; Althaus, *Theology of Martin Luther*, p. 82.

[21]*LW*, 22, 218.

[22]Ibid., 219.

[23]Cited by Reu, *Luther and the Scriptures*, p. 85.

[24]Rogers and McKim, *Authority and Interpretation*, p. 88.

[25]*WA*, 33, 144, cited by Kooiman, *Luther and the Bible*, p. 235.

[26]John Calvin in *Library of Christian Classics*, vol. 23, p. 70 as cited by John H. Leith, "John Calvin—Theologian of the Bible," *Interpretation* 25 (1971): p. 341.

[27]John Calvin, *Institutes of the Christian Religion*, ed. John T. McNeill, trans. Ford Lewis Battles, *Library of Christian Classics*, vols. 20 and 21 (Philadelphia: Westminster, 1960) (hereafter cited as *Inst.*), I, vii, 1.

[28]*Inst.* IV, viii, 9.

[29]Ibid., III, ii, 6.

[30]John Calvin, *Commentary on the Book of Psalms*, vol. 4 (Grand Rapids: Baker, 1979), p. 480.

[31]John Calvin, *New Testament Commentaries*, ed. D. W. and T. F. Torrance, vol. 10 (Grand Rapids: Eerdmans, 1964), pp. 329–30. Calvin is not denying here the use of human authors of Scripture nor is he teaching a mechanical dictation theory of inspiration. He is saying that every part of Scripture is ultimately of divine origin and that every

part is to be received as one would receive God Himself. He is rejecting any notion of human error in the Bible.

[32]*Corpus Reformatorum: Joannis Calvini Opera Quae Supersunt Omnia*, ed. Guilielmus Baum et al., vol. 55 (Brunsvigae: Schwetschke, 1863–1897) (hereafter cited as *CR*), col. 441, cited by Leith, "John Calvin...," p. 343.

[33]Calvin, *Comm. on Psalms*, vol. 5, p. 20.

[34]Rogers and McKim, *Authority and Interpretation*, p. 99.

[35]Ibid., p. 108.

[36]Ibid., p. 109

[37]Ibid., p. 110.

[38]Ibid., p. 112.

[39]Ibid., p. 110.

[40]Calvin, *New Testament Commentaries*, vol. 6, p. 182. That Luke cannot be the subject of the crucial clause is obvious from the Latin: "*in nomine Abrahae erratum esse palam est*" (*CR*, 26, Acts 7:16 ad loc.). The older translation also makes this clear: "It is manifest that there is a fault [mistake] in the word Abraham" (John Calvin, *Commentary upon the Acts of the Apostles*, vol. 1 [Grand Rapids: Baker, 1979], p. 265). The source of Rogers and McKim's quotation is unclear, since neither the newer nor the older English translations have it as they have cited it. Perhaps Rogers and McKim are depending on John T. McNeill's statement, "In Acts 7:16 Luke has 'made a manifest error' ..." (J. T. McNeill, "The Significance of the Word of God for Calvin," *Church History* 28 [1959]: 143) although they do not cite that work at this place. If this is their source, Rogers and McKim have just repeated McNeill's error.

[41]Ibid., pp. 181–82.

[42]Rogers and McKim, *Authority and Interpretation*, p. 116.

[43]For other discussions of Calvin's view of Scripture, see Kenneth Kantzer, "Calvin and the Holy Scriptures," in *Inspiration and Interpretation*, ed. John F. Walvoord (Grand Rapids: Eerdmans, 1957); John Murray, *Calvin on Scripture and Divine Sovereignty* (Grand Rapids: Baker, 1960); J. I. Packer, "Calvin's View of Scripture," in *God's Inerrant Word*, ed. J. W. Montgomery.

[44]Leith, "John Calvin—Theologian," pp. 337–38.

[45]It is not clear what Leith has in mind when he refers to modern views of inerrancy. It is amazing how otherwise learned men can misunderstand the doctrine of inerrancy. John T. McNeill, an eminent Calvin scholar, is an example. He assumes that the doctrine of inerrancy is equivalent to an extreme, mechanical dictation theory of inspiration that allows no significant role for the human authors of Scripture. (See McNeill, "Significance," pp. 139–40, and *Inst.* IV, viii, 9, n. 9.) But very few if any proponents of inerrancy have ever held such a view.

[46]As in the case of Luther, Rogers and McKim wrongly attribute this dualism to Calvin (p. 111). Charles Partee shows how Calvin bound the pastoral and the scholarly, the functional and the formal, together in a quotation from Calvin: "None will ever be a good minister of the word of God except that he be a first-rate scholar" (cited by Partee, *Calvin and Classical Philosophy* [Leiden: Brill, 1977], p. 146).

[47]John Calvin, *Theological Treatises*, trans. J. K. S. Reid (Philadelphia: Westminster, 1954), p. 130.

[48]The French Confession of 1559, Article 5. This and all the following quotations from confessions or catechisms are from Philip Schaff, *Creeds of Christendom*, vol. 3 (Grand Rapids: Baker, 1977).

[49]Belgic Confession, Article 4.

[50]Ibid., Article 7.

[51]Ibid., Article 5.

[52]Zacharias Ursinus, *The Commentary on the Heidelberg Catechism*, trans. G. W. Williard (Grand Rapids: Eerdmans, 1954), p. 108.

[53]Ibid., p. 111.

[54]Rogers and McKim, *The Authority and Interpretation*, pp. 200–202.

[55]Rogers and McKim betray a fundamental misunderstanding when they simply say that "The Church of England stood between Roman Catholic and Protestant" (p. 200), an assessment that does not reflect the real Protestant theology of the Anglican church expressed in the Thirty-nine Articles, for example. So too they argue curiously that the English civil war retarded the growth of scholasticism (p. 247) when on the other hand they assert that scholasticism was triumphant on the continent long before the civil war.

[56]At the Synod of Dort the English delegate Samuel Ward represented a Puritan perspective.

[57]David Sabean, "The Theological Rationalism of Moise Amyraut," *Archiv für Reformationsgeschichte* 55 (1964): 213.

[58]Ibid., p. 204.

[59]William Ames, *The Marrow of Theology*, 3rd ed. and trans. J. D. Eusden (Boston: Pilgrim, 1968), p. 186.

[60]Rogers and McKim, *Authority and Interpretation*, chap. 3: "Concern for Literary Form in the Post-Reformation Period," pp. 147–99.

[61]This entire chapter of Rogers and McKim's book needs a thorough review because it is not at all reliable as a guide in the matters it discusses. For example, their three paragraphs on the Synod of Dort (pp. 164–65) contain several errors. They speak of Dort producing a "confession," but the Synod actually adopted only certain canons as the authoritative interpretation of some of the articles of the Belgic Confession and the Heidelberg Catechism. They claim that Dort "purported to define the essential elements of Calvinism," but the Canons were never conceived of as more than specific Reformed answers to the five errors of Arminianism. They were never intended to be a summary of Calvinism in its essential elements. Rogers and McKim call the Synod hyper-Calvinist and scholastic, though even they admit that the moderate Calvinism of infralapsarianism was dominant at the Synod. Also the Canons were written clearly in pastoral and not scholastic language. Rogers and McKim assert that Dort fixed continental Reformed theology in a "scholastic mold" and offer as one piece of evidence the claim that Dort taught eternal reprobation while Calvin did not. But Calvin clearly teaches eternal reprobation, see *Institutes*, III, xxii, 11 and III, xxiii, 1, 3.

[62]Rogers and McKim, *Authority and Interpretation*, p. 147.

[63]Rogers and McKim have a strange insensitivity to the reality of historical threats to the authority of the Bible. This naïveté is also manifested in the remarkable judgments that they make in the introduction to their book. There (p. xxiii) they seem to underestimate the threat posed by modernism to biblical Christianity and see scholasticism as the principal threat to the Reformed tradition in America.

[64]Rogers and McKim, *Authority and Interpretation*, pp. 174–75. The only evidence offered to support this statement is that Turretin did not quote Calvin in his section on Scripture.

[65]Rogers and McKim do not show any first-hand knowledge of Turretin's *Institutio*. They appear to depend entirely on Leon McDill Allison, "The Doctrine of Scripture in the Theology of John Calvin and Francis Turretin," a 1958 Th.M. thesis written at Princeton Theological Seminary. But even a cursory look at Turretin demonstrates serious problems with their characterization of Turretin.

[66]Rogers and McKim, *Authority and Interpretation*, pp. 176, 179, 182.

[67]Francis Turretin, *Institutio Theologiae Elenctiae*, 1674, trans. George M. Griger, in a

manuscript at Princeton Theological Seminary (hereafter cited as *Inst. Theo.*), II, 2, 9. (Since this chapter was written, an English translation on Scripture has been published: Francis Turretin, *The Doctrine of Scripture*, ed. and trans. John W. Beardslee III (Grand Rapids: Baker, 1981).

[68]Ibid., 4, 9.

[69]Rogers and McKim, *Authority and Interpretation*, p. 176.

[70]*Inst. Theo.*, II, 4, 1 and II, 5, 1.

[71]Ibid., 6, 5.

[72]Ibid., 4, 6.

[73]Ibid., 4, 7.

[74]Ibid., 4, 8.

[75]Ibid., 4, 9.

[76]*Inst.*, I, vii, 4.

[77]Ibid., viii, 1.

[78]Ibid., 3, 5, 12, 13.

[79]Ibid., vii, 5.

[80]Ibid., 2.

[81]Ibid., viii, 1.

[82]*Inst. Theo.*, II, 4, 13. Rogers and McKim (p. 177) quote only part of this statement and give a distorted picture of Turretin's position here.

[83]Rogers and McKim, *Authority and Interpretation*, pp. 176–77.

[84]Ibid., pp. 174, 177.

[85]*Inst. Theo.*, II, 19, 18.

[86]Ibid., 5, 11.

[87]Rogers and McKim allege this in *Authority and Interpretation*, pp. 180–81.

[88]*Inst. Theo.*, II, 5, 3.

[89]From Canon II of the Formula Consensus Helvetica as printed in A. A. Hodge, *Outlines of Theology*, enlarged ed. (Grand Rapids: Zondervan, 1972), p. 656.

[90]John Bowman, "A Forgotten Controversy," *The Evangelical Quarterly* 20 (1948): 55.

[91]Canon III, Formula Consensus Helvetica, in A. A. Hodge, p. 657.

[92]Rogers and McKim, *Authority and Interpretation*, p. 177.

[93]*Inst. Theo.*, II, 19, 8.

[94]Ibid., III, 10, 14.

[95]Ibid., III, 11, 11.

[96]Rogers and McKim, *Authority and Interpretation*, p. 187.

[97]*Inst. Theo.*, I, 7, 2.

[98]Ibid.

[99]Ibid., 6.

THE PRINCETONIANS AND BIBLICAL AUTHORITY:
AN ASSESSMENT OF THE ERNEST SANDEEN PROPOSAL

John D. Woodbridge and Randall H. Balmer

pages 251–79

[1]A few segments of this chapter appeared originally in John Woodbridge, "Biblical Authority: Towards an Evaluation of the Rogers and McKim Proposal," *Trinity Journal* 1 (Fall 1980): 165–236. Reprinted with permission of the editor, D. A. Carson. Several segments of this chapter also appeared in John Woodbridge, *Biblical Authority: A Critique of the Rogers and McKim Proposal* (Grand Rapids: Zondervan, 1982).

[2]George Marsden's study *Fundamentalism and American Culture: The Shaping of Twentieth Century Evangelicalism 1870–1925* (New York: Oxford University Press, 1980) also constitutes a very significant milestone in the study of Fundamentalism. Marsden apparently views his work as supplanting Sandeen's study. Thus he interacts with Sandeen's arguments at length, sometimes in an approving way and sometimes in a critical fashion. We refer to Marsden's study later in this chapter. Other important interpretations of Fundamentalism include Stewart G. Cole, *The History of Fundamentalism* (1931; reprint, Hamden, Conn.: Archon, 1963); Norman Furniss, *The Fundamentalist Controversy, 1918–1931* (New Haven: Yale University Press, 1954); Louis Gasper, *The Fundamentalist Movement* (The Hague: Mouton, 1963); George Dollar, *A History of Fundamentalism* (Greenville, S.C.: Bob Jones University Press, 1973); C. Allen Russell, *Voices of American Fundamentalism* (Philadelphia: Westminster, 1976).

[3]Sandeen writes, "Fundamentalism of the late nineteenth and early twentieth centuries in America was comprised of an alliance between dispensationalists and Princeton-oriented Calvinists, who were not wholly compatible but who managed to maintain a united front against Modernism until about 1918" (*The Origins of Fundamentalism: Toward a Historical Interpretation* (Philadelphia: Fortress, 1968), p. 24; consult also Ernest Sandeen, *The Roots of Fundamentalism* (Grand Rapids: Baker, 1978), pp. 130–31). See also his "Fundamentalism and American Identity," *The Annals of the American Academy of Political and Social Science* 387 (January 1970): 57–65.

[4]Ibid., p. 25. Basing his analysis on a study by Elwood Wenger (1973), Marsden notes that the greatest concentration of Fundamentalists in the 1920s was found in the Middle Atlantic and East-North-Central states (Marsden, *Fundamentalism and American Culture*), p. 258, n. 2.

[5]John Garraty, *The American Nation: A History of the United States* (New York: Harper and Row, 1966), p. 703.

[6]Sandeen writes: "Fundamentalism originated in the metropolitan areas of the northeastern part of the continent, and it cannot be explained as a part of the Populist movement, agrarian protest. or the Southern mentality" (*Origins of Fundamentalism*, p. 26).

[7]Marsden, *Fundamentalism and American Culture*, p. 5.

[8]George Marsden, "Defining Fundamentalism," *Christian Scholar's Review* 1 (Winter 1971): 141–51; see also Sandeen's reply in *Christian Scholar's Review* 1 (Spring 1971): 227–32.

[9]Marsden, "Defining Fundamentalism," 144–45.

[10]For worthwhile criticisms of Sandeen's earlier work, see Le Roy Moore, Jr., "Another Look at Fundamentalism: A Response to Ernest R. Sandeen," *Church History* 37 (June 1968): 195–202. George Marsden offers few correctives to Sandeen's treatment of the nineteenth-century Princetonians' attitudes concerning biblical authority. His own work on that subject appears quite indebted to an uncompleted doctoral dissertation by John W. Stewart, "The Princeton Theologians: The Tethered Theology" (Marsden, *Fundamentalism and American Culture*, p. 260, n. 3). Marsden does point out that sources other than the Princetonians' writings may have contributed to the belief in inerrancy among some Fundamentalists.

[11]Sandeen suggests that millenarians' sentiments about the interpretation of the Bible accorded with the emerging theory of inspiration at Princeton Seminary (*Roots of Fundamentalism*, pp. 111–14).

[12]James Barr, *Fundamentalism* (Philadelphia: Westminster, 1978), p. 274. Barr particularly recognizes his debt to Sandeen on page 354, note 9. Jack Rogers and Donald McKim refer to Sandeen in *The Authority and Interpretation of the Bible: An Historical Approach* (New York: Harper and Row, 1979), notes on pp. 311–12, 314–15, 376, 401. Rogers and McKim modify some of Sandeen's judgments in their exposition. Nonetheless they follow him closely on others.

[13]Sandeen, *Roots of Fundamentalism*, p. x.

[14]Ibid.

[15]Ibid., p. 106.

[16]Ibid., p. 123. Sandeen bases this judgment on this statement of Archibald Alexander: "In the narrative of well-known facts, the writer did not need a continual suggestion of every idea, but only to be so superintended, as to be preserved from error; so in the use of language in recording such familiar things, there existed no necessity that every word should be inspired; but there was the same need of a directing and superintending influence, as in regards to the things themselves" (*Evidences of Authenticity, Inspiration and Canonical Authority of the Holy Scriptures* [Philadelphia: Presbyterian Board of Publications, n.d.], pp. 226–27). But Alexander clarifies this position a few pages later in his "true definition of inspiration" (p. 230). Sandeen's interpretation of Alexander is understandable if one refers only to the passage he cites, without looking at the broader context for the statement.

[17]Sandeen, *Roots of Fundamentalism*, pp. 125–26.

[18]Charles Hodge, *Systematic Theology* (New York: Scribner, 1871), 1: 170.

[19]Sandeen, *Roots of Fundamentalism*, p. 128.

[20]Ibid.

[21]Ibid. A touch of inappropriate sarcasm unfortunately bestirs Sandeen's prose as he discusses the Princetonians' views of Scripture.

[22]Sandeen, *Origins of Fundamentalism*, p. 14. Sandeen attempts to moderate this claim in note 39: "I am not ignoring the Lutheran and Reformed dogmatic tradition of the sixteenth and seventeenth centuries. I have shown in my article in *Church History* . . . that Princeton began as the offspring of that tradition and developed from that point, in the course of the nineteenth century creating something unique." The article to which Sandeen alludes is his "Princeton Theology: One Source of Biblical Literalism in American Protestantism," *Church History* 31 (September 1962): 307–21. Given his references to the Lutheran and Reformed dogmatic tradition of the sixteenth and seventeenth centuries, one would expect to find a detailed exposition of that "tradition" in the article. In fact, the article contains only a few comments that have any bearing on that topic. Sandeen's claim, "I have shown . . . ," is an overstatement of considerable magnitude.

[23]Sandeen, *Roots of Fundamentalism*, pp. 120–21.

[24]Sandeen, *Origins of Fundamentalism*, p. 13.

[25]The problem of selecting representative spokesmen emerges when one treats so broad an expression as "Reformed thought" or the "Reformed tradition." Rogers and McKim's study *The Authority and Interpretation of the Bible* (1979) contains a serious conceptual flaw because the authors do not elucidate the criteria by which they select representatives of the "historic position of the Church" concerning biblical authority. For bibliographical background on the history of biblical authority, see Woodbridge, *Biblical Authority: A Critique*.

[26]We have selected William Whitaker and William Ames as viable representatives of the "Reformed tradition" because their contemporaries viewed them as influential

spokesmen for that tradition, because they saw themselves as disciples of Calvin and Augustine, and because few modern commentators have deemed them to be "scholastics." They belonged to a pre-Westminster strain of Reformed thought that cannot be discounted because it was allegedly overwhelmed by "Aristotelian" tendencies (although Whitaker did not dismiss Aristotle). Sandeen rules out so-called scholastics as legitimate representatives of the Reformed tradition, as do Rogers and McKim. Like Robert Godfrey in this volume, we hare argued elsewhere that Rogers and McKim misunderstand in a significant fasion the relationship between the Reformers' attitudes and those of the "Orthodox" toward Holy Scripture (see Woodbridge, *Biblical Authority: A Critique*, pp. 177–200). Sandeen makes relatively few comments about what he means by the word *scholastic*. And yet he freights the word with negative connotations as he applies it to the Princetonians. It is interesting that Charles Hodge himself criticized "the tincture of scholasticism" on occasion.

[27] Richard Simon, *Histoire critique du Vieux Testament* (Rotterdam: Reinier Leers, 1685 [1678]), p. 472.

[28] On the dispute concerning biblical authority between Roman Catholics and Protestants in the latter half of the sixteenth century, see Richard Popkin, *The History of Scepticism: From Erasmus to Descartes* (New York: Harper and Row, 1968), pp. 67–68; Woodbridge, *Biblical Authority: A Critique*, pp. 188–92.

[29] William Whitaker, *A Disputation on Holy Scripture*, ed., William Fitzgerald (1588; reprint, Cambridge: Cambridge University Press, 1849), p. x. This edition includes both Whitaker's 1588 and 1594 apologetic works on Scripture.

[30] Philip Edgcumbe Hughes, *Theology of the English Reformers* (Grand Rapids: Eerdmans, 1966), p. 16.

[31] On William Whitaker, see Sidney Lee, ed., *Dictionary of National Biography* (New York: Macmillan, 1900), 61:21–23; H. C. Porter, *Reformation and Reaction in Tudor Cambridge* (Hamden, Conn.: Archon, 1972).

[32] Whitaker, *Disputation on Holy Scripture*, pp. 36–37. The passage Whitaker cites is drawn from Augustine's *De Cons. Ev. Lib.* II. c. 12. It should be pointed out that Whitaker, a theologian with Puritan sympathies, believed that Augustine advocated complete biblical infallibility. The thesis that Rogers and McKim attempt to establish—namely, that both Augustine and the English Puritans were committed to limited biblical infallibility—does not appear convincing in view of both Augustine's comments and those of Whitaker. On Augustine's stance concerning biblical infallibility, see Woodbridge, *Biblical Authority: A Critique*, chap. 2; A.D.R. Polman, *Word of God According to St. Augustine* (Grand Rapids: Eerdmans, 1961), pp. 56, 66. In discussing Augustine, Warfield approvingly cites Whitaker's *Disputation on Scriptures* (*Calvin and Augustine*, ed. Samuel Craig [Philadelphia: Presbyterian and Reformed, 1956], pp. 461–62).

[33] Whitaker, *Disputation on Holy Scripture*, p. 37.

[34] Ibid. To track down the attitudes of Erasmus and Jerome toward biblical infallibility is a difficult task. Jacques Chomaret suggests that Erasmus did not believe in biblical inerrancy ("Les *Annotations* de Valla, celles d'Erasme et la grammaire," *Histoire de l'exégèse au XVIe siècle*, ed., Olivier Fatio and Pierre Fraenkel [Genève: Droz, 1978], pp. 209–10). However, when some Spanish monks accused Erasmus of destroying biblical authority by admitting that the authors of Scriptures could err, Erasmus apparently retorted that his admission had been "per fictionem." He wanted to defend the Bible in such a way that, if small errors were discovered within it, its entire authority would not be undone. As for himself, said Erasmus, he believed in complete biblical infallibility. The case of Jerome is just as complex. Augustine challenged Jerome's supposition that the apostle Paul "did not speak the truth" when he found fault with Peter (Letter 28). Augustine, the younger man, sparred with Jerome on this point for several years. Jerome apparently conceded some years later that Augustine's position was correct (J. N. D. Kelly, *Jerome: His Life, Writings, and Controversies* [New York: Harper and Row, 1975], p. 272, n. 41).

[35]Whitaker, *Disputation on Holy Scripture*, p. 38. See Robert Godfrey's discussion of Calvin's comment about this difficult passage (Acts 7:16). It is remarkable that scholars as knowledgeable as John McNeill, Jack Rogers, Donald McKim, and R. Hooykaas have assumed that Calvin believed an error existed in the original text of this passage of Scripture.

[36]Ibid., pp. 294–95.

[37]Ibid., p. 148.

[38]Ibid., p. 160.

[39]On the career of William Ames consult Keith Sprunger, *The Learned Doctor William Ames: Dutch Backgrounds of English and American Puritanism* (Urbana: University of Illinois Press, 1972) and the many books of Perry Miller.

[40]William Ames, *The Marrow of Sacred Theology*, ed. John Eusden (Boston: Pilgrim, 1968), pp. 185–86. John Eusden describes Ames's influence in these words: "Despite his array of personal misfortune, Ames's voice was still one of the most influential in the theological development of the Puritan and Reformed churches in England and the Netherlands" (ibid., p. 6). Ames's thought was also very well received in New England.

[41]Ibid., pp. 188-89. On the concept of "originals" in the sixteenth- and seventeenth-century disputes between Roman Catholics and Protestants, see Jacques Le Brun, "Sens et portée du retour aux origines dans l'oeuvre de Richard Simon," *XVIIe Siècle* 131 (Avril-Juin 1981): 185–98; Don C. Allen, *The Legend of Noah: Renaissance Rationalism in Art, Science, and Letters* (Urbana: University of Illinois Press, 1949), pp. 41–65.

[42]In his *Scripture in the Westminster Confession* (Grand Rapids: Eerdmans, 1967), pp. 90–95, Jack Rogers argues that the thought of William Ames helped set the stage for the work of the Westminster divines. If this is so, then it is difficult to understand how Rogers can posit the hypothesis that the Westminster divines did not believe in complete biblical infallibility and did not make a distinction between the original autographs and the Hebrew and Greek texts that they possessed. See Roger Nicole's comments about Jack Rogers's interpretation of the Westminster Assembly: Archibald A. Hodge and Benjamin B. Warfield, *Inspiration*, ed. Roger Nicole (Grand Rapids: Baker, 1979), Appendix 6, pp. 97–100. Consult also Woodbridge, *Biblical Authority: A Critique*, chap. 6, for a lengthy discussion of these issues.

[43]Ernest Sandeen, Jack Rogers, and Donald McKim label many Protestant theologians "scholastics" and thereby disqualify them as authentic representatives of the Reformed tradition. For this reason it is important to speak about Whitaker and Ames, who were not scholastics and yet advocated complete biblical infallibility.

[44]William Whitaker described the debates between Roman Catholics and Protestants in this fashion: "But our adversaries allow what the fathers write of the authority of the originals was true indeed formerly; and they would not deny that we ought to do the same, if the Hebrew and Greek originals were still uncontaminated. But they maintain that those originals are now corrupted, and that therefore the Latin streamlet is deserving of more regard than the ancient well-spring. Hence it is now the earnest effort of the popish theologians, and the champions of the Council of Trent, to persuade us of the depravation of the original scriptures" (*Disputation on Scripture*, p. 157). As we saw, Whitaker did not exclude the possibility that the canonical books of Scripture had been erroneously copied on occasion. The biblical critic Richard Simon (1638–1712) assumed that Augustine held to the original documents' premise: "But because men were the depositories of the Sacred Books, as well as the other books, and because the first originals have been lost, it was in some regards impossible to avoid several changes, due more to the passage of time, than to the negligence of copyists. It is for this reason that St. Augustine above all recommends to those who wish to study the Scripture, to apply themselves to the Criticism of the Bible, and to correct the mistakes in their copies" (*Histoire critique du Vieux Testament*, p. 1). In their fideistic apologetic for the church's authority, some Roman Catholics argued that because the originals had been lost, Protestants could never recreate a completely infallible text. Concerning Augustine's stance

see Letter 82 and *Doct. Christ.*, lib. 2. Augustine was prepared to correct the Latin text with the Septuagint, so taken was he by its supposed divine inspiration. Later he moderated his commitment to the Septuagint's inspiration. Bruce Metzger suggests that the quest to establish "the original text of the New Testament" began in the late second century (*The Text of the New Testament: Its Transmission, Corruption, and Restoration* [New York: Oxford University Press, 1968], p. 150).

[45]Patristic scholars generally agree that the church fathers believed in biblical inerrancy. Bruce Vawter, no friendly partisan of the belief, writes, "It would be pointless to call into question that biblical inerrancy in a rather absolute form was a common persuasion from the beginning of Christian times, and from Jewish times before that. For both the Fathers and the rabbis generally, the ascription of any error to the Bible was unthinkable; . . . if the word was God's it must be true, regardless of whether it made known a mystery of divine revelation or commented on a datum of natural science, whether it derived from human observation or chronicled an event of history" (Vawter, *Biblical Inspiration* [Philadelphia: Westminster, 1972], pp. 132–33). J. N. D. Kelly concurs, although he does not favor the concept of inerrancy. Speaking of the Latin fathers, he writes, "First, they were hampered by an altogether too narrow, too mechanical conception of inspiration; and they drew from it the fatal corollary of the absolute inerrancy of Scripture in all its parts" (*The Church's Use of the Bible Past and Present*, ed. D. E. Nineham [London: SPCK, 1963], p. 53). See also Jaroslav Pelikan, *The Christian Tradition: A History of the Development of Doctrine* (Chicago: University of Chicago Press, 1971), vol. 3: *The Growth of Medieval Theology (600–1300)* (1978), pp. 40–42, 121–24, 221–23. For a critique of Rogers and McKim's analysis of this topic, see Woodbridge, *Biblical Authority: A Critique*, pp. 172–92.

[46]Sandeen believes that the emphasis of the Dispensationalists on a "literal" interpretation of Scripture made them susceptible to the doctrine of inerrancy. But it was the Princetonians who particularly innovated by defining the teaching with care.

[47]We are not denying that this article received much commentary, particularly some ten years after its publication. We are taking issue with Sandeen's contention that it represented an essentially "new formulation of the doctrine of the Scriptures."

[48]Sandeen, *Roots of Fundamentalism*, p. 126. Sandeen refers to the analysis by Lefferts Loetscher, *The Broadening Church: A Study of Theological Issues in the Presbyterian Church Since 1869* (Philadelphia: University of Pennsylvania Press, 1954), p. 30. Loetscher notes that Charles Hodge did intimate "a distinction between the existing text of Scripture and the original text or autographs" (ibid., p. 24).

[49]Randall Balmer has surveyed some of the correspondence of A. A. Hodge and B. B. Warfield in the 1870s and 1880s in an attempt to determine their perceptions of the article "Inspiration." Concerning Robertson Smith, see Donald Nelson, "The Theological Development of the Young Robertson Smith," *The Evangelical Quarterly* 45 (1973): 81–99; Warner Bailey, "William Robertson Smith and American Biblical Studies," *Journal of Presbyterian History* 51 (1973): 285–308. In 1875 Smith wrote for the *Encyclopaedia Britannica* an important article ("Bible"), which provoked a series of heresy trials in the Free Church of Scotland. Smith and Charles Briggs began to correspond with each other in the late 1870s. A. A. Hodge and B. B. Warfield did indicate that they had a better grasp on the concept of inspiration than some of their predecessors. A key letter (October 22, 1880) in which Warfield describes to Hodge his thinking about the essay is unfortunately difficult to decipher at points.

[50]Sandeen, *Roots of Fundamentalism*, p. 120.

[51]Ibid., p. 127.

[52]We are not denying that Evangelical Protestants perceived threats to biblical authority in the 1870s and 1880s stemming from higher criticism and "science." Rather we are questioning Sandeen's proposal that these threats provoked a significant modification of the Princetonians' attitudes toward biblical authority. They had faced serious challenges to complete biblical infallibility in the first half of the nineteenth century.

Even such a notable work as Jerry Wayne Brown's *Rise of Biblical Criticism in America, 1800–1870: The New England Scholars* (Middletown, Conn.: Wesleyan University Press, 1969) is deficient in its treatment of several of the serious attacks against biblical authority in the antebellum period. For example, Brown makes no mention of Coleridge's *Letters of an Inquiring Spirit*, a volume that directly attacked complete biblical infallibility. His only reference to Coleridge concerns the "important influence" of the Englishman on certain aspects of Horace Bushnell's thought (p. 177). It is true that pressures on the faith of evangelical Christians did mount in the second half of the nineteenth century. Consult Paul Carter, *The Spiritual Crisis of the Gilded Age* (DeKalb: Northern Illinois University Press, 1971); Owen Chadwick, *The Secularisation of the European Mind in the Nineteenth Century* (London: Cambridge University Press, 1977); James Moore, *The Post-Darwinian Controversies* (Cambridge: Cambridge University Press, 1979).

[53]*Plan of the Theological Seminary of the Presbyterian Church in the United States, Located at Princeton, New Jersey* (Philadelphia: William S. Martien, 1850), p. 14. On the founding of Princeton Seminary, see Mark Noll, "The Founding of Princeton Seminary," *The Westminster Theological Journal* 42 (1979): 72–110. It is difficult to know what form of biblical criticism the charter was specifically targeting.

[54]The initial detractors were apparently "deists," some unitarians, "infidels," neologians, and particularly David Hume. See Noll, "Founding of Princeton Seminary," pp. 93–94, about the deep concerns of Samuel Miller, Ashbel Green, and Archibald Alexander.

[55]See Leonard Trinterud, "Charles Hodge (1797–1878)," in *Sons of the Prophets: Leaders in Protestantism From Princeton Seminary*, ed. Hugh Kerr (Princeton: Princeton University Press, 1963), p. 24.

[56]Letter from Archibald Alexander to Charles Hodge, 24 March 1827, File D. Princeton Theological Seminary, Princeton, New Jersey. This letter has been cited in several secondary sources.

[57]Charles Hodge, "Inspiration," 23 September 1850, Alumni Alcove, Princeton Theological Seminary, Princeton, New Jersey.

[58]In his *Sixty Years With the Bible: A Record of Experience* (New York: Scribner, 1910) William Newton Clarke described the multiple factors that led him to give up biblical inerrancy in the 1870s, the decade *before* Sandeen indicates that the doctrine came into vogue: "I have dated this conviction against the inerrancy of the Bible here in the Seventies, and here it belongs" (ibid., p. 108). Clarke's doubts stemmed from many issues, not simply from teachings concerning human origins and textual criticism. He assumed that the standard belief in his youth was what he called "the ancient theory of dictation, or verbal inspiration" (ibid., pp. 41–42).

[59]In the writings of American Evangelicals one also finds complaints about "deists," German "neologians," the disciples of Coleridge or of Schleiermacher, many of whom denied the absolute infallibility of Holy Scripture. On German and English literature in America, see Philip Schaff, "German Literature in America," *Bibliotheca Sacra and Theological Review* 4 (1847): 503–21.

[60]Samuel Taylor Coleridge, *Confessions of an Inquiring Spirit* (Boston: James Monroe, 1841), pp. 79–80.

[61]Ibid., p. 81. In 1893, the Englishman Thomas Huxley declared, "The doctrine of biblical infallibility . . . was widely held by my countrymen within my recollection" (cited in John C. Greene, "Darwin and Religion," in *European Intellectual History*, ed. W. Warren Wagar [New York: Harper and Row, 1966], pp. 15–16).

[62]Coleridge, *Confessions*, p. 51.

[63]Ibid., p. 113.

[64]Ibid., p. 69. On Coleridge's religious beliefs, consult David Pym, *The Religious Thought of Samuel Taylor Coleridge* (New York: Barnes and Noble, 1979).

[65]Cited in William Lee, *Inspiration of Holy Scripture*, p. vii.

[66]Noah Porter, "Coleridge and his American Disciples," *Bibliotheca Sacra and Theological Review* 4 (1847): 156. See also another lengthy article devoted to Coleridge: Lyman Atwater, "Coleridge," *Biblical Repertory and Princeton Review* 20 (1848): 143–86. James Marsh published the first American edition of Coleridge's *Aids to Reflection* in 1828 (Herbert Hovenkamp, *Science and Religion in America 1800–1860* [Philadelphia: University of Pennsylvania Press, 1978], pp. 50–52).

[67]Porter, "Coleridge and His American Disciples," pp. 167–71.

[68]Noah Porter, later a president at Yale, described Thomas Arnold in this way: "Such a man was the late Dr. Arnold, an eminent and inspiring example to all scholars and all teachers, the record of whose life should be held in the memory of all such, till a brighter example shall arise" ("The Youth of the Scholar," *Bibliotheca Sacra and Theological Review* 3 [1846]: 121).

[69]Cited in Basil Willey, *Nineteenth Century Studies: Coleridge to Matthew Arnold* (New York: Harper and Row, 1966), p. 264.

[70]On Thomas Arnold and biblical authority, see Willey, *Nineteenth Century Studies*, pp. 64–69.

[71]J. D. Morell, *The Philosophy of Religion* (New York: D. Appleton, 1849), p. 149. (English edition: London: Longman, Brown, 1849).

[72]Ibid., p. 167 (American edition).

[73]Henry B. Smith, *Introduction to Christian Theology* (New York: A. C. Armstrong, 1882), p. 208. On the theology of Henry B. Smith, see George Marsden, *The Evangelical Mind and the New School Presbyterian Experience: A Case Study of Thought and Theology in Nineteenth Century America* (New Haven: Yale University Press, 1970), pp. 157–81. Smith, a respected leader of the New School Presbyterians, believed in complete biblical infallibility (ibid., pp. 169–72). Sandeen does not observe that other Presbyterians besides Old Schoolers held that position.

[74]Theodore Dwight Bozeman, *Protestants in an Age of Science: The Baconian Ideal and Antebellum American Religious Thought* (Chapel Hill: University of North Carolina Press, 1977), p. 135. See, for example, "Transcendentalism," *The Biblical Repertory and Princeton Review* 11 (1839): 37–101.

[75]The author of the article "Transcendentalism" was also worried about attacks against the Scriptures issuing from these writers (ibid., pp. 81, 95). Professor John Vander Stelt distinguishes between the influence of German philosophical and theological thought before the Civil War (*Philosophy and Scripture: A Study in Old Princeton and Westminster Theology* [Marlton, N.J.: Mack, 1978], p. 151). At least Old School Presbyterians sensed theological dangers to be associated with certain German and English "philosophical" writings.

[76]Lee, *Inspiration of Holy Scripture*, p. iv.

[77]Ibid., p. viii.

[78]Ibid., p. ix.

[79]Ibid., pp. ix, 35–41.

[80]Charles Hodge, "Short Notices," *Biblical Repertory and Princeton Review* 29 (1857): 328–29; "Inspiration," pp. 660–98.

[81]Hodge, "Short Notices," 329. Ironically, Lee was associated with the very theory that he was trying to modify.

[82]Hodge wrote, "Geology has of late asserted her claims and there are the same exultations and the same alarms. But any one who has attended to the progress of this new science, must be blind indeed not to see that geology will soon be found side by side with astronomy in obsequiously bearing up the queenly train of God's majestic word" (Hodge, "Inspiration," p. 683). Theodore Bozeman's excellent study *Protestants in*

an Age of Science (1977) describes the concord Old School Presbyterians believed existed between scriptural teachings and diverse "sciences" during the antebellum period. See also E. Brooks Holifield, *The Gentlemen Theologians: American Theology in Southern Culture 1795–1860* (Durham, N.C.: Duke University Press, 1978), pp. 96–100. In a similar fashion early "scientists" in the sixteenth and seventeenth centuries frequently sought to demonstrate an accord between biblical infallibility and the findings of their investigations (see Richard Popkin, "Scepticism, Theology and the Scientific Revolution in the Seventeenth Century," in *Problems in the Philosophy of Science,* ed. I. Lakatos and Alan Musgrave [Amsterdam: North Holland, 1968], 3:21–25). See also Walter Schatzberg, *Scientific Themes in the Popular Literature and the Poetry of the German Enlightenment* (Berne: Herbert Lang, 1973), pp. 64–86.

[83]Hodge, *Systematic Theology,* 1:168.

[84]Ibid., pp. 173–80.

[85]T. F. Curtis, *The Human Element in the Inspiration of the Sacred Scriptures* (New York: D. Appleton, 1867), p. 20. Curtis discusses Coleridge's *Letters of an Inquiring Spirit* at length.

[86]Ibid., p. 19. Noted Curtis: "Few men have been more influential in forming the present state of religious thought in England, than the late Dr. Arnold, of Rugby" (ibid., p. 103).

[87]Ibid., p. 37.

[88]Ibid., p. 13.

[89]In his *Plenary Inspiration of the Holy Scriptures* (New York: Randolph, 1858), Eleazar Lord put the state of the question in this way: "No question concerning Revealed Religion is of higher importance in itself, or in its bearings at the present time, than that which immediately respects the plenary Inspiration of the Holy Scriptures. What is the nature of that Inspiration by which the Divine thoughts are so conveyed to man and so expressed in human language, that the words of the sacred Text are the words of God?" (p. 9). Lord disliked the distinction several theologians (e.g., Horne, Doddridge, Pye Smith, Dick, Daniel Wilson) were making when they spoke of different kinds and degrees of inspiration (ibid., pp. 10–12).

[90]These Evangelicals generally defined biblical infallibility in a similar fashion as later Evangelicals defined inerrancy: the Bible does not wander from the truth in anything it affirms or says when properly interpreted. They did enter into sharp debate over the issue of plenary inspiration. Consult Ian Rennie, "Mixed Metaphors, Misunderstood Models and Puzzling Paradigms" (an unpublished response to Jack Rogers's essay, delivered at the conference "Interpreting an Authoritative Scripture," June 22, 1981, held in Toronto, Canada).

[91]*The Union Bible Dictionary* (Philadelphia: American Sunday-School Union, 1839), p. 256. See also the article "Inspiration" in *A Dictionary of the Holy Bible* (New York: American Tract Society, 1859), pp. 208–9. For England, consult "Inspiration," *Berton's Bible Dictionary* (London: Ward, Lock, n.d.), p. 117: "When this influence is so exerted as absolutely to exclude uncertainty and all mixture of error in a declaration of doctrines or facts, it is called a plenary or full inspiration." The editor of this popular work claimed that he had excluded anything "approaching sectarianism by any denomination of Evangelical Christians" (from the preface).

[92]*Union Bible Dictionary,* p. 4.

[93]Sandeen uses unnuanced dichotomies in his analysis. He plays the lack of a "fully integrated theology of biblical authority" against the existence of a "great deal of popular reverence for the Bible" (*Roots of Fundamentalism,* p. 106).

[94]Sandeen on occasion confuses his own judgment of a volume's worth with the judgment contemporaries made of the same volume. For example, he dismisses the value of Louis Gaussen's *Theopneustia* as a competent defense of verbal inspiration (*Roots of Fundamentalism,* pp. 113–14). Because Sandeen does not appreciate its argu-

ments, he apparently assumes that nineteenth-century Evangelicals had the same opin-ion and turned to the Princetonians to find a better defense. In point of fact many Evangelicals, ranging from Baptists to Methodists, cited Gaussen's work and William Lee's *Inspiration of Holy Scripture* as those theology texts that sustained their commit-ment to complete biblical infallibility, without referring to the Princetonians (see, for example, Bruce Shelley, "A. J. Gordon and Biblical Criticism," *Foundations* 14 (January–March 1971): 77, n. 33). In 1868 the *Methodist Quarterly Review* described Gaussen as "the ablest writer of our age on the subject." The Princetonians also read many authors on the Scriptures including the same Louis Gaussen and William Lee. Their thinking was not determined in a monocausational way by the writings of Francis Turretin, as several historians have argued in a surprisingly reductionist fashion.

[95]Charles Elliott, "The Subjective Theory of Inspiration," *The Princeton Review* (July–December 1881), pp. 193–94. Elliott commented about the longstanding commit-ment of the church to the absolute infallibility of the Holy Scriptures: "From the Refor-mation until that time [the days of Jean Le Clerc, 1657–1736] distinct theories of inspira-tion were scarcely known in the church. The assertion of the absolute infallibility of the Holy Scriptures and the denial of all error in them rendered any theory except that of plenary inspiration unnecessary" (ibid., p. 192). Concerning Jean Le Clerc, consult Annie Barnes, *Jean Le Clerc (1657–1736) et la République des Lettres* (Paris: Droz, 1938). See the 1981 M.A. thesis in church history by Martin Klauber (Trinity Evangelical Divinity School) about Jean Le Clerc's debate with Richard Simon (1638–1712) over questions of biblical authority. As late as the early eighteenth century Oxford professor Jonathan Edwards claimed that all Protestants held to a position of complete biblical infallibility (see his *Preservative against Socinianism* [Oxford: Henry Clement, 1703], part 4, p. 19). In the colonies the American Jonathan Edwards held just that stance. Concerning John Wesley's viewpoints on religious authority, see the forthcoming M.A. thesis in church history by Timothy Wadkins (Trinity Evangelical Divinity School). Sandeen has few re-marks about the issue of biblical authority in the thirteen colonies. But this American context should not be neglected.

[96]Ernest Sandeen, "The Princeton Theology: One Source of Biblical Literalism in American Protestantism," *Church History* 31 (1962): 314; also cited in Sandeen, *Roots of Fundamentalism*, p. 123.

[97]Alexander, *Evidences of Authenticity*, p. 230. For the context of this definition, see note 16 above.

[98]Ibid., p. 112. Alexander continued, "It is impossible for men [transcribers] to write the whole of a book without making mistakes; and if there be some small discrepancies in the gospels with respect to names and numbers, they ought to be attributed to this cause."

[99]Ibid., p. 306.

[100]Archibald Alexander, "Review of Woods on Inspiration," *Biblical Repertory and Theological Review* 3 (January 1831): 10.

[101]Alexander, *Evidences of Authenticity*, p. 230. See also Dennis Okholm, "Biblical Inspiration and Infallibility in the Writings of Archibald Alexander," *Trinity Journal* 5 (1976): 79–89.

[102]Hodge, *Systematic Theology*, 1:169–70.

[103]Charles Hodge, Lecture Notes, File D, Princeton Theological Seminary, Princeton, New Jersey.

[104]Charles Hodge, Lecture on "Biblical Criticism," November 1822, File D, Princeton Theological Seminary, Princeton, New Jersey. In another lecture entitled "Integrity of the Hebrew Text" he advanced the view that the present Hebrew text "has neither been entirely preserved from errors . . ." (Hodge, Lecture Notes, File D, Princeton Theological Seminary, Princeton, New Jersey). Hodge continued, "That the present Heb. text is not immaculate is proved by the following arguments: 1. From the nature of the case and

human imbecility it is impossible without a perpetual miracle that the Old Testament should have been transcribed so frequently without some mistakes occurring; 2. All experience shows that every ancient work is more or less injured in its transcription from one age to another" (ibid.).

[105]C. Beck, "Monogrammata Hermeneutics N.T.," *Biblical Repertory and Theological Review* 1 (1825): 27.

[106]As we indicated earlier, the concept that only the biblical autographs were infallible was a familiar piece of European theological furniture, particularly for textual critics. It is true that in the seventeenth century a good number of Christians esteemed that the Bibles they had in their hands were infallible.

[107]Hodge, *Systematic Theology*, 1:170.

[108]Sandeen, *Roots of Fundamentalism*, p. 128.

[109]Hodge, *Systematic Theology*, 1:170.

[110]Ibid., p. 182.

[111]Hodge, "Inspiration," *The Biblical Repertory and Princeton Review* 29 (1857): 687. In this article Hodge refers to the very same objection concerning the "twenty-three thousand versus the twenty-four thousand slain" accounts used in the "flecks in the Parthenon marble illustration." And once again Hodge discusses the objection in the context of his commitment to complete biblical infallibility.

[112]B. B. Warfield, *The Inspiration and Authority of the Bible*, ed. Samuel Craig (Philadelphia: Presbyterian and Reformed, 1964), pp. 220–21.

[113]John C. Vander Stelt argues that Charles Hodge began to stress the biblical infallibility of the original autographs in 1878, but that in the 1820s he had believed that the Bible "as we have it now" was infallible (*Philosophy and Scripture* [Marlton, N.J.: Mack, 1978] p. 141, n. 353). Vander Stelt is apparently unfamiliar with the sources we cited earlier in this chapter (see, for example, note 104 above).

[114]Francis L. Patton, *The Inspiration of the Scriptures* (Philadelphia: Presbyterian Board of Publication, 1869), p. 112.

[115]Ibid., pp. 112–13.

[116]L. Loetscher indicates that Patton's "defense of Scripture" followed the same pattern as that of A. A. Hodge (*Broadening Church*, p. 25). In fact Patton's discussion of the infallibility of the biblical autographs predated A. A. Hodge's 1879 edition of *Outlines of Theology* by ten years.

[117]Our contention that other nineteenth-century Protestants spoke about the infallibility of the original autographs is discussed in the next section of the present essay.

[118]It would be interesting to determine if the promulgation of the doctrine of the pope's infallibility in the early 1870s had any bearing on some Protestants' use of the word *inerrancy*.

[119]See B. B. Warfield's reply to his conservative critics in this regard (Hodge and Warfield, *Inspiration*, Appendix 1, Appendix 2, pp. 73–82).

[120]Sandeen, *Origins of Fundamentalism*, p. 14, n. 40; Sandeen, *Roots of Fundamentalism*, p. 130.

[121]Sandeen, *Roots of Fundamentalism*, p. 118.

[122]Sandeen describes the results of this adaptation as "a wooden, mechanical discipline as well as a rigorously logical one" (ibid.). It is true that Charles Hodge spoke of theology as a "science." Mark Noll and George Marsden have studied the complex relationships between the Princetonians' Baconianism and their perceptions of doing theology.

[123]Bozeman, *Protestants in an Age of Science*, p. 209, n. 12.

[124]Sandeen, *Roots of Fundamentalism*, p. 119.

[125]Hodge, *Systematic Theology*, 1:153.

[126]Philip Schaff, ed., *The Creeds of Christendom* (reprint ed., Grand Rapids: Baker, 1969), 3:602.

[127]Chapter I, section V of the Westminster Confession (which Sandeen does cite) reads, ". . . yet, notwithstanding, our full persuasion and assurance of the infallible truth, and divine authority thereof, is from the inward work of the Holy Spirit, bearing witness by and with the Word in our hearts" (ibid., p. 603).

[128]Hodge, "Inspiration," p. 661. Hodge's essay on inspiration should be studied with care.

[129]Hodge, *Systematic Theology*, 1:16.

[130]Hodge, *Conference Papers*, ed. A. A. Hodge (New York: Scribner, 1879), p. 159.

[131]Charles Hodge distinguished between the inspiration of the biblical writers and the spiritual illumination that allows Christians to grasp the Bible's authority and to understand biblical truths. See Hodge's discussion, "Spiritual Discernment," delivered on April 8, 1855 (*Conference Papers*, pp. 176–77) and his *Systematic Theology*, vol. I, pp. 154–55. See also Archibald Alexander's discussion of illumination and inspiration (*Evidences of Authenticity*, pp. 223–24).

[132]A. A. Hodge, *The Confession of Faith* . . . (1869; reprint ed., London: Banner of Truth Trust, 1958), pp. 36–37.

[133]On the other hand Warfield did not neglect the importance of the Holy Spirit as Sandeen and others have proposed. The Princetonian declared, "It lies more fundamentally still in the postulate that these Scriptures are accredited to us as the revelation of God solely by the testimony of the Holy Spirit—that without this testimony they lie before us inert and without effect on our hearts and minds, while with it they become not merely the power of God unto salvation, but also the vitalizing source of our knowledge of God." (*Calvin and Augustine*, ed. Samuel Craig [Philadelphia: Presbyterian and Reformed, 1956], p. 115). See also: John Gerstner, "Warfield's Case for Biblical Inerrancy," *God's Inerrant Word*, ed. John W. Montgomery (Minneapolis: Bethany, 1974), pp. 115–42.

[134]Basil Hall describes the quest for the "originals" during Calvin's day: "The desire of the biblical humanists had been to arrive at an authentic text of the Hebrew and Greek originals, which they believed to have greater authority than the Vulgate since it was taken for granted that this version came later in time than the others" ("Biblical Scholarship: Editions and Commentaries," *The Cambridge History of the Bible: The West From the Reformation to the Present Day*, ed. S. L. Greenslade [Cambridge: Cambridge University Press, 1976], 1:63).

[135]An extensive listing is available in Randall Balmer, "The Princeton Doctrine of Original Autographs in the Context of Nineteenth Century Theology" (M.A. thesis in church history, Trinity Evangelical Divinity School, 1981). For a general background on the doctrine of Scripture in the nineteenth century, see, among others, Hans Frei, *The Eclipse of Biblical Narrative: A Study in Eighteenth and Nineteenth Century Hermeneutics* (New Haven: Yale University Press, 1974); H. D. McDonald, *Ideas of Revelation: An Historical Study, A.D. 1700 to A.D. 1860* (London: Macmillan, 1959); J. T. Burtchaell, *Catholic Theories of Inspiration Since 1810* (Cambridge: The University Press, 1969). For the impact of historical criticism on biblical studies see Klaus Scholder, *Ursprünge und Probleme der Bibelkritik im 17 Jahrhundert* . . . (München: Kaiser, 1966); Peter H. Reill, *The German Enlightenment and the Rise of Historicism* (Berkeley: University of California Press, 1975); Edgar Krentz, *The Historical-Critical Method* (Philadelphia: Fortress, 1975); Gerhard Maier, *The End of the Historical-Critical Method* (St. Louis: Concordia, 1977); Peter Stuhlmacher, *Vom Verstehen des Neuen Testaments* (Göttingen: Vandenhoeck und Ruprecht, 1979), pp. 134–49.

[136]John Dick, *An Essay in the Inspiration of the Holy Scriptures of the Old and New Testament* (Edinburgh: J. Richie, 1800), p. 239.

[137] John Dick, *Lectures on Theology*, 2 vols. (Philadelphia: Desilver, Thomas & Co., 1836), vol. I, p. 124.

[138] Ibid., p. 234.

[139] There is reason to believe that the author of the articles is Leonard Wood (cf., *Biblical Repertory* 3 [January 1831]: 5).

[140] "The Inspiration of the Scriptures," *Spirit of the Pilgrims* 1 (December 1828): 628–29.

[141] "Inspiration of the Scriptures," *Christian Review* 9 (March 1844): 16.

[142] Ibid.

[143] Gilbert Haven, "The Divine Element in Inspiration," *Methodist Quarterly Review* 50 (April 1868): 183.

[144] Louis Gaussen, *Theopneusty, or, the Plenary Inspiration of the Holy Scriptures*, trans. Edward N. Kirk, 3rd ed. (New York: John S. Taylor, 1845), pp. 44–45.

[145] Ibid., p. 80.

[146] See our discussion of Sandeen's treatment of Gaussen's volume (note 94 above).

[147] "Lee on Inspiration," *Bibliotheca Sacra* 15 (January 1858): 34.

[148] Alexander Carson, *The Inspiration of the Scriptures* (New York: Fletcher, 1853 [1830]), p. 136.

[149] David Dyer, *The Plenary Inspiration of the Old and New Testaments* (Boston: Tappan, Whittmore & Mason, 1849), p. 57.

[150] J. C. Ryle, *Expository Thoughts on the Gospels*, 7 vols. (New York: Robert Carter & Brothers, 1866 [1856–1869]), 1: v, viii.

[151] "Ryle on Inspiration," *The Truth: or Testimony for Christ* 1 (1875): 246–48.

[152] Lemuel Moss, "Dr. Curtis on Inspiration," *Baptist Quarterly* 2 (1868): 106. This review concerns T. F. Curtis, *The Human Element in the Inspiration of the Sacred Scriptures* (1867). See notes 85–88 above.

[153] Alvah Hovey, *Manual of Systematic Theology and Christian Ethics* (Philadelphia: American Baptist Publication Society, 1877), pp. 77–84. An article in the January 1855 issue of the *Freewill Baptist Quarterly* notes, "The inspiration of the Scriptures relates to the original production of the books of Scripture, and denotes the divine superintendence of their production which secured them from error" ("Inspiration of the Scriptures," *Freewill Baptist Quarterly* 3 [January 1855]: 34). A subsequent article in the same journal reviews some of the numerical discrepancies found in surviving Old Testament manuscripts and concludes, "These examples are enough to show how the numbers of the Bible might become confused by the copyist during the ages which have passed since they were written, and by frequent transcribing, cease to stand in perfect agreement with the original or its own several parts" ("The Word of God," *Freewill Baptist Quarterly* 14 [July 1866]: 294). Norman Maring observes, "In the 1860's Baptists shared a predominant belief in the inerrancy of the Bible" ("Baptists and Changing Views of the Bible, 1865–1918," *Foundations* I [October 1958]: 52). See also the New Hampshire Confession (1833), an important Baptist document.

[154] A. H. Kremer, "The Plenary Inspiration of the Bible," *Reformed Quarterly Review* 26 (October 1879): 569. See also "On the Correctness of the Common Bible," *Utica Christian Repository* 3 (1824): 294, reprinted in the *Calvinistic Magazine* 1 (November 1827): 323.

[155] D. A. Whedon, "Greek Text of the New Testament," *Methodist Quarterly Review* 50 (April 1868): 325.

[156] Henry Boynton Smith, *Inspiration of the Holy Scriptures* (Cincinnati: Herald and Presbyter, 1891), p. 1.

[157] "Inspiration of the Scriptures," *Southern Presbyterian Review* 5 (July 1851): 75.

[158]Ibid., p. 79.

[159]Sandeen, *Roots of Fundamentalism*, p. 130.

[160]Ibid., p. 126.

[161]Archibald Alexander, "Review of Woods on Inspiration," *Biblical Repertory and Theological Review* 3 (January 1831): 10. The careful reader will note the similarity between Alexander's statement and the following one that appeared in the 1881 article on inspiration and is quoted by Sandeen: "A proved error in Scripture contradicts not only our doctrine, but the Scripture claims and, therefore, its inspiration in making these claims" (*Roots of Fundamentalism*, p. 126).

[162]Alexander, *Evidences for Authenticity*, p. 228. Alexander continues, "No evil or inconvenience would result from this hypothesis, if the line could be definitely drawn between the parts of the book written by inspiration and those in which the writers were left to themselves. But as no human wisdom is sufficient to draw this line, the effect of this opinion is to introduce uncertainty and doubt in a matter concerning which assurance is of the utmost importance" (pp. 228–29).

[163]Ibid., p. 229.

[164]Ibid.

[165]Samuel Wakefield, *A Complete System of Christian Theology* (Cincinnati: Cranston and Stowe, 1869), p. 77. Wakefield designed his study as an introductory theological text to supplement "Watson's Theological Institutes" used by "mature theologians" (from the preface). It is remarkable how several current-day Wesleyan scholars ignore Wakefield and earlier Methodist authors in their attempt to demonstrate that Methodists have not held a belief in complete biblical infallibility. Paul M. Bassett begins his analysis of Methodist theologies in the 1870s (the works of Miner Raymond and W. B. Pope) rather than with earlier Methodist authors such as Watson and Wakefield ("The Fundamentalist Leavening of the Holiness Movement, 1914–1940; The Church of the Nazarene: A Case Study," *Wesleyan Theological Journal* 13 [Spring 1978]: 68). Following Sandeen's argument, Bassett speaks of the "Princeton mutation" concerning the doctrine of Scripture. Wesley himself made comments like these, and Timothy Wadkins is attempting to study them in their contexts: "Nay, will not allowing there is any error in Scripture, shake the authority of the whole way?" "Nay, if there be any mistakes in the Bible, there may as well be a thousand."

[166]Cited in Kurt Marquart, *Anatomy of an Explosion: A Theological Analysis of the Missouri Synod Controversy* (Grand Rapids: Baker, 1978), p. 45. On Walther, see Robert Preus, "Walther and the Scriptures," *Concordia Theological Monthly* 32 (November 1961): 669–91. For criticism of Sandeen's analysis from a Lutheran perspective, see Leigh Jordahl, "The Theology of Franz Pieper: A Resource for Fundamentalistic Thought Modes Among American Lutherans," *The Lutheran Quarterly* 23 (May 1971): 127–32.

[167]Cited in G. F. Wright, *Charles Grandison Finney* (Boston: Houghton Mifflin, 1891), pp. 182–83. Finney affirmed complete biblical infallibility: "There is a real substantial agreement among all the writers, and that when rightly understood they do not in any thing contradict each other. It implies, that the several writers always wrote under such a degree of divine illumination and guidance, whether of suggestion, elevation, or superintendence as to be infallibly secured from all error" (Finney, *Skeleton Lectures* [1840; published in 1841], p. 52). The authors are indebted to David Callen for the Finney materials.

[168]See note 34 above.

[169]It should be pointed out that B. B. Warfield flatly denied that he founded the "whole Christian System" on the doctrine of plenary inspiration: "We found the whole Christian system on the doctrine of plenary inspiration as little as we found it upon the doctrine of angelic existences" (See B. B. Warfield, *The Inspiration and Authority of the Bible*, 2nd ed. [Nutley, N.J.: Presbyterian and Reformed, 1948], p. 210).

[170]Professor Sandeen's study contains few intimations of the author's methodology for ascertaining "doctrinal developments."

[171]Clarke wrote, "I have dated this conviction against the inerrancy of the Bible here in the Seventies, and here it belongs ..." (*Sixty Years with the Bible*, p. 108).

[172]See, for example, Marsden, *Fundamentalism and American Culture*, pp. 242–43, n. 7.

[173]Ibid., pp. 113–14. Marsden's understanding of the Princetonians tends to be monocausational in orientation (e.g., the impact of Common Sense Realism). It does not do full justice to the complex factors that influenced their attitudes toward Scripture. This is a surprising feature of Marsden's brilliant analysis. As we suggested earlier, Christians throughout the ages had emphasized the importance of the words of Scripture, thinking that the Bible itself underscores the significance of its own words. Moreover, the fact that Christians did understand the words of Scripture to be important did not necessarily lead them to minimize the importance of the Holy Spirit in confirming the authority of the Bible (Westminster Confession I, v.) or to deny the validity of understanding its authority through spiritual illumination (rightly defined). Marsden attempts to explain the attitudes that developed in the Holiness tradition toward women partially on the basis of what he calls "Baconian Biblicism," an infelicitous and reductionistic expression (ibid., p. 250, n. 40). For insightful criticisms and appraisals of Thomas S. Kuhn's *Structure of Scientific Revolutions*, a book whose "paradigm" motif apparently undergirds a portion of Marsden's analysis, see Gary Gutting, ed., *Paradigms and Revolutions, Appraisals and Applications of Thomas Kuhn's Philosophy of Science* (Notre Dame: University of Notre Dame Press, 1980). For an important critique of Kuhn's work see Frederick Suppe, *The Structure of Scientific Theories* (Urbana: University of Illinois, 1977), p. 648. On Common Sense Realism, consult Sydney Ahlstrom, "The Scottish Philosophy and American Theology," *Church History* 24 (September 1955): 257–72.

[174]John Vander Stelt, George Marsden, and Ernest Sandeen could well have profited from a reconsideration of Charles Hodge's pusthumous *Conference Papers* (1879) in which the Princetonian made statements about the Holy Spirit, "truth," the fallibility of reason, and conscience. These statements do not accord easily with their perception of the effects of Common Sense Realism on this Princetonian. Marsden and Vander Stelt do take note of the important studies by Andrew Hoffecker concerning the Princetonians and piety. See Steve Martin's forthcoming M.A. thesis in church history (Trinity Evangelical Divinity School) on Charles Hodge's concept of religious authority.

[175]For more background on the clash between Coleridge's conception of truth (as it influenced Bushnell and Protestant liberalism) and Evangelicals' conceptions of Scriptural authority, see the older study by Walter Horton, *Theology in Transition* (New York: Harper and Brothers, 1943), part 2, pp. 26–32.

[176]Many Evangelicals assumed that their belief in biblical infallibility was based on the Scripture's witness to its own authority, not on the teachings of theologians either past or present. Their understanding also needs to be evaluated in that light (see chapter 1 by Wayne Grudem). Washington Gladden, no friend of biblical inerrancy, noted in the 1890s that most American Protestants believed that the Bible was "free from all error, whether of doctrine, of fact, or of precept" (Charles Hodge's expression). He wrote, "Such is the doctrine now held by the great majority of Christians. Intelligent pastors do not hold it, but the body of the laity have no other conception" (*Who Wrote the Bible? A Book for the People* [Boston and New York: Houghton, Mifflin, 1891], p. 357).

[177]Shelley, "A. J. Gordon and Biblical Criticism," p. 77, n. 33.

[178]A. A. Hodge intimated that the Princetonians believed some form of reconciliation was possible. In the preface to his father's *Conference Papers*, A. A. Hodge described the Sunday afternoon sessions between students and faculty at Princeton: "The dry and cold attributes of scientific theology, moving in the sphere of the intellect gave place to

the warmth of personal religious experience, and to the spiritual light of divinely illuminated intuition" (preface, p. iii).

[179]Several tools should be considered: (1) those developed by historians of the book trade (consult the studies of Robert Darnton, Henri-Jean Martin, and Raymon Birn, among others) and (2) those developed by historians of popular religion, of "secularism" and "dechristianization" (see the studies of Andrew Greeley, David Martin, Michel Vovelle, and Gabriel Le Bras, among others). See also the studies of Timothy Smith's students concerning the Bible and American culture. Technical analyses are needed on individual Princetonians. Their published and unpublished volumes and correspondence should be carefully assessed as the backdrop for these analyses. Several older theses on the Princetonians have become outdated.

[180]In this essay we are not attempting to defend every emphasis of the Princetonians' thought about Holy Scripture. Their discussion of theology as a science is unnerving. We do want, however, to counter misrepresentations of their views and of themselves.

THE BIBLICAL CONCEPT OF TRUTH
Roger Nicole
pages 287–98

[1]Charles Malik, "Fallacies of the Age," *Inform*, vol. 58, no. 4 (July 1981), p. 1.

[2]This is reflected in the word 'om^{e}nôt (2 Kings 18:16), denoting the pillars supporting the door of the temple (NIV, "doorposts").

[3]Perhaps as a reflection of these perfections in the Godhead, mercy and truth are also used in combination with respect to human activity (Gen. 24:49; 47:29; 2 Sam. 15:20; Prov. 3:3; 14:22; 16:6; 20:28).

[4]Psalm 45:4 perhaps should be listed in this context, but the text is rather obscure and the connotation of 'emet in it not manifest.

[5]A few lines must be devoted also to the word '^{e}mûnah, a cognate of 'emet. This word appears some forty-nine times in the Old Testament and is usually rendered by words relating to the idea of faithfulness. In the LXX it is translated more than half the time by alētheia (truth) or cognates. In the KJV, while "faithfulness" preponderates as the translation, "truth" (or a cognate) is used fifteen times. In the NIV "truth" is used as the translation of '^{e}mûnah eight times only. It is probably safe to say that the idea of faithfulness is the dominant connotation of this word, but that the idea of "truth," "truthfulness," "integrity," being closely related to, although not identical with faithfulness, is nevertheless always close at hand.

The same may be said for the cognate 'ēmûn "faithful," "truthful," which appears only five times in the Old Testament (Deut. 32:20; Prov. 13:17; 14:5; 20:6; Isa. 26:2).

The Hebrew word 'āmēn, strangely enough, occurs more often in the Greek New Testament than in the Hebrew Old Testament. There it is mostly used as the expression of emphatic religious assent, sometimes with repetition: "Amen, Amen" ("truly, truly"). One notable exception is found in Isaiah 65:16, where God is named "the God of Amen," the God of truth, a form of language that reminds us of the expression "God of *truth*" ('emet) discussed above.

[6]This may perhaps provide the explanation of the apparent contradiction between 2 Samuel 24:1 and 1 Chronicles 21:1. Satan is the one who incited David to take the census (2 Samuel) out of pride and vainglorious confidence in numbers, but God was in control and permitted this activity on Satan's part in order to fulfill His own purposes (cf. Job 1).

[7]J. H. Vrielink, *Het Waarheidsbegrip* (Nijkerk: Callenback, 1956), p. 6.

[8]Proverbs 3:3; 14:22, 25; 16:6; Jeremiah 28:9; 32:41; 33:6.

[9]An accurate count is especially difficult here because of textual variations. In the *textus receptus* there are 152 occurrences of *amen*, a number of the additional instances occurring at the end of the various books.

[10]This may well be the case also for 2 Corinthians 1:20, not counted in this number.

[11]This figure is reached as follows.

alētheia: truth, 109 times
alēthēs: true, 26 times
alēthinos: true, truthful, 28 times
alēthōs: truly, 18 times
alētheuō: speak, do the truth 2 times

The writings of John (Gospel, epistles, and Revelation) show a special emphasis here, with 93 occurrences. The recorded words of Jesus in the days of His flesh have it 45 times. To this should be added the 75 occurrences of His use of "amen."

[12]Matthew 14:33; 26:73; 27:54; Mark 14:70; 15:39; Luke 9:27; 12:44; 21:3; John 1:47; 4:42; 6:14; 7:26, 40; 8:31; 17:8; Acts 12:11; 1 Thessalonians 2:13; 1 John 2:5.

[13]Matthew 22:16; Mark 12:14, 32; Luke 4:25; 20:21; 22:59; Acts 4:27; 10:34; 12:9; Philippians 1:18; Colossians 1:6; 1 John 3:18; 2 John 1, 3; 3 John 1.

[14]John 5:31, 32, 8:13, 14, 17; 19:35; 21:24; Titus 1:13; 3 John 12; Revelation 3:14.

[15]Mark 5:33; 12:32; John 4:18; 8:40, 45, 46; 10:41; 16:7; 19:35; Acts 26:25; 2 Corinthians 6:7; 7:14; 12:6; Galatians 4:16; Ephesians 4:15; 2 Timothy 2:15.

[16]Romans 9:1; 1 Timothy 2:7.

[17]In 1 John 5:20 it is difficult to distinguish with assurance what is said of the Father, and what applies to the Son. I have opted here to apply the statement "He is the true God" to the Father.

FAITH, EVIDENCE, AND THE SCRIPTURES

Paul Helm

pages 303–20

[1]Joseph Butler, *The Analogy of Religion* (New York: Ungar, n.d.); John Locke, *Essay Concerning Human Understanding*, Book IV, chaps. 18–19; Thomas Aquinas, *Summa Contra Gentiles*, Book I, chap. 6.

[2]Archibald Alexander, *Evidences of the Authenticity, Inspiration, and Canonical Authority of the Holy Scriptures* (1836; reprint ed., New York: Arno, 1972), p. 61.

[3]Ibid., p. 64.

[4]Alvin Plantinga, "Is Belief in God Rational?" in C. F. Delaney, ed., *Rationality and Religious Belief* (Notre Dame, Ind.: University of Notre Dame Press, 1979). In a later version of this paper Professor Plantinga develops his views in a direction that appears to be more in accord with the argument of the present chapter. See section III of his "Rationality and Religious Belief" in *Contemporary Philosophy of Religion*, ed. Steven M. Cahn and David Shatz (New York: Harper and Row, 1982).

[5]For similar criticisms from a contemporary philosopher see Keith Lehrer, *Knowledge* (New York: Oxford Univeristy Press, 1979).

[6]Plantinga, "Is Belief in God Rational?" pp. 24–25.

[7]Ibid., p. 26.

[8]Augustine, *Confessions*; John Calvin, *Institutes of the Christian Religion*, Book I, chap. 1.

[9]Lehrer, *Knowledge*.

INFALLIBLE SCRIPTURE AND THE ROLE OF HERMENEUTICS

J. I. Packer

pages 325–56

[1]Carl F. H. Henry, *The Christian Century*, vol. 47, no. 35 (November 5, 1980), p. 1062.

[2]See, for instance, A. A. Hodge and B. B. Warfield, *Inspiration*, ed. R. R. Nicole (Grand Rapids: Baker, 1979; reprint of an article published in 1881); B. B. Warfield, *The Inspiration and Authority of the Bible* (Philadelphia: Presbyterian and Reformed, 1948; reprints of articles published between 1892 and 1915); W. Sanday, *Inspiration* (New York: Longmans, Green, 1896); J. Orr, *Revelation and Inspiration* (London: Duckworth, 1910).

[3]See, for instance, the composite volume *Revelation*, ed. J. Baillie and Hugh Martin (London: Faber, 1937); J. Baillie, *The Idea of Revelation in Recent Thought* (New York: Columbia University Press, 1956); H. R. Niebuhr, *The Meaning of Revelation* (New York: Macmillan, 1941). The energy of Barth's insistence that God is not knowable apart from revelation brought about this change of focus.

[4]See, for instance, J. Smart, *The Interpretation of Scripture* (Philadelphia: Westminster, 1961); J. Bright, *The Authority of the Old Testament* (Philadelphia: Westminster, 1967); I. Howard Marshall, ed., *New Testament Interpretation* (Grand Rapids: Eerdmans, 1977); David Stacey, *Interpreting the Bible* (London: Sheldon, 1976); Brevard S. Childs, *Biblical Theology in Crisis* (Philadelphia: Westminster, 1970). The debate arising out of Bultmann's article of 1941 in which he called for a program of demythologizing served to trigger this development.

[5]For a catalog and conspectus of evangelical responses to Barth, see Gregory G. Bolich, *Karl Barth and Evangelicalism*, especially part 2 (Downers Grove: InterVarsity, 1980). Discriminating analyses of Barth's doctrine of Scripture are given in Klaas Runia, *Karl Barth's Doctrine of Holy Scripture* (Grand Rapids: Eerdmans, 1962) and (briefly) by G. W. Bromiley, *Introduction to the Theology of Karl Barth* (Grand Rapids: Eerdmans, 1979), pp. 34–44.

[6]See, for instance, Francis Schaeffer's critique of Barth, *The God Who Is There* (Downers Grove: InterVarsity, 1968), pp. 52ff.; Barth, *Church Dogmatics*, I.ii (Edinburgh: T. & T. Clark, 1956), pp. 514–26.

[7]See, for instance, Clark Pinnock, *Biblical Revelation* (Chicago: Moody, 1971), pp. 218ff.; Robert D. Knudsen in Philip E. Hughes, ed., *Creative Minds in Contemporary Theology* (Grand Rapids: Eerdmans, 1966), pp. 131–59.

[8]The self-consciously embattled stance of the fundamentalist constituency has often obscured the pastoral and doxological motivation of its testimony and literature. Harold Lindsell's *Battle for the Bible* and *The Bible in the Balance* (Grand Rapids: Zondervan, 1976, 1979) could be cited as cases in point.

[9]See, for instance, George M. Marsden, *Fundamentalism and American Culture: the Shaping of Twentieth Century Evangelicalism, 1870–1925* (New York: Oxford University Press, 1980), pp. 43ff., 72–101, and passim; Steven Barabas, *So Great Salvation: the History and Message of the Keswick Convention* (London: Marshall, Morgan and Scott, 1952); Oliver R. Barclay's history of the Cambridge Inter-Collegiate Christian Union, *Whatever Happened to the Jesus Lane Lot?* (Leicester: Inter-Varsity, 1977). The titles of two of Lindsell's books are *When You Pray* and *The World, the Flesh and the Devil*.

[10]See, for instance, John W. Montgomery, ed., *God's Inerrant Word* (Minneapolis: Bethany Fellowship, 1974); James M. Boice, ed., *The Foundation of Biblical Authority* (Grand Rapids: Zondervan, 1978); Norman L. Geisler, ed., *Inerrancy* (Grand Rapids: Zondervan, 1979); idem, *Biblical Errancy: An Analysis of Its Philosophical Roots* (Grand Rapids: Zondervan, 1981); R. R. Nicole and J. R. Michaels, eds., *Inerrancy and Common Sense* (Grand Rapids: Baker, 1980); J.I. Packer, *"Fundamentalism" and the Word of God* (Grand Rapids: Eerdmans, 1958), *God Has Spoken* (Downers Grove: InterVarsity, 1979), *Beyond the Battle for the Bible* (Westchester: Cornerstone, 1980). The International

Council on Biblical Inerrancy exists in order to establish this precise point.

[11]See, from among textbooks that Evangelicals treat as standard, Louis Berkhof, *Principles of Biblical Interpretation* (Grand Rapids: Baker, 1950), pp. 82ff.; Bernard Ramm, *Protestant Biblical Interpretation* (Boston: Wilde, 1956); A. B. Mickelson, *Interpreting the Bible* (Grand Rapids: Eerdmans, 1963); Milton S. Terry, *Biblical Hermeneutics* (New York: Hunt and Eaton, 1883).

[12]Cf. Hans-Georg Gadamer, *Truth and Method* (London: Sheed and Ward, 1975), p. 275; cf. pp. 290–305; cf. also Gerhard Ebeling in James M. Robinson and John Cobb, eds., *The New Hermeneutic* (New York: Harper and Row, 1964), pp. 107ff. Test questions on the transcultural application of biblical principles would include how far to apply in the modern West the directives that women should pray with their heads covered (1 Cor. 11:5–15), whether we should wash each other's feet (John 13:14–15), and how far to approve J. B. Phillips's substitution of a "handshake all round" for the "holy kiss" in his New Testament paraphrase (Rom. 16:16; 1 Cor. 16:20; 2 Cor. 13:12; 1 Thess. 5:26; 1 Peter 5:14).

[13]Cf. J. I. Packer in *God's Inerrant Word*, pp. 55ff. Sample systematic theologies by which the claim in the text can be tested are those of John Calvin (1559), J. Wollebius (1626), F. Turretin (1674), Charles Hodge (1872–73), W.G.T. Shedd (1888), A. H. Strong (1907), F. Pieper (1917–24), W. B. Pope (1875), E. A. Litton (1882–92), W. H. Griffith Thomas (1930), H. Bavinck (1895–1901), H. C. Thiessen (1949), and J. O. Buswell (1962–63).

[14]See, for example, Kenneth S. Kantzer and Stanley N. Gundry, eds., *Perspectives on Evangelical Theology* (Grand Rapids: Baker, 1979).

[15]Cf. Robert Johnson, *Evangelicals at an Impasse: Biblical Authority in Practice* (Atlanta: John Knox, 1973).

[16]J.D.G. Dunn, *Unity and Diversity in the New Testament* (London: SCM, 1977), leans in this direction; most other writers today go much further, James Barr, for example. See his *Old and New in Interpretation* (London: SCM, 1966) and *The Bible in the Modern World* (London: SCM, 1973), with evaluation by Paul Ronald Wells, *James Barr and the Bible: Critique of a New Liberalism* (Phillipsburg, N.J.: Presbyterian and Reformed), chapter 4, especially pp. 267–75, and J. I. Packer in *God's Inerrant Word*, pp. 58–59. In part 3 of his valuable study, *The Uses of Scripture in Recent Theology* (Philadelphia: Fortress, 1975), David H. Kelsey appears to assume biblical pluralism as axiomatic, a fact that may help to explain how the classic Freudian misprint, "Theology is 'done' as one of the activities compromising the life of the Christian community" (p. 212), got past the proofreader's eye.

[17]So Dennis Nineham, most fully in *The Use and Abuse of the Bible* (London: Macmillan, 1976); criticized by Ronald H. Preston, "Need Dr. Nineham Be So Negative?" *Expository Times* 90 (June 1979): 275–80, and Anthony Thiselton, *The Two Horizons: New Testament Hermeneutics and Philosophical Description With Special Reference to Heidegger, Bultmann, Gadamer and Wittgenstein* (Grand Rapids: Eerdmans, 1980), pp. 52–60, 70–74. Nineham's scepticism about the possibility of understanding what came from a different culture seems to have sprung directly from his meditations on Troeltsch, but it has evident affinities with the "radical historicism" in literary interpretation against which, along with other underminings of the knowability of authors' meanings, E. D. Hirsch, Jr., wrote his magisterial *Validity in Interpretation* (New Haven: Yale University Press, 1967).

[18]Those of Jesus' parables that end startlingly, contradicting the expectations of His hearers (e.g., the publican being justified rather than the Pharisee, Luke 18:14) tend now always to be invoked as paradigms of the encounter with all Scripture, as if the essence of that encounter is not so much the realizing of how permanently given truth applies to one as just the radical changing of one's mind from whatever one thought about God before. Cf. W. Wink, *The Bible in Human Transformation: Toward a New Paradigm for Biblical Study* (Philadelphia: Fortress, 1973); R. W. Funk, *Language, Hermeneutic and Word of God* (New York: Harper and Row, 1966); D. O. Via, Jr., *The Parables: Their Literary*

and Existential Dimension (Philadelphia: Fortress, 1967); J. D. Crossan, *In Parables: The Challenge of the Historical Jesus* (New York: Harper and Row, 1973); Anthony Thiselton, "The New Hermeneutic" in *New Testament Interpretation*, ed. I. Howard Marshall (Exeter: Paternoster, 1977), pp. 320–22.

[19]Cf. such samples of unitive biblical theology as E. C. Hoskyns and F. N. Davey, *The Riddle of the New Testament* (London: Faber, 1931); A. M. Hunter, *The Unity of the New Testament* (London: SCM, 1943); A. G. Hebert, *The Bible From Within* (London: Oxford University Press, 1950); Leon Morris, *The Cross in the New Testament* (Grand Rapids: Eerdmans, 1965); R. A. Ward, *The Pattern of Our Salvation* (Waco: Word, 1978).

[20]On the situational particularity of Barth's account of God's command, cf. J. I. Packer in B. N. Kaye and G. J. Wenham, eds., *Law, Morality and the Bible* (Leicester: Inter-Varsity, 1978), p. 154. Kelsey acutely describes the way Barth uses biblical narrative to build up his account of God and of Jesus Christ as "rendering an agent" in the way that novelists do by narrating actions that cohere in patterns revealing character (see *Uses of Scripture*, pp. 39–50). Barth's methodological commitment to treating the historic canon of Scripture as a theological unity (the commitment producing what he called "theological" and B. S. Childs calls "canonical" exegesis) serves to safeguard the consistency that his rejection of the category of general principles would otherwise endanger.

[21]Kelsey, *Uses of Scripture*, p. 163.

[22]Cf. Luther's response to Erasmus's generalization that Scripture contains obscurities: "I certainly grant that many *passages* in the Scriptures are obscure and hard to elucidate, but that is due ... to our own linguistic and grammatical ignorance; and it does not in any way prevent our knowing all the *contents* of Scripture.... If words are obscure in one place, they are clear in another.... I know that to many people a great deal remains obscure; but that is due, not to any lack of clarity in Scripture, but to their own blindness and dullness" (*The Bondage of the Will*, trans. J. I. Packer and O. R. Johnston [Old Tappan, N.J.: Revell, 1957], pp. 71–72). See G. C. Berkouwer's chapter on "Clarity," in *Holy Scripture*, trans. Jack B. Rogers (Grand Rapids: Eerdmans, 1975), pp. 267–98.

[23]H. J. Cadbury illustrates this by citing an absurd account of Jesus as, in effect, a modern American achiever: "Jesus exemplifies all the principles of modern salesmanship. He was, of course, a good mixer. He made contacts easily and was quick to get *en rapport* with his 'prospect.' He appreciated the value of news, and so called his message 'good news.' His habit of rising early was indicative of the pressure of the 'go-getter' so necessary for a successful career ..." (*The Peril of Modernizing Jesus* [reprint; London: SPCK, 1962] p. 11).

[24]See *The Use and Abuse of the Bible*, especially chapters 1, 5, 10, 11; and the comments of Thiselton, *The Two Horizons*, pp. 52–60, 70–74.

[25]For positive arguments on the possibility of divine communication through Scripture, see J. I. Packer, "The Adequacy of Human Language," in N. L. Geisler, ed., *Inerrancy*, pp. 197–226.

[26]T. H. L. Parker, *Calvin's New Testament Commentaries* (London: SCM, 1971), p. 66: Hunnius spoke disparingingly of *Calvinus Judaizans*.

[27]See James M. Robinson and John B. Cobb, Jr., *The New Hermeneutic* (New York: Harper and Row, 1964), pp. 1–7; Richard E. Palmer, *Hermeneutics: Interpretation Theory in Schleiermacher, Dilthey, Heidegger and Gadamer* (Evanston: Northwestern University Press, 1969), pp. 12–32; cf. pp. 33–71.

[28]The first book to use the word in its title was J. C. Dannhauer's *Hermeneutica Sacra, sive methodus explicandarum Sacrarum Literarum* (Strasbourg, 1654). Until Schleiermacher, hermeneutics meant "interpretation of the Scriptures according to either the Roman or the Protestant understanding of dogma" (Alan Richardson, *Religion in Contemporary Debate* [London: SCM, 1966], p. 90).

[29]Alan Richardson summarizes Dilthey's approach thus: "The historian ... can project himself into the experience of others.... Historical understanding means to re-live *(nacherleben)* the past experience of others and so to make it one's own" *(History Sacred and Profane* [London: SCM, 1966], p. 163). Dilthey himself says, "Understanding is a rediscovery of the I in the Thou.... The subject is here one with its object" (quoted from H. A. Hodges, *Wilhelm Dilthey: An Introduction* [London: Kegan Paul, Trench and Trubner, 1944], p. 114). On Schleiermacher's anticipations of this, see H. Kimmerle, "Hermeneutical Theory or Ontological Hermeneutics," *Journal for Theology and the Church,* 4 (1967): 107–21; R. E. Palmer, *Hermeneutics,* pp. 84–97.

[30]See Packer, *God Has Spoken,* pp. 52–53, 74–80.

[31]Acts 9:4ff.; 10:13ff.; 18:9–10 (cf. 12:7ff.); 27:23–24; 2 Corinthians 12:9–10 (cf. Revelation 1:17ff. and passim).

[32]Cf. Matthew 19:4–5; Acts 4:25ff.; 28:25ff.; Romans 15:3–12; 1 Corinthians 10:6–11; Hebrews 1:5–13; 3:7ff.; 10:15ff.; 12:5–6.

[33]Warfield, *Inspiration and Authority,* pp. 145, 152, 348; Augustine, *Confessions,* CIII.29.

[34]See Thiselton, "The New Hermeneutic," in *New Testament Interpretation,* pp. 308–33.

[35]As they do; see, for instance, Louis Berkhof, *Introduction to Systematic Theology* (reprint; Grand Rapids: Baker, 1979), pp. 146–50.

[36]This rather unpleasant patronizing of Jesus is logically inseparable from the Schleiermacherian approach, for Jesus' entire self-understanding and ministry, even His courting of death in Jerusalem, rested on His certainty that the Scriptures were divine instruction (cf. Matt. 4:4, 7, 10; 5:17–19; 26:53–56; Mark 12:10, 24; Luke 18:31ff.; 22:37; 24:25ff., 44ff.; John 5:39, 45ff.; 10:35), and the Schleiermacherian approach is made possible only by declining to take seriously the obvious implication of Jesus' certainty for Christian theological method.

[37]Cf. Gerhard Ebeling: "The primary phenomenon in the realm of understanding is not understanding OF language, but understanding THROUGH language" *(Word and Faith* [London: SCM, 1963], p. 318).

[38]See P. Tillich, *Systematic Theology* (Chicago: University of Chicago Press, 1951–63); K. Hamilton, *The System and the Gospel: A Critique of Paul Tillich* (London, SCM, 1963).

[39]See M. Wiles, *The Remaking of Christian Doctrine* (London: SCM, 1975) and the critique by Paul Wignall in S. W. Sykes, *The Integrity of Anglicanism* (London: Mowbrays, 1978).

[40]See G. W. H. Lampe, *God as Spirit* (Oxford: Clarendon, 1977).

[41]See Thiselton's masterly critique, *The Two Horizons,* pp. 205–92.

[42]See Norman Pittenger, "Process Theology," in *A Dictionary of Christian Theology,* ed. Alan Richardson (London: SCM, 1969); the critiques by N. L. Geisler *(Tensions in Contemporary Theology,* ed. Stanley N. Gundry and Alan F. Johnson [Chicago: Moody, 1976], pp. 237–84); Bruce A. Demarest *(Perspectives on Evangelical Theology,* ed. Kenneth S. Kantzer and Stanley N. Gundry [Grand Rapids: Baker, 1979], pp. 15–36).

[43]The divergences regularly reflect different forms of reductionist thinking, thus, for example, Fuchs "tends to see the translated message of the New Testament itself in narrowly selective terms. In the end, almost everything in the New Testament can be translated into a call to love ..." (Thiselton, in *New Testament Interpretation,* p. 324).

[44]See Gadamer, *Truth and Method* pp. 217ff.; Thiselton, *The Two Horizons,* pp. 303–10, cf. pp. 149–68.

[45]Cf. note 18 above.

[46]Thiselton's comments on the parable of the Pharisee and the publican illustrate

excellently what is involved here at the level of communication *(The Two Horizons,* pp. 12–16).

[47] Cf. note 23 above.

[48] See, on this, Thiselton, "The New Hermeneutic," in *New Testament Interpretation,* pp. 308–33 and *The Two Horizons,* pp. 334–35, 342–56; Robinson and Cobb, eds., *The New Hermeneutic:* P. J. Achtemeier, *An Introduction to the New Hermeneutic* (Philadelphia: Westminster, 1969); Alan Richardson, *Religion in Contemporary Debate,* pp. 81–101; Cornelius Van Til, *The New Hermeneutic* (Nutley, N. J.: Presbyterian and Reformed, 1974). The main relevant works by Ebeling in English are *Word and Faith* and *Introduction to a Theological Theory of Language* (London: Collins, 1973); those by Fuchs are his essays, "The New Testament and the Hermeneutical Problem in Robinson and Cobb, eds., *The New Hermeneutic,* pp. 111–45, 232–43 and *Studies of the Historical Jesus* (London: SCM, 1964). Fuchs's *Hermeneutik,* 4th ed. (Tübingen: Mohr, 1970), remains untranslated, as does Ebeling's important article "Hermeneutik" in *Die Religion in Geschichte und Gegenwart,* 3rd ed. (Tübingen: Mohr, 1959), 3: 242–62.

[49] See, on Heidegger, Thiselton, *The Two Horizons,* pp. 143–204, 327–42; Mazda King, *Heidegger's Philosophy: A Guide to His Basic Thought* (Oxford: Blackwell, 1964); John Macquarrie, *Martin Heidegger* (Richmond: John Knox, 1968); Howard M. Ducharme, Jr., "Mysticism: Heidegger," in *Biblical Errancy,* pp. 205–27. Heidegger's *Being and Time,* written in 1927, appeared in English in 1962 (Oxford: Blackwell). Important for his later thought are his *an Introduction to Metaphysics* (New Haven: Yale University Press, 1959), *On the Way to Language* (New York: Harper and Row, 1966), and *Discourse on Thinking* (New York: Harper and Row, 1972).

[50] *On the Way to Language,* p. 85.

[51] William Barrett, in the preface to his anthology of D. T. Suzuki's writings (Suzuki is a leading exponent of Zen Buddhism), tells of a friend of Heidegger's who once heard him say, "If I understand this man [Suzuki] correctly, this is what I have been trying to say in all my writings" *(Zen Buddhism: Selected Writings of D. T. Suzuki* [Garden City: Doubleday, Anchor, 1956], p. xi). Heidegger thought that being "speaks" with great authenticity through poets such as Sophocles and Holderlin (see Thiselton, *The Two Horizons,* p. 339) and adapted his concept of *Gelassenheit* ("receptive yieldedness," Thiselton, *The Two Horizons,* p. 340; "releasement," Ducharme, "Mysticism: Heidegger," p. 219) from Meister Eckhart.

[52] Thiselton, *The Two Horizons,* p. 341

[53] It must be realized that the later Heidegger was polemicizing against the traditional Western type of metaphysics with its static concept of being and its objectifying of concepts in a subject-object epistemological frame. He saw his own radical activism (i.e., his view of being's existence, not as an ultimate reality that is constantly "there" to be grasped, but as consisting entirely in the event of its self-disclosure on each occasion) as "overcoming" metaphysics. See Richardson, *Religion in Contemporary Debate,* pp. 85–87.

[54] Ibid., p. 88.

[55] "Fuchs refused to define the content of faith.... He is afraid of the word as convention or as a means of conveying information.... Fuchs carries this so far that revelation, as it were, reveals nothing ..." (Amos N. Wilder, "The Word as Address and Meaning," in Robinson and Cobb, eds., *The New Hermeneutic,* p. 213). Fuchs follows in Bultmann's footsteps at this point.

[56] *New Testament Interpretation,* p. 324.

[57] Cf. Thomas C. Oden, *Agenda for Theology* (San Francisco: Harper and Row, 1979), chapter 7, "The Expurgated Scripture," pp. 130–47. Oden shows the link between the systematic depreciation of the Pastoral and Catholic epistles in the New Testament criticism of such as Bultmann, Käsemann, and Bornkamm and today's conventional depreciation of the idea of orthodoxy (given truth, right belief, the pattern of sound

words), which is so basic to the concept of faith that these letters teach. He rightly diagnoses both depreciations as expressions of the same liberal-existentialist a priori, which appeared most clearly in Bultmann's work. Fuchs, as one of Bultmann's epigoni who, like his mentor, doubles in the roles of exegete and theologian, takes this a priori for granted and sees himself as carrying on in hermeneutics where Bultmann left off.

[58]Achtemeier, *Introduction to the New Hermeneutic*, p. 162.

[59]"Each science orients itself to its subject matter. In this case [hermeneutics] the subject matter is you yourself, dear reader" (Fuchs, in *The New Hermeneutic*, p. 141). "In the new hermeneutic ... the text, rather than being the object of interpretation, as with Bultmann, becomes an aid in the interpretation of present existence" (John R. Cobb, in Robinson and Cobb, eds., *The New Hermeneutic*, pp. 229–30).

[60]Pinnock, *Biblical Revelation*, p. 226.

[61]Thiselton in *New Testament Interpretation*, p. 323.

[62]Cf. Thiselton, *Two Horizons*, p. 343.

[63]Cf. J. I. Packer, "Preaching as Biblical Interpretation," in Nicole and Michaels, eds., *Inerrancy and Common Sense*, pp. 187–203, especially pp. 189–92.

[64]Thiselton in *New Testament Interpretation*, p. 324.

[65]J. C. Weber, "Language-Event and Christian Faith," *Theology Today* 21 (1965), p. 455.

[66]Books giving such an account include those listed in note 11 above, plus, at a more popular level, A. M. Stibbs, *Understanding God's Word*, rev. D. & G. Wenham (London: Inter-Varsity, 1976), and R. C. Sproul, *Knowing Scripture* (Downers Grove: InterVarsity, 1977). Cf. J. I. Packer as cited, note 63 above, and "Inerrancy and Biblical Authority" in E. R. Geeham, ed., *Jerusalem and Athens* (Philadelphia: Presbyterian and Reformed, 1971), pp. 141–53. As Henry Krabbendam of Covenant College shows in his excellent unpublished syllabus, "Towards a Biblical Hermeneutics," ch. III, the Puritan John Owen produced an archetypal and classic account of evangelical hermeneutics, in which the individual's spiritual understanding of what is given in Scripture is the central notion, as long ago as 1677. This was his *Causes, Ways and Means of understanding the Mind of God, as revealed in his Word, with Assurance therein. And a Declaration of the Perspicuity of the Scriptures, with the External Means of the Interpretation of them* (W. Goold, ed., *Works*, vol. 4 [London: Banner of Truth, 1967], *Calvin's New Testament Commentaries*, pp. 118–234).

[67]Cf. T. H. L. Parker, pp. 60–68; R. P. C. Hanson in A. Richardson, ed., *A Dictionary of Christian Theology* (SCM, 1969), pp. 4–5; Beryl Smalley in ed. G. W. H. Lampe, *The Cambridge History of the Bible*, vol. 2 (Cambridge: Cambridge University Press, 1969), pp. 212–20.

[68]The common formula, that the "literal" meaning of Scripture is what the human writer "intended," opens the door to the idea that what he meant differs from what he actually said, due to his imperfect mastery of the verbal medium. Since that idea is a false trail both as interpretation (cf. J. W. Montgomery on the "intentionalist fallacy," *God's Inerrant Word*, pp. 29–31) and as theology (cf. 2 Peter 1:19–21; Heb. 3:7–11; 10:15–17, et al.), it is better to avoid the formula altogether.

[69]On the idea of canonical exegesis, cf. B. S. Childs, *Introduction to the Old Testament as Scripture* (Philadelphia: Fortress, 1979), pp. 71–83.

[70]This can be seen at once by examining the classic expositions of Scripture by Matthew Henry (1708–10) and Thomas Scott (1788–92) and the contemporary New London and Tyndale (Eerdmans) commentary series.

[71]Ebeling, *Introduction to a Theological Theory of Language*, p. 17.

[72]On the "magic-word" idea in relation to Scripture, cf. Thiselton, "The Supposed Power of Words in the Biblical Writings," *Journal of Theological Studies* 25 (1974): 283–99.

[73]In Berkhof's *Principles of Biblical Interpretation*, for example, there is not a single reference to the Spirit save in connection with the inspiration of the text (see pp. 41–46).

[74]The conservative Reformed theological tradition, from Calvin through Owen and Kuyper to Van Til, has most to say on this subject, and on the enlightening work (the "internal witness") of the Spirit whereby we are enabled to discern the reality of divine things and the divinity of two fully human realities, Holy Scripture and Jesus of Nazareth. See, for a full exposition, Bernard Ramm, *The Witness of the Spirit* (Grand Rapids: Eerdmans, 1959).

[75]After Owen's *Causes, Ways and Means of Understanding the Mind of God....*, the only evangelical treatment known to me that integrates the Spirit's ministry with the following of interpretative rules is the nontechnical but weighty discussion by Arthur W. Pink, *Interpretation of the Scriptures* (Grand Rapids: Baker, 1972).

[76]Cf. Packer, *Beyond the Battle for the Bible*, pp. 11–36.

[77]On Heidegger's view of the circle, cf. Thiselton, *The Two Horizons*, pp. 104–5, 166, 196–97. For Bultmann's view, cf. W. Schmithals, *An Introduction to the Theology of Rudolf Bultmann* (Minneapolis: Augsburg, 1968), pp. 243–48, and Bultmann's own article, "Is Presuppositionless Exegesis Possible?" in Schubert M. Ogden, ed., *Existence and Faith* (London: Hodder and Stoughton, 1961).

[78]H. Kimmerle, in *Journal for Theology and the Church* 4 (1967): 107; cf. Richardson's remark cited in note 28 above.

[79]This conception of hermeneutics as the handmaid of accepted orthodoxy hardly squares with the freedom and integrity of Calvin's exegesis or with Owen's stress on the sovereignty of the Holy Spirit as teacher and the inexhaustible riches of the scriptural revelation of God that seekers are enabled to understand. When both these men embrace the principle of harmony (supposing this to be what ἀναλογία τῆσ πίστεως in Romans 12:6 signifies: see Calvin, *Institutes of the Christian Religion*, ed. J. T. McNeill [Philadelphia: Westminster, 1960] I.12–13; Owen, *Works* IV.198–99), their commitment is to a method, not an orthodoxy as such; and full recognition must be given to the good faith and honesty of men like B. B. Warfield, who once said that he subscribed to the Westminster Confession not because he could make the Bible teach it, but because he could not make the Bible teach anything else.

[80]Charles Hodge's constant claim that what he teaches in a divided Christendom is the "church doctrine" (*Systematic Theology*, passim) and Warfield's conservative triumphalism as a debating style are certainly among the evidences for the assertion in the text.

[81]Cf. Packer in *Jerusalem and Athens*, pp. 146–47.

[82]Cf. Warfield, *Inspiration and Authority*, passim.

[83]On the logic of the theological language found in Scripture and echoed in the church, cf. Ian T. Ramsey, *Religious Language* (London: SCM, 1957), *Models and Mystery* (London: Oxford University Press, 1964); Basil Mitchell, ed., *Faith and Logic* (London: Allen and Unwin, 1957); Frederick Ferré, *Language, Logic and God* (London: Collins, 1970); William Hordern, *Speaking of God* (London: Epworth, 1965); John Macquarrie, *God-Talk* (London: SCM, 1967).

[84]On the semantics of Scripture, see Anthony Thiselton, "Semantics and New Testament Interpretation" in *New Testament Interpretation*; G. B. Caird, *The Language and Imagery of the Bible* (Philadelphia: Westminster, 1980); James Barr, *Semantics of Biblical Language* (London: Oxford University Press, 1961).

[85]Cf. Nicole and Michaels, eds., *Inerrancy and Common Sense*, pp. 168ff. (Gordon D. Fee), 193ff. (J. I. Packer).

[86]For a modern restatement of what is essentially Luther's position, see Gustav Wingren, *The Living Word* (Philadelphia: Muhlenberg, 1960).

[87]Timothy R. Phillips, in "The Argument for Inerrancy; an Analysis" (*Journal of the*

American Scientific Affiliation, vol. 31, no. 2 [June 1979], pp. 80–88) maintains that the "true" inerrantist has an a priori commitment to "foundationalism," that is, a Cartesian view of knowledge as clear and indubitable certainty, linked to a Cartesian insistence that theology must have a foundation that yields this kind of certainty. To set Scripture, as the *principium* of knowledge, in this frame of reference is to require it on a priori grounds to be epistemologically definitive on every matter of fact to which it refers. That some inerrantists in and since the seventeenth century have embraced this bit of natural theology is evident, but it is also evident that many who affirm the totally error-free character of Scripture have not done so (Kuyper, for instance); so it is misleading, to say the least, for Phillips to describe such a person as "not a true inerrantist" (p. 87, n. 33). Cf. Paul D. Feinberg, "The Meaning of Inerrancy," in N. L. Geisler, ed., *Inerrancy*, pp. 267–304.

[88]Cf. J. I. Packer, *God Has Spoken*, pp. 110–14; idem, *Beyond the Battle for the Bible*, pp. 37–61.

[89]Cf. G. Tavard, *Holy Church or Holy Writ? The Crisis of the Protestant Reformation* (New York: Harper and Row, 1959).

[90]Barth, *Church Dogmatics*, I.ii, 620–60.

[91]See, for presentations of it, Warfield, *Inspiration and Authority*; J. W. Wenham, *Christ and the Bible* (Downers Grove: InterVarsity, 1973); idem, "Christ's View of Scripture," and Edwin A. Blum, "The Apostles' View of Scripture" in *Inerrancy*, pp. 3–36; 39–53; and chapter 1 by Grudem in this volume.

[92]Cf. note 16 above.

[93]Cf. J. W. Montgomery, ed., *God's Inerrant Word*, pp. 145ff. (Clark Pinnock) and 263–81 (J. W. Montgomery).

[94]Cf. Hendrikus Berkhof, *Christian Faith* (Grand Rapids: Eerdmans, 1979), pp. 84–86; Kelsey, *Uses of Scripture*, pp. 103–8 and passim.

[95]Cf. Colin Brown, *Karl Barth and the Christian Message* (London: Inter-Varsity, 1967); G. C. Berkouwer, *The Triumph of Grace in the Theology of Karl Barth* (Grand Rapids: Eerdmans, 1956).

[96]Cf. Bruce Demarest, "Process Trinitarianism," in *Perspectives on Evangelical Theology*, pp. 15–36. "The God of process theology is shorn not only of personality, but also of aseity, eternity, infinity, omniscience and omnipotence. The process Deity is not the causative agent of creation, nor the sovereign sustainer of the universe, nor the providential protector of human destiny. In short, the God of process theology is not the God of the Bible" (p. 33).

[97]For Heidegger's contribution here, cf. Palmer, *Hermeneutics*, pp. 155–61; for Gadamer's, cf. pp. 167–76; and see pp. 237–41.

[98]This is shown in Heidegger's case by Ducharme, in *Biblical Errancy*, pp. 221–27, and in Gadamer's by Hirsch, *Validity in Interpretation*, pp. 245–64. Thiselton lets Gadamer down very lightly, saying only, "It *may well be* that, in contrast to the undue pessimism of the later Heidegger, Gadamer himself is too optimistic about the capacity of language, tradition and temporal distance to filter out what is false and leave only what is true" (*The Two Horizons*, p. 314). In fact, the verdict seems inescapable.

Abbreviations

Jos.	*On Joseph*
Q. Gen.	*Questions on Genesis*
Quis Her.	*Who Is the Heir*
Spec. Leg.	*On the Special Laws*

RABBINIC LITERATURE

b.	*Babylonian Talmud*
Ber.	*Berakhoth*
Cant. Rab.	*Midrash Rabbah on Song of Songs*
Est. Rab.	*Midrash Rabbah on Esther*
j.	*Jerusalem Talmud*
Lev. Rab.	*Midrash Rabbah on Leviticus*
m.	*Mishnah*
Midr. Ps.	*Midrash on Psalms*
Nid.	*Niddah*
Num. Rab.	*Midrash Rabbah on Numbers*
Ros Has.	*Rosh Hashanah*
Sanh.	*Sanhedrin*
Sota	*Sota*
t.	*Tosefta*
Yebam.	*Yebamoth*
Yoma	*Yoma*

EARLY CHRISTIAN LITERATURE

| Ign. *Eph.* | Ignatius, *To the Ephesians* |

Index of Persons

Abrahams, I., 363
Achtemeier, P. J., 342, 416, 417
Ackroyd, P. R., 360, 384
Aeschylus, 147, 332
Ahlstrom, Sidney, 409
Aland, Kurt, 110, 112, 376
Albright, W. F., 360
Alexander, Archibald, 253, 259, 265, 266, 268, 270, 275, 305, 306, 308, 310, 312, 318, 397, 401, 404, 406, 408, 411
Allcock, P. J., 365
Allen, Don C., 399
Allen, Leslie, 364
Allison, Leon McDill, 394
Althaus, Paul, 229, 391
Amamus, 241
Ambrosiaster, 365
Ames, William, 235, 236, 254, 256, 257, 264, 271, 394, 397, 399
Amyraut, Moyse, 236, 285, 394
Anderson, Bernhard W., 359
Aquinas, Thomas, 304, 308, 352, 411
Aristotle, 148, 235, 240
Arminius, 235
Arndt, W., 39, 364
Arnold, Matthew, 261 402
Arnold, Thomas, 260, 262, 263, 265, 402, 403
Athanasius, 10, 199, 202
Athenagoras, 204
Atwater, Lyman, 402
Augustine, 11, 200, 204, 205, 206, 207, 209, 210, 213, 214, 215, 220, 226, 255, 256, 257, 271, 276, 277, 311, 335, 365, 389, 398, 399, 400, 406, 411, 415
Aune, David, 368

Bahr, Gordon J., 112
Bailey, Warner, 400
Baillie, J., 412
Baker, J. A., 360

Balmer, Randall H., 249, 396, 400, 406
Balnsen, Gregory L., 112
Banks, R., 128, 130, 371, 380
Barabas, Steven, 381, 412
Barclay, Oliver R., 412
Barclay, W., 377
Barnes, Annie, 404
Barr, James, 20, 139, 140, 189, 252, 353, 359, 368, 380, 385, 397, 413, 418
Barrett, C. K., 158, 159, 160, 371, 384, 385
Barrett, William, 416
Bartsch, H.-W., 387
Barth, Karl, 10, 178, 182, 220, 325, 326, 329, 330, 335, 345, 349, 351, 353, 387, 412, 414, 419
Barth, Marcus, 386
Basil of Caesarea, 390
Basset, Paul M., 408
Battles, Ford Lewis, 392
Bauer, Walter, 39, 66, 71, 72, 94, 364, 368, 370
Baum, Guilielmus, 393
Baur, F. C., 110, 180
Bavinck, H., 413
Beardslee, John W., III, 395
Beasley-Murray, G. R., 111, 376
Beck, C., 266, 405
Bellarmine, Robert, 237, 254–55, 256
Berkhof, Hendrikus, 220, 418, 419
Berkhof, Louis, 413, 415
Berkouwer, G. C., 10, 39–40, 297, 361, 362, 366, 414, 419
Bernard of Clairvaux, 333
Best, E., 375, 379
Betz, Otto, 363
Beza, Theodore, 391
Birn, Raymon, 410
Bjornard, R., 359
Blank, Sheldon H., 359
Bloch, Renée, 386
Blocher, Henri, 297
Bloesch, Donald G., 375

The editors would like to thank Mark Seifrid for his time and careful industry in helping with the compilation of the indexes.

Index of Subjects

Accommodation: of God's language to human error, 53–57, 366n76, 367nn81 and 82; in Luther's understanding, 228–29; in Turretin's understanding, 242–43

Alexander: views of Scripture in, 265–66, 397n16

Allegorizing: in the Fathers, 214–17; perniciousness of, 187–88. See also Hermeneutics; Paul: his use of the Old Testament.

Amanuenses, 106–9, 111

Ames: views of Scripture in, 256–58

Analogia fidei, 91–93, 208–9, 375n121, 418n79

Anonymity. See Pseudonymity.

Apostles: authority of, 366n71; errors and sins of, 364n58; relation to the canon in the views of the Fathers, 202; role regarding the Scriptures, 46, 47. See also Paul; Hermeneutics: the possibility of copying the New Testament writers' hermeneutics.

Atonement theology: in Luke/Acts, 75–76

Authenticity: of Jesus' teaching, 124–25, 137–40, 380–81n62; of Matthew 5:17–20, 128–30

Authority: and finality, 29–30; problem of, in every ecclesiastical communion, 211–12; of prophets, 21, 22–25; rise of church authority, 209, 210, 217–18; of royal decree formula, 21–22

Autographs: and concern for "originals" in the 19th century, 406nn134 and 135, 407n153; importance of, 192, 405n106; inerrancy of, in American and European thought, 271–75; problems of identification of, 381n1. See also Textual criticism; Textual corruption.

Bible: authority of, according to the Fathers, 207; defensiveness concerning, 193–94; divine origin of, recognized by the Fathers, 204–5, 218; as God-breathed; human origin of, recognized by the Fathers, 205–7, 217; humanness of, 101, 362n34; imprecise language and free quotations of, 51–52; inerrancy of, according to the Fathers, 204–5, 398n34, 400n45; judged as a nonauthoritative model for faith, 180; nature of, as foundational to what divides Evangelicalism, liberalism, and Catholicism, 326; not the preserve of the specialist, 176–77, 218–19; phenomenological language of, 52–53; and relation to apostolic tradition according to the Fathers, 208–12; self-presentation of, 19–59; truthfulness of, 19, 58, 79, 361n27; univocal meaning of, 328–32; as viewed in Jewish intertestamental literature, 36–37; as Word of God, 19–36. See also God; Words.

Biblical theology: definition of, 69; problems in, 67

Botenspruch, 20–21

Calvin: his view of Scriptures, 230–34, 392–93n31, 393n40

Canon: criticism, 68; diversity of, 73; origins of, 49; role of the church in recognizing, 199–203. See also New Testament; Old Testament.

Canon within the canon, 67, 73, 93.

Catholic epistles, 105–6, 111

Chalcedon, 188–90

Christology: explanation of Matthew 19:16–21 parallels, 134–35; hermeneutical control of, 212–14; model for understanding the nature of the Bible, 191–94; role of, in early ecclesiastical debates, 189–90; subordinationist, 75–76

Holy Spirit: role of, in bringing a person to accept the truthfulness of the Bible, 312–13; role of, in understanding the Bible's meaning, 214; view of, in the writings of the Princetonians, 269–71, 406n133. *See also* Hermeneutics.

Incarnation: denial of, 183–84
Infallibility: and inerrancy, 403n90; and omniscience, 382n16; of the Scriptures, 58. *See also* Bible; God; Truthfulness.
Inspiration: affirmed by Finney, 276, 408n167; affirmed by Wesley, 408n165; definition of, according to Alexander, 265; as God-breathed, 39, 40; importance of, 403n89; limits of, 161–62; method of, 40, 57–58, 363n47, 366n76, of New Testament Scriptures, 46
Irrationalism, 313

Jesus: as itinerant preacher, 126; as unifying theme of the New Testament, 68, 71, 72–73
Jonah: historicity of, 364n52
Josephus: his view of Scripture, 36–37

Kerygma: found in Acts, 75–76; multiplicity of in the New Testament, 74; preached by Jesus, 74

Letters: in antiquity, 101–2; form of, 103; in the New Testament, 101; relation between "epistles" and "true letters," 102–3; tractate letters, 104–6
Logic: ambiguity of terminology, 375n127; in Calvin, 80–81; universal applicability of, 80–81
Luther: his view of Scripture, 227–30, 414n22

Manuscript evidence: abundance of, for New Testament documents, 148
Masoretes: general reliability of, 151–52
Merit theology, 136–37
Midrash, 386n51
Muratorian Canon, 201–2
Mustard seed: parable of, 367n81, 383n21

New Testament: assigning authority even to words and letters of the Old Testament, 40–41; authority and truthfulness of, 45–49; canon, 200–203; perspectives on the Old Testament, 37–45; treatment of historical details in the Old Testament, 41–44; use of the Old Testament, 157–61. *See also* Bible; God; Hermeneutics: of New Testament writers; Word of God.
New Testament theology: alleged mutual incompatibility of New Testament theologies, 72–73; diversity of idiosyncratic styles and interests of the New Testament writers, 89–90; diversity of pastoral concerns of the New Testament writers; recent study and definition of, 67, 70–71
Nicea, 188–89
Nonnegotiables, 141–42

Old Testament: authority and truthfulness of, 19–44; canon, 199–200. *See also* Bible; God; Hermeneutics; Word of God.
Orthodoxy: alleged late development of, 71–72, 184; constant line of, 188–89; in the first century, 72–73; overreactions of, 190–94; in the second century, 66

Paul: development of thought of, 84–86; diversity of circumstances of, 88; emphases of, in Galatians and 1 Corinthians, 86–87; flexibility of, 174–75; letters of, 102–4, 111; as preacher, 87; resurrection in the thought of, 85–86; towering over theological landscape, 68; his use of the Old Testament, 157–61
Pesher, 386n55
Philo: his view of Scripture, 37, 363n44
Princeton Seminary: biblical infallibility at, 265–69
Princetonians: view of Scripture in, 258–71, 397n22, 408n165, 409–10n178. *See also* Holy Spirit.
Progressive revelation: definition of, 82–83; implications of, for systematic theology, 83–86; in the understanding of the Fathers, 212–13
Proof-texting: among the Fathers, 216

Index of
Scripture References